Enterprise-wide Strategic Management

In today's highly competitive and dynamic business environments, corporations can no longer afford to rely on the static strategic management constructs of the past. *Enterprise-wide Strategic Management* is a leading-edge work that shows how business leaders can take better advantage of their opportunities by taking a broader perspective of the world in which they operate. David Rainey advocates a holistic approach to the business environment, arguing that managers must work with all stakeholders, both internal and external, to create long-term success. Including numerous case studies featuring global corporations and small and medium-sized enterprises (SMEs), the book provides guidance and support in formulating, developing, and implementing business strategies and action plans. It also includes advice on how to develop and deploy strategic management systems, management constructs, and organizational structures. This gives executives, strategic leaders, professionals, and practitioners the tools they need to create value and achieve sustainable success.

David L. Rainey is Professor of Management at the Lally School of Management and Technology, Rensselaer Polytechnic Institute, USA. He is the author of *Product Innovation* (Cambridge University Press, 2005) and *Sustainable Business Development* (Cambridge University Press, 2006).

Enterprise-wide Strategic Management

Achieving Sustainable Success through Leadership, Strategies, and Value Creation

David L. Rainey

CAMBRIDGE
UNIVERSITY PRESS

CAMBRIDGE UNIVERSITY PRESS
Cambridge, New York, Melbourne, Madrid, Cape Town, Singapore, São Paulo, Delhi

Cambridge University Press
The Edinburgh Building, Cambridge CB2 8RU, UK

Published in the United States of America by Cambridge University Press, New York

www.cambridge.org
Information on this title: www.cambridge.org/9780521769808

First published 2010

Printed in the United Kingdom at the University Press, Cambridge

A catalogue record for this publication is available from the British Library

ISBN 978-0-521-76980-8 hardback

Contents

Part I: Context: Laying the foundation and the underpinnings of ESM

Part II: Strategic management: Formulation and implementation

Figures

Tables

Boxes

Abbreviations

AMD	Advanced Micro Devices
AOL	America Online
AT&T	American Telephone and Telegraph
B2B	Business to business
B2C	Business to customer
B/C	Benefit–cost
BCG	Boston Consulting Group
BOP	Bottom of the pyramid
BPR	Business process reengineering
BRIC	Brazil, Russia, India and China
BSR	Business for Social Responsibility
C2B	Customer to business
CD	Compact disc
CEO	Chief executive officer
CFC	Chlorofluorocarbons
CNN	Cable News Network
CSR	Corporate social responsibility
CUP	Cambridge University Press
DAD	Decide, announce, and defend
dad	Discuss, analyze, and decide
DOS	Disk operating system
ESL	Enterprise-wide strategic leadership
ESM	Enterprise-wide strategic management
EU	European Union
FMC	Ford Motor Company
HDI	Human development index
HP	Hewlett-Packard
GATT	General Agreements on Tariffs and Trade
GDP	Gross domestic product
GE	General Electric

GM	General Motors
GUI	Graphical user interface
IBM	International Business Machines
ICT	Information and communications technologies
IPD	Integrated product development
ISO	International Organization for Standardization
IT	Information technology
JV	Joint venture
KRA	Key result areas
LCA	Life-cycle assessment
LCD	Liquid crystal displays
M&A	Mergers and acquisitions
MIT	Massachusetts Institute of Technology
MNC	Multinational corporations
NAFTA	North American Free Trade Agreement
NCR	National Cash Register
NGO	Non-governmental organization
P&G	Procter & Gamble
PC	Personal computer
PPPUS$	Purchasing power parity in US dollars
R&D	Research and development
RCA	Radio Corporation of America
RoHS	Restrictions on hazardous substances
SBD	Sustainable business development
SBP	Strategic business planning
SBU	Strategic business unit
SD	Sustainable development
SEC	Securities and Exchange Commission
SME	Small and medium-sized enterprise
SMS	Strategic management system
SOA	Sarbanes-Oxley Act of 2002
SSA	Sub-Saharan Africa
SUV	Sports utility vehicle
SWOT	Strengths, weaknesses, opportunities, and threats
TPS	Toyota Production System
TQM	Total quality management
TV	Television
UN	United Nations
UNDP	United Nations Development Programme

UNEP	United Nations Environmental Programme
UPS	United Parcel Services
USPS	US Postal Services
USX	US Steel Corporation
UTC	United Technologies Corporation
VCR	Video cassette recorder
VOC	Volatile organic compounds
VoIP	Voice of Internet Protocol
WBCSD	World Business Council for Sustainable Development
WEEE	Waste from electrical and electronic equipment
WRI	World Resources Institute
WTO	World Trade Organization
WWII	World War II

Introduction

Businesses across the world are engaged in the relentless struggle to stay ahead of social, economic, environmental, technological, and market changes that seem to expand and accelerate as time moves forward. Business executives, strategic leaders, management professionals, and practitioners must confront the overwhelming challenges of exceeding the increasing demands and expectations of customers, stakeholders, shareholders, and other constituents, and deal with the growing complexities of the global business environment. Customers in the developed countries expect and demand customized products and services having high value, six-sigma quality, and superior performance that are affordable, reliable, and easy to use. Stakeholders want improved social, economic, and environmental outcomes from businesses and reductions in defects, burdens, and negative impacts. And, shareholders expect improved business performance, wealth creation, and sustainable success.

With globalization, increasing social, environmental, and regulatory mandates, complex economic forces, rapid technological developments, and the rising power of customers and stakeholders, the global business environment is more complicated, interdependent, and less predictable than just a decade ago. Today, customers and stakeholders have more power and influence than ever before because they have access to more information and data via the Internet and more leverage in their choices. However, these changes should not be viewed as negatives from a strategic perspective. On the contrary, they represent incredible opportunities for businesses to excel and achieve success, creating even more exciting opportunities and enhanced realities and results.

Strategic leadership and business management in the twenty-first century involve building solid foundations, creating innovative solutions, and making dramatic improvements across the whole spectrum of the business landscape and time horizon. Business success depends on having a holistic perspective on the business environment and creating an effective business enterprise with great solutions and solid relationships with customers, stakeholders, supply networks, producers and providers of complementary products and services, and all other contributors. Achieving sustainable success demands excellence from every perspective. Strategic leaders of today have to integrate their businesses internally and externally to ensure that all efforts are aligned and that the maximum performance and outcomes are realized. They cannot tolerate compromises, piecemeal approaches, or narrow perspectives.

Over the last few decades, large multinational corporations and small and medium-sized enterprises (SMEs) have become more adept at developing and commercializing new technologies and products, improving business operations and processes, and creating exciting marketing campaigns for inducing customers to buy their products and services. The business literature is replete with success stories like Intel, Microsoft, Wal-Mart, Apple Inc., Google, eBay, Toyota, Samsung and LG. Yet, despite all of the improvements, many businesses are struggling to maintain their market positions, financial performance, and enduring success. Many executives and strategic leaders are having difficulties adapting their businesses and strategic management systems to the changing business realities of the twenty-first century.

Too many business leaders concentrate on the inner workings of the organizations, their direct relationships with customers, suppliers, and distributors, and how to beat competitors. They are still thinking in terms of company-centric business concepts and approaches. While such thinking considers other entities such as governments, financial institutions, and the media, the connections and relationships are typically based on transactional linkages and imposed requirements (mandates) instead of having a comprehensive and inclusive strategic framework that considers all direct and indirect relationships, connections, and responsibilities.

The older, often obsolete strategic management approaches were based on twentieth-century realities, not the complexities and challenges of globalization and today's social, economic, and environmental realities. The business world has changed, but to a large extent, strategic management concepts and approaches have not kept pace with the new realities.

Most companies and SMEs still have management constructs, strategic management systems (SMSs), and organizational structures that are rooted in the past and are not in sync with the mandates, requirements, and expectations of the present, never mind the future. While managing change is difficult and necessitates ongoing strategic thinking and action, it also presents enormous opportunities for improving strategic and operational positions and performance. Higher levels of achievements can be realized by integrating the knowledge, competencies, capabilities, and resources of the entire business enterprise through strategic leadership, strategic direction, and value creation. While there are numerous reasons for the growing challenges associated with leading, managing, and developing large corporations, especially multinationals and SMEs, many of the main challenges and difficulties are related to the outmoded and ineffective management constructs used by strategic leaders for leading change in complex and dynamic business situations. Many of the traditional constructs and approaches focused on a narrow perspective and a relatively short time horizon.[1]

Most business situations have radically changed over the last three decades. Companies have dramatically expanded the scope of their product lines and served markets to diversify their businesses, improve their financial performance, and mitigate the inherent risks associated with technologies, products, processes, and operations. They have created more sophisticated operating systems and decentralized their organizational structures as well, moving from vertically integrated structures to more horizontal ones using the constructs of the management system and process management. While the strategic leaders of most businesses believe that they are making progress, many large companies and SMEs are unsuccessful in making enhancements, improvements, and developments that are significant enough to keep pace with the demands, expectations, and realities of the global business environment.

One of the main premises of this book is that many strategic leaders and their companies are using obsolete strategic management constructs – those that are unable to realize today's business opportunities and challenges resulting in poor solutions, inadequate outcomes, and inferior performance. The most important premise is that strategic leaders of businesses must adapt more innovative and holistic strategic management system(s) to achieve sustainable success.

Enterprise-wide Strategic Management: Achieving Sustainable Success through Leadership, Strategies, and Value Creation describes and explores how an "enterprise view" of the business environment, strong strategic management, and exceptional strategic leadership can create extraordinary business value and sustainable success. The "enterprise view" is a more comprehensive business framework that involves strategically connecting all of the driving and supporting forces in the business environment and the business enterprise with the strategic and operating management systems. An enterprise view involves more than just examining the direct production and consumption linkages; it requires strategic thinking about all of the linkages, relationships, actions, and inter-temporal effects of business strategies and operations and their causes and effects, especially those that have long-term impacts and consequences. For instance, an enterprise view of petroleum involves perspectives on exploration, refining, distribution, marketing, use, and depletion among numerous other considerations including increasing demand in the Pacific Rim and development of renewable energy sources. The quantity and quality of petroleum resources depend on existing reserves and the capabilities of the oil companies to explore, recover, and deploy additional resources from existing and new sources of petroleum. These factors also affect the rate of depletion of petroleum reserves. But, users rarely think about the implications of oil depletion because the effects are spatially upstream of their applications and the impacts are expected to be the most profound in the future. Moreover, the most significant concerns related to the use of petroleum products, like climate change or air pollution, are difficult to fully appreciate and understand, especially for those users who lack the knowledge to assess the impacts on the natural environment and the social world.

A modern company, whether a multinational or SME, is a complex business enterprise. It includes all of the internal management levels (the corporate, strategic business units, and operating systems) within the company and all of its external, direct, and indirect relationships with contributors and recipients. Some of the key relationships include the customers, stakeholders, supply networks, partners and allies, governments, and supporting and constraining entities that the business interfaces with directly and indirectly as it sustains its missions and achieves its vision and objectives for the future. These include suppliers of suppliers, customers of customers, logistical support entities, related industries, and those involved with end-of-life considerations. It also includes all of the critical external dimensions of the business environment that are affected by or involved in the company's strategies, action plans, and operations. All of the direct and indirect entities are the parties to the real world of business strategies, actions, transactions and outcomes. This broader perspective of business with all of its linkages is often referred to as an "extended enterprise."

To manage this extended enterprise with its broader scope and time horizons and to realize its full potential for creating and achieving sustainable solutions, extraordinary value creation, and outstanding business performance, strategic leaders must integrate the numerous disparate participants (the contributors to and recipients of the solutions) into an effective strategic management framework. This requires a new strategic management archetype, herein called enterprise-wide strategic management (ESM).

ESM involves defining, developing, and deploying a richer, more comprehensive strategic management framework that stretches from the origins of the raw materials and the supply of externally produced parts and components to the far-flung customers, stakeholders, and providers of end-of-life solutions along with all of the complementary providers of products and support services. Although ESM takes a strategic perspective of a company, an SME, or a large multinational corporation, especially ones with many strategic business units (SBUs), it mainly pertains to strategic management at the business unit or business enterprise level. In all cases the focus is on the SMS and its extended enterprise, the strategic leaders thereof, and all of the related contributors to and recipients of sustainable solutions and success. It includes the associated internal operating systems and the external value delivery system with all of the direct and virtual relationships with customers, stakeholders, supply networks, partnerships, alliances, and other entities in the value-producing networks. It involves strategically examining all inputs, outputs, and effects, assessing and managing the impacts and consequences of production and consumption, and linking all of the participants and activities in the extended enterprise from cradle to grave.

Traditional business and economic models focus on the relationships between buyers and sellers (customers and producers). Customers want to satisfy their needs and expectations. Producers want to design, produce, and market their products and services to derive revenues and profits. Market demand for existing products and services drives producers to seek cost-effective, market-related solutions that are competitive and profitable. Supply and demand determine price levels and production volumes. The quantities demanded are functions of the value created, the benefits obtained, and the prices paid.

These traditional (supply and demand) models usually concentrate on the primary considerations of capabilities, resources, products, distribution channels, and markets. Suppliers provide inputs to the producers who create and produce products that flow through distributors to customers. Customers buy and use the products during their useful life and are responsible for the applications, use, ownership, maintenance, and disposal. The producer's responsibilities are typically limited to production and sale, contractual transactions, and products liabilities. Note that there are many variations to the general theme. For example, Amazon.com sells its goods directly to customers using the Internet. Barnes and Noble sells through the Internet and retail stores. eBay provides an information technology (IT) system that allows clients to make exchanges that would be cost prohibitive without its system.

While this may be an oversimplification of complicated interactions, the underlying contention is that the main premise of many of the traditional management constructs (models) is to keep the perspectives simple. In attempting to reduce complexities, most such constructs only include the primary elements. The related approaches often examine the competitive landscape as the primary consideration rather than the primacy of market spaces and customers. Moreover, many strategic leaders tended to examine reality in terms of what was happening instead of exploring the possibilities of what should be happening or what might happen in the future. While strategic leaders explored conditions and trends in the business environment and markets, the focus was on the direct entities (competitors and customers) and the short-term implications. There were few attempts to determine whether the underlying management constructs and ways of strategic thinking were still relevant. While such concepts, constructs, and models were generally useful during the slow-paced realities of the early to mid twentieth century they have become less effective if not obsolete in the fast-paced world of the twenty-first century.

Today, the scope of business units and their SMSs, their operations and processes, actions and activities, flows of goods and services, information, and money must be more comprehensive and inclusive. They must also include all of the social, economic, environmental, political, technological, ethical, and market-related perspectives. Such views must include not only the primary considerations (products and services), but also the secondary effects such as the residuals of production and use (pollution, discards, and other waste streams) and broader effects, such as the long-term implications of social and environmental impacts. Social and environmental impacts are important considerations in determining the economic viability of products, services, and processes.

As a result of these driving forces, leading companies are transitioning their strategic management constructs and SMSs into more innovative, inclusive, and sophisticated frameworks that include the design and development processes, cradle-to-grave implications of inputs and outputs, supply and delivery considerations, the implications of consumption and application, and end-of-life considerations (reuse, refurbishment, recycling, and/or proper disposal of residuals). For instance, end-of-life considerations are becoming increasingly important considerations in the European Union (EU). The EU is aggressively developing legislative initiatives to address many of the end-of-life problems associated with product discards.[2] The new frameworks are based on the realities of the present and the expectations of the future.

Executives, strategic leaders, operational managers, and professionals must understand and manage the whole extended enterprise and not just the company and its strategic business units, operating systems, and functional areas. They must possess broad knowledge about every facet of the business environment and market spaces, including the underpinnings and relevant factors pertaining to the social/human world and the natural environment. They must be able to craft business strategies, manage the operations, lead change, and make effective decisions that improve the prospects of their business enterprises faster than competitors are improving theirs and ahead of the expectations of customers and stakeholders.

While the traditional strategic management focus has been on competition, markets, operations, and financial outcomes, today's business leaders must also focus on discovering and exploiting opportunities to create extraordinary value, achieve sustainable advantages, and ensure enduring (sustainable) success. They must think outside of the normal purviews of markets and customers and discover new opportunities in the broader social, economic, and environment underpinnings of the business world. This requires extraordinary leadership capabilities, outstanding management skills, exceptional competencies and knowledge, and innovative strategic thinking. Strategic leaders must have a mindset for accepting challenges, thinking more holistically, dealing with uncertainties, crafting outstanding strategies and solutions, and developing outstanding SMSs. Today's strategic leaders have to welcome complexities and hard work, and enjoy opportunities and challenges for creating value for everyone, building solid relationships with all of the essential entities and people, and achieving sustainable success.

Successful business leadership and superior strategic management focus on achieving outstanding business performance and financial results in both the short term and the long term and across the whole extended enterprise. The overarching goals are the creation of extraordinary value for shareholders of the company and everyone else involved in the extended enterprise and to sustain success over time. It is folly to maximize profits in the present and give the gains back through poor strategic performance in the future.

The concept of an extended enterprise is still in its infancy. The strategic management of the whole extended enterprise, ESM, is an evolving management construct. In many cases it is an informal system yet one that is gaining importance. For example, Mercedes' automobile-related business unit in Stuttgart, Germany has linked its IT systems with all of its suppliers and suppliers of suppliers seven tiers deep in the supply networks.[3] It has linked most of the upstream side of the value delivery system into a fully integrated supply network.

ESM provides a strategic management framework that includes all of the essential external and internal dimensions and elements and ensures that they are covered in the analyses of the business environment and the formulation and implementation of business strategies. It sets the stage and provides the means and mechanisms for a descriptive, analytical, and structural under-standing of the needs, expectations, requirements, and specifications of the business environment, the market spaces, and the extended enterprise and how to realize the opportunities and meet the challenges. It specifically involves crafting, selecting, and implementing the business strategies and action plans of the business unit whether an SBU, an SME, or a single line of business or company.

The focus of the book is on strategic management in the context of a defini-tive business or an SBU and how strategic leaders develop and execute their strategic roles and responsibilities and lead change. The emphasis is on how business unit leaders formulate and implement business strategies and action plans. Moreover, the overarching perspective is on achieving sustainable suc-cess through enterprise-wide strategic leadership (ESL) and value creation. SBUs are generally the business units of large corporations. For example, United Technologies Corporation (UTC) is a $30 billion multinational cor-poration with many semi-autonomous business units that have their own strategic leaders and SMSs. UTC's SBUs include Pratt & Whitney, Hamilton Sundstrand, Sikorsky Aircraft Carrier Corporation, Otis Elevator, and Chubb. Each SBU is responsible for formulating and implementing business strategies and action plans and achieving sustainable results.

A fully articulated ESM framework may take several decades to come to fruition. It represents the next wave in developing business strategies and action plans that reflect a more comprehensive view of the realities of the business world. ESM focuses on finding innovative solutions that create extraordinary value, exceeding customer and stakeholder needs and expec-tations, and achieving sustainable success in the future. The power of ESM lies in how strategic leaders think innovatively, contemplate possibilities, and invent new solutions that may not be highly profitable in the short term, yet are desirable and worthwhile in the long term. Such strategic leaders think in terms of what is necessary, desirable, and sustainable. They carve out their own unique perspective on leadership, strategies and value cre-ation instead of simply following the pack or the prevailing views. The num-ber of financial institutions that lost billions of dollars in the "sub-prime" mortgage debacle is a testament to the lack of wisdom in following rather than leading.

Plato discussed such outrageous ideas in the context of a dream of the perfect answer of which reality is an imperfect copy. In the same way, ESM is about what should or could be instead of what is. ESM focuses the aspirations of strategic leaders and their dreams about exciting opportunities, unrealized possibilities, and new business solutions as well as making dramatic improvements to the prevailing realities.

To get there, the dreamer (strategic leader) merely has to think about what could or should be done without limiting his or her thinking with existing constraints and realities. One of the most famous examples is John F. Kennedy's goal of going to the moon by the end of the 1960s. In William Manchester's book, *The Glory and the Dream: A Narrative History of America 1932–1972*, Manchester discusses President Kennedy's address to Congress on May 25, 1961 and the "urgent national needs" that the President identified. In that address, Kennedy made the following comment: "I believe that this nation should commit itself to achieving the goal, before the end of this decade is out, of landing a man on the moon and returning him safety to earth." Surely Kennedy realized that the US did not have the means to get to the moon in 1961. In reality, his address was intended to reinvigorate a sense of national pride and change the temper of the political debates at that time. Still, the idea of going to the moon might have been viewed as an impossible dream. The US did not have the rockets, the guidance systems, or the technology to land on the moon and return to Earth safely. Thousands of technologies, products, processes, and new capabilities would have to be developed to transform the idea into a new reality. Nevertheless, the dream was realized on July 26, 1969 when Neil Armstrong took "one small step for man and one giant leap for mankind."

For a growing number of global businesses, ESM can be the dream and the means, providing insights about managing today and ways for discovering the great promises of tomorrow. ESM has to be very clearly understood by everyone in the organization and the extended enterprise(s) based on fully articulated goals and strategies that are embraced by everyone – the dream of getting a man on the moon was something everyone could understand and get behind. It united people and gave them a sense of purpose and direction.

ESM necessitates business leaders with an entrepreneurial mindset – strategic leaders with the willingness and commitment to create great solutions, to develop the requisite means and mechanisms, to improve the systems and structures, to develop and exploit the opportunities, and to exceed expectations. It includes the traditional concepts of efficiency (doing more with less), effectiveness (doing the right things), and social and environmental consciousness (exceeding expectations and eliminating waste and harmful impacts) and also the broader management constructs of being inclusive, open, innovative, and sustainable. More efficient approaches reduce costs, save resources and money, and create opportunities, thereby mitigating risks and negative impacts. Enhanced effectiveness improves business performance and reduces problems and defects. Being socially and environmentally conscious also saves time and money by reducing resource utilization, lessening environmental impact, and making outcomes more valuable.

Whereas ESM builds upon traditional concepts, it also moves strategic thinking from the older paradigms of "supply and demand" and "production and consumption" into a new world of value creation, enterprise-wide strategic leadership, balanced and innovative solutions, enduring relationships, and sustainable success. ESM focuses on crafting and implementing powerful strategies and initiatives, the sustainability of investments and performance, and most importantly, the elimination of non-value added activities and effects, and the reduction of the related economic and environmental wastes. It focuses on creating value for the greater good and success of the business, and the primary and indirect contributors and recipients.

This book examines how strategic leaders can take better advantage of their opportunities by having a broader perspective of their business world. It discusses the principles, philosophies, perspectives, processes, and practices of ESM and how businesses and strategic leaders can create extraordinary value and exceed expectations using strategy formulation and implementation. It defines and explores the importance of creating and using more effective and innovative business frameworks for companies and SMEs in the twenty-first century. It examines the relationships of SBUs with their enterprise partners, customers, stakeholders, and constituencies. It offers insights into what leading companies are doing to create extraordinary value and how they provide benefits for their customers, shareholders, employees, stakeholders, and other constituents. It includes many examples of how leading businesses are integrating their business units with their enterprise partners.

The book includes practical and achievable ESM constructs and business strategies and action plans for leading change and achieving sustainable success. It avoids being prescriptive and instead explores the formulation and implementation of leading-edge management constructs and SMSs, and the creation, development, and deployment of business strategies, processes, and practices. Moreover, the perspectives may be viewed as the early stages of leading change that is expected to continue to evolve over the next several decades.

The book is divided into two parts:

Part I: Context: Laying the foundation and the underpinnings of ESM – Part I introduces ESM in relation to strategic management, the extended enterprise, management frameworks, strategic leadership, the business environment, market spaces, and value creation. It examines the underpinnings of strategic management and strategic leadership. It includes how to discover and exploit opportunities in the natural environment, the social/human world, the business environment, and market spaces. It explores the foundation upon which the extended enterprise is laid and the driving forces of change. The discussions also include the importance of principles, values, ethics, corporate governance and social responsibility.

Part II: Strategic management: Formulation and implementation – Part II includes the constructs of strategic management process, sustainable success, and roles and responsibilities of strategic leaders. The focus is on strategic management frameworks, SMSs, and the processes thereof. This includes formulating and implementing business strategies and action plans. The discussions include topics pertaining to strategic analysis, strategic formulation and implementation, and execution. It also includes discussions on risk assessment, risk mitigation, performance measurements, and action programs and initiatives. The concluding chapter reflects on the discussions through the book and provides concluding comments.

The history of business is full of stories of great companies that failed to keep pace with change or those that lacked the strategic leadership and management capabilities to sustain themselves. Unfortunately, in the long term, most companies struggle to survive and many, if not most, fail. It takes exceptional strategic leadership to continuously formulate, implement, and execute great business strategies and action plans as well as develop and deploy innovative technologies, products, and processes. Business is not just about maximizing profits or making money – it is also about being successful and spreading this success across the business landscape. Sustainable success is predicated on making others successful. For example, Intel's success with microprocessors has contributed to the success of people around the world. Intel is successful because it made people successful.

The discussions and suggestions in this book are based on what real companies have done and are doing, especially some of the leading-edge businesses. The trends are generally positive. Global companies are becoming more connected and integrated with their business environment and market spaces. Given the state-of-the-art strategic management theories and practices, this book represents the beginning of the dialogue on twenty-first-century strategic management constructs, models, methods, and techniques that focus on the realities of the present and the opportunities of the future. In general, strategic leaders are innovating, developing, improving, growing, and sustaining success, or they are moving toward oblivion.

The book is intended to enable strategic leaders, professionals, and practitioners to be more effective in leading their SBUs and organizations to create extraordinary value. It is especially intended for today's MBA students who will become tomorrow's business leaders.

NOTES

1 It can be assumed that perspectives also fit SMEs when the terms corporations and companies are used throughout the book.
2 The trend is toward mandating highly prescriptive "take back" requirements and systems.
3 The model focuses on supply systems management for the Mercedes-Benz production.

Part I

Context: Laying the foundation and the underpinnings of ESM

Enterprise-wide Strategic Management: Achieving Sustainable Success through Leadership, Strategies, and Value Creation presents a comprehensive, state-of-the-art framework for formulating, implementing, and executing business strategies and leading change in complex and challenging business environments. Enterprise-wide strategic management (ESM) focuses on creating value for everyone engaged in the enterprise and sustaining success over the long term. It is an exciting and inclusive strategic management construct that executives, strategic leaders, and business professionals can use for dealing with the multiplicity of driving forces, requirements, mandates, and expectations in the more complex world of the twenty-first century. As the rate of change in the business environment accelerates, business leaders across the world must become more knowledgeable, innovative, adaptive, and sophisticated. Most importantly, they have to embrace change and take advantage of the ever-present opportunities and challenges.

The extended enterprise and enterprise-wide strategic leadership (ESL) are relatively new management constructs in the vocabulary of contemporary strategic management. The concept of a business enterprise, also called the extended enterprise, includes the internal strategic business unit(s) (SBUs) and their value delivery systems linked with all of the value-added entities of the supply networks, related industries, partners, and all of the relationships with customers, stakeholders, and other constituents in the value networks. The term "extended enterprise" is an accurate reflection of what a business enterprise of today really is. The "extended enterprise" has the same connotation as a concept of a multiple-dimensional enterprise as presented in my book, *Product Innovation: Leading Change through Integrated Product Development*. The added descriptor "extended" is really unnecessary since the enterprise involves all of the direct and indirect participants, operations, processes, and activities. The notion of what an enterprise is has not changed; businesses have changed.

ESL involves leading change across the business environment and providing strategic leadership of the business unit(s) and their extended enterprise(s). Leading large companies and small and medium-sized enterprises (SME) require highly competent, innovative, selfless, and technologically sophisticated strategic leaders who have the vision, insight, imagination, and innovativeness to think broadly about opportunities and to create new landscapes for meeting the needs and dreams of all customers, stakeholders, shareholders, employees, and society. The depth and breadth of strategic leadership within an organization are two of the most important factors for achieving sustainable success.

Strategic leaders are ultimately responsible for everything from the foundation of the whole enterprise to its integration with the natural environment, social/human world, and business environment. This includes strategic management systems (SMSs) and their value chains and value systems, the strategies of business units, and the strategic actions across the enterprise.

Strategic management involves ensuring that the business unit and its enterprise(s) have the right perspectives and proper strategic direction for achieving success in the future. It includes transitioning and transforming the existing capabilities, resources, and knowledge into more powerful realities and creating the best strategies, systems, structures, and solutions necessary for leading change in today's complex world.

Part I includes the following chapters:
- Chapter 1: Enterprise-wide strategic management: Underpinnings and context
- Chapter 2: Strategic management: Historical aspects and contemporary perspectives
- Chapter 3: Enterprise-wide strategic leadership: Creating value and sustainable success
- Chapter 4: The business environment: A global perspective on leading change
- Chapter 5: Market spaces: The intersections of economic and business forces

Chapter 1 examines how ESM can be used by large companies and SMEs to reinvent their strategic management frameworks and to link the SMSs with the business environment and the real world in order to achieve long-term success. The chapter focuses on the underpinnings and context of ESM.

Chapter 2 discusses the historical aspects of strategic management and how strategic leaders make decisions. Strategizing focuses on making decisions today that affect the strategic direction and future success of the company. The chapter involves strategic decision making about creating, developing, and building sustainable positions that are dynamic in space and time. It also describes and evaluates various strategic management constructs.

Chapter 3 discusses ESL and sustainable success. It also examines the essential elements of strategic leadership and decision making, core capabilities and learning, the cultural aspects of organizations, and the constructs for leading and managing change.

Chapter 4 discusses the business environment and its related opportunities and challenges. The business environment is a dynamic reality of customers, stakeholders, the public, people in general, and all of the external forces impinging upon the corporation. It includes social, economic, political, ethical, technological, environmental, and market forces. The business environment also includes the external dimensions of markets, stakeholders, competition, related industries, supply networks, and the infrastructure that are directly linked to the corporation through its extended enterprise.

Chapter 5 examines markets, stakeholders, and the economic forces. Markets and customers are among the most important dimensions of business enterprises. Businesses are economic entities that clearly have to engage in some form of commercial activities to make money and sustain their well being. This includes developing economic solutions, making investments, covering expenses, and achieving positive returns. While there are many ways in which businesses can make money, including licensing technologies, renting property, and earning interest among numerous others, most businesses depend on the sale of goods and services to sustain their success. The exchange of goods and services for money can be characterized as market spaces where producers and customers have the opportunity to interact to achieve positive outcomes.

1 Enterprise-wide strategic management: Underpinnings and context

Introduction

The global business environment has changed dramatically over the last decade. This is due in large measure to globalization, the power of new technologies and products, the intensity of customer expectations for low-priced, high-quality products and services, the expansion of extreme competition, and the proliferation of information and data, especially via the Internet. While such changes provide new opportunities and challenges, they are making the global business environment more complex, interconnected, interdependent, and turbulent.

The business world is undergoing spectacular upheavals. To meet the new challenges, cutting-edge business organizations are transitioning into more sophisticated and integrated business enterprises that are more cost-effective, performance-oriented, competitive, profitable, and sustainable.

Over the last decade many large companies and small and medium-sized enterprises (SMEs) have merged and/or acquired competitors to achieve the size, strength, and position that they assume is necessary to succeed in a demanding world full of world-class competitors. Today's business entities run the gamut from powerful global giants of the developed countries to highly aggressive, fast-paced emerging companies in the developing countries who vie to be the business leaders of tomorrow. The business landscape is also characterized by the tens of thousands of SMEs and entrepreneurial companies across the world that are trying to expand their presence and positions by taking advantage of globalization and the interconnectedness of the business environment.

Enterprise-wide strategic management (ESM) involves establishing a holistic management framework for strategic thinking, strategic management, strategic planning, and high-level decision making for leading and managing change and integrating the full spectrum of the business reality from spatial and temporal perspectives. This includes strategic perspectives on natural environment, the social/human world, and the business environment with all of its social, economic, technological, environmental, market, and competitive considerations and implications. ESM also includes the strategic leadership, the strategic direction, strategic formulation and implementation, and governance of the company, the business units, and the value delivery systems associated with their operations and processes.

The chapter includes the following main topics:

- Understanding the global business context.
- Identifying the historical roots of the notion of an enterprise and discussing the foundation of the extended enterprise.
- Describing the overarching perspectives of ESM, strategic leadership, and value creation.
- Articulating the management framework for ESM and its linkages to the natural environment, social/human world, and the business environment.

An overview of business context

Today's business leaders realize that rapidity of change necessitates creating extraordinary value and achieving success for their businesses and customers, stakeholders, supply networks, supporting entities, and shareholders at speeds greater than the underlying rate of change in the business environment. The underlying business philosophy among the strategic leaders of leading companies is that a business organization must continuously innovate to stay ahead of the changes in the business environment. For example, Apple's iPhone is being replaced by new versions in little more than a year after its launch. A fundamental belief is that business organizations must make significant improvements and even radical developments in their strategic positions, value creation, organizational capabilities, and physical resources.

The consolidation of many of the global competitors in various industries and the rise of emerging companies in the Pacific Rim and elsewhere are related phenomena, yet may be viewed as opposing forces. Many of the large global corporations in the developed countries (especially in the US, European Union, and Japan) are attempting to reinvent themselves and to become more competitive through entrepreneurial thinking, visionary leadership, and strategic innovation. Simultaneously, emerging companies in the rapidly developing countries (especially in Brazil, Russia, India, and China, also known as BRIC) are taking advantage of the opportunities to provide raw materials, parts, components, selected goods and services, processes, and even end products to global corporations and larger SMEs in the developed countries. Many of these emerging companies seemingly have the wisdom and patience to acquire the know-how, experience, and requisite capabilities necessary to become powerful global leaders of the future. Currently, they are concentrating on becoming the giants in their home markets in the short term and then competing on the world stage in the long term. For example, Lenovo, a Chinese company, acquired IBM's personal computer business to gain the status of being China's prime producer of personal computers and to give it credibility in world markets. In the short term it is satisfied to be a key player; eventually, it wants to be the global leader.

Today, many large global companies, their business units, and/or operating systems are outsourcing a significant part of their processes and manufacturing requirements to become more cost-effective, productive, agile, and flexible in serving the established markets in the developed countries. They are seeking every avenue possible to improve their competitive positions, especially through outsourcing, reductions in product cost structures, and by avoiding large capital investments. They are also attempting to be less vulnerable to the technological, social, economic, and political changes that are reshaping their business environment on a daily basis. These approaches focus on being more successful in meeting the demands and expectations of customers, stakeholders, and shareholders in the short term while finding new opportunities for achievement in the long term. While the underlying strategic logic for such approaches appears to be fundamentally sound, being engrossed on outsourcing and cost reductions is troubling, since the results are often skewed toward making short-term improvements to the prevailing situation and not making dramatic developments for long-term success. Moreover, any short-term strategic advantages may be quickly lost as increases in the costs of logistics, wage escalations, currency re-evaluations, and new competitors erode the assumed improvements. Indeed, the rapid increases in petroleum prices in this decade has subverted the assumption that transportation costs are marginal considerations.

Moreover, strategic management thinking over the last few decades has focused mainly on the pursuit of continuous improvements and incremental innovations for enhancing business prospects and obtaining financial rewards. While the logic of continuous improvements and incremental innovations is sound and appropriate for managing the short term, in today's business world just making small improvements may actually result in just maintaining the status quo. If peers and competitors are also making the same incremental improvements, then everyone is improving at the same rate and none are gaining advantages. In such situations, strategic leaders believe they are making gains, but in reality they are just keeping pace with parity among the peers and competitors. Worse still, there are usually aggressive business leaders like those at Toyota who are capable of outpacing change, thus obtaining significant advantages over time. Toyota's success is predicated on creating more value, building excellent customer relationships, and ensuring that customers are successful. It provides good solutions that are based on an enterprise-wide value system.

The lessons learned over the last decade suggest that businesses and their strategic leaders have to develop a comprehensive understanding of the business realities as well as the future expectations. They must develop innovative management constructs, methods, and techniques to achieve successful outcomes and sustain success in the future. The business world is dynamic. For example, Yahoo! was a great success several years ago until Google entered with its powerful software. Now, Yahoo! is fighting for its survival as an independent company. Microsoft wanted to acquire it. While Microsoft was not successful in its first attempt, Yahoo! is not safe from such quests.

Strategic leaders cannot assume that a new opportunity like e-business or a phenomenon like outsourcing will automatically materialize into successful results. For instance, the 'dot.com' business successes and failures of the 1990s are vivid reminders that success depends on having a comprehensive and future-oriented business framework and the proper mindset for creating value. Success also depends on strategic leaders who have the vision, entrepreneurial spirit, willingness, and exceptional talents to lead strategic change. Strategic leaders must have a great sense of what is theoretically possible and an understanding of trends and future expectations, yet have the pragmatism to deal with the realities involved. For example, companies like General Motors (GM) and the Ford Motor Company (FMC) have many products that were designed under the assumption that fuel costs and climate change issues were not significant consumer considerations. However, over the last five years such issues have now become primary concerns.

Today's strategic leaders and business managers have to continually test their assumptions about the external business world. They have to thoroughly examine what they believe to be true, as well as what they think the risks and uncertainties are, especially those associated with making dramatic changes. Most importantly, they have to think beyond the mainstream and create multi-dimensional business frameworks that include critical aspects of the natural environment, social/human world, and the business environment. Such management constructs must be broad and inclusive of the forces of change. For instance, strategic leaders cannot assume that natural resources and raw materials like water and petroleum will always be readily available at reasonable prices or that they will be able to control the flow and use of such resources. Most importantly, they have to be sure that decisions made today will continue to be viable in the future.

Many of the most important business opportunities are often discovered during bleak times when strategic leaders and innovators explore the prevailing situations from new perspectives and envision what could be or should be instead of what is. For example, high crude oil prices make many of today's products and processes like automobiles and power plants more costly to operate and less attractive to buy and own. However, such conditions present opportunities for providers of alternate energy sources like wind farms, photovoltaic, biomass, and fuel cells to become more economical and desirable.

Conversely, many long-term problems are created during boom periods when strategic leaders focus on exploiting the short term and neglect the long-term implications of their decisions. For instance, many global companies are facing major business problems and expenses associated with the defects and impacts of their past or existing technologies, product lines, and/or business methods. Paying for recalls, addressing past product liabilities, and eliminating environmental impacts cost large sums of money. For instance, the remediation of a hazardous waste landfill is expensive and is of little value to future operations, yet expenditure in such situations is absolutely necessary due to regulatory mandates. Moreover, many companies in the US and elsewhere have huge unfunded pension and health care programs for retired employees that are costing them millions or billions of dollars. Large companies like GM, US Steel Corporation (USX), and United Airlines are experiencing financial difficulties and management constraints today due to deferred expenses and liabilities based on poor decision making in the past. While such obligations are clearly a social responsibility and a business commitment, the strategic implications of such expenses and liabilities have profound effects on the sustainable success, financial viability, and the ability of such corporations to survive. Clearly, it is better to address such issues in real terms on a real-time basis.

The concept of the company or corporation has changed significantly over the last several decades. The business enterprise has changed from the heady days of the vertically integrated corporation like GM and FMC of the 1950s and 1960s to those of today that are more dependent on the whole business enterprise. For example, Nike, Inc. is a market share leader in footwear and sports apparel, yet it primarily engages in product design and marketing activities. It depends heavily on hundreds of other companies around the world to actually produce the products that Nike sells to its customers. Nike is often cited as one of the best examples of a virtual enterprise, one that is linked with global suppliers in developing countries.

The modern company is no longer a self-sufficient entity that engages in business transactions using mostly its own resources and capabilities with only a few dependencies. On the contrary, it has become more and more dependent on external entities to fulfill the economic missions and achieve the desired outcomes. Based on the concept of the business enterprise, it follows that companies/corporations and their business units create their own business enterprises by their choices of customers, supply networks, partners, allies, related industries, and the like. Each business enterprise may be significantly different than those of its main competitors or industry participants.[1] A corporation/company may create specific relationships with strategic suppliers who manage entire functional requirements of the supply of materials, parts, components, and products. It may establish partnerships with key distributors to assure the flow of products to customers. For example, Dell Computer depends on FedEx and UPS to package Dell products and deliver them directly to customers. FedEx provides the inventory and logistical support services for many businesses that want to ensure that customers can take delivery of critical parts in one day. As companies outsource more and more of these functions, processes, and operations to vendors and partners, the business enterprise expands dramatically and managing the enterprise becomes a critical responsibility of strategic management. This means that strategic leaders have to think and strategize in terms of the whole business enterprise, not just their organization.

ESM involves a holistic view of a business that transforms last century's "supply and demand" strategic thinking into a more sophisticated strategic management framework based on enterprise-wide strategic leadership (ESL), strategic innovation, value creation, sustainable development, social responsibility, and other cutting-edge constructs for achieving sustainable success. ESM also involves openness, integrity, transparency, and accountability. ESM focuses on how strategic leaders and senior professionals create sustainable solutions that are based on the strategic perspective of the whole business enterprise and not just on the needs and expectations of producers and customers. The mindset of strategic leaders shifts from focusing on short-term financial rewards to more balanced perspectives that include making money, ensuring customer and stakeholder success, learning, promoting business development, encouraging ethical behaviors, mitigating risks, and eliminating negative impacts. Strategic leaders must embrace ESL.

ESL concentrates on the business environment and market spaces, not just on the competitive scene. It seeks to achieve success through the networks of partners, allies, and other contributors and by having an exciting vision for the future and a fully articulated strategic direction. It seeks to create extraordinary value and make people successful. But, extraordinary value is difficult to define and often depends on the context of the whole enterprise. It involves developing innovative technologies and products, satisfying customers and stakeholders, creating wealth for shareholders, and a myriad of other strategic goals.

Singular goals like profit maximization usually involve trade-offs that may result in short-term gains but often make the company and its business units less successful and more vulnerable in the long term. Maximizing short-term gains at the expense of long-term success is foolish; it often consumes valuable resources and capabilities in less than fully productive and rewarding outcomes. Moreover, maximizing profits, though easy to define in the short term, becomes more nebulous in the long term. Conversely, creating extraordinary value is hard to define in the short term, but can be become easier to understand in the long term through the growth, improvements, and sustainable development.

ESM advances a very healthy strategic balance by subordinating the notions of maximizing profits and money making as being subsets of the overarching goals of maximizing value creation and achieving sustainable success. And so, ESM involves linking people, data, information, technologies, products, processes, and decision making to solve social, economic, environmental, and business problems and challenges in ways that are in the best interest of all participants, customers, stakeholders, employees, and shareholders.

ESM requires senior management's commitment and dedication. Good intentions are not good enough. Strategic leaders must be authentic and committed to exceeding the expectations of shareholders, superiors, subordinates, customers, and other stakeholders. They must lead by example not just through dictates and commands. "Walking the talk" is critical if strategic leaders want operating managers and employees to create a more fruitful future. It takes exceptional strategic leaders to transform these broad goals into realities through an exciting vision, broad perspectives of the business environment, holistic philosophies, and balanced values and objectives. In fact, exceptional strategic leadership is one of the most important factors for achieving sustainable success.

The business enterprise and the extended enterprise

A brief historical perspective of the enterprise

The term "enterprise" has had many meanings over the last two centuries. At the beginning of the industrial revolution, it was synonymous with a business, a firm, or even a manufacturing plant. It was usually a self-contained business operation engaged in farming, mining, manufacturing, construction, or the production of wood and wood products. Most such businesses were family operations or closely held partnerships. They tended to be small and focused on commodity-type products. They were also dependent on suppliers of raw materials and the numerous intermediaries and agents in the long distribution channels that were required for getting the products to markets and customers.

According to business historian and scholar, Alfred Chandler, Jr., until the 1840s, enterprises remained small. Owners and/or operators had little difficulty managing their businesses.[2] The larger, more complicated enterprises were often owned and operated by the government, typically for the manufacture of military goods and hardware. In the US, the federal government's Springfield Armory became world famous in the 1850s when it developed the capability to manufacture interchangeable parts (and their associated products) and began producing guns in batches rather than one at a time. The "American System" of production dramatically improved production volumes and the economics of scale. While innovations such as improved steam engines and new manufacturing techniques made large production facilities possible, the majority of the enterprises in the US and Europe at the time were still relatively small and devoted to one or two products.

According to Chandler, in the 1840s and 1850s, the railroads became the first modern enterprises to employ networks of technological resources and organizational capabilities.[3] He suggested that earlier entities in private or public transportation businesses such as canals or turnpikes focused on a single endeavor like providing the right-of-way. Such enterprises were limited in scope and complexity. The railroads, on the other hand, were large, complex, and varied organizations that required extensive knowledge, managerial expertise, sophisticated technologies (steam engines, bridges, and telegraph), and huge investments of financial capital. They epitomized the notion of a modern enterprise in the nineteenth century. The critical requirements for their growth were administrative knowledge and the talent to manage the railroads and the complicated inter-company arrangements necessary for the efficient and safe transport of goods and people. For instance, effective railroad management and operations were highly dependent on the telegraph to provide information and keep the railroads on schedule and safe from collisions.

Railroads were more than just companies or single businesses. They were industrial enterprises that depended on land, labor, managerial capabilities, technologies, and inter-company transactions in order to function properly and achieve useful outcomes. Railroads required enormous amounts of land and raw materials (wood) for laying their tracks, building bridges, and constructing stations. They consumed vast quantities of natural resources from water to wood and later, coal. They also required trained workers and administrators to build the networks and operate the systems. The specialized managers and employees often worked at some distance from their homes. Tremendous capital, including real estate, buildings, equipment, and money, was needed to establish and sustain them.

The founders and initial owners of these enterprises usually did not have the requisite financial capital, so they needed external sources of financing. Thus, the stock corporation became a necessity to acquire the financial capital. Moreover, the railroads depended on many other enterprises such as telegraph companies like Western Union to provide communication and information to control schedules and the flow of goods, and provide information about emergencies. All of these external support mechanisms had to be integrated into the large operating systems that were the railroads. They also involved enormous sophistication in administrative and managerial capabilities of the leaders to manage the complexities of the entire enterprise. The railroad companies were truly the central ingredients of much larger enterprises that included everything necessary to make the systems work, including communications and logistics.

Thus, the concept of the enterprise expanded during the second half of the nineteenth century to include most large transportation, distribution, and manufacturing companies. The connotation included building an operating system using technology and trained labor, raising capital to finance the operations, growing the resource base of raw materials and manufacturing facilities, and distributing products to customers. While the railroads were the early leaders, manufacturing companies followed, borrowing technical and managerial capabilities and methods from the railroads and others.

Companies like the Singer Sewing Machine Company and the Pullman Company (railroad cars) were "integrated, multifunctional and often multinational enterprises that surpassed the railroads in size and in complexity and diversity of operations."[4] These large enterprises were the cutting-edge companies of the time that extended beyond the implied definition or earlier perspectives pertaining to limited liability corporations. They expanded their business implications to include having influence and direct effect on customers, suppliers, and employees. For instance, Singer had take-back systems for old sewing machines which it then redistributed to people in Latin America. Pullman organized housing and community support structures for its employees. Though both of these companies had strategic reasons for reaching beyond the traditional scope of businesses at the time and many actions and activities were controversial, Singer and Pullman operated as extended enterprises in the modern sense.

According to Chandler, the paradigm of mass production and mass distribution offered new opportunities for manufacturers to lower costs and increase productivity using more effective administration.[5] In *The Visible Hand: The Managerial Revolution in American Business*, Chandler discussed the importance of the effective administration of industrial enterprises during the last quarter of the nineteenth century. While there were many other forces that drove the creation of large enterprises, Chandler viewed the managerial roles and the contributions of the strategic leaders as pivotal.

The notion of an enterprise was used extensively during the late nineteenth and early twentieth century. Most of the large, product-producing companies at that time considered themselves to be industrial enterprises. They usually focused on production, but many of the larger companies were also dominant forces in selling products and in leading organizational change. They had the size, power, and the drive to become modern, complex, efficient, and administrative organizations with effective strategic leaders and administrators who planned and coordinated the activities that distinguished their corporation. In Chandler's book, *Strategy and Structure: Chapters in the History of the American Industrial Enterprise,* he defines the term industrial enterprise as follows:[6]

Used in a broad sense, it [enterprise] means a large private, profit-oriented business firm involved in the handling of goods in some or all of the successive processes from the procurement of the raw material to the sale to the ultimate customer. Transportation enterprises, utilities, or purely financial companies are not included in this study, while those firms concerned with marketing and with the extraction of raw materials as well as those dealing with processing or manufacturing do fall within this definition. An industrial enterprise is thus a subspecies of what Werner Sombart has described as capitalistic enterprise, which as "an independent economic organism is created over and above the individuals who constitute it. This entity appears then as the agent in each of these transactions and leads, as it were, a life of its own, which often exceeds in length that of its human members."[7]

While the notion of an industrial enterprise persisted through the post-World War II period, the rise of the large modern corporation (multinational) during the early part of the twentieth century had a profound effect on the connotation of the term, enterprise. The large enterprises became big businesses. Big business meant large corporations with huge operations and significant market shares, who were self-reliant and had few dependencies. USX epitomized this scenario. In 1901, the three largest steel producers in the US – Carnegie, Federal, and National Steel – merged to form US Steel under the control of J. P. Morgan. It became the world's first billion dollar corporation, capitalized at $1.4 billion. It was a vertically integrated corporation that "controlled" more than 60 percent of the steel business in the US. Moreover, it had vast reserves of iron ore, over 50,000 acres of coking-coal lands, natural gas and limestone properties, over 1,000 miles of railroads, and a fleet of 112 lake steamers and barges.[8] While the evolutionary process of acquiring and owning the resources of production and distribution unfolded over several decades, USX was one of the first corporations to become vertically integrated. It was self-sufficient in the essential ingredients of steel production and the distribution channels to its customers. USX had become a self-contained extended enterprise with the capital, land, equipment, resources, and people to control its own destiny.

The phenomena of mergers, acquisitions, consolidations, and vertical integration expanded during the first half of the twentieth century in the US and Europe. Automobile companies, in particular, grew through mergers and acquisitions and became the quintessential examples of vertically integrated organizations. In the US, GM and FMC evolved from entrepreneurial companies to large corporate entities that controlled most aspects of the supply, production, and distribution of automobiles within the domains of the corporation. Vertical integration involves the principal becoming more independent of external supply networks by performing a larger and larger share of the value-added in-house using the businesses' own operations and resources.

Henry Ford was the genius who understood that millions of automobiles could be sold to farmers and people living in rural areas if he could produce them cost-effectively and sell them at low prices (around $500). He realized that standardization, affordability, and reliability were the critical elements of the solution. His Model T (circa 1907 through 1927) became one of the most important solutions of the early twentieth century that drove much of the US economy during the 1920s. Ford believed that success depended on mass production, the control of resources and product specifications, and advantageous production costs. Ford integrated the fabrication and assembly of the Model T and controlled the fabrication of parts, the manufacture of steel and glass, and almost everything except the tires. FMC became one of the most vertically integrated companies in the world.

Like Ford, Alfred P. Sloan, Jr., CEO of GM from 1923 to 1946, recognized the enormous opportunities for selling automobiles to the masses if the cars were affordable.[9] He created an organizational structure and the administrative capability at GM to replicate Ford's cost-effective and affordable car and its mass production system. During the 1920s, Sloan integrated the means of production and created a more advanced low-cost car, the Chevrolet. He went beyond Ford's approach with the concept of creating "a car for every person and purpose."[10] This was the underlying concept of GM's structure of product divisions, Chevrolet, Pontiac, Oldsmobile, Buick, and Cadillac. Chevrolet was the product for the common person, while Cadillac was the car for the elites. But, the higher end cars were also desired by many people in the demographic chain who tried to garner sufficient disposable income or aspired to own an Oldsmobile or a Buick and eventually a Cadillac if they were so fortunate. Moreover, in 1923, Sloan created General Motors Acceptance Corporation to provide financial mechanisms for offering credit to customers. Sloan's innovation enhanced people's ability to buy a car since they did not have to pay cash. Sloan understood that the solution was more than just the product; it included all aspects of designing, producing, selling, buying, and owning the product as well.

However, Ford failed to continue to be innovative during the late 1920s. He refused to make changes and his beloved Model T became obsolete when strategic leaders at GM introduced their "closed coupled" cars that were superior to Ford's automobile and only slightly more expensive. Ford lost market share leadership to GM in 1927. FMC was able to survive the closing of its plants to develop the Model A, but it was never able to regain leadership in the affordable car category. GM's success in dominating automobile production and sales continued through the 1960s.[11] It was unrivaled until the Japanese and European car manufacturers made significant inroads in the US market during the 1970s.

During the mid twentieth century, internal business integration and organizational structure became the overarching management constructs and themes as many corporations followed the initiatives and actions of USX,

GM, and FMC. Many corporations became decentralized organizations of product-related divisions focusing on production, marketing, and finance. The divisions (business units) integrated their resources around the mission and objectives of the organization and were typically led by general managers.

The vertically integrated corporation slowly replaced the notion of an industrial enterprise. While the term industrial enterprise was still commonly used during the 1960s, as evidenced by Chandler's books, the concepts of the corporation and the industry usurped the meaning of an enterprise. An industry is a group of producers and marketers that provide common products, goods, services, and/or outputs (solutions) to markets and customers that have similar needs and expectations. It includes corporations that are providing similar products and/or services from an economic perspective and are, therefore, often viewed as competitors.

The vertically integrated corporation included most of the resources and capabilities to provide solutions for the marketplace. The corporation provided the innovations, resources, operations, and control mechanisms of the products and processes. Moreover, it assumed the risks and problem-solving requirements. Strategic leaders of such organizations concentrated on producing and marketing products and services and ensuring that the financial mechanisms were controlled and that financial performance met expectations.

The large corporation or "Big Business" as Peter Drucker suggested in his *Concept of the Corporation* became the focus of management constructs during the latter half of the twentieth century.[12] Large corporations became important economic and social forces. They were the sum of all of their businesses, usually defined as strategic business units, and the supporting functional aspects. They were legal entities created for perpetual life, a totality of strategies, operations, products, processes, and activities.

As global forces impacted large corporations, the concept of vertical integration gave way to a more horizontal perspective with suppliers and allies providing some of the inputs and value-added. During the early 1980s, Michael Porter, world-renowned management professor at Harvard Business School, developed the concepts of the value chain and the value system based on the fundamental changes occurring in the business world. These constructs dramatically shifted the mainstream management frameworks from a vertical organizational approach to a system approach with horizontal processes.[13] The value chain involves the "collection of activities [and processes] that are preformed to design, produce, market, deliver, and support its products."[14] The value chain includes the internal process necessary to satisfy customer

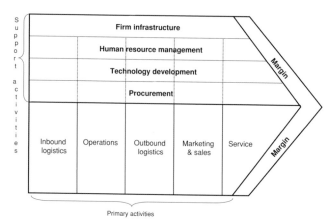

Figure 1.1   Porter's generic value chain

needs and expectations. Figure 1.1 shows Porter's generic value chain; the actual value chain of an organization depends on its scope of activities and its decisions about operations and outsourcing.[15]

Porter's generic value chain was instrumental in establishing process management as the main construct for managing the functional and operational aspects of the corporation, especially those of the business units. It linked the flow of activities within the operations and started the transition to a more holistic perspective on creating value within the firm based on process management using an integrated approach. Porter articulated the primary activities from the flow of materials and parts into the operations using inbound logistics to the actual in-house operations involving production and assembly of products or operational elements for services. He linked the marketing and sales efforts of the upstream elements of operations with the downstream aspects of services and customer support. Porter suggested that the successful integration and execution of the activities created margins and financial rewards. Success was based on the total flow of activities and information not just based on the separate contributions of functional areas.

One of Porter's greatest contributions was his construct of the "value system." The value system included the upstream value chains of suppliers and the downstream value chains of distributors and customers. The value system includes all of the interrelated entities that contribute to value creation and value delivery. They include all of the partnerships, alliances, supply networks, and customer and stakeholder relationships. The value system is a more inclusive view of the horizontal integration of the contributors and recipients of the solutions that create value. In this text, the term value delivery system is used in the context of the value system except it is more inclusive than Porter's value system. It includes all of the entities of the extended enterprise as well.

Most vertically integrated corporations started to shift toward value systems thinking during the 1980s. Global competition in many industries, especially the automobile industry, forced strategic leaders to reexamine their business strategies, processes, and methods as well as their organizational designs and structures. The demands for improved product quality, the pressures for cost reduction, the intensity of global competition, the needs for dramatic innovations, the changes in the social, economic, environmental, and technological dimensions, and the need for greater flexibility, taken together, demanded new ways of strategic thinking. The most important needs were for more creative strategies and more flexible organizational structures.

During the late 1980s, the concept of business process reengineering (BPR) became a leading management construct for making improvements, especially to systems and processes. The focus generally was on improving the quality and the performance of operations and products. Moreover, BPR sought to make radical improvements in how businesses created value and it drove changes from the bottom-up. While there were many advocates of BPR, Michael Hammer and James Champy were among the BPR leaders who advocated radical redesign of business processes, organizational structure, and culture. In *Reengineering the Corporation: A Manifesto for Business Revolution*, the authors discussed the need for radical improvements in organizational design, management thinking, and process flow.[16] The focus was supposed to be on process improvements for making operations more effective and in discovering best practices. However, many strategic leaders used BPR to reduce the layers of management in their organizational structure and to focus on obtaining competitive advantages. Middle management ranks were often the targets for reductions and in many situations the incumbents were usually moved aside, fired, or reduced in rank.

While the intent of BPR was to find best practices through benchmarking similar processes of world-class corporations and to make improvements at every level, the actual results for most companies were mixed. The great criticism was that many companies and their strategic leaders used BPR to justify downsizing their organization and cutting costs without achieving the targeted dramatic improvements in operations, quality, and performance. While BPR lost momentum by the mid-1990s, the transformation toward process management and the outsourcing of parts fabrication, tangential activities, and many support functions of large corporations reduced vertical integration and made many business units and their operations more dependent on supply networks and external entities. Indeed, BPR and other prevailing management constructs like core competencies, and competitive advantage of the 1980s and 1990s shifted organizational thinking from vertical integration to process management (horizontal) using extended external capabilities and resources for achieving outcomes and securing competitive advantages.

During the 1990s and the early part of the twenty-first century, Wall Street and shareholders drove senior management to concentrate on customer satisfaction, and the core competencies and strengths of the organization. These perspectives were reinforced by the management theories of Gary Hamel and C. K. Prahalad in their book, *Competing for the Future.*[17] Hamel and Prahalad suggested that core competencies, not business units, set the stage for strategizing and establishing direction, and organizing operations and activities. As strategic leaders followed their suggestions, focusing on core competencies evolved as one of the most important "generic defaults" for strategic decision making. Operations, processes, and activities that were determined to be core competencies were maintained and improved. Others that did not seemingly fit as core competencies were often outsourced. Outsourcing became a mainstream strategic initiative. While there were many variations on the theme and it is difficult to prove generalizations, business operations, especially manufacturing, became more reliant on external suppliers, partners, and support entities.

Competitive pressures on a global basis forced many companies to improve their effectiveness and reduce the manufacturing costs of their products. Business leaders were driven by improving their costs structures and their desire to improve gross margins, cash flow, and overall profit. Many of the initiatives had a sound strategic logic but they were implemented poorly based on the narrow criteria of making money. In many cases, strategic leaders missed the more profound perspectives to enhance strategic positions, improve their market standings, and the long-term prospects for being successful.

The story of outsourcing is complex and involves many variables. However, it is obvious that many large corporations have used or are using outsourcing as a key mechanism to improve their strategic positions in today's business environment. The literature is replete with examples. The question remains: Is simply outsourcing activities and operations a true strategic action that improves performance or is it a short-term tactic that provides short-term benefits at the expense of increasing long-term vulnerabilities?

Moreover, there are concerns about focusing too much on core competencies as well. One of the main concerns about relying too heavily on the concept of core competencies is that it tends to be a static view. Core competencies in the present may become irrelevant in the future or vice versa. Business units and their business enterprises have to continuously reexamine the required competencies and capabilities and acquire and develop new ones before they are required or update old ones to suit new requirements and conditions. For example, Kodak was a world leader in chemical-based photography. But, those competencies are less meaningful in a business world dominated by digital technologies, especially digital cameras and customer-based applications.

The business of today is one with ongoing changes and improvements. The strategic logic for making changes includes positioning for innovations, improving flexibility, reducing risks, concentrating internal capabilities and activities based on the inherent strengths of the organization, and augmenting weaknesses using the resources and capabilities of external entities. It is the never-ending quest for perfection through continuous improvements and developments, and strategic innovations. The underlying theoretical foundation is based on the perspective of achieving outstanding performance in the short term and building new capabilities, technologies, and products for the future.

Most businesses have disintegrated their vertical structures and today they much more depend on the resources, capabilities, and contributions of suppliers, distributors, logistical support providers, and others in the extended enterprise. These changes renew the notion that corporations are industrial enterprises with many external supporting entities that provide the means and mechanisms to create and deliver the most beneficial solutions. This expansion extends the concept of the business enterprise to include all of the key contributors on the front-end processes of the value delivery system as well as all of the entities necessary for fulfilling customer satisfaction on the back-end. The latter includes customers, stakeholders, and other constituencies. Thus, the business enterprise includes the company/corporation and its business units and all of the contributors to and recipients of the value creation and value delivery processes. It moves beyond the focus on core competencies and internal organizational structure. The view must include the core capabilities and their effectiveness for the whole enterprise and all of the interfaces and relationships between the entities and the individuals involved. It is a more complex and sophisticated structure that provides greater flexibility and enhanced capabilities to do more with lower investments and risks.

The notion of a business enterprise

Historically and in today's perspectives, the concept of a business enterprise has multiple connotations. In its simplest form, an enterprise is a single large innovative project with a scope that covers many business functions and sweeps across the entire business environment. A business enterprise is typically a self-contained business unit that is adapting new approaches or reinventing its mission or a new venture that focuses on a specific agenda. It has sufficient resources, capabilities, and strategic leadership to achieve its goals, and enjoys a modicum of independence and innovativeness. Clearly, starting a new business venture fits the definition. Today, a business enterprise may also be the entire company with all of its capabilities and resources along with those of its support entities, serving customers and stakeholders, and other beneficiaries. A business enterprise is generally a horizontal management system or value delivery system. It stretches across reality to include all of the dimensions, forces, and factors that affect and impact the business environment, the company, the leadership, and the decision-making processes.

A narrow perspective of an enterprise encompasses just those entities involved in undertaking innovative and untried initiatives that are based on new-to-the-world or highly innovative technologies, products, processes, and/or practices. This may be viewed as the entrepreneurial side of an enterprise and the management system thereof. It is often viewed from the perspective of the small company. The notion of enterprise also involves large companies or business units as they engage in significant developments, improvements, investments, and innovations, most of which affect the value delivery system and operating system. This is particularly the case with IT initiatives that focus on linking the company and the entities within the enterprise via operations management and information systems. Mercedes-Benz's supply system management is an example of a fully integrated IT system that links all of the suppliers seven deep in the supply chain.

The broader perspective of a business enterprise focuses on the business units of large corporations and the businesses of SMEs. The initiatives usually involve radical technological innovations, entrepreneurship, and/or even creating new business frameworks for reinventing the purpose, strategic logic, principles, and perspectives of the company or the business units. The underlying approach is to radically change value creation provided to external entities and shareholders, creating new knowledge, intellectual capital, and learning, and sustaining performance and success in the future.

The broader concept of a business enterprise today takes the form of the *extended enterprise* that includes all of the appropriate and necessary external relationships that are part of the value delivery system and are required to provide sustainable solutions for customers, stakeholders, and other constituencies. An extended enterprise uses inter-company relationships to create and deliver solutions and achieve success. The perspective is based on the realization that large companies as well as SMEs are dependent on a myriad of support entities or systems including suppliers, distributors, technology providers, logistics, and external infrastructure to name a few. It involves broader views than Porter's value system or just examining the participants in the industry.

An industry is a relatively narrow perspective that understandably focuses on what similar companies are producing and selling. Industry participants (competitors) typically provide an array of similar products that enhances the choices for customers but they often fail to provide the solutions desired. For instance, today's automobiles are a vast collection of hardware and software that include steel, rubber, electronics, computers, programs, navigation systems, and safety devices. Yet, most of the competitive forms of automobiles in a market segment are very similar to each other that fail to offer significant alternatives in terms of fuel efficiency, pollution control, and affordability. Many people really want devices that get 100 miles to the gallon and zero emissions among other requirements.

An extended enterprise, in contrast, includes resources and capabilities that vary greatly from those of the traditional industry participants and include inputs, transactions, and outputs from many industries, complementors, and other contributors. In addition, the extended enterprise includes virtual players who provide direct or indirect contributions and often function independently of the prime activities of the company or its business units. For instance, eBay has achieved phenomenal success because it has millions of individuals who use its system to buy and sell products or even to create their own businesses. eBay depends on these relationships even though most of them are temporal and tangential to the strategic management of the company. eBay's extended enterprise is unique and enhances its solutions. The strategic leaders of an extended enterprise embrace change as opportunities and endeavor to create uniqueness and provide the best customer-driven solutions.

While in the traditional sense an enterprise is a project, venture, or business organization, it also connotes participation in any undertaking for making improvements and radical developments. In the modern sense, a business is an ongoing venture that is continuously being changed, developed, and improved. It has informational, transactional, physical, virtual, and intellectual connections with its supply networks, customers, stakeholders, related industries and infrastructures. It involves broad participation of many entities across space and time. It is an ever-evolving physical and managerial construct for understanding, managing, and changing the prospects of the company and its relationships.

The twenty-first-century framework of the extended enterprise

In *Leading the Revolution*, Gary Hamel describes the future of strategic management as the "age of revolution." He suggests that the most significant opportunities and challenges for change exist at the higher levels of the corporation:[18]

Industry revolutionaries take the entire business concept, rather than a product or service, as the starting point for innovation. Revolutionaries recognize that competition is no longer between products and services, it's between competing business concepts.

Hamel's insights provide a solid foundation for thinking about creating new business frameworks and management constructs that embody inclusiveness, connectedness, responsiveness, innovativeness, leanness, effectiveness, productiveness, cleanness, and openness. Today, and in the future, businesses compete on the basis of their extended enterprise and all of the strategic resources and core capabilities of the entities within that enterprise. The intellectual capital and core competencies of the whole define the capabilities, strengths, and advantages. Hamel maintains that business concept innovation is a critical strategic management role and responsibility. Business concept innovation involves redefining the mission and purpose of the business and creating more effective and sustainable business frameworks and management constructs.

Extended enterprise-wide thinking, ESM, and ESL are leading-edge business concepts and management constructs. One of the most important strategic challenges of the twenty-first century is to invent improved strategic management frameworks that reflect the realities of the business world and the significant changes that have occurred in recent times. The business environment has changed dramatically due to phenomena like globalization and the Internet yet many corporations/companies and business units continue to follow their old paradigms.

Competition is more intense, and customers and stakeholders are more demanding. Product life-cycles are declining. Technological innovations are more pervasive and have created powerful new technologies that are changing industries and the world. As discussed, digital camera technologies have wiped out Kodak's huge strategic advantages in film-based photography and have introduced cleaner and more effective product forms for customers.

Customers and stakeholders expect and demand dramatically improved products with more benefits, lower costs, and fewer defects and burdens. They seemingly want perfection. Additionally, outsourcing is more prevalent. Many large companies are making strategic determinations about what operations, processes, and activities they should perform and what to have others do.

The general strategic thinking still prevalent at many large companies and SMEs is that strategic leadership and the organization should focus on areas where they enjoy competitive advantages and outsource everything else. However, there are many concerns about such strategic thinking. Strategic leaders have to make sure that they are optimizing their systems and the effectiveness of their operations and processes. Businesses need to be cost-effective which may favor outsourcing, especially to low-cost countries, yet strategic leaders have to protect their knowledge and ensure that proprietary information and know-how are closely held within the organization. The strategic management framework has to provide broad perspectives as well as the means and mechanisms for understanding the new realities and for formulating and implementing strategies and initiatives for creating extraordinary value and outperforming competing enterprises.

In the book *Lean Enterprise Value,* members of MIT's Lean Aerospace Initiative provide an innovative and inclusive definition of an enterprise:[19]

The *enterprise* perspective we bring makes it possible to see entire "value systems" as well as the interconnected levels of activity that reach across national and international boundaries. That perspective stands in sharp contrast to "lean" as narrow change efforts in only one part of an organization, such as manufacturing or supply network.

Their view of enterprise includes three enterprise levels: program, multi-program, and national/international, reflecting a view of the product, the business unit, and the whole business environment, respectively. The critical and dramatically changed views of an enterprise are articulated in the following:[20]

Remember, "enterprise" is contextual. In its simplest form, a business enterprise could consist of a single division or business unit of a firm . . . The unit might produce an entire product, portion of a product, or contribute to multiple units . . .

It is unusual to extend the concept of enterprise beyond the multi-program level, but we find it helpful to do so as we address the challenges aerospace enterprises face on the journey to lean. In our context, the collection of all entities that contribute to the creation and use of aerospace products, systems or services can be seen as national or international enterprises...

For each of these three enterprise levels, a distinction exists between what we term the core and the extended enterprise. The core enterprise consists of entities tightly integrated through direct or partnering relationships. Less tightly coupled customers, suppliers, government agencies encompass the extended enterprise – all of the entities along an organization's value chain, from its customer's customers to its supplier's suppliers, that are involved with the design, development, manufacture, certification, distribution, and support of a product or family of products.

The concepts of the core enterprise and extended enterprise were developed as a means to define, understand, and link the e-commerce, e-business, and IT initiatives of the 1990s. Operational areas and the need to integrate processes from cradle to grave drove these initiatives. They focused on the informational and transactional flows. The definitions of core and extended enterprises are critical to the discussions in this book and are directly related to the constructs of ESM and ESL. In simple terms, the core enterprise includes the corporation and its primary participants, and the extended enterprise includes all of the direct and indirect relationships (second, third tiers, and beyond) that are embedded within the complex nature of business today.

Overarching perspectives of ESM

Philosophical perspectives and underpinnings

The philosophical perspectives of ESM derive from strategic thinking and leadership about integrating the extended enterprise, creating new opportunities, developing innovative solutions, maximizing value creation, and investing into the future. ESM is not about "winning" the competitive battles and maximizing short-term profits, but succeeding across space and time and providing the best possible solutions that are socially responsible, economically sound, and environmentally compatible. It involves ensuring that contributing entities, partners, employees, and stakeholders are like-minded and are properly compensated for their efforts and intellectual considerations. While many business leaders have adapted the perspective of "winning" as articulated most vociferously by Jack Welch in his book, *Winning*, the philosophical underpinnings of ESM articulate a higher level of strategic thinking that focuses on succeeding and sustaining success instead of just "winning."[21]

Winning is often a zero-sum game; the winner gets the rewards, and the loser is vanquished. It is critical to recognize that business is not about winning at all costs; it is not intended to be a win-lose situation. ESM is about achieving sustainable success.

As an aside, sport is about winning and not winning. People expect that sports teams engaged in games or matches will either emerge victoriously or suffer the pangs of defeat. Everyone at the beginning of the game or match knows one team will win and one team will lose in most situations. Businesses on the other hand are not engaged in zero-sum games. Business is about succeeding on an ongoing basis, making participants successful, and supporting and rewarding the efforts of those who contribute to success.

Moreover, business is a social construct about serving and satisfying people. Outstanding business leaders and great companies create successful management systems and structures based on cooperation and collaboration with many entities and partners, not just based on their own assets and organizational capabilities. For example, it can be argued that Apple Inc.'s closed architecture restricted the market's ability to exploit opportunities in personal computers (PCs) in the 1970s. Therefore, IBM and subsequent IBM-clone manufacturers were able to capture strategic advantages by having more powerful networks and exploit the broader opportunities because there were many more entities that gained from the more open processes. Likewise, Sony had seemingly technological and commercial advantages with its Betamax videocassette recorder technology in the early 1980s, but it was unable to achieve long-term success because competitors and customers wanted a more open structure with more options and lower prices. Business people in the industry were concerned that Sony would dominate the opportunities and keep them out; they wanted to avoid a Sony wins, others lose scenario. Most such examples involve complicated phenomena and outcomes are usually not just based on a single factor. However, it is apparent that the more people who have opportunities to gain from the economic and social activities of an organization, the more likely such approaches will be favored over the alternate approaches. From a different view, think about Intel's success over the last several decades and the large numbers of businesses and people who have shared in the success.

While there are ongoing debates about the purposes and strategic objectives of large companies and SMEs, business enterprises are really people-centric entities. They have explicit and implicit duties to create wealth for shareholders, provide benefits for customers and stakeholders, take good care of their employees, and enhance the viability of the whole business environment to the extent they can. Business is about broad-based succeeding, not narrow perspectives like winner takes all.

The philosophical underpinnings of ESM is based on the recognition that the business environment has changed dramatically over the last decade and that many companies and SMEs and their strategic management frameworks, management constructs, and methods have not evolved sufficiently to meet the demands and expectations of the real world. Many business leaders continue to focus too much on the internal aspects of their businesses and the financial objectives rather than on the external needs and expectations and the creation of extraordinary value and enduring success. For instance, many strategic leaders still focus on how to exploit their existing core competencies, resources, and assets as primary means to success. Rather than first determining that strategies and capabilities should be based on external context and on an assessment of the business environment and future expectations, many strategic leaders concentrate on their internal strengths and competencies. They still measure success based on return on investment or shareholder equity rather than on a more balanced perspective of external objectives of customers and stakeholders, on enhancing internal knowledge, learning, and future capabilities, and on achieving business objectives and financial rewards. From an ESM perspective, strategic leaders should also evaluate their contributions to the improvements in the quality of life, the success of their customers and partners, and the creation and distribution of wealth around the world. While the latter is more complex and more difficult to measure, the broader perspectives offer opportunities to create more balanced and enduring outcomes.

Historically, many strategic leaders thought in terms of the limits of their responsibilities and actions rather than expanding the scope of their business frameworks to be more inclusive and responsive to all of the entities and constituencies involved in their businesses. Such strategic thinking focused on what the company had to do instead of what it should do. While the prevailing philosophical perspectives of keeping things simple and narrowly focused seem sound, such beliefs are often inconsistent with the complexities and challenges of a global and fast-paced business world. Managing complexity is both an essential requirement in today's more complex business world and a source of sustainable advantage for those who are capable, willing, and committed. For example, Wal-Mart has outperformed its competitors in the US for more than two decades because it used an integrated system for managing all of the flows of goods, transactions, information, and relationships with suppliers and customers. Its success can be attributed to its integration of the whole business enterprise, the power of its strategic and operating management systems, and its willingness to assume responsibilities for its strategic actions and business operations.[22] While there are many detractors of Wal-Mart today, historically its broader perspectives of the social, economic, and business environments gave it a good understanding of what the company had to do. During its formative years, especially during the strategic leadership of Sam Walton, Wal-Mart had to develop most of the capabilities necessary to assure the success of its expanding operating system of its retail stores and distribution outlets because it had an isolated location in Bentonville, Arkansas. The limitations of the support industries in that region of the US, which were initially a big problem, later proved to be a huge benefit to Wal-Mart. Executives and strategic leaders at Wal-Mart recognized that they had to expand their capabilities if it was going to be successful. Ultimately, a limitation became one of Wal-Mart's great strengths. It developed a holistic strategic management framework that exploited the contributions of supply networks, the logistical support entities, and its own operating systems to meet the needs and expectations of customers. Wal-Mart realized that everything was important and that strategic advantages are achieved through integrating the systems and doing everything as well as possible. The whole is greater than the sum of the parts.[23]

ESM focuses on making dramatic changes, improvements, and developments to the underlying foundation of the business through strategic innovation. Gary Hamel in his book, *Leading the Revolution,* suggests that business concept innovation is the realm of strategic management that includes the whole business, not just technologies or products.[24] Hamel defined business concept innovation:[25]

Business concept innovation is the capacity to imagine dramatically different business concepts or dramatically new ways of differentiating existing business concepts. Business concept innovation is thus the key to creating new wealth. Competition within a broad domain . . . takes place not between products or companies but between business models.

New business models can render old business models obsolete . . . More often, new business models don't destroy old models they just siphon off customer demand, slowly deflating the profit potential of the old business model . . . The goal of business concept innovation is to introduce more strategic variety into an industry or competitive domain.

New or dramatically improved management constructs focus on radically changing strategic positions and ways of conducting business. This involves investing in inventing a more sustainable future and transforming the existing strategies, operations, processes, and practices into value-added approaches that enrich the organization and its business enterprise. Table 1.1 identifies the underpinnings of ESM.

Table 1.1 The philosophical underpinnings of ESM

Element	Underpinnings
Value creation	Value is the overarching perspective. People want value and solutions, not products and services. They want the maximum benefits and the fewest defects and burdens possible.
Inclusiveness	The strategic management framework should include all of the critical entities of the external world from the natural environment and the social/human world to the business environment and extended enterprise. This includes the integration of the internal strategic and operating systems with their external partners, allies, supply networks, customers, stakeholders, related industries, infrastructure, and other support relationships.
Connectedness	The management systems have to be connected to all of the external entities in the extended enterprise, and those connections should be linked to each other at all of the appropriate levels. Businesses depend on people for success; therefore, connectedness involves building enduring relationships with all of the external and internal participants from customers to suppliers and from the bottom to the top.
Responsiveness	Strategic leaders must take responsibility for their actions and ensure that external needs, requirements, mandates, and expectations are fulfilled. Outcomes must bring satisfaction, success, and rewards to all of the participants. Such rewards include tangible aspects (money, value, products, promotion, etc.) and intangible aspects (status, prestige, reduction in risks, etc.) as appropriate.
Innovativeness	The leadership and people within the organization must assess and understand the business environment and market spaces and create innovative management constructs and new solutions. This is achieved through new creations of systems, technologies, products, processes, and practices that enrich the future and create more with less. Such innovations include new business concepts, management constructs, and approaches for creating sustainable solutions.
Effectiveness	Effectiveness involves selecting the right management systems, leadership methods, business strategies, innovation programs, and processes to investigate, analyze, and implement change. It includes allocating the proper resources to achieve the desired results and inspiring people to obtain sustainable success.
Productiveness	The organization must be able to carry out its mission and meet objectives productively using only the resources and capabilities that are commensurate with the requirements and balanced with respect to the outcomes.
Leanness	Management and the organization must focus on value-added strategies, systems, operations, products, and processes that efficiently use resources, money, and time to generate long-term value and minimize economic, social, and environmental waste. Lean involves using resources wisely and effectively.
Cleanness	Businesses must provide solutions that are inherently positive, minimizing wastes and impacts on the business environment. All products and processes should be based on the best available technologies to reduce or eliminate wastes and impacts.
Openness	Strategic leaders must be open and honest in all of their relationships and ensure that they employ best policies, processes, and practices. Company philosophies and principles must build trust, integrity, and awareness across the extended enterprise. They must provide assurances to the stakeholders and society through reporting mechanisms and communications that the strategic leaders and their lieutenants are fulfilling their social, economic, and environmental responsibilities. Non-confidential information and data must be shared with all constituencies to ensure that plans, actions, and outcomes have peer review and are generally acceptable both internally and externally.

With ESM, the strategic focus is on value creation, maximizing positive aspects of valued-added strategies, operations, and activities and minimizing if not eliminating the non-productive and destructive ones. Fundamentally, ESM is about using capabilities and resources efficiently and effectively so that the organization can realize gains and rewards in the near term, make new investments for the future, and create the necessary transformations to a richer reality. ESM depends on strategic leadership for integrating all of the entities in the extended enterprise and leading change by creating innovative ways for improving the underpinnings of the business and its extended enterprise, and developing new solutions through innovative technologies, products, and processes.

These underpinnings are the springboard for contemplating and articulating the future and the strategic management framework used for strategic decision making. The framework should be inclusive and have both extensive breadth and depth. The breadth involves all direct and indirect entities that participate in the value-added activities over time. The depth involves the integration of the organization from the top to the bottom and from the beginning to the end of the extended enterprise.

Connectedness means linking all entities and establishing relationships with the principals and main players of each organization. It involves ensuring that there are linkages with and between all of the contributors and recipients. Responsiveness is the call to action. It transforms the strategic management framework into a dynamic construct that continues to develop and improve over time. It means providing solutions when and where they are required. Innovativeness involves seeking opportunities to develop, improve, expand, and sustain the businesses and the extended enterprises. It involves creating new means and mechanisms to transform the old into the new. It requires creativity and an entrepreneurial mindset. Effectiveness simply means having the best strategies, solutions, and systems and implementing the most appropriate strategic actions. It involves doing the right things, and doing them well. Productiveness means being efficient in creating solutions and matching those solutions to the needs and expectations. Leanness means achieving the best performance and results with the fewest resources and least waste possible. Cleanness means avoiding the creation of negative impacts and their consequences. Impacts detract from value creation and, in many cases, shift the burdens of production and consumption to society. Openness demands honesty, integrity, ethics, social responsibility, and fairness. It implies that everything pertinent to outside observers is obvious and clear, that nothing is concealed or obfuscated, and that business leaders behave and operate as if everything they decide and do is being made public. Simply put, frankness and truthfulness abound. Moreover, openness means taking proactive steps and actions to provide disclosures to the public on relevant non-confidential information and data including positive and negative aspects of the business and the enterprise.

These philosophical underpinnings guide strategic leaders in their decision-making processes, providing a sense of what's right, what ought to be done, and how to behave properly. The philosophical underpinnings outlined above lay the foundation for the vision, objectives, strategies, and behaviors and determine how strategic leaders, professionals, and practitioners within the strategic and operating management systems should respond to situations. They are intended to provide the basis for appropriate, balanced, and advantageous decision making.

New ways of thinking strategically

Today, strategic management is evolving from simple management constructs that focus on the business unit and its value systems to more elegant constructs that examine the global business environment, the extended enterprise, and the implications, impacts, and consequences of business decisions. Some of the more profound management constructs include the notion of the enterprise-wide strategic leadership, value creation, and the concept of the "balanced scorecard."

Enterprise-wide strategic leaders are the pivotal individuals for leading corporate and business unit change. They are responsible for integrating the organization and the extended enterprise into a cohesive force that creates exciting opportunities and achieves sustainable success. Success depends heavily on ESL to guide, encourage, and inspire people. ESL creates an atmosphere in which people are empowered to translate resources into outcomes that exceed expectations in the most efficient and effective way possible.

To do so, strategic leaders must become the architects of change and the masters of inter-disciplinary and inter-company innovations, initiatives, programs, and actions. Dynamic strategic leaders have to be able to orchestrate the design and development of new paradigms for proactively inventing the future. They are responsible for setting the strategic direction, determining the principles and policies, establishing the values, and for providing governance, reporting, and guidance for everything related to the company and its business units and their extended enterprises. Moreover, strategic leaders have the overall responsibility for ensuring that the whole company, the business units and their extended enterprises meet their objectives, performance criteria, and social and economic responsibilities. They must become enterprise leaders who integrate the whole extended enterprise into an effective and successful system.

For more than a century, the economic underpinnings of capitalism and the overarching objective of profit-oriented businesses have been to maximize profits and shareholder wealth. While there is an implicit sensibility to this concept, such thinking has fundamental flaws from a strategic perspective. Firstly, it is difficult to define exactly what maximizing profits means and how to achieve it in the long term. It is relatively easy to suggest that increasing revenues and decreasing costs will increase profits. However, the business world is dynamic, and the interrelationships are complex. For instance, increasing prices to improve profits in the short term may cause customer backlash, reducing customer loyalty and decreasing market share in the long term. Secondly, shifting certain costs into future liabilities only improves the financial picture for a relatively short period of time.

The renaissance of economic thinking involves value creation and value maximization. It is value that drives the economics of supply and demand. Customers and stakeholders seek solutions that exceed their needs and expectations. Supply networks and producers also seek value creation in terms of their own improvements, growth, and financial success. Businesses that deliver extraordinary value are generally rewarded by the loyalty of customers, the knowledge and learning gained through investments and experiences, the ongoing growth of their businesses, and positive long-term financial performance. Profits are important, and cash flow is deemed to be even more critical. However, they are usually the results of effective strategies and well-tuned management systems that convert inputs into outputs and create value and wealth. Profits are derivatives of effective strategies, operations, and outcomes, not strategic targets that can be selected.

From a strategic perspective, improving value across the extended enterprise and enhancing the market acceptance of solutions and the value delivery systems are critical factors for achieving balanced and sustainable outcomes. Over the last decade, Robert Kaplan and David Norton have advocated management constructs that focus on balanced outcomes for all customers, stakeholders, suppliers, employees, shareholders, and others. According to Kaplan and Norton, an organization must use what they call a "balanced scorecard" when making decisions.[26] They suggest that business organizations balance their strategies and objectives by including in them financial considerations, customer satisfaction, organizational learning, and internal business improvement.

ESM incorporates "balance scorecard" thinking. Businesses must build all of the balanced scorecard factors into every product and service, every process, every activity, and every solution. This perspective allows businesses to solve problems and create sustainable advantages through reduced impacts and costs, increased benefits, improved margins and brand images, and improved market positions.

ESL is ultimately responsible for creating new business frameworks and constructs and for leading change. In a dynamic and complex world, improvements, developments, investments, growth, and learning are essential for staying ahead of change. Resting on past successes is a prescription for disaster.

The imperative of value creation

Value creation includes enhancing the positives and eliminating the negatives. The positives are the value-added primary effects and outcomes that support the enterprise. They are the primary effects that are positive benefits provided by the extended enterprise through the technologies, products, and services of the solutions. The imperative of value creation is to maximize the primary effects and reduce the non-value-adding ones. Primary effects are directly related to determining, developing and implementing the present and future objectives, strategies, and positions that are necessary for innovative, responsive, effective, productive, and sustainable solutions. There are three main categories of primary effects: developments and investments in a better and more sustainable future; the transformations and transitions of the business framework and strategic management systems to achieve significant advancements through valued-added strategies, systems, networks, processes, and practices; and the operational activities required to deliver the solutions to the market spaces.

Table 1.2 provides examples of primary and secondary effects. The former add value and the latter do not. Moreover, the latter often detract from value creation. Many of the listed effects are discussed throughout the book.

The first two categories of the primary effects involve investing in the future of the businesses and fulfilling the implicit and explicit intent of the vision and strategic direction. They involve creating the future. Investments and developments focus on creating knowledge and capabilities, creating new

Table 1.2 Examples of primary and secondary effects

Primary effects (value-added)

Investments/developments

Creating new businesses	Building production facilities
Inventing new technologies	Creating an enterprise
Developing new products	Establishing strategic management systems
Acquiring intellectual property	Developing leaders and people
Acquiring other companies	Building core competencies
Building information system	Acquiring new capabilities

Transformations/transitions

Leading change	Crafting solutions
Selecting business strategies	Establishing new paradigms
Determining policies and ethics	Learning new knowledge
Improving the business framework	Structuring value networks
Creating new processes	Creating alliances and partners
Managing innovations	Enhancing relationships

Operational activities

Satisfying customers and stakeholders	Supporting cash flow
Improving process capability	Selecting best practices
Selecting markets to serve	Enhancing quality
Providing products/service	Building core capabilities
Selecting supply networks	Training and rewarding people
Building relationships	Controlling operations
Reporting performance openly	Evaluating performance
Protecting society	Protecting employees
Providing information	Protecting assets
Ensuring compliance	Dealing with competition

Secondary effects (non-value-added)

Avoidable expenditures

Buying non-productive assets	Having unnecessary purchases
Owning luxury or extravagant goods	Having unfunded benefits
Having non-value-added activities	Providing excessive executive compensation
Having excessive supporting personal staffs	Creating waste streams
Providing excessive perks to executives	Creating product liabilities

Legacy problems and unexpected mistakes/blunders

Paying for externalities	Paying for accidents and spills
Cleaning up pollution	Paying penalties and fines
Managing defects and burdens	Correcting inaccurate reporting
Paying for remediation	Tracking hazardous wastes
Paying for unfunded retirement benefits	Managing waste streams

businesses and opportunities, acquiring new knowledge, developing future leaders, and creating new enterprises. For instance, developing new technologies and products creates powerful means to enhance value for customers and stakeholders, to sustain the success of the organization, and to support positive cash flow for future investments and shareholder wealth. Transformations and transitions focus on radically changing the prevailing businesses and dramatically improving them, respectively. They include crafting innovative strategies and solutions, determining policies and ethics, improving the business frameworks and management constructs, and achieving extraordinary results.

The third category involves the operating core of the businesses and enhancing the ability to achieve superior results and success in the future. The prime approaches are to enhance external results like satisfying customers and stakeholders. This includes enhancing the capabilities of the operating systems to deliver extraordinary performance. Improved systems, operations, and processes result in better outcomes for the entire enterprise. For instance, improving quality enhances the organization's ability to satisfy customers while at the same time reducing its vulnerabilities due to defects and problems. For example, General Electric's drive toward six-sigma quality is predicated on the principles that high quality lowers the cost of doing business, enhances the value delivered to customers, and reduces the overall risks associated with serving customers and conducting business operations. Toyota developed lean business practices to maximize the benefits of its resources and capabilities through more effective processes and activities. It focuses attention on maximizing the good and minimizing the bad across the whole extended enterprise.

The list of primary effects is extensive. There are numerous value-added actions and activities that are important for success. Strategic leaders have to determine their own set of critical value-added elements that are necessary for success.

The secondary effects are non-value-added actions, activities, behaviors, defects, and burdens that diminish the business's ability to perform and achieve extraordinary results. They are the acquisition and/or deployment of tangential or non-critical assets, the expenditures of money on unnecessary actions and activities, and the waste of resources on approaches that do not contribute to sustainable success. They include all forms of economic and environmental wastes that are unnecessary and avoidable for the most part. The first category of secondary effects involves the expenditure of resources and capabilities on non-productive and wasteful activities. They reduce power and divert resources from the goals and tasks of enhancing business performance and achieving positive outcomes. For example, buying non-productive assets like palatial headquarters reduces the resources (financial capital) available for making investments in new technologies, products, and other more productive assets. Non-productive assets require ongoing support expenditures and management attention that are usually not rewarded through positive financial performance or sustainable success.

The secondary effects and related non-valued-added considerations should be scrutinized to determine whether they are absolutely necessary and what alternatives are available to achieve the desired outcomes and results. Most importantly, every decision related to this category should undergo rigorous analysis to determine the long-term viability of the proposed action and the long-term need for the use of the resources and/or commitments. For instance, large global corporations often have huge corporate offices. The purchase of such facilities is typically justified based on the prevailing conditions and scope of the corporation's activities. However, such investments often cannot be supported if the fortunes of the corporation change and the size and scope of the corporation shrink. For example, executives at the old AT&T believed that they needed and could afford the corporate headquarters at Basking Ridge, New Jersey. The facility may have been a necessary and suitable option when AT&T was a giant with more than one million employees. However, as AT&T spun-off businesses and became a much smaller entity, the cost of such an extensive headquarters became an expensive proposition that was difficult to maintain.

The second category involves those actions and activities that detract from value creation in the present or future but are necessary because of government mandates or due to past difficulties that were not resolved during earlier times. Many businesses have created liabilities that they are currently paying for and must continue to do so. They are the legacies of the past. Such effects cost money to manage and remedy, and usually take time and resources away from the primary effects and the potentially positive contributions. For instance, the generation of hazardous wastes from past and present operations usually requires resource deployments in the future to remediate the problems. Such deployments of time, money, and people do not provide additional benefits to the business in the future but the actions are absolutely necessary because of laws and regulations and other government mandates. They negatively impact value creation and diminish the resources and capabilities of the organization. For instance, waste management and remediation projects to cure past problems drain capital and do not contribute to creating new opportunities.

They are usually the legacies of the previous strategic leaders and are often the result of poor decision making. Nonetheless, laws and regulations mandate that such problems be addressed and resolved. While such projects are critical for ensuring the survival of the corporation, they often consume the time, talent, and contributions of some of the best management and professional leaders of the corporation. The return on such investments is typically negative.

The purpose of this section is not to precisely define and delineate all of the effects that might fit into each category but to provide examples to stimulate strategic thinking. Moreover, there may be many business situations in which owning non-productive assets may be justifiable and necessary due to the unique aspects of the businesses and enterprises. Again, as discussed earlier, the approach in this book is not to be prescriptive in what to do and/or not to do but to suggest a general management framework for strategic thinking about alternatives and ways for leading change and managing strategically.

Outstanding ESL focuses on increasing the primary effects and reducing, if not eliminating, the secondary ones. While the latter may be impossible in the short term, strategic leaders should be aiming to move toward that end in the long term. Moreover, ESM involves both investing in creating a more sustainable future and transforming and/or transitioning existing positions, strategies, systems, operations, processes, and practices into more and more value-added approaches.

Framework for enterprise-wide strategic management

The overarching perspectives of the natural, social, and business worlds

ESM as a management framework is intended to function in the real world and provide a platform for strategic decision making. It starts with the whole and works across the enterprise and down the organization to the operating and functional areas. While this is not a radical concept, the scope of an enterprise-wide strategic perspective represents a significant change from conventional strategic management approaches. It is a strategic management framework for understanding and assessing reality and identifying the available opportunities and challenges and how to exploit them in positive ways.

Figure 1.2 provides an embedded perspective of the company/corporation/SME and the connections between the natural world, the social/human world, the business environment, and extended enterprise.[27]

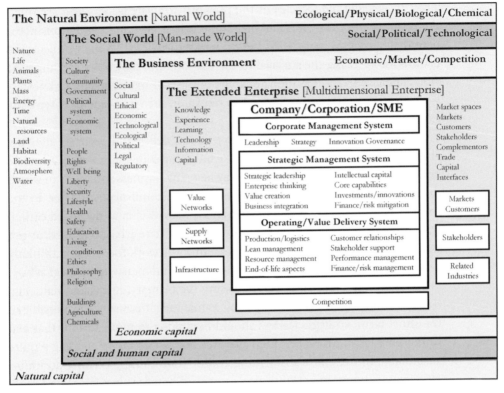

Figure 1.2   The overarching framework of ESM

Clearly, such broad perspectives involve incredible complexities that are usually beyond the traditional purview of business and strategic management. However, in a more complex and global world strategic leaders have to take broad perspectives and understand the dynamics of the whole business world not just their little piece of it. The natural environment and the social/human world are not superfluous or merely tangential perspectives for determining the purposes, aims, roles and responsibilities, and strategies of businesses and their enterprises. Rather, they are the essential forces that must be considered in formulating and implementing strategies and action plans. Most importantly, they are the overarching forces that drive the business environment and markets in which the corporation, its SBUs and their enterprises exist and must excel.

While the book focuses primarily on the business environment, market spaces, the extended enterprise, the company, and the business unit, it is important to acknowledge that the influences of and impacts on the natural environment and the social/human world are critical considerations with powerful consequences for the business environment and businesses themselves. The business environment is a microcosm of total reality and it includes many elements of the natural and social worlds. It includes the external forces – social, economic, political, technological, environmental, ethical, and market-impinging upon the corporation. It also includes the external dimensions of stakeholders, competition, related industries, supply networks, and the infrastructure. While it is appropriate to focus on the primary driving forces in the business environment, great care must be taken to ensure that all necessary considerations are taken when developing a strategic management framework and crafting and implementing strategies and action plans. Moreover, many of the latent opportunities that manifest themselves in the business environment over time are foreseeable in the broader perspectives, especially in the social/human world. For instance, climate change is a critical issue that governments and scientists try to understand. It is also a profound business challenge regardless of whether the strategic leaders believe that it is critical.

John Elkington's "triple-bottom line" reflects the importance of including the social, economic, and environmental considerations in managing businesses.[28] The social aspects include considerations that provide opportunities for businesses to develop, build, and enhance customer and stakeholder relationships, and ultimately, company reputation, image, and success. Relationship management involves being in sync with broader considerations and factors of external customers, stakeholders, and other constituencies and building trust among the external entities and individuals. The challenge is how to exceed customer and stakeholder expectations using cutting-edge methods and techniques in order to differentiate the reputation and image of the organization and to build a sustainable position.

Economic factors revolve around value creation, production, distribution, consumption, and waste management. The global economy is a vast array of physical, financial, and informational transactions, connections, and relationships through which goods and services, money, and information flow in order to increase social, economic, and environmental "good" and value creation. Economic considerations include the actual distribution of goods and services. In simple terms, economic factors pertain to costs and revenues, supply and demand, and the related activities. Costs include all of the costs to acquire the means of production, to produce, store, transport, and manage the product, process, or service, and to use, maintain, improve, and dispose of it, accounting for recycling, disposal, and residuals. They encompass the culmination of all costs from the cradle to the grave, direct and indirect, private and external, obvious and hidden, and short term and long term. Primary economic considerations also include the revenues, cash flows, and profits generated through the exchange of goods and services, and how investments translate into transformational capabilities and outcomes.

Ecological/environmental considerations are among the broadest and include a myriad of factors that cover nature, the physical world, mass, energy, time, and all of the implications, impacts, and their consequences. Driven by a dramatic increase in the number of environmental laws and regulations, environmental considerations have evolved over the last thirty years in most of the industrialized countries from simply achieving compliance with the laws and regulations and addressing waste problems to the development and deployment of sophisticated environmental management systems focusing on external drivers and internal capabilities. The maturation process has been difficult for most businesses involving complex requirements for managing the residuals from the value systems. For instance, environmental management was not an essential part of the business strategy during the 1970s and 1980s. It was viewed as a necessary, but unwanted aside. Now, it is an essential part of strategic thinking and management. Moreover, many of the stakeholders focus on environmental issues from climate change and toxic substance to protecting endangered species and the quality of air and water.

The natural world is a source of phenomenal capital for businesses and their extended enterprises. Enterprises depend on the natural world for resources and infrastructure ranging from water for food and beverage companies and wood for lumber and paper companies to land and waterways for roads and transportation. The list of natural capital is so extensive that it is impossible to describe its full importance. It is estimated the natural capital provides trillions of dollars worth of benefits to businesses each year, much of which is free. For instance, bees pollinate plants used in agriculture free of charge. Such services are not only essential but are the reason why food crops are so economically viable.

The social/human world is likewise pivotal in providing capital. The essence of all enterprises is human capital that includes knowledge, insights, creativity, and productivity. Human resources are central to finding and implementing effective solutions for meeting the needs of society and markets. Businesses are social entities. Instruments of the social world, they are people working to serve people. Much of the knowledge comes from the broad domains of human activities. Again much of it is free. For instance, large research universities engage in basic knowledge that supports the success and well being of all people and business entities. They also provide the means and mechanisms to transfer knowledge from one generation to the next through education. Businesses would be seriously disadvantaged if they had to pay for such expenses.

The global business environment

The global business environment provides context for the corporation and its extended enterprise. The scope of the business environment for most corporations has expanded dramatically over the last several decades. At the end of World War II, most large corporations were primarily engaged in serving their own national markets and focused extensively on the conditions and trends in those limited business environments. Exceptions like Coca-Cola, GM and IBM derived a significant portion of their revenues outside of their home markets. However, such business endeavors were said to be doing business in foreign markets or exporting to international markets instead of being global corporations with business units and operations throughout the world. The management perspective was still on the indigenous markets and corporate identity was based on being an American, French, German, Japanese, etc. company. Today, almost everything has changed. Most global corporations think in terms of global opportunities and requirements, not national. They are transnational corporations that have operations in multiple countries. Indeed, many of these companies base their strategic thinking in global terms, not national, and some are so diverse like ABB that it is becoming more difficult to identify their home base.

Historically, most strategic management frameworks focused mainly on the direct relationships between the producer and its suppliers and distributors and the intended customers. As discussed earlier, Porter characterized such relationships as the value chain for the value-added activities within the business entity and the value system as the linked value chains of suppliers, producer, distributors, and buyers. In his book, *Competitive Advantage: Creating and Sustaining Superior Performance*, Porter discusses the competitive scope that shapes the economics of the value chain.[29] He identified four dimensions of scope that characterized value chains:[30]

- Segment scope. The product varieties produced and the markets and buyers served.
- Vertical scope. The extent to which activities are performed in-house instead of by independent firms.
- Geographic scope. The range of regions, countries, or groups of countries in which a firm competes with a coordinated strategy.

- Industry scope. The range of related industries in which the firm competes with a coordinated strategy.

While Porter's view focused on production and consumption of products and services, it provided significant insights into how to determine a strategic perspective of the business environment. He clearly articulated the importance of scope and identified the crucial characteristics for determining what is relevant. His work laid the foundation for a broad view of the business environment and an early version of the extended enterprise. His value system of upstream suppliers linked with the value chain of the producer and the producer's linkages with the downstream value systems of customers and market-related aspects include many of the entities of the extended enterprise.

The global business environment extends beyond the value system and includes the external social, economic, political, technological, environmental, and competitive forces and ethical aspects. The global business environment also includes extended enterprises and the external dimensions of markets, stakeholders, competition, related industries, supply networks, and the infrastructure. Most importantly, however, the global business environment contains the thousands of other enterprises that are competitors, supporters, partners, or unrelated entities. The latter consists of entities in other industries and business areas that have limited if any connection with the corporation and its enterprise.

Most business situations today involve many interactions and connections with networks of players who directly or indirectly provide solutions to existing or latent needs of the external dimensions. Moreover, most business situations are complex, affected by market conditions and trends that involve intensive customer demands and hyper-competition. The interrelationships are complex, with many of the suppliers and distributors providing materials, parts, components, and goods to myriad competitors and other industries. Most relationships are built on a transactional basis. There are relatively few exclusive arrangements and most of the relationships within an enterprise are open-ended.

Historically, most businesses focused on the economic, market, legal and regulatory, and competitive forces as primary considerations in managing their businesses. Early strategic management frameworks attempted to simplify the business environment by concentrating on what the strategic leaders and other strategists deemed to be the primary considerations – markets and competitors. While such views facilitated analysis and strategy formulation, they often led to an incomplete picture of reality. Some of those frameworks are discussed in the next chapter.

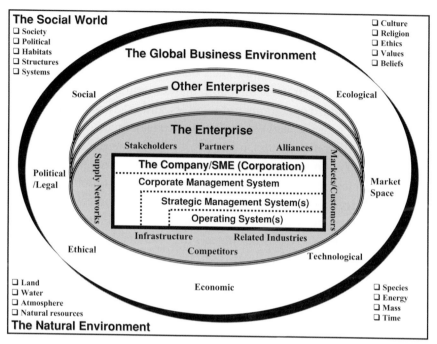

Figure 1.3   A simplified framework of the business environment

Today, the forces driving the global business environment require businesses and strategic leaders to become more connected with their customers, stakeholders, suppliers, distributors, and other partners. Connectedness in thoughts and actions is now crucial for staying in touch with reality and understanding rapidly changing needs, wants, expectations, and mandates. In a slow-paced world, business leaders had the time to watch events unfold, contemplate strategies, and then respond in deliberate fashion. In today's more turbulent times, corporations must be proactive in analyzing and understanding the business environment, market and stakeholder expectations, and future requirements in order to be prepared for action regardless of what unfolds.

Figure 1.3 provides a high-level perspective of the global business environment, including the forces driving the social, political, economic, technological, competitive, ecological, and ethical dimensions.[31] It also depicts the enterprise and other enterprises that affect and impact the corporation's or business unit's enterprise.

The depicted framework is intended to provide a more inclusive look at the business environment. Still, it is impossible to portray all of the interconnections between suppliers, distributors, customers, service providers, competitors, and other constituencies that make up all of the enterprises that may influence and impact the corporation and its business units. The corporation is depicted at the center of the framework because its strategic leaders largely determine their business environment by the decisions they make about strategic direction, markets and customers, geographical reach, value-added operations and activities, and externally sourced support, among many other aspects. Theoretically, strategic management selects customers, suppliers, distributors, related industries, and even competitors as it formulates and implements corporate and business strategies. Indeed, strategically selecting the players in the business environment is one of the most critical of all executive responsibilities. The intent of the framework is to provide a more balanced perspective of the business world and the critical factors that have to be considered during strategic decision making. The details of the business environment are articulated throughout the book, especially in Chapter 4.

A framework of the business unit and the extended enterprise

The company/corporation is the legal entity that assumes responsibility for the actions and transactions with customers and stakeholders and all of the supporting players. During the early twentieth century, vertically integrated corporations produced most of the materials, parts, components, and products in the world and provided a significant percentage of the value added that customers received. As discussed earlier, Henry Ford's production and distribution of the Model T is a good example. As a vertically integrated company, FMC controlled most of the fabrication and production using its internal value chain.

Today, most businesses have become more horizontal with large extended enterprises to support their operations. Global corporations have shifted their emphasis from owning and controlling the means of production and leveraging their resources across as many markets as possible to exploit their intellectual capital, technological and market know-how, financial strengths, and management savvy. There has been a subtle change in emphasis from focusing on physical resources to intellectual capital, from tangible production capabilities to intangible management competencies and business models.

Today, businesses have vast networks of horizontally distributed resources and capabilities that extend well beyond the boundaries of the organization. They have expanded and diversified by integrating the resources and capabilities of suppliers and their suppliers, distributors, retailers and their customers, their own customers and customers of those customers, and the providers of logistical support including end-of-life considerations. Global corporations are complex organizations that use and depend on the resources of thousands of entities through commercial, technological, and financial relationships.

These networks and relationships, both direct and indirect, form the basis of the enterprise. As such, the enterprise is a dynamic construct that is constantly improving as customers and stakeholders demand more value and fewer problems. Businesses compete, not just as individual entities, but also on the basis of the inclusiveness, connectedness, and innovativeness of their enterprises. The power and capabilities of the enterprise are often more important than the strengths and weaknesses of the business units themselves. For instance, a business unit having high-quality production may actually exhibit weak manufacturing and product quality due to defects and burdens associated with its suppliers. For example, Airbus has had significant difficulties delivering its A380 Superplane because of late deliveries from its suppliers. In reality, business units compete against their rivals based on the quality and capabilities of their extended enterprises and the strengths and weaknesses of the integrated whole. While this is not a new phenomenon, the power and importance of enterprise-wide integration is gaining recognition and understanding as a strategic management construct. Strategic management perspectives are evolving from company-centric approaches to holistic frameworks based on ESM with global implications.

Figure 1.4 provides an overview of the essential elements of the enterprise and their connection with the company or business unit.[32]

The horizontal structure of the enterprise consists of the entities of the value networks that define, develop, produce, and use the value that implicitly establishes the underlying purposes. The enterprise contains the traditional primary participants of the value system, the supply networks and customers as well as the broader connections to all of the entities that provide value (i.e. the partners, allies, and other supporters).

The dimensions of the enterprise include the implications and impacts of the entire business environment on the social, economic, and the natural worlds from the origin of raw materials to the end-of-life considerations.

The enterprise is defined by the supporting structures, means, and mechanisms of related industries that provide complementary products and services for customers, offer supplementary information and intellectual resources to enhance the value provided, and complete the package of resources, capabilities, knowledge, and related services that makes a sustainable solution

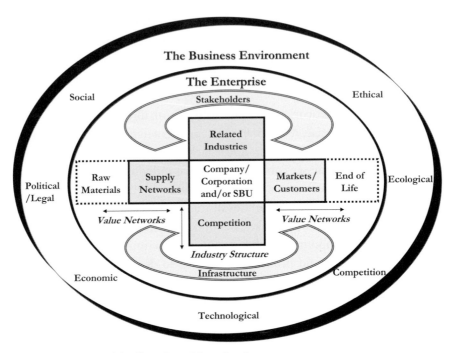

Figure 1.4   A simplified overview of the dimensions of the enterprise

possible. This includes training and education, repair and maintenance services, informational and analytical services, and a plethora of products and
services that customers and stakeholders need and expect to provide total
satisfaction.

The enterprise includes all of the stakeholders influencing or impacted by
the products, processes, operations, and activities of the enterprise. Stakeholders include all of the individuals and groups that are directly or indirectly affected by the products, programs, processes, and/or systems, but
do not directly benefit as economic participants as customers or suppliers.
Stakeholders include government agencies, interest groups, communities, and
society.

The enterprise includes the competitors in the form of other enterprises or
on the basis of the industry structure in the traditional sense of production
and consumption. While competitors are often viewed as adversaries that
vie for customers and take away market share, they may be beneficial to the
whole by providing options and choices for customers and creating industry
power that creates barriers for new entrants or makes it difficult for alternate
technologies or substitutes to gain an economic foothold. For instance, many

inventors and entrepreneurs have tried with limited success to commercialize new automobile types or replace internal combustion engine technologies. It might have been possible to overcome the competitive advantages of a single producer in the automobile industry, like Volkswagen or Honda, but it is extremely challenging and expensive to defeat the combined strengths and financial resources of the major competitors of the global automobile industry. While the competitors are clearly competing for customers, revenues, and profits, they also share many common objectives such as the stability and survival of the economic aspects and industry structure, and protection from new rivals or technologies from outside the prevailing structures. For example, individual companies like Toyota and Honda enjoy the current market conditions in their segments of the automobile industry. They want to maintain the competitive positions. But, they also generally support initiatives that maintain the economic stability of the industry.

The enterprise consists of the external infrastructure(s) that support and facilitate commercial activities and the applications of products and services. The external infrastructure includes Internet communications, telecommunications, energy systems, the airways, the roads, the waterways, and atmosphere, etc. These networks and resources add value by facilitating the movement of goods, information, data, waste, and energy to and from the supply networks, producers, and customers.

The enterprise is a complex management construct that can be viewed from the company/corporation or business unit perspectives as well as the value delivery system. It is difficult, if not impossible, to completely map out the whole of an enterprise for a large business organization since it comprises thousands of networks, connections, and relationships.

The embedded corporate strategic management framework

As stated earlier, large companies/corporations, especially those that were vertically integrated, used a hierarchical structure as the predominant business model. They generally employed top-down approaches that included strategic business management at the top, general management of business units in the middle, and operations and functional management at the lower levels. Most such management constructs limited the purview of the business units to the direct transactions and responsibilities associated with producing products and serving customers. While there were significant variations to the management constructs, most simplified their strategic management framework to facilitate analysis, strategy formation, decision making, and implementation.

The prevailing view, which still permeates business thinking today, was to keep it simple.

Senior management controlled their corporation and implemented strategies through decision making, reporting relationships with subordinates, information flows, and other control mechanisms via a vertical structure. The approaches required many interactions between levels of management up and down the chain of command. The methods were usually thorough, but extremely slow, consuming enormous amounts of time and resources. The strength of the methodology was the ability to focus on the specific strategies and actions and achieve results. Typically, the main strategies focused on competitive forces, market-related initiatives, and financial performance. The operating and functional areas were the central or core parts of the structure but were deemed to be subordinate. Each part was developed and optimized as if it was an independent component. While examining the parts separately facilitated decision making, the integration of the parts into a truly or fully integrated management system was challenging. The strength of the approach became the weakness. Due to the lack of integration at the operating level, strategic leaders had to play a significant role in resolving difficulties that existed within the hierarchy of the company/corporation. While this is a broad brush of the historical situation, it is clear that most businesses optimized the operating and functional areas and had difficulties integrating the whole.

The embedded corporate strategic management framework consists of three levels:

- *Corporate management system* – focuses on the long-term strategic positions and direction relative to the global business environment and on formulating and implementing corporate vision, grand strategies, objectives, and initiatives for leading change and sustaining the future through visionary leadership.
- *Strategic management system (SMS)* – focuses on the missions and intermediate term of the strategic business unit (SBU) and its strategic positions relative to the business environment and the enterprise and on formulating and implementing business strategies, objectives, and initiatives for achieving dramatic improvements and outstanding performance through integration and innovation.
- *Operating system or value delivery system* – focuses on satisfying customers and stakeholders through outstanding value-added solutions and on implementing and executing strategies, objectives, and initiatives for achieving dramatic improvements and near-term performance and results.

The business environment with its needs and requirements drives the corporate management system. Corporate executives protect the present, create an enhanced future, and sustain value creation across the whole enterprise and up and down the organization. Most importantly, executives must focus on the future rather than just managing the present.

The focus of the book is on business units and operating systems. The SMSs of the business units involve the strategic logic and direction of the businesses and their missions. The construct is similar to the corporate management system except that strategic leaders of the business units concentrate on the missions and business strategies, objectives, and action plans for their units. The SMS then links and aligns the core operating level at the base of the system, linking the operating system with the business environment and markets. It involves strategic thinking about innovation and creating innovative solutions for the future. While corporate management is concerned about the complexity of the business environment and the vision for the future, strategic leaders and general managers of the business units contemplate the strategic implications of change and develop strategies to achieve positive outcomes. They examine and analyze the business environment and market spaces to discover opportunities and understand challenges.

The operating system, also called value delivery system, is the core operating level. It concentrates on the existing conditions and meeting the market, production, technical, and financial requirements of the organization. It is usually supported by the product and process capabilities for updating and improving performance. The focus is on output and results.

A management construct that produces results through well-defined processes drives the core operating level. Historically, that construct focused on the resources deployed within the system and the organizational elements engaged in converting inputs into outputs. The embedded corporate management model sets the stage for a descriptive, analytical, and structural view of the opportunities and challenges. The details of the embedded management system are discussed throughout the book.

The strategic management system

The evolution and development of the SMS is central to the successful strategic management. The SMS focuses on the strategic logic of the organization and its mission. It connects the business units with the global view of the entire enterprise. It integrates the objectives, strategies, concerns, and directives of the corporate executives with the management of operations. SMS integrates the organization's processes and resources into a comprehensive framework for formulating and implementing business strategies including those related to technology and new product development.

Strategic leaders must ensure that management systems are functioning properly, that all requirements are understood and met, and that value delivery systems are appropriate and effective. SMSs include the intellectual capital, assets and resources, and the interests of shareholders, society, customers, stakeholders, employees, partners, and all constituents. Learning and knowledge are critical but less tangible elements for building for the future. Some of the most important and innovative management constructs related to improving organizational capabilities include knowledge management, lean business management, and sustainable business development (SBD).

Knowledge management involves identifying, developing, and improving the competencies, skills, know-how, and knowledge of an organization. It also involves enhancing the organization's rate of learning and developing its abilities to learn. Rapid change necessitates rapid learning. Knowledge management requires people who can think "outside-the-box" to develop new knowledge and capabilities to enrich the organization.

Lean business management is one of the most profound changes in management thinking of the latter part of the twentieth century. Lean business thinking embodies philosophical, theoretical, and practical concepts and mechanisms to reinvent and reinvigorate the corporation and its organizational structure. Being lean involves using resources in the most efficient and effective ways. It combines improving economic performance and reducing environmental impacts. Organizations in a dynamic business world have to be lean. They also must be flexible and agile. Lean corporations can move quickly in new directions, and flexibility allows an organization to transform existing core capabilities into new ones that better respond to new realities. Lean organizations are more likely to encourage change and to discover new opportunities than to think about their vulnerabilities. This way of thinking enhances the corporation's ability to satisfy expectations in the most suitable and effective way. Lean business management has been deployed effectively at the operating levels of the corporation. The concepts, methods, and techniques are now being expanded to include strategic thinking and management.

SBD involves creating economically sound, socially responsible, and environmentally conscious businesses, technologies, products, and processes that maximize value creation, enhancing the benefits and minimizing degradation of human health and the natural environment, the depletion of resources, and negative impacts from wastes and pollution. It also involves life-cycle thinking and management about all of the effects, impacts, and consequences from cradle to grave. It involves achieving sustainable outcomes that balance the performance objectives of the present with the needs and expectations of the future.

SBD examines all of the inputs and outputs in qualitative and quantitative terms and links products and processes to all of their precursors and outcomes. The focus is the identification of the materials and energy incorporated in products, the quantities used and their social, economic, and environmental implications, and the determination of the effects and impacts that the products and processes have over their life cycles. This includes avoiding or minimizing the use of toxic substance, eliminating hazardous wastes, and reducing residual waste streams and byproducts. SBD is discussed in more detail in Chapter 2.

The strategic management process

Strategic management involves extremely complicated management constructs that often involve high-level strategizing, decision making, and oversight among a myriad of methods and approaches for leading change and managing the affairs across the whole corporation. Strategic leaders are responsible for everything that happens or fails to happen properly. Their roles and responsibilities are open-ended and it is virtually impossible to map out everything.

Strategic management of the business units involves definitive management constructs for providing strategic direction, formulating and implementing strategies, and enduring success. It includes establishing a framework for mapping out the strategic management process for strategic business planning and strategic implementation. The framework establishes the management approaches for decision making and the actions for achieving outcomes.

Strategic analysis of the external business environment and internal dimensions of the organization and enterprise provides strategic leaders with the exciting opportunities and challenges for succeeding and realizing the strategic direction of the company and the missions of the business units. It allows strategic leaders to identify the options and formulate objectives and strategies. The business strategies are translated into action plans and initiatives that are implemented by the organization.

Strategic implementation involves developing the systems, structures, and programs for ensuring positive outcomes. It also involves allocating resources

and building capabilities with the enterprise to assure success. While implementation deals with the means and mechanisms for translating strategies
into action, the actual execution involves getting everyone in the enterprise to
carry out the strategies to obtain the desired results. The details are covered
in Part II.

Summary

ESM involves integration, innovation, and leadership of the business unit,
the extended enterprise, and all of the management systems and processes
from the origins of the raw materials to production processes, customer
applications, and the end-of-life considerations. It can bring about dramatic
improvements and continuous development to the full scope of relationships
and capabilities with customers, stakeholders, supply networks, and support
service providers. It can bring about sustainable outcomes that balance the
business objectives of the business units with the needs and expectations of the
enterprise.

Business is not about winning the battles in the short term at the expense
of destroying relationships in the long term or failing to sustain success. ESM
focuses on finding unique opportunities and creating innovative solutions
that are more attractive and enduring from business and market perspectives as well as economic, social, technological, and environmental ones.
It is about leading, creating, developing, integrating, building, deploying,
and succeeding. It also involves the search, discovery, and cure of weaknesses, defects, problems, burdens, and negative impacts across the extended
enterprise.

Most importantly, ESM focuses on how strategic leaders create business
frameworks, management constructs, and innovative ways of achieving sustainable success. It also focuses their efforts on finding and making dramatic
changes to affect the entire enterprise instead of just the corporation/company
and its business units, operations, and products. It is intended to be holistic
in scope, audacious in innovation, enduring over time, and persistent in creating new solutions and extraordinary value. It invokes a new mindset among
strategic leaders and professionals that is entrepreneurial in spirit, collaborative in nature, participatory in style, ambitious for the whole, and win–win
attitude. The grand objective is to continuously create extraordinary value
across space (the enterprise) and time (future generations). Such strategic
thinking transcends the concepts of "winning the battle" and "defeating the

competitors" to move a business unit toward inventing solutions that are sustainable, beneficial, and rewarding to the entire enterprise.

Great leaders are those that achieve sustained performance and success and enrich all contributors, customers, stakeholders, and shareholders. They relentlessly pursue continuous improvements, sustained developments, and extraordinary results. And, they ensure that good leaders are developed to follow in their footsteps.

ESM incorporates many of the principles, processes, and practices of SBD.[33] ESM focuses on the strategic design, development, and enhancement of the business unit, SMS, and the enterprise. SBD focuses on the design, development, validation, and commercialization of new and improved technologies, products, processes, and operations. Both have the same underpinnings and principles and long-term strategic objectives: to enhance the positives, eliminate the negatives, and ensure long-term success. Both involve strategic undertakings to create value. Both involve risks and rewards. The great reward is sustainable success. It is not just maximizing the present that drives strategic leaders but perpetuating success across space and time.

References

Chandler, Jr., Alfred (1962) *Strategy and Structure: Chapters in the History of the American Industrial Enterprise.* Cambridge, MA: MIT Press

(1977) *The Visible Hand: The Managerial Revolution in American Business.* Cambridge, MA: Harvard University Press

Drucker, Peter (1946, 1972) *Concept of the Corporation,* 1972 edition. New York: The John Day Company

Elkington, John (1997) *Cannibals with Forks: The Triple Bottom Line of Sustainable Development.* Oxford, UK: Chapstone Publishing

Hamel, Gary (2000) *Leading the Revolution,* Boston, MA: Harvard Business School Press

and C. K. Prahalad (1994) *Competing for the Future.* Boston, MA: Harvard Business School Press

Hammer, Michael and James Champy (1993) *Reengineering the Corporation: A Manifesto for Business Revolution.* New York: Harper Business

Kaplan, Robert and David Norton (1996) *The Balanced Scorecard: Translating Strategy into Action.* Boston, MA: Harvard Business School Press

Lawrence, Paul R. and David Dyer (1983) *Renewing American Industry.* New York: Free Press

Murman, Earll, Thomas Allen, Kirkor Bozdogan, Joel Cutcher-Gershenfeld, Hugh McManus, Deborah Nightingale, Eric Rebentisch, Tom Shields, Fred Stahl, Myles Walton, Joyce Warmkessel, Stanley Weiss, and Sheila Widnall (2002) *Lean Enterprise Value: Insights from MIT's Lean Aerospace Initiative.* New York: Palgrave

Porter, Michael (1985) *Competitive Advantage: Creating and Sustaining Superior Performance.* New York: Free Press

Rainey, David L. (2006) *Sustainable Business Development: Inventing the Future through Strategy, Innovation, and Leadership.* Cambridge, UK: Cambridge University Press

Sloan, Jr., Alfred P. (1964) *My Years with General Motors.* Garden City, NY: Doubleday & Company, Inc.

Welch, Jack (2005) *Winning.* New York: Harper Business

NOTES

1 Note that each of a corporation's business units may have its own enterprise which is specifically selected to meet the requirements of the businesses.

2 Alfred Chandler, Jr., *The Visible Hand: The Managerial Revolution in American Business* (Cambridge, MA: Harvard University Press, 1977, p. 50).

3 *Ibid.,* p. 81.

4 *Ibid.,* p. 289.

5 *Ibid.,* p. 287.

6 Alfred Chandler, Jr., *Strategy and Structure: Chapters in the History of the American Industrial Enterprise* (Cambridge, MA: MIT Press, 1962, p. 8).

7 Chandler provided the following note: Werner Sombart, *Encyclopedia of the Social Sciences,* "Capitalism" (New York: 1930, p. 200). Sombart (1863–1941) was a German economist and sociologist during the early twentieth century.

8 Paul R. Lawrence and David Dyer, *Renewing American Industry* (New York: Free Press, 1983, p. 62).

9 Alfred P. Sloan, Jr., *My Years with General Motors* (Garden City, NY: Doubleday & Company, Inc., 1964, p. 3).

10 *Ibid.*

11 Alfred Chandler, Jr., *Strategy and Structure: Chapters in the History of the American Industrial Enterprise,* p. 6. In 1959, General Motors and Ford were listed as second and fourth of the seventy largest industrials based on assets.

12 Peter Drucker, *Concept of the Corporation,* 1972 edition (New York: The John Day Company, 1946, 1972, p. 4). Drucker discusses the terms for a corporation but admits that the meanings are difficult to define.

13 Michael Porter, *Competitive Advantage: Creating and Sustaining Superior Performance* (New York: Free Press, 1985, pp. 33–61).

14 *Ibid.,* p. 36.

15 *Ibid.,* p. 37.

16 Michael Hammer and James Champy, *Reengineering the Corporation: A Manifesto for Business Revolution* (New York: Harper Business, 1993).

17 Gary Hamel and C. K. Prahalad, *Competing for the Future* (Boston, MA: Harvard Business School Press, 1994).

18 Gary Hamel, *Leading the Revolution* (Boston, MA: Harvard Business School Press, 2000, pp. 61–131).

19 Earll Murman, Thomas Allen, Kirkor Bozdogan, Joel Cutcher-Gershenfeld, Hugh McManus, Deborah Nightingale, Eric Rebentisch, Tom Shields, Fred Stahl, Myles Walton,

Joyce Warmkessel, Stanley Weiss, and Sheila Widnall, *Lean Enterprise Value: Insights from MIT's Lean Aerospace Initiative* (New York: Palgrave, 2002, p. 3).

20 *Ibid.*, p. 161.

21 Jack Welch, *Winning* (New York: Harper Business, 2005, p. 3).

22 These points are not to be construed as suggesting that Wal-Mart is perfect or its business model should be emulated as an example of the ideal. Moreover, Wal-Mart like all corporations has challenges.

23 Wal-Mart is used as an example of a corporation that has an inclusive, innovative, responsive, effective, and productive management system. Wal-Mart like most companies has pluses and minuses.

24 Gary Hamel, *Leading the Revolution*, pp. 61–131.

25 *Ibid.*, p. 66.

26 Robert Kaplan and David Norton, *The Balanced Scorecard: Translating Strategy into Action* (Boston, MA: Harvard Business School Press, 1996, pp. 7–18).

27 The elements in each of the boxes are some of the essential aspects but they do not provide a comprehensive view of the perspectives.

28 John Elkington, *Cannibals with Forks: The Triple Bottom Line of Sustainable Development* (Oxford, UK: Chapstone Publishing, 1997).

29 Michael Porter, *Competitive Advantage: Creating and Sustaining Superior Performance*, pp. 33–61.

30 *Ibid.*, pp. 53–54.

31 David L. Rainey, *Sustainable Business Development: Inventing the Future through Strategy, Innovation, and Leadership* (Cambridge, UK: Cambridge University Press, 2006, p. 79). The framework is the same as in my book on SBD and adapted from it. The framework also depicts the extended enterprise.

32 *Ibid.*, p. 89. Same comments as above.

33 Rainey, *Sustainable Business Development: Inventing the Future through Strategy, Innovation and Leadership* examines the principles, theories, strategies, processes, and practices of SBD when applied in concert with enterprise-wide thinking as the means for creating innovative solutions to the social, economic, environmental, and business challenges in today's turbulent business environment.

2 Strategic management: Historical aspects and contemporary perspectives

Introduction

Strategic management is a high-level management construct that is well defined and understood by most executives, strategic leaders, strategists, practitioners, and business scholars. It initially focused on strategic leadership, business policies, and long-range planning. It evolved from the poorly articulated management constructs involving business policy during the 1950s and earlier to the more formal strategic management methodologies of the 1970s. Kenneth Andrews (1916–2005) of Harvard Business School and H. Igor Ansoff (1918–2002) of Massachusetts Institute of Technology were two of the renowned pioneers of strategic management and strategic business planning (SBP). Today, strategy management is one of the most well-known and frequently used constructs in business management. Andrews defined it thus:[1]

Corporate strategy is the pattern of decisions in a company that determines and reveals its objectives, purposes, or goals, produces the principal policies and plans for achieving those goals, and defines the range of businesses the company is to pursue, the kind of economic and human organization it is or intends to be, and the nature of the economic and non-economic contribution it intends to make to its shareholders, employees, customers, and communities. In an organization of any size or diversity, "corporate strategy" usually applies to the whole enterprise while "business strategy," less comprehensively defines the choices of product or service and market of individual businesses within the firm. Business strategy is the determination of how a company will compete in a given business and position itself among its competitors. Corporate strategy defines the businesses in which a company will compete, preferably in a way that focuses resources to convert distinctive competence into competitive advantages.

Andrews regarded economic and non-economic considerations as important elements of strategic management. He clearly discerned the differences between corporate strategy and business strategy, the former being the high level about the choices of businesses and strategic direction and the latter about how the company positions itself in the markets it selected and how well it performs against competitors.

Ansoff was one of the first to be concerned with the dynamics of the business environment and the implications of technological change. He advocated that companies conduct a comprehensive strategic analysis of the business environment to identify, define, articulate, and exploit the available opportunities and to mitigate or neutralize the threats. He realized that change was ever present and a critical factor in strategic management. Intriguingly, both Andrews and Ansoff believed that strategy formation was best when based on a comprehensive understanding of the business environment and that strategies should focus on the whole business environment rather than just on markets and competitors. Andrews also talked about the whole enterprise and its contributions to communities and society, not just customers and markets. While their perspectives are about forty years old, they are reincarnated in some of the more sophisticated strategic management frameworks of today.

Strategy focuses on making decisions today that affect the strategic direction and future success of the company. It involves strategic decision making about creating, developing, and building sustainable positions and achieving success in the business environment and markets. It also involves creating value for the whole enterprise through strategic leadership and sustainable solutions. Strategies and the related decision-making processes must be based on a multifaceted assessment of the business environment, a clear understanding of the opportunities and challenges in the market spaces of today, and the potential ones for tomorrow, and comprehensive perspectives about the capabilities, resources, capital, and leadership of the organization.

The mindset of the strategic leadership must envision what could be and seek to find and create opportunities. Strategic leaders in crafting strategies must be mindful of both the positives and negatives in the business environment, and work to enhance the positives and convert negatives into positives. One of the most critical challenges is that of integrating the entire extended enterprise into an efficient and effective strategic management system (SMS) and value delivery system that can exploit opportunities, eliminate threats, and choreograph the many forces affecting the enterprise to achieve extraordinary value and sustainable results.

The embedded corporate management system and extended enterprise are central to the development of an effective strategic management framework for coping with today's complex business world and for leading change in it. That framework is the enterprise-wide strategic management (ESM) framework as introduced in Chapter 1.

This chapter starts with a brief historical overview of the development of the most significant management constructs of the last century and how they have evolved. It also provides a contemporary perspective of the development of strategic management and SBP. It elaborates on the management constructs discussed in the first chapter and how they fit into a holistic strategic management framework. Special topic includes how sustainable business development (SBD) and ESM are connected.[2]

The chapter includes the following main topics:

- The historical development of management constructs and strategic management.
- A contemporary perspective on strategic management.
- Reflections on the strategic management model.
- SBD and its connections with ESM.

Management theories and strategic management constructs

A brief historical perspective

Management theories and practices have been studied for more than a century. They have evolved steadily from simple concepts used to explain a single phenomenon to more elaborate theories about the purposes, philosophies, principles, policies, and processes of business and the concepts of free enterprise. While great strides in analysis and understanding were made during the nineteenth century, most management constructs of the time were practitioner oriented and machine centered. The theories and practices concentrated on production and operations, machines and workers, and sales and finance. They were based on the prevailing realities which focused extensively on production and operations. Companies produced the goods and found entities to sell them in order to generate revenues and profits. The most critical management challenges and approaches centered on improving the efficiency and productivity of operations, manufacturing activities, and workers. Efficiency was expressed in terms of machines and production layouts, and productivity was defined based on the interfaces between workers and the machines.

Improvements were made slowly in the form of incremental changes to the established operations, processes, activities, and practices. Essentially, practice led theory. Mainstream management theories and constructs developed from trial and error, experiments, and the proven practices of innovative companies and their enlightened strategic leaders.

During the late nineteenth century and the early part of the twentieth century, academic scholars and business practitioners focused on the essence of management and tried to explain the meaning and flow of work activities, and the roles and functions of the manager. Frederick Winslow Taylor (1856–1915) established time and work studies to optimize activities based on what he called scientific methods. In *Principles of Scientific Management*, Taylor applied scientific thinking to management and analyzed work functions in detail to determine the best practices for improving performance.[3] Taylor used objective criteria to establish the most appropriate practices. While there are significant criticisms about Taylor's scientific management, including its simple constructs and its lack of attention to planning and worker influences, Taylor was one of the first management gurus to think about management theories that could be used by managers in multiple settings and not just in the operations being studied. He made management more broadly based, more scientific, and somewhat more theoretical. Taylor sought to improve practices based on research, analysis, and decision making. He was a major early contributor to the generalization of management constructs and a broader adaptation of the most widely used approaches.

During the same time frame, Frank (1868–1924) and Lillian Gilbreth (1878–1972) established many principles of industrial psychology and were among the first business scholars to think about work simplifications that would benefit both the companies and the workers. Their perspectives were early examples of a more humane and balanced view of work and management. They tried to balance the forces in the workplace and establish fair and appropriate solutions. They were the innovators of the notion of best practice.

Henri Fayol (1841–1925) was a French management guru who described the fundamental functions of organizations and management activities. He characterized the main categories as: technical, commercial, financial, security (protection of assets and personnel), accounting, and managerial. His most famous contribution, which was recognized only after his death, was the identification and definition of the specific functions of management. He defined management in terms of planning, organizing, commanding, coordinating, and controlling.[4] These functions are still fundamental to management thinking today. Moreover, Fayol's general principles of management, which he defined in 1908, laid the foundation for a more theoretical basis of business management. Some of Fayol's general principles of management include division of labor, discipline, unity of command, unity of direction, order, equity, and initiative.[5] His principles established some of the timeless, theoretical aspects of management that still resonate.

Mary Parker Follett (1868–1933) applied social science to the study of the management of industrial organizations.[6] Her contributions included the concepts of employee engagement, cross-functional involvement, and direct communications. Follett's ideas seemed radical during the early twentieth century, but are now mainstream thinking. Her view of management as a social process is fundamental to our contemporary view of managing people and building effective relationships with entities and individuals. She maintained that work environments had human problems and interactions with psychological, ethical, and economic perspectives. She suggested the management should engage in strategic thinking about vision, empowerment, and relationship management. She also advocated the importance of the whole rather than focusing only on the specific. The latter was the most prevalent approach during her time. Follett's contributions were significantly ahead of the mainstream thinking during her life; however, she left an enormous legacy for other scholars and business leaders to follow.

Elton Mayo (1880–1949) was the famous interpreter of the Hawthorne experiments at Western Electric's plant near Chicago during the 1920s. Mayo concluded that job satisfaction increased as workers were given more self-determination in establishing work conditions and standards of production.[7] He also found that interaction and cooperation enhanced group cohesion, and that job satisfaction and output depended on an individual's sense of worth and importance. Mayo established the importance of social research in making determinations about effective practices in the workplace. Unlike some of his predecessors, his work was well known and formed a basis for management thought in the US. He led the way toward the philosophy that business administration was more than just managing resources and that leadership and people were among the most important aspects of managing enterprises because people are the essential ingredient for achieving success.

Much later, during the second half of the twentieth century, Peter Drucker (1909–2005) became one of the most influential management gurus to date. Drucker's contributions included the concept of the corporation, the practice of management, and his articulation of the tasks, responsibilities, and practices of management. In the *Concept of the Corporation*, Drucker challenged many of the prevailing practices and the underlying management perspectives. He studied operations at General Motors (GM) and suggested that many processes were inefficient and that management should focus on managing people, not just the machines. Drucker was a leader in establishing management as a discipline in its own right. Moreover, he was an innovative thinker who viewed business in the broader context of the whole business environment. The following reflects Drucker's views, ones that still resonate today:[8]

Harmony also [must] exists between the interest of society in a clear and carefully planned corporation policy and the interest of the corporation itself. If the corporation does not have a clear policy and a definite organ of policy decision, its actions and behavior become unpredictable. This must introduce elements of insecurity into the economic life which directly threaten social stability. Society has an overriding interest in predictable pricing policies, predictable employment and personnel policies, and predictable business practices, which can be obtained only through managerial policy decisions.

Drucker encouraged senior management to think about social and environmental responsibilities as well as the economic ones. He was keenly concerned about the relationships between management and the individual workers.

In his second book, *The Principles of Management*, published in 1954, Drucker established his famous eight key result areas (KRA) for selecting objectives. They include market standing, innovation, productivity, physical and financial resources, profitability, managers' performance and development, workers' performance and attitude, and public responsibility.[9] Drucker used KRA as a basis for determining the primary concerns that senior management should include in strategy development and implementation. He wanted business leaders to take a broader perspective in establishing strategies and objectives. Most importantly, he wanted senior management to focus on market position and innovation. While his KRA are not exactly the same as the primary areas of the balanced scorecard (financial, internal business process, learning and growth, and customer), the underlying theoretical theme is similar.[10]

Drucker was a theoretical strategists and management construct innovator who articulated what the management should be focusing on and doing instead of just trying to reflect on the prevailing practices of the day. For instance, many business scholars during those days were simply trying to convey to strategic leaders and practitioners what the GM, DuPont, and US Steel (big businesses) approaches were. They simply endorsed the prevailing practices rather than critically evaluating them. On the other hand, Drucker was critical of many of the prevailing approaches and suggested how companies might improve their management constructs. He was intellectually honest and did not fear being on the leading edge of management thinking or opposing mainstream perspectives. Moreover, he did not worry about criticizing many of the commonly held perspectives and existing practices, even those of the business giants – the most successful companies and strategic leaders.

Drucker focused much of his work on what good management should be. He put the strategic leaders at the forefront, not just the company. Indeed, he identified that good management should include "seven new tasks":[11]

- Manage by objectives;
- Take more risks and look further ahead. Push risk-taking decisions into lower levels in the organization;
- Be able to make strategic decisions;
- Be able to build an integrated team, each member of which is capable of measuring their own performance and results in relation to common objectives;
- Be able to communicate information fast and clearly . . . and be able to motivate people . . . to obtain responsible participation;
- Be able to see the business as a whole and to integrate an individual's function within it;
- Be able to relate the product and industry to the total environment, to find what is significant in it and to account for that in decisions and actions . . . Increasingly, the manager will have to learn to see economic, political, and social developments on a worldwide scale and to integrate worldwide trends into decisions. This perspective must encompass developments outside of the company's particular market or country, and the manager must begin to see the economic, political, and social developments on a worldwide scale.

Drucker's insights about the tasks included many elements of contemporary management theories. In fact, his recommendation to promote risk-taking at lower levels of the organization is being relearned in many businesses today in the form of empowerment. His perspectives on viewing the whole business and integrating the entire organization with its external dimensions are essential elements of ESM as discussed throughout this book.

The theories, concepts, and practices that Drucker articulated during the 1950 and 1960s, including the broader corporate responsibilities in the social, economic, and political realms, are central to many of our modern concepts of strategic management. For instance, he stated in 1954 that "management is also responsible for making sure that the present actions and decisions of the business enterprise will not create future [negative] public opinion or demands and policies that threaten the enterprise, its freedom, and its economic success."[12] Many of his comments have become the underlying premises of ESM and the principles of SBD and corporate social responsibility (CSR).

Drucker was instrumental in changing the pre-World War II view of management that focused on hierarchical structure to a more global perspective of best practices and well-defined roles and responsibilities of managers. Drucker has had a great influence on the discipline of management and on strategic thinking and management in particular. It is difficult to say what his most definitive work and contributions are. One of Drucker's most widely used books that helped to establish the roles and responsibilities of managers and leaders was *Management • Tasks • Responsibilities • Practices.* In this book, he defines the essence of management:[13]

Management is a social function and embedded in a culture – a society – a tradition of values, customers, and beliefs, and in governmental and political systems. Management is – and should be – culture-conditioned; but in turn, management and managers shape culture and society . . .

Management is tasks. Management is a discipline. But management is also people. Each achievement of management is the achievement of a manager. Every failure is a failure of a manager. People manage rather than "forces" or "facts." The vision, dedication, and integrity of managers determine whether there is management or mismanagement.

His greatest achievement may have been in changing the mindset about what management is from a narrow perspective dealing with the immediate situation and the short term to a broader perspective of the global business environment and a more inclusive view of both the short term and the long term. He viewed short-term wins as meaningless if they made the company more vulnerable in the future. His holistic thinking included:

The tasks – economic performance: making work productive and the worker achieving; managing the social impact and social responsibilities; and doing all of this in balance between the demands of today and the demands of tomorrow – are the things in which the public at large has a stake. The public has no concern with – and only mild interest in – what managers have to do to accomplish their tasks. It is rightly concerned with its performance.

Drucker based his management constructs on the idea that businesses are social organizations obligated to achieve performance in each of the social, economic, and environmental dimensions and to provide balanced outcomes and ongoing success. He advocated that successful companies had to be successful across the broad spectrum of the business environment, and all of the internal and external dimensions, and had to ensure that such success would endure over time.

In the 1960s, Douglas McGregor (1906–1964) wrote about the *Human Side of Enterprise*.[14] McGregor's Theory X and Theory Y laid the foundation for expanding the importance of employees of an organization and changing management thinking about the roles and contributions of individuals in organizations. Theory X assumes that people dislike work and they must be controlled and directed by management to ensure that results are achieved.[15] Theory Y assumes that people enjoy work and naturally engage in productive activities. It holds that people exercise self-direction and self-control and are committed to achieving organizational objectives.[16] While there has been much debate about McGregor's theories, he clearly was a leading determinant of strategic management thinking, using theories rather than examining prevailing practices to determine what would be most effective and suitable for the mainstream.

In the 1960s, Theodore Levitt (1925–2006) became famous when his article, "Marketing Myopia" appeared in *Harvard Business Review*.[17] While his work focused on the importance of marketing and the need for innovation in marketing, he challenged the shortsightedness of conventional management thinking that focused on production and the prevailing market situation rather than on developing a broader, strategic view of the business realities and market opportunities.[18] He suggested that organizations must learn to think in terms of markets, not just products, and in terms of opportunities, not just making money. He warned against complacency and suggested that management should think about what business they should be in rather than assume the narrow focus of the prevailing case (the business that they are in). While Levitt made his mark on marketing, he also had a great influence on strategic thinking about what could be instead of what is. Implicit in his work is the notion that changes in the business environment and market spaces force management to think about theoretical and "outside-the-box" solutions as well as those based on the realities of the time. As the world changes, the old practices become less relevant and new theories and practices have to be conceived and constructed to fit the new realities. These concepts resonate well in today's more complicated and turbulent times.

At the same time, Alfred Chandler, Jr. (1918–present) helped to transform many of the largest corporations from centralized organizational structures to decentralized ones. In his book, *Strategy and Structure: Chapters in the History of the American Enterprise*, Chandler promoted the strategic management theory that structure is driven by strategy.[19] He emphasized the importance of external forces as opportunities for change and the concomitant actions of setting direction and strategic decision making. Chandler championed a broader theoretical perspective of management that included strategic decision making and leading change.

Henry Mintzberg (1939–present), Cleghorn Professor on Management Studies at McGill University in Montreal, focused on the organizational aspects of management and the roles and responsibilities of managers. Mintzberg is a radical thinker who looked at the nature of managerial work as a determinant of strategy. He classified the different types of organizations, and in his 1979 book, *The Strategy of Organizations*, he discussed the entrepreneurial organization, the machine organization, the diversified organization, the professional organization, the innovative organization, and the missionary organization.[20] He examined organizational design and the best ways for managers to accomplish their ends. Mintzberg developed an organizational construct consisting of "six basic parts of the organization."[21] The six parts included the primary level of the operating core, the middle line, the strategic apex, the support structure of the supporting staff, the "techno-structure," and the ideology.

The strategic apex comprises of senior management and the strategic direction of the organization. It is the domain of the strategic leaders and senior executives. Middle line connects the linkages between the higher levels of senior management and the lower levels of functional management. It provides stability and control and facilitates the flow of information and decision making. The operating core involves the basic operations, functions, and activities of the organization. It involves the design, development, production, marketing, distribution, and delivery of the products and services. Techno-structure is the staff analysts who design the systems and processes and provide the technical expertise and control mechanisms. The supporting staff includes the specialists like data management, accounting, human resource management, and numerous others who support the middle line and the core. The ideology involves the beliefs, values, philosophies, traditions, and culture of the organization. Figure 2.1 depicts Mintzberg's construct.[22]

Michael Porter (1947–present), one of the leading management gurus of the late twentieth century, reinvented many of the constructs of strategic thinking and management. In his 1980 book, *Competitive Strategy: Techniques for Analyzing Industries and Competitors*, Porter articulated five forces that he contends drive industry competition: the power of buyers, the power of suppliers, the threat of substitutes, potential new entrants, and rivalry among

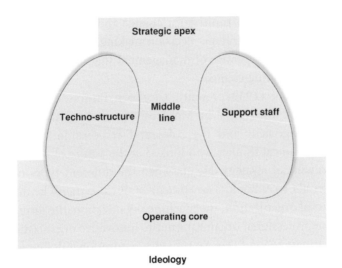

Figure 2.1   Mintzberg's six basic parts of the organization

existing firms. He also identified his famous generic strategies: cost leadership, differentiation, and focus.[23] Subsequently, in his 1985 book, *Competitive Advantage: Creating and Sustaining Superior Performance*, Porter analyzed in detail the value chain and value system concepts. His thoughts on the value chain and value system are still some of the most prevailing views of the essential relationships in the value delivery system.[24] His models examine product delivery, industry structure, and competitive aspects. They also include a comprehensive analysis of the suppliers, distribution channels, and customers as part of the value system. His models were discussed in the previous chapter.

During the early 1980s, W. Edwards Deming (1900–1993) brought back to the US his theories on quality management that he had so successfully embedded into the management culture of many Japanese companies. Deming and other quality management gurus, like Joseph Juran (1904–present), helped to transform Japanese manufacturers from the low quality producers to world-class corporations.[25] In his book, *Out of the Crisis*, Deming articulated a powerful message that all corporations could reform their management style to include the importance of quality, productivity, continuous improvement, and the transformation of the management system.[26] He emphasized that it is management's responsibility to ensure quality and continuous improvement, and he articulated fourteen total quality principles focusing on management commitment and involvement, employee training, and continuous improvement.[27] He was an advocate of process analysis for problem solving and decision making. Most importantly, he argued that ninety percent of all problems are due to the management system, not the people involved.

Deming's philosophies were pivotal and now serve as the foundation for contemporary strategic thinking about leading change. Deming was a true theoretical strategist who understood that developing, producing, and marketing high-quality products was inherently correct. He realized that there was no way to prove his theories empirically before strategic leaders committed to quality initiatives because most companies at the time had poor quality methods and generally produced thousands of defects per million opportunities for defects. Deming suggested that strategic leaders make the improvements and the proof would follow. History has proven his theories to be correct; today, the prevailing quality mantra is six-sigma thinking (3.4 defects per million opportunities).[28]

Deming's greatest contribution in the long term may be his notion of using theory rather than practice as the rationale for leading change and developing strategic action plans. His philosophies and principles may be applied to many other areas, most importantly to ESM and SBD, where executives often ask for proof instead of using the underlying principles, philosophies, and beliefs. Deming would say to initiate the management constructs because the underlying aspects are inherently sound and correct. It is impossible to prove that the benefits will be achieved until the company commits to the strategies and action plans and achieves sustainable success. For instance, Toyota transformed its product delivery system to just-in-time and lean production and has achieved great success over the last four decades. The strategic leaders at the time did not ask for proof because there were no examples of management constructs which would prove that the changes would be successful. They simply had the courage, confidence, and commitment to implement the necessary actions because they knew that inherently the constructs were proper; better quality is always better. Moreover, they knew that doing nothing was unacceptable. They refused to let the prevailing competitive forces dictate the company's destiny. They were too disadvantaged in the global business environment because of the low volume at the time; they had to do something dramatic and they did just that.

Kenichi Ohmae (1943–present) expanded the concepts of strategic management by incorporating Japanese thinking into the formulating and implementing of business strategies. In his 1982 book, *The Mind of the Strategists: The Art of Japanese Business*, Ohmae challenged business leaders to think in broad terms when developing strategy.[29] He advocated dynamic interaction with the business environment as a means of finding new opportunities not being exploited by the competition or other industries.

Toward the end of the 1980s, business process reengineering became a prevailing management approach for managing change as discussed in Chapter 1. The original intent of reengineering, which was made popular by Michael Hammer and James Champy in their book, *Reengineering the Corporation*, was to make quantum leaps in performance through innovative processes and new business structures. They defined it as:[30]

Reengineering is the fundamental rethinking and radical redesign of business processes to achieve dramatic improvements in critical, contemporary measures of performance, such as cost, quality, service, and speed.

While reengineering was intended to be a critical examination of the fundamental strategies and positions of businesses to make dramatic improvements, it was generally misapplied. Many companies decimated their middle-management ranks, laid off workers, and focused on short-term, cost-cutting efforts. Profits improved in the short term, but many of the companies suffered in the long term. While the theoretical foundation had merit, the practical applications missed the mark.

In 1990, Peter Senge influenced strategic management thinking by introducing new concepts about systems thinking and adaptive change. He also popularized the notion of mental models. In his book, *The Fifth Discipline*, Senge defined mental models as "deeply ingrained assumptions, generalizations, or even pictures of images that influence how we understand the world and how we take action."[31] He examined the learning organization and questioned how people could use their imagination to create a better future. Imagination involves mental models of what could be or what it really is. Senge's work on developing models is a precursor to the constructs of the extended enterprise and the crafting business strategies and solutions for twenty-first-century companies so that they may better manage complexity and lead change.

C. K. Prahalad and Gary Hamel published *Competing for the Future* in 1994.[32] In it they argued that strategy was intended to be broad and adaptive and that businesses should determine the underlying conditions and respond with strategic intent and architecture. They view strategy to be complex, robust, and based on the core competencies of the organization and on ways to exploit the business context, especially internal capabilities and external opportunities. While there are significant disagreements about the importance and applications of core competencies, Prahalad and Hamel's theories have driven the strategic thinking of many corporations over the last decade.

Robert Kaplan and David Norton have also been pivotal contributors to the discourse on business strategy, promoting balanced constructs that cut across the business environment and the value delivery systems of the organization. In their 1996 book, *The Balanced Scorecard*, they set forth perhaps the greatest single philosophical modification in management thinking in recent times. They argue that financial success depends on more than just making money.[33] They assert that business success derives from a balanced management system that focuses on long-term investments in customers and employees (people), product innovation, and the whole value system. Their perspectives connect distributed thinking about making money for the corporation to extended enterprise-wide thinking about creating value for all of the internal and external participants.

Today, Gary Hamel, one of the leading authorities on business concept innovation suggests that in an age of non-linear change, insights provide opportunities for dramatic innovation, not just knowledge. In *Leading the Revolution*, Hamel asserts that business concept innovation is the next level to be explored in creating new possibilities and opportunities. Hamel believes business concept innovation is a rare occurrence within organizations, but one that offers exciting opportunities for outpacing competition and creating new market spaces. His view is that "unless you and your company become adept at business concept innovation more imaginative minds will capture tomorrow's wealth."[34]

Strategic management constructs have evolved dramatically over the last half century, yet many businesses and academic institutions lag significantly behind in their articulation of strategic management. Many business schools still focus on industry settings, competitive warfare, and profit making above everything else. One of the problems for many companies is that their employees are learning old theories when they attend business school. Strategic leaders then have to convert such thinking into what the company is doing in the real world.

The development of selected strategic management models

Strategic management and SBP have evolved incrementally over the twentieth century. The underlying constructs changed from administrative policy formation to long-range planning during the 1950s and to the origins of strategic management developed at Harvard Business School during the early

1960s. During those times, strategic management and planning models were typically based on the prevailing business situation and the development of competitive strategies, especially those pertaining to products and markets. When developing business strategies, the focus was to exploit and/or improve the competitive positions within the company's served markets or its industry. The main areas of concern and interest were typically on finding or expanding opportunities for making money and converting the internal resources into external outcomes.

As the management construct matured, leading scholars developed numerous strategic management and planning models to guide business leaders and strategists in their quest to formulate and implement strategies. F. F. Gilmore and R. G. Brandenburg created a fairly elaborate top-management planning framework in 1962.[35] It included an appraisal of operating results, competitive actions, economic trends, and technological developments that would identify problems, indicate opportunities, and define threats. Based on the strategic analysis, their model presented a process flow that would provide the means and mechanisms for the development of a new economic mission, competitive strategy, and a program of actions that would lead ultimately to a new master plan.[36]

H. Igor Ansoff, considered one of the founders of strategic planning, wrote *Corporate Strategy* which was published in 1965. He mapped out the Ansoff Model of Strategic Planning.[37] It was a detailed flow chart of analysis, gap identification, and strategic decision making. It flowed from the specific external industry and economic questions to the narrow internal objectives and product–market strategy. While Ansoff intended to articulate a strategic planning process, he really focused on a very specific range of strategies dealing with the expansion of the product–market dimensions and options relating to diversification.

One of Ansoff's most famous constructs was the Ansoff matrix for selecting business (marketing) strategies. The matrix was a simple product–market decision framework that provided four strategic choices for addressing product and market opportunities. Strategic choices included market penetration of existing products in existing markets, product expansion via new products for existing markets, market expansion of existing products for new markets, and diversification via new products for new markets.[38] His view of strategic thinking about product–market choices was used extensively for decades. While the Ansoff Model was narrow in scope, it did set the stage for further development of strategic planning. The focus was mainly on the value delivery system and the action plans that the strategic leaders of the business units had formulated.

Many of the strategic management models today are still based on the fundamental concepts and methods developed by Andrews, Ansoff, C. R. Christensen, Drucker and others during the late 1960s and early 1970s. While there have been many refinements and modifications, the generic models of today still have many elements in common with the early models. For instance, Edmund Learned, C. R. Christensen, K. R. Andrews, and W. D. Guth developed a simple model in the mid-1960s that contained the underpinning of early strategic management. The main propositions were:[39]

- Strategy involves the pattern of objectives, purposes, or goals and major policies and plans for achieving those goals, stated in such a way to define what business the company is in or is to be in and the kind of company it is or is to be.
- Strategy entails two equally important and interrelated tasks: strategy formulation and strategic implementation.
- The formulation of strategy requires the general management to create a fit among:
  - the opportunities in the external industry environment,
  - the strengths and weaknesses of the firm,
  - the personal values of the key implementers, and
  - the broader societal expectations of the firm.

Mintzberg called this the core "Design School" model because it was created at Harvard and it was based on the concept that strategy formulation and implementation was a process.[40] It is also called the strengths, weaknesses, opportunities, and threats (SWOT) model. It simply analyzed the key internal capabilities and external factors. The main questions it asked were what business are you in and what are your goals and plans. It was a static view of the realities of the business world. It reflected on the conditions and trends in the markets and competitive spaces and examined the opportunities and risks in terms of internal resources and processes. It focused on what was, not what could be.

Andrews added sophistication to the basic SWOT model with the addition of a formulation stage that was linked to the development of the corporate and business strategy and an implementation stage that connected strategy to organizational processes and leadership. Figure 2.2 is a representation of Andrews' model and a view of SBP circa 1970.

Andrews' model included a situation analysis of the external opportunities and risks and the internal capabilities and resources of the organization. It

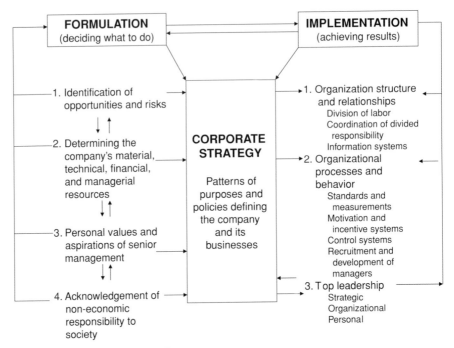

Figure 2.2   Andrews' strategic planning model[41]

included an assessment of the personal values of senior management and of the social climate of the organization. It is interesting to view how Andrews included in his model the notion of non-economic responsibilities to society. Andrews was not the first to suggest the notion of social responsibilities, and there remain critics today that challenge whether businesses even have any social responsibilities. His model followed Chandler's view that strategy leads structure.

George Steiner developed a "flow-type" model for strategic planning in 1969. He was a business scholar and professor of management at the University of California, Los Angeles. In his book, *Top Management Planning*, he mapped out the strategic planning process from establishing the fundamental purposes, identifying the basic values, and evaluating the SWOT to crafting the strategic plans, the medium-range plans, and the tactical plans and implementation actions.[42] While his model had less detail than the Ansoff or Gilmore and Brandenburg models, Steiner did distinguish between high-level corporate plans, business unit level strategies, and lower-level tactical plans.

Steiner's model divided the process into three stages: premises, planning, and implementation and review. While there are many similarities to earlier

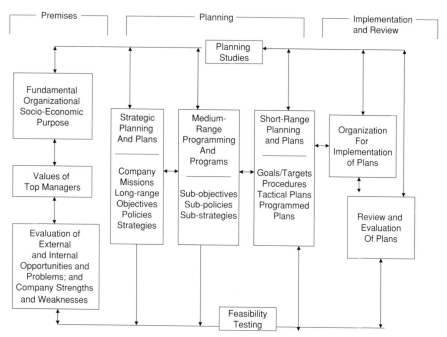

Figure 2.3   Steiner's structure and process of business planning model

models, he emphasized the review of outcomes and the evaluation of the current and previous plans. This review established an ongoing process of strategic thinking and planning rather than a linear process or annual planning cycle. What was once task oriented became result oriented as the focus shifted from developing business plans to crafting strategies, implementing them, and managing results.

Figure 2.3 shows Steiner's structure and process of business planning model.

In his 1994 book, *The Rise and Fall of Strategic Planning*, Mintzberg challenged the prevailing views of strategic management and SBP and argued that strategic management should be more open-ended and based on insights and imagination rather than solely on data and analysis.[43] He also called for strategists to actively engage in the dynamics of their businesses and not be so detached from the real world.[44] He said they should "craft strategies" rather than plans. His work lays the foundation for the modern view of strategic management and the inclusion of the extended enterprise in strategic planning.

Based on the contributions of these scholars and others, strategic management and SBP have evolved over the decades to include the concept of vision and mission, the analysis of the business environment, an assessment of core

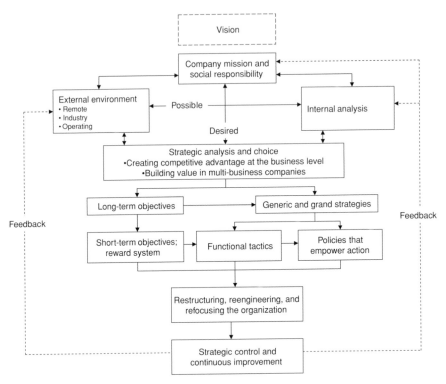

Figure 2.4   A generic strategic management model

competencies and resources, and the selection of strategies and action plans, and implementation. In fact, the generic model for strategic management and planning today is still heavily influenced by Porter's perspectives on the five forces driving industry competition (power of buyers, power of suppliers, threat of substitutes, potential new entrants, and rivalry among existing firms), his generic strategies (cost leadership, differentiation, and focus), and his value chain and value system concepts. These concepts still focus on existing industry settings and assume that the best way to "win" is to defeat the competitors. That perspective is narrow and fails to benefit from a more innovative view of what could be or should be. Figure 2.4 depicts one of the standard strategic management models of today.[45]

The concept of a vision for the future was not in the authors' model but was added because most contemporary models include the notion of vision. Note that the vision is generally determined by corporate executives, not the strategic leaders of business units. The model depicts nine critical tasks:[46]

1. Formulate the company's mission, including broad elements about its purpose, philosophy, and goals.
2. Conduct an analysis that reflects the company's internal conditions and capabilities.
3. Assess the company's external environment, including both the competitive and the general contextual factors.
4. Analyze the company's strategic options by matching resources with the external environment.
5. Identify the most desirable options by evaluating each in light of the company's mission.
6. Select the set of long-term objectives and grand strategies that will achieve the most desirable results.
7. Develop annual objectives and short-term strategies that are compatible with the selected set of long-term and short-term objectives and grand strategies.
8. Implement the strategic choices by means of budgeted resource allocations to support the matching tasks, people, structures, technologies, and reward systems.
9. Evaluate the success of the strategic process.

The contemporary model retained many elements of earlier models. The addition of philosophy, however, is critical for establishing sustainable enterprises. Most approaches would suggest that the strategic analysis of the external business environment should precede the assessment of the internal capabilities and resources. Moreover, the selected strategic options should be based on a match between the external and internal factors, while recognizing the changes and improvements to internal capabilities that have to be made. Core competencies and capabilities are not static, but are dynamic realities and should be always in the state of development and improvement. The selection of strategic options should also be based on the vision for the future and follow the grand strategy of the corporation that sets the overall strategic direction. For instance, a grand strategy might focus enterprise-wide strategic leadership (ESL) on making the corporation a six-sigma quality company across its business units and a sustainable enterprise using the principles and practices of SBD.

The model highlights several key aspects of implementing strategies and action plans. It discusses some, but not all, of the means and mechanisms for executing strategies. One of the most important is the allocation of resources and the identification of incentives for achieving the desired short-term and long-term objectives. The evaluation of success and outcomes is likewise critical to sustainable success. The feedback mechanisms provide management with information and understanding about the adjustments and improvements that they have to make on an ongoing basis to perpetuate the process and realize positive outcomes. However, the notion of an annual cycle may not be appropriate in a fast-paced world. These concepts will be explored in greater detail in subsequent chapters.

The models discussed in this section were originally intended to provide a framework for the strategic management of the corporation. But given their limited scope and lack of sophistication from a contemporary perspective, they are more suitable for small companies. They focus on the strategic management of the business units rather than the strategic management of the whole corporation.

A synopsis of the strategic management model

Reflections on reality

Strategic leaders and business scholars have been searching for the all-encompassing strategic management construct and/or strategic management model for decades. Porter's five forces of industry structure has been one of the most often referred to models over the last twenty-five years; however, its strength is its limitation. It is relatively simple and includes only the main elements of the value system or extended enterprise; it focuses on competitive spaces rather than market spaces. Moreover, it is based on the idea that the competitive space is the main arena and agenda. The focus is narrow and the scope is limited to only economic considerations. It is easy to understand and characterize any competitive situation using the model. However, it does not include the broader elements of the business environment and the social and natural worlds.

Porter's model, while useful in competitive setting, especially those where the competitive forces are severe, must be expanded to fit the realities of the twenty-first century. Today, the competitive scene is often more intense than when Porter conceived his model, and competition will most likely intensify as emerging companies from China, India, Brazil, and others become global players. Some of those companies have the potential to develop, produce, and sell products on scales that are five to ten times greater than those historically enjoyed in the developed countries. For instance, the economic power of the US increased dramatically at the end of the nineteenth century because it had a unified market established by the commerce clause of the US Constitution and connected by a vast transportation system (the railroads). This approach, open and free markets, has since been expanded to include "free trade" in

North America and the common market of the EU. However, those markets are much smaller than the potential markets in China and India. China is expected to have approximately 500 to 600 million households within a decade, while the US is expected to have about 125 million households. The opportunities in these "new market spaces" are enormous, as are the challenges associated with designing, developing, producing, and marketing the solutions.

Competition is a primary consideration, but just one of many that must be made in developing an innovative strategic management model. The development of such a framework for understanding the business world is a precursor to developing business models for specific companies and individual situations or for crafting and implementing strategies.

A strategic management model is a broad mapping of the essential elements that should be incorporated in real-world management constructs and business models that corporations use to develop and deploy business strategies and achieve their objectives. The strategic management model serves as a platform for fine-tuning the elements and creating the actual methods for transforming or transitioning the corporation into a more effective, desirable, and sustainable entity.

The efforts are unending as management constructs continue to be transformed in response to changes in the business environment. Each business may have its own unique management constructs and strategic management model based on its view of reality and strategic direction, with strategic management processes within the overall SMS, and sub-systems within systems.

The whole system of strategies, action plans, and processes for D-Day (June 6, 1944) during World War II is an example of a system with many sub-systems. The Allies created a system with many components in preparing and executing D-Day. Success was achieved because the SMS worked exceptionally well. However, there were many difficulties and failures within the sub-systems, and not everything worked according to plans. But, because General Eisenhower and his strategic leaders focused on the whole and integrated the plans and operations into an overarching system, they were successful. It was their attention to the whole system and the imagination, ingenuity, and commitment of the whole enterprise that led to success. Of course, success was also due to the millions of individual contributors who gave their full efforts and even their lives to the cause.

The strategic management model and SMS can be articulated in many different ways, and there are numerous sub-systems, sub-structures (platforms) and processes that can be included. Platforms are the critical areas or the building blocks that can be easily modified to create a unique approach. The most important of the platforms include:

- **Strategic leadership** – providing vision, strategic direction, perspectives, values, policies, and business models for leading change through innovation, integration, and inspiration, and for achieving sustainable success.
- **Strategic management** – analyzing the business environment to find opportunities and mitigate vulnerabilities, crafting and implementing strategies to create value for customers and stakeholders and outperforming competition, and leading the enterprise.
- **Market and customer success** – discovering and providing markets, customers, and stakeholders with the solutions they need, require, and expect to be successful in their endeavors.
- **Enterprise-wide integration** – structuring an effective extended enterprise(s) with solid relationships, linking the enterprise with its business environment and market spaces, and connecting the processes in a seamless holistic system with effective and efficient sub-systems.
- **Value proposition** – providing the desired benefits, positive effects, and knowledge in terms of the investments made by all of the constituents and similarly, reducing all of the costs, defects, and burdens associated with the situation; maximizes the positives and minimizes the negatives.
- **Value innovation** – identifying new opportunities and developing them into new realities, creating value for the business environment through new technologies, products, processes, and most especially business frameworks, and transforming the extended enterprise, the organization, and all of the people therein through learning.
- **Value creation and delivery** – creating new solutions and building positive relationships in the market spaces, envisioning and delivering products and services to customers, satisfying stakeholders and constituents, and achieving performance and objectives.
- **Competitive forces** – preempting the competition through sustainable solutions, outpacing it through innovation and substitution.

While other sub-systems and sub-structures may pertain in specific situations or industries, those suggested embody the general approaches and elements that are important to most companies and businesses. They provide broad perspectives so that strategic leaders have the foundation necessary to create, reinvent, or reinvigorate their own strategic management constructs and frameworks.

The idea is to expand strategic thinking, management, and planning to be more inclusive, innovative, and connected, and not necessarily to develop a grand unified theory of strategic management. While the latter might be desirable, such a goal is most likely not within reach for most companies or not within the realm of the academic theories of today. It is more of a dream for tomorrow than a possibility for today. As in transforming a three-sigma quality company to six-sigma quality, there are many phases and steps to be taken, actions to be initiated, and lessons to be learned that cannot be skipped over. Moreover, it takes time and a lot of learning to make the transitions and transformations to new realities.

Strategic leadership and strategic management cut across all levels of the company, but represent the most crucial considerations for the strategic leaders for strategic business units (SBUs) and small and medium-sized enterprises (SMEs). Innovation and integration are also important across the entire enterprise, but are of primary concern for the strategic management of the business units. In turn, value creation and value delivery are generally the domain of functional management and the operating units. Functional and operational management address the needs and expectations of the customers and stakeholders. Competition is usually perceived as adversarial, causing conflicts and rivalries. While this can be true, the most effective way to deal with competition is to preempt it by creating sustainable solutions that are affordable with maximum benefits and minimum negative aspects.

Strategic leadership and management

Every leader within the embedded strategic management system must have the capability to be a visionary leader that understands the big picture and a strategic leader that leads change and gets results. Moreover, every leader must be able to inspire people to become part of the solution and take aggressive actions so that the positive changes and dramatic improvements are realized. Strategic leaders must instill optimism and dedication in people and get them to reach out beyond the norm to create a richer reality and more sustainable future.

The highest level strategic leaders create the vision for the future and work to translate the vision into reality through strategic direction and grand strategies. They provide the big picture, the perspective, or mental model of the future for the company and make the strategic direction understandable and desirable. Visionary leaders also provide the sense of purpose and broad philosophies, principles, values, and ethics.

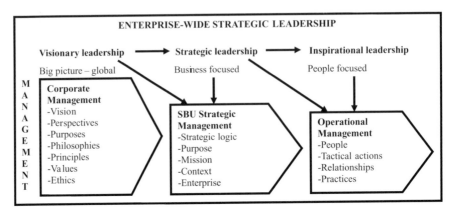

Figure 2.5   The overlapping aspects of ESL and embedded strategic management

Strategic leadership at the business unit level (often referred to as SBUs) involves crafting business strategies and ensuring that implementation plans are appropriate and actionable. Moreover, it requires a steadfast dedication to execution and action. Operational and functional leadership which is usually subordinate to the strategic leadership involves gaining acceptance of the strategic direction and getting people across the organization to align the capabilities and resources of the corporation and its enterprise(s) and to enthusiastically execute initiatives and programs. Still, operational management and functional leaders at lower levels must also think in strategic terms. People at each level within the organization have influence and therefore, the responsibility and ability to move the organization toward its vision and the strategic direction. Many great strategies fail because of the lack of commitment and poor execution.

Strategic leadership occurs throughout all levels of the organization's management. Figure 2.5 depicts the overlapping aspects of forms of leadership and the embedded corporate management systems.

Typically, executives and high-level senior management devote a majority of their intellectual capital, time, and efforts to thinking about the future and crafting and ensuring the strategic direction of the company, its SBUs, and their extended enterprises. They should take a broad perspective of the business environment and work on discovering new opportunities and creating new business ventures. They also provide for the proper governance of the corporation and ensure that the vision, purposes, philosophies, principles, values, and ethics of the corporation are well established, succinct, and articulated to everyone, up and down and across the corporation and all that it reaches.

Strategic management and the strategic leaders at the next level, in turn, are involved in constantly reexamining the strategic positions of the SBUs to find and take advantage of opportunities and to mitigate challenges and vulnerabilities. Strategic leaders of the business units articulate the strategic logic of the businesses, explaining who they are, what they are doing, and what they want to become. They express and communicate the purpose and mission of the business units and the operating systems. They develop pathways to success and ensure that strategies and action plans are implemented and the desired performance is achieved based on context of the external business environment. They also connect the people of the organization with the executive management of the corporation and link the businesses with their extended enterprises. SBU strategic leaders are the general managers who typically spend half of their time on strategic concerns and initiatives and half on the proper performance of the operations and functional aspects. Thus, SBU strategic leaders focus on business-related strategies and action plans.

Finally, operational management devotes a relatively small portion of time and effort to strategic considerations and most of its time to the day-to-day execution of the businesses strategies and operational aspects. Operational management and functional leaders are at the forefront of actions and tactics. They are engaged in encouraging people within the organization and in the extended enterprise(s) to achieve results and become committed to obtaining positive outcomes. They are the inspirational leaders who are dedicated to achieving positive outcomes and supporting the employees.

The overlapping construct suggested in Figure 2.5 bridges the tangible roles and responsibilities of the management levels in an organization with intangible aspects such as the visionary leadership's view of the future and the inspirational leadership's more down-to-earth view of creating excitement about how to improve the present. The most important message of the construct, however, is that outstanding leaders at all levels have to think about how to create the future and achieve extraordinary results in the present, that is, they must think and work strategically. ESL is critical from the high level to the lowest as leaders across the whole organization build bridges to the future through innovation, integration, and value creation. More details about ESL are provided in Chapter 3.

Innovation and integration

Creating a sustainable enterprise involves integrating and linking together the embedded corporate management system and all of the systems within it and linking them from the origins of the raw materials and energy sources to customer applications and end of life. This includes linking the company's micro-environment with its suppliers and partners to the macro-environment of customers and stakeholders, market spaces, the business environment, and the social and natural worlds. From an enterprise point of view, strategy formulation and implementation must be based on an integrated system approach that includes the micro and the macro. However, the realities of the business world may force strategic leaders to focus more on the present or even on the past than on the prospects for the future. It is often easier to think about the prevailing situation and all of the challenges that have to be dealt with than to contemplate how to extricate the business from its difficulties. When in trouble, many business leaders simply do more of the same with more intensity. For instance, companies having problems with profitability often pressure their suppliers to cut the prices in belief that such actions will improve the situation. But, it usually does not solve the problems because they have not addressed the underlying causes of the difficulties. Such actions usually lead to a disintegration of the interests of the whole enterprise rather than an integration of two of the essential entities: producer and suppliers.

Two of the most critical management constructs involve strategic innovation and systems integration that focus on resolving embedded problems between the entities of the enterprise or with the technologies, products, processes, and operations (i.e. the solutions). Strategic innovation involves how strategic leaders plan to make the requisite transformations, transitions, developments, and improvements. Systems integration pertains not just to the company but to the extended enterprise(s) as well. While the management constructs of strategic innovation and systems integration include the micro-environment of the firm, the discussion herein covers the broader aspects related to the enterprise perspective, not just those that pertain only to the operational aspects.

In general, the strategic approaches to innovation and integration involve continuously working to create new solutions and to integrate the existing systems into more sustainable enterprises with solid linkages with all of the entities and everyone understands the relationships and works toward the common good. The best way to do this depends on the situation. The business environment changes rapidly, and it is often necessary to innovate as quickly as possible and to take on as many initiatives as are reasonably possible. It is important to recognize that too many innovations may result in many ongoing programs that are in progress, but not contributing to success. Having too many programs may frustrate the organization's ability to achieve its desired outcomes, resulting in few actual improvements. The intentions are good, but the results are fragmented. Strategic gains are made when businesses build upon ongoing success where the new gains are compounded with previous successes. On the other hand, if strategic management is too cautious and selects only those programs that they know can be achieved, they may underperform, fail to keep pace with change, and are unable to sustain success.

Business success depends on intellectual, physical, and financial capital that must be integrated in a succinct way. The business leaders of today owe a debt to their predecessors and to the other leaders and contributors in the arts, science, and technology who laid the foundation of knowledge that provides our high level of sophistication. The work of these pioneers has resulted in physical resources, capital assets, management constructs, knowledgeable people, and a lot of goodwill in the market spaces and the social world. The knowledge and experiential bases are enormous and growing daily through research and development, experimentation, and millions of other contributions. It is estimated that humankind's overall intellectual wealth doubles approximately every seven to nine years.[47] Therefore, learning is one of the most effective ways to achieve extraordinary value and high levels of performance.

While business leaders and people in general enjoy the benefits provided by their predecessors, current strategic leaders also have to rectify the problems created by poor decisions in the past and ensure that improvements are made and old problems are eliminated. For instance, product defects may result in liabilities that cost lives and money. Environmental problems like the inadequate or improper disposal of hazardous waste or spills of toxic substances require huge remediation projects often involving expenditures of capital that could have been used to pursue market space opportunities. Chemical companies in the US spent more money on environmental remediation projects during the 1990s than they invested in research and development for new technologies and products.

Figure 2.6 depicts the overlapping aspects of innovation and integration and identifies the typical initiatives to achieve extraordinary results at that level.

Knowledge is essential for creating new solutions through innovation. Such innovations involve the whole ESM framework at the macro-environment level using business concept innovation, technological innovations at the enterprise level, and product and process innovation generally at the microenvironment level. There are overlaps and each type of innovation can occur at the various levels.

The business concept is the platform upon which everything is organized, structured, and managed. It is an overarching ESM framework that provides

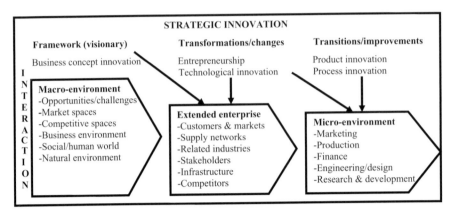

Figure 2.6   The overlapping aspects of strategic innovation and integration

strategic leaders, professionals, and practitioners across the enterprise with a sense of direction, understanding, and focus. It makes the complexities of the business environment easier to understand, appreciate, and deal with over time. Business concept innovation examines the corporation, business units, and their enterprises and develops new ways to integrate the whole into a more effective and efficient system for creating, delivering, and sustaining value and success.

At the macro-environment level, the business world is driven by opportunities and challenges. Most companies focus on finding opportunities with the present customers and in the existing markets. While there are many variations to purchasing patterns, businesses rely heavily on the loyalty of repeat customers. For example, Procter & Gamble and Unilever rely on customers to buy their soap, toothpaste, and many other household products on a regular basis. Obviously, the patterns vary for industrial and government markets and for business-to-business transactions.

Businesses have to identify, analyze, and deal with the challenges that exist in the markets. Those challenges may be caused by problems created by the companies when they create products and processes with defects, burdens, and impacts. Customers may be satisfied with the products that they buy, while stakeholders are unhappy with the implications. Cigarettes are a good example. Tobacco companies have loyal customers, but extremely unhappy stakeholders who want to restrict the use of the tobacco products and even eliminate their sale. Challenges also result from competition or technological changes that induce customers to change their behavior. The cell phone, for instance, has radically changed how people view telephones and the benefits that they provide.

But opportunities and challenges extend beyond current customers and stakeholders. The theories espoused in this book and those related to enterprise-wide strategic thinking involve broadening the normal purview of existing markets and customers to include the whole available market space(s). The market space includes potential customers who currently cannot buy the product for a variety of reasons. The many reasons usually include affordability and lack of the necessary support mechanisms. For instance, most of the available products in the world today have been designed by and for people in high-income countries (average incomes over PPPUS$20,000).[48] However, most such products are not suitable for people in low-income counties. Not only do the people lack the income necessary to buy the products, many of the products require support systems or infrastructures that do not exist in their locations. For these reasons, companies must understand the needs and expectations in the market spaces if they are to realize the opportunities. When this is done, extending the ESM framework to include the entire business environment, the social world, and the natural environment opens the door to many additional opportunities. Billions of people exist on only marginal income (i.e. one to four dollars per day). They need affordable products. Product designers should be asking themselves if and how they can provide products that represent real solutions for the needs of these people. Market space factors and considerations are discussed further in Chapter 5.

On the micro scale, systems integration involves linking the operations of the company with supply networks to identify opportunities to improve cost structures and overall effectiveness. Eliminating economic and environmental wastes is a critical factor in making products and services more affordable and attainable for people across all spectrums. While a lot of attention has been given to reducing costs through the use of low-wage locations like China and India, there are many other ways to reduce costs, including integrating the entire extended enterprise from the mining, extraction, and refining of raw material to the fabrication and production of parts and final products. Improved integration reduces redundancies, defects, and wastes by assuring that the work is performed efficiently, effectively, and correctly during each stage of production. For example, Wal-Mart has become a low-cost retailer by integrating the flow of goods from the beginning of its supply networks to delivery to its customers. It focuses on the effective and efficient flow of goods, information, finances, and decision making, minimizing costs and transactions within the system and the logistical support required to connect the suppliers and partners. Early strategic leaders at Wal-Mart, especially

Sam Walton, recognized that there are no "magic formulas" for achieving extraordinary outcomes. It takes strategic innovation and systems integration.

Sustainable outcomes are not the results of doing one thing exceptionally well, but rather, they are the results of doing everything as well as possible. It is the sum of all gains through the entire extended enterprise that leads to extraordinary success. Moreover, sustainable success is achieved by creating the means and mechanisms to take advantage of opportunities and mitigating challenges. Much of Wal-Mart's past success was due to its ability to attract people (customers) with marginal disposable incomes and satisfy their needs better than other retailers. It expanded the ability of its customers to buy more products and to repeat their success via shopping at Wal-Mart.

Transformations and transitions are the preemptive approaches for changing the foundation of the enterprise and creating the potential for sustainable success in the near and long terms. Transformations typically involve the more radical innovations that change the very nature of the businesses. They include new technologies and new-to-the-world products used to create and deliver value. Transitions usually involve product and process innovations that tend to be more incremental.

Technological innovation involves the discovery, development, demonstration, and deployment of new-to-the world technologies and the associated changes to the enterprise that are required to transform the old realities to ones that are more appropriate for the new situations. It often involves modifications to the enterprise from supply networks to customer relationships to incorporate the requirements of the new technologies. Entrepreneurship typically results in new, more sustainable solutions. It may include the development of clean technologies having fewer negatives and better benefits.

Transitions are incremental changes within the existing business framework (model) and strategic direction. They include improvements to existing technologies. Generally, they involve creating a new technology platform that is superior to the previous one. The Intel Pentium platforms are good examples of technology transitions that dramatically improve existing technology and ultimately become the next generation of related technologies. In transitions, the technologies change, but much of the extended enterprise stays the same. Such changes are not considered radical.

Likewise, product innovation, unless it is linked to radical technological innovation, involves evolutionary changes to existing products and replacing some of them with improved versions. It involves identifying, selecting, planning, implementing, and integrating new product development programs, understanding the latent needs and expectations of potential customers and stakeholders, improving supply networks and logistics, and solving end-of-life considerations. It usually incorporates the existing technologies and requires few changes to the extended enterprise.

The selection of effective new product development programs depends on the capabilities, skills, knowledge, desires, and resources of the corporation. It includes methods and analytical techniques that link product development and process improvement to the strategic direction of the enterprise. Considerations include the mandates and standards of the business environment, the underlying social, economic, and environmental concerns, and the identifiable needs and wants of customers and stakeholders.

Value networks and competitive forces

Creating value is driven by technological and product changes, improved solutions, and system enhancements. As discussed in the previous section, more effective and efficient systems lead to less waste. Value creation may also be enhanced as new competitors expand the options for customers and stakeholders. In some cases, the offerings are identical, especially if the products are essentially commodities. In other cases, each competitor attempts to differentiate its products and services so that it can gain a competitive advantage. Such advantages vary from an intangible advantage like the power of a brand name, such as the status associated with owning a BMW, to a tangible advantage like the better fuel efficiency of a Toyota Camry.

Value creation drives the value system and value delivery. Value creation focuses on innovation and mostly on the upstream side of the value system. It involves designing, developing, and producing solutions. Value delivery focuses on the downstream side of the enterprise: the delivery of products and services to customers and their customers and the transactions of goods and services in exchange for revenues and profits. It also includes end-of-life considerations and waste management. Value creation and value delivery also include the options that customers have in satisfying their needs through other means and mechanisms. Today, there are many non-traditional alternatives available through the Internet that did not exist ten years ago. People can easily buy previously owned products and services, and product reuse has expanded over the last decade with the advent of eBay and others. Moreover, the "eBay" phenomenon has turned some of one's previous customers into competitors. Now, there are eBay businesses that sell previously owned products of all kinds.

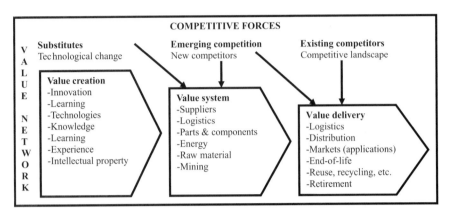

Figure 2.7   The overlapping aspects of value networks and competitive forces

Figure 2.7 depicts the overlapping aspects of value networks and competitive forces.

New competition is also found in emerging companies in developing countries. The emerging companies often have differential advantages like low-cost labor and no negative legacies to be concerned about. Substitute products, usually offered by corporations outside the traditional market space and its boundaries influence the economics and competitive positions of players in an industry. For instance, plastics have replaced steel in many applications and aluminum-can producers have captured most of the market space for beverage containers. And, there are thousands of other examples.

The framework presented in Figure 2.7 is similar to Porter's five forces. (Porter's forces include the producers, suppliers, buyers, new entrants, and substitutes.)[49] The major difference is that Porter focused on rivalry among industry competitors while the focus of an ESM perspective is on value creation, value system, and value delivery. The basic goal is not to defeat the competition, but to outperform customer and stakeholder expectations and achieve sustainable success for everyone. It is not to avoid dealing with competitors, but to make them less relevant to the strategic actions of the company.

Strategic leaders can do so by taking preemptive strategies and initiatives to assure that customers, stakeholders, supply networks, and other constituents achieve their objectives and are commensurately rewarded. Such actions do not eliminate competitive forces, they simply shift the emphasis from beating the competitors to preempting their actions by being more aggressive and successful with respect to markets and customers. The focus is where it should be (i.e. on markets and customers and the positive relationships that create value).

Successful strategic leaders understand that they cannot waste time and effort engaging in pitched battles with competitors in which no one wins and both parties are likely to become damaged or even destroyed. Analogously, in the natural world successful predators at the top of the food chain like lions instinctively know that they cannot waste too much energy on powerful prey animals or become engaged in battles where there is likelihood that they may be hurt; simple injuries may lead to catastrophic consequences. Even the top predators realize that it is not advantageous to waste energy or risk injury.

While there are numerous business scholars and strategic leaders who advocate winning the battle or gaining power over customers and suppliers, such thinking usually plants the seeds for future difficulties. The problem is that the countervailing forces may respond in the same ways. Business history is replete with stories about powerful companies who exploited their positions only to create animosity and bad will amongst their customers and suppliers. For instance, US Steel established pricing schemes during its dominance in which it controlled the pricing of steel products across the US industry. Such schemes worked effectively for US Steel in the short term but were unfavorable to its customers and many of its competitors. As long as US Steel had the power, customers had little choice but to pay what the company demanded. However, customers sought other options and eventually discovered that buying products from Japanese and Korean companies was more affordable even though US Steel operations were closer than those of the Pacific Rim companies. Eventually, US Steel lost market share and its dominance because it took a narrow perspective of how to conduct business. It attempted to win even though such actions meant that customers would lose. Today, very few companies have such overwhelming power, and those that have power may easily lose it as technologies and market forces change rapidly. Indeed, the more a corporation attempts to exploit its customers and/or suppliers, the more likely those entities will try to find alternatives so that they are less vulnerable and have a better chance of achieving sustainable success.

SBD and its connections with ESM

The principles of SBD

The notion of sustainable development (SD) originated in the 1987 Brundtland Report entitled "Our Common Future" prepared by the World Commission on Environment and Development for the General Assembly of the

United Nations.[50] The report defined SD as development and growth that "meets the needs of the present without compromising the ability of future generations to meet their needs."[51] SBD, the business-oriented perspectives of SD, involves creating economically sound, socially responsible, and environmentally conscious products and processes that maximize value creation and benefits, and minimizes degradation of human health and the natural environment, the depletion of resources, and negative impacts from wastes and pollution.

SBD is a parallel management construct to ESM that focuses on creating extraordinary value through preemptive strategies and value innovation in business settings. SBD involves moving toward more ideal solutions with greater benefits for customers and stakeholders, lower costs and enhanced affordability, and fewer deficiencies and impacts affecting the social, economic, and environmental dimensions. The objective of SBD is to create the best possible solutions for customers, stakeholders, and society. SBD imbues an aspiration to create a better future with improved and enduring outcomes.

Using the principles of SBD, strategic leaders become the architects of change and the masters of inter-disciplinary and inter-organizational action. Dynamic strategic leaders must have the knowledge and capabilities to orchestrate the design and development of new paradigms for proactively inventing the future of the organization.

SBD and ESM involve creating the vision of the future, positioning the organization to realize that vision, and inspiring the people to transform the existing capabilities into world-class competencies. Strategic leaders must engage people throughout the organization to become aware of and accept the principles and objectives of SBD and ESM, and to build the knowledge, capabilities, and actions necessary to support the transition to a richer reality.

SBD is principally concerned with innovation using product and technology developments to design clean technologies and innovative products. It includes the identification, selection, planning, implementation, and integration of development programs. SBD innovation programs are based on life-cycle thinking and management.

Life-cycle thinking is a leading-edge philosophy about how to progress from achieving satisfactory results and continuous improvement to creating extraordinary value while at the same time eliminating the causes of business problems at their source. The focus is on creating value streams that are strategically aligned and functioning effectively over time so that negative consequences are minimized and positive benefits and implications endure over time, justifying the investments of time, money, and resources. SBD innovations depend on people who have the intellectual capacity to think "outside-the-box" and create new knowledge and capabilities that enrich humankind and all that surrounds us.

The philosophical underpinnings of SBD

SBD is based on philosophical underpinnings concerning leading change through strategic innovations and creating harmony between business endeavors, human activities, and the natural world. The overarching principles include honesty, integrity, ethics, social responsibility, and fairness. The most significant principles also include inclusiveness in scope and strategic analysis, innovativeness in design and development, connectedness with customers, stakeholders, and partners, and openness in communications, reporting, and decision making. The philosophy is to create value for all based on social, economic, and environmental considerations. All of these principles guide strategic decision making. They lay the foundation for the vision, objectives, strategies, and behaviors of business leaders, professionals, and practitioners within the strategic and operating management systems.

SBD is based on real-world logic and uses fair and effective processes and approaches. It focuses on producing stability within the business environment, providing companies and their enterprises with effective use of resources and capabilities, achieving outstanding performance, and meeting the needs and wants of constituents. While these requirements may seem to be impossible to obtain simultaneously, the principles and philosophies of SBD maintain that they represent the path to the greatest results in the long term. Specifically, SBD focuses on creating sustainable outcomes using the following criteria:[52]

- *Value creation* – Value creation involves moving toward ideal solutions with greater benefits, fewer deficiencies, and reduced impacts. The objective is to create the best possible solutions for customers, stakeholders, and society, solutions that maximize gains and minimize losses. Such solutions are sustainable solutions.
- *Insightfulness* – Information, data, and analysis drive solutions. Solutions originate in the real world of the twenty-first century and are not just hypothetical or theoretical constructs. Insights gleaned from analogous solutions set the stage for improvements in the future. Most importantly, initiatives and programs of other global corporations serve as evidence of what is doable and advantageous.
- *Equity* – Good solutions are not compromises where one group wins and another loses. The social, economic, and environmental factors all have to

be addressed. Compliance with laws and regulations, pollution prevention, stewardship, and enterprise-wide strategic thinking are inherent elements of any satisfactory solution. Equitable consideration of all impacts to all parties is critical in achieving balanced and sustainable outcomes.

- *Balance* – The transition from current processes and practices to more sustainable ones has to be orchestrated within a framework that achieves the social, economic, and environmental goals in concert with business objectives and realities. Solutions have to be based on the needs of the business environment and the corporate structure and have to be achievable and sustainable.
- *Stability* – Sustainable business development involves systematically creating a better future through evolutionary and even revolutionary changes that produce stable and sustainable outcomes. In essence, if solutions are totally disruptive, gains in one arena may be losses in another. For example, a wholesale change of conventional automobile technologies to fuel cell-based automobiles within a short time frame would have dramatic impacts on the viability of the automobile industry and related industries, making it an unstable and unsustainable solution.

These principles focus on social, market, customer, and stakeholder considerations that provide opportunities for corporations to develop, build, and enhance customer and stakeholder relationships, and ultimately, corporate reputation and image. The principles and management constructs of SBD are used to position products and services in the most favorable light with respect to social issues and market conditions and trends and to create powerful brand images that reflect positive attributes and mitigate negative ones.

The basic SBD framework describes the way businesses can develop innovative processes and deploy effective practices. The central focus is on the "why" and "how" questions. In dealing with complex, diverse, and innovative situations, it is imperative that the business leaders, strategists, developers, and practitioners understand the dynamics of the enterprise and discover theories and insights pertaining to the realities of the world.

Box 2.1 World Business Council for Sustainable Development (WBCSD)

WBCSD is a collation of global corporations working together to develop new business models, methods, and approaches for creating tomorrow's business opportunities. WBCSD focuses on the following key objectives:[1]

- Business leadership – to be a leading business advocate for sustainable development;

1. Understand what drives value in your business;	2. Recognize that different people are accountable for different things;	3. Connect the functions that contain identified value drivers;	4. Leverage the effort that is going into straightforward compliance; and,	5. Tell people what you think accountability means to you.

Figure 2.1A The five fundamentals for creating value from accountability

- Policy development – to help develop policies that create framework conditions for the business contribution to sustainable development;
- The business case – to develop and promote the business case for sustainable development;
- Best practice – to demonstrate the business contribution to sustainable development and to share best practices among members;
- Global outreach – to contribute to a sustainable future for developing nations and nations in transition.

WBCSD advocates that challenges can be turned into market opportunities. Moreover, it suggests that corporations can manage SD challenges, create new venues for creating value, and reduce business risks. It argues that the boundaries that divide the role of business from those of governments and non-governmental organizations are blurring and shifting.[2] WBCSD maintains that successful global business leaders of the future will:[3]

- take responsibility for understanding the significance of global issues for their individual companies and sectors;
- search for business opportunities that help to address them;
- direct their core business strategies to align them with the opportunities arising from major global issues;
- make judgments that incorporate long-term measures into their definition of success.

WBCSD promotes market-based solutions for managing many of the global issues and advocates holistic approaches for solving problems. In "a manifesto for tomorrow's global business" WBCSD leaders articulate the belief that "the leading global companies of 2020 will be those that provide goods and services and reach new customers in ways that address the world's major challenges – including poverty, climate change, resource depletion, globalization and demographic shifts."[4] Travis Engen and Samuel DiPiazza in "Beyond Reporting: Creating Business Value and Accountability" identified five fundamentals for creating value from accountability within a company. They are outlined in Figure 2.1A.[5]

Understanding what drives value is a critical fundamental regardless of the approach. The integration of SD with ESM and operations of the company focuses the essential for achieving success. Customer satisfaction and success are irrefutable primary drivers that align the internal functions with external issues and needs recognizing that different people within the organization contribute to success in different ways. Each person is accountable in some way for achieving the success of the company. Each plays a role in influencing outcomes and contributing to the positive results. Connecting the organization and the functions with what drives value and integrating the efforts into a comprehensive system leads to success. It is the whole that makes success possible, not the pieces. Leveraging efforts into broader gains that go beyond simple compliance can contribute to long-term success. Doing more than expected when compounded over time provides competitive advantages through performance and standards that exceed what peers and competitors are doing. Telling people what you have done and expect provides guidelines for acceptable behaviors and actions. It also involves communicating with them to make clear expectations. Finally, communicating with others gives a sense of accomplishment. WBCSD is a rich source of information for managing SD programs. It facilitates the learning processes with tools and techniques associated with training people about SD.

Notes

1. Travis Engen and Samuel DiPiazza, "Beyond Reporting: Creating Business Value and Account-ability," June 2005, p. 22.
2. WBCSD brochure, "From Awareness to Action."
3. *Ibid.*
4. WBCSD brochure, "From Challenges to Opportunity: The Role of Business in Tomorrow's Society."
5. Travis Engen and Samuel DiPiazza, "Beyond Reporting: Creating Business Value and Account-ability," p. 11.

Summary

Strategic management has evolved from simple constructs focusing on the strengths and weaknesses of the organization and opportunities and threats in the business environment to much more sophisticated management con-structs. ESM involves that next level of sophistication in strategic management in which strategic leaders preempt the opportunities and challenges and lead change. The discussions are derived from theory and practices of leading large companies who are already employing elements of such thinking as their framework for achieving success. ESM provides a strategic view of what is needed to formulate and implement business strategies for leading profound change.

Leading global companies in the developed countries are transitioning and transforming their strategic management models from narrow perspec-tives to highly interactive strategic management constructs framed in the global business context of the twenty-first century. The underlying theoretical perspectives focus on holistic approaches for solving problems, discovering opportunities, and exploiting the capabilities and resources of the strategic management systems. These companies have developed their own form of ESM. ESM is not just a linear extension of strategic management models of the twentieth century; it is a radical change about the scope and role of businesses. It involves all of the people affected by the business enterprise and focuses on achieving the best outcomes and sustainable success. The essential ingredients include systems integration of the SMS with the external dimensions of the business environment, strategic innovations to discover and develop new solutions, technologies, and products, and strategic leadership that provides the vision, strategic thinking, and inspiration for people to be the best.

Markets and customers in particular demand a lot from businesses and people in general expect even more. To meet these challenges, many leading companies in the industrialized world are using SBD principles to create, develop, and apply highly interactive management constructs. SBD provides the management thinking and constructs for creating innovative solutions to social, economic, environmental, and business challenges.

References

Andrews, Kenneth R. (1980) *The Concept of Corporate Strategy*, revised edition. New York: Irwin

Ansoff, H. Igor (1965) *Corporate Strategy*. New York: McGraw-Hill
  (1957) "Strategies for Diversification," *Harvard Business Review*, vol. 35, September–October, pp. 113–124

Chandler, Jr., Alfred (1962) *Strategy and Structure: Chapters in the History of the American Enterprise*. Cambridge, MA: The MIT Press

Delavigne, Kenneth T. and J. Daniel Robertson (1994) *Deming's Profound Changes*. Englewood Cliffs, NJ: PTR Prentice Hall

Deming, W. Edwards (1982) *Out of the Crisis*. Cambridge, MA: MIT Center for Advanced Engineering Study

Drucker, Peter (1973, 1974) *Management ● Tasks ● Responsibilities ● Practices*. New York: Harper & Row, Publishers
  (1954) *The Principles of Management*. New York: Harper & Row
  (1946, 1972) *Concept of the Corporation*. New York: The John Day Company, Inc.

Fayol, Henri (1984) *General and Industrial Management*, revised edition. New York: IEEE

Follett, Mary Parker (1941) *Dynamic Administration*. New York: Harper & Row

Gilmore, F. F. and R. G. Brandenburg (1962), "Anatomy of Corporate Planning," *Harvard Business Review*, vol. 40, no. 6, November–December 1962, pp. 61–69

Hamel, Gary (2000) *Leading the Revolution*. Boston, MA: Harvard Business School Press
  and C. K. Prahalad (1994) *Competing for the Future*. Boston, MA: Harvard Business School Press

Hammer, Michael and James Champy (1993) *Reengineering the Corporation: A Manifesto for Business Revolution*. New York: Harper Business

Kaplan, Robert S. and David P. Norton (1996) *The Balanced Scorecard: Translating Strategy into Action*. Boston, MA: Harvard Business School Press

Kurzweil, Ray (2005) *The Singularity Is Near*. New York: Viking-Penguin Group.

Learned, Edmund, C. R. Christensen, K. R. Andrews, and W. D. Guth (1965) *Business Policy: Text and Cases*. Homewood, IL: Richard D. Irwin

Levitt, Theodore (1962) *Innovation in Marketing: New Perspectives for Profit and Growth*. New York: McGraw-Hill

(1960) "Marketing Myopia," *Harvard Business Review*, July–August 1960, pp. 45–56

McGregor, Douglas (1960) *The Human Side of Enterprise*. New York: McGraw-Hill Book Company

Mayo, Elton (1945) *The Problems of an Industrial Civilization*. Andover, MA: Harvard University

Mintzberg, Henry (1994) *The Rise and Fall of Strategic Planning*. New York: Free Press

(1979) *The Strategy of Organizations: A Synthesis of the Research*. Upper Saddle River, NJ: Prentice Hall

Ohmae, Kenichi (1982) *The Mind of the Strategists: The Art of Japanese Business*. New York: McGraw-Hill

Pearce II, John and Richard Robinson, Jr. (2005) *Strategic Management: Formulation, Implementation and Control*. New York: McGraw-Hill Irwin

Porter, Michael (1985) *Competitive Advantage: Creating and Sustaining Superior Performance*. New York: Free Press

(1980) *Competitive Strategy: Techniques for Analyzing Industries and Competitors*. New York: The Free Press

Quinn, James Brian, Henry Mintzberg, and Robert M. James (1988) *The Strategy Process: Concepts, Context and Cases*. New York: Prentice Hall

Rainey, David L. (2006) *Sustainable Business Development: Inventing the Future through Strategy, Innovation and Leadership*. Cambridge, UK: Cambridge University Press

Senge, Peter M. (1990) *The Fifth Discipline: The Art and Practice of the Learning Organization*. New York: Currency/Doubleday

Steiner, George (1969) *Top Management Planning*. London, UK: Macmillan

Taylor, Frederick Winslow (1911) *The Principles of Scientific Management*. New York: Harper & Row

Watkins, Kevin (2005) *Human Development Report 2005: International Cooperation at the Crossroads; Aid, Trade and Security in an Unequal World*. Oxford, UK: Oxford University Press

World Commission on Environment and Development (1987) *Our Common Future*. Oxford, UK: Oxford University Press

NOTES

1 Kenneth R. Andrews, *The Concept of Corporate Strategy*, revised edition (New York: Irwin, 1980, pp. 18–19). Andrews was a leading scholar in strategic management and the concept of business strategy at Harvard Business School.

2 David L. Rainey, *Sustainable Business Development: Inventing the Future through Strategy, Innovation and Leadership* (Cambridge, UK: Cambridge University Press, 2006). The book provides the essence of sustainable business development and the management constructs used by selected global corporations to achieve sustainable success.

3 Frederick Winslow Taylor, *The Principles of Scientific Management* (New York: Harper & Row, 1911).

4 Henri Fayol, *General and Industrial Management*, revised edition (New York: IEEE, 1984).

5 The following are Fayol's principles:

• Division of labor	Specialization of labor provides the individual to become more expert and productive.
• Authority	Provides the right to issue commands along with the appropriate responsibility.
• Discipline	Employees obey orders only if managers play their part by providing good leadership.
• Unity of command	One man, one boss with no other limiting lines of command.
• Unity of direction	Staff involved in the same activities should have the same objectives.
• Subordination of individual interest to the general interest	The good of the organization must come first over any group, just as the interests of any agreed team should come first over the individual.
• Remuneration	Should be fair and equitable, encouraging productivity by rewarding well-directed effort; it should not be subject to abuse.
• Centralization	There is no formula to advocate centralization or decentralization; much depends on the optimum operating conditions of the business.
• Scalar chain	Although hierarchies are essential, they do not always make for the swiftest communications; lateral communication, therefore, are also fundamental.
• Order	Avoidance of duplicate and waste through good organization.
• Equity	A combination of kindliness and justice in dealing with employees.
• Initiative	Encouraging people to use their initiative as a source of strength for the organization.
• Esprit de corps	Management must foster and develop the morale of employees and encourage each person to use his or her abilities.

6 Mary Parker Follett, *Dynamic Administration* (New York: Harper & Row, 1941).

7 Elton Mayo, *The Problems of an Industrial Civilization* (Andover, MA: Harvard University, 1945).

8 Peter Drucker, *Concept of the Corporation* (New York: The John Day Company, Inc., 1946, 1972, p. 176).

9 Peter Drucker, *The Principles of Management* (New York: Harper & Row, 1954, p. 63).

10 Robert S. Kaplan and David P. Norton, *The Balanced Scorecard: Translating Strategy into Action* (Boston, MA: Harvard Business School Press, 1996, p. 9). Market position depends on building customer relationships and satisfying customers and stakeholders. Innovation depends on people, knowledge, and learning. Productivity depends on having outstanding internal business processes. Profitability depends on financial aspects and the other

scorecard considerations. Managers' performance and development and workers' performance and attitude depend on learning and growth. Public responsibility depends on a broader interpretation of customer.

11 Peter Drucker, *The Principles of Management*, pp. 372–373.

12 *Ibid.*, p. 385.

13 Peter Drucker, *Management • Tasks • Responsibilities • Practices* (New York: Harper & Row, Publishers, 1973, 1974, pp. xii–xiii).

14 Douglas McGregor, *The Human Side of Enterprise* (New York: McGraw-Hill Book Company, 1960).

15 *Ibid.*, p. 33.

16 *Ibid.*, p. 45.

17 Theodore Levitt, "Marketing Myopia," *Harvard Business Review*, July–August 1960, pp. 45–56.

18 *Innovation in Marketing: New Perspectives for Profit and Growth* (New York: McGraw-Hill, 1962).

19 Alfred Chandler, Jr., *Strategy and Structure: Chapter in the History of American Industrial Enterprise* (Cambridge, MA: The MIT Press, 1962).

20 Henry Mintzberg, *The Strategy of Organizations: A Synthesis of the Research* (Upper Saddle River, NJ: Prentice Hall, 1979).

21 James Brian Quinn, Henry Mintzberg, and Robert M. James, *The Strategy Process: Concepts, Context and Cases* (New York: Prentice Hall, 1988, pp. 277–279).

22 *Ibid.*, p. 332.

23 Michael Porter, *Competitive Strategy: Techniques for Analyzing Industries and Competitors* (New York: The Free Press, 1980, pp. 4 and 35).

24 Michael Porter, *Competitive Advantage: Creating and Sustaining Superior Performance* (New York: Free Press, 1985, pp. 33–61). Porter's value system includes suppliers, the firm's value chain, the distribution channel, and the buyers. His generic value chain depicted inbound logistics, operations, outbound logistics, marketing and sales, and service as the primary internal activities.

25 Joseph Juran developed the concept of "fitness for use" as a definition of quality. In his construct, quality depends upon the application of the product or service. Juran suggested a "quality trilogy" that includes quality planning, quality control, and quality improvement.

26 W. Edwards Deming, *Out of the Crisis* (Cambridge, MA: MIT Center for Advanced Engineering Study, 1982, p. 19).

27 *Ibid.*, pp. 23–24. Kenneth T. Delavigne and J. Daniel Robertson, *Deming's Profound Changes* (Englewood Cliffs, NJ: PTR Prentice Hall, 1994, pp. 265–268). Deming's fourteen points are:

   1. Create constancy of purpose for the improvement of products and service.
   2. Learn the new philosophy; teach it to employees, customers, and suppliers; put it into practice.
   3. Cease dependence on mass inspection and testing: much better to improve the process in the first place so you don't produce so many defective items, or none at all.
   4. End the practice of awarding business on the basis of the price tag alone; instead minimize total cost in the long run.
   5. Improve constantly every process, whether planning, production, or service.

6. Introduce training for skills, taking into account the differences among people in the way they learn.
7. Adopt and institute principles for the management of people, for recognition of different abilities, capabilities, and aspirations.
8. Drive out fear and build trust.
9. Break down barriers between staff areas – in other words build a system in which everyone wins.
10. Eliminate slogans, exhortations, and targets – asking for zero defects and new levels of productivity.
11. Eliminate numerical goals and quotas for everybody.
12. Remove barriers that rob people of the joy in their work.
13. Institute a vigorous program of education and self-improvement.
14. Accomplish the transformation and continue to study the new philosophy; develop a critical mass in your organization that will bring about the transformation.

28 Six-sigma thinking is more than a quality methodology; it is a business philosophy and a way of managing processes for production, operations, or product development. It focuses on achieving "world-class" performance and distinction by eliminating defects and problems. Six-sigma quality means producing fewer than 3.4 defects per million opportunities for defects.

29 Kenichi Ohmae, *The Mind of the Strategists: The Art of Japanese Business* (New York: McGraw-Hill, 1982)

30 Michael Hammer and James Champy, *Reengineering the Corporation: A Manifesto for Business Revolution* (New York: Harper Business, 1993, p. 32).

31 Peter M. Senge, *The Fifth Discipline: The Art and Practice of the Learning Organization* (New York: Currency/Doubleday, 1990, p. 8).

32 Gary Hamel and C. K. Prahalad, *Competing for the Future* (Boston, MA: Harvard Business School Press, 1994).

33 Robert S. Kaplan and David P. Norton, *The Balanced Scorecard: Translating Strategy into Action*, pp. 4–19. The authors argued that a balanced perspective that includes financial, customer, internal business process, and learning and growth aspects are critical for linking measures to strategy.

34 Gary Hamel, *Leading the Revolution* (Boston, MA: Harvard Business School Press, 2000, pp. 62–66).

35 F. F. Gilmore and R. G. Brandenburg, "Anatomy of Corporate Planning," *Harvard Business Review*, vol. 40, no. 6, November–December 1962, pp. 61–69.

36 *Ibid.*

37 H. Igor Ansoff, *Corporate Strategy* (New York: McGraw-Hill, 1965, pp. 202–203).

38 H. Igor Ansoff, "Strategies for Diversification," *Harvard Business Review*, vol. 35, September–October 1957, pp. 113–124.

39 Edmund Learned, C. R. Christensen, K. R. Andrews, and W. D. Guth, *Business Policy: Text and Cases* (Homewood, IL: Richard D. Irwin, 1965).

40 Henry Mintzberg, *The Rise and Fall of Strategic Planning* (New York: Free Press, 1994, p. 36).

41 Kenneth R. Andrews, *The Concept of Corporate Strategy*, revised edition, p. 28.

42 George Steiner, *Top Management Planning* (London, UK: Macmillan, 1969, p. 33).

43 Henry Mintzberg, *The Rise and Fall of Strategic Planning*, pp. 323–416.

44 *Ibid.*, pp. 254–294.

45 John Pearce II and Richard Robinson, Jr., *Strategic Management: Formulation, Implementation and Control* (New York: McGraw-Hill Irwin, 2005, p. 2).

46 *Ibid.*

47 Ray Kurzweil, *The Singularity Is Near* (New York: Viking-Penguin Group, 2005, p. 512).

48 Kevin Watkins, *Human Development Report 2005: International Cooperation at the Crossroads; Aid, Trade and Security in an Unequal World* (Oxford, UK: Oxford University Press, 2005, p. 222).

49 Michael Porter, *Competitive Advantage: Creating and Sustaining Superior Performance*, p. 6.

50 World Commission on Environment and Development, *Our Common Future* (Oxford, UK: Oxford University Press, 1987).

51 *Ibid.*, p. 8.

52 David L. Rainey, *Sustainable Business Development: Inventing the Future through Strategy, Innovation and Leadership*, pp. 97–98.

3 Enterprise-wide strategic leadership: Creating value and sustainable success

Introduction

Enterprise-wide strategic leadership (ESL) and sustainable success are two relatively new constructs of engaging in contemporary strategic management that are easy to understand but difficult to define. Strategic leadership has been in use for many decades, usually among the higher levels of management such as corporate executives, senior group management, and general managers of strategic business units (SBUs) and small and medium-sized enterprises (SMEs). It may also include the general management of the value delivery systems in large corporations. These are the business leaders responsible for setting vision and/or strategic direction, establishing principles and values, crafting objectives and strategies, determining high-level policies and behaviors, and assuring governance, reporting, and ethical practices among many other aspects.

ESL involves all aspects of strategic leadership, except that the perspectives are broader and include strategic thinking and management of the company and its SBUs as well as the extended enterprise(s). It includes leading change within the company, linking the SBUs with their extended enterprises, ensuring that the whole enterprise is functioning properly, and achieving success across the business environment. The same is true for SMEs.

ESL requires a mindset that envisions a more assertive and inclusive vision for the future based on the underpinnings and perspectives of enterprise-wide strategic management (ESM), the principles of sustainable business development (SBD), and an architectural blueprint that integrates the value delivery system. It focuses on enhancing the capabilities and resources necessary to create a new reality and on inspiring people at all levels of the organization and across the extended enterprise. It engages people in designing, developing and implementing solutions that create extraordinary value. It defines what is good, what is right, and what is expected.

ESL necessitates comprehensive strategic management that ensures that real value is created and sustained. Moreover, it ensures that the enterprise collectively creates new solutions to maximize the benefits, exceed the needs and expectations of the internal and external participants and constituencies, and minimize the negative aspects. It also concentrates on ensuring that decisions are based on sufficient research and analysis to ensure that the solutions of today do not become the problems of tomorrow.

ESL involves understanding opportunities and challenges from the strategic perspective as well as at the ground level. It involves differentiating between what is an impossible dream and what can and needs to be done. It creates positive outcomes in the present and transforms the foundation, systems, and structures of the company and its enterprise(s) to take advantage of opportunities and create a more positive future. It uses resources and creates new resources, and mitigates burdens and impacts.

ESL involves creating an innovative strategic management framework and sustainable success and ensures that risks and problems are mitigated to the greatest extent possible. Sustainable success, in turn, involves envisioning what the business(es) should become and what it has to do to achieve ongoing success. It involves creating a realistic vision for the future, leading change to realize the implicit and explicit objectives, transforming the systems and structures to implement necessary actions, and continuously measuring results. It also involves creating the means and mechanisms to sustain extraordinary performance and success. It is an endless pursuit of excellence, one that is difficult to define and even more difficult to truly obtain.

Sustainable success is a multi-sided management construct that focuses on radically improving social, economic, and environmental benefits and on significantly decreasing the cost structures and eliminating hidden defects, burdens, and negative impacts. While most strategic leaders have historically concentrated on creating or improving management systems, technologies, products, services, and processes, sustainable success requires strategic leaders to think beyond just the tangible realities of today and explore the best strategic direction for assuring success in the future as well. While it is always difficult to define what the long term is, generally most strategic leaders would like to look out ten to twenty years and be confident that their businesses will still be successful over that time frame. Sustainable success involves realizing the vision, achieving the overarching objectives, facilitating the "lifestyle" of the enterprise, and attaining extraordinary performance.

Enterprise-wide strategic leaders of companies and SBUs are the architects of their enterprises. They establish the foundation of the organizational architecture, ensure that the management systems and structures are solid and support strategies and objectives, and provide the whole enterprise with enduring knowledge, capabilities, and resources. It is akin to building a modern dome stadium. The stadium provides the foundation, system, and structure so that the games can be played and that everyone involved is able to participate successfully. But, success also depends on the coaches and managers who ensure that the process is dynamic and that real-world outcomes are achieved. While sports are zero-sum games, business is not; business is about achieving ongoing wins for everyone and it is clear that both stadiums and corporations are sterile without strategic leaders who orchestrate the game plan and provide the resources and facilitate success. Leadership is the difference.

This chapter describes and evaluates the notions of ESL and sustainable success. It also examines the essential elements of strategic leadership and decision making, core capabilities and learning, the cultural aspects of organizations, and the constructs for leading and managing change. The chapter includes the following main topics:

- ESL qualities that are necessary for leading change in a sustainable enterprise.
- The precepts and principles of ESL.
- The strategic leadership mindset.
- The meaning of sustainable success.

Enterprise-wide strategic leadership qualities

Strategic leadership in the twenty-first century

Traditionally, the executives, especially the chief executive officer, were the main strategic leaders working with the board of directors to establish the desired vision, orchestrate strategic direction, set overarching objectives, formulate grand strategies, and develop appropriate action plans. Generally, executives and their boards of directors focused on how to be financially successful. However, this perspective was usually narrow, based on the organization and its direct relationships with customers, suppliers, and only the most critical stakeholders. Today, executives and boards of directors have to think about all the relationships of the company, SBUs, and extended enterprise(s) that are necessary for success. The list is extensive, including suppliers' suppliers, customers' customers, waste treatment providers, and logistical support companies, to name but a few.

ESL goes beyond merely satisfying customers. For example, IBM works with its customers to develop solutions that will help them to become even more successful. It is engaged in discovering solutions for its customers, not just selling hardware and software. The underlying approach is to discover what is required for customer success and to find a way to obtain it. This is a radical change from the methods used by many manufacturers and service providers who are just trying to sell their wares. ESL also involves being creative and providing new solutions that are fully articulated and analyzed from both the positive side and the negative side of the value proposition.

Effective strategic leaders have to be aggressive, yet skeptical about any proposed solutions until there is sufficient analysis, evidence, and/or fundamental logic that the proposed actions make economic, social, environmental, technological, and market sense. For instance, there are many projects now focusing on developing bio-fuels from agricultural raw materials like corn or sugar beets. While these technological innovations may make economic sense, it is not clear that there are sufficient reserves of agricultural land, nutrients, and water to turn farmlands into energy projects. Sugar beets, in particular, tend to degrade farmlands quickly. To recover, the land requires time and more resources. Moreover, farmlands may be too valuable for food production and for human health and well being to be used for renewable energy development. This example also indicates how enterprise-wide strategic leaders must think about achieving both internal (corporate and SBUs) and external (business environment and extended enterprise) successes in both the short term and the long term. They have to design, produce, and market products and services and ensure that those products and services are used effectively, safely, and productively for as long as possible and ones that do not degrade into future problems.

ESL derives from the underlying values and beliefs of strategic leaders, and it becomes manifest in the principles and philosophies exhibited in the core culture of the organization. It requires strategic leaders at all levels to understand what is required to achieve sustainable success and to think in terms of what should be instead of what is or what maximizes one's own position. Good strategic leaders think about the whole, not just their own personal or business-related positions and expected outcomes.

In 2001, Jim Collins wrote the book, *Good to Great*. Collins identifies the process that successful business leaders employ to build a great company. While it is always difficult to describe exactly what makes a great company,

Collins suggests that success derives from having leaders and people who are disciplined in their thoughts and actions.[1] It would follow then, that the most critical element for developing a great company is to develop great leadership. Collins identifies "Level 5 Leadership" as the highest level of management development and thinking. He describes "Level 5 Leadership" as the starting point in the process to becoming great.[2]

Level 5 leaders channel their ego needs away from themselves and into the larger goal of building a great company. It's not that Level 5 leaders have no ego or self-interest. Indeed they are incredibly ambitious – but their ambition is first and foremost for the institution, not themselves.

Level 5 leaders are fanatically driven, infected with an incurable need to produce sustained results. They are resolved to do whatever it takes to make a company great, no matter how big or hard the decisions.

"Level 5-type" strategic leaders are critical for building a sustainable enterprise and achieving sustainable success. Without strategic leaders who are committed to the principles of ESM, ESL, and SBD, and are able to lead positive change for the whole enterprise, sustainable success may remain elusive. For success is not just based on the financial or market success of the company, the wealth of the shareholders, or the rewards that executives receive, it is based on creating value and success for the external entities and internal contributors. Financial rewards for the internal participants and strategic leaders should be derived from the positive outcomes that are created in the real world for people. Financial success of the business is a derivative of great strategies, actions, and outcomes; it is not the driving force.

The history of business is replete with stories of businesses that were exceptionally successful from financial and/or market perspectives during earlier times only to create difficulties and resentments that diminished their future prospects and led to decline. For example, General Motors (GM), US Steel, and Pan Am were industry leaders who were financially successful during the post-World War II period. However, as customers gained more options from new producers and suppliers, especially foreign companies with new technologies, products, and business approaches, many companies were unable to keep pace with the changes, and their fortunes declined. GM has suffered many declines over the last several decades. Pan Am went out of business. On the other hand, companies like Procter & Gamble, formed in 1837, DuPont, established in 1802, and Siemens, started in 1847, have been successful for most of their existence. Siemens, in particular, is a great example of enduring success. It was decimated after World War II when most of its facilities were destroyed and patent positions were confiscated by the Allies. Yet, it was able to survive and successfully regain its technological and business prominence. Why? – because it focused on creating value and making people successful.

What differentiates these companies and their strategic leaders? Why are some businesses able to recreate successful outcomes decade after decade and to continuously reinvent strategic leaders within the company when others are not able to do so? A critical difference involves the philosophical thinking of the strategic leaders and their perceptions of what is most important in fulfilling their responsibilities. Great strategic leaders focus on making other people successful and sharing the rewards with all of the contributors. Many strategic leaders, shareholders, and stock market analysts believe that the "prime directive" is to maximize profits. However, ESL focuses instead on fulfilling the desires of shareholders and their financial success by ensuring outstanding enterprise-wide performance and sustainable success through strategic investments, development programs, and transformations of the company, the enterprise, and the people to be more capable and agile. The intent is to develop an organization and extended enterprise that can achieve above-average financial performance and sustained outcomes. Astute strategic leaders intuitively understand that business enterprises are long-term ventures that have to be nurtured day after day, week after week, month after month, and year after year. They realize that the ultimate objective is sustainable success and not just achieving "windfall" profitability in the short term. Bill Gates and Warren Buffett have articulated the importance of the long term. One of Buffett's famous business tenets about what is considered to be good investment is: "the business has favorable long-term prospects."[3]

Today, enterprise-wide strategic leaders have to think outside-the-box just like the inventors, innovators, and technical specialists involved in creativity, research and development, and strategic innovation. Strategic leaders who wish to move their organizations from good to great must relentlessly pursue sustainable outcomes. It is critical for strategic leaders to focus on the business challenges and opportunities within the business environment, the social world, and the natural environment in both the present and the future. It is of little good to achieve great success during good times only to fall victim to recessions or industry downturns. The primary obligations of enterprise-wide strategic leaders are to protect and preserve the well being of the company, discover new opportunities, develop and grow the capabilities and intellectual capital of the enterprise, ensure good governance and performance of the corporation, and create sustainable success.

Prime directive for strategic leaders

The primary roles and responsibilities of executives and other strategic leaders have profoundly changed from the strategic management of the organization to strategic leadership of the enterprise. In the 1800s the development of the railroads brought business to a new level of complexity and dramatically changed the roles and responsibilities of management as discussed earlier. While the actual experiences varied considerably from company to company, strategic leaders had to concentrate on the big picture, manage far-flung operations, and understand the long-term implications. They focused on laying the foundation, building the system and the enterprise, expanding opportunities, and meeting challenges and necessities. They had to delegate most of the actual operations to subordinates. The scope of activities and the distances were too large for any one person to personally manage and control. Moreover, strategic leaders had to think about the future requirements significantly ahead of the time in which they were required. Laying tracks, building bridges, and creating a railroad took years to complete. Planning became essential.

The evolution of the large corporations during the early part of the twentieth century followed a similar course. Successful strategic leaders began to create strategic direction and orchestrate development of the assets, capabilities, and the offerings of the businesses. While strategic leaders paid attention to operations and financial performance, increasingly they had to prepare for the future. They had to contend with growing their businesses as opportunities became available, deal with new competitors as companies expanded, and ensure that products and services were provided to customers over increasing larger areas.

Today, the strategic leaders, especially those of global corporations, have to tackle even broader responsibilities. They can no longer focus solely on producing products and satisfying customers or ensuring that profits expectations are realized. Now, they must take a broader perspective on leading change and achieving sustainable success. To do so, they focus on setting strategic direction, managing growth, and dealing with a broad array of shareholders and external customers and stakeholders from consumer groups, government officials, bankers, and the investment community among many others. They must reach out to the whole world and think about creating solutions that are not only comprehensive, but that provide the means and mechanisms for everyone to be successful. And, they must tirelessly continue to sustain success decade after decade.

Some of the main goals of ESL are to discover and take advantage of opportunities, to improve an imperfect business world, and to mitigate challenges and vulnerabilities. Enterprise-wide strategic leaders can reinvent their businesses by understanding the external world and inspiring those within the corporation and its enterprise with a new mindset that provides dramatically improved perspectives. Strategies to get to that future must be framed in reality to create success across the enterprise. They must be inclusive and not limited to the direct beneficiaries of the companies and their strategic leaders.

Enterprise-wide strategic leaders can begin the process by conceiving a mental picture of what the business and its enterprises can be or should be. Their perspectives should include the needs of future leaders and owners, the values and principles of the organization, the overarching ethics and moral behavior of the whole enterprise, and the governance provided by the board of directors and executives. The transformation of a large company or SMEs to the envisioned sustainable enterprise requires commitments to the relentless pursuit of excellence and the acceptance of nothing less than the best. Committing to the creation of extraordinary value through excellence, high quality, and outstanding performance is one of the initial steps.

High quality and the commitment to excellence can and should be attributes of the entire enterprise as well as of the products and processes of the operations. From a systems perspective, pursuing high quality means that everything is important, especially the inputs from the supply networks and the value and effectiveness of the outputs in the hands of customers. For instance, Boeing produces and sells highly regarded airplanes like the Boeing 777 and 787 that are affordable, fuel-efficient, low in emissions, reliable, and easy to use and maintain. Its suppliers are an essential part of the enterprise and are provided with the information and knowledge necessary to enhance their performance, and are guided in their contributions to the enterprise. Boeing and its suppliers, especially the main contributors like Mitsubishi Heavy Industries, are interdependent on each other to ensure that quality and performance are at the highest level. In other words, Boeing's success is not just built on product attributes or on the excellence of its own operations, but also on the interrelationships and interfaces that exist within the whole enterprise. This multifaceted system is difficult to create and even more difficult for others to duplicate. Competitors can copy quality initiatives or product attributes but it is much more complicated to duplicate an entire system of processes, interactions, and positive relationships.

Good strategic leaders have to have multifaceted abilities to think about what should be done, and then develop the strategies and initiatives and implement the actions required to get there. They must use insight and imagination to set a course toward creating improved realities. They also have the ability to operate at the ground level of the company and its enterprise and ensure that ongoing performance exceeds expectations. Great strategies require great implementation.

Great strategists who are slow to implement strategies usually fail. For instance, during the American Civil War General George McClellan, commander of the Army of the Potomac in 1862, was viewed by military historians as one of the great military strategists of the period but he often failed to take decisive actions.[4] Ultimately, President Lincoln removed McClellan. Robert E. Lee on the other hand was a good strategist and a great implementer. He won many battles in which his forces were inferior to those of his adversaries.

A grandiose vision and aggressive strategies are meaningless unless there are commitments, dedication, and ongoing performance of the organization to generate the financial capital, promote the intellectual capital, and provide the rewards to all of the participants so that the enterprise is sustained in the near term and over time. Sustainable success is not a future event, nor just a long-term goal. It is the unceasing realization and commitment to the strategic vision, the enduring pursuit to realize the interrelated objectives of the whole enterprise, and the unending quest toward perfection. It is about creating extraordinary value, not just short-term profits. It is about ensuring that everyone in the enterprise gains and that the negative effects and impacts are minimized if not eliminated.

The precepts and principles of enterprise-wide strategic leadership

Philosophical aspects and precepts

The requisite roles and responsibilities of executives and strategic leaders have been characterized and debated by scholars and business leaders over the last 100 years. Ever since the birth of scientific management and the theories of Frederick Winslow Taylor, most management constructs, especially American ones, were based on observation, measurement, analysis, and supposedly rational decision making. The process was viewed as scientific because "Taylorism" as it was called required that decisions be made on the basis of science not opinion. While upholding scientific principles is appropriate and the fundamentals are sound and sensible, the practice of scientific management generally followed a micro view rather than a holistic view (macro and micro). Scientific management approaches focused on the parts, the individual practices, the work methods, and the management of the activities. Its main strength was its biggest weakness. The methods attempted to optimize individual operations and processes, and not the business enterprise and its embedded systems. This theoretical error led to many of the problems that plagued many companies during the twentieth century, especially conflicts like the quality versus costs debates. Management styles were narrowly focused. The attempts to optimize a process led to many trade-offs. For instance, during most of the twentieth century, optimizing productivity and cost structures often caused the quality of the products and processes to suffer. Quantity, which impacted costs and profits, was usually favored over quality, at least by many American companies.

Scientific management tended to stifle innovation, especially more radical innovations, because to be acceptable, approaches had to be based on scientific methods and observations, not on imagination, insight, or individual initiative. They had to be provable, which favored experimentation with existing processes and practices rather than making wholesale changes even when it was clear that the existing approaches were obsolete. Creating new approaches would require stringent validation. They would have to be statistically analyzed and validated. While it is relatively easy to validate the merits of incremental changes since they are based on existing approaches, it is much more difficult to verify, justify, and gain acceptance of more radical departures from the prevailing situation since the proof of the decisions lie in the future.

Today, most strategic leaders use more sophisticated management constructs and methods for decision making. Yet, with all of the sophistication, some of the historical conflicts still exist. Most relate to philosophical views that are rooted in the educational background and experiential perspectives of the strategic leaders. It is often difficult for individuals to validate change or to obtain approval for more radical change. This is based on the fact that many of the existing approaches and practices are accepted by most people and they fit their fundamental beliefs and are seemingly validated by their experiences. While this is not to suggest that most strategic leaders are driven by "Taylorism" or that their thought processes have not evolved over time, it does suggest that strategic leaders still want overwhelming proof of the validity of proposed plans before they approve the selection and implementation of the new initiatives. They most often want financial justification for decisions and evidence that the proposed actions will be financially sound and make money. Such strategic leaders were trained to justify decisions based on financial analysis and conventional perspectives. While traditional thinking is rational and even prudent, it is most appropriate for operational aspects or near-term programs and constructs (less than five years). However, such thinking may be less effective and more limited for strategic or future-oriented situations. Moreover, most traditional approaches were derived during a slow-paced world where incremental changes were usually adequate for staying competitive and being successful. Today, many decisions, especially those pertaining to radical change and new paradigms, have to be made on the basis of the underlying principles and philosophies and implemented quickly with courage and conviction.

The basic questions for strategic leaders pertaining to ESM and the overarching philosophies and the principles involve how to decide what is appropriate and necessary. Strategic leaders have to think about the methods and techniques they use to make strategic decisions. They have to ensure that they are using the leading-edge strategic management constructs. What could be appropriate for low levels of management, such as focusing on the present or near term, may not be philosophically and strategically correct for strategic leaders. Indeed, one of the problems of today's strategic management may be that most of them think and act like operational types rather than strategic leaders. They function at the level of their subordinates instead of truly leading change, creating value, and developing a richer future. Strategic leaders, regardless of their positions within the company or SME, have to establish the strategic direction, lead change, and invent the future. They have to determine the principles, objectives, strategies, and action plans. They establish the policies and set the rules and guidelines for the company based on the socially accepted norms, laws and regulations, and the overarching ethical principles and practices. Strategic leaders also ensure performance, proper governance, and correct the mistakes of the past. They are not engaged in making trade-offs, but in ensuring that everything is considered when strategizing, leading change, and implementing action plans. Operational management, in turn, ensures that the present requirements, mandates, and expectations are fulfilled. They also correct the mistakes of the past and prevent them from occurring in the future.

The precepts of ESM are deeply embedded with social, economic, and environmental considerations as well as in the more traditional perspectives of strategic management. The overarching perspectives are to improve the company's strategic, market, financial, and competitive positions and its relationships in the business environment and beyond, and to invent new solutions for dramatically enhancing the positive and eliminating the negative. This also includes building relationships with all of the participants. The overarching aspects of ESM as articulated in Chapter 1 are critical for leading change and creating value. The most critical are inclusiveness, openness, and innovativeness.[5]

Inclusiveness means involving everyone in the enterprise in strategic formulation and strategic implementation so that a broad array of knowledge and experience is brought to bear on decisions and actions. This broad scope helps to avoid mistakes in which important elements are missed because they are outside of the normal thinking of the people involved. For instance, it is difficult for a person living in a high-income country to contemplate the latent needs and desires of poor people living at the margins of life. Moreover, people who are not part of the indigenous situation tend to make assumptions that are true in their realm, but not in the realities of a developing country. For instance, American and European business leaders might assume that the transportation system is adequate to provide the ways and means to get their products to the customers. Such assumptions are usually correct in the developed countries. However, a poor farmer or a merchant in sub-Saharan Africa cannot assume that there are roads or waterways to reach beyond the local markets. Strategic leaders have to open up to new ideas and be open to sharing the information about their corporation and its intentions and actions.

Openness and transparency are essential precepts of ESL.[6] They involve being honest and forthright in decision making and making full disclosures about the social, economic, and environmental performance of the corporation. This includes reporting appropriate information and data about systems, technologies, products, processes, practices, and the underlying operations and decision making.[7] When decision makers realize that customers and stakeholders may scrutinize the results of their decisions and that outsiders might have the background information necessary to understand the reasoning involved, they are more likely to take a balanced perspective. Moreover, if they make decisions that are open to full scrutiny, they are more likely to make good decisions. While such open communications are critical for involving the multiple constituencies of the business environment, openness and transparency also facilitate good decision making from an internal perspective. Good solutions are more likely to be developed when there are balanced inputs from many contributors and the decisions are made on the basis of satisfying the requirements of the whole enterprise. Good solutions are also innovative ones that create more value and provide more success than their predecessors.

Innovativeness is central to making progress for the corporation and for all its constituents. It involves discovering opportunities to solve old problems, improve strategic positions and operating outcomes, and invent future clean technologies, products, processes, and services. Innovation also includes creating new business models that change the way corporations manage their enterprises. Currently, leading corporations are changing their management thinking to a more global perspective of the interactions between the competing needs and expectations of a multifaceted constituency.

Value creation is the pivotal ESL construct. People want valuable and sustainable solutions. They want their interactions with businesses and the products and services they buy to make them more successful. As this happens, they are able to buy more products and services in the future.

Tomorrow's leaders will have to have even a broader perspective. The world is becoming ever more complex and more difficult to understand. While such comments may cause concern, there are many exciting positive aspects as well. The opportunities for expanding business fortunes are incredible. Most global corporations have only reached out to people in the developed countries or approximately twenty percent of the world's population. There are numerous untapped opportunities in the developing countries.

The underlying principles of good leadership

Many of the principles of ESM spring from timeless values. While the business environment is constantly changing, there remain many important underlying axioms. One of the primary ones is that strategic leaders have to protect and preserve human rights and the well being of their businesses and people. A derived axiom is that leaders have to provide the best solutions possible that sustain success for all. Moreover, the axioms assert that decision makers have an inherent responsibility to consider the effects, impacts, and consequences of their decisions and have a duty to mitigate negative impacts and their consequences.

Good strategic leaders also build trust and integrity into everything they do. Trust binds people together across the enterprise in the knowledge that the proper actions are being taken and all precautions have been considered. Integrity is essential for preserving the corporate image and reputation.

Strategic leaders subordinate their own objectives and rewards to those of the organization and its employees, customers, stakeholders, and other constituencies. Their own success is predicated on the sustainable success of the whole, and their rewards derive from the success that they and other contributors create in the market spaces and the broader business environment. Great strategic leaders realize that they are an important part of the whole, but they are not arrogant enough to think they are the only reason for success. Instead, they are responsible for the success of others and ensure that others have the means to become successful. They must put the interests of others ahead of their own.

Good leaders do not take rewards when the company is having difficulties and not even when it is enjoying extraordinary financial success. They should share success with others and ensure that everyone gets his or her fair share of the rewards. They should treat people with respect and recognize their achievements. They should obtain a diverse set of views so that strategies, objectives, and action plans are balanced and inclusive of minority or alternate perspectives. They must create stability. Stability involves balancing the needs of present customers and constituents, meeting the goals for the future, and ensuring continuity over time. For instance, investors provide capital assets and other resources because there is evidence and a belief that the anticipated rewards justify the commitments to the future. If the company has a high level of variability of negative aspects, investors and other supporters are less likely to make the ongoing commitments.[8]

People expect better and better business performance year after year. They expect outstanding quality and great solutions. They want their lifestyles and living conditions to be improved without having to make compromises in their choices. They expect that companies and their suppliers and partners will police themselves to ensure that best practices are employed and that individuals, groups, departments, business units, and entire organizations act and behave in a responsible, prudent, and safe manner. Moreover, they expect that businesses will achieve extraordinary financial performance as a derivative of providing great solutions and outcomes.

Leading strategic change of the enterprise

ESL is fundamentally different than the traditional strategic management of a company. As discussed, traditional strategic management was usually company-centric, focused on how to achieve strategic and financial rewards based on the resources, capabilities, and intellectual capital of the organization. It viewed customers as sources of revenue and consumers of goods and services, and suppliers as the means to acquire the necessary inputs. However, customers and suppliers were viewed as outsiders who had their own objectives and self-interests. Customers wanted the best products at the lowest possible prices. And, they wanted products that would last forever, thereby decreasing opportunities to sell additional products in the future. Suppliers, on the other hand, wanted to enhance their positions and profits by charging the most that they could for their products and delivering goods that met the minimum specifications, not the most stringent ones. Many business leaders thought that the objectives of customers and suppliers conflicted with those of the company and it was in the company's best interest to use its power to maximize its position. The prevailing theories evoked the notion that everyone was watching out for their own self-interest.

Strategic leaders during much of the twentieth century were predominantly concerned with managing their organizations, engaging competition, and maximizing financial performance. They were usually preoccupied with their own success and that of their businesses. They tended to focus their attention on the inner workings of their systems, operations, and processes. They also wanted to exhibit some control over the served markets, competitive landscape, and the entities that were directly related to their success. The concept might be described as survival of the fittest. While the strategic perspective was often stated in terms of satisfying customer needs and wants, the underlying strategic aspects typically reflected the personal ambitions of the strategic leaders and the external pressures from stock markets or impatient shareholders who wanted to improve their financial returns.

As a result, many leaders acted in their own self-interest or that of their organizations and not for the greater good of the enterprise. Customers and suppliers responded similarly, and a vicious cycle was perpetrated. Customers who lacked leverage or power had to endure poor quality goods and pay high prices. In the latter part of the twentieth century, however, customers in general gained more power by having more choice from global sources, through technological advances and widespread communications, and through government actions like product recalls. This allowed them to demand better products and to expect producers to pay for mistakes when they occurred. For instance, over the last ten or so years, car buyers have been able to obtain information from the Internet about the quality and reliability of various car models. This information has put them in a better position to choose the models and options that best fit their needs.

Suppliers faced the same problems. However, some suppliers have also improved their strategic positions by having a broader array of producers to deal with. In short, power has become more widely distributed. However, there are exceptions. For instance, ExxonMobil still has significant influence in the petroleum industry and makes enormous profits via its assets, power, and market position. Wal-Mart has incredible power over its suppliers because of its share of the consumer market, sales volume, and purchasing positions. In the short term, its suppliers may have few options and have to accede to Wal-Mart's dictates and demands. In the long term, customers and suppliers attempt to find ways to extricate themselves from their weak positions.

While such broad generalizations are always difficult to prove, and there are many exceptions, the focus of this discussion is about the future, specifically, what the strategic leaders of sustainable enterprises need to consider. The growth of outsourcing, the accelerating power of the Internet, the connectedness of the global economy, and the rapidity of technological change have changed the business world dramatically over the past ten years. With these kinds of changes, the theories, concepts, and practices of ESL are now even more critical and demanding. Like never before, companies and SBUs have become subject to scrutiny and debate, especially large ones that are easy targets for public review.

Strategic leaders must adapt to this new world. Insular thinking limits the scope of opportunities and creates conflict instead of harmony. Over time the causes and effects of discords may become obscure and the difficulties persist. The questions today include how can strategic leaders avoid such thinking and traps that go with it and think about solutions that are favorable to suppliers and customers as well as the companies and SBUs, and how to preempt their competitors so that their strategies and actions are less relevant to the businesses. Eliminating discord and promoting common good usually enriches all the participants in the enterprise.

Building sound and sustainable relationships across the enterprise is one of the most critical functions of strategic leaders. It requires creating links that are based on more than short-term economic benefits and developing mechanisms that allow parties to be mutually successful. They must move toward becoming direct or indirect partners instead of transactional entities, each with its own objectives and strategies for achieving success. And the success of a relationship must be judged on the basis of satisfaction in the short term and sustainable success in the long term.

Strategic leaders at every level have to ensure that relationships are built on a solid foundation, that exchanges are fair and mutually beneficial, that financial, economic, social, and environmental rewards are commensurate with each party's contributions, that value is created across the enterprise, and that advantageous and profitable outcomes are created in the short term and enduring success over the long term.

Rethinking the mindset of strategic leadership

The changing aspects of strategic management thinking

Defining strategic management thinking in the early twenty-first century is very challenging because of the scope and sophistication of most large companies and the variations of their approaches. In many cases, large companies and even SMEs are using much more sophisticated approaches than those taught in business schools through the world. Nevertheless, most of the prevailing strategic management thinking is still based on survival of the fittest and winning competitive battles. Many of the constructs used in recent decades centered on the strengths and weaknesses of the businesses and on the opportunities and threats in the business environment. While such thinking makes good sense when examining one's place *vis-à-vis* the competition or in light of the needs and expectations of the business world, such perspectives are self-centered. The perspective is typically based on who you are instead of what you should be or would like to be.

One example of this narrow focus was the absorption with the notion of the primacy of a company's core competencies that was prevalent throughout most of the 1990s. At that time, it was thought that strategic management should concentrate on business units, technologies, products, etc. that enjoyed core competencies or core capabilities that were superior to those of the competitors. The theory was to capitalize on strengths and minimize those areas affected by intractable weaknesses. Strategic leaders were encouraged by shareholders and stock market analysts to focus their attention on the competencies of the organization and reduce the importance of those areas that were deemed to be weak. The latter could be accomplished by outsourcing the areas affected. Proponents of the theory argued that it was logical, as businesses should build on their strengths.

However, it can be argued that such thinking worked when the opportunities within the company domain were to some extent "controlled" by the company. In the US during the early part of the twentieth century, US Steel could control pricing in the steel industry; Pan Am had significant influence on international air travel; and GM had incredible power over the automobile industry. In most situations, the leading corporations had many strengths and relatively few weaknesses. Moreover, many of those leaders were able to compel market forces to favor the company's powerful positions and limit the impact of any weakness. For example, during the 1960s GM was very powerful in the large car segment of the industry and was very weak at designing, producing, and marketing small, more affordable automobiles. Rather than finding ways to overcome its weaknesses, GM's strategic leaders decided to encourage people to buy its bigger cars, especially in the segments where it made good profits.[9]

The major shortcoming pertaining to the theories surrounding the notion of core competencies was that the approach takes a static view of business environment, the markets, and customer perceptions. It assumes that the prevailing situation would continue for a reasonably long period of time, say ten years. Such assumptions may have been close to reality fifty years ago when the underlying business environment changed much more slowly, but at the beginning of the twenty-first century the rapidity of change has made such thinking obsolete, if not perilous. The business world has become much more dynamic, requiring agility, flexibility, and "rapid response" capabilities to deal with change. Moreover, in some situations strengths can quickly become weaknesses as the changes in the business environment shift the preferred position toward new directions. For example, Amazon.com made buying books online easy, enjoyable, and a richer experience because it also provides a plethora of information that is not available in a bookstore. Amazon, Barnes and Noble, and a few others reshaped the industry and customer expectations. Customers could get the requisite information about the books that they wanted via the Internet. The cost of having a retail location became a liability. Many smaller shops went out of business. The core requirements of the industry changed, thus changing the power of certain competencies. The "knowledgeable" bookseller became less important and the information system became the primary source of advantage.

New technologies, innovative business methods, and even novel business models can rapidly replace the older paradigms. These changes empower markets and customers. Changes and improvements in the overall business environment or markets often mean that customers, stakeholders, and other constituencies do not have to put up with weaknesses or tolerate poor performance or behaviors of the prevailing producers. Moreover, the core competencies of a company often become commonplace over time, negating the competitive advantages that were once so powerful. For instance, GM in the 1950s and 1960s was like a basketball team with twelve eight-foot (approximately three meters) players playing against teams that had twelve six-foot players. Over the last half of the twentieth century many of the other teams also acquired the stature analogous to having eight-foot players. Whether or not GM actually declined, it is clear that companies like Toyota and Honda have grown significantly and are world-class competitors. In most situations, the underlying forces are dynamic and core competencies are quickly emulated by others or made irrelevant by the driving forces of change.

In the face of such dramatic changes, the enormous advantages provided by core competencies, for many, faded away into oblivion. For instance, electronics made many previously powerful mechanical devices obsolete and seriously affected the fortunes of some of the most powerful companies of yesteryear. The same can be said of certain chemical processes. For instance, digital camera technology supplanted chemical-based technology and rendered Kodak's strengths and once-powerful market position in film-based, chemical process photography a thing of the past. Kodak must now compete in the photography industry with many other companies like Sony, Nikon, Minolta, and Canon and new competitors like Samsung are selling products that include cameras in cell phones. This is akin to changing the game from basketball to soccer. The old competencies related to physical size and strength are not as relevant as the new requirements for speed and agility.

Focusing on strengths and weaknesses and core competencies and capabilities may still be appropriate in certain settings, especially those that are not as dynamic as electronics, telecommunications, and computers, but great care must be used to ensure that the conclusions are correct and relevant. It may be more applicable to think in terms of the advantages and disadvantages of the options available and to understand what the intellectual capital of the business has to have instead of what it is; again, the critical aspects are the future requirements, not present positions, power, and influence.

Focusing on customer satisfaction was also a major theme during the last decade and one that paid off for many businesses. It is an inherently proper concept, but one that may be limited as well. The logic behind the importance of customer satisfaction is obvious since customers are the primary source of revenue and are often the principal driving forces. The concept may actually be viewed as an extension of the total quality management (TQM) movement of the 1980s and effects of high-quality products from global competitors. As customers gained more power and had more options via purchasing products from international sources having equal or better products to those of the national competitors, customer expectations changed from simply requiring that companies meet product specifications to demanding that producers and marketers ensure positive outcomes. Customers expected the best solutions available. For example, Toyota is enjoying increased market share in the US for many of its models because its products are more reliable and valuable over a longer period of time. It also has a sophisticated production system that is difficult to fully emulate. The point is, it is crucial to think about strategic management from the customers' point of view as well. What they perceive and how they decide and act are critical to business decision making. Customer satisfaction is not just about what happens at the point of purchase, but what occurs over the life of the products and the end-of-life considerations.

Still, as more changes unfold and the rate of change increases over the next few decades, the ability to lead, to adapt to a changing business world, and to provide total satisfaction and success for customers, stakeholders, shareholders, and all of the other constituents may become the primary strategic advantages. The business world is most likely transitioning from the concept of "survival of the fittest" to the archetype of "rapid adaptability" where strategists attempt to lead change more quickly than the changing requirements of the business environment. Those that can adapt may obtain the advantages.

The theory of customer satisfaction worked well when the main concerns were those related to markets and competitors. One of the prevailing beliefs during the 1990s was that if business leaders failed to maintain or achieve competitive prominence, their corporate and/or SBU positions would erode. In today's more complex business world characterized by social change, economic disruption, environmental problems, market upheavals, the emergence of radical new technologies, new competitors from developing countries, and innovative new business models, it is much more difficult to conclude that customer satisfaction alone will lead to success or that competition remains the most important force. While competition is intense and is expected to become even more so, strategic leaders have to examine the whole business landscape to discover opportunities and challenges and to make changes rapidly to accommodate a broad array of needs, expectations, requirements, and mandates. They have to adapt to new ways quickly, make adjustments, test the validity of the new approaches, and seamlessly implement them across the enterprise. Upon or even before completion they have to be ready for the next wave of changes, to adopt best theories and management constructs, and make ongoing adaptations. It is complex and dynamic, but it is also exciting and reinvigorating. Ultimately, the agile and flexible businesses will have a good probability of succeeding and the intransigent and rigid ones will have difficulty maintaining their strategic positions.

While such a business world appears daunting, it may actually be easier for many businesses to lead change and proactively adapt to the changing business environment. In such situations, strategic leaders have the ability to orchestrate what happens to some degree. They can be the architects. Think about the complexities of trying to reinvent a large company once it has been overtaken by a plethora of difficulties and problems. For example, imagine what the strategic leaders at GM and Ford Motor Company (FMC) have to do to solve all of the strategic challenges and operational difficulties necessary to restore those companies to their former greatness. In contrast, it might seem relatively easier for companies positioned on the cutting edge to make ongoing changes before they are forced to do so, especially in the case of new companies like eBay and Google. Though challenging, these approaches may be achievable using the theories and concepts of ESM and ESL.

Staying ahead of the expectations of the changing business world may be the best answer to the questions of competencies, customer satisfaction, competitiveness, stakeholder acceptance, and shareholder wealth creation. While leading change is not yet the norm for most businesses, it is gaining acceptance from some of the most sophisticated corporations, especially those that recognize the complexities of governing and managing large corporations in today's global business environment. Assuming that successful corporations have to achieve success across a broad front of challenges, it makes good strategic sense to preempt the requirements and provide outstanding answers before the questions are asked, the issues are addressed, or the problems are made apparent.

Strategic thinking has to reflect the whole business environment. It has to provide answers to the present challenges and assure the sustainable success of the enterprise over time. It goes beyond solving problems and includes preventing problems in the first place and leading change that creates opportunities for everyone.

A strategic–entrepreneurial mindset

Strategic leaders have to have an entrepreneurial as well as strategic perspective. They must possess the intellectual capital and leadership capabilities to reinvigorate, reinvent, and reconstitute the corporation and integrate its strategies and action plans with the rest of the enterprise to create a holistic value system. They must be the creators of the management frameworks and business model(s) that link the people of the enterprise with the business environment in a way that sustains success. While traditional entrepreneurs usually create and develop SMEs, strategic leaders of large companies face much more complicated situations. They must strive to successfully meet the objectives of the near term and transform businesses with all of their historical legacies, rigidities, and vested interests into dynamic entities connected to their extended enterprise(s), market spaces, and business environment. And, they must be prepared for the future. As they do so, their mindset must value the basics of protecting the health, safety, and well being of people and preserving and protecting the natural environment.

A business leader with this kind of strategic–entrepreneurial mindset realizes that success is an ongoing challenge that depends on the collective contributions of many people from the top of the organization to the bottom. Even Henry Ford, lauded for his technical and marketing genius, failed to maintain his company's leadership in affordable automobiles because he did not allow others in the organization to contribute to the necessary transformation of FMC during the late 1920s. He became rigid and was convinced about the power of his Model T and the customer satisfaction that it had provided for more than twenty years. But, times changed.

The best strategic leaders realize the dual importance of their leadership at the top and their involvement and contributions to all levels of the organization. They deal with the big picture and engage in the realities as well. As they think about their own success, they must think about how they can help others in the enterprise to be successful.

In the same vein, strategic leaders have to develop the next generation of leaders. Historically, many company failures were due to the inability of the leaders to do this. For example, David Sarnoff was an innovative leader who created great technological and financial wealth for the shareholders of RCA. Sarnoff was an entrepreneur and pioneer in radio and television technologies. However, the choice of his son, Robert W. Sarnoff, as successor was based on the narrow perspective of having his own son carry on with his life's work.[10] The younger Sarnoff did not have the skills and capabilities of his father and the fortunes of RCA declined significantly during his tenure. Eventually, RCA was acquired by General Electric (GE) and disassembled. On the positive side, Thomas Watson, Sr. prepared the way for his son, Thomas Watson, Jr., to be very successful well before the latter assumed the leadership of IBM. The son took the strategic underpinnings that his father provided and created an even more successful corporation that was an innovator and market leader in mainframe computers and many other technologies.

As business leaders develop new leaders, they must instill in them the mindset necessary for being successful. The strategic–entrepreneurial mindset seeks to engage people throughout the enterprise to realize their potential and achieve their goals and dreams. It seeks to make customers successful, not just satisfied, and suppliers successful, not just the winners of contracts. The mindset envisions dynamic processes that allow other leaders and people across the enterprise to transform their situations into richer, more successful realities on an ongoing basis.

The strategic–entrepreneurial mindset focuses on people and their success.

The theoretical proposition behind this mindset is that if customers, suppliers, employees, and other constituents are successful, the company will be more successful. Thus, the strategic leaders can create extraordinary value across the enterprise, enabling it to achieve sustainable success. For example, Dell Computer (Dell) has done just that during its rise to prominence in the personal computer (PC) business. Its suppliers are linked to a valuable supply network that enjoyed a steady stream of customer orders. Customers realize the benefits of the latest technologies at affordable prices and use the PCs they bought to become even more productive and capable. But, the challenges are ongoing; Dell must continue to adapt and improve to sustain success.

James M. Kouzes and Barry Z. Posner, authors of *The Leadership Challenge*,[11] identify five fundamental practices of exemplary leadership: challenge the process; inspire a shared vision; enable others to act; model the way; and encourage the heart. These practices are at the intersection of ESL and strategic–entrepreneurial thinking. Enterprise-minded leaders must think about new processes that effectively link the whole and minimize negative outcomes. They have to inspire people to think outside-the-box in creating solutions and forming cross-company teams to improve processes and outcomes. They must create synergy and engender passion for excellence and achievement. Kouzes and Posner capture the essence of leadership thus:[12]

Most of us can agree on what we want from our leaders. We want them to be credible, and we want them to have a sense of direction. Leaders must be able to stand before us and confidently express an attractive image of the future – and we believe that they have the ability to take us there.

The strategic–entrepreneurial mindset that looks at the whole is based on openness, cooperation, and collaboration, and strives for innovativeness and continual improvements and developments. These aspects are essential for creating a desirable and attractive future, one in which all participants succeed and success is sustainable.

Strategic leaders are usually ambitious and tenacious, but they do not all achieve sustainable success. While self-centered business leaders may be successful for a time, their narrow mindset determines and often limits their destiny. They may be arrogant and dictatorial and put themselves ahead of everyone and everything else. And they often play zero-sum games in which they attempt to win even if it means many others lose. These kinds of leaders do not usually tolerate criticism. They base their strategies and actions on their perceptions, not on those of the broad organization and generally accepted principles. They consider a narrow perspective and often reject other points of view.

Strategic leaders with an entrepreneurial–strategic mindset that focus on sustainable success are typically just the opposite. They are open-minded, engaging, and selfless individuals who put the objectives of the organization/enterprise ahead of their own. They invest in promoting the success of other individuals and the greater organization. They listen to those from the highest levels of senior management to the grass roots of the organization. They are open to constructive criticism and realize that learning is a critical part of the strategic process and that no one person has all the right answers. They empower people to participate and share in recognition and rewards. Their view of the world is broad, and they are open to innovative ideas and new ways of doing things. They believe that if everyone succeeds, they will succeed. They do not attempt to obtain personal glory or financial rewards, but focus on achieving sustainable success, success that continues for the long term, even decades after they have left or retired. Great business leaders think about others and inspire others to think about everyone else as well.

Sustainable success

Determining what sustainable success means

The notion of sustainable success is almost impossible to define without understanding the context of the business environment. Slow-paced industries like the petroleum industry based on the supply of commodity products underpinned by large economic, social, and technological forces take decades to change and the driving forces usually involve incremental changes. For instance, there are more than 200 million vehicles in the US that require petroleum-based fuels for their engines. The capital investments of the global petroleum industry involve trillions of dollars, euros, or yen that are fixed and depend on the ongoing extraction, refining, and delivery of petroleum products. It will take decades to convert all of those investments, capital assets, technologies, products, and operations into more sustainable solutions. Yet, if the industry's global corporations do not recognize the need to change, they may one day find the reserves of crude oil evaporating, rendering their strategic positions untenable and their investments worthless. For a time, large petroleum companies like ExxonMobil, Chevron, BP, and Shell may be able to generate record profits, increase their market capitalizations, and make significant contributions to shareholder wealth while their strategic leaders increase corporate vulnerabilities by depleting the very resources that the corporations depend on.

The slower the change mechanisms, the more difficult it is to perceive the importance of strategic change and to understand the true meaning of sustainable success. In such cases, the strategic leaders may assume that they are on the road to sustainable success and that prevailing management constructs are adequate to maintain financial performance. They may be right in their assumptions, but only for a relatively short time frame.

In fast-paced industries like electronics, telecommunications, personal computers, and software, it is virtually impossible to stipulate the life cycle of the prevailing markets, technologies, products, and business conditions. Technological innovations across such business sectors cannibalize powerful strategic positions and make existing products and services obsolete within months. For example, Motorola was the market leader in cell phones during the early 1990s; it lost the lead and is making huge investments to recapture its earlier strategic position. On the other hand, Siemens sold off its cell phone business because it could not or did not want to keep making huge investments without achieving any sense of sustainable success in the markets. Rapid changes give strategic leaders a much better understanding of the need to secure sustainable success because it is readily apparent that financial and even market success is fleeting. The turbulence in the markets and business environment makes it difficult to predict what can to be done to create sustainable success.

Businesses have to think in terms of strategic success across the enterprise. They have to create strategic platforms of technologies and products that allow the gains made during one generation of technology to be easily transferred and captured in the next. This focus on enterprise-wide or strategic success involves developing and building resources, capabilities, and physical assets that can be remolded to fit the needs of the next generation. The bottom line is that sustainable success cannot be defined in simple terms of years or strategic positions. Rather, it has to be defined by the vision of the organization, the strategic direction, the business strategies and objectives, and the capabilities to create extraordinary value. Parallel to the concept of continuous improvement at the operating level, sustainable success can be defined in terms of the long-term approaches to continuously reinventing the company and its businesses and to keep on the track for success.

Strategic leaders must discover new opportunities for innovation, development, improvements, investments, and growth. They must ensure that there are more resources, capabilities, and prospects for future generations, and must not simply exploit the wealth of the existing situations to achieve short-term objectives. They must make capital and intellectual investments and ensure that strategic development programs and operational transactions are appropriate for current and future generations. This also includes the individuals involved, the owners and leaders of the corporations, the customers, stakeholders, and constituents as well as society in general. Most importantly, they must leave behind a positive legacy for future success. In his book, *Collapse*, Jared Diamond discusses the demise of the population of Easter Island through the depletion of natural resources, especially deforestation.[13] He questions the legitimacy of the profits gained by the person who cut down the last tree in light of the huge losses that the society suffered because it no longer had materials for boats and houses, firewood, watershed protection, natural habitat, and thousands of other requirements. One person's gains should not translate into losses for everyone else. Likewise, business success should not be achieved in this manner.

Sustainable success is an overarching construct that provides guidance for strategic direction and an intangible metric for leaders and practitioners. It can instill an organization with courage and confidence that it can be vital and capable of change and it can affirm the validity of the business model and management systems. The notion of business success can be subdivided into four main realms within which organizations can seek and attain success: (1) enterprise-wide; (2) strategic; (3) market; and (4) financial. Each category has its own meaning and connotation. The key question involves whether the type of success is sustainable.

The enterprise-wide category takes a broad perspective of the whole extended enterprise and explores how to ensure that success is across the whole spectrum. The strategic success category is slightly less broad and examines success from the perspective of the company and its SBUs. The market success category is even more limited in scope. It is a more traditional perspective focusing on how the company or SBU can achieve success in the targeted markets and with the served customers. It also looks at competitive advantages and the business's standing within the competitive landscape. The financial success category concentrates on making money and how the company is able to do that. It generally has a very narrow perspective. There are obviously other categories that could be included. For the sake of simplicity, these four are discussed.

While the theoretical underpinnings suggest that organizations can achieve success in all four realms, sustainable success implies that the broader perspectives (i.e. enterprise-wide success and strategic success) are more likely to enable the organization to be successful over the long term. Table 3.1 lists some salient characteristics and main focuses of each.

Table 3.1 Salient characteristics of the different realms of success

Realm	Salient characteristics	Main focuses	Main concerns
Enterprise-wide success	Providing solutions; creating value; building networks that produce sustainable outcomes; integrating the extended enterprise to discover opportunities; building solid relationships; creating partnerships; building a sustainable business model; transforming and transitioning business units; leading change; focusing on the long term to ensure sustainable success.	Value creation; sustainable success; customer and stakeholder success; reputation enhancement; knowledge; learning; capabilities; resources; openness; inclusiveness; innovativeness; social responsibility; waste elimination; strategic success; market success; financial success.	Dramatic changes in business environment; radical, unpredictable, and totally disruptive change; difficulties in integration and innovation; failure to build enduring relationships.
Strategic success	Finding opportunities in market space; crafting strategies and action plans; implementing initiatives for developing new technologies and products; forming new business units; acquiring companies; creating new ventures; leading change; building customer loyalty; focusing on the long term.	Successful business units; customer and stakeholder success and satisfaction; core competencies; innovation successes; strategic success; market success; financial success; survival.	Dramatic changes in value systems; poor leadership; poor growth potential; lack of opportunities; new competitors; radical new technologies; lack of innovation. Vulnerabilities include all of those in the other categories.
Market success	Achieving success in markets; selling products and services; building market acceptance and customer loyalty; creating marketing programs; producing cost-effective products; building supply networks; focusing on the intermediate term to ensure revenues and cash flow.	Market share; customer satisfaction; revenues; gross margins; profits; product platforms; number of products; new technologies; new products; market success; financial success.	Poor customer loyalty; technological change makes existing products obsolete; low margins; commoditization; new competition; severe business conditions. Vulnerabilities include all of those in the other categories.
Financial success	Achieving financial rewards; making money and profits; maximizing shareholder wealth.	Profitability; return on investment; return on equity; financial success.	Changes to business; new technologies; customer disloyalty; social and environmental problems.

Enterprise-wide success involves ongoing transformations and transitions to keep the strategies, management constructs, technologies, products, and processes on the cutting edge and in concert with the business environment, market spaces, and all of the strategic entities and resources necessary to be socially responsible, economically viable, and environmentally sound. It is a broad perspective and includes the whole extended enterprise and focuses on the long term. The main motivation for focusing on the perspective of enterprise-wide success is the desire to increase opportunities and reduce vulnerabilities. Enterprise-wide success also includes many of the salient characteristics of the other realms.

Strategic success involves the ongoing development of strategic initiatives and action plans to reinvent the company and business units and their prospects for success through new strategies, innovation, and integration. It is a relatively broad perspective and includes focusing on the value delivery system and the long term. This kind of success is motivated by the desire to increase competencies and capabilities and to take advantage of opportunities in the business environment and market spaces. The vulnerabilities include the need to develop new strategic leaders and create innovations before they are necessary.

Market success involves focusing the portfolio of products and services and marketing products and services to customers. The focus is on the markets and customers, building customer awareness and acceptance, and the sale and purchase of goods and services. It relies on the functional capabilities of the business and its supply networks, especially on marketing and production. Market success involves a more limited perspective, including the market positions and the near-term functional strategies and tactics. Increasing revenues and finding more customers are the primary motivations. Radical new technologies and products created by competitors, customer dissatisfaction, obsolescence, and radical market changes are some of the worrisome vulnerabilities.

Financial success involves making money through supply and demand constructs. It often is a company-centric approach that focuses on short-term financial outcomes. The desire to sell products, generate revenues, and earn profits motivates financial success. The vulnerabilities include radical changes in markets, technologies, and products.

Short-term success can be achieved using any one of these main types. But sustainable success involves being successful in all four realms. The theoretical perspective suggests that companies focusing on enterprise success are more likely to succeed over the long term than those simply relying on, or motivated by, financial success. There are numerous examples that fit each category, and there are many ways to achieve success. Moreover, corporations may be able to sustain success for a long period of time if they have overwhelming financial resources. For example, ExxonMobil might fit into the realm characterized as financial success. However, it has incredible financial resources that might allow it to transform itself to something deemed to be more sustainable in the long term even if it waits until petroleum reserves become depleted and its current business model is obsolete. On the other hand, Siemens is taking positive actions everyday to reinvent itself and become broader and more sustainable. It focuses on creating new innovations and discovering new opportunities for achieving long-term success.

Assessing sustainable success

In the grand scheme of strategic thinking and objectives, sustainable success is at the pinnacle of the desired outcomes. People invest in companies and start new ventures to enjoy a return on their capital, to realize their objectives and aspirations, and to contribute to the greater social good among numerous other reasons. Whether the capital is financial, physical, intellectual, or all three, investors expect to be rewarded with ongoing returns, not just a single payback. While there are investors who buy and sell their stock positions to make short-term gains, the companies themselves are expected to be ongoing concerns. Even in the case of stock traders, the value of their holdings would be significantly less if there was an end point to the companies that they hold stocks in. The prospect of future earnings contributes significantly to the value of a company or a new venture.

The value of most successful companies is based on the culmination of the successes that it has realized over its history. While there are ups and downs in the market capitalization of most companies, the wealth created by successful businesses for their shareholders is based on sustaining success year after year, decade after decade. Corporations like GE (founded in 1892) have achieved long-term success by employing a succession of strategic leaders who understood that two of the most important primary objectives were to assure the health and well being of the organization and to translate opportunities and investments into enduring realities and sustainable success. While some leaders like Jack Welch (GE's CEO from 1981 through 2001) made significant contributions to market capitalization in a relatively short amount of time, most successful companies generally achieve financial success by the ongoing accumulation of profits and rewards. For example, Intel began its foray into microprocessor technologies in 1971 with its 4004 and had many successes with its later versions, 8088, 80286, 80386, and 80486, during the 1980s and early 1990s. Still, Intel did not realize extraordinary results until it launched the Pentium processor platform in 1993. Its strategic leaders had to have patience and fortitude to make ongoing investments in intellectual properties, technology developments, and operating systems to build great financial wealth and sustainable success. But, the story goes on. Current strategic leaders at Intel must continue to reinvent the corporation as competitors like AMD challenge it with new products, enhanced capabilities, and market success.

While technologies, products, and processes are important, ongoing success is based on having a solid strategic management framework, an outstanding business concept, and solutions, systems, and structures that support the vision, strategic direction, and realities of the company. Businesses and their enterprise(s) must also have resilience and the flexibility to accommodate change. Periodically, the framework, business models, systems, and structures have to be reinforced and modified, and occasionally, replaced. Strategic leaders can measure the ability of the company to maintain and achieve sustainable success by examining the following critical factors:

- The ability of enterprise partners and customers and stakeholders to enjoy positive results and to succeed in their objectives.
- The capabilities of the strategic leaders of the whole enterprise to solve legacy problems, to resolve current issues and concerns, and to mitigate or eliminate the negative aspects in the enterprise that inhibit future success.
- The innovativeness of strategic leaders as they expand the enterprise into new market spaces and find new opportunities for growth and development.
- The ability of the organization to learn at rates faster than the changes that are occurring in the business environment and to lead change to exceed the needs and expectations of the customers, stakeholders, and constituents.
- The innovativeness to create effective management constructs and solutions.
- The energy available to transform the company into a new reality of what the shareholders, strategic leaders, and employees would like to be instead of what it is.

Sustainable success is difficult to determine in the short term, and the metrics required for measuring it have not yet been fully developed. When they are, they are more likely to be more qualitative than quantitative. Measuring this kind of success will require judgment and a keen understanding of how small changes can translate into large opportunities and challenges and what they mean over the long term.

Sustainable success of a business and its enterprise benefits everyone – producers, customers, stakeholders, suppliers, distributors, and other constituents – through the integration of systems and processes and innovations that affect the whole. One way to judge the sustainable success then is to determine how well each of the participants is achieving its long-term objectives and strategies. A successful business enterprise is dynamic, but also stable and fruitful. The benefits of its success, both those that are tangible and those that are not, should be distributed fairly, although not necessarily evenly, among the participants, including the customers, stakeholders, employees, and other constituents.

Another measure is the ability of strategic leaders to lead change and to make dramatic improvements in the social, economic, environmental, market, and financial underpinnings of the enterprise. Strategic leaders across the enterprise have to create value and reduce the vulnerabilities of the enterprise. Often, as the enterprise expands, the associated concerns and problems expand as well. In many cases, the latter expand at a greater rate than the enterprise itself (i.e. the vulnerabilities increase faster than the strategic leaders can handle them). When the problems become difficult to address, or strategic leaders are not paying attention to them, a crisis can occur.

The prospects for sustainable success can also be measured by tracking the number of unresolved problems and difficulties in the enterprise. While it only gives a relative sense of how well the enterprise is succeeding, it can provide an early warning that the enterprise is becoming more vulnerable to external forces. This view is analogous to the model used during the late 1990s by Procter & Gamble (P&G) in managing critical business issues. Dr. Deborah D. Anderson, P&G's former Vice President of Worldwide Quality, described the logic of the company's anticipatory issues management construct as taking all appropriate actions during the emergence of an issue so that it does not become a critical problem for the corporation.[14] P&G tracks the most critical issues and intervenes in the process as early as possible to ensure that a triggering event does not occur. A triggering event is one in which the issue escalates from one that can be resolved at a low cost using few resources and having minimal repercussions into a crisis involving extraordinary costs and liabilities and requiring extensive resources to resolve. Such crises dramatically increase the vulnerability of the corporation and can threaten sustainable success. It is much more effective to monitor the performance of the enterprise and to nip any negative issues "in the bud." Figure 3.1 depicts P&G's anticipatory issues management process.[15]

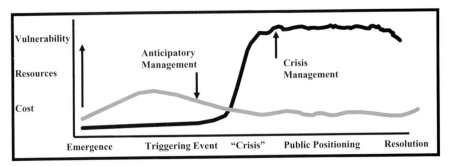

Figure 3.1   Procter & Gamble's anticipatory issues management process (circa 1999)

Sustainable success can also be measured according to the probability of a company continuing to be successful for an extended period of time. For instance, the strategic leaders of P&G might determine that the key businesses have a 95% probability of being successful and financially viable over the next quarter century. Alternatively, executives at ExxonMobil might calculate that the corporation is expected to be financially successful using its current business model until say 2025 at which point petroleum reserves may become severely challenged and unpredictable.

While sustainable success may be open-ended and difficult to define, strategic leaders intuitively understand what it means and what they have to do to become more sustainable. It is not the end point that is meaningful, but the journey. Great companies will establish the game plan for making the journey even though they realize that it may take forever to get there. Along the way, the corporation will improve its positions so that it becomes more sustainable each day and ultimately more successful. Having a vision, a game plan, and dedicated people will lead to transformation and extraordinary outcomes.

Box 3.1 Toyota Motor Company and its focus on enterprise-wide success

In 1937, Kiichiro Toyoda founded the Toyota Motor Company (Toyota) to develop trucks and passenger cars designed for the domestic market based on Japanese management and control.[1] The challenge was enormous since at the time, GM and FMC dominated the Japanese market. From the early days Toyoda realized that he had to design a unique system if Toyota was to successfully compete against its more formidable competitors. He avoided replicating their standard "lot production system." Given that Toyota did not have the capital or warehouses for parts, he developed a flow-type system that he referred to as the "just-in-time" concept. According to Eiji Toyada, the concept was a way to produce products and sell them before the accounts had to be paid.[2]

World War II disrupted Toyota's plans to become a viable player in the industry. More-over, the early 1950s were turbulent for Toyota as management crises and labor disputes took their toll.[3] But Toyota's strategic leaders prevailed. During the mid-1950s, government policy encouraged domestic production. Initially, the primary demand was for trucks and buses to rebuild the national transportation and distribution infrastructure that was devastated during the war. Although the Japanese market was small, the demand structure was a major challenge to Toyota. The economic situation was tight, and customers wanted low-cost vehicles. The high gasoline prices also made fuel efficiency a significant concern for Japanese consumers. Toyota responded by focusing on value, quality, and reliability. Toyota's capacity and output and that of the Japanese automobile industry grew dramatically between 1950 and 1975 with a hundredfold in annual production.[4]

From the very beginning, Kiichiro Toyada took his father's (Sakichi Toyada) philosophy of being innovative and creating radical solutions. The philosophy became a standard for action. To succeed in a competitive industry with complex products and enormous investments in plants and equipment, Toyota's leaders realized that they had to set ambitious goals, concentrate organizational resources, and focus on specific opportunities.

Based on its philosophy of leading change, Toyota explored ways to improve its competitive position in relation to the major producers of the 1950s and 1960s. It was convinced that the key to success was to invest into a new production system having the productivity advantages of mass production, but which could achieve high quality and remain flexible enough to produce low quantities of each of its different models. At the time, Toyota did not have the financial strength or the market position to support the large-scale facilities suited to mass production. Mass production was too rigid to accommodate the relatively small market potential of the Japanese market and its wide variation of product offerings. Principally due to the contributions of Eiji Toyada and Taiichi Ohno, the chief production engineer, the Toyota Production System (TPS) was developed.[5] TPS focused on the whole value system and how to satisfy customer needs in the most efficient and effective way possible. The philosophy was to determine exactly what customers needed and to deliver the right product at the right time, to meet market demand, not to anticipate market requirements and build inventory for expected demand. With TPS, each process produced only those parts or products that the downstream process or customer required for the next sequence. TPS is the "just-in-time" system. Ohno described it as a "pull system" as opposed to the "push system" of mass production.[6] The reduction in inventory across the system significantly reduced operating costs and provided the flexibility to produce exactly what customers wanted. TPS also has the capability to detect abnormalities and take corrective action immediately, thus improving quality at the source of the difficulty.

Quality control is built into TPS, rather than affected by a small cadre of quality control professionals who determine quality assurance and stop production when defects are found. The approach, called "Total Quality Control," depends on the entire workforce to prevent defects from progressing from one step to the next by determining the quality achieved at each step. The quality check avoids waste and minimizes the impacts of problems as it finds defects and cures them before additional steps are performed.

Standardized work and kaizen, a Japanese word meaning "continuing improvement," are the "dual dynamics" of TPS. Discovering the most efficient work flow to achieve the quality, quantity, safety, and cost objectives of the system leads to standardized work. The goal is to achieve an optimal workload and to provide workers with the opportunity to rearrange and improve the work process using their experience and creativity. Employees are given significant responsibility and authority.

What makes TPS successful is more than its emphasis on quality and productivity. It is its philosophy of involving people in the solution mechanisms, identifying waste and eliminating it, and striving for continuous improvement. Eliminating waste is pivotal since waste causes environmental concerns, economic losses, quality problems, safety issues, deterioration of customer value, and complexity. Minimizing waste reduces or eliminates economic and environmental problems producing a lean, simple, clean, and agile system.

TPS is not the only competency contributing to Toyota's strategic success. The company has established a successful new product development process that reduces the time for developing new models to twenty-four months. This agility gives Toyota a competitive edge in markets driven by significant changes in market trends and government mandates. Toyota's product strategy is to develop a platform and derive different models using common parts and resources. Its shortened development cycle is even more powerful considering the state of flux in the underlying technologies.

In 1996, Hiroshi Okuda, President of Toyota, developed the company's strategy for sustainable growth in the twenty-first century. It included balancing the needs of people, society, and the global environment. Toyota's concerns include:[7]

- societal concerns and attitudes about the environment, pollution, wastes, and climate change;
- more stringent regulations worldwide pertaining to automobile emissions and increased concerns about their effect on the environment and the health and safety of the general population;
- wide fluctuation in the economics of the automobile, principally driven by the uncertainties associated with fuel prices and availability;
- the increasing turbulence and risks created by rapidly evolving technologies both within the industry and in other sectors;
- expansion in the number of market segments in response to the wants and needs of various customer groups, especially in developing countries; and
- globalization and its influence on the industry.

Based on these concerns, Toyota designs its vehicles to have reduced environmental impacts and burdens throughout their life cycle. Its priorities are to conserve resources and energy, minimize waste, and recycle whenever possible. This approach extends across the entire system from development and manufacturing to use and waste management. The company strives to provide customers, stakeholders, and society with the best solutions possible.

TPS is a world-class management system that is synchronized with market needs and society's expectations. Toyota's model focuses on achieving enterprise-wide success by linking its value system so that everyone is successful. The company has a rich tradition of providing its customers with exceptional value through outstanding product delivery. It believes good solutions are those that generate customer value, minimize negative impacts, conserve resources, protect the environment, and make money. Such solutions meet the strategic objectives and allow Toyota to enjoy great relationships with customers, and provide financial rewards to make further improvements.

Notes

1. Eiji Toyoda, *Toyota: Fifty Years in Motion* (New York: Kodansha International/USA Ltd., 1987, p. 52).
2. *Ibid.*, p. 58.
3. Koichi Shimokawa, *The Japanese Automobile Industry: A Business History* (London, UK: The Athlone Press, 1994, pp. 31–41).
4. *Ibid.*, p. 9.
5. James Womack, Daniel Jones, and Daniel Roos, *The Machine that Changed the World* (New York: HarperPerennial, 1991, pp. 48–69).
6. Toyota Production System, publication of Toyota Motor Corporation, Toyota City, 1992.
7. Toyota Motor Corporation, "CARe FOR THE EARTH: Toyota Automotive Eco-Technologies," p. ii.

Summary

The primary objective of strategic leaders is to create successful businesses and enterprises that enjoy sustainable success over the long term. James C. Collins and Jerry I. Porras characterized the role of strategic management in their book, *Built to Last: Successful Habits of Visionary Companies.* They discussed some of the underpinnings for achieving long-term success. Some of their comments include:[16]

Visionary companies, we learned, attain their extraordinary position not so much because of superior insight or special "secrets" of success, *but largely because of the simple fact that they are terribly demanding of themselves* . . . we found substantial evidence that the visionary companies invested for the future to a greater degree than the comparison [less successful] companies . . . The essence of a visionary company comes in the translation of its core ideology and its own unique drive for progress into the fabric of the organization – into goals, strategies, tactics, policies, processes, cultural practices, management behaviors, building layouts, pay systems, accounting systems, job design – into everything that the company does . . . For it is through the power of the human organization – of individuals working together in common cause – that the bulk of the world's best work gets done.

ESL is one of the most essential aspects of ensuring sustainable success. Choosing strategic leaders is one of the most important strategic decisions that fiduciaries like boards of directors have to make. These strategic leaders are ultimately responsible to shareholders, employees, customers, stakeholders, and society to ensure that the enterprise is successful both in the short term and in the long term. They are the ones that must translate corporate success into mutual gains for everyone. They are not above everyone else, but rather, are subservient to the whole. Strategic leaders are the entrusted individuals who are supposed to subordinate their own personal gains for the benefit and well being of the organization and the external business environment. They must play to win, but ensure that their success is not at the expense of customers, stakeholders, partners, or employees.

Sustainable success is the never-ending challenge of developing people, technologies, solutions, systems, structures, and relationships, and investing for the future. It means leading change and being ahead of expectations. It means engaging everyone and ensuring that they are treated fairly and justly. It means discovering and translating opportunities into successful realities, and it means dealing openly with issues, difficulties, and problems as soon as possible. Outstanding strategic leaders do all these things as they guide their organizations toward improvements, new developments, growth, and extraordinary results. They integrate the entire enterprise into a seamless whole that functions for the benefit of each and every participant. They continuously transform the organization into a more capable and sustainable position for the future and transition the competencies and strengths of the enterprise into greater value.

References

Abernathy, William J., Kim Clark, and Alan Kantrow (1983) *Industrial Renaissance: Producing a Competitive Future for America.* New York: Basic Books

Anderson, Deborah D., Dr. (1999) *Tools for Managing Environmental Progress in a Global Consumer Goods Company*, Rensellaer Polytechnic Institute, Troy, NY, June 14, 1999

Collins, James C. and Jerry I. Porras (1994) *Built to Last: Successful Habits of Visionary Companies.* New York: HarperCollins Publishers

Collins, Jim (2001) *Good to Great: Why Some Companies Make the Leap . . . and Others Don't.* New York: Harper Business

Diamond, Jared (2005) *Collapse: How Societies Choose to Fail or Succeed.* New York: Penguin Books

Hagstrom, Robert (2001) *The Essential Buffett.* New York: John Wiley & Sons

Kouzes, James M. and Barry Z. Posner (1995) *The Leadership Challenge.* San Francisco, CA: Jossey-Bass

Lyons, Eugene (1966) *David Sarnoff: A Biography.* New York: Harper & Row

Rainey, David L. (2006) *Sustainable Business Development: Inventing the Future through Strategy, Innovation and Leadership.* Cambridge, UK: Cambridge University Press

Wilson, Woodrow (1901) *A History of the American People*, volume IV. New York: Harper & Brothers Publishers

NOTES

1 Jim Collins, *Good to Great: Why Some Companies Make the Leap . . . and Others Don't* (New York: Harper Business, 2001, p. 142).

2 *Ibid.*, pp. 21 and 39. While some of the concepts discussed in *Good to Great* fit the constructs of sustainable enterprise management, the premise of success using Collins's methods depended on meeting financial objectives rather than achieving multifaceted outcomes.

3 Robert Hagstrom, *The Essential Buffett* (New York: John Wiley & Sons, 2001, p. 79).

4 Woodrow Wilson, *A History of the American People, Volume IV* (New York: Harper & Brothers Publishers, 1901, pp. 226–229).

5 David L. Rainey, *Sustainable Business Development: Inventing the Future through Strategy, Innovation and Leadership* (Cambridge, UK: Cambridge University Press, 2006, p. 9). The critical principles are: *Inclusiveness*: Sustainable enterprise that integrates the internal strategic and operating systems with their external partners, allies, supply networks, customers, stakeholders, related industries, infrastructure, and other support relationships based on a holistic understanding, analysis, and execution of all of the systems processes involved from the raw materials to the disposal of the residuals and waste streams. It includes the natural environment, the social/human world, and the business environment. *Openness*: Corporate philosophies and strategic leaders that believe in building trust, integrity, and awareness across the extended enterprise. Most importantly, this includes human rights considerations that are an essential part of being open. Stakeholder perspectives must also be included in the discussions and decision processes as soon in the processes as reasonable. Information and data must be shared with all constituencies to ensure that plans, actions, and outcomes have peer review and are generally acceptable both internally and externally. *Innovativeness*: An innovation management system that includes incremental improvements to existing technologies, products, and processes and radical new inventions and discoveries for exciting solutions through clean technologies and new products that meet the needs and expectations of customers, stakeholders, and constituents.

6 Global Reporting Initiative (GRI), Sustainability Reporting Guidelines, 2002, p. 24. GRI suggests that the principles of transparency and inclusiveness represent the starting point and are woven into the other principles.

7 David L. Rainey, *Sustainable Business Development: Inventing the Future through Strategy, Innovation and Leadership*, pp. 264–265.

8 Examples are not used in this section because the goal is to reflect on what the principles and practice should achieve and not to castigate individuals or companies.

9 William J. Abernathy, Kim Clark, and Alan Kantrow, *Industrial Renaissance: Producing a Competitive Future for America* (New York: Basic Books, 1983, pp. 51–57).

10 Eugene Lyons, *David Sarnoff: A Biography* (New York: Harper & Row, 1966, p. 352).

11 James M. Kouzes and Barry Z. Posner, *The Leadership Challenge* (San Francisco, CA: Jossey-Bass, 1995, p. 9). Kouzes is the CEO of the Tom Peters Group/Learning Systems. Posner is Dean of the Leavey School of Business and Administration at Santa Clara University.

12 *Ibid.*, p. 29.

13 Jared Diamond, *Collapse: How Societies Choose to Fail or Succeed* (New York: Penguin Books, 2005).

14 Dr. Deborah D. Anderson, *Tools for Managing Environmental Progress in a Global Consumer Goods Company*, Rensselaer Polytechnic Institute, Troy, NY, June 14, 1999.

15 *Ibid.*

16 James C. Collins and Jerry I. Porras, *Built to Last: Successful Habits of Visionary Companies* (New York: HarperCollins Publishers, 1994, pp. 188, 192, 201, 218).

4 The business environment: A global perspective on leading change

Introduction

Strategic management has become much more complex than it was just a decade ago.[1] The dramatic rate of industrialization in China and India, globalization in general, improved transportation systems, advances in information and communications technologies, and the ubiquitous Internet are among the many forces of change that have increasingly connected people, businesses, and societies around the world. Over the last twenty years, many of the economic limitations of the business world like distance and cost have been dramatically diminished by technological advancements and more sophisticated management constructs. For instance, new transportation technologies have made it possible to move huge quantities of freight around the world at a very low cost. Today, consumer and industrial products can be produced in China and shipped to customers in Europe or the US within days without adding significantly to the unit cost. Transportation costs have been reduced by 50% in many cases to approximately 10% of the total product costs. Because of this globalization, businesses today must adopt a more inclusive perspective of their business environment. A much broader set of conditions and trends is now relevant and must be included in strategic thinking, strategic analysis, strategizing, and decision making.

The business environment is a dynamic reality of customers, stakeholders, the public, and all of the external forces impinging upon businesses. Those forces are social, economic, political, ethical, technological, and environmental considerations and the market and competition-related factors. The business environment also includes the external dimensions of related industries, supply networks, and the infrastructure that are directly linked to the company or business unit through its extended enterprise. These external forces and dimensions provide opportunities, challenges, limitations, and vulnerabilities to the fortunes of the corporation and its prospects for sustainable success.

What strategic leaders include in their strategic thinking and the strategic analysis of the business environment determines their understanding of reality and influences their ability to achieve the desired results. If strategic decision makers have an inclusive framework for analyzing and understanding the business environment, it is more likely that they will have a sound foundation for making good strategic decisions.

The traditional constructs of strategic management and planning are generally focused on the direct effects of value systems of the business units and the production and consumption of products and services. While customers, stakeholders, suppliers, and other entities of the extended enterprise play a critical role in shaping the strategic direction, creating value, and achieving extraordinary outcomes, the critical forces and elements of the business environment and underlying fundamentals of the natural and social worlds have significant influences on strategic direction as well. Effective strategic thinking, analysis, and decision making necessitate an examination of all of the relevant external forces. In order to make informed and good decisions, business leaders of today have to include in their decision-making processes considerations of the natural environment (the ecosystems) and the social/human world as discussed in the previous chapter, and the driving forces of the business environment. Those that limit the scope of their strategic analysis may suffer the consequences of their narrow perspective.

Enterprise-wide strategic management (ESM) requires an expanded view of the business environment. It involves integrating the organization and its enterprise with its business environment and creating innovative ways for solving problems, discovering new opportunities, and creating new, cleaner, and more valuable solutions across the entire business landscape. When practiced, it finds corporations on the cutting edge of proactive change addressing and resolving many of the social, economic, environmental, and market-related problems and creating extraordinary value for shareholders and the corporation and its enterprises in the process. The goals are to ensure that natural, human, and economic capital and resources are used efficiently, effectively, and fairly. ESM improves the positive side of the value creation by developing sustainable solutions and maximizing benefits. It also mitigates the negative side by minimizing the adverse effects and impact and reducing or eliminating resource depletion, environmental degradation, social and economic disruptions, and social, economic, and environmental wastes.

The chapter includes the following main topics:
- The global forces affecting trade and complexity.
- The underpinnings and dynamics of the business environment.

Selected forces affecting business

Globalization

Globalization is the seemingly pervasive, hotly debated phenomenon that appears to be driving the global economic, social, and market forces today and those over the last few decades. It encompasses the full scope of social, cultural, ethical, economic, political, technological, environmental, and market forces affecting the natural environment, the social/human world, and business environment. In today's context, globalization is the merging of national economies into regional and ultimately a single global economy. It is the notion that the world economies are shifting toward a borderless economic structure in which nation-states are less relevant and global corporations vie to satisfy customer demand based on both standardized ("globalize") and customized products and services and more homogenized approaches. Space and time are compressed and geography is less of a critical factor than it once was.

After World War II, twenty-three major trading countries, especially, the US, the UK, and France, established the General Agreement on Tariffs and Trade (GATT) to develop multilateral agreements promoting freer trade. GATT was replaced by the World Trade Organization (WTO) in 1995 to regulate trade and provide mechanisms within an organizational structure to adjudicate problems and disagreements. WTO expanded representation to 132 countries and established rules for handling trade and trade disputes.

During the 1990s, the major political and economic powers, known as the G7 countries, supported reducing tariffs, quotas, and other trade barriers and creating free-trade zones to enhance trade and globalization.[2] Freer trade makes the exchange of goods, services, and capital less complicated and costly and allows companies to have more open access to resources and markets. The establishment of free-trade agreements among major trading countries has been pivotal in opening up markets and trade. The following are examples of changes in political thinking that were initiated in 1993 to improve connectedness:

- The North American Free Trade Agreement (NAFTA) between the United States, Canada, and Mexico opened the borders by eliminating tariffs and other barriers.
- The European Union (EU) replaced the European Economic Community, establishing free trade and eliminating border restrictions among member countries.

The trend toward free trade and greater linkages between countries and support for the relationships between suppliers, producers, and customers characterizes globalization today. But, globalization also affects intangible changes that influence customer behaviors and attitudes. Ideally, it will benefit all producers, consumers, intermediaries, stakeholders, and other trade constituencies.

Today, economic trends indicate that international trade is expanding and that understanding the global business environment and the influences of all of the key participants are critical for making sound strategic decisions. However, the process is evolutionary and circuitous. The global economy is still undergoing change and rapid development. While some global trends are contributing to an improved world economic order, most of the significant changes have occurred on a regional basis as indicated by the NAFTA and the EU. Most large corporations still focus their strategies on selected markets, business sectors, and geographical regions. Many companies are powerful in certain regions like North America and weak in other areas like the Pacific Rim. For example, General Motors (GM) derives more than 70% of its automotive revenues from North America.[3] It has a North America market share of 26.7% but its global share is 14.5%.[4] In reality, GM is a regional player and a relatively weak global one.

The mega trend toward a global economy is clearly a phenomenon that was evolving even before John Naisbitt suggested it in his 1982 book, *Megatrends: Ten New Directions Transforming Our Lives*,[5] and it will continue for decades in the future. The process unfolds unevenly, usually revealing the strategic perspectives like outsourcing that are viewed as the most critical at the time. The global challenge is to make significant economic gains for industrialized nations and the developing countries concurrently and to maintain economic stability on a global basis. For instance, the major trend today is to outsource the fabrication and even the production of commodities and highly competitive products to China. Much of the strategic thinking behind the decisions of many strategic leaders pertaining to outsourcing is cost minimization in order to improve product margins and business profits. While the underlying theory seems to be rational, the actual consequences require significant analyses to ensure that the strategic logic is sound. If such decisions de-stabilize the economic well being of workers in the developed countries, products and services may be more cost-effective, but less affordable because a larger percentage of people simply do not have the economic means to purchase goods.

Globalization and managing complexity

Globalization is an ill-defined phenomenon that engenders a vision of a unified world economic order, a global economy with global products and standards characterized by innovative technologies. While the notion of globalization is far from reality, information and communications technologies (ICT), especially the Internet, inexpensive transportation technologies, the development of radical technologies, and customized products are driving the world toward a single global economy. The expanding physical and informational links between distance markets have spawned an increasing understanding of cultural and regional similarities and differences among people. The political will in the industrialized countries to eliminate historic barriers to free trade and commerce also contributes to common markets, and globalization is bringing about freer access to raw materials, resources, intellectual capital, and investment opportunities. Still, the realities fall short of the ideal. China, for instance, is using its financial resources to capture, or at least control, certain strategic resources and raw materials like copper and iron. It may be trying to create barriers to others in certain industries who depend on obtaining the same raw materials. Petroleum prices have skyrocketed making logistics more costly.

But, globalization is more than geography, politics, and trade. Strategic leaders have taken or are taking a more global perspective of their business environment in crafting and implementing the strategies and action plans. Their strategic thinking finds them examining the whole context of reality (inclusiveness), formulating outside-the-box solutions (innovativeness), building enduring and trust-based relationships with customers, stakeholders, partners, and others (connectedness), communicating and sharing information with all constituencies (openness), and ultimately, sustaining success over time (effectiveness). To do this, they have had to develop an open mindset that recognizes cultural differences, contemplates non-traditional and countervailing perspectives that reveal new opportunities, and understands the needs of the future as well as the expectations of the present.

Globalization can be viewed as part of the evolutionary track of expanding opportunities and trade, opportunities that form the basis for economic and social imperatives at all levels: local, national, regional, and global. It is a result of goods and services becoming more affordable and companies being more effective, productive, and responsive in satisfying wants, needs, and expectations. Worldwide momentum toward creating more value through efficient, effective, responsive, flexible, and integrated production, distribution, and service support of products and the related processes is also contributing to globalization.

Value creation through lower costs, reduced defects and burdens, customization, and other product and process attributes can expand the reach of businesses into new markets and new applications. The history of personal computers (PCs) is a good example of the effects of value creation on a broad scale. The early devices based on Intel's 8088 and 8086 microprocessor technologies were extremely expensive, costing between $5,000 and $7,000 for a very limited device (basically a word processor). As a result, the PC market of the early 1980s was generally limited to large companies that could afford the prices and had applications suitable to justify the investments. Contrast that situation with today's PC market where millions of ordinary customers can buy a Pentium-based PC or equivalent for less than $250. The PC example is indicative of the global trend in technologies and products. Ongoing changes and improvements in value creation and outcomes have eliminated the notion of the status quo. During the early stages of a new technology and related product developments, the technology platform tends to be weak with limited positive attributes. Prices tend to be high. However, over time the situation quickly changes if the new technology is successful. The technology becomes more powerful and sophisticated with many positive attributes, and prices drop dramatically. When this occurs, there are many implications. One of the most important implications is that as the requirements for being successful increase the number of successful competitors tends to decline. Again, the number of producers of PCs fit the case. In the 1980s, there were hundreds of PC manufacturers who believed they could make staggering profits because of the high gross margins. However, most of the companies failed to keep pace with the declining prices and profits and had ineffective business models for managing change. Dell Computer (Dell), on the other hand, enjoyed success because it focused on creating an innovative business approach that was responsive and flexible. Dell continues to stay ahead of change by continuously reexamining its management approaches and strategies. Yet, Dell may also be vulnerable to change if it cannot quickly interpret new market requirements and adapt accordingly.

Globalization requires companies to examine their management constructs and ensure that their strategic management models consider the right forces driving change on a global basis and adapt the right strategies for outpacing the expectations. A global perspective is inherently more complex than managing nationally or even regionally. Global markets are not homogeneous, and one product typically does not fit every situation. While there are exceptions like cola soft drinks, even Coca-Cola and PepsiCo adapt their marketing messages and tailor their production process and distribution channels to meet local and regional conditions. The complexity cuts across every aspect of business, from customers and stakeholders to the acquisition of resources and the production of products and services. Managing on a global scale involves thousands of variables. For instance, determining whether or not to operate or do business in the Pacific Rim and China, in particular, depends in part on the company's dynamics and the importance of Pacific Rim countries and the businesses and markets therein.

The underpinnings of the business environment

A general perspective

The business environment is a complex web of interconnected forces affecting social, political, ethical, economic, technological, environmental, and market dimensions of our world. Because of the breadth and depth of these dimensions as they relate to and are affected by businesses, it is often difficult to ascertain exactly what dimensions business leaders have to focus on and what the relevant and important aspects are. In general, strategic leaders focus on the primary forces within the business environment that affect their businesses and operations. And, they also monitor the most critical elements of the natural environment and the social/human world to understand potential opportunities, concerns, and their consequences. It might be viewed as a "balancing act" in which it is impossible to consider every possible element. Still, vulnerabilities arise if too many assumptions are made which limit the scope of the strategic management model as it pertains to the business environment. The basic construct is to expand the dimensions included so that a comprehensive view of reality is available to strategic decision makers. As new information becomes available and/or as changes occur in the business environment, new elements can be added or elements that are no longer relevant can be discarded.

The business environment includes the following primary dimensions: (1) social; (2) political; (3) ethical; (4) economic; (5) technological; and (6) ecological/environmental. (Please note that market considerations are also critical elements, but they are covered separately because of their primacy.) Each can be divided into two or more subdivisions. The business environment also includes the market spaces of customers, non-customers, stakeholders, and competitors. Of particular importance is the category of non-customers who could or would be linked to the company and its extended enterprise if the solutions provided by the enterprise were appropriate and offered a means of satisfaction. Market space actually lies between the business environment and the extended enterprise. It is clearly the primary focus pertaining to social and economic interactions between businesses, societies, and people. Customers are the economic drivers, and stakeholders are the link to the social dimension. Competitors are other corporations and their enterprises that have similar objectives and generally participate in the same market space.

In conventional strategic management models, the business environment is regarded as the external environment or the macro-environment. These terms are used interchangeably. Market space is of primary importance because it is directly linked to the enterprise and indeed, is part of it. The external dimensions are often viewed as a secondary focus to market spaces because they typically have indirect effects. And the natural environment and the social/human world are often viewed as subordinate to the business environment because most of their critical factors are not directly or even indirectly related to the strategies and actions of the businesses and their extended enterprises.

Figure 4.1 depicts the interrelationships between the natural environment, the social/human world, and the business environment. The former can be viewed as general external considerations that business leaders should be aware of, while the latter are the specific opportunities, challenges, concerns, issues, requirements, and vulnerabilities that drive strategic direction and decision making.

Businesses generally try to think broadly about all of the critical elements of the external world and then develop more focused approaches for understanding and dealing with the primary dimensions of the business environment, particularly those that have direct and indirect impacts on the business units and their extended enterprise. The most critical elements are the ones that represent opportunities, challenges, threats, or vulnerabilities. Each dimension of the business environment is impacted by the broader natural environment and social/human world. Likewise, each dimension affects the market space and the internal dimensions of the business and its enterprise.

For any given element, there are often many overlapping considerations that drive changes downstream and become more specific for the business and its extended enterprise. For instance, as more people move to urban areas, vehicular congestion tends to increase. These conditions affect the business environment for car makers and for providers of mass transit services.

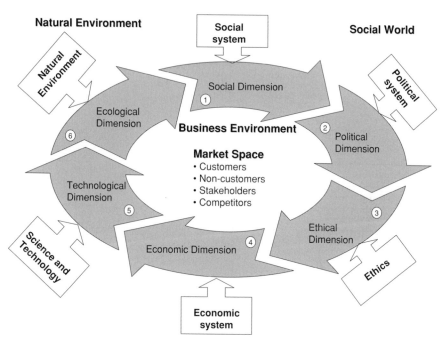

Figure 4.1   The business environment and its linkages

Changing business conditions affect the market space for automobiles and other types of vehicle, which may give rise to opportunities for more fuel efficient and less polluting automobiles like Toyota's hybrid, the Prius, which is specifically designed to be more fuel efficient in heavily congested traffic. It also may become a future threat to automobile manufacturers as customers in the market space move from being customers to non-customers as they select alternative forms of transportation.

Figure 4.2 is a graphical representation of the interfaces between the business environment, the market spaces, and the business unit and its extended enterprise.

It shows the market space as a primary focus of the business unit. The construct provides a customer or market-centric perspective. It also shows the competition as part of the extended enterprise, but not as the center of strategic thinking.[6] The competitors generally have their own extended enterprise that may also be serving the market spaces.

In the case of the automobiles, concerns about air quality and resource depletion (specifically petroleum) drive governments, stakeholders, and markets to seek improvements and new options. Moreover, the limitations of the infrastructure (roads) and the changing social dynamics (population density)

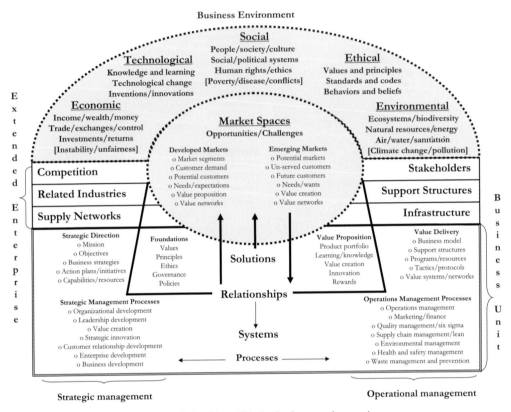

Figure 4.2   An example of the interrelationships within the business environment

of the social/human world necessitate adaptations in the social systems. The markets and customers respond to the changing conditions in the business environment by rethinking their needs and expectations for products and services. If significant changes have occurred, people seek new options to satisfy a revised view of their needs and expectations. Thus, innovative companies respond with new solutions that eliminate the difficulties and limitations.

The conventional approach for scanning the business environment is to examine the primary considerations only to the extent necessary to understand the direct requirements of customers, the mandates of government, and the implications of competition. The focus on competition sets the stage for understanding what competitors' strategies and action plans are for obtaining market share, achieving market performance, and what the company has to do in response. While this is a simple and manageable approach, it leaves many exciting opportunities unexplored, which ultimately may be addressed by new competitors or new entrants in the market space. By just focusing on markets, customers, and competitors, the company narrows its perspective, and often fails to examine all of the opportunities in the market spaces and the business environment. Indeed, the greatest opportunities may lie with the non-customers. Why don't we have a business relationship with them? What is necessary to establish the relationships? Asking these questions shifts the focus from what the company is doing and how well it is doing it to what it should be doing and determining what the essential requirements, needs, and expectations are for success.

The more inclusive and expansive approach involves delving into the business environment to determine what customers are seeking and to explore the underlying reasons for their needs and expectations. This requires digging deep to determine what is causing change and understanding the underlying factors. It also involves analyzing the market space of the non-customers to ascertain why they have made other choices and what the implicit and explicit aspects are. Some of the reasons why non-customers may select other options include changes in lifestyle, government mandates or restrictions, ethical perspectives, affordability constraints, new technological alternatives, and ecological considerations. Companies should explore as many of the reasons as possible, drilling deeply into the business environment, the natural environment, and the social/human world.

Scanning the business environment can start with looking at the business and its extended enterprise and working backward to examine the causes of change (causes of change in society, the business environment, or the market space). The alternate method is to start with the fundamentals of the natural environment and the social/human world and look specifically at the influence on the business environment, market space and ultimately, the company and its enterprise. The alternate approaches are explored in more detail in Chapter 5. Regardless of the approach, however, it is imperative to identify and map out the primary dimensions of the business environment.

Social dimension

Overview

The business environment is really all about people. Businesses are social entities. They are part of the social structure that is theoretically designed to benefit people and sanctioned through public discourse, policy, and acceptance. Businesses find their purpose and opportunities in the social dimension.

Conventional strategic management models examined the social dimension primarily in terms of downstream entities like customers, stakeholders, and interest groups and only examined those upstream elements that included direct relationships. This limited scan of the social dimension was easy to execute and made sense to the business leaders of the time because the general focus was on what was perceived to be most important – the markets, customers, and revenues. Indeed, limited scope is still used by companies that concentrate on the short term. If changes in the business environment progress slowly, and the business leaders focus on exploiting the present market opportunities, they generally make incremental improvements to the prevailing situation.

From a strategic management perspective, however, the narrow focus tends to reinforce basic assumptions about the social dimension. It examines reality from the business's existing strategies and attempts to discover opportunities within that well-defined context. However, this shortsighted approach often fails to uncover less defined or deeper opportunities and it is one of the reasons why many businesses only achieve small improvements in their performance. The better approach is to scan the whole business environment including particular sub-elements and even the broader context of the interfaces of the business with the social/human world. This kind of perspective sheds light on new opportunities derived from the entire social dimension. It examines reality from the perspective of the external world, not just from that of the prevailing business situation.

The digital camera phenomenon evolved rapidly during the 1990s. Initially, demand was minuscule because the technology was limited and the quality of the pictures was inferior to those of film-based cameras. A narrow perspective would indicate a limited opportunity for camera and film manufacturers. However, a broader perspective that included the expansion of home-based computers and printers, the increased power of those devices, the exponential growth of the Internet, and the rapid developments and improvements in digital technologies would have provided evidence that the digital cameras and their related products were on the verge of becoming the dominant product forms.

The purpose of research into the broader social dimension is not necessarily to determine specifics about market space, but to obtain a sense of what people think about and what they believe reality is. It also examines people's perceptions, especially about the future. In the short term, people buy the existing products in the marketplace because they do not have any alternatives. But, as new solutions become available people often switch to the superior choices. The aim of such research is to understand the ideas, ideals, perceptions, impressions, and skepticisms of people – specifically their latent desires. It also assesses public awareness and understanding of critical issues and concerns. It explores the rational and objective views that people have of the business world as well as their underlying feelings that may not be based in reality. Moreover, people may live within the reality of the world, but not like it. They make choices for themselves from options that were decided upon by powerful social, political, and/or economic forces. Often what they really desire – better solutions and outcomes – are not available. For instance, in US elections voters can choose either the Democrat or the Republican candidate. They select one candidate over the other, when, in reality, they may not particularly like either one. This is often referred to as "choosing the lesser evil." The same is often the case in business.

The impressions that people have about their reality are often based on a multiplicity of inputs and thoughts. In most cases, they are based on personal experiences. Some impressions are accurate and based on solid evidence and facts. However, many others are based on limited information, personal opinions, and faulty conclusions. Such impressions may be skewed due to a lack of understanding and misguided beliefs. For instance, many people think that ethanol fuel is a way to solve the world's energy problems without thinking about the implications that ethanol production, especially from corn feed stocks, would have on food prices.

Perceptions are also very important and are similar to impressions, except that perceptions are usually powerful views that take time for people to acquire and even more time to change. If they are positive with respect to businesses, then the effects can have long-term benefits in supporting the strategies and actions of the businesses and their enterprises. On the other hand, if perceptions are negative and not based on the facts, it may take huge efforts to reverse them and create more favorable views.

Understanding the depths of the social dimension allows strategic leaders to develop a more realistic framework for linking their businesses with the market spaces and the business opportunities. It gives them the ability to assess reality, find better alternatives, and craft better solutions. Without carefully examining this dimension, businesses risk the consequences of a limited view. Wal-Mart is an example of a company trying to understand the realities of the social dimension. Its belief that customers are principally driven by "low prices" causes Wal-Mart to reduce costs and expenses across the whole spectrum of its operations. Yet, the number of court cases involving unfair labor practices at Wal-Mart is an indication that the leadership may have an incomplete picture of its social dimension. It needs to better understand the importance of its employee contributions to the success of the company. Good decisions regarding the social dimension go beyond just customers.

An inclusive perspective of the social dimension would encompass primary social factors pertaining to people, their human rights, and the prevailing conditions and trends as well as demographics, economic circumstances, lifestyles, cultures, the makeup of local, regional, and global communities, and the concerns and perceptions of specific stakeholders.

Social factors

Most business opportunities depend on the social characteristics of people: who they are, where they live, what they need, what perceptions they have, how they behave, and how they change. Without their connection to people, businesses, technologies, and products are less relevant, possibly even meaningless.

The social factors are the objective characteristics of populations and people. While these characteristics may be deterministic, they are also dynamic and difficult to precisely map out given the large numbers of people in a given society. For instance, in 2003 the US population was approximately 292.6 million people.[7] However, the population is far from being homogeneous. It is a matrix of demographic segments having differing lifestyles and ethnic and cultural backgrounds. Indeed, the population of the US is a rich mosaic representing people from all over the world. This is also true for the largest cities in the US like New York, Los Angeles, San Francisco, and Miami. The diversity is both a challenge for business leaders attempting to understand the underlying social factors and an opportunity for them to find ways to differentiate their strategic positions and systems and structures and to provide the best possible solutions.

Demographics characterize the human population, usually according to age, geographic distribution, ethnic mix, and income levels. They identify the number of people in certain age groups, usually in five-year increments, and break the population down into categories based on geographical or political location, sex, family, income, occupation, education, religion, race, and nationality.

The age distribution and life-cycle stages are critical demographic factors that help identify the needs, wants, and expectations of people. Each age group tends to exhibit certain patterns of behaviors. While it is difficult to generalize, especially on a global basis where culture is a crucial factor in determining behavior, there are certain characteristics that tend to be true for certain age categories in most cultures and societies. For instance, new-born children require nurturing, protection, and basic physical and social needs. Also, young children have to be educated and/or trained and grow in stature and esteem with respect to the hierarchy of their society and their peers. Young adults create households and usually build families and/or other social relationships. As young adults mature they try to become a more important part of the prevailing social structure and become contributors to the social and economic underpinnings of their society. Middle-aged people tend to focus on reinforcing their positions in the communities and society. They often expand their participation in the social and economic well being of the society to achieve status and recognition. In their later years, people think about retirement and how they will be able to take care of themselves as their productivity and interests change. While there are more exceptions to behaviors than common elements, over the course of a human life the basic needs can be characterized to some extent.

Societies and/or countries with large numbers of young people (e.g. developing countries) typically have to focus a large portion of their resources on education and caring for young children. On the other hand, societies and/or countries with a significant elderly population tend to focus more resources on health care and social benefits. Still, it can be risky to generalize. For instance, the US might be viewed as a mature society with a more uniform distribution of people in the various age categories. Yet, the US has one of the largest immigrant populations in the world. In 2000, the US had approximately thirty-five million foreign immigrants.[8] With a population that is approximately 12% immigrants, mainstream demographics mask the implications of these new segments of the population which are typically younger and less affluent. This sets the stage for a possible dichotomy within the general population making it a little more difficult to characterize the whole. Yet, there may be undiscovered opportunities to fulfill the needs and expectations of the people in these expanding segments. For example, Wal-Mart has been very successful in serving less affluent people who need to spend less when making purchases. Costco, the wholesale club, has been very successful serving the more affluent people who have the disposable income to save money by purchasing in larger quantities. The strategic leaders of both companies understand the underlying needs of the people they serve.

It is important to realize that the purpose of understanding social factors is to determine the needs, wants, and expectations of society and not just to identify good customers and their needs. The objective is to build an awareness and understanding of the broad opportunities and challenges so that appropriate business direction can be formulated and implemented. The focus is on lifestyle considerations, consumption patterns, cultural aspects, and many others.

Lifestyle is a nebulous term that is used to characterize how people live. It pertains primarily to people in high-income countries – those who have many choices in what they do and how they do it. It describes the general patterns of behavior and attitudes about living. Understanding lifestyle considerations means understanding patterns of living including household formation, education levels, work, and leisure time activities. In contrast, in developing countries, the focus is usually on living conditions, especially in situations where people are surviving at the subsistence level.

Consumption is likewise a key variable in describing lifestyles. People in most developed countries have high consumption levels. However, consumption patterns also indicate lifestyle demands as people may buy goods and services to save time and effort. They purchase convenience foods and time-saving devices because their family demands, work schedules, educational needs, and leisure time consume and/or constrain much of their free time. Moreover, as more women enter the workforce or seek educational opportunities, the use of disposable, single use products and services has increased. As the basic necessities of life become more easily obtained, lifestyle, health, safety, security considerations, and personal satisfaction become more critical to achieving a sense of well being and happiness.

Culture is critical as well. On a global basis, and even within countries, culture is a key variable that has to be considered when making strategic decisions. As the populations in the developed countries change and they become less homogeneous, the business environment in those countries is expected to change as well. For example, EU countries like Germany and France have large immigrant populations that have their own ethnic and cultural identities. Germany has a large Turkish population who immigrated as guest workers over the last three decades. France has many ethnic groups from its former colonies of North Africa. Understanding the historical basis of the major cultural groups within a country or region is an important determinant for understanding the true business environment and the underlying opportunities and challenges.

Businesses can improve their standing in society by ensuring that they deal with people across the spectrum of the social dimension in the best ways possible. To do so, strategic leaders must understand and reflect on a broad range of social factors as they create their framework for formulating and implementing strategies. Strategic leaders and strategists need to know how people behave in various situations and ensure that businesses' interfaces and interactions are positive and promote the social good. Moreover, businesses have to realize that social factors are dynamic and are positively and negatively influenced by what the businesses and their extended enterprises do.

Community involvement

Communities are groups of individuals living together in some form of social and/or political arrangement. Community members generally have common interests in many social, economic, and political factors. For instance, people living in a geographic area surrounding a manufacturing plant or in a specific section of a city may form a basic type of community; it is often referred to as a neighborhood. These people may have common interests in the proper operation and maintenance of the plant and its effects on them and their lives. Some of the effects may be negative, but others such as employment opportunities, commercial activities, and greater influence in economic and political affairs may be viewed as positive. For instance, Cambridge, Massachusetts, home of Harvard University and the Massachusetts Institute of Technology, is a community with many biotechnology companies that offer high-tech jobs, research projects for the universities, and enormous prestige and political influence. People in these situations are also interested in how the government responds to their needs and in the related distribution of services and social programs provided.

Local communities are often the smallest political units of the overall political structure of a region or country. They have a governmental form that facilitates the control and maintenance of the social and political affairs of the people living in the locality. While there are many forms of local communities from hamlets and villages to towns and cities, local communities usually share common traits that can be identified and characterized so that an understanding of how to deal with the community can be determined.

Obviously, communities vary in size and scope. Each has its own opportunities and challenges. The complexity of understanding a given community expands as the size and scope increases. For instance, it is much more difficult to understand Shanghai, China than it is Oxford, UK. The former has a diverse population of thirteen million people with many foreigners.[9] It is the center of China's social, economic, and political expansion with a global perspective. The latter is a fairly homogeneous population of approximately 60,000 people that are focused on the academic and social life of Oxford University.

Community involvement from a business point of view includes understanding the underpinnings of life within that community and ensuring that any contributions are positive. It involves making relevant information about the corporation and its operations available to the community and allowing key community leaders to have input into the critical decisions pertaining to operations and processes that affect the community. It means ensuring that community issues and concerns are resolved to the satisfaction of both the community and the strategic interests of the corporation.

Stakeholder groups

Stakeholders are individuals or groups that are directly or indirectly affected by the products, services, processes, programs, and/or systems of businesses, but who do not share in any direct economic benefits or participate directly in economic processes as do customers or suppliers. Stakeholder groups are usually organized into informal structures and formal organizations to study, promote, and/or control certain interests or concerns, especially those pertaining to businesses, technologies, products, operations, and processes. They are typically the supporting, challenging, confronting, and/or controlling external entities that affect the affairs of the companies and their extended enterprises. Stakeholders include the public, consumers in general, environmental activists, government agencies, the media, financial institutions, nongovernmental organizations (NGOs), political interest groups, and other constituencies. The discussion herein applies only to stakeholder groups that affect businesses and their extended enterprises.

Stakeholders may support and facilitate the strategies and actions of the businesses or may be opponents of them. For instance, the public may encourage the development of new transportation technologies that reduce a country's dependence on petroleum. On the other hand, stakeholders may resist the introduction of certain new products that exasperate existing problems. For instance, there is an underlying belief in many countries that sport utility vehicles (SUVs) are too inefficient and that manufacturers should be forced to achieve a certain standard for fuel efficiency. There are groups that are working on banning SUVs in countries like the US or in countries of the EU.

Government agencies often promulgate regulations requiring businesses to obtain permission, approvals, and certifications to develop and sell a new product or before building new faculties. They may set constraints on operating conditions, establish rules for disclosures, and determine protocols for ensuring that technologies, products, and services are safe and meet the specifications promised to customers. There may be hundreds of such agencies within any given country, each having numerous regulations, directives, and protocols that must be understood and incorporated into the processes of the corporations.

NGOs are usually voluntary, non-profit organizations that focus on enhancing the public good or a specific subset of it such as protecting the environment, promoting social justice, developing economic opportunities for the disadvantaged, or a host of other concerns. The typical NGO focuses on a relatively small number of selected issues that establish its purpose, mission, and agenda. NGOs often track the activities of industries and corporations and disseminate information and data along with their analysis and interpretation of the implications and impacts. Political interest and environmental groups are similar except that they focus on political or environmental agendas, respectively. Some support the industry or corporations, but most don't. Other constituencies include the capital markets, financial institutions, and the related organizations like Dow Jones that provide the funding sources for corporate equity and debt instruments. The media also have interests in following corporate activities and developments. It is their job to inform the public. There are numerous tracking and information processing organizations like J. D. Powers and Innovest that provide assessments of companies and their performance.

Businesses should ensure that stakeholders and stakeholder groups are properly informed and have an accurate understanding of the corporation's reality. Moreover, as much as possible, stakeholder management constructs should ensure that stakeholders are involved in the decisions that affect them. Their involvement will add to the complexity of the processes, but can result in a more sustainable outcome. Moreover, stakeholder involvement provides a high probability that nothing has been overlooked and that the best decisions are made based on both internal and external perspectives. The importance of stakeholder involvement has increased during the last decade as the number of stakeholder groups has grown significantly and the number of social, environmental, health and safety, and liability issues has escalated.

Stakeholder management is the ongoing effort to understand, characterize, and respond to the most important issues to improve positive outcomes from social, economic, and market perspectives and to reduce the negative impacts and consequences of corporate decisions on the business environment. The Aspen Institute is one of the most important advocacies for stakeholder-based management methods and practices.[10]

Political dimension

The political dimension deals with the affairs of government, politics, and public policy. Governments are formal structures that provide the proper functioning of a political entity (i.e. a state, province, or country). Politics pertains to the activities of the officials responsible for governing and setting public policy and the processes of selecting those officials. Laws and regulations typically determine public policy. They are enacted by governments and enforced and interpreted by various segments of the legal system.

The political dimension is extremely complex as there are many forms of national governments, political subdivisions, and political structures. Nations are sovereign states that are independent and theoretically free to determine their own social, political, and economic systems. They may change their systems, structures, and governance as they wish. While such changes are rare, they do happen. There are also limits on governments based on their relationships with other countries and the global community. For instance, countries with heavy debt burdens are often forced into stringent spending policies by the World Bank or the International Monetary Fund.

Trying to understand the various political systems and structures for all of the countries in the world is a daunting challenge. Keeping track of the potential changes and political events is time consuming and requires resources be dedicated to continuously scan and monitor the political environment.

A desirable political environment is one that is stable, free of conflict, and incorporates basic human rights and freedom. In most democratic countries, changes are typically slow and managed within the architecture of the political system, which is often based on a constitution or some other guiding foundation. Radical shifts are rare, and the basic philosophies of government are understandable and predictable. Most of the developed countries have enjoyed this kind of stable political system for most of the latter part of the twentieth century.

In less than ideal situations, however, the government is unstable and often controlled by a ruling political party or individual(s) that has usurped most of the political power. The many dictatorships around the world are indicative of such situations. Even in countries where control is broader, political power is often held by less than 10% of the population, a small power base that has overwhelming influence in setting the political agenda, enacting laws, and promulgating rules and regulations.

In analyzing the political dimension, there are many factors that have to be examined including: the influence of nationalistic groups that exert huge political and economic power; hostility toward foreigners or other political groups; the lack of an open forum for discussing and debating policy issues; and the potential for the government to confiscate property and restrict rights. There are numerous other concerns as well. In countries that lack political stability, businesses must watch for corruption, lop-sided regulations that favor indigenous companies, and the potential for unfavorable changes in rules and regulations.

Regulations pertaining to business are often promulgated to establish policies and practices within an industry, set standards for performance and outcomes, require business reporting and information disclosures, and provide incentives and disincentives. They often seek to control or balance relationships in various business settings, especially between businesses and society. For example, there are many powerful corporations that have overwhelming advantages. Governments may attempt to restore balance within the business environment by regulating how the industry participants operate. These kinds of regulations attempt to level the playing field between the interests of businesses, customers, stakeholders, and other constituencies. Regulations also establish the expected outcomes for certain activities, performance criteria, and behavior. For instance, the governments of most developed countries prescribe limits on automobile emissions such as those established under the Clean Air Act Amendments of 1990 in the US and promulgated by the US Environmental Protection Agency (EPA). Regulations also require strategic leaders (companies) to disclose information about their businesses, operations, processes, and products. There is a growing trend toward more openness and reporting of information from financial details to environmental discharges. Regulations also may reward socially desirable behavior and punish undesirable activities through fees, fines, and penalties. For instance, governments may impose a tax on carbon dioxide production.

Business leaders often see regulations as having negative effects or involving adverse control on corporations. While there are situations where regulations make doing business more costly, regulations may also stabilize the business environment and make it easier for well-intentioned, honest companies to deal with not-so-honest and ill-behaving businesses. Regulations may raise the standards of acceptable practices and behaviors and make it more difficult for negative elements to sustain their operations. This is particularly important in developing countries where the standards of proper business behavior are ill-defined and there are wide variations between the best and the worst businesses. However, even with the best laws and regulations, dishonest and criminal behaviors still exist.

Ethical dimension

The ethical dimension is a non-traditional, more intangible perspective of the business environment that focuses on the principles and standards of proper behavior and practices regardless of the political or regulatory mandates. These standards of behavior are based on underlying human rights and generally accepted principles and practices. While it is difficult to precisely define universal principles, there is a trend toward articulating standards of conduct that apply to all companies and small and medium-sized enterprises (SMEs) regardless of who they are, their home country, or where they operate. For example, in 1999, the Secretary-General of the United Nations formulated the Global Compact, a set of principles to guide and integrate business, labor, and society in the quest toward ethical behavior and social responsibility. While there are debates about the rationale behind the UN Global Compact, the principles are similar to other multinational agreements that are recognized as a foundation for ethical behavior. The Principles of the Global Compact are:[11]

Human rights
- *Principle 1*: The support of and respect for the protection of international human rights;
- *Principle 2*: The refusal to participate or condone human rights abuses.

Labour
- *Principle 3*: The support of freedom of association and the recognition of the right to collective bargaining;
- *Principle 4*: The abolition of compulsory labor;
- *Principle 5*: The abolition of child labor;
- *Principle 6*: The elimination of discrimination in employment and occupation.

Environment
- *Principle 7*: The implementation of a precautionary and effective program to address environmental issues;
- *Principle 8*: Initiatives that demonstrate environmental responsibility;
- *Principle 9*: The promotion of the diffusion of environmentally friendly technologies.

Anti-corruption
- *Principle 10*: The promotion and adoption of initiatives to counter all forms of corruption, including extortion and bribery.

The principles combine codes of conduct and statements of intent. They may be viewed as standards of business behaviors that transcend laws and regulations in cases where the laws and regulations do not adequately provide for proper behaviors or the protection of society and the natural environment. They set the philosophical foundation for conducting business and are especially important in some of the least developed countries that do not have stringent laws and regulations.

Protection of human rights is clearly a universal requirement regardless of the political structure or laws and regulations. Companies and SMEs also have an ethical responsibility to ensure that labor practices are fair, open to scrutiny, and devoid of discrimination and bias. They must use best practices to design, produce, sell, and service their products, to manage their operations and processes, and to eliminate or minimize waste streams and the environmental impacts of their products from cradle to grave. Most importantly, they have a fiduciary responsibility to eliminate all forms of corruption and improper behaviors within their extended enterprise and to avoid dealing with corrupt governments, agencies or organizations.

While most of the these obligations are usually part of the underlying principles and common practices guiding a global corporation within its home country, occasionally companies have some difficulty deciding what to do when they are operating in developing countries that do not have stringent laws and regulations, or standards for governmental or corporate behavior. The challenge arises in highly competitive situations where the lack of legal and ethical standards allows unscrupulous companies to gain economic advantages. For instance, if one or more competitors do not comply with generally accepted practices and ethical behavior and gain an economic advantage because they have lower costs, some strategic leaders do not know how to compete against them. The right answer is to take the high ground, adhere to ethical operations, and work to require the competition to behave according to ethical standards of the global community. Such situations should be exposed to the global community and the offending companies should be forced to comply with generally accepted behaviors. While many people would view this as idealistic, it is actually the most pragmatic approach. Given that one of the most serious risks that all companies face is damage to their reputations, it is imperative that they promote high ethical standards. Corruption distorts the competitive landscape in the short term and increases the costs of doing business in the long term. Corruption, bribery, and other forms of distortion siphon some of the capital required to build a sustainable future.

The simplest philosophical and ethical approaches for large companies and SMEs are to simply adopt universally the standards, behaviors, and practices that meet the most stringent laws, regulations, and requirements. This means that strategic leaders would not exploit the social, economic, and environmental dimensions in countries with less stringent laws and regulations, but would use the mandates and standards that they recognize as critical for success in the developed countries.

This is not a radical concept, but rather, part of the foundation of philosophical, intellectual, and rational thought. Immanuel Kant (1724–1804), the great eighteenth-century German philosopher, stated that: "there is only one categorical imperative and it is this: act only according to the maxim whereby you can at the same time will that it should become a universal law [absolute moral obligation], and act in such a way that you treat humanity, whether in our person or in the person of another, always at the same time as an end, and never simply as a means [practical imperative]."[12] This is often translated as "do unto others as you would have them do unto you." Kant considered this an ethical and moral duty, a duty that ought to be acted upon regardless of the legal mandates or lack thereof.

This categorical imperative requires businesses and strategic leaders to always follow the most stringent mandates that apply when conducting business regardless of location. This is not only founded on an ethical perspective, but it also involves practical considerations in that exploiting the social world and the natural environment usually has repercussions in the future. For example, during the mid-1990s, Shell Oil damaged its international reputation with its conduct and behavior in Ogoniland, Nigeria. According to Ogbonna Ike, associate faculty member of the Lagos Business School of the Pan-African University and an affiliate of the Business Ethics Network, Africa, Shell Petroleum Development Company of Nigeria (SPDC), a subsidiary of Shell Oil, did not exercise proper responsibility for its operations in Nigeria even though Shell had extensive experience in oil development and used proper protocols elsewhere. Ike's assessment of the situation suggested:[13]

The accusation against Shell is that its operations have had side effects that it could have avoided if it had taken a more responsible approach to its operations. The side effects include harm to the environment, pollution, and harm to the human population. Critics claim that Shell did not apply suitable environmental standards. Shell is also accused of complicity with human rights abuses of the government in power at the time.

The Shell example demonstrates how a lack of government requirements does not alleviate the duty to act responsibly. Note that Shell has since made dramatic improvements in view of its corporate responsibilities.[14] Today, Shell is recognized as one of the best performing energy companies, but it has a long way to go to correct the mistakes and blunders of the past. It has made a remarkable transformation from a laggard to a leader by demonstrating a new commitment to a sustainable future.

While the social and political dimensions revolve around human rights and the human condition, and man-made laws and regulations respectively, the ethical dimension of the business environment derives from the transcendental ethic of correct behavior and proper decision making. Individuals, business leaders, their companies, and other entities of the extended enterprise are obliged to produce positive outcomes and eliminate harmful effects and impacts regardless of whether or not laws and regulations require them to do so. Oddny Wiggen and Lene Bohmann-Larsen, researchers associated with the United Nations University and the University of Oslo, respectively, have studied the implications of the negative side-effects of business and suggest that business leaders have an ethical responsibility and duty to mitigate the side-effects.[15] They call the occurrence of side-effects as the "double effect."[16]

A double effect refers to the fact that actions often have more than one outcome (i.e. actions may produce side-effects). The phenomenon of the double effect becomes a moral problem when the side-effects are not desirable, especially when they are harmful to those affected. Actors [business leaders] are responsible for such side-effects when these are foreseeable and they still choose to proceed. Actors are blameworthy for harmful side-effects when they allow them to happen even if they could have been prevented, or when they make no, or only insignificant attempts to minimize them.

The side-effects or double effect are discussed through this book in the form of "dual-sided perspective and/or management." It is based on the implicit and explicit responsibilities of business leaders to improve the positives and eliminate the negatives.

One of the other main underpinnings of the ethical dimension is the precautionary principle. It obliges business leaders to ensure that their actions are safe and appropriate and that they are not risking the health, safety, and well being of people or involve damage and/or destruction of the natural environment. The precautionary principle advocates taking preventive measures when there is good reason to believe that potential danger, harm, or negative impacts exist even before there is conclusive evidence about the causes and effects. It maintains that the most reasonable course of action is to err on the side of safety and protection of people and the natural environment. Business is full of stories in which companies created dangers and societal risks that ranged far from their capital structure and organizational resources.[17] While it can be argued that businesses have the right to risk their capital, they clearly do not have the right to risk the health, safety, and well being of people or to damage the natural environment. They have an absolute duty to ensure that they do not produce harmful effects and impacts.

Considering the ethical dimension reinforces the notion that businesses are responsible for the effects and impacts of their operations. It further suggests that businesses have an absolute duty to adopt a holistic perspective for their strategic decision making and commit to resolving potential problems during strategic analysis, strategy formulation, and program development rather than during implementation or execution. It presumes that strategic leaders have performed the requisite strategic analyses and are confident that they have mitigated the negative effects and impacts to the extent possible.

Economic dimension

The economic dimension refers to the macroeconomic conditions and trends of the marketplace, national economies, and global economy. The economy, whether national or global, consists of the aggregation of the exchange of goods and services, the availability and use of resources, and the application of labor. When examining the business environment, the general economy involves broader considerations than the needs and wants of customers in the market spaces. The traditional view of the macro-economy, which still dominates economic perspectives, however, focused on production and consumption of goods and services. As the global economy expands, and more national economies become increasingly linked to the global economy, the ability to discern economic causes and effects becomes more challenging.

The concept of supply and demand has been central to economic theory for centuries. It derives from the principle of resource scarcity and examines how companies make decisions when confronted with scarce resources, especially insufficient time, capital, energy, or natural resources, to meet the needs and wants of everyone. It assumes that decisions must reflect trade-offs either on a micro or macro scale. It also assumes that the trade-offs are best resolved using cost–benefit analysis. In reality cost–benefit analysis is better conveyed as benefit-to-cost since the driving factors really pertain to the benefits. Benefit–cost (B/C) analysis, using a B/C equation, depicts the sum of the benefits of a course of actions relative to the sum of the costs. The equation can be expressed as: $B/C = \sum benefits\ (B) \div \sum costs\ (C)$. It is a ratio of expected beneficial outcomes to expected costs.

Traditional economics also focused on the principle of comparative advantage. It suggests that individuals, groups, and countries do well when they concentrate on activities in which they have inherent advantages over others, either in costs, benefits, or both. For instance, the Province of Quebec, Canada has an overwhelming advantage in North America in aluminum production because it has extremely low electricity costs due to the large number of hydro-electric power plants there. Given that electricity requirements account for approximately 40% of the cost of primary aluminum, having a ready supply of low-cost electricity provides an incredible comparative advantage. Again, even in these cases, supply and demand are pivotal in establishing economic decision making. If the demand is high and the supply is low, prices increase until an equilibrium point is reached. Actual supply and demand phenomena are more complicated due to the elasticity of demand, and there are many distortions in the markets around the world created by government subsidies, costs paid by society, the excessive power of producers, consumers, or owners of capital and land, and taxation and other forms of government intervention.

The economic dimension involves many other factors like the state of the economy, economic growth, living standards, people's income and savings, international trade, foreign exchange, concentration of wealth, land ownership, the availability of capital and labor, and the application of investments. The state of a given economy depends on these factors and is the critical question relating to the economic dimension. Recessions and expansions are part of the normal cycles of macroeconomic conditions. Improved productivity and financial capital contribute to stability and growth, and long-term improvements generally help to reduce unemployment and lower inflation. Improved standards of living and human happiness are also important factors within the economic dimension.

The ultimate purpose of economic activity is to satisfy the needs and wants of humankind. While some producers may believe that the purpose is to make profits, and consumers may think in terms of consumption, the economic dimension is really a complex array of transactions, interactions, and relationships aimed at producing the means and mechanisms for people to satisfy their needs and create an acceptable standard of living and to provide investors and shareholders with rewards that compensate them for their contributions and risks. In simple terms, customers and employees seek a reasonable degree of economic stability. Owners of capital, land, natural resources, and production capacity seek an adequate return on their investments and uses of resources.

In developed countries, consumers generally drive the economy through the choices they make as they seek to meet their basic needs, support their lifestyle commitments, and exceed their economic aspirations. Needs and wants for food, shelter, and clothing involve both required expenses and discretionary spending. If economic conditions are positive, people tend to increase spending on discretionary goods. For instance, automobile purchases are typically cyclical with higher demand during good economic times and lower demand during recessions. Consumer confidence in the economic system and the prospects for the future are important factors in having positive economic conditions in the developed countries.

In developing countries, economic conditions usually revolve around fundamental human needs and the supply and demand of basic goods. Traditional economies in many of the least developed countries depend on non-monetary exchanges of the basic requirements for subsistence. People often fulfill their basic needs, wants, and expectations through barter systems that have elaborate methods for establishing fair value. While it is true that approximately 2.6 billion people earn less than $5 per day and that 3.5 billion people in low-income countries earn less than 20% of the world's income, in many such countries a majority of the economic activities may not be accounted for in the gross domestic product (GDP).[18] Making comparisons becomes difficult in these situations. Nevertheless, there are billions of people living on the margins.

Whether developed or developing economies, economic growth is fundamental to positive conditions and stability. It is often measured in terms of the increase in GDP. While GDP measures the value of all of the goods and services produced by an economy, including the contributions of government, it is an imprecise measurement since it does not discern the quality of the outcomes. For instance, when the *Exxon Valdez* spilled 10.8 million gallons of crude oil into Prudhoe Bay, Alaska, it created employment opportunities for thousands of people. While the people who earned income were positive contributors and their incomes and the purchases with their earnings added to the GDP of the US at the time (1989), it is impossible to say that such events or situations are desirable and really improve the overall economic conditions of a country.

Still, despite the difficulties in measuring it, economic growth and improved GDP provide the means for human development and enhanced living standards. In the developed countries a significant portion of the economies depends on growth-related activities like construction, housing, and other developments. Businesses such as those in the construction industry, producers of capital equipment, architectural firms, and land developers are usually greatly affected by the economic conditions and often suffer severely during recessions. If there is no growth at all over long periods of time, as in some of the least developed countries, growth-dependent companies in these sectors would evaporate.

Economic growth also depends on population growth and on increasing affluence which triggers more demand and consumption. In high-income countries, population growth has been relatively low over the last quarter century (0.7%), and it is expected to actually decline to 0.4% by 2015.[19] In these countries, economic growth has come to depend less on population growth and more on consumption growth. With greater affluence, people buy more, consume more, and seek more time-saving products and services. Consumers and producers have shifted toward using greater quantities of short-term products that result in high levels of resource utilization and waste generation. The economies of the high-income countries of Europe, Japan, and the US are shifting from the production focus to consumption- and service-based economies.

While there have been significant debates about the limits to such growth and the sustainability of the business world, the central challenge may be the viability of the economic systems – specifically how political and social leaders and economists view value creation and how well they are able to develop more sophisticated ways to measure progress. At least from the perspective of the developed countries, improved economic models are necessary to provide a better balance between the economic benefits of providing more goods and services to fuel affluence and the need to achieve sustainable development by ensuring that resources are used wisely and that waste is eliminated if possible from every point in the life cycle, from production, though consumption and the end-of-life.

The new economic models have to be integrated with the social systems to create more comprehensive solutions that address social problems, environmental pollution, educational imbalances, social injustice, and other challenges in the path toward broader social and economic progress. The greatest challenge may be wealth distribution and ensuring that the "underclass" in a society is treated fairly and obtains the same opportunities as the privileged. This may become an absolute necessity for the continuation of affluence as the rich in the developed countries get older and the young become poorer. Currently, the lack of education often limits the potential of young people in both developed and developing countries, leaving them unable to understand and work with sophisticated technologies and business practices. In the developed countries, in particular, opportunities for entry level employment continue to decline as automation, technological change, and outsourcing reduce manual labor positions. Many of these problems have to be addressed comprehensively from individuals taking the initiative to political entities finding new solutions to age-old problems.

Economic growth in developing countries derives from providing the basic requirements of life and building the knowledge and know-how. While economic factors are important and necessary, human development is also critical for developing countries to make their way in a complex world of powerful economic forces. Ending hunger and poverty, building adequate housing, providing proper health care, preventing and curing diseases, finding solutions to educational problems, providing good public transportation, and creating political stability are fundamental requirements for improving their economic systems. It is difficult for people in developing countries, especially those in sub-Saharan Africa, to concentrate on moving toward an income-based economic system when there are so many barriers to economic progress. They need support from global corporations and NGOs if they are to participate in the global economy. This includes the production of goods and services, not just financial aid or philanthropy.

Production usually requires some labor which, in turn, generates income for the people that provide it. Income allows people to enjoy a better standard of living and to improve their quality of life. The economic system links producers and consumers and provides a sense of equilibrium as production of goods produces more income for people to buy more goods. While this view is simplistic, it does indicate that such processes generally work to benefit producers, consumers, and workers. While perfect balance is rarely achieved, in most developed countries there is generally economic stability. And, while distortions like subsidies and protectionism have muddled the picture, economic growth over the last fifty years in most countries has been based (both in theory and practice) on the creation of value for everyone. Earnings provide employees with the monetary resources to afford the products and services they need and desire. Producers need adequate numbers of customers to buy their products and services that allow for the recovery of their invested capital and a reasonable return. This kind of stability is critical for the proper functioning of the economic systems and for growth. Capital is only rewarded when the economic systems are in balance, that is when people earn money and spend it on products.

The expansion of international trade has been a boon to most of the developed countries and some developing countries like China and India. In 2002, the total value of exports for all countries was $6.4 trillion in goods and $1.6 trillion in services (US dollars), respectively.[20] There has been a threefold increase since 1980, with a 6.8% and 8.1% rate of growth for goods and services, respectively.[21] Developed countries currently account for 65% of exports measured in US dollars. However, the share of exports deriving from developing countries is growing. International trade and its implications have dominated the economic dimensions over the last five years. The production of commodities is shifting from the high-wage, industrialized countries to low-wage, developing countries. Again, China and India have benefited significantly as large companies and SMEs attempt to exploit the comparative advantages of low wages, marginal benefits, and the lack of stringent regulations. With the reduction in costs, consumers in the developed countries can purchase goods at a lower price and consume more because prices are low. The people in the developing countries, in turn, obtain employment based on production of large quantities of goods most of which are for export. Most of these workers would not have been able to earn the same level of income if the production was based on product demand in their home country because there is insufficient means (disposable income) to buy the products. Therefore, exports make the development of manufacturing capacity and industrial output in the developing countries possible.

While this seems a sensible approach for making large companies more cost competitive, the ramifications are far-reaching and more complex than the simple economic construct of supply and demand. There are many concerns. As employment opportunities for manufacturing and select service jobs shift to the developing countries, this may leave more people in the developed countries looking for adequate employment at least in the longer term. Most importantly, if the aggregate net income available to households in the developed countries declines in real terms, it is not clear that the disposable income of people in the developing countries will increase quickly enough to continue to drive the global economy. The low wages paid to people in countries like China and India may be insufficient to provide the economic development necessary to grow their economies. Moreover, the loss of jobs in the US and the EU may cause economic slowdowns. If there is an economic decline in the developed countries, there may be a global decline. If unemployment rises and people do not have sufficient incomes, it may not matter how cost-effective products are. There may not be enough people to buy the available products regardless of the low costs due to the reduction in disposable income on a global scale.

In addition to these economic concerns, there are social and human rights issues about the fairness of the low wages and benefits paid to workers in China and India. While low wages are not considered to be exploitation in those countries by many business leaders, it is clear that such conditions would not be tolerated by national governments in the EU, Japan, and the US or by various interest groups or labor unions, etc. if such conditions were prevalent. For example, Wal-Mart is the largest private employer in the US with many low-wage employees by American standards. And, it generally pays above the minimum wage set by the federal government. However, numerous advocacy groups still question the fairness of the wages and benefits that Wal-Mart gives to its employees. Several states are working on legislation to impose requirements for companies with more than 10,000 employees to have health care programs for their employees or contribute to the programs run by the state government. If below par employment conditions are not acceptable in the developed countries, one must wonder why or for how long they should be deemed acceptable elsewhere.

International trade is one of the biggest issues of the early twenty-first century as businesses and countries try to find new strategic advantages in a more complex world. Great care has to be taken to discern the economic conditions and trends and to ensure the pathways taken are sustainable and meet the standards of human rights and the global community. Again, prosperity involves everyone. The goal is to improve human development and not to create winners and losers.

Foreign exchange problems and currency valuation are also huge concerns as certain countries try to maintain a cost advantage by deliberately undervaluing their currency in world markets. This distorts the economic analysis done by business leaders who believe that the low-cost structures in countries like China and India will continue in the long term. Currency values affect the balance of payments between countries like the US and China. Any adjustments in these payments could have severe consequences on the ongoing exchange of goods and services.

Another critical issue is the concentration of economic power and wealth across the world in the hands of the wealthiest individuals and corporations. Moreover, in many countries land ownership is held by a minority of the people, making it difficult for the poor to improve their economic status due to a lack of tangible assets. This inequality of income and assets translates into tension between the rich and poor and between countries. For instance, per capita income measured in PPP US dollars was 29,898 in 2003 for high income countries and only 6,104 and 2,168 for middle income and low income countries, respectively.[22] Moreover, in the US in 2000, the richest 10% of the population had a 29.9% share of income or consumption, while the poorest 10% had only a 1.9% share.[23] These situations require additional studies to determine global trends and to see if people are becoming more affluent or if only certain individuals are.

Finally, the availability of capital and labor is also critical for long-term development. Capital usually chases the highest returns. While trying to achieve the highest returns is seemingly a sensible criterion for investment, the underlying social, political, and economic health aspects are also important in determining whether or not to invest in a country or company.

Technological dimension

The technological dimension includes technical and economic considerations of the complex array of technologies, technological change, and technological innovations that continuously affect humankind's interactions with the natural, social, political, and economic dimensions. It includes all of the knowledge, scientific methods, devices, and apparatuses that enrich people's lives, support our social and economic systems, and create better solutions for people and the natural environment. Technology includes art, science, engineering, as well as the devices, methods, and know-how that can be applied in a beneficial manner.

Technological change occurs with the discovery, invention, and development of new technologies, knowledge, and mechanisms for providing improved solutions for customers, stakeholders, society, and the natural environment. Technological innovation includes the systematic creation of new-to-the-world technologies that are superior to the prevailing technologies, the invention of new technical approaches and devices, and dramatic improvements in existing technology platforms. Technological innovation also occurs when improvements are made in the way we use existing knowledge or when technological sophistication and learning are advanced.

Being optimistic, technologies are developed to make improvements and enhance the quality of human life and the well being of the social and natural worlds. Still, most technologies have both positive aspects and negative ones. There are always side-effects that have to be mitigated or controlled. People generally seek to have their wants and needs satisfied, not technologies themselves. They want solutions that are positive and ones that maximize value. Moreover, people do not want to make trade-offs like accepting the risks of cancer to enjoy high-tech products.

Technologies are often manifested in the form of the body of knowledge, the hardware and the software that are used to create commercial equipment, devices, products, and processes. They encompass the competencies, capabilities, experiences, and processes of the social and economic systems and include the contributions of supply networks, customers, stakeholders, related industries, other enterprises, and technology partners.

The technological dimension is tangible and real, but elusive and difficult to define definitively. It is the vast array of science, engineering and technology, knowledge, know-how, methods, and techniques that exist in the public domain and are open to everyone who wants to take advantage of them. The technological dimension also includes new innovations that are being discovered, created, and developed as part of technological change. These are most often the intellectual property of the inventor, researcher, and/or investor who usually has proprietary rights to the technology through patents or trade secrets.

Technological change occurs in the business environment when actions are taken to improve the technological dimension. In the broadest sense, it is the ongoing accumulation of new knowledge, new methods and techniques, the developments of new technologies, and new-to-the-world products and processes. Technological change usually involves multifaceted interactions with equally complex implications. For instance, digital camera technology has radically changed how people engage in photography, has contributed to a significant reduction in environmental impacts by eliminating chemical processing, and has improved the economics of taking pictures because users only have to pay for good pictures. Some of the major areas of technological change include:

- ICT including microprocessors, electronics, computers, telecommunications, fiber optics, the Internet, and all of the related software and protocols.
- Biotechnology and genetic engineering including new products for pharmaceuticals, food, health care, agriculture, and environmental protection and remediation.
- Nanotechnology and advanced materials science including lightweight, molecular-based building blocks and environmentally friendly materials that have fewer impacts.
- Advanced automation including smart devices, chips, radio-frequency IDs, sensors, security devices, and totally integrated processes.
- Sustainable/clean technologies including solar energy, hydrogen-based technologies like fuel cells, smart houses, energy-saving devices, and new-to-the-world technologies that minimize resource depletion, waste generation, and energy consumption.

These areas are just a microcosm of the exciting possibilities for new technologies that promise substantial improvements for the future. Behind each is the objective of doing more with less. If the quality of life worldwide is going to improve substantially over the next several decades and people in the developing countries are going to have greater opportunities for a higher standard of living, future technologies will have to be more efficient, effective, and use fewer resources while causing fewer negative impacts and related consequences. It will take the combined efforts of researchers and technologists at universities, government research laboratories, and agencies, private organizations, and corporations to make this possible.

Technological change is driven by the needs, wants, expectations, and mandates of the other dimensions. As the social requirements grow as the population of the world expands, new technological solutions will have to be developed to provide the basic necessities and ensure that the social systems across the world are sustainable. Political and regulatory changes also demand new and improved technologies. They often establish the rules for the development processes and specify the desirable outcomes. Deregulation may have similar challenges as the elimination of rules and constraints opens the door to new competition and new approaches. Economic considerations are also influenced by technological change, especially if the new technologies have non-linear improvements on the economic underpinnings of the business environment. Dramatically reduced costs expand the opportunity for new customers to enjoy the benefits of the technologies and the products. For instance, very few individuals could afford an LCD or plasma TV for their home in the late 1990s when the prices for such TVs were $5,000 to $10,000. However, less than ten years later, such devices are becoming standard TV sets given that people can buy the state-of-the-art technologies for about $500 to $1,000. The shifting economics has altered the value proposition, the affordability, and the demand.

Technology is central to the dynamics of the business environment, and the implications of new technologies can be far-reaching. It is important that business leaders are not blind-sided by unexpected technological change. They must keep track of all changes, not just those that are part of the foundation of a given corporation or its extended enterprise. For instance, microprocessor technologies from Intel, AMD, and others have influenced almost every sector of the business environment from automobiles and appliances to buildings and defense systems.

Technological innovation focuses on how to discover, assess, select, develop, commercialize, and manage emerging technologies based on the needs of the global business environment and the competencies, capabilities, and creativity of the organization. Business leaders invest in specific technological innovation programs to create sustainable value and obtain competitive advantage. The focus is on the effectiveness and performance of knowledge and how to transition to richer levels of sophistication.

Environmental dimension

The environmental dimension centers on connections between business and the natural environment and it is interconnected with all of the other dimensions of the business environment. It includes a complex array of forces affecting the health, safety, and well being of people and nature, and the environmental conditions and trends that either impact businesses or are caused by businesses. It involves those subsets of the natural environment and the social world that businesses must consider and address.

The environmental dimension is multifaceted. It is also very challenging for business leaders to comprehend the magnitude of the many driving environmental forces and how best they should respond to the challenges these forces impose. These challenges require strategic leaders to consider and deal with how pollution and waste streams from their businesses negatively affect the business environment. The main considerations are the degradation and destruction of the natural world, the disruptions on people and businesses, and the depletion of resources.

The direct environmental effects caused by businesses are relatively easy to identify. They include air emissions, waste water discharges, production of solid and hazardous wastes, the use and disposal of synthetic chemicals, accidents and spills, and the health and safety of workers, contractors, and the general public. Laws and regulations generally address these effects in most developed countries. However, in countries where they are not specifically covered, the environmental dimension would still call for best practices to be used to ensure that degradation, destruction, disruption, and depletion problems are eliminated or at least mitigated to the greatest extent possible. As discussed above, the ethical dimension would also assert that business leaders have a duty of care to employ the most stringent approaches in every situation regardless of where it occurs. The environmental dimension explores the needs and expectations of society, customers, and stakeholders and focuses the attention of business leaders on what the solutions should be instead of on what exists.

The possible destruction of the natural environment is perhaps the most worrisome of the environmental problems because the consequences are severe, affect everyone, and most likely are irreversible. The potential consequences of environmental impacts like climate change, eutrophication, acidification, ozone layer depletion, toxic contamination, habitat loss, and catastrophic illnesses require companies and business leaders to develop sustainable solutions.[24] Again, the precautionary principle must be invoked. If there is uncertainty, then strategic leaders have a duty to ensure safe and appropriate outcomes. Moreover, sustainable solutions are in the self-interest of companies since the negative impacts generally make businesses less successful. Think about how the litigation involving asbestos workers resulted in the bankruptcy of the Johns-Manville Corporation, what happened to Union Carbide as a result of the catastrophe at Bhopal, and what businesses could have done with the billions of dollars spent on remediation projects over the last quarter century.

Environmental disruption and resource depletion have local and regional impacts, but are also profoundly capable of affecting the whole business environment including the ecosystems and the entire biosphere. Disruption is a broad category that includes relatively simple impacts such as those of traffic congestion and noise as well as broader concerns about the loss of biodiversity and the negative impacts on the balance of nature. It also includes the compounding effects and impacts of such issues as deforestation and the loss of natural habitat. For instance, deforestation is itself an impact, but it also leads to other impacts such as loss of watershed, degradation of land resources, and the loss of flora to absorb carbon dioxide, something that could potentially exacerbate climate change.[25] Disruption of the natural world often has far-reaching future effects that are usually difficult to calculate in the near term. For example, erecting large dams like the Three Gorges Dam in China can have many disruptive effects on the natural environment and the people who live in the affected areas. Typically, strategic decisions to build such structures are based on simple economic models, using cost–benefit analysis without a clear understanding of the long-term detrimental effects and impacts on the other critical factors. Some of the effects are felt immediately. The flow of the river is disrupted, and the natural habitat downstream is significantly altered. However, most of the effects and impacts often take many decades to manifest themselves. Many of the native species will fail to thrive in the radically changed environment and the new conditions may lead to the proliferation of diseases, the infestation of non-native species, and other environmental problems affecting humankind and nature.

Depletion of natural resource is another ill-defined subject, and one that typically lacks the depth of research necessary to truly understand the effects and impacts. Usually, business leaders and strategists determine whether there are sufficient resources to meet their requirements into the foreseeable future or at least throughout their normal planning horizon of five to ten years. But, resource depletion has far-reaching consequences including the loss of economic viability of the business activities, the necessities to develop alternate technologies and resources, the increase in costs to use the existing products, and the acceleration of negative economic and environmental impacts and consequences when it becomes more difficult to obtain the remaining resources. For example, as petroleum resources become depleted, petroleum companies expand their exploration for oil into more marginal areas or they use more destructive approaches to exploit the remaining resources.

Some of the most critical resources include clean air and water. These resources are ubiquitous affecting everything in nature, life, and the economy from human survival itself to our systems for supporting manufacturing processes for producing high-tech products like microprocessors. Yet, when technologists discuss the possibility of converting petroleum-based automobiles to ethanol-based vehicles, they calculate the acreage required to produce the sugars or starches needed for ethanol production, but typically fail to consider the vast quantities of water required to grow the crops. They underestimate the importance of land and water, its scarcity in many countries, and the fact that it is expected to become even more limited as the world's population grows to more than nine billion people in 2050.

Diminishing biodiversity due to human and industrial activities is another grave concern. It is impossible to understand all of the interconnections and interrelationships in nature that will determine the ultimate impacts and consequences of declining diversity. Humankind may be losing valuable resources and innovative solutions for future needs without even realizing the effects and consequences as the human activities overwhelm the natural world in many locations. In many situations, the focus is on the immediate need for resources without any consideration about the long-term effects of the natural world.

Interrelationships among the dimensions

The examination and understanding of the business environment is complicated because most of the dimensions are interrelated. It is difficult to simply say that a phenomenon fits exactly into a given dimension or even into just two of the dimensions. For instance, the environmental dimension is one of the most complicated because of its connections to the other dimensions of the business environment.

The economic and social dimensions often have significant effects and impacts on the environmental dimension. The impacts and their consequences on the environmental dimension are central to determining the true value and viability of many of the economic decisions. The associated environmental requirements are complicated and represent tremendous challenges, but also significant opportunities for making better decisions and obtaining better solutions than those made in the past. Business leaders should view environmental issues and concerns in positive terms, not simply as negative impacts and their consequences. They often are opportunities for

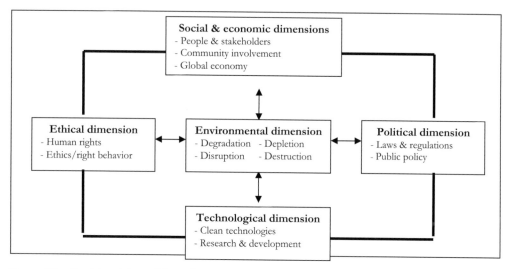

Figure 4.3   The interrelations of the environmental dimension

outperforming competition exceeding the expectations of the social and political dimensions.

Figure 4.3 depicts the interrelationship of the environmental dimension and the other main dimensions.

The ethical dimension reinforces the environmental dimension. Many environmental impacts are directly related to the human condition and the rights that everyone has for the protection of their well being and for a safe, secure, and healthy life. Examining what ethical, social, and business behaviors would mandate and then following the requisite approaches can often shed new light on how to deal with the complex environmental situations. Moreover, being ethical and following best practices can lead to the means and mechanisms for addressing complex problems and finding the most appropriate solutions.

Many of the environmental problems in the business environment are due to inefficiencies and ineffectiveness of products, processes, or operations. In most cases, efficiencies and effectiveness can be much improved. The answer is to address the problems and find dramatic improvements using the best solutions possible from the technological dimension. There are cleaner technologies being created every day, technologies that eliminate many of the problems of the past. Leadership must strive to discover those cleaner technologies and acquire ways to use them.

Ultimately, the social and economic dimensions determine what the perceptions and expectations are and what has to be done to conform to requirements. People usually do not prescribe specific environmental solutions per se, and unfortunately, most expectations are not fully manifested in the present and become obvious only in the future when it may be too late to respond adequately. Here is where the broader philosophies and perspectives of ESM pay dividends. By including the whole of the business environment when examining reality, strategic decisions are made on the basis of all of the inputs and implications. While there are few if any perfect solutions, the broader considerations generally lead to better outcomes.

The political dimension often has a direct relationship with the environmental dimension. Obviously, laws and regulations spell out what has to be done, and there is often limited flexibility once the regulatory requirements are promulgated. The better scenario is to participate in the development of public policy to help orchestrate solutions that are fair and balanced from ethical, social, economic, technological, and environmental perspectives. As always, looking upstream for ways to address concerns may lead to more options and better solutions. Moving upstream reveals opportunities to eliminate the causes, effects, and impacts of problems. In these situations, simplicity often leads to complexity, and intricacy back to simplification. For instance, a combustion process that generates enormous quantities of air pollutants and carbon dioxide and is devoid of sophisticated clean technologies and pollution abatement equipment is simple to design, construct, and operate. Moreover, the process economics are simple as well. However, the lack of clean technologies and uncomplicated process equipment results in significant environmental degradation which triggers regulatory requirements, social concerns, stakeholder responses, ethical issues, and additional costs in the future to pay for externalities, liabilities, and lost opportunities. The simple approach becomes complex. On the other hand, deploying more sophisticated clean technologies from the start, while more costly, complex, and expensive to operate, can simplify the resulting outcomes. With fewer defects and burdens and less pollution, the ultimate costs of the process are lower, and the downstream impacts are less. The complex approach becomes the simple.

Technological change and the changing global landscape have moved, responding to today's business environment and managing the implications beyond the reach of simplistic approaches, to a broader world where opportunities abound. When examining the business environment, the key questions pertain to what should be instead of what is. The focus is on understanding the depth of the needs and expectations and translating that understanding into sustainable business opportunities. But, the perspective can change still further from finding opportunities to creating them, from satisfying demand to providing solutions, and from realizing internal objectives to achieving short- and long-term outcomes that create value for everyone. While these are far-reaching and obviously challenging goals, the opportunities of the future clearly lie in the unmet demand in the business environment and not just in the stated demand of the marketplace. For instance, the vast majority of people in this world have yet to enjoy the social and economic benefits that businesses provide or could provide.

Box 4.1: eBay and its influence on change

eBay is one of the most successful startup companies in the annals of American business. While it had a relatively slow beginning, eBay has accelerated into the forefront of American business and is one of the largest "retailers" in the world. eBay was founded by Pierre Omidyar in 1995 to facilitate peer-to-peer trading. Initially, Omidyar allowed free access of his "electronic Bay" website to San Francisco area residents who engaged in the auctions of personal goods. As its success grew, eBay expanded that site and charged a small fee for each transaction. Clients were more than happy to pay a modest fee to be able to transact their business. They carried out transactions that would not have been possible without eBay. In 1996, Jeffrey Skoll joined his friend, Omidyar, in the business. Being a Stanford MBA Skoll brought a sense of professional management to the equation. However, neither of them really wanted to run the business, so Margaret Whitman, head of Hasbro Inc.'s preschool business, was hired in late 1997 to become president and CEO. With an MBA from Harvard and plenty of leadership experience, she added the management and marketing expertise necessary for expanding the operations and building a senior management team.

eBay expresses its mission and business purpose of service and commitment to the broader communities. As stated in its Form 10-K, 2006, its purpose is:[1]

to pioneer new communities around the world built on commerce, sustained by trust and inspired by opportunity. To achieve our purpose, we operate three primary business segments: Marketplaces, Payments and Communications. We provide online marketplaces for the sale of goods and services, online payments services and online communication offerings to a diverse community of individuals and businesses. Our Marketplaces segment enables online commerce through a variety of platforms, including the traditional eBay.com platform and our other online platforms, such as Shopping.com, classifieds websites and Rent.com. The wide array of websites that comprise our Marketplaces segment bring together millions of buyers and sellers every day on a local, national and international basis. Our Payments segment, which consists of PayPal, enables individuals and businesses to securely, easily and quickly send and receive payments online. Our Communications segment, which consists of Skype, enables VoIP calls between Skype users, and also provides Skype users with low-cost connectivity to traditional fixed-line and mobile telephones.

eBay brings millions of people together each day to conduct their business or personal agendas for trading, exchanging, selling, or buying products and services. It provides a low risk, convenient, cost-effective, and relatively secure means for its customers to fulfill their objectives. eBay establishes the rules, standards, and procedures for the transactions and monitors ongoing results. It provides powerful business platforms and mechanisms for making its customers successful. Its success is predicated on the success of its users. Its power is derived from its tremendous reach into the world of its customers. It has over 82 million active users according to a recent 10-K report:[2]

Our success has resulted largely from the growth of our community of confirmed registered users, which has increased in size from approximately two million at the end of 1998 to approximately 222 million as of December 31, 2006. As of December 31, 2006, we had approximately 82 million active users on the eBay.com platforms, compared to approximately 72 million at the end of 2005.

In 2005, eBay's customers accounted for $44.3 billion in gross merchandise volume representing a 30% increase over the previous year.[3] eBay's marketplace strategies include identifying selected product categories to participate, determining the formats for exchanges (i.e. traditional auction listings, "Buy-It-Now" feature, fixed-price sales, "Dutch Auction" format, which allows a seller to sell multiple identical items to the highest bidders, and eBay Stores enable sellers to show all of their listings and to describe their respective businesses through customized pages) and geographies involving communities in more than twenty countries.[4] eBay's power comes from its extensive customer base, many of whom are running their own businesses using the eBay platforms.

eBay has enjoyed phenomenal success leveraging the interactions of its customers. It charges listing fees, transactional fees, and other charges. eBay's gross margins are incredible. It has been able to use the resources and efforts of its customers to obtain financial success. Revenue growth has been tremendous. Its gross margins are about 80%. Its revenue growth is outstanding even though the rate has decreased slightly in recent years.

eBay has an exciting past, a bright present, and an uncertain future. Sustaining success is the biggest challenge. Strategic leaders have taken a global perspective to lead change. Strategic leaders at eBay have accepted the concept of leading change and have created new opportunities and new ways for people to enjoy success. eBay has provided people with a format and the means to sell and buy goods that might have gone to waste. But, it has to continue to innovate and to think about its value proposition and how it creates and sustains success over time without exceeding its capabilities and the needs and expectations of the market spaces. The challenges are enormous, but the opportunities are great.

Notes

1. eBay Form 10-K 2006, p. 1.
2. *Ibid.*, p. 2.
3. eBay Form 10-K 2005, p. i.
4. *Ibid.*, p. 4.

In exploring problems, challenges, opportunities, and expectations, the best solutions are found where people's needs, desires, adequate safeguards, and the means and mechanisms converge. This convergence requires astute business leaders – those who understand the broad nature of the business environment and have a comprehensive perspective of the many elements that make up reality.

Summary

The business environment includes phenomena that provide both direct and indirect business opportunities and challenges. Generally, the dimensions of the business environment are broader than those affecting the extended enterprise. They often foretell of trends that may materialize into business realities in the long term.

Strategic leaders have to focus on understanding the realities of the business environment and discovering and creating opportunities to expand the reach of the enterprise. However, most companies are finding it difficult to grow successfully through existing markets and customers. At the same time, we know the world is full of people with wants and needs that are unfulfilled. To the forward-thinking strategic leaders this spells incredible opportunities to expand. And, business leaders that can look "outside-the-box" can decide how to realize those opportunities.

The discussions in this chapter have examined the broader dimensions of the business environment. Those dimensions are linked upstream to the natural environment and the social/human world. They are linked downstream to the market spaces and the extended enterprise, and there are numerous instances of overlap. The exact elements within the dimensions of the business environment that are relevant depend on the businesses involved. However, in every case, understanding reality and knowing the driving forces and factors are essential attributes of ESM because opportunities, strategies, and action plans are derived from knowledge, understanding, and capabilities.

Understanding the business environment is central to effective strategic leadership and management in the fast-paced world of the twenty-first century. As the rate of change accelerates, businesses and their enterprises have to be leading change from a perspective that is as far upstream as possible. For instance, changes in customer preferences are usually manifested much earlier in the social dimension of the business environment. The changing demographics in the developed countries are creating new opportunities for products related to the facilitating the well being of the elderly while at the same time reducing the demand for more traditional products like automobiles and furniture. This does not mean that automobiles will disappear or that the elderly will become the most important segment. It does mean that there are fundamental shifts that can be anticipated in customer thinking and behavior. Business leaders and strategists must understand these general tends as well as the specific requirements of the marketplace.

References

Bohmann-Larsen, Lene and Oddny Wiggen (2004) *Responsibility in World Business: Managing the Harmful Side-effects of Corporate Activity.* New York: United Nations University Press

Edwards, Paul (1967) *The Encyclopedia of Philosophy,* volume three. New York: Macmillan Publishing Co., Inc. & The Free Press

Harremoes, Paul, David Gee, Malcolm MacGarvin, Andy Sterling, Jane Keys, Brian Wynne, and Sofia Guedes Vaz (2002) *The Precautionary Principle in the 20th Century.* London, UK: Earthscan Publishing Ltd.

Naisbitt, John (1982) *Megatrends: Ten New Directions Transforming Our Lives.* New York: Warner Books

Rainey, David L. (2006) *Sustainable Business Development: Inventing the Future through Strategy, Innovation and Leadership.* Cambridge, UK: Cambridge University Press

United Nations Conference on Trade and Development (2001) *World Investment Report 2001.* New York: United Nations

   (2004) *Development and Globalization 2004: Facts and Figures.* New York: United Nations Publications

United Nations Environmental Programme (2005) *Global Environmental Outlook 3.* London, UK: Earthscan Publications Ltd.

United Nations Human Settlements Programme (2004) *The State of the World's Cities 2004/2005: Globalization and Urban Culture.* London, UK: Earthscan

Watkins, Kevin (2005) *Human Development Report 2005, International Cooperation at the Crossroads: Aid, Trade and Security in an Unequal World.* New York: United Nations Development Programme and Oxford University Press

NOTES

1 Most of the discussions in the chapter are taken from the perspective of the global corporation. However, many of the concepts, constructs, and comments also apply to SMEs, especially the larger, more sophisticated ones. In order to keep the flow of the text easier to follow, the reference to SMEs is not always included.

2 The G7 is the group of seven major industrial countries established in 1985 to discuss the world economy and to promote economic development. It includes Canada, France, Germany, Italy, Japan, the UK and the US. The G8 is the G7 with inclusion of Russia.

3 General Motors Corporation 2004 Annual Report, pp. 96–97.

4 *Ibid.,* p. 45.

5 John Naisbitt, *Megatrends: Ten New Directions Transforming Our Lives* (New York: Warner Books, 1982, pp. 55–77).

6 Please note that the graphical representation is not intended to depict any actual situation and there are many variations to the layout. It is almost impossible to generalize the complexities involved.

7 Kevin Watkins, *Human Development Report 2005, International Cooperation at the Cross-roads: Aid, Trade and Security in an Unequal World* (New York: United Nations Development Programme and Oxford University Press, 2005, p. 232).

8 United Nations Human Settlements Programme, *The State of the World's Cities 2004/2005: Globalization and Urban Culture* (London, UK: Earthscan, 2004, pp. 77–78).

9 *Ibid.*, p. 16.

10 Judith Samuelson and Bill Birchard, "The Voice of the Stakeholder", www.strategy-business.com/press/article/03311. The Aspen Institute is a strong advocate of stakeholder-based management methods and practices.

11 www.un.org/Depts/ptd/global.htm.

12 Paul Edwards, *The Encyclopedia of Philosophy, Volume Three* (New York: Macmillan Publishing Co., Inc. & The Free Press, 1967, pp. 305–324).

13 Lene Bohmann-Larsen and Oddny Wiggen, *Responsibility in World Business: Managing the Harmful Side-effects of Corporate Activity* (New York: United Nations University Press, 2004, p. 138).

14 Shell has had a number of significant miscues in the past. In particular, it had many problems in Nigeria. Nigeria is an oil-rich country. Shell acquired development rights and partnerships to exploit the oil reserves. Nigeria did not have sophisticated political, regulatory, or social mandates pertaining to oil exploration and production. Although there were a few regulations, oil companies were allowed to use their own standards and practices. Without governmental constraints, Shell experienced oil spills, oil leaks, pipeline problems, and other operating difficulties affecting the indigenous population. The impacts included polluted water and contaminated land that affected drinking water, food resources, and natural habitat resulting in social and political unrest. In 1997, Shell took action to move toward SBD in order to preempt difficulties and problems.

15 Oddny Wiggen is an Academic Programme Associate of the Peace and Governance Programme, United Nations University in Tokyo, Japan. Lene Bohmann-Larsen is a researcher with Ethics, Norms, and Identities Programme, International Peace Research Institute, Oslo, and research fellow, Department of Philosophy, University of Oslo, Norway.

16 Lene Bohmann-Larsen and Oddny Wiggen, *Responsibility in World Business: Managing the Harmful Side-effects of Corporate Activity*, p. 4.

17 Paul Harremoes, David Gee, Malcom MacGarvin, Andy Sterling, Jane Keys, Brian Wynne, and Sofia Guedes Vaz, *The Precautionary Principle in the 20th Century* (London, UK: Earthscan Publishing Ltd., 2002, pp. 49–63, 170–184).

18 United Nations Environmental Programme, *Global Environmental Outlook 3* (London, UK: Earthscan Publications Ltd., 2005, pp. 35, 222, 235). In 2003, low-income countries had a population of 2.6 billion people who had an average GDP per capita of PPPUS$2,168.

19 Kevin Watkins, *Human Development Report 2005, International Cooperation at the Cross-roads: Aid, Trade and Security in an Unequal World*, p. 235.

20 United Nations Conference on Trade and Development, *Development and Globalization 2004: Facts and Figures* (New York: United Nations Publications, 2004, pp. 48–49).

21 *Ibid.*

22 Kevin Watkins, *Human Development Report 2005, International Cooperation at the Cross-roads: Aid, Trade and Security in an Unequal World*, p. 269.

23 *Ibid.*, p. 270.

24 David L. Rainey, *Sustainable Business Development: Inventing the Future through Strategy, Innovation and Leadership* (Cambridge, UK: Cambridge University Press, 2006, pp. 255–264).

25 *Ibid.*

5   Market spaces: The intersection of economic and business forces

Introduction

Markets and customers are among the most important dimensions of business enterprises. Businesses are economic entities that clearly have to engage in some form of commercial transactions to make money and sustain their well being. This includes developing economic solutions, making investments, covering expenses, obtaining cash flow, and achieving positive returns. While businesses can make money in many ways including licensing technologies, renting property, and earning interest, ultimately most businesses depend on the sale of goods and services to sustain their success. The exchanges of products and services for money can be characterized as markets where producers and customers interact to achieve positive and mutually beneficial outcomes.

Markets are broad generalizations about commercial exchanges, purchasing patterns, buyer behaviors, and many other facets pertaining to the sale and purchase of products and services. They are the pivotal spaces where the economic forces of business enterprises intersect and create the realities of the commercial and financial worlds. During most of the last century economists usually had fairly precise definitions about specific markets and economic exchanges. They were often characterized in terms of government classifications and industry structures based on data collection and analyses. Today, many markets are fragmented and it is becoming more and more difficult to identify and classify exactly what the markets are and how they behave. Market characteristics can change quickly and new aspects take hold. For instance, the markets for cell phones have splintered into many segments and many of those segments overlap with other market segments such as those pertaining to digital cameras and other devices.

The traditional economic basis for market generalizations has been the products and services that companies sell to specific groups of customers. As the world moves toward mass customization[1] and beyond, markets are becoming more difficult to define accurately, and demand is fragmented into many specific "product–market" segments and the trend is toward even more segmentation. Mass customization suggests that there are uniquely designed, produced, and delivered products for each customer. The notions of markets and industries may eventually give way to the concept of customer-based solutions or the concept of sustainable solutions based on what customers expect rather than what producers provide. While products are broad producer-centered means to satisfy customer needs and wants, solutions are specific, customer-based, and stakeholder-based outcomes that focus on what is expected and how to more precisely meet the needs without wastes and burdens. Such solutions are theoretically more affordable and desirable because they are tailored to specific requirements, rather than the general perspectives of markets. For instance, many people in the developing countries need products like refrigerators or even personal computers but they cannot afford the devices sold in the developed countries nor can they use all of the functions and features. Moreover, they may not have access to electricity, making the devices unusable. Solutions have to be tailored to the conditions, needs, requirements, and expectations of the people involved and designed and configured on the basis of the prevailing situations. In many developing countries people need simple devices that provide basic outcomes, meet fundamental needs, are affordable, and require very little support.

The notion of market space is a theoretical view of all of the markets plus the potential ones that could be developed if the right solutions were available. It includes the existing market segments as traditionally defined per geographical, demographical, behavioral, and other categories and the underlying potential markets that are inadequately served or not served at all. From a strategic perspective of market spaces, the opportunities and challenges involve finding what the needs, wants, and expectations are before others do and determining how to meet the requirements ahead of the competition or others. This is usually difficult because people often do not have an exact sense of what the solutions should be. Even in the developed countries where people have a fairly sophisticated sense of their expectations, people have latent needs that they are unable to articulate until businesses develop and offer new solutions. For instance, plasma and LCD televisions are all the rage but how could the average person know that such technology was possible. Most of the existing products and services of today satisfy customers in the short term if they meet the general expectations and requirements. However, business history tells us that there are often new technologies and new approaches just across the business horizon which may lead to better solutions. People want the best solutions possible, not just products and services.

Stakeholders drive the solutions as well. The myriad of needs and wants of customers, stakeholders, related industries, and other constituencies ultimately determine specifications of the solution. Strategic leaders have to ensure that the solutions represent the best combination of all of the specifications. The mandates of governments are especially important.

The chapter portrays the pivotal nature of business connections and links with the markets, customers, and stakeholders. It discusses the relationships within the enterprise and its markets and customers. It focuses on how the strategic leaders of business units and their strategic management systems (SMSs) realize opportunities and meet challenges in the market spaces. Moreover, it provides insights about how enterprise-wide strategic management (ESM) makes achieving sustainable success possible. The chapter includes the following main topics:

- Perspectives on markets, customers, and the value proposition
- Concepts and realities of market space
- Business opportunities in space and time
- Perspectives pertaining to external context.

Perspectives on markets, customers, and the value proposition

The traditional view of markets and customers

Traditional business transactions are usually based on the primary relationships between buyers and sellers (customers and producers). Customers want to satisfy their needs and expectations through products and services provided by companies. Companies desire to design, produce, and market their products and services to achieve customer satisfaction and generate revenues and profits.

Markets consist of groups of similar customers who are seeking to satisfy their needs and wants in specific ways. The historic basis for market generalizations has been the products and services of the companies and/or businesses. Market demand for existing products and services is typically one of the most important drivers for strategic decision making. Demand for existing products and services is relatively easy to determine because there are

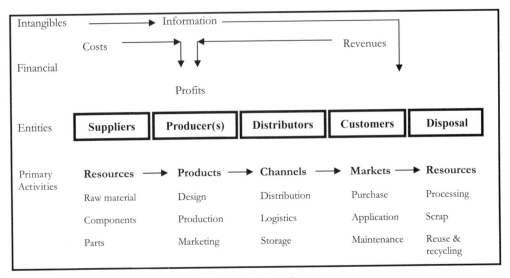

Figure 5.1 Traditional model of supply and demand structures[2]

usually vast quantities of data and information available about markets and customers' actions at least in the developed countries. In countries like the US, the UK, Germany, France, and Japan, various government agencies compile and analyze markets and economic activities, and prepare periodic reports on market conditions and trends. The economics of supply and demand typically determines price levels, quantities sold, and the long-term market potential. The quantity demanded is usually a function of the benefits obtained by customers, the prices paid, and the quantities available.

Traditional economic models and/or management frameworks focus on resources, products, channels, markets, and demand among other characteristics. Figure 5.1 depicts an expanded view of the conventional supply and demand model. Here suppliers provide inputs to the producer who creates and produces products that flow through distributors to customers. Customers buy and use the products during their useful life and are responsible for their maintenance and ultimate disposal. The producers' responsibilities are limited to the actual transactions involving the exchange of goods for money. They may be liable for certain product defects and failures depending on the laws of the country.[3]

The traditional model also included considerations about competitors that delivered similar products and services. It is based on the generic value chain and value system. It includes the primary internal dimensions (inbound logistics, operations, outbound logistics, marketing and sales and service) and the support activities (firm infrastructure, human resource management, technology development, and procurement) required for delivering value to customers.[4] The value system links the internal value chain with the value chains of the suppliers, channels, and buyers (customers) to provide a system of upstream contributors and downstream recipients.[5] The value chain and value system were discussed in Chapter 1.

The producers established the value systems and selected the suppliers and distributors who supported the producers' capabilities to obtain raw materials, parts, and components of the upstream side of the value system and to deliver products and services to the ultimate customers on the downstream side. Distributors might take ownership of the products until their sale to the end customer, provide information and marketing promotion, and logistical support among other services depending on the nature of the market and demand.

Customers would purchase the products that were available, choosing from a relatively limited array of product forms. They might increase the number of choices by seeking alternative products from competitors. Customers were responsible for the applications and most importantly for the costs associated with the installation, maintenance, use, and disposal of the products. Each of the entities in the value system operated independently of the others and most of the activities and actions where guided or mandated through the industry standards, commercial codes, and laws and regulations. The entities of the value system usually operated at arm's length from each other. Some of the participants established relationships with their upstream and downstream entities, but the norm was typically one of cordial arrangements with mostly professional and formal ties. However, the relationships between the parties were very weak and often adversarial.

The prevailing market perspectives

Many strategic leaders still think in the narrow terms of selling products and services to customers and fending off the advances and impacts of competition. They identify their strategic positions based on competitive space rather than market space. Moreover, many strategic leaders are often more concerned with the strategies and actions of the main competitors than they are about providing the best solutions for their customers and customers of customers and keeping stakeholders satisfied as well.

The theory of competitive space examines the industry and its participants from the perspective of the producers. This seems to make intuitive sense because the producers are often the decision makers who design, manufacture, deliver, and market the products and services. They have the knowledge about the technical details and the linkages across the extended enterprise. Moreover, the actions of competitors are typically perceived to be the barriers to success. It is also easy to orchestrate because the "centroid" of the model involves the producers who are relatively easy to understand especially if many of the producers (competitors) are alike.

This perspective also fits the historical relationships between producers and customers. In the early years of the twentieth century producers had enormous influence on the options that customers had about satisfying their needs. Producers made decisions about the products that they would develop and offer, and customers would have to choose from a limited number of choices. They would select the ones that fit their needs, but those might not necessarily be the optimum choices. Many strategic leaders developed their marketing themes based on the perspectives of what the competitors were doing rather than examining what customers really wanted. While it would be an overstatement to suggest that customer inputs were neither sought nor used, and there are many examples of businesses that successfully incorporated customer requirements in their strategic thinking, the mainstream approach was to think about competitive space instead of market space.

The notion of competitive space was best typified by Porter's most famous model pertaining to industry rivalry. His model of the "five competitive forces" of industry structure defined competitive space. It included buyers, suppliers, industry competitors, substitutes, and potential entrants.[6] The perspective was based on the producers' view of reality. The basic model assumed that there would be rivalry among the competitors and, to a large extent, the outcomes were determined on the basis of power and influence. Likewise, the relationships between producers (competitors) and their suppliers and customers depended on the power that the entities enjoyed in the competitive situation. If there were few producers and many customers, or customers had few options for fulfilling their needs and expectations, then producers would have the power. If there were many products available in the markets and few potential customers willing to buy the products, then the customers would have the power. For instance, there is serious competition in many industries, including high-tech cell phones, because the producers can manufacture and deliver many more products than there are customers willing to buy them. If suppliers provided strategic materials that were in short supply, they might have the power. Using the same logic, the positions of power could change depending on the dynamics of the industry and who holds the most power and influence.

In Porter's model, customers would use the existing market structure to satisfy their short-term needs and requirements and attempt to find better solutions in the long term. Competitors would fight for sales, profits, and market share in the short term and design and develop new technologies, products, and processes to build competitive advantages in the long term. Successful companies used their advantage to outperform the competitors, to leverage their core capabilities and resources to achieve superior financial results.

During the 1980s and 1990s, the strategic logic of the underlying models pertaining to competitive space was to provide customer satisfaction, maximize profits, and improve one's advantage over the competition. It was based on the relentless struggle to stay at or near the top of the competitive pyramid. Business relationships were often built on single-sided objectives and actions, mistrust, and manipulation. Producers tried to be successful and win the competitive battles. While there were winners, there were also many losers. Many producers went out of business or were taken over by bigger, more successful competitors. Many customers suffered with inferior products and services and with the associated defects and burdens that created problems instead of providing solutions. Many suppliers were forced by producers to sell the materials and parts at a marginal gain or no gain at all. The focus was on exploiting the perceived opportunities of customer demand rather than on creating new opportunities and achieving sustainable success through improving existing products and services and developments of new technologies and new-to-the-world products that solve the underlying problems. While it cannot be said that the theoretical basis was just short-term oriented, it is appropriate to suggest that the primary attention was on products, markets, and demand, and not on solutions, relationships, long-term expectations, and successful outcomes. While the business world is changing and many strategic leaders are taking on more sophisticated perspectives, there are still many companies operating on the basis of competitive space and how to capture superior positions and defeat competitors.

Over the last ten years, cutting-edge corporations have made dramatic improvements in their strategic positions and the way they do business. By focusing on the management systems, processes, and capabilities, they have produced significant gains in quality management, lean business practices, just-in-time production, and technological and product innovations. The notion of continuous improvement is now firmly rooted in the mindset of most operational and functional management. Many businesses have improved quality, affordability, reliability, efficiency, and usefulness.

They have also solved customer-related problems like end-of-life product disposal.

Market dynamics, economic fluctuations, technological change, and continual changes in the competitive landscape prevent global corporations from resting on their laurels. People in the developed countries have become wealthier and more sophisticated over the last several decades and have many more options available to them for satisfying their wants, needs, and expectations. For instance, they can buy products and services via the Internet from just about any place in the world. They can buy from large global corporations or from individuals who sell one item at a time using eBay and other technological outlets. Customers have more power, information, and selections. Their choices are almost endless.

Despite these dynamic changes, many companies and their strategic business units still focus on the narrow perspectives of the product–market interfaces rather than taking a broader perspective of the whole market spaces and beyond to discover opportunities and provide the best solutions. Moreover, business leaders often think in terms of products and competitors instead of looking for ways to frame the business environment and market spaces to create and/or develop new opportunities and to mitigate existing problems. They focus on selling products, satisfying customers, and outperforming competitors instead of making people successful and providing the best solutions possible.

Value proposition

Customers seek the most value when selecting the best solutions. They want the benefits derived from those solutions and to obtain positive outcomes with the minimal negative aspects. Similarly, the entities of the extended enterprise seek value and expect a balanced portfolio of positive rewards. They expect that outcomes are positive and that no entity or individual suffers because of the solutions (i.e. the transactions, processes, and products). While there are always some negative aspects in any system or solution, outstanding value propositions maximize the positives and minimize the negatives, and ensure that they are not lumped at any point in the value system. For instance, nuclear power has many positive aspects including no carbon emissions and reduced dependence on petroleum; however, the security and end-of-life problems pertaining to plant safety, nuclear fuels, and plant decommissioning remain as major hurdles for its broader applications.

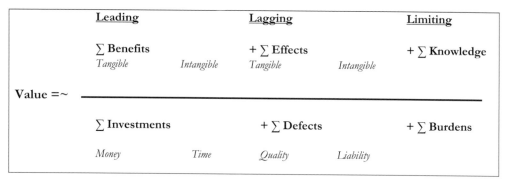

Figure 5.2   Value equation from an enterprise perspective

The value proposition can be expressed in terms of the value equation. This examines the short- and long-term benefits and knowledge gained about the enterprise in terms of the investments made by all constituents and the negative aspects of defects and burdens. Figure 5.2 depicts the general form of the value equation from an enterprise perspective.[7] Please note that it is a ratio that depicts relationships and relative positions. An improved ratio suggests enhanced value. While this equation provides a broader perspective of the value proposition, it is often impossible to map out all of the implications of what value means in a given situation.

The prevailing view of most business leaders is the simplified version of the value equation expressed in terms of performance ($\sum$Benefits) to price ($\sum$Investments). Per this version, value is improved by increasing performance or decreasing price or both. Performance is improved by enhancing the benefits, both the tangible and intangible ones. Tangible benefits are the direct outcomes that meet the needs of customers, stakeholders, and/or other constituents. Intangible benefits are the psychological effects. For instance, the tangible benefit of an automobile is mobility; the intangible benefit may be the pleasure produced by driving the car. During most of the last century, the mindset for making improvements was to increase performance at a rate greater than the associated increase in the price.

The sum of the benefits (the positive outcomes) represents the leading effects that are sought at the creation of the solutions and at their delivery. The leading effects are the primary benefits that are usually apparent and are based on what is desired and expected by the recipients (principally customers) of the solutions. The value of the benefits is established by the investment of time and money to acquire the benefits. Money might be viewed as the tangible aspect, since it represents actual resources, property, or physical goods. Time might be viewed as intangible, since it cannot be captured or stored. Time may be just as critical as money in the determination of the investment, given that time can never be recovered. The leading effects are usually apparent when determining whether a project, program, product, etc. is worthwhile and usually the required investment(s) is apparent as well with the exception that the time required may exceed expectations.

Lagging effects and defects are a little more difficult to ascertain. They are often discovered at a much later time frame. Lagging effects are considered to be positive and provide additional benefits over time. For instance, the enhanced reliability of Toyota's products and their sustained value in the secondary markets provides Toyota and its customers with long-term benefits. Customers enjoy more residual value and Toyota enhances its reputation. Moreover, certain devices become more valuable as more people have them. For example, Microsoft's operating systems are very successful because most people want to be connected with their colleagues and a standardized system provides the solution. Defects are often not apparent at the beginning, but manifest themselves over time. They include early failure due to quality defects in design or manufacture and possible product liabilities that cost money after the failures occur. Lagging effects are actually benefits that were not contemplated. Defects are often hidden and are not detected until there are significant problems.

Burdens include all of environmental problems. Pollution is an obvious example. There are many social and economic burdens as well. Many burdens are not readily apparent at the inception of the product, process, or business. While burdens may be difficult to determine during the early stage of an endeavor, it is imperative that a continuous evaluation be made to discover and mitigate such impacts. Learning how to use complicated devices or software may be fun for some people, but many people view such efforts as a burden. For instance, during the days of MS-DOS, users of personal computers had to devote a lot of time to learning the routines. Windows eliminated the burden of knowing what routine to use by making the operating system user friendly. Indeed, the notion of "ease of use" is very familiar to most people today and is often one of the key attributes of the solutions that people demand.

The long-term trend is to significantly increase the top of the line and reduce the bottom of the line. Great value is achieved when the negative aspects are eliminated, especially defects and burdens. Moreover, using the value equation it is apparent that the customer could pay more for great solutions if defects and burdens are reduced or eliminated and still have better value.

Concepts and realities of market spaces

The concept of market space

The concept of market space takes the notion of market segmentation and reverses the perspective. Market segmentation is the categorization of the whole market into definitive segments that exhibit homogeneous characteristics. It is used to target a group of customers having common needs, wants, and expectations that are identifiable and clustered by behavior, geographic, demographic, psychographic, etc. Market space examines the whole first and then drills into the details including all of the specific product–market segments.

Market space includes all of the product–market segments across the multiple dimensions of space and time. It is the sum of the market segments from all of the possibilities. Defining the product–market segments depends on the type of markets and the needs and expectations of the customers and stakeholders. The standard market categories of consumer, industrial, and government can be further subdivided into specific product–market segments.

Consumer markets are typically segmented according to demographic aspects, behavioral/psychological, and/or geographic situation. Demographics play a powerful role in predicting how potential customers perceive the product and how they shape their basis for decision making. People can be categorized by age, household circumstances, and education. These variables play a role in what people seek and how they make decisions. Behavioral variables include the psychographic profile of individual customers, his or her values, disposable income, and purchase behaviors. There are numerous interrelationships and interactions among the variables. While it is useful to perceive the notion of certain market segments in the realities of today, it is becoming more and more difficult to articulate what a given market segment really is.

Industrial markets are segmented by applications and buyer behavior. Government markets are usually defined in terms of purchasing protocols established by the governmental entity or by very specific mandates that have to be followed.

The notion of market space also has gloabal implications since customers across the world and those in specific countries do constitute purchasing power and do buy real products and services. Market spaces include the whole universe of markets and customers with all of the real and potential transactions. Specific markets and market segments are the subsets of the whole. For instance, each country has identifiable markets that can be viewed as the market space of that country (i.e. the US consumer market or the US car market). Market spaces are occupied by people who buy, or want to buy, products and services. They are characterized in terms of the numbers of people involved, their social and economic situation, the money that they have available to spend and/or do spend, and how the people make decisions about what they buy and use.

The focus of market space is on the customers and stakeholders, and what they want to accomplish, not just on the producers and/or competitors and what they want to sell. Market space has a higher level of primacy than the prevailing notion of competitive space because it pertains to the needs, wants, and expectations of customers, potential customers, and emerging customers. The focus is on what people want to buy and use, not on what producers and competitors want to sell.

A framework of market space

Market space can be perceived to be the entire world of people taken from multiple dimensions. It can be divided using traditional variables including the specific country (geography), the industry, customer characteristics, purchasing power, revenue for products and services, etc. Market space is central to the economic and business forces. It is the reason for economic activity and is the primary focus for most businesses.

The market space can be theoretically divided into two major categories: inner (defined) market space and outer (open) market space. The inner market space is typically the strategic focus of businesses, business units, and their value delivery systems. It includes the market segments addressed by the businesses and the customers served by the products and services. Figure 5.3 depicts the business unit and its value delivery system with its market spaces and the overarching business environment. While it shows the value delivery system as the central focus, in reality, the inner and outer market spaces are pivotal in determining strategic perspectives and positions. From the perspective of the strategic leaders, the business unit and/or the value delivery system can be superimposed over the market space since the framework is intended for decision making by business leaders not customers. Please note that the perspectives in Figure 4.2 correctly portray market spaces as the center of the framework.

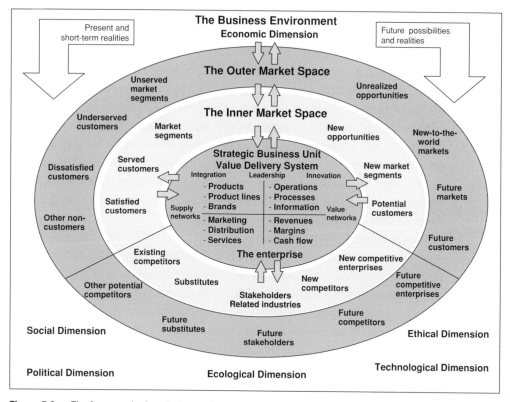

Figure 5.3   The framework of market space from an SBU perspective

The left side of Figure 5.3 showing the inner market space indicates the prevailing situation with existing customers, stakeholders, and competitors. It represents the near-term realities. Assuming that the inner market space is stable, customers are generally satisfied and usually continue to buy products and services from the existing producers. Even though there may be some switching to competitors or the occasional purchasing of substitutes or new products, the relationships are typically well established and continue for a long time. However, the flow is dynamic and ever-changing.

The right side of the inner market space can be characterized as the potential expansion of the prevailing inner market space based on innovations, new technologies, and new-to-the-world products. It presumes that there are prevailing opportunities that are not being addressed or developed by the business unit(s) or its competitors – opportunities that can be exploited, especially through enterprise-wide strategic leadership (ESL) and strategic innovations. While existing customers are often satisfied with the existing portfolio of products and product lines, potential customers often seek different (better) solutions to meet their needs and expectations. However, potential customers are not just waiting around for new solutions. They may have found other approaches that work, but not as well as they would like. Through technological and product innovations, new solutions can be created that increase the inner market space of customers and potential customers, thereby creating new opportunities to create value, make money, and satisfy additional customers. While there is much evidence that it is cheaper to keep existing customers happy than to develop new customers, the commoditization of technologies and products often means that revenues, margins, and profits decline over time. For instance, plasma and LCD TVs are today selling at half the price that they were several years ago.

Managing the known portions of the inner market space is typically based on conventional thinking about the value chain and functions of the organization including product management, program management of product lines, brand management, marketing, distribution, services, operations, production processes, information flow, and financial management considerations. These internal dimensions and functions are well articulated and normally very sophisticated, especially in global corporations. For instance, large companies are often marketing products with six-sigma quality, operating under lean production practices and methods, and creating value for customers and suppliers through integrated value networks.

The most important perspective of the framework is that the primary focus is on markets, customers, and stakeholders, and not on competitors. Strategic analysis and decision making are usually driven by the prime factors, conditions, trends, and realities of the market spaces. Some of the most important additional considerations are how to improve relationships with customers and stakeholders and build new relationships with those that are not being successfully served. Competitive aspects are important and require due consideration. They are part of the economic equation, but strategic decisions should be based on an analysis and understanding of the markets and customers. Markets and customers are the primary driving forces followed by competition, not the other way around. This may be a significant shift in strategic thinking for many business leaders who were historically driven primarily by the forces of competition.

The best opportunities to create sustainable advantages are where customers seek new solutions. Taking advantage of the new opportunities in the inner market space through strategic innovations is usually more difficult than satisfying existing customers and managing the key dimensions of the value delivery system because there are many more unknowns, uncertainties, and risks. Creating new solutions typically involves venturing into the realm of innovation and entrepreneurship. Latent customer needs and expectations are not always obvious and in many cases, the potential customers themselves cannot articulate with any precision the specifications of the solutions they seek. Managing the process for developing innovative solutions is inherently more challenging and risky. Still, it is often much more rewarding, especially if the new solutions expand the inner market space and allow for encroachment into the outer market space. For instance, today's PCs are more affordable and usable than their predecessors of the1980s and early 1990s. The earlier devices were expensive and so had more limited market potential, but users had to learn difficult software and protocols like MS-DOS. The market space for the purchase of personal computers has expanded from a few million per year in the early 1980s to hundreds of millions in recent years.

Technological and product innovation provide the means and mechanisms to reshape the market space, increasing the opportunities to sell new, more exciting products and, in many cases motivating existing customers to upgrade. This opens the door to exceptional customer satisfaction which, in turn, can lead to greater rewards for producers and customers. This "creative–destruction" process – discovering new opportunities and developing new solutions – enriches everyone who is willing to think outside-the box and create new value. The modern pathway to market success involves discovering how to make customers successful and developing the means and mechanisms to deliver that success. For example, BASF, the largest chemical company in the world, established four strategic guidelines for its long-term success: (1) help our customers to be more successful; (2) ensure sustainable development; (3) form the best industry team; and (4) earn a premium on our capital.[8] BASF recognizes that its success is dependent on making its customers successful.

The outer market space also offers exciting possibilities for expanding opportunities and eliminating the structural boundaries of the prevailing conditions and trends. Structural boundaries that prevent the expansion of business success are often characterized by social, political, and economic constraints. For instance, people in developing countries do not have the money to buy products from large companies that are designed to meet the requirements of more affluent people. In certain countries there are no mechanisms to extend credit to people without property or those who do not have any means of collateral. The outer market space is generally made up of emerging markets with potential customers whose wants and needs are not being served. For instance, people in developing countries would like to own many of the products that are routinely used in high-income countries, but they simply cannot afford to buy them. There are enormous market opportunities, but the prevailing products that exist in the inner market space are often not well suited for the potential customers in the outer loop. The products may be too large, too expensive, require too much support, and take too many resources. American cars, for example, are typically large, costly, have poor fuel efficiency, and require sophisticated equipment to diagnose problems. These limitations may not be a barrier to ownership in the US where there are approximately 800 cars per 1,000 people and about 150,000 gas stations and support facilities. However, in developing countries such requirements and/or conditions limit the size of the market for these cars. The answer for developing the outer market space lies in identifying the solutions required for satisfying the needs and wants of the populations and providing people with specific solutions that fit their realities. One of the best examples of this was how Canon developed small copiers for the home and home office. Canon strategists realized that a small copier had to be affordable and reliable with great quality and outstanding performance. The product had to be priced in the several hundred dollar range and function for years without requiring repair or service. Canon's small size copier has been successful because its specifications and designs were uniquely selected based on the market conditions and not on the prevailing design specifications used in the large copier segment.

The emerging markets typically have large segments of the population that do not have access to sophisticated or expensive products because the people lack the means, knowledge, and infrastructure to buy and use such products. The lack of affordability, the poor links with reality, and cultural fabric are some of the main reasons why many of the existing products in the world do not fit such people; therefore, they do not or cannot participate in the inner market space. C. K. Prahalad argues that product–market thinking must be reshaped for expanding business opportunities to the 5 billion people at the bottom of the pyramid (BOP).[9] Prahalad identified twelve principles for innovation for BOP markets.[10] Table 5.1 lists the principles with comments about the outer market space.

The list could be even more comprehensive for turning limitations and constraints into new solutions. Stuart Hart, professor and head of Cornel University's Sustainable Enterprise Initiative suggests that businesses take "the great leap downward" and discover how they can expand their opportunities by "driving innovation from the BOP."[11] Hart believes that the "indigenous enterprise" is the next wave of sustainability. It involves creating a road map for meeting the needs at the BOP and broadening the scope of participation

Table 5.1 Prahalad's principles for BOP markets

Prahalad's principles	ESM and outer market space connection
1. Price performance	In accordance with the main premise of ESM, products must not only be affordable, they must have a superior value proposition for both customers and the enterprise.
2. Innovation-hybrids	Outer market space customers and BOP opportunities can be driven by advanced technologies that provide superior solutions and eliminate problems.
3. Scale of operations	Solutions have to be provided on a broad scale focusing on billions of similarly situated people who need innovative approaches.
4. Sustainable development and eco-friendly	Solutions cannot deplete resources or cause degradation and destruction. Benefits have to be increased dramatically, and impacts have to be minimized.
5. Identifying functionality	Designers must understand the basic needs and expectations of the users and design in the proper functionalities.
6. Process innovation	Processes must be suited for the available infrastructure or the lack thereof. Products must be cost-effective and affordable.
7. Deskilling the work	The work and tasks required for producing the products must be simplified and achievable based on indigenous capabilities.
8. Education of customers	Customers must have access to the educational opportunities required for producing and using the products and processes.
9. Designing for hostile infrastructure	Given the poor or absent infrastructure, products must be useful in a broad array of conditions.
10. Interfaces	Learning curves for using the products and processes must be short and achievable and companies should have links with customers.
11. Distribution	Distribution channels have to be enriched or developed if they do not exist.
12. Challenge conventional wisdom in delivery	Emerging markets require innovative solutions for transforming opportunities into realities.

by stakeholders.[12] An indigenous enterprise is one that involves "the true voices of those who have previously been bypassed by globalization, and by learning to co-develop technologies, products, and services with nature and local people."[13]

The outer market space may include customers from the inner market space who have dropped out because of dissatisfaction. They are the people who no longer participate in the markets or who do not buy the existing products. For instance, there are a small, but growing, number of people who will not buy food products produced using artificial chemicals or manufactured using non-natural compounds. Such people are willing to pay more for organically grown food or grow their own food products. Similarly, there are people who are opposed to the sale and use of luxury cars or sports utility vehicles. Also, non-customers may be unaware of many of the existing products, do not have the education or knowledge to use them, or are unable to use them because they lack the infrastructure or required complementary products. They may also lack the acceptance of the products and their logic or fit into the individual's world. There are a whole host of additional reasons including religious, cultural, and moral ones. For instance, many religions forbid certain foods like pork or have restrictions against using certain medical procedures that are based on stem cells from fetuses.

The outer market space also has the right side of unrealized opportunities that represent the future. Again, people have latent needs and desires that could lead to substantial markets and customer purchases if there were the means and mechanisms to provide the requisite solutions. For instance, there are billions of people in the developing countries who would like to have such devices as refrigerators, washing machines, and PCs, but they cannot afford to buy or use the appliances that are sold to people in the developed countries. Those devices are too sophisticated and too expensive to buy and operate. Imagine the number of stoves or washing machines that could be sold if producers could manufacture a standard high-volume version that would sell for under $50. Such products might quickly become the global products of their type with sales of several hundred million units per year. This sort of phenomenon has already happened with such mainstream products as PCs, DVD players, and cathode ray tube-type televisions. They have experienced significant price declines by factors of ten to twenty over the last several decades. The key difference would be that prices would have to start low, and manufacturers would have to assume that they can achieve high volume and dramatically lower the product costs. The experiences of the Ford Model T and the Volkswagen Beetle demonstrate that this phenomenon is indeed possible. As the rate of adoption of new technologies increases and the time required for commercial applications of the inventions declines there is a dramatic reduction in the time required to achieve very low costs per devices. Ray Kurzweil, one of the world's leading inventors, suggests in his book, *The Singularity Is Near*, that it should take less than ten years for 25% of a population to adapt a new technology.[14] It is actually expected to be less time in the next several decades. Moreover, prices are expected to drop quickly from the initial high price to less than half in two to three years.

New, cleaner and more cost-effective technologies promise to create new-to-the-world markets for products and services that are hard to even dream about in the present. They usually evolve slowly at the beginning but rise quickly to prominence. For instance, in *The Singularity Is Near* Kurzweil outlines the increase in cell phone subscribers in the US from less than one million in 1985 to over 100 million in 2000.[15] At their origins new technologies are imperceptibly obscure in most cases and only become obvious after they reach some prominence due to the extraordinary value being created. It is similar to trying to detect the effects of non-native species in an ecosystem. For instance, the negative effects of the introduction of rabbits into Australia were only appreciated after millions of the animals overwhelmed the capability of humankind to control them. On the positive side, new-to-the-world products and markets can make real changes and improvements to the prevailing conditions. However, it is often difficult to measure and determine the long-term effects of such changes during the early stages. For example, the essence, importance, and benefits of eBay's trading system during its initial launch in San Francisco in 1998 were so small and localized that it seemed to be just another dot.com in a world full of such technologies and companies. However, as eBay improved its software and its system, it created new market mechanisms that permitted individuals to trade with each other in a cost-effective way, independent of distance. It broke out of the old paradigm that required individuals to meet face-to-face to carry out transactions or they had to advertise their products in static forms like magazines. eBay created new market spaces that are virtual yet real – those that utilize many of the elements and resources of traditional markets. Even though eBay is not exactly a BOP example, it follows many of Prahalad's principles and the precepts of the value proposition. Transactions have incredible price-to-performance ratios, costing only a small percentage of the value of the exchange. eBay uses advanced technologies to link individuals to effect one transaction at a time. There are currently billions of such transactions each year. The transactions are eco-friendly and promote the reuse of products that might otherwise be discarded or have little further economic value, at least to the owner. eBay and its customers use the existing infrastructure and distribution channels for shipping the goods, especially through companies like UPS and FedEx. Most importantly, the system is easy to use and broadly available to people connected to the Internet. It makes such exchanges possible at very low costs, costs that are a fraction of what they would be without eBay's system and the supporting structures.

The point is: the market space is dynamic. While most of the focus historically has been on market conditions and trends, attention has to be given to future markets and customers and how to expand market space or how to create new market spaces. The focus needs to be on facilitating the changes that are coming in these areas. In today's business world, it is safe and even wise to presume that products and markets will change and that most of the products and technologies will be replaced by more exciting, cleaner, better, and more affordable solutions.

Likewise, the competitive landscape is changing dramatically as well. New competitors with new technologies, capabilities, and/or advantages are entering the market spaces. Older, less effective competitors are being absorbed by their competitors or simply fading into oblivion. Today, there are no guarantees that any corporation will survive, much less prosper. The number of major companies producing cars provides a sense of the changes in competition over the last four decades and the prospects for the future. The number of major producers declined significantly from thirty-five in 1970 to thirteen in 2000. This is most likely a result of the competitive pressures and the increasing sophistication of the products, production requirements, and value delivery systems. Yet, with the growing economic improvements and power of companies in China and India, now there are about seven to ten new entrants who are planning to take advantage of the unrealized opportunities in China, India, and several other developing countries. These new entrants are focusing on future customers who are gaining economic power as they join the ranks of the middle class.

The world of the future will have technological substitutes that are not even contemplated today. Many of the technologies are now in research and development at major universities, government facilities, and companies around the world. Nanotechnologies and biotechnologies are just two areas with the potential to radically change the business world. Just as digital cameras and the related computer technologies have changed the world of photography within a decade, new technologies and potential competitors from outside existing industry structures have the potential to open new market spaces and radically alter the business environment and the nature of business.

ESM implications of market space

ESM cannot create markets or market demand. They exist in the business environment and are generally beyond the direct control of businesses. However, strategic leaders and marketing executives can select market spaces that are most advantageous for their businesses and develop plans that expand the potential of the market spaces by leading change and responding to the opportunities and challenges. Strategic leaders can think outside-the-box (i.e. they can think about how to create the required and desired solutions and systems). They can create business strategies and models that are more effective than those of the competition. Many business leaders believe that their problems are due to a lack of customers or resources, or that there is a failure to communicate effectively with markets, potential customers, or even employees. However, while some of those problems may exist, one of the major limitations of strategic management is the failure of strategic leaders to think about what is possible and how to alleviate the limitations of the prevailing situations.

For many decades, strategic leaders believed that there had to be rivalry amongst competitors. And it is true; there are significant competitive pressures on a global basis, and the intensity of competition is likely to increase during the next decade as companies in the developing world gain footholds in global markets and leverage their inherent advantages in their home markets. For instance, the global products of the future are more likely to be Chinese than American, European, or Japanese simply because of the greater number of Chinese households. By 2010, China is expected to have more households than the total number in the developed countries.[16]

Today, large companies must change their strategic thinking and discover strategic moves that go beyond the fray of battle. They must preempt the business environment and the market spaces with extraordinary solutions. W. Chan Kim and Renee Mauborgne in their book, *Blue Ocean Strategy: How to Create Uncontested Market Space and Make Competition Irrelevant*, discuss how businesses can break the vicious cycle of fighting competitive wars and create new market spaces while discouraging others from imitating them.[17] Blue ocean refers to market spaces that are free of the bloody conflicts between corporations and are built on positive buyer–seller relationships with win–win value propositions. For instance, Siemens produces electrical devices that are intended for extreme conditions (plus 140°F or minus 20°F). It is the only producer of much of the equipment it sells in these categories. The product specifications are so demanding and complex that other manufacturers have chosen not to participate in that market space. Dr. Helmut Ludwig, President of Systems Engineering at Siemens, said "We love complexity because it provides a sustainable advantage that others can not duplicate."[18] Siemens has found a way to create a blue ocean market for its products.

Kim and Mauborgne suggest six principles for obtaining a "Blue Ocean Strategy":[19]

1. Reconstruct market boundaries.
2. Focus on the big picture, not the numbers.
3. Reach beyond existing demand.
4. Get the strategic sequence right.
5. Overcome key organizational hurdles.
6. Build execution into the strategy.

Their principles advance many of the management constructs of ESM. Two of its main premises are to expand the framework of the extended enterprise and to think holistically about the business environment, the market space, and about how the extended enterprise can create extraordinary value for everyone. ESM integrates the dimensions of the enterprise into an effective strategic team that improves the benefits and reduces the costs and eliminates defects, burdens, and impacts wherever possible. In doing so risks are mitigated, and organization and the extended enterprise are enriched.

Markets are the domain of the business environment, but market space is the domain of the extended enterprise. Companies choose the market spaces that they want to serve. They can structure the boundary conditions by selecting the scope and scale of their enterprise. They can define their solutions in terms of what they do for people and not entirely in terms of how much money they make. Market space is how and where companies choose to create enduring outcomes and success for customers and stakeholders. It means going beyond just meeting demand and satisfying customers.

Kim and Mauborgne suggest that: "It is not enough to maximize the size of the blue ocean you are creating. You must profit from it to create a sustainable win-win outcome."[20] One of the most important fundamental aspects of the strategic management of a corporation and its enterprise is finding new ways to enhance value creation in the market spaces or to create new market spaces that are unique and represent opportunities to capture sustainable advantages without destructive competitive fighting. It is easy to engage in destructive behaviors. It is more difficult to develop those win–win business strategies and approaches that provide customers and stakeholders with cost-effective, differentiated, high-quality, value-driven solutions and allow the businesses to succeed and continue providing those solutions. These topics will be developed further in Part II dealing with business strategies and action plans.

Uncovering business opportunities in space and time

Perceiving broad-based opportunities

The most wonderful aspect of fast-paced changes in market spaces is the proliferation of exciting new business opportunities. However, these opportunities are not always readily apparent to strategic leaders, especially those who take a narrow perspective or who spend their time exploring opportunities in the known market spaces. Their strategies and actions are similar to those of gold miners of yesteryear who continued to pan for gold in areas like California in the 1850s or those in Alaska in the early 1900s after thousands of their compatriots had exploited the readily available opportunities. Their continuing efforts seemed logical because others had been successful in finding and extracting gold, but over time the opportunities became fewer and fewer and the efforts required to be successful became more and more arduous.

Likewise, many of today's business leaders spend most of their time trying to dig deeper and deeper into what they perceive to be known business opportunities. While it may be sensible for lower-level strategic management, even more so for the operations management whose missions are to explore, evaluate, and exploit known market spaces, strategic leaders and their professional staff have to expand their thinking beyond the known or historical perspectives and examine other possibilities for discovering new opportunities. They should think about expanding the dimensions of their business world and their strategic management frameworks and move beyond their known situations to the distant possibilities that are untouched, or those that lack the perceived underpinnings for achieving financial success.

As an aside, in theoretical physics scientists try to understand the multiple dimensions that are beyond the obvious three dimensions of space and the fourth dimension of time. They discuss the complexities involved in interpreting spatial realities that are difficult to contemplate using our standard view of the world via Euclidian geometry and calendar time. The concept of a "flatlander" is used to portray the inability to visualize and understand broader realities if one's perception is based on a limited view of just two spatial dimensions.[21] Flatlanders live in a two-dimensional space with limited comprehension of a third spatial dimension. The flatlanders perceive the world to be flat and all of the perspectives and opportunities are based on what such people (flatlanders) visualize in the two dimensions. There are enormous opportunities in the third dimension as we know, but the flatlanders cannot contemplate them. They are beyond their reality. The flatlanders would have to move into three-dimensional space to expand their opportunities dramatically.

Likewise, business leaders are often caught in their own constrained views of reality and perceive only what is apparent from their limited perspectives. From such perspectives, people within the organization, especially those focused only on current products and services and on serving customers and existing markets, are often constricted with respect to opportunities that are outside of their "two-dimensional" world. Their business situation blinds them to the other dimensions and possibilities. They can only perceive a limited view of reality. Indeed, there is a much richer world in the other dimensions that have multiple times (hundreds, thousands, and more) the existing opportunities that they do not or cannot realize. However, it is not their fault. It is typically the constraints of the management systems, the limits on the scope of creativity, and the pressing requirements to meet the existing strategic and operational objectives that hamper their thinking. If they are fulfilling the missions, then it is incumbent on the higher level of strategic leaders to ensure that the "other worlds" of opportunities are addressed and properly considered for building the future of the company. This kind of strategic thinking is an essential part of ESM.

Assuming that these premises are correct, it suggests that discovering, developing, and exploiting new-to-the-world or new-to-the-business opportunities necessitates people who are unconstrained by specific missions of value delivery systems. It takes unencumbered people at the higher levels of the organization to explore the vast reaches of space and time, to gain insights into what the corporation can do in addition to what it is doing. It also requires that strategic leaders have a business framework or business models to reach out beyond the existing space and time continuum to incorporate additional realities that exist but may not be palpable because of the constraints of the SMSs. For example, ExxonMobil appears to be highly focused on its petroleum businesses ranging from the exploration and recovery of crude to production, distribution, and marketing of the related products to customers around the world. Its strategic management model has a broad geographic scope covering most of the countries in the world with an enterprise mindset. Yet, in reality the scope of ExxonMobil's SMSs may be very limited from the perspective of alternate energy, renewable energy, and clean technologies. It might be characterized as a two-dimensional approach that lacks the richness of all of the possibilities of the broader world of energy and the related opportunities and challenges. ExxonMobil may have optimized its present position, especially considering its stature as one of the largest corporations in the world and its enviable financial success, but is the corporation well positioned for the future? On the other hand, Statoil of Norway is also a very successful petroleum company, yet it is a much smaller business. It is expanding its reach into the broader field of providing energy solutions. While most of Statoil's assets and operations are dedicated to petroleum, it has made investments into alternate energy technologies like photovoltaic and wind energy. The strategic direction toward the "third dimension" (sustainable energy) opens the way for many exciting new possibilities and ultimately provides the platform for achieving sustainable success after all the petroleum has been depleted. However, these statements do not mean to suggest that Statoil has done everything right and that ExxonMobil is headed into oblivion.

Strategic leaders and their support staff are akin to cosmologists who explore the outer reaches of the very large as well as nanotechnologists who explore the inner reaches of the very small. They seek opportunities in the broader reaches of space and try to determine and understand what the possibilities are and how to take advantage of the opportunities.

Discovering broad-based opportunities

Discovering opportunities outside the known market spaces of the business enterprise is a huge challenge that is difficult to characterize and map out. It usually involves unprecedented approaches, considering reality from different perspectives and making judgments about what the situation could be instead of what it appears to be. For example, Bill Gates and Paul Allen recognized that software (the operating system) represented a significant money-making opportunity in the early days of the PC revolution when most other companies, including IBM and Compaq, believed the golden opportunities were in hardware. Another more poignant example is how Toyota in the late 1940s and early 1950s turned a huge disadvantage in car production into one of the most important strategic advantages of the twentieth century. At the time Toyota lacked the market power and manufacturing volume to use mass assembly techniques that made GM and Ford powerhouses, so it created just-in-time production and lean manufacturing processes to produce a wide variety of low-volume cars that also enjoyed low-cost positions similar to those enjoyed by GM and Ford in their mass production approaches.

Discovering opportunities also involves insightfulness, imagination, and quick learning with respect to chance discoveries and good luck, or even perceived mistakes or problems. Per the examples above the key is to understand what the true value is and how to realize the value and benefits that can be derived. For instance, Columbus's voyage in 1492 was based on the mistaken belief that he could find a new route to India by sailing directly west. He was looking for one thing and found something else, the "New World." Whereas Columbus and his supporters (the King and Queen of Spain) clearly understood the potential riches involved in discovering a shorter route to the Pacific, they did not understand the true potential of the New World and were ill-prepared for dealing with the realities that they discovered. They continued to think about the opportunities from their narrow perspectives rather than the broader perspectives of building new relationships with the native people and establishing mutually beneficial approaches to the social and economic wealth that existed. While Columbus's discovery changed life in Spain and Europe and made Spain a rich country for several centuries thereafter, his exploits and those who followed him are both controversial given the negative impacts on the indigenous population in the colonized areas of Central and South America and a failure in terms of not realizing the true opportunities. The Spanish sought riches that they understood which included cherished gold and other European treasures. However, they failed to understand the vast opportunities to enjoy the natural resources of the lands and improve the social and economic conditions of the populations in the Americas, and how that could benefit people in the Americas as well as those in Europe. They obtained the gold but could not sustain their political and social power in the world, especially after the colonies successfully regained independence.

Likewise, the British suffered similar difficulties with their colonies in North America. Instead of developing the vast social, economic, and environmental opportunities, they used the colonists to get at raw materials and as lock-in customers for their manufactured products.[22] In hindsight, it is always easy to be critical. The colonists also tried to take maximum advantage of the immediate situation rather than viewing the broader perspectives and the long-term gains and successes.

While it is often difficult, if not impossible, to determine what the potential is during the early development of most situations, strategic leaders have to try to envision what the opportunities really are and how to properly characterize them. It is a huge challenge but the rewards can be great as well. For instance, it would have been almost impossible to think about the US as a great economic power in the early days after the American Revolution. Who could have foreseen the enormous potential of the new landscape of the eastern US with a sparse population and the lack of an extensive infrastructure? However, less than 100 years after the Declaration of Independence, the US was on the verge of becoming a world-class economic power. While there are many reasons for such limited perspectives and failures over the course of human history, one of the most prevalent causes is viewing opportunities from one's own traditional perspectives rather than from the perspectives of the broad context of the external aspects of the many dimensions involved – social, economic, etc. This statement is not intended to criticize historical figures or the countries involved, but it is meant to suggest that there are complexities in dealing with such opportunities especially those that are outside of the normal realm of the people concerned.

Strategic leaders usually find that it is relatively easy to understand the needs and wants of customers in the current markets and market segments. However, it is far more complicated to find new opportunities outside of the existing market spaces and to truly understand their potential implications. It is particularly difficult to consider all of the critical factors and potential for those that exist in the broader business environment and beyond, or even those that might develop in the future and become more apparent over time. Most business leaders can think about the market space of realities but are usually ill-equipped to deliberate on future possibilities. It is even more difficult to think about latent opportunities. Think about what eBay did in creating new market space for improving the mechanisms for people, especially individuals, to exchange goods. Of course, having the courage to take the appropriate actions is of paramount importance.

Inventing new ways of creating value from natural, social, economic, and intellectual capital, meeting latent needs and expectations, solving the underlying challenges of the human condition and well being, and/or preserving, protecting, conserving, and sustaining the business environment and the market spaces necessitates thinking in terms of the long term, decades into the future. It involves understanding the trends and changes that are likely to occur and envisioning the solutions that are necessary to sustain success. It also determines how the current businesses and extended enterprises can be linked together more effectively and efficiently to improve capabilities, enhance outcomes, and reduce waste. Even with the incredible innovations of the last few decades many businesses and enterprises still suffer from poor coordination, collaboration, and communication.

Broad-based business opportunities can be developed using a myriad of methods from traditional brainstorming to more radical approaches like questioning the company's fundamental beliefs and actions or examining basic assumptions about the business environment including the notion of the scarcity of economic resources and the concept of industry structure. Given the open-ended and presumed novelty of such endeavors, one cannot specify a process for finding new opportunities that are outside traditional businesses activities. The methods may have to unfold through exploration and engagement, especially through the involvement of strategic leaders who have to dedicate their time, knowledge, and intellectual creativity to explore the possibilities for today and those of tomorrow.

Interestingly, many of the precursors of the changes in the market spaces that may occur in the future already exist in the present. Indeed, since all changes and innovations take time to develop and come to fruition, nothing in the business environment appears instantaneously. Strategic leaders are occasionally caught off guard by threats or they fail to identify significant opportunities because they were not paying attention or did not appreciate the meaning, significance, and implications of the dynamics involved. They often prefer to continue exploiting the present conditions based on short-term beliefs rather than exploring potential changes. While opportunities and threats are often viewed as different constructs, the former being mostly positive and the latter being mostly negative, they may also be viewed as interrelated as there are enormous challenges in realizing many of the most exciting new opportunities, and enormous opportunities in responding to challenges. For instance, moving outside of the known market spaces requires exploration, discovery, and investment to understand the possibilities and bring them to fruition. These challenges precede obtaining knowledge about the opportunities. Some of the methods that could be used to discover new business opportunities include the following:

- *Alternatives within the market spaces* – undertake a detailed examination of the external dimensions covered or influenced by the company and its business units and identify everything that is significantly less than desirable and determine what options are available to rectify the situation or undesirable aspects. For instance, petroleum prices are skyrocketing in every sector; how can energy consumption be reduced? How can energy be made more affordable? What can be done to make alternate energy sources and technologies more viable?
- *Possibilities outside the market spaces* – start by exploring the untapped reaches of the outer market spaces. Often the constraints and restrictions of the real world limit opportunities. Determine the constraints in the outer market spaces which limit the potential for people there to enjoy the solutions that the business could provide. For instance, lack of property ownership and financial collateral, and the inability to obtain credit severely

restrict the purchasing power of people in many of the developing countries, therefore limiting the potential for business enterprises to establish credit lines for potential customers. Eliminating such constraints could open the doors to the outer market spaces.

- *Alternatives within the external dimensions* – think about the opposites of what the company or the vast array of competitors focus on and reflect on the possibilities associated with the countervailing approaches. For example, Wal-Mart realized during its early years that most discount retailers in the US served middle-class customers who lived in or near the large metropolitan areas. Wal-Mart took the opposite approach, building its stores in rural areas and serving people whose primary concern in buying retail products was satisfying their basic needs via high-quality, low-cost products.
- *Possibilities outside of the business environment* – create new solutions that reach out beyond the normal business environment via the underpinnings of the social world and the natural environment. This follows one of the underlying theories of ESM – that broader perspectives provide additional opportunities. For instance, the availability of clean, fresh, and safe water is a natural resource that is fundamental to human well being. GE is creating new businesses based on providing water in various modes in many countries around the world. They realize that water is the strategic resource of the future.
- *Alternatives to expanding endogenous technological change* – invest in and invent new technologies that depart from the prevailing approaches. These examine the worlds of science and engineering to discover new opportunities for technological innovation. For instance, biotechnology was born in the research labs and incubators of universities such as MIT and Stanford. This expanded into the business world with the help of funding from pharmaceutical companies and venture capitalists.
- *Possibilities from externally developed technological solutions* – keep ahead of new technologies. Externally developed technologies represent new possibilities that may change or even replace current approaches. Astute business leaders explore and try to understand innovations regardless of where they are developed and see them as opportunities, not threats. The threats are if the strategic leaders are passive and fail to recognize the potential opportunities. For instance, microprocessors were initially viewed as devices that were integral to computers, but today they are used in all types of products from cars to steam irons. Think about what the Internet has done for business!

- *Alternatives to achieve desired outcomes* – generate ideas to achieve more affordable and sustainable outcomes. This relates to reconfiguring what is into more powerful and economical, social, and environmental more successful outcomes. While such approaches do not have to be internally based, the focus may be on how work is done and how outcomes are achieved. Many of the great "solutions" of the past followed this thinking. For instance, Adam Smith's notion of the division of labor created a more efficienct manufacturing process that became apparent in the American System for the batch production of guns at the Springfield Armory in the 1850s. Henry Ford took that concept to the next stage with the development of the assembly line. Toyota took the linear flow of Ford's mass production and linked it with the value system to create a three-dimensional flow of lean production, which again improved efficiencies and effectiveness.
- *Possibilities through knowledge and understanding* – understand the fundamentals underpinning the business world, searching for the deep driving forces or even trying to envision what is missing or what could become a roadblock in the future. Most people know more about their world today than the elites of previous centuries knew about theirs. The changing space–time aspects of life represent shifts toward more information and knowledge which operate on a global basis and twenty-four/seven (24/7). Wealth is being created not just in the domains of knowledge but within the multiple intersections of knowledge. For instance, the mid-nineteenth century was a mechanical world; and the late-twentieth century was an electronic world. Today, the world is multifaceted with a rich mosaic of understandings and knowledge from many overlapping fields. Biotechnology and nanotechnology focus on creating value from the building block of genes and molecules, respectively. The focus has shifted from producing goods by taking vast quantities of materials and drilling down to a paradigm of building products from the base upward.

The intention of this discussion is not to outline a comprehensive list of what strategic leaders should be looking for or what they should seek to find, but to suggest a broader perspective for thinking about business opportunities that are beyond the normal scope of traditional strategic thinking. While business leaders have to exhibit ESL to discover new-to-the-world opportunities, they can engage others throughout the organization to participate in the discovery process (i.e. the responsibility can be delegated to the strategic management professionals and to the general managers and their staff).

The discovery of new business opportunities is often delegated to marketing executives. In the case of high-level opportunities as discussed above it is critical that executives, strategic leaders, their professional staff, and many others take on a holistic, multidisciplinary approach that covers the broader perspectives of the organization and the enterprise. Discovering opportunities is not just a marketing exercise. Indeed, marketing professionals who normally focus on customers and markets may be the wrong individuals to engage in the process. Their perspectives are usually narrow – they are concerned with customers and markets. Sometimes the most radical people in the organization are the ones that have some of the most exciting insights and concepts for exploiting out-of-the-box opportunities.

Great discoveries usually involve great leaders and extremely talented people who can think about the richness of the world. They have the intellectual capacity to handle complexity and to think beyond the obvious. They have to have a mindset that enjoys uncertainties and open-endedness. Moreover, they should have the imagination and the creativity to contemplate all the potential alternatives to today's reality and to envision all of the possibilities for tomorrow's initiatives. The aspirations for a better world and future may not be realized unless there are strategic leaders who have the courage, conviction, and confidence to think beyond the prevailing conditions and trends and discover the exhilarating opportunities to change the world.

The implicit process for finding new opportunities

The discovery of anything new is usually an open-ended process that is ill-defined and often involves examining conditions and trends in a changing world, while at the same time hunting for new possibilities. While there are many examples of strategic leaders stumbling across new opportunities and being in the right place at the right time, good luck and fortuitousness cannot be relied upon to ensure that new opportunities are discovered, examined, developed, and exploited on a systematic basis; it takes a concerted effort to understand reality and create new possibilities. The best time to start the journey toward new discoveries is when the company is enjoying success in its market space. However, during such times many strategic leaders are usually content to enjoy their short-term success or focus on growing the business in conventional ways. They are often too busy exploiting the present to think too far into the future. Moreover, they may believe that there are not compelling reasons to seek out new-to-the-world or new-to-the-company opportunities; they are happy to exploit the opportunities in their market spaces. For instance, ExxonMobil has achieved record annual profits

($39 billion in 2006 and $44 billion in 2007) in its petroleum-related businesses because of the high prices for crude oil ($80 to $100 per barrel in 2007); it is difficult to imagine finding new opportunities that would result in better financial outcomes. However, there are always questions about sustainable success and how long the prevailing situation will continue. The time to start is now when there is money available. Again, there are no guarantees.

Discovery actions go beyond the "known world" of markets, customers, competitors, and even enterprises. They involve intellectual exercises and physical efforts to explore, find, interpret, and develop unrealized opportunities that could lead to future businesses and sources for sustainable success. The approaches include many broad steps that establish the foundation and management systems for new discoveries but cannot ensure that discoveries will be made. The general steps include:

- Determining the spatial and temporal scope of the searches; how far out into space do researchers and leaders look and what is the expected time horizon?
- Identifying the key objectives of the searches and defining new opportunities.
- Selecting the best people within the organization and extended enterprise(s) and establishing their roles and responsibilities.
- Developing and providing training modules so that individuals and teams are prepared to perform their roles.
- Establish the systems, processes, and protocols for capturing the information and data, performing the analyses, determining the insights, creating support mechanisms, and developing reporting schemes so that new opportunities, ideas, and concepts can be evaluated on a systematic basis.
- Establishing high-level appraisal mechanisms to separate the feasible and desirable new opportunities from those that do not fit the strategic direction of the organization or are outside its realm of possibilities.
- Deciding how they fit into the SMSs for crafting strategies and implementing action programs and making decisions about each of the viable opportunities.

The scope of the search should be at least as extensive as the spatial dimensions of the extended enterprises. Moreover, there are reasons why it should actually be greater than that as most businesses are trying to broaden their understanding of reality so that they can make more significant contributions to their social, economic, and environmental goals. Likewise, the time horizon should be equal to or greater than the general time horizon of planning models used by strategic leaders. Since opportunities take time to translate into strategies and action plans and then into realities through implementation and execution, it makes sense to have a longer time horizon. Remember, most new opportunities involve developing the means and mechanisms to translate the vision and strategic direction into what the company wants to become. Many of these opportunities relate to the future, not what it is happening today; therefore, strategic leaders have to create the systems and structures to support the realization of the new opportunities that ultimately enhance their ability to lead change.

Identifying the objectives of the searches is difficult because the general purpose is to think "out-of-the-box" and find new ways to expand the reach and growth potential of the businesses. The strategic direction of the company can provide guidance, as the new opportunities should resonate with plans for its long-term future. For example, BP Plc wants to be an energy company; therefore, it is logical to presume that most of the new opportunities that it might be seeking are likely to be in the areas of sustainable energy and renewable energy technologies. Without constraining the searches for new opportunities, the vision, strategic direction, and strategic fit help to define what opportunities make sense in the context of the external world and the aspirations of the organization. Some of its goals and desires may be to find a given number (say five) of new opportunities per year, one or two of which could be translated into new businesses within a five- to ten-year time frame. For instance, fuel cell technology could potentially be used to distribute electricity to private residences, but such technologies require substantial investment to build the necessary systems and processes.

Strategic leaders may engage others within the organization and enterprise to support such actions, but it is very important that the people involved are open-minded and unbiased about the potential impact on existing businesses. Those who view new opportunities as a threat to existing businesses, technologies, or products are not good candidates. Limited thinking often results in limited results. Some people believe that change will "cannibalize" the success of the existing business units and other internal strengths, rather than thinking about the potential to make a significant difference in improving the external world and sustaining the overall success of the company. Candidates should have both the breadth and depth of knowledge in the appropriate fields of study and should be willing to learn quickly about the topics that they are exploring. While it is important that the people have a positive mindset and take a broad perspective, they should also be skeptical about the new opportunities that they find and/or are working on. There are often reasons why certain opportunities have not been exploited in the past. There may be hidden defects or problems. For instance, producing bio-fuels (ethanol) from corn and other food crops may seem like a good idea, until one examines the concept from a holistic perspective and explores the economics of the future and not just the present. What happens to corn prices as ethanol production increases in the out-years? Is there enough water to grow the crops in areas with significant soil degradation? What about soil depletion? Indeed, a quick assessment of the various feed stocks for ethanol production indicates the switch grass produces approximately 1,150 gallons per acre while corn-based ethanol is only one-third as efficient. Moreover, from a societal point of view, is it acceptable to create potential food problems to solve energy problems? Do energy suppliers want to compete with food producers?

The selected candidates should represent a cross-section of the fundamental disciplines and should be balanced in terms of their relationships within and outside the corporation. Discovering new opportunities is more than just exploring and assessing. It is about understanding what one finds and making valid interpretations about facts and truths gleaned during the discovery process. Teams are useful for engendering new ideas and concepts since the collective wisdom of the whole is usually significantly greater than the sum of the individuals. They should be cross-functional, cross-level, and even cross-company. One person's idea triggers thoughts and insights in others who fuel creativity. Teams also have the capability and expertise to translate concepts into a broad-based understanding of opportunities and how to define and articulate what they represent. This may require business people to think like scientists, physicians, lawyers, news reporters, and others who try to make sense of information, data, evidence, and even symptoms. It may require specialists who are trained in seemingly unrelated fields to shed light on realities, possibilities, and perceptions from a business perspective. For example, Michigan State University hired anthropologists in its quest to obtain evidence about the underlying needs of customers, stakeholders, and society and their views on potential solutions to business problems in the quest to understand the potential of innovative technologies like nanotechnology. Likewise, companies have used forensic scientists to piece together clues about the needs, desires, and expectations of customers and stakeholders.

Training and education are essential for strategic leaders, professionals, and others engaged in exploring new opportunities. Training modules should be both instructive and share ideas and concepts about the methods to be used. Again, the approaches are intended to be open-ended.

For most business people, dealing with new opportunities may be outside their normal roles and responsibilities. They have to understand the logic and rationale behind the quest for new opportunities and dealing with challenges. They need guidance and direction from the strategic leaders and strategists. Yet, they need the freedom to determine their own courses of action so that creativity, imagination, and insights are not stifled.

Establishing a protocol for the search for opportunities can actually precede the training modules or may follow them based on the benefits of having more input and reflection from a broader group of participants. The searches are empirical inquiries that investigate contemporary phenomena within a real-life context using multiple sources of evidence. Discovering new opportunities involves complex, diverse, and novel situations that are dynamic. The protocols also establish objectives, techniques, and the criteria required to meet the rigors of scientific standards. The effectiveness of the information and data can be judged using the following criteria: validity and reliability. The analysis should follow scientific methods, incorporating both inductive and deductive reasoning.

In addition to having a general protocol, criteria must be established to evaluate new opportunities to determine which fit the strategic direction and are feasible and desirable. Generally, most new opportunities are ill-defined, with long time horizons, so conventional assessment criteria like discounted cash flow analyses do not work. Indeed, most of the conventional techniques used to assess long-term opportunities discount the potential to the point where even the most exciting ideas would be discarded. For instance, in the 1970s what methods and techniques would the typical business leader have used to understand, characterize, and evaluate the potential of PCs? Who would have been able to forecast and assess the enormous growth during the 1980s and 1990s? A few people at Apple, IBM, and Intel might have been able to understand the implications for the future, but the vast majority of the business leaders engaged in electronics, office products, and related devices were unable to perceive the opportunities until there was widespread interest and early adaptation of the technologies and products. The appraisal techniques have to be based on the broader economic, social, political, environmental, and technological underpinnings. Moreover, judgments should be based on holistic perspectives underpinned by sustainable solutions, not on an individual basis. Decisions should be determined in the aggregate, not with specific aspects like financial analysis.

Great opportunities often have significant weaknesses and shortcomings which might eliminate further consideration if the protocols only focus on near-term benefits and financial rewards. For instance, most companies examine the market demand for a potential new product before deciding to invest in product development programs. They also use financial criteria like internal rate of return to judge financial viability. These well-established techniques make good sense when making decisions about product innovations that have short development cycles if the cycles are long, they may result in a great opportunity being screened out.

The best criteria include value creation and the potential to create new-to-the-world businesses. Value creation cuts across most of the key elements of the business environment resulting in the potential for positive gains for many participants from customers to partners and society. The PC revolutionized working conditions, lifestyles, and income generation for millions around the world. It enhanced productivity and reduced costs. It made life easier and more productive – it epitomizes the notion of win–win. The potential to create something new from a business perspective is always intriguing. Being on the ground floor of a new market, industry, or technology gives early innovators and adopters the ability to set the stage and achieve uncontested wins. While there are no guarantees that early participants will continue to be successful, they at least have the capability to chart their own destiny. In many cases the early innovators are able to orchestrate the flow of events. For example, DuPont was a leader in chlorofluorocarbons from their invention in 1929 until it closed the business because of the government mandates pertaining to ozone-depleting materials. Grumman was the dominant designer and producer of aircraft for the US Navy because it understood the rigors and stresses of landing a plane on an aircraft carrier and the extensive maintenance requirements in hostile marine environments.

Great care has to be used when making judgments. Other criteria include the resources and intellectual capital necessary to take advantage of the new opportunities. Bill Gates and Paul Allen were able to create a software giant by bootstrapping knowledge and learning into success after success. On the other hand, global corporations typically are more concerned about the size and potential of the opportunities rather than the capability or learning necessary to exploit them. While it is sensible to assess the exact potential, it is often difficult early on to establish what precise outcomes might be and what the long-term prospects are.

Exploring new opportunities in many businesses is an *ad hoc*, or informal process at best. These explorations can be a continuum in some cases or they may be episodic events that are supported by a professional staff to examine the implications. Regardless, the outcome is a decision whether or not to proceed. The judgments are often made based on how the new opportunities would fit the strategic direction and realities of the company. If strategic leaders agree that further efforts are appropriate, funding may be provided and more formal initiatives and action plans developed. Certain new opportunities, especially those that are not linked to any of the existing business units, are continued through the resources and capabilities of the corporate management system. For example, new-to-the-company initiatives might be assigned to the corporate research and development department for further development. On the other hand, if there is a link with one of the business units, corporate strategic leaders may provide additional funding to lower levels so that they can further develop the opportunities using their facilities, resources, intellectual capital, and business acumen.

Business perspectives pertaining to external context

Most business leaders typically assume that the conditions and trends of the natural environment and the social/human world are beyond the scope of their primary roles and responsibilities. Still, most companies are indirectly influenced by the realities of the broader world. Today, as the rate of change accelerates and the interconnectivity of the natural, social, and business worlds increases, astute strategic leaders have to be mindful of the forces of change affecting the global landscape. As globalization expands and the impact of business decisions increases across many spheres, distinguishing between what is business related and what is not becomes more difficult. Moreover, indirect forces that seemingly have little impact on business activities today may quickly (in just one or two years) become critical concerns affecting business economics, market viability, resource availability, and even the strategic direction and sustainable success of corporations. For example, in the wake of Hurricane Katrina and the record number of hurricanes in 2005, weather-related phenomena are much greater concerns. Katrina not only shut down the city of New Orleans and caused billions of dollars of damage; it impacted businesses across the region and country. It also had a global impact as the loss of 3 million barrels per day of Gulf Coast production sent oil prices on world commodity markets soaring.

As the world changes and businesses respond, it is imperative that business leaders think in broader terms and keep pace with changes in the natural environment and social world. Prudent leaders will consider making this a priority and decide on appropriate approaches based on the perceived opportunities and vulnerabilities of their corporate situations. The analysis of the natural environment and the social world includes identifying, quantifying, and evaluating the driving forces of change and how they might influence and impact the corporation. The overall objective is to discover opportunities or difficulties as soon as possible and to take whatever actions are necessary to exploit or mitigate them.

Companies should develop their own methods and techniques to deal with the realities of the broader context of the natural environment and the social/human world. The approach should be tailored to the strategic direction of the corporation and its extended enterprise. The analysis should be based on providing tangible benefits to the corporation and insights for its strategic leaders, insights that can be used to more accurately define the business environment and the extended enterprise. The analysis of the natural environment and the social/human world helps to determine what is critical for long-term success. It can be viewed as the precursor to understanding the business environment and the strategies and action plans that are necessary to stay on the cutting edge.

Given the scope of the natural environment and the social world it is impossible to identify all of the critical elements that should be examined. The complexities of human existence and human systems make it impossible to identify and discuss all of the critical elements. Strategic leaders should reflect on their own local, regional, and global social landscapes and determine the salient factors that they should include in their analysis. The template also provides a general outline of some of the more critical issues that strategic leaders face.[23] The business implications vary from the fundamentals of protecting human rights which are the obligation of all business leaders to ensuring that the best interests of the corporation are protected and preserved. In most situations, protecting the fundamentals of human existence also protects the most profound interests of the company.

In a world that is more integrated and connected through social institutions, global economics, and communication, thinking outside-the-box about the roles of strategic leaders and the scope of their strategies and actions creates opportunities for exceeding expectations and building more viable and vibrant businesses and sustainable success. Great strategic leaders are respectful of the world in which they live and work. They are mindful of their broad responsibilities to their companies, the extended enterprise, civil society, and the common good. They try to maximize the benefits derived from their strategies and actions, and from their products, services, and operations. They also try to minimize the negative effects and impacts. Ultimately, they seek to create a better world.

Box 5.1 Siemens and its focus on market space

Siemens is one of the leading knowledge management and innovation corporations in the world. It was founded in 1847 by Werner von Siemens and has a long history of developing new technologies that change the face of its enterprise and making extraordinary contributions to its customers and society. Werner von Siemens based decision making on solid business principles and the philosophy of ethics and creating value. One of his famous sayings was: "I won't sell the future for a quick profit."[1] His brother, Carl von Siemens who became the chief executive in 1890, said, "I've always placed the interests of the business above my own."[2] These comments resonate well in terms of sustainable success and ethical behaviors.

Siemens is a global corporation with over 416,000 employees in 190 countries. It had sales of €75 billion in 2005 with a net income of €3.1 billion.[3] Siemens has six major lines of business including automation and control, information and communications, medical, power, transportation, and services.[4]

Former CEO Dr. Heinrich V. Pierer stated that the "surest way to predict the future is to create and shape it yourself."[5] For Siemens, inventing the future means identifying customer needs, developing new technologies, recognizing technological breakthroughs, and creating new business opportunities, products, and solutions.[6] Strategic leaders have initiated a new game plan for creating the future called "Fit4More."[7] It has four main pillars:[8]

- *Performance and portfolio*: We are committed to achieving profitable growth by growing our sales at least twice as fast as global GDP and ensuring that every one of our groups achieves its margin targets. Strengthening our portfolio is an ongoing process that includes continuous adaptation and acquisitions.
- *Operational excellence*: We are committed to executing the *top+* Siemens Management System with its sharp focus on innovation, customer focus and global competitiveness, including finding the most strategic fit in today's ever-changing global supply chain.
- *People excellence*: We are working to create a uniform high-performance culture company-wide, one that motivates our people to excel at everything they do. After meeting with countless employees worldwide, I know our employees are excited about our people excellence programs. We are also increasing our global talent pool, establishing career tracks for specialists and offering a new curriculum for our Siemens Leadership Program.
- *Corporate responsibility*: We are committed to being an active and responsible member of every community where we do business worldwide and we've set the goal of becoming best-in-class in corporate governance, business practices, sustainability and corporate citizenship.

Fit4More is a plan that sets the stage for the long-term transformation of Siemens into a world-class company. Siemens views social, economic, and environmental challenges as opportunities to excel. It identifies several mega-trends that will shape the opportunities and challenges that lay ahead. They include the increasing need for reliable and affordable healthcare, the importance of accessible fresh water and wastewater treatment systems for proper sanitation, the growing demand for power, the constraints and pollution associated with the desire for mobility, the expanding requirements for security of buildings, facilities, and people, and the expansion of communications, automation, and lighting.[9] Siemens is looking beyond traditional customers to discover ways to grow its businesses and meet the demands of the world's population. Strategic leaders believe that people make the difference in achieving sustainable success based on well-established principles. Siemens' management and employees are the guided by the following principles:[10]

- We strengthen our **CUSTOMERS** – to keep them competitive. Our success depends on the success of our customers. We provide our customers with our comprehensive experience and solutions so they can achieve their objectives fast and effectively.
- We push **INNOVATION** – to shape the future. Innovation is our lifeblood around the globe and around the clock. We turn our people's imagination and best practices into successful technologies and products. Creativity and experience keeps us on the cutting edge.
- We empower our **PEOPLE** – to achieve world-class performance. Our employees are the key to our success. We work together as a global network of knowledge and learning. Our corporate culture is defined by diversity, open dialogue and mutual respect, and by clear goals and decisive leadership.
- We embrace corporate **RESPONSIBILITY** – to advance society. Our ideas, technologies and activities help to create a better world. We are committed to universal values, good corporate citizenship and a healthy environment. Integrity guides our conduct toward our employees, business partners and shareholders.
- We enhance company **VALUE** – to open up new opportunities. We generate profitable growth to ensure sustainable success. We leverage our balanced business portfolio, our business excellence and synergies across all segments and regions. This makes us a premium investment for our shareholders.

Siemens' primary mechanisms for meeting its principles and vision are business excellence and corporate citizenship. Business excellence involves supporting customers with "right-fit" solutions and environmentally compatible products. Most importantly, Siemens' focus is not just on satisfying customers, but on making them successful. Successful customers enhance the company's prospects for being successful and enhance loyalty and sustainable relationships. Siemens' business conduct guidelines include:[11] (1) mutual respect, honesty, and integrity; (2) behavior which abides with the law; (3) abiding by fair competition and anti-trust legislation; (4) rules against corruption; (5) rules for awarding contracts; (6) donations; (7) confidentiality and insider trading rules; (8) data protection and data security; (9) policies for protecting environment, health and safety; (10) procedures for addressing complaints and comments; (11) implementing and controlling. Corporate responsibility helps build trust with stakeholders, government agencies, and society.

Siemens works with 9,000 strategic partners and suppliers worldwide. It requires suppliers to do business in accordance with the fundamental laws and principles of the international community. It expects them "to compete fairly and with integrity and also to protect the environment, to be socially responsible, and to have appropriate employee-oriented policies."[12]

The most important factor in Siemens' transformation to sustainable success is its management leadership and organizational structure. In 2004 Siemens introduced the Siemens Management System.[13] It contains three permanent company programs: customer focus, innovation, and global competitiveness.[14] This customer focus program examines mega-trends in the business environment at their early stages to discover opportunities to help customers and non-customers with innovative solutions to their needs. This involves the cross-company synergies of bundling Siemens' expertise and knowledge in new ways to create comprehensive solutions, especially for large-scale infrastructure projects like hospitals, airports, and sports stadiums.[15] Customer satisfaction is important, but building enduring customer relationships that provide customers success in the future is the essence of Siemens' framework for success.

Siemens' technological edge has created enormous value and represents competitive advantages for the future. Its R&D strengths lie at the center of its success, and innovation is foremost among its activities. It has 47,000 researchers in 150 centers in over 38 countries. The total R&D budget for 2005 was €5.2 billion.[16] The various R&D centers created more than 8,800 inventions and produced 5,700 patent applications in 2005.[17]

Siemens' quest for leading-edge innovation is an excellent example of an ESM construct. It uses two complementary perspectives to determine its vision for the future. One is obtained using extrapolations into the future based on the world of today and Siemens' relationships with products, technologies, and customers; the other is obtained through strategic thinking about the desired future state and working back to the present. The latter involves envisioning possibilities in the future and drawing upon their implications for today. It looks out ten, twenty, and even thirty years to find new opportunities. Siemens follows this dual-sided approach for examining and selecting opportunities. One involves improving the current capabilities and approaches through transitions; the other thinking about how to invent the future to create new markets, customers, and technologies. Strategic leaders believe that both approaches are essential to discover true potential. Short-term objectives are based on an extrapolation of the present; long-term objectives are based on inventing the future. Like many companies in recent times Siemens has had problems. While failing to uphold one's principles usually leads to difficulties, strategic leaders should learn from mistakes and redouble their efforts to achieve sustainable success.[18] Nevertheless, Siemens continues to focus on its potential and sustain success.

Notes

1. www.w4.siemens.de-siemens.
2. *Ibid.*
3. www.siemens.com/index.jsp?sde, Letter to Our Shareholders, 2006, p. 1 of 6.
4. *Ibid.*
5. www.siemens.com "Key Figures."
6. *Ibid.*
7. www.siemens.com/index.jsp?sde, Letter to Our Shareholders, 2006, p. 2 of 6.
8. *Ibid.*
9. *Ibid.*, p. 3 of 6.
10. www.siemens.com "Our Principles."
11. www.siemens.com "Business Excellence Programs."
12. www.siemens.com/index.jsp?sde_pft55mls6u20o1235613i123.
13. www.siemens.com/index.jsp?sde_p=ft4mls4uo130578i130579, p. 2 of 5.
14. *Ibid.*

15. *Ibid.*
16. www.siemens.com/index.jsp?sde_p=ft4ml1s7uo1182521n11, p1 of 1.
17. www.siemens.com/index.jsp?sde_p=fdpFEcfi11839041mno1182, p. 1 of 1.
18. Siemens has had legal problems with its contracts for systems relating to the Olympics in Greece. There are allegations about the appropriateness of certain corporate financial practices and accounts. Since these problems are being handled by the governments and the story is currently unfolding, they are not discussed here.

Summary

Market space approaches involve constructs that the company and its business units must use to address opportunities and challenges in the market spaces. Strategic leaders decide on the scope and intensity of their participation in the market spaces as they create solutions that maximize value for all parties and reduce, if not eliminate, defects, burdens, and impacts. The new perspective for strategic management involves this dual-sided thinking: maximize the positive, and minimize the negative.

Today, there are numerous market space opportunities that could be realized if businesses adopted a broader perspective. Moreover, there are many untapped opportunities that are available, but are not being addressed because they lie outside the parameters of the normal market. For instance, there are billions of people around the world that would like a device to help cook their meals. They don't necessarily need and perhaps wouldn't even want many of the benefits of products sold in the developed countries. They could really use simpler and more affordable devices. Imagine the hundreds of millions of such products that could be sold if companies could design a simple product that is inexpensive and reliable.

The dual-sided approach of ESM also asks strategic leaders to rethink competition. Competitors may be more than mere rivals. They may be serving market space that your company does not want to address or alternatively, leaving a segment of the market space available that your company can focus on and excel in. Moreover, by responding to competition, companies may improve their own performance to the extent that their competitors become irrelevant. The bottom line for this new management thinking is discovering opportunities to enrich businesses and all of their external relationships. It is creating win–win environments that are as comprehensive as possible, yet balanced over time as corporations achieve extraordinary performance and outcomes in the present and prepare for an even more exciting future through investments in people, systems, technologies, and products. The desire is to create an even more positive future with better solutions than today, and to do so through strategic leadership and creative thinking.

References

Hart, Stuart (2005) *Capitalism at the Crossroads: The Unlimited Business Opportunities in Solving the World's Most Difficult Problems.* Upper Saddle River, NJ: Wharton School Publishing

Kaku, Mickio (1994) *Hyperspace: A Scientific Odyssey through Parallel Universes, Time Warps, and the Tenth Dimension.* New York: Anchor Books

Kim, W. Chan and Renee Mauborgne (2005) *Blue Ocean Strategy: How to Create Uncontested Market Space and Make Competition Irrelevant.* Boston, MA: Harvard Business School Press

Kurzweil, Ray (2005) *The Singularity Is Near.* New York: Viking-Penguin Group

Pine, II, J.B. (1993) *Mass Customization.* Boston, MA: Harvard Business School Press

Porter, Michael (1985) *Competitive Advantage: Creating and Sustaining Superior Performance.* New York: Free Press

Prahalad, C. K. (2005) *The Fortune at the Bottom of the Pyramid: Eradicating Poverty through Profits.* Upper Saddle River, NJ: Wharton School Publishing

Rainey, David L. (2006) *Sustainable Business Development: Inventing the Future through Strategy, Innovation and Leadership.* Cambridge, UK: Cambridge University Press

Watkins, Kevin (2005) *Human Development Report 2005, International Cooperation at a Crossroads: Aid, Trade and Security in an Unequal World.* New York: United Nations Development Programme and Oxford University Press

NOTES

1 J. B. Pine, II, *Mass Customization* (Boston, MA: Harvard Business School Press, 1993). Pine describes mass customization as customers having the economic benefits of mass production and the selectivity of a custom producer. The title conveys the topic introduced by S. Davis in 1987 in his book, *Future Perfect.*

2 J. B. Pine, II, *Mass Customization* (Boston, MA: Harvard Business School Press, 1993).

3 *Ibid.,* p. 241.

4 Michael Porter, *Competitive Advantage: Creating and Sustaining Superior Performance* (New York: Free Press, 1985, p. 37).

5 *Ibid.,* pp. 34–35.

6 *Ibid.,* pp. 4–10.

7 David L. Rainey, *Sustainable Business Development: Inventing the Future through Strategy, Innovation and Leadership* (Cambridge, UK: Cambridge University Press, 2006, p. 102).

8 Magdalena Moll and Lother Meinzer, "Sustainable Development: A Key to Creating Value", Faire, Paris, June 25, 2004.

9 C. K. Prahalad, *The Fortune at the Bottom of the Pyramid: Eradicating Poverty through Profits* (Upper Saddle River, NJ: Wharton School Publishing, 2005).

10 *Ibid.*, pp. 25–27.

11 Stuart Hart, *Capitalism at the Crossroads: The Unlimited Business Opportunities in Solving the World's Most Difficult Problems* (Upper Saddle River, NJ: Pearson Education, Inc./Wharton School Publishing, 2005, pp. 107–133).

12 *Ibid.*, pp. 22, 219–221.

13 *Ibid.*, p. 219.

14 Ray Kurzweil, *The Singularity Is Near* (New York: Viking-Penguin Group, 2005, p. 512).

15 *Ibid.*, p. 49.

16 www.china-embassy.org/eng/gyzg/t179428.htm.

17 W. Chan Kim and Renee Mauborgne, *Blue Ocean Strategy: How to Create Uncontested Market Space and Make Competition Irrelevant* (Boston, MA: Harvard Business School Press, 2005, pp. 186–187).

18 Personal discussion with Dr. Ludwig and from his presentation at a joint seminar with Siemens Systems Engineering and the Technical University of Munich, June 23, 2004, Fürth, Germany.

19 W. Chan Kim and Renee Mauborgne, *Blue Ocean Strategy: How to Create Uncontested Market Space and Make Competition Irrelevant* (Boston, MA: Harvard Business School Press, 2005, p. 21).

20 *Ibid.*, p. 115.

21 Mickio Kaku, *Hyperspace: A Scientific Odyssey Through Parallel Universes, Time Warps, and the Tenth Dimension* (New York: Anchor Books, 1994, pp. 46–48, 70–74).

22 This statement should not be misconstrued to suggest that colonialism is acceptable, but unlike the Spanish conquest of indigenous populations, most American colonists considered themselves to be subjects of the Crown. They simply wanted fair treatment and the capability to pursue their dreams. Like most of these stories the situations were complex, and it is impossible to rewrite history or to discuss what could have been.

23 Kevin Watkins, *Human Development Report 2005, International Cooperation at a Crossroads: Aid, Trade and Security in an Unequal World* (New York: United Nations Development Programme and Oxford University Press, 2005). *The Human Development Report 2005* provides details about social development on a geographical regional basis.

Part II

Strategic management: Formulation and implementation

Part II includes the following chapters:
- Chapter 6: Strategic management framework and strategic analysis
- Chapter 7: Strategic formulation – options, mission statements, and objectives
- Chapter 8: Strategy formulation – business strategies and action plans
- Chapter 9: Strategic implementation and execution
- Chapter 10: Reflections and concluding comments

Chapter 6 focuses on how strategic leaders translate the company's vision and strategic direction into business strategies that are actionable and result in desired outcomes. Strategic leaders have to have the intellectual capacity to determine the scope of their businesses and extended enterprises, analyze and understand the business environment and market spaces, and establish a framework for formulating strategies and objectives, implementing the strategies and actions plan, evaluating outcomes, and leading change. They also have to engage in organizational dynamics and help people within the organization to achieve extraordinary outcomes.

Chapter 7 examines how to take the implications of the strategic analysis and develop strategic options. The options are than translated into business objectives and strategies. Some of the main categories involving strategic options include growth, development, improvements, and investments. They also include potential divestitures. The main perspectives focus on closing the gap between the opportunities and challenges and the organization's capabilities and resources to take advantage of the current and future situations. The chapter includes a discussion about the selection of business objectives.

Chapter 8 involves crafting business strategies and allocating resources to enhance the future of the SBU. Strategy formulation also involves strategic business planning and the intellectual contributions and activities necessary to develop new or revised mission statements, formulate new business strategies, and decide on the action plans and initiatives that set the stage for strategic implementation.

Chapter 9 discusses how strategic leaders implement strategies and action plans. It discusses the most important means and ways for executing strategies. These include the allocation of resources, the identification of incentives, and the evaluation of ongoing results. The evaluation of success and outcomes provides leaders with the knowledge to make adjustments and corrections. Feedback mechanisms provide management with information and understanding about the requisite improvements that they have to make on an ongoing basis to perpetuate the process of realizing positive outcomes.

Chapter 10 reflects on how strategic leaders can integrate their extended enterprise into a strategic management system that includes all of the entities and relationships in a mutually beneficial way that leads to sustainable success. The chapter ends with concluding comments.

6 Strategic management framework and strategic analysis

Introduction

The more specific and tangible aspects of enterprise-wide strategic management (ESM) involve the strategic management systems (SMSs) of business units. The strategic business units (SBUs) translate the vision and strategic direction of the company/corporation into executable missions, business strategies, action plans, and operating results. They focus on the market spaces, competitive landscapes, and specific business/product portfolios. Whereas corporate strategic leaders focus on crafting and implementing high-level, future-oriented grand strategies, SBU leaders manage the SMSs and concentrate on developing the game plans providing means and mechanisms necessary to take advantage of business opportunities and deal with challenges. They concentrate on achieving balanced and broad-based, near-term objectives and long-term sustainable success. SBU leaders play more specific roles in managing the affairs of the business units than corporate executives. They are responsibile for formulating and implementing business strategies and ensuring that functional and operational management performs in accordance with the strategic direction of the company and overall objectives.

For some companies, especially small and medium-sized enterprises (SMEs), the corporate level management system and the SMS are merged into a single, embedded system. Here, corporate executives also function in the roles of SBU leaders with narrower perspectives, well-targeted market spaces, and definitive product portfolios. In such cases, there may still be distinctions between corporate roles and responsibilities and those of the SBU leaders as articulated in this chapter. It is imperative that business leaders understand the differences and act accordingly. This distinction helps to avoid confusion and complications and supports the development of separate management systems if the situation warrants it in the future. These distinctions become more important as the company grows, especially as new businesses are added.

Historically, an SBU is a well-defined semi-independent business unit, division or even a subsidiary of a large corporation/company with the responsibility to establish its own SMS, craft strategies and action plans based on the company's overall vision, strategic direction, and leadership, and ensure proper implementation. It is, or can be, a grouping of related business platforms and/or operating systems. While the connotation today is much broader than the original definition used in the 1970s by General Electric (GE), a SBU is characterized by its mission(s), a defined business environment, served markets and business strategies, and actions. Being a subset of the company, it is generally narrower in scope than the corporate management system.

In today's context, an SBU is often a relatively self-contained SMS and/or organizational unit with a definitive strategic perspective. It employs available resources and capabilities, and has strategic leaders who are responsible for the businesses which formulate and implement their own business strategies and actions. An SBU has one or more value delivery systems that design, develop, and deliver products and services to selected markets and customers. The value delivery systems depend on their SBU leaders for strategic direction, resource allocations, and oversight.[1] The value delivery systems are dependencies since they focus on operational tactics and activities to execute the business strategies and objectives.

SBU leaders are accountable for their strategic decisions, the organizations and their capabilities, the resources they deploy and use, and the results they obtain. Some of the typical objectives include: (1) revenue generation, cash flow, and profitability; (2) business growth, development, and improvements; (3) customer and stakeholder satisfaction and success; (4) organizational capabilities and learning; and (5) strategic transitions and transformations.

Most of the prevailing academic strategic management theories are designed for SBUs and their leaders. Constructs like Michael Porter's three generic competitive strategies (cost leadership, differentiation, and focus) and five forces (discussed in previous chapters) are business unit strategies and constructs that address industry perspectives and competitive forces. As discussed previously, while these appear to be a sensible construct, they tend to view competition as the prime motivation for strategic action, and ignore broader aspects of the business environment and markets spaces. The difficulty with such thinking is that strategic leaders box themselves in in a narrow field. Options often become reduced to fighting it out with competitors based on low costs or differentiated products. While the realities of the business world may force strategic leaders to fight or die, the aspirations associated with ESM include developing sustainable strategic positions that are defensible if not invulnerable for a reasonable period of time, acquiring long-term advantages that are difficult to emulate, and achieving sustainable success through value creation and positive relationships.

SBU leaders are general managers who translate the corporate strategic direction into strategies and actions that yield results. Their perspectives are usually easier to define than those of corporate leaders. They develop and improve the systems and processes, control and evaluate outcomes, and lead change. Most importantly, they engage people through organizational dynamics and inspire people to achieve extraordinary outcomes.

While corporate leaders are the architects required to create the overall vision and strategic direction of the whole, SBU leaders incorporate corporate strategies into their own business strategies and create plans for implementation and execution. From theoretical and practical perspectives, corporate leaders articulate and orchestrate the "big picture" from a global perspective like a satellite orbiting the Earth at 100,000 feet (about 30,000 meters) whereas SBU leaders operate between 33,000 feet (10,000 meters) and ground level. They run the gamut from crafting business strategies and overseeing that the organization has clear direction to ensuring that people on the ground are engaged and successful. They are not middle management per se, but are strategic leaders connected and occupied with the realities of the business world. SBU leaders have to achieve targeted results in the present and near term, at the same time supporting the transformations and transitions necessary to achieve the desired future state as well. This duality makes leading change and managing the SBUs complex and challenging, requiring exceptional preparation and competencies.

ESM involves ensuring that the SBU and its enterprise(s) understand and execute the current and future mission(s), the strategic direction, and make improvements to tangible resources, capabilities, products, processes, and operations, especially those related to the value delivery systems. SBU leaders preempt challenges and threats and encourage change within the organization to outpace the dynamics of the business world.

SBU leaders have many similar responsibilities with corporate leaders except that their focus is more specific and definable. They determine policies, scope, strategies, objectives, and organizational design within their domains. They deal with governance, control, and evaluation. The key differences include more attention on market spaces, customers, and competition. They have to integrate the enterprise, build relationships with partners, customers, and stakeholders, and achieve short-term as well as long-term objectives.

This chapter includes the following main topics:

- Identifying the key aspects of strategic business planning (SBP) and the strategic management process.
- Developing a strategic framework for scrutinizing prevailing conditions and trends in the global business environment, determining the scope or domain of the business unit, translating corporate vision and strategic direction into reality, and selecting the appropriate strategic management process, management constructs, and business models to achieve sustainable outcomes and success.
- Conducting a strategic analysis of the external landscape to identify opportunities and challenges in the business environment and market spaces, and of the internal capabilities and resources for exploiting opportunities or mitigating threats and vulnerabilities. This includes mapping out the most crucial prospects for achieving success and identifying special issues that have critical strategic significance.

Developing the strategic management framework is a precursor to the strategic management process and SBP. It may be viewed as part of the strategic foundation upon which the strategic management process lies. It is examined, reviewed, and determined periodically.

Strategic business planning and strategic management process

Historical and contemporary perspectives

SBP has been in vogue for more than forty years. It implies both the crafting of the strategic moves and the implementation of the required actions. It has a history of many positive outcomes and some negative ones as well. The notion of SBP implies a dynamic process that focuses on determining the best courses of action and transforming the organization into a more effective and successful entity through sustained efforts, commitments, contributions, and leadership. The main critics of SBP over the years have suggested that too much emphasis is placed on the "strategic plan" instead of analyzing the business environment, strategizing, implementing actions, and defeating competitors; and too little attention given to determining ways to make customers successful through sustainable solutions.

The notion of a strategic plan often conveyed a static view of preparing written documents that convey good intentions but lacked the mechanisms to invoke actions. For instance, when Jack Welch became CEO of GE he changed the strategic management paradigm from planning to action. While planning is important, plans are useless unless strategies are translated into immediate action and intended outcomes. Often a significant amount of time is lost between the planning stage and the implementation phases.

SBP and the strategic management process focus on strategic analysis, business strategies, objectives and actions of the SBU and its SMS, and the necessary organizational and enterprise-wide interfaces and activities required to obtain the achievements. The focus is on making decisions today to produce favorable outcomes in the future. It is about creating strategic positions in which the business units can become what they want to be and can obtain sustained improvements, developments, and growth without damaging the natural environment or the social/human world, or becoming vulnerable to the winds of change. SBP and the strategic management process are means to an end, not the end itself. They include: (1) establishing a management framework; (2) analyzing the business environment, market spaces, the extended enterprise, and the organization; (3) crafting objectives, strategies, and action plans; and (4) implementing and executing plans and programs.

The strategic management process is a pivotal construct. It helps strategic leaders to orchestrate the flow of the required elements. The front end, strategic analysis and strategy formulation, tends to be intellectual exercises performed by the strategic leaders, their staff, and other senior professionals. These are usually carried out in controlled settings with a relatively small number of people. While limiting the number of participants in the process is not necessarily desirable, it is often done to keep the information and decisions confidential and to keep competitors and others from discovering the strategies and intended actions. The back end, implementation and execution, tends to be the most difficult part of the strategic management process because it involves many more people and it is often difficult to coordinate and integrate the efforts and actions of the multitude. It can be argued that everyone in an organization and the extended enterprise eventually becomes involved or engaged in the implementation and/or execution. Businesses have a difficult time implementing strategies effectively and proficiently when they fail to include a diverse number of participants during the formulation stage. People are more likely to commit to strategies and engage in implementation when they have participated in the upstream stages of the process.

SBP and the strategic management process are not single-sided aspects, where the strategic leader can be a great planner but a poor implementer, or vice versa. Moreover, strategic decision makers have to use their knowledge, expertise, insights, and imagination to examine the most appropriate options and select the best choices for their organizations and enterprises – ones that fit their strategic needs and objectives as well as empower, support, and reward the people engaged in the actions. Great strategies are meaningless if they are not implemented properly. Effectiveness depends on an ongoing evaluation of the whole strategic management process. Otherwise, the strategies become those of the senior leaders instead of the organization.

Strategic leaders must have a strong will and the courage to entertain criticisms as well as compliments. They must have or develop a multifaceted leadership style that includes the ability to think strategically and tactically, globally and locally, broadly and narrowly, business-related and people-related, and short term and long term. They need to be able to craft and implement strategies. Most importantly, ESM requires strategic leaders who have brilliance and tenacity. They have to be *brilliant* in strategic analysis and strategy formulation. And, they have to have *tenacity* to implement the strategies and execute the action programs.

ESM and the strategic management process

The underlying intent of the strategic management process is to make good strategic decisions based on a comprehensive understanding of reality and future prospects. Achieving sustainable success and realizing the full potential of the organization are the primary aims. There are often many ways to fail, but it requires a widely understood systematic process to succeed. In *Anna Karenina*, Leo Tolstoy begins the book with one of the most famous quotes in literature: "Happy families are all alike; every unhappy family is unhappy in its own way."[2]

Similarly, it takes a systematic and well-honed approach to realize strategic success that can be replicated over time. Great companies and SBUs that are successful over many decades (if not centuries) have developed strategic leaders and strategic management processes to ensure that strategic decisions are made based on the whole enterprise and on its long-term future – not just its current bottom line. Moreover, successful strategic leaders solicit and listen to input from corporate leaders, peers, subordinates, and other leaders of the extended enterprise. The process involves many iterations and numerous modifications to keep the process up-to-date, and consistent with the needs of the business.

A systematic strategic management process helps strategic leaders avoid trial and error approaches that produce good results occasionally – and bad ones as well. As the rate of change increases, the implicit requirement to reinvent the businesses and develop new strategies and action plans also increase. As strategic leaders play the strategy game over and over again, they not only have to ensure good outcomes through effective strategy formulation and implementation, but they also have to improve the strategic management process as well. There are numerous examples of how successful corporations achieved success early on, only to eventually fail to keep pace with change and become unsuccessful. Companies like Pan Am, RCA, NCR, and British Steel went from the pinnacles of success to the depths of annihilation. Stories about how giant companies failed to continue to succeed provide scholars and business leaders with insightful case studies that describe how even market share leaders eventually became just one of many, because their strategic leaders were not aggressive, and failed to outpace market expectations and the competition. For example, many of GM's divisions and brands were leaders in their sectors. Cadillac was once the undisputed leader in the luxury car sector. However, over the last three decades it relinquished its leadership and is now just one of the pack.

Businesses can make improvements, but if they are not sufficiently aggressive, the strategic leaders may find that they are falling behind as others catch up and even overtake them. At one time, American basketball players dominated the Olympic Games – until the last few Olympiads. The difficulty is not that the American players are less skilled at playing the game; the fact is that other teams have gotten much better. Like any comparison the story is complex and there are many reasons for this change in fortunes. But it is clear in today's business world that very little stands still. Small companies can become giants and vice versa. Wal-Mart was once just a speck in the competitive space of retailing. Twenty-five years ago, few people could have imagined its growth and dominance. Likewise, few can envision a challenger to Wal-Mart's preeminent position today. Yet, such changes have frequently occurred. There are no guarantees of success. Strategic leaders have to create their own sustainable success.

Strategic leaders of the SBU and its SMS have the critical roles and responsibilities to make the strategic management process work for their organization. They have to select the strategic management framework/process, determine its scope, and decide how to formulate and implement business strategies and action plans.

The strategic management process is driven by external forces of the business environment, executives of the corporation, and the strategic leaders of the SBU/SMS. Strategic leadership at both levels continuously influences the process of developing and executing strategies. The strategic management

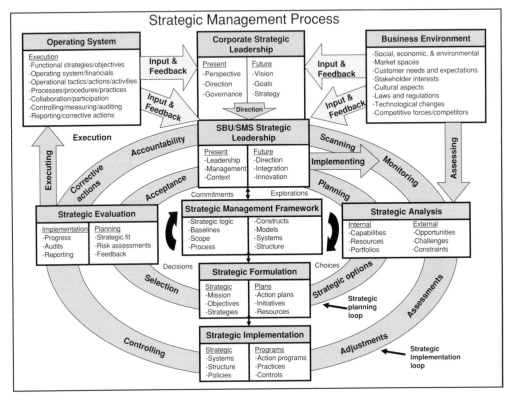

Figure 6.1   The strategic management process

process is usually mapped out by a strategic management framework which provides the sense of connectedness among the entities of the corporation, SBU(s), the extended enterprise(s), and the business environment. The strategic management framework is at the center of the process, and links the realities of the company and the SBUs with the requisite elements of the process.

Figure 6.1 graphically portrays this comprehensive strategic management process. It is based on the more sophisticated and holistic thinking of strategic management of the SBU from an ESM perspective.

The strategic management process links senior management thinking and leadership, both corporate and SBU, with the elements necessary to determine proper strategies and how best to implement those strategies in the context of the business world. The process can be envisioned as a continuous double-loop cycle consisting of two prime flows, one loop involving strategy formulation and the other loop involving strategy implementation

This strategic management process is obviously more complicated than the traditional models discussed in Chapter 2. However, there can be many variations to fit the specifics of a business situation. Some companies have even more complicated and sophisticated processes devised to suit the demanding requirements of their businesses. The strategic management process shown in Figure 6.1 maps out the essential elements for determining and deploying what is necessary to formulate and implement business strategies.

The inner loop focuses on formulating new strategic moves using the intellectual capital of the leadership of the organization, the key strategists, and supporting professionals and all of the contributing internal and external individuals and entities. The inner loop may also be referred to as the "SBP loop." The outer loop focuses on implementing strategies and action programs to achieve short-term and long-term results using economic, technological, and human capital. It may also be referred to as the "strategy implementation loop." Both involve the ongoing transformations and transitions of the organization into a more effective, efficient, productive, capable, and rewarding entity.

The formulation loop involves SBU leaders engaged in analysis, strategy formation, and decision making. It includes strategic analyses of the external context and the internal capabilities and resources; the identification of strategic options; and the formulation of strategies, objectives, and action plans. It also involves evaluating the choices selected, and commits to specific strategic action plans.

The implementation loop involves how SBU leaders and operational management implement and execute action plans and keep themselves current and effective via ongoing analysis. It involves executing the strategies, crafting the desired solutions, obtaining the expected results, and ensuring that progress is made across the SBU and its value delivery systems. It also involves reinforcing the management systems and the organizational structure to ensure that strategies can be implemented. It includes ongoing strategic evaluation to ensure that progress and outcomes are realized.

The process is non-linear with both loops functioning in parallel. As new strategic moves are being crafted, the organization is often working on carrying out existing programs developed during previous cycles. For instance, Toyota initiated the design and development of its hybrid drive system and related products during the early 1990s. However, hybrid technology has only been extended to the other product lines in the last few years. The implementation across value delivery systems has taken more than ten years. Occasionally, strategies are implemented earlier in the new cycle, since many of the action plans and programs take years to complete and integrate into the operation.

The strategic management process is not just a typical series of elements, tasks, or functions that lead to a set of outcomes, like producing a product via a manufacturing process. It involves strategic thinking and insights about what could be done and/or must be done. It also involves strategic decision making that is based on informed and logical (objective) choices and a pattern of interconnected actions with numerous iterations. Moreover, the strategic management process tends to be open-ended with many unknowns, uncertainties, and a lot of risks. Perfect information and knowledge about all of the variables and choices are impossible. Ultimately, strategic leaders have to make decisions about strategies and actions based on their creativity, personal knowledge, and experience.

The strategic management process has to be robust, but it is often imprecise and circuitous. SBU leadership is pivotal in overcoming the inherent uncertainties involved and some of the open-endedness of the strategic management process. Strategic leaders make the whole process work. It is their leadership and judgment that create and sustain positive outcomes. They integrate planning with implementation and execution. Great strategies, in concept, are useless without proper execution. Many businesses have the capability to formulate exciting strategies but cannot get the organization to support their implementation and execution. Failures occur because the process is not properly carried out. Some of the main reasons for failures include lack of integration, lack of knowledge, poor leadership, poor planning, poor execution, and too many barriers to success.

Sustainable success requires contributors at every step to participate fully, to complete their assignments and reach valid results. It is critical that every leader of the SBU and value delivery systems provides input and that they are significant contributors in decision making. In most large companies and SMEs, the actual execution takes place at the operating system level, especially those involving tactical aspects (i.e. day-to-day operations).

The details of the strategic management process are covered in the rest of this chapter and in Chapters 7, 8, and 9. They are provided in the context of the strategic management framework as discussed in the subsequent section.

Strategic management techniques and life-cycle management

Strategic management constructs involve extensive analysis that depend on analytical techniques and methods for understanding reality, and making determinations about proper strategies and actions. Strategic decision making constructs include: (1) qualitative and quantitative techniques for finding opportunities and challenges; (2) making investments and financial decisions; and (3) handling the numerous strategic decisions that have to be made. Strategic decisions are always difficult because of the complexities of the situations, the risks involved, the uncertainty and lack of complete information, and often conflicting short-term and long-term objectives.

Many of the analytical techniques used are mainstream management approaches, including financial management techniques. Discounted cash flow, internal rate of return analysis, and statistical methods for analyzing data and information are commonplace. These techniques are well grounded in management practice, and are not covered in this book.

Life-cycle assessment (LCA) is a relatively new technique that can help strategic decision makers make better decisions. LCA is a systematic methodology which is used to identify and evaluate impacts and burdens associated with products, their related processes, supply and distribution requirements, and applications. LCA uses scientific principles and technical rigor to ensure the validity of assessments and the appropriateness of steps taken to make improvements. LCA examines the existing situation and explores the possibility to make improvements using new designs, developments, and deployments. It is a multi-stage, input/output model that analyzes all of the inputs and outputs, their impact – including materials, products, wastes, and emissions – and the possible options for improving the value proposition of products and processes. LCA is covered in detail in my book, *Sustainable Business Development: Inventing the Future through Strategy, Innovation and Leadership*.

Strategic management framework: Logic, scope, direction, and constructs

Strategic logic

Strategic logic defines the purpose of the SBU and the rationale for its existence. It addresses the "why" question. It defines what the business units are trying to accomplish, and why such accomplishments are important. It provides the rationale for the businesses, their missions, and the strategic actions for transitioning and transforming them into more successful organizations. The most important perspective of the strategic logic is to discover and define how the SBU creates value for customers, stakeholders, shareholders, employees, and society. This includes: (1) discovering opportunities; (2) translating those opportunities into business realities that make money; and (3) providing success and satisfaction for the contributors and recipients in the value delivery system.

The strategic logic provides an understanding of how the SMS of the SBU fits with the overall strategic direction of the company. The strategic logic is a precursor to strategy formulation and lays the foundation for strategic thinking by the SBU leadership. It sets the stage for determining the strategies and objectives of the business units by linking the corporate vision, grand strategies, and goals to the expressed missions of the SBUs.

Strategic logic of the SBUs defines who they are and what they intend to be. It involves purpose and aims, connections to the overall company and the external world. It establishes the underpinnings of the SBUs from the company point of view so that SBU leaders can establish their strategic framework for the scope, processes, and constructs of their strategic management. The strategic logic of the SBUs is based on the realization that strategic choices are dependent on the business situation, the vision, and strategic direction of the whole company. Therefore, the business strategies that are ultimately selected should fit the context of the external realities, and be based on the existing and/or enhanced capabilities and resources of the organization developed to implement the strategies.

While businesses can develop new capabilities and expand existing ones, being realistic is a critical factor. Grandiose schemes that fall outside a logical perspective of the business units, or those that cannot be supported by the fundamentals of the businesses, are usually not viable options if they are not aligned with the strategic logic of the organization. For instance, it has taken almost a decade for the strategic leaders of Chrysler to understand they did not fit within the larger Daimler Chrysler organization. On the other hand, Nissan became much more successful once its leaders developed a better sense of its fit in the car industry, and assumed a strategic alliance with Renault.

Strategic logic helps decision makers understand how they fit into the strategic management of the SBUs and what they have to do to be successful. It includes the principles, values, beliefs, and ethics of the corporation, and the needs and requirements of the businesses. It establishes or provides the baselines for analysis and decision making. Baselines are the high-level targets that companies seek, or that they use, to form comparisons between what the company wants to be and what others have done. Baselines can be broad perspectives on what are desirable or specific requirements that define the thresholds of the company. For instance, a simple baseline may be, "that all business will be conducted openly and honestly to build integrity and trust among all relationships across the enterprise."

A slightly more complicated baseline might be, "to achieve six-sigma outcomes in every product design, development, and delivery." Baselines provide guidance for decision makers, and a means and mechanism for analyses and evaluation during the strategic management process. Further discussions on baselines are covered under the section of strategy formulation in the next chapter, as many of the baselines are reinforced as new objectives are formed and articulated.

Scope of the strategic management framework

Most SBU leaders have predetermined missions that evolve over time and have strategic direction and guidance from the top to help them make changes and improvements. In sophisticated companies there is usually some form of strategic management framework to link the corporate management system with the SBUs and its external business environment. While not all SBUs have an articulated strategic management framework they may still have an implicit identification of the intended scope of the SBU and its relationship with the corporate management system and the external business environment.

The strategic management framework includes the domain of the SBU, strategic direction from corporate, the implicit or explicit business models used to link the extended enterprise into a value system for achieving outcomes, and the management constructs for strategic decision making. It sets the stage for strategic analysis, formulation, implementation, and evaluation. It may be viewed as Level "0" because it is part of the embedded corporate management system, part of the structure for leading and managing the SBU, and the precursor to the steps in the process for formulating and implementing business unit strategies. Corporate management may play a critical role in determining the elements of the strategic management framework and making strategic decisions about many of the inputs into the strategic management and SBP, especially those that pertain to the vision and grand strategies of the corporation. Developing an explicit framework is one of the most critical elements in making strategic management and planning more accessible and understandable by managers and professionals within the SBU and for providing guidance and a sense of linkage to everyone involved.

SBU leaders are also architects, planners, strategists, and implementers who conceive innovative ways to: (1) create what is desirable and possible; (2) strategize on how such outcomes can be achieved; (3) devise the means and mechanisms to realize them; (4) provide the necessary resources for the solution; and (5) ensure that success is realized and sustained. They have to plan for the future, craft and implement new business strategies and action plans, develop new technologies, products, and process and sustain the investments thereof, and manage these programs to achieve the return on investment and enhance future positions. At the same time, they have to ensure that the existing businesses and their value delivery systems and operations perform in accordance with the prevailing governance of the company. They must meet or exceed expectations across the whole spectrum of external driving forces. While it is not exactly a fifty-fifty proposition, SBU leaders should spend about half of their time dealing with the short term and about half thinking about the long term. Seen another way, they should also spend half of their time dealing with internal organizational and strategic requirements and half dealing with external opportunities, needs, expectations, and issues.

Determining the scope of the strategic management framework of the SBU and its SMS is one of the most critical decisions that strategic leaders make. The scope can be based on a philosophical view of the SBU's business world and what it must include in its strategic decision making to realize the corporate vision and the SBU's mission. It should embrace a preliminary understanding of the opportunities and challenges facing the SBU and achieve success in both the long and short term. The former is more of a theoretical approach originated through the underpinnings of the organization (principles, beliefs, etc.) while the latter is more of a practical approach grounded in the realities of the business environment, market spaces, and what the SBU must do based on opportunities and challenges. In the real world of the SBU, strategic leaders usually select frameworks that are combinations of the two approaches and modify them to meet their specific needs.

Determining the scope involves defining/establishing the boundaries of the value delivery system and the extended enterprise. While a holistic perspective includes cradle-to-grave thinking, practical considerations may necessitate a more definitive and less expansive view of the external dimensions, especially for the short term. Strategic leaders may decide to limit the scope to suppliers and suppliers of the suppliers on the upstream side of the value system, and customers, customers of customers, and certain end-of life considerations that the company can effect and control on the downstream side.

Many SBUs have an extremely large business environment making strategic analysis and strategy formulation and implementation almost impossible to accomplish in a timely fashion. Limiting the scope of the strategic framework by establishing more definitive boundaries makes business sense if the underlying goals are to make the process more doable, and more likely to be successful, as long as the boundaries selected are rational and not biased by avoiding unpleasant realities. For instance, the selected boundaries should not limit the scope to exclude geographical areas or global issues that have many difficulties or undesirable effects and impacts that the company does not want to shed light on like the implications of climate change. Some strategic leaders fail to explore the challenges associated with doing business in developing countries or dealing with the effects and impacts of the production processes that are not based on accepted norms or standards (e.g. many companies were not proactive in ensuring that the goods made in China were not contaminated with lead paint or that food products were free of microorganisms).

The establishment of the boundaries should be based on logical and defendable criteria that any similarly placed company would use, or that any independent standards organizations such as the International Organization for Standardization (ISO) or appropriate government agency might suggest as appropriate. The more objective the basis of the selection, the easier it is to defend the choices made. Moreover, the boundaries should be expanded by logical increments at the end of each cycle. This approach makes the framework more inclusive and less constrained over time.

The strategic management framework can be defined for each SBU. The scope can be determined using the following perspectives:

- The inclusiveness of upstream and downstream entities in the extended enterprise, and the specific value networks that add value, including critical perspectives on market spaces and competitive spaces.
- The expansiveness of geographic areas, including regions of the world, countries, and locations, including specific parts thereof; or other important considerations.
- The extensiveness of the time horizon used in analysis of opportunities and challenges; determining the strategic direction, expressed in the number of years into the future the strategic perspective should go.
- The soundness of the internal systems and structures that support the formulation and implementation of strategies, objectives, and strategic decision making.

Defining the scope of the strategic management framework is always a difficult proposition with few easy answers. The general philosophical perspective is based on holistic thinking. One of the most important questions connected to the scope of the strategic management framework involves to what extent the

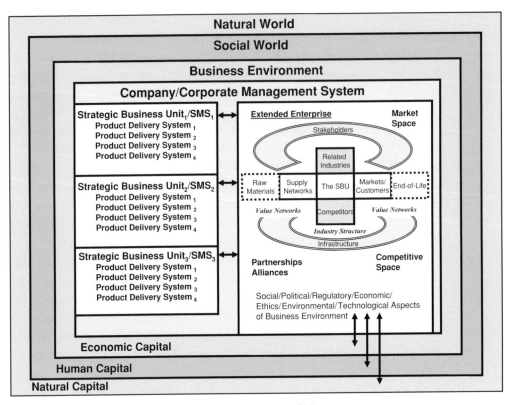

Figure 6.2   Example of a strategic management framework and SBU

essential elements of the natural environment and the social/human world are included. Strategic leaders in their deliberations may decide to include only specific ecosystems or social concerns. While certain elements must be included because of laws and regulations, most of the indirect natural and social aspects that should be included might be selected on the basis of their potential impact on the vision of the company, the mission of the businesses, and the realities of the business environment.

Each SBU is connected to the business environment, the social world, and its natural environment, and to the corporate level and other SBUs. Each SBU has one or more operating systems engaged in the production and delivery of the products and services. Figure 6.2 depicts linkages of the company with its external world and that of its SBUs. The graphic cannot represent all of the complexities involved. The operating system is called the product delivery system – also called the value delivery system.

Limiting the scope of the strategic management framework and under-reaching potential opportunities and challenges may leave the business vulnerable to more aggressive and far-reaching adversaries who have the courage and conviction to integrate their whole enterprise and the business environment. Likewise, businesses have to be careful not to take steps that are too radical from the organization's normal perspective, steps that may increase vulnerabilities by trying to do too much, too soon. It is usually preferable to expand the strategic management framework using logical steps, adding new elements each time questions on scope are revisited. While it is difficult to stipulate what the preferred scope must be, it is clear that it should include all of the basic elements of the extended enterprise (customers, supply networks, stakeholders, infrastructure, related industries, and competition). Indeed, it should include the next levels upstream and downstream, including the next level of depth of potential or emerging stakeholders, related industries, and competition. Moreover, it should include potential new customers in the outer market space, and the inclusion of new partnerships and alliances.

The geographic space can also be expanded to include new areas that pose potential challenges or represent opportunities for expansion before the company actually decides to start doing business there. Business can expand nationally or internationally. The former is often based on a logical progression. The latter is more complicated. As a rule of thumb, new countries (markets) might be considered for inclusion one planning cycle or five years before the actual actions are considered. Not only does this provide time for strategic leaders to analyze the situation in depth without risks and to sort out potential strategies and actions, but it also gives sufficient time for the business leaders across the organization to understand some of the possible interactions with or within other geographical areas. For instance, if the SBU plans to expand its operations into China, this may have implications for other operations in the US or Europe. Or, if the business unit wishes to sell products in certain Spanish-speaking countries in South America, it might want to leverage its knowledge of certain markets in California where there is a large Spanish-speaking population. Moreover, time allows the strategic leaders to understand the essential requirements for doing business. For example, Wal-Mart was unsuccessful in Germany; it may have implemented its expansion strategy before it had all of the requisite know-how.

The planning time horizon can also be expanded as the strategic leaders become more capable of assessing and dealing with the long term. Many companies and businesses use a five- or ten-year planning horizon. This means that they look out five or ten years, analyze the expected business situation during that time frame, and formulate objectives and strategies that cover the planning horizon. The choice of the planning horizon is dependent on many factors, including stability or turbulence in the business environment, the overall rate of change in business conditions, and the aggressiveness of the strategic leaders.

The greater the rate of change, the more likely the planning horizon is to be short (say five years). However, short planning horizons usually require short planning cycles. The planning cycle describes how frequently strategic leaders formulate new strategies and objectives. For instance, in the consumer electronics industries products have a life cycle measured in months. The rate of change is fast. Most companies may have a five-year planning horizon, but they also have a six-month planning cycle. With such a fast rate of change it becomes more and more difficult to envision what the business world will look like more than five years out; there may be three or four new generations of products during this time interval. To compensate for this short time horizon, strategic leaders generally have to spend more time on strategic analysis and strategy formulation and implementation.

Inclusiveness is not only a function of the external world, it applies to the internal management systems, operations, and functions of the SBU. It should include the people, capabilities, resources, and knowledge of the organization. It should also include the business portfolios, technologies, products, and brands. The more extensive the considerations the more likely it is that new strategic insights and innovative solutions will be discovered. Sound management systems are a critical factor in achieving success.

The strategic management framework is intended to be a dynamic view of the business world that provides a sense of what can be done in addition to what is happening. It gives strategic leaders a frame of reference and provides all participants in the strategic planning process with an overarching view of the existing and expected business situation. It helps to clarify complexities and maps out perspectives for decision making.

Understanding corporate strategic direction

A company's strategic direction is one of the preeminent management constructs driving change. Corporate strategic leaders receive inputs from the board of directors, the whole organization, selected external stakeholders, and even shareholders to decide how aggressive they want to be in orchestrating change, and preempting the needs, wants, and expectations of the business environment and market spaces. The strategic direction is the broad road map to the desired future of the corporation and all of its SBUs and their extended enterprises. It highlights the long-term targets (strategic positions and capabilities) that are seemingly unobtainable in the short term, but offer superior and sustainable advantages in the long term. It is a unifying and integrating construct that puts everyone in the corporation on an equal footing in terms of understanding what is desirable, where they are going, and how to make good decisions along the way.

The vision and the vision statement delineate executive management's aspirations for changing the company from "what it is" to "what they want to be" through transformations, transitions, and innovations. In well-managed companies and SMEs, the vision statement is developed through a consensus-building process in which many people have participated, and significant dialogs have resulted in desirable, feasible, discernible, and flexible statements about realizing sustainable success. Moreover, people in the SBUs must understand that the vision is an ambitious dream that requires ongoing updating as gains and improvements are made, and new opportunities and challenges arise.

Strategic leaders at the SBU can reinforce the vision through specific details that make the vision more understandable and actionable. Moreover, the strategic leaders are often the decision makers who have to make the vision real and communicate it across their organization. They have to explain the vision and its strategic logic, and then inspire people to personalize the vision and embrace the efforts and actions necessary to realize it.

Strategic management constructs

The purpose of strategic management constructs, like frameworks and management constructs, is to facilitate some understanding of the linkages, relationships, and interfaces between the company, its SBUs, and the external world. It includes the processes, actions, and decisions required within the SMSs to ensure that the essential requirements are covered and carried out. The notion of a business model has gained significant importance over the last decade as many successful businesses have used specific frameworks to link the external and internal dimensions into an integrated force for sustaining outcomes. The business model provides the logic and framework on how the elements fit together and what people have to do to be successful.

Gary Hamel, a visiting professor at the London Business School, one of the leading authorities on business model innovation, suggests that the business model is the critical management construct for creating value and wealth. In *Leading the Revolution*, Hamel defines the meaning and discusses the importance and implications of business models. He states:[3]

In the new economy, the unit of analysis for innovation is not a product or a technology – it's a business concept. The building blocks of a business concept and a business model are the same – a business model is simply a business concept that has been put into practice. Business concept innovation is the capacity to imagine dramatically different business concepts or dramatically new ways of differentiating existing business concepts. There are many ways of describing the components of a business model. I have created a framework that is complete, yet simple. A business concept comprises four major components: Core strategy; strategic resources; customer interfaces; and value networks.

Hamel's core strategy includes the business mission and the product–market scope. The basis for differentiation and strategic resources include core competencies, strategic assets, and core processes.[4] The link between strategy and customers are the benefits that are provided and enjoyed. People want benefits and solutions, not products. The link between strategy and resources is configuration or the way in which the elements are linked and interrelate with each other.[5] The link between resources (internal) and value networks establish scope and boundaries. Of course, value networks include the entities of the extended enterprise, especially suppliers, partners, and alliances. Company boundaries establish the perceived scope of the business model.

Hamel notes that the outcomes of business model thinking are incredible. According to him, many of the success stories like Wal-Mart, Home Depot, and eBay are due to their unique business models. He also invokes a new way of thinking about business strategy by expanding the view of the business arena from focusing on competitive spaces to a more holistic view of the whole value system (the extended enterprise). The strategic management framework and a specific business model provides a sense of integration, and an understanding of how the critical elements are connected. Business success depends on more than just defeating the competition, and business models include ways to think about the broader context and how to circumvent competition. For example, Canon developed a very elaborate business model focused on satisfying the basic needs of customers using the most cost-effective means to link its production system from the suppliers of suppliers – to the delivery of the products – to customers and the service of the products during their useful life.

The business model is intended to simplify the complexities involved in mapping out all of the elements in the extended enterprise. The power of business model innovation involves creating and articulating the means and mechanisms for all those engaged in the enterprise to visualize and deal with the linkages and interactions. Most of the older management constructs tried to deal with the complexities of the business world by simplifying the scope of the strategic management framework and defining narrow overarching perspectives. For instance, the concept of profit maximization may be easy to understand because the focus is on making money. But the simplicity of these objectives often made the lives of the implementers very difficult because they could not actually determine how to maximize profits and achieve all of the requisite objectives that were included. Strategically and philosophically, the underlying approach of strategic management thinking is to handle complexity during strategy formulation, and simplify strategy implementation through business models that make strategy execution easier. Larry Bossidy and Ram Charan, authors of *Confronting Reality*,[6] suggest that a "business model is a new name for an ancient analytical tool." They suggest a business model that is:[7]

a robust, reality-based process for thinking about the specific of your business in a holistic way. It shows you how to tie together the financial targets you must meet, the external realities of your business and the internal activities including strategy, operating activities, selection and development of people, and organizational processes and structure.

While it can be argued that there are many "targets" including social and environmental imperatives and other economic objectives, the notion that a business model involves the means and mechanisms to tie the enterprise together and have it function strategically is appropriate and important. Moreover, the business model depicts reality and allows strategic leaders to develop ways to connect the internal and external dimensions, understand what has to be included in the strategic analysis of the business environment and internal organization, and how to lead change and manage from a strategic perspective.

An effective business model outlines the framework and analytical techniques used to formulate and implement strategies and action plans. A business model may be synonymous with the construct of an SMS since they have similar purposes, except a business model generally focuses on implementation. The concept has undergone significant modifications over the last decade as more corporations try to determine what their business model should be and how to use it to capture sustainable advantages.

Strategic analysis: External context and internal capabilities

Overview

Strategic analysis involves an assessment of the current business situation in light of conditions, trends, opportunities, challenges, capabilities, and the resources of the organization. Exploring the external business context should precede the examination of the internal aspects. The meaning, value, and usefulness of the latter are dependent on the former. Great strengths and powerful competencies are meaningless in a business environment that no longer values their importance. For instance, in today's digital world of microelectronics and the Internet, many of the older analog technologies are on the wane. Most of the analog products have little value in comparison to the more powerful, cost-effective, and smaller digital devices that are easier to use, less expensive, and more reliable. Picture a cell phone of today versus the analog phones ten years ago that were the size of a laptop computer.

External context includes all of the dimensions associated with the business environment, market spaces, competitive spaces, and the associated opportunities and threats. Moreover, almost everything has to be defined in terms of the circumstances in which it exists. The external business world provides strategic leaders with an understanding of what context means, and defines opportunities and challenges. For instance, the fuel efficiency of cars did not seem very important in the late 1990s when crude oil was $10 per barrel. But, less than ten years later, following wars in the Middle East, it is a critical factor for success. Companies with more fuel efficient cars are better aligned within the context of markets and realities than those with gas guzzling vehicles.

Most factors are interrelated and are not only dependent on circumstances, but also on time. Remember that context involves space and time. What is a positive aspect today could be a negative one in the future. Likewise, what is a current threat could become an opportunity in just a few months from now. For instance, digital camera technology threatened Kodak in the 1990s, but now Kodak is taking advantage of the customer needs for digital prints, and has formed a new business unit to exploit these opportunities. Therefore, great care must be used to understand context in terms of the external world, not just from a company's existing perspectives. Most external factors are neither inherently good nor bad. Prevailing conditions and trends present opportunities and challenges.

Even so, there are situations and circumstances that are always undesirable, inherently dangerous and harmful. Catastrophic accidents, extreme weather events, the depletion of resources, pandemic diseases, wars and conflicts, among many others, are part of the realities of the world that no one would view as beneficial to business success. While it is clear that certain industries profit by selling products and services that respond to such circumstances, most people hope to eliminate the impacts of adverse situations. While such conditions and situations present business opportunities in the short term, most business leaders would prefer to focus on more positive ones.

When strategic leaders understand the business environment from the broader perspective and decide what it means, not the reverse, they have developed one of the keys to success. Opportunities and challenges drive strategic thinking, decision making, and action plans; therefore, strategic analysis should focus on what reality is and how it is expected to change over the time horizon (five, ten, or even twenty years from now). As previously stated, corporations and SBUs usually specify a time horizon that depends on the strategic nature of their businesses and what they are trying to accomplish.

Strategic analysis of the external context is based on the defined scope of the strategic management framework. One of the key questions during the initial phase is to determine what dimensions have to be examined and to what extent. Generally, businesses examine the most powerful direct factors and influences in the extended enterprise and market spaces. This approach starts with the external dimensions in terms of direct effects, impacts, and consequences – then drills deeper to understand the causes and the fundamental driving forces in the business environment. However, it can be argued that reversing the flow makes strategic sense as well. Starting with the broader dimensions of social, economic, environmental, technological, ethical, competitive, and market forces may provide a better understanding of the phenomena in the extended enterprise which make the strategic analysis of the other elements much easier to determine. Again, it is the context that sets the stage. In some business situations it is sensible to start with the extended enterprise and market spaces because they define what has to be explored in the business environment. For instance, retailers like Wal-Mart, Costco, Macy's, Carrefour (France), Marks and Spencer (UK), and METRO AG (Germany) have such an extensive customer base that they have to understand who they are serving before they can determine social and economic implications. Each of these retailers has a different clientele with different demographics and lifestyles. Knowing who the customers are is critical in determining the other facets of the business environment. Alternatively, in situations where radical new technologies may play a dominant role in the market spaces it usually necessitates a broad perspective about the changes occurring before one can drill into the specifics. Both approaches are correct, especially if the strategic analysis is completed within a reasonably short time.

Strategic analysis of internal aspects follows an understanding of the external realities. The power of capabilities and resources and even of product portfolios are a function of what they mean in context of the businss world. There are few inherently useful core competencies that are independent of the business realities. Analysis of the internal dimension is critical for determining what is possible and desirable. It is also a precursor to discerning what initiatives have to be taken to develop or augment internal capabilities and resources. The stage for formulating strategies is set by the total context of the business, not just the prevailing core competencies.

Strategic analysis: The external context

Assessing the business environment

Given the critical nature of the business environment, the strategic analysis of the external dimensions of the SBU involves an ongoing effort to provide an understanding of the forces impinging on the business. In corporations with related business units, monitoring and assessing the business environment can be done at the corporate level or centralized for multiple business units. For instance, car companies can perform strategic analysis at the corporate level for their truck and car divisions because they exhibit many common elements, and tend to be interrelated. On the other hand, more diversified corporations like GE and United Technologies Corporation (UTC) may organize such analyses by formal divisions or informal sectors. They then have a common effort to do the work for each division or sector. For example, UTC might combine the efforts of its SBUs whose focus is aircraft into an overarching sector that has one group doing analysis for its Pratt & Whitney, Hamilton Sundstrand, and Sikorsky Aircraft divisions. In corporations with mostly unrelated diversified businesses, each unit may have to undertake the efforts themselves. Obviously, leveraging efforts saves money and enriches the outcomes. Such collaboration may include working with other corporations who have similar business environments in which the players are not competitors. Hewlett-Packard, Electrolux, Braun, and Sony formed an alliance in the European Union (EU) to comply with its directives. Their electronics businesses face many of the same opportunities and challenges. Such companies could also participate in sharing information, data, and efforts on the strategic analyses of the business environment.

SBU leaders generally focus on the more specific elements of the business environment than corporate leaders. While they should also take a broad perspective, it makes sense that the strategic leaders concentrate on specific opportunities and challenges that directly impinge on the success of the SBU and its mission. Moreover, the time horizon is often shorter. While the corporate view may extend ten to thirty years into the future, the SBU's time horizon may be only five to fifteen years out.

Any assessment of the business environment can be divided into four areas that form a matrix based on time and implications. While there are other approaches, the following categories can help strategic leaders characterize their business environments as they relate to the SBU:

- Long term involving change – approximately ten to twenty-five years into the future where the effects, impacts, and implications would imply a shift in the mission and/or radical changes in the business strategies of the SBU.
- Long term involving stability – approximately ten to fifteen years into the future where the effects, impacts, and implications would not necessitate a shift in the mission and/or radical changes in the business strategies of the SBU.
- Near term involving change – approximately five to fifteen years into the future where the effects, impacts, and implications would imply a shift in the mission and/or radical changes in the business strategies of the SBU.
- Near term involving stability – approximately five to ten years into the future where the effects, impacts, and implications would not necessitate a shift in the mission and/or radical changes in the business strategies of the SBU.

While the selected time horizon is somewhat arbitrary, it may force strategic thinking about the long term, and the emerging trends in the business environment that may have significant consequences in the future. The key is to identify the existing opportunities, challenges, and threats and discover the less obvious ones that could make a significant difference in how the SBU thinks about its future mission and business strategies.

Strategic leaders and analysts have to be careful not to take a static view of the business environment. They must characterize and think about long-term effects and their implications. Indeed, from a strategic perspective, the assessment should focus on the SBU's opportunities, threats, challenges, and vulnerabilities of the future not just the present.

The dynamics of change in the business environment are significant driving forces, and the assessment must be framed in the context of the overall economic, social, political, legal, ecological, and technological conditions and trends. Anticipating trends before they become part of the mainstream provides a mechanism for determining new opportunities and potential challenges. The driving forces are often the precursors for identifying significant new product opportunities.

Table 6.1 covers the primary business factors with key considerations for each factor.

These elements provide a broad assessment of external factors in terms of conditions, trends, opportunities, and threats. The most important perspectives are the identification of the essential elements for analysis and a determination of their impact on forming new strategies and action plans. The questions listed provide a sample of the questions that may be asked. The actual list of questions is dependent on the SBU, the industry and markets served, and the strategic position of the organization.

The questions in Table 6.1 are not comprehensive, and represent only a small fraction of those that could, or should, be asked. It is imperative that strategic leaders think about these questions and the implicit need to find ways to turn problems into opportunities – and opportunities into action plans yielding positive results.

The ultimate objectives are to discover opportunities for enriching the SBU's prospects for the future and to mitigate potential threats and vulnerabilities. Such objectives are good for the businesses and good for the broader business environment as well. This is one of the main premises of the notions of what holistic thinking is, and what sustainable solutions are. Each of the questions can be based on how to create sustainable outcomes that enhance the wealth, longevity, and success of the SBU and its external relationships.

Assessing market spaces

Market spaces provide most of the direct opportunities for SBUs. Obviously, these opportunities revolve around the products and services that the SBU produces and markets, and the even better solutions that it is developing for its future positions. From a strategic perspective, market spaces and customers define market opportunities and challenges, not competitors.

Markets are generally characterized in traditional ways. These include industry structure, government classifications, and/or product–market types. The market definition is a primary consideration requiring thoughtful examination. Definitions that are either too general or too specific can distort the picture of true opportunity and lead to faulty conclusions. The market or market segment can be characterized as the total number of potential users of

Table 6.1 Scanning the business environment – selected questions pertaining to opportunities and threats

Factors	Conditions and trends	Opportunities/threats
Overall factors	What are the most significant driving forces? What are the causes of change? Is the business environment stable or turbulent?	What are the most important changes? What is the degree of uncertainty? What are the most important opportunities? What are the most critical threats?
Economic Business cycle Growth rate Stability Inflation	What are the general economic factors? Is the economy expanding or contracting? Is there overall economic stability? What are the effects of globalization? What is the inflation rate?	Are the current levels sustainable? What are the prospects for growth? Are monetary funds available at a low cost? Are there downward pressures?
Social Stakeholders Demographics Behavior Attitudes	What are the social norms and trends? How is consumer behavior changing? What are the demographic shifts? Have people changed their attitudes and behaviors?	What are the favorable /unfavorable changes in demographic? Are there opportunities and challenges associated with stakeholders? What are the new attitudes?
Political Political groups Public policy Legislation Regulation Stability	Who are the most powerful interest groups? How stable is government action? What are the new public policy issues? What new laws are anticipated? What are the regulatory mandates? Is the political climate stable?	What does government policy favor? What are the major changes? What are the opportunities due to changes? What are the negative consequences? What are the impacts of new laws? What are the positive and negative effects?
Ethical Principles Practices	What are the right behaviors? What are the proper ways of making decisions? How can negative effects/impacts be reduced?	What are the proper decisions when others are not acting responsibly? What are the best practices?
Technological Technologies Rate of change Inventions	What are the most important innovations? What are the rates of technological change? Are there new materials or substitutes? What are the sources of technology?	What technologies create new ways? What are the impacts of the change? Are life cycles declining? What are implications of the new inventions?
Environmental Degradation Depletion Destruction Disruption	What are the most costly regulations? What resources are threatened by depletion? What are the most destructive processes and the ones with the greatest risks and dangers? What are the effects and impacts on the natural environment and social world?	How can the negative effects be eliminated? What substitutes can be used that are more plentiful and less costly? How can such vulnerabilities be reduced? What are the means and mechanisms to eliminate threats, risks, and impacts?

the products and services – the served markets, the segments currently using the products and services, and the potential markets.

A market space assessment provides a broad analysis of key market factors, and their potential to provide opportunities for businesses. It is a technique used to discover opportunities and threats in market spaces, and to determine how attractive they are, or how negative they may be. It is used to identify the primary opportunities that are available for serving customers and satisfying needs, wants, and expectations in new and exciting ways. This broad assessment provides definition, and determines what markets and segments to address. The assessment examines prevailing conditions and trends, their importance, and what their potential consequences are. Subsequent examinations focus on how those opportunities are related to the capabilities and resources of the SBU, or those that have to be developed to take advantage of emerging opportunities.

Generally, the market space assessment is performed on each market segment, especially if they are large and/or represent significant opportunities. It is also done on the basis of market segments, especially when the overall market is fragmented into many pieces. For instance, the car industry has many different segments: from trucks and sports utility vehicles (SUVs) to cars and motorcycles. While each segment is different there are many overlapping factors, and customers may move easily from one to the other. On the other hand, the insurance industry is divided into many categories including property, health care, life, and liability. While a given customer may participate in several segments, customers do not move from segment to segment when shopping for a specific outcome. For instance, one does not buy flood insurance to provide protection against catastrophic health problems.

The analyses examine market opportunities, determine the key characteristics of the markets and their segments, and understand the overall requirements for being successful. At the SBU level, broad opportunities are examined so that effective strategies can be developed to create solutions and achieve sustainable advantages in the market spaces. Specific marketing strategies are typically developed at the product delivery level where the action plans are carried out. Remember, market space assessment is about understanding external realities, and techniques for taking advantage of the opportunities, not about marketing strategies.

Table 6.2 provides a template for conducting market space assessment. It includes many of the essential elements, and highlights some of the critical questions pertaining to the conditions, trends, and potential opportunities and threats facing the strategic business unit.

Table 6.2 Market space assessment – selected questions on conditions, trends, opportunities, and threats

Primary factors	Conditions and trends	Opportunities/threats

Market factors
Location
Size
Potential
Growth rate
Seasonality
Life cycle
Stability
	What or where is the market space?
	How large is the market space?
	What are the main markets and segments?
	What is each segment's potential size?
	How fast are they growing?
	Is market demand seasonal?
	What is the stage of its life cycle?
	Is demand stable?
	What is the risk of decline/obsolescence?
		Where are the markets? Emerging
		  markets?
		What are the major forces influencing
		  demand?
		What are the needs and wants?
		What are the main attributes required?
		Are there segments that are not being
		  served?
		What is the demand structure? Where?
		What is the long-term potential?
		What are the long-term opportunities?
		What are the long-term vulnerabilities?

Market aspects Variety Differentiation Legal Regulatory Price sensitivity Scale/volume	How are the markets segmented? How is the value proposition defined? How are products differentiated? What are the legal requirements? What are the regulatory mandates? What are the economic factors? How is market share distributed?	What determines value? What is the solution sought? What are the latent needs? Are there wants and needs that are not being served? Are there regulatory barriers? What are the absolute requirements? What is the available share?

Customer aspects
Satisfaction
Purchasing
  patterns
Applications
Pace of change
	What determines customer satisfaction?
	What are the critical factors for success?
	How is the product purchased?
	Who are the buyers of the product?
	Who uses the product?
	Do people have the money/resources to
	  buy?
	What are the change mechanisms?
		What are the essential benefits sought?
		What are the required features and
		  functions?
		How can relationships be built and
		  enhanced?
		How do people buy and use products?
		What are their most critical expectations?
		What contributes to customer success?
		How can credit become available?

Cultural aspects
Lifestyle
Norms
Support systems
Language
Sensitivities
	What are the most important cultural
	  aspects?
	What are the main social institutions?
	Are the living conditions satisfactory?
	Are the support systems stable and
	  working?
	Are the minimal human needs being met?
	Are language differences a barrier?
	What are the main sensitivities?
		What are the required new solutions?
		Can social institutions support the
		  solutions?
		How can the living conditions be
		  improved?
		What is necessary to improve the systems?
		What can be done to meet the basic
		  needs?
		How can language differences be handled?
		Can sensitivities become differentiators?

Market space assessment is also intended to find new ways to exploit existing positions, and discover new means and mechanisms for becoming more successful in the future. Opportunities are the underlying circumstances for future growth and success. More and more companies are viewing the success of their customers as the pivotal means for creating success within their corporations. Business success depends on the success of their customers and strategic partners. For example, BASF appears to understand that positive earnings and growth depend on making its customers successful in their businesses. Moreover, financial success is predicated on sustainable success across the enterprise. It also depends on having the best people possible in orchestrating that success. Enduring success involves making customers and partners successful.

Market space assessment is a critical part of a complex puzzle. It provides a sense of the most important opportunities for realizing the aspirations of the businesses and strategic leaders. Market space opportunities, especially those involving open space where there is not a lot of competition, as in many of the developing countries, are the precursors to other analyses for determining exactly what the SBU should focus on. The results are examined based on the capabilities and resources as discussed in the next section, and they fit into an overall context based on how they fit the strategic direction and the business portfolio.

Identifying opportunities and vulnerabilities in stakeholder space

Stakeholders require special considerations because of the diversity of the factors and considerations and the important roles they play in determining opportunities and vulnerabilities.[8] This topic was discussed in Chapter 4.

Stakeholder assessment involves identifying the most significant stakeholders across the extended enterprise of the SBU, and determining their importance to the success of the enterprise. It is more open-ended than market space assessment because it is not always apparent who the stakeholders are, or their interests. Stakeholder assessment includes the general interests of society, the social aspects, and special critical factors influenced by governments and NGOs. It includes many of essential elements, and highlights some of the critical questions pertaining to the conditions, trends, and potential opportunities and vulnerabilities facing an SBU. Critical stakeholder factors require ongoing attention and assessment. As in Procter & Gamble's anticipatory issues management approach discussed in Chapter 3, it is easier to identify and deal with issues early on, rather than trying to manage a crisis in full bloom.

Table 6.3 Stakeholder assessment – selected questions pertaining to conditions, trends, opportunities, and vulnerabilities

Primary factors	Conditions and trends	Opportunities/vulnerabilities
Social aspects Watchdogs Trade unions Religious groups	Who are the activists or watchdog groups? What are the agendas of the trade unions? What do the religious organizations advocate? What are the main social issues?	How can the agendas of activists be turned into advantages? Eliminating the issues? How can social aspects become opportunities? How can social problems be mitigated?
Critical factors Government agencies Industry standards NGOs Special interest groups Local communities	What are the laws and regulations that have to be complied with? What are the industry standards? Who are the key stakeholders? What are the special interest groups' agenda? Are there risks that are imposed on society? What are the needs and expectations of the local communities?	Are there stakeholder issues that can be reduced or dissolved? Can major constraints be eliminated? Are there laws and regulations that can be eliminated by new strategies and actions? How can risks be mitigated? How can local communities become more involved in creating solutions?
Financial groups Social investors Investment managers Media	What criteria are used by investors for making investment decisions? Who are the critical influencers in the decision-making processes in the financial communities?	How can openness and reporting translate into improved shareholder success? How can the media obtain accurate information that present a fair picture?

Stakeholder assessment is a relatively new approach in strategic management that is still being formalized in the mainstream of strategic thinking. Introduced by R. Edward Freeman, in *Strategic Management: A Stakeholders' Approach* in 1984,[9] he included customers, suppliers, and competitors as stakeholders; but they are really direct participants in the extended enterprise. However, constructs associated with stakeholder analysis are pivotal in understanding stakeholder issues, concerns, and interactions. They provide critical inputs for determining the true nature of the opportunities, threats, and/or vulnerabilities.

Early identification and definition of stakeholder-related situations are essential for understanding what the opportunities really are, or for eliminating threats or vulnerabilities. Like the assessment of the business environment, it is difficult to articulate a comprehensive list of all of the elements that any given business faces. Table 6.3 is a template for conducting stakeholder assessment. The questions are indicative of the areas that might be explored.

Assessing the intensity of the competitive landscape

Competitive space is a derivative of market space as discussed in Chapter 5. Competitive space is a perpendicular construct to that of the market space. Large companies often think in terms of beating the competition as the first order of importance. They then think about what is necessary to create unique and/or sustainable advantages in the market spaces. But, competition can be positive as well as negative. Competition may offer alternatives that expand market space for all of the contenders. A company or its competitors may discover ways that provide avenues for many others to follow. It is difficult to keep great opportunities a secret and even the most well-positioned company usually cannot exploit every possibility. While it can be argued that businesses can create market space through discoveries and innovations, in most cases the latent needs and requirements already existed in the market spaces, the potential customers were just waiting for the new solutions. This is an important distinction since it indicates that the primary way to overcome intense competition is to focus on the expectations of the market space first, and then to concentrate on how to engage competitive forces.

The central theme of many of the older, but still prevalent, strategic management constructs is rivalry among the industry competitors. As discussed in previous chapters, Porter's theory of five forces is among the most famous and well-known models for assessing competition. His is one of the most often quoted management constructs, and appears in most academic texts on strategic management. His model assumes rivalry and conflict but competition can be positive as well.

Competition can help build critical mass within an industry. Competitors may offer alternate and/or complementary products and services that complete the package of requirements to meet consumer needs.[10] The converse can become a problem. Limited customer options often open the door to alternatives or substitutes. While these actions are usually based on a variety of reasons, the trigger point that leads to new sources may be due to the limited actions of the competitors in the industry. In such cases, competitors act independently, but focus on maximizing their own positions instead of creating value across the enterprise to reduce the options and advantages for customers. For example, the US steel industry declined during the 1970s and 1980s as customers sought less expensive solutions from plastics, aluminum, and other materials. While the story is complex and involved technological obsolescence, international competition, and the inherent economic advantages of the alternative materials, the competitors in the steel industry focused too much on rivalry among themselves rather than solving the problems and creating better solutions for their customers. The principal players wasted their resources on industry conflicts instead of building harmony with customers. At the same time industry leaders and company executives fought with labor unions to the demise of both.

The degree and intensity of competition are critical factors in determining strategic positions and actions. During the mid twentieth century many industries and companies enjoyed a relatively calm competitive situation with a minimum of predatory behavior. Many industries were oligopolies with only a couple of competitors or had a few powerful companies, who often segmented the markets so that each was a principal in a given segment and had competitive advantages that were difficult to duplicate in the short term. For instance, the aluminum industry has only eight major participants. The industry leaders like Alcoa and Alcan focus on specific markets for achieving success. The former supplies semi-finished and finished products and the latter provides basic aluminum forms such as ingots and logs. This phenomenon was prevalent in the US and European countries where the indigenous corporations had tangible and intangible advantages like low logistics costs, high customer loyalty, and government support and protection. However, as globalization increased and competitive landscapes became global, competition increased as global companies became more forceful. This reduced the ability of competitors to gain sustainable advantages.

Richard D'Aveni, renowned professor of business strategy at Dartmouth College, says that companies gain competitive advantages through the following arenas: (1) cost and quality; (2) timing and know-how; (3) strongholds; and (4) deep pockets.[11] He suggests that competitors "drive costs down and quality up until the industry approaches the point of ultimate value."[12] His view of costs and quality is exactly on target – companies have to improve both so that value is enhanced. Timing and know-how are directly related to leading change and providing innovative solutions where the leaders generally have the advantages of setting the stage and determining the rules of the game and the standards for the solutions, at least as long as they are able to lead. Strongholds are preemptive positions, usually garnered by industry leaders that create huge difficulties for the other competitors. For example, Microsoft has a powerful position in software because people want interconnectivity and standard protocols. And, eBay has exceptional power due to the depth and breadth of its connections with millions of individuals who want to engage in business transactions with others, even for a single exchange. D'Aveni suggests that the giants can also rely on their financial clout to avoid competition or minimize it. ExxonMobil and Wal-Mart are good examples of companies with substantial resources and strategic positions that make it difficult for others to compete. Even the most successful of the competitors like Target and Costco have concerns when competing in retail spaces dominated by Wal-Mart. Moreover, the more strategic the advantage, the more powerful it is. For example, it is difficult to overcome Siemens' technological advantage built upon its 40,000 patents. It is a technology leader with a relatively long time horizon based on proprietary positions and the unique solutions it has for customers.

As national markets become increasingly infiltrated with global competitors, profits generally erode. The once dominant competitors often exhaust the positive means to differentiate their offering, or simply become less effective as others copy the successful approaches that created the competitive advantage in the first place. Remember, competitive advantages are time dependent, especially those involving products, processes, operations, and marketing.

As suggested earlier, the halcyon days of oligopolies have given way to the hyper-competition of the 1990s and 2000s. Hyper-competition negatively affects margins and financial performance. This hyper-competition described by D'Aveni has some of the following characteristics:[13]

- Firms aggressively position against one another by attempting to disadvantage opponents.
- Firms create new competitive advantages which make obsolete or match the opponents' advantage in one or more of the four arenas (per above).
- Firms attempt to stay ahead of their competitors in one or more of the four arenas.
- Firms create new competitive advantages that make the opponents' advantages irrelevant by moving to compete in another arena.
- Temporary advantages and short periods of profits are achievable until competitors catch up with or outmaneuver the aggressor's last competitive move.

It is expected that global competition will intensify as powerful new global competitors emerge from countries like China, India, Brazil, and Russia. Some of these companies have the capability to enjoy competitive advantages on the world stage due to the size of their home markets and/or their ability to design, produce, and market high-volume, low-cost products.

Battles are continuously fought, and new moves are initiated, but in the longer term few companies gain enduring advantages. Ultimately, everyone competes on the basis of price, and no one is able to obtain more than "normal profits" or in some cases, like the airline and automobile industries, most competitors struggle to be profitable if not to just survive. In certain cases, strategic leaders, especially those of the large companies, give up, sell and/or spin off the affected business. For example, IBM quit the personal computer business, Siemens sold its cell phone business, and Sears and K-Mart joined forces.

When aggressive competitive forays are the primary strategic approach, they usually result in outcomes that are typified by "sometimes you win and sometimes you lose." Moreover, even the big winners may lose in the longer term because they often exhaust resources fighting battles rather than creating real value. As existing competitors get worn down, new competitors emerge to take their place. For instance, competition in the global car industry is again on the rise as emerging companies in China and other developing countries replace older, ineffective competitors.

Competition can be categorized using numerous constructs to determine the imprint on the business landscape. Competition is the broad perspective on opposing forces in the market spaces vying for revenue, market share, and customer loyalty. They include existing competitors, new entrants, substitutes, and a myriad of alternative choices that are available to existing and/or potential customers. The main focus is usually on existing competitors, their strategic positions and capabilities. They are the frontline opposition typically viewed as the countervailing force to the success of the business unit and its value delivery system. Such views are generally correct because existing competitors normally have the biggest short-term impacts on market and financial performance. Customers often compare and contrast the offerings of existing competitors, and make their choices based on the most advantageous fit, even if they are far from perfect. This is especially the case when customers require an immediate solution and they have to make a decision, despite their dissatisfaction with the options available. This phenomenon often misleads all of the competitors to think that they have the means to satisfy customers when in reality the opposite is true. As the dissatisfaction grows, the existing competitors may become even more aggressive in competitive terms rather than becoming more aggressive in market terms.

These situations allow new entrants to become players even in highly competitive markets. One of the most important venues for new entrants is their emergence from non-market spaces or non-traditional markets into those occupied by the major competitors. New entrants usually have unique positions and offer certain benefits currently unavailable through the entrenched competitors. They typically use one or more new strategic advantages to make their presence felt and to gain market share. For example, Wal-Mart silently gained on the giants in the retail industry like Sears and K-Mart during the 1980s by using its low-cost structure to provide customers with more afford-able branded (high quality) products, especially for those people at the lower end of the economic structure.

Substitutes are competition from other sources or even industries. They provide alternate solutions in the form of different products and/or materials that satisfy basic customer needs and requirements. Such changes are often driven by technological innovation. Some of the classic substitutes include plastics for steel (as the former is lighter and more affordable), natural gas for powering electric generators in lieu of fuel oil because it is cleaner and easier to use, and cell phones versus wire-based telephones because they are flexible and mobile.

Assessment of the competition pertains to identifying the most significant competitors, new entrants, and potential substitutes. The primary purpose of competitive assessment is to discover ways to satisfy customers more effectively and to ensure that the company and its SBUs outpace existing competitors, new entrants, or potential substitutes in providing solutions to their customers. The focus is on making customers successful. It is not just about defeating competitors in the battle for market share and revenues.

The initial step is to identify and describe the key competitors. While this might include an exhaustive list of competitors who are part of the industry structure and serve some of the same markets that the business unit serves, the most typical competition assessment focuses on primary competitors, new entrants, and substitutes who pose the most significant threats and challenges to the actions of the SBU.

Knowing who the present or future competitors are is only part of the picture. It is critical to have a strategic profile of the competition across the board, and an understanding of their capabilities, strategies, and expected actions and responses to the SBU's strategies and action plans.

An overview of a competitive assessment is provided in Table 6.4. It high-lights some of the critical questions pertaining to the conditions, trends, potential threats, and/or vulnerabilities facing the SBU.

Competitor assessment requires accurate information and data about each of the major competitors. It is relatively easy to get information about existing competitors, but much more difficult to research new entrants and substitutes, especially in small companies with new-to-the-world technologies, products and materials. For existing competitors, information and data are gener-ally available from primary and secondary sources. Primary sources, such as company reports, Internet web pages, brochures, etc. are widely available,

Table 6.4 Competition assessment – selected questions pertaining to conditions and trends, and challenges and/or vulnerabilities

Primary factors	Conditions and trends	Challenges/vulnerabilities
Competitors Market share leaders Low-cost providers Differentiated players Niche players Imitators	Who are the most significant current competitors in the selected markets and/or product/market segments? How intense is competition? Who are the market share leaders? What are their visions, missions, objectives, and strategies? What are their core competencies/ capabilities and their strengths/ weaknesses? What are their current/anticipated strategies?	What are the advantages and disadvantages of the key competitors? What is their value proposition? What are the key differences and similarities? How do they differentiate their positions and products? What are the most likely competitive responses? Who are their strategic partners? What are their relationships?
New entrants Certain suppliers Unhappy customers Global corporations Emerging companies in developing countries	Who are the most significant potential competitors? What are the open opportunities for new entrants? What are their visions, missions, objectives, and strategies? What are their core competencies/ capabilities and their strengths/ weaknesses? What are their current and anticipated strategies?	What are the means and mechanisms available for new entrants? What are the barriers? What are the critical factors for success? What knowledge is required to new entrants to participate? How can they gain a foothold? What are their unique advantages, if any? Do they have strongholds in other markets? Do they have deep pockets?
Substitutes New technologies New products New materials	What are potential substitutes? What are the most likely sources? How can they influence customers? What is the expected timing of such substitutes?	What are the means and mechanisms available? What are the barriers? What are the critical factors for success? What knowledge is required? How can they gain a foothold? What are their unique advantages, if any? Do they have strongholds in other markets? Do they have deep pockets?

providing rich sources of information. Secondary sources include articles in trade journals, investment houses, case studies, trade shows, industry conferences, etc. A basic literature search should assess past history, the financial record of each competitor, and a current profile of their capabilities, positions, strategies, and initiatives.

As stated above, information and data on new entrants and substitutes are much more difficult to glean. New entrants can keep a low profile for many years until they have the means and mechanisms prior to bursting on the scene and making a run for market share. The story of Toyota is a good example. During the 1950s and 1960s it was an obscure provider of niche products to Japanese customers. Even after it entered the US market it was an insignificant blip on the competitive scene. Yet within three decades it was a significant player. In 2007, it became the number two car maker.

By the time the major competitors realize the threats posed, successful new entrants have often gained a foothold that provides a solid foundation for ongoing success. Moreover, they often have significant advantage because they invested in crafting solutions and building value systems that are superior and modern. For example, Nippon Steel was able to take on the American giants like US Steel because it had the advanced technologies (basic oxygen) and modern manufacturing equipment and plants. In many of these kinds of situations, the prevailing competitors often exhaust their strengths and resources fighting what they perceive to be the main competitive battles. In many such cases, the competitive forays simply result in losses for everyone. It is akin to the battles of the First World War in which the armies on both sides suffered horrendous losses with few prospects of winning. Only when after the US entered the war did the tide turn in favor of the Allies.

The threat of substitutes can be even more insidious since it is difficult to determine their origin, or predict expected effects, impacts, and implications. Main sources include new technologies, new value systems and/or value chains, enhanced value propositions, and improved product characteristics and/or solutions among many others. The most obvious is the potential impact of technological change on the prevailing competitive scene. New technologies can disrupt the entire competitive landscape creating not only new-to-the-world products and processes, but new competitors from outside the original industry. Business history is replete with stories of wholesale substitution from the wooden ships to powered steel-hull vessels for ocean travel, to the jet engine replacing piston radial engines, and personal computers devastating the businesses of producers of typewriters and other mechanical devices.

Substitution also occurs when innovators improve their value chain and value delivery system making them more efficient and effective. For instance, the internet has had a dramatic effect on how to market, sell, and deliver books and other more complicated products that require a lot of information for customers to understand what they are buying. The Internet allows the dissemination of large quantities of information that is both cost-effective and easy to manage. It is now essential for success in many product–market categories, especially for disseminating information and providing access to specialty products. With new means and mechanisms, non-traditional competitors arise, able to compete in market spaces that would have been difficult to enter because they could not match the scale and reach of the established companies.

Substitution simply involves alternate ways to accomplish the desired end – *the solution*. For example, Amazon eliminated the need for huge investments in retail bookstores by selling its products online. It by-passed the conventional industry structure that presented significant disadvantages and barriers to entry by start-ups. Because of the efficiency and effectiveness of the innovative business model used by Amazon, many existing competitors like Barnes and Noble established their own websites. Others who were unable to follow, especially the smaller bookstores, went out of business. Moreover, the online information wiped out the competitive advantage of expert booksellers and his or her knowledge of books.

Radically improving the value proposition is another form of substitution that is less apparent, but often more effective. Recycled materials or remanufactured products are examples of how the end products remain the same, but the means and mechanisms are substantially different. A recycled aluminum can is a good example of the former. The final material is the same, but it costs less to produce and the capital equipment requirements are about one-tenth of the investment required for a state-of-the-art modern smelter. The cost saving associated with using remanufacture and/or refurbished equipment is an example of the latter. Xerox makes more money selling refurbished copiers than new ones. It is more cost-effective and profitable to upgrade the electronics and replace only the worn parts than it is to produce a new machine.

Substitution can also occur when the existing products and processes are simplified. Microsoft's Windows' graphical user interface (GUI) dramatically changed the PC market by enabling many more people to use PCs because GUI made using a PC easy. While Microsoft was not the first or only adapter of GUI, the company popularized it, and set the standard. Its less complicated applications allowed individuals to prepare their own documents using desktop software like MS Word or PowerPoint. The software was not only easier to use, it made correcting mistakes easy – one of the big limitations of typewriters. Microsoft transformed the world of specialists who knew how to use typewriters or the early word processors using complicated software into the world of the everyday person.

As stated above, the competitive landscape is actually a subset of the market spaces. It is based on the producers' perspective of the products and services provided rather than the customers' perspectives and demand side of what customers desire and expect. Great care has to be used to ensure that the focus remains on the markets and customers, not just on the rivalry among the competitors.

Assessing supply networks

Supply networks include those suppliers and distributors who support the production and distribution of products and services. Supply networks involve the flow of materials and finished goods, information and relationships from suppliers through production, the distribution channels to customers. Supply networks are becoming more dynamic and important because many global corporations and even SMEs are outsourcing many of the fabrication requirements and production requirements. Moreover, six-sigma quality initiatives and the demand for high-quality inputs have made selecting qualified suppliers and distributors more difficult to execute and more important for achieving sustainable success.

Supply network assessment includes the identification, understanding, analysis, and the determination of the physical, managerial, informational, and systems requirements and their effectiveness. The assessment involves a comprehensive analysis of capabilities of the supply networks, their resources, and performance. Moreover, the assessment involves determining how the relationships are working, and that the products, processes, practices, and behaviors meet industry standards, government mandates, and customer expectations. Some of the most important items are to:

- determine critical strategic supply networks, and their related materials, resources, products;
- identify the main strategic suppliers and distributors;
- prioritize requirements in order of importance to the success of the business:
  - strategic materials that are critical for design decisions, or proper production flow;
  - expensive or long lead-time items that are critical for production;

- ○ standard materials, parts, and components that are not critical for product development or production;
- ○ commodities that are always readily available;
- determine vulnerabilities and sources of alternatives;
- determine how well the products, processes, practices, and behaviors meet expectations;
- assess risks to the business and the corporation's reputation due to the actions of supply networks.

It is often difficult to determine the critical providers of suppliers, requiring an in-depth understanding of the flow of goods and information from cradle to grave. It also necessitates an understanding of the embedded relationships within the supply networks. This involves identifying the critical strategic suppliers and distributors, and knowing who the most important contributors are. While there are certain strategic goods or critical items that are easy to determine, many of the raw materials, parts, components, and other inputs require more extensive analysis to identify the critical items and what has to be tracked. For instance, while most PC manufacturers and/or assemblers know that Intel and AMD are critical suppliers, it may not be as apparent where the vulnerabilities lie for their other strategic resources. Copper wire may become the scarcer resource in the future.

Disruptions on manufacturing operations in many of the developed countries occurred during the late 1970s due to problems associated with the oil crises. During normal times, companies make assumptions about the flow and availability of upstream goods and energy that are generally correct; but nevertheless these are assumptions. More recently, Hurricane Katrina not only had devastating effects on New Orleans and the Gulf Coast, it caused disruptions in the flow of petroleum, and brought those assumptions into question.

Even in good times there may be difficulties with the supply networks. Both Airbus and Boeing have had problems getting suppliers fully integrated into their systems so that components were always available to assemble the final products. Airbus's A380 and Boeing's 787 are both behind their schedules because of constraints in the supply channels.

Determining and prioritizing the most critical requirements of the supply networks requires a tailored framework for each company/SBU based on its specific situations. The framework should focus on the specific materials, resources, and products of the supply networks that might impact strategies and action plans. This includes determining what is strategic or what has long lead times that might disrupt production or sale of products. The assessment should examine the benefits of outsourcing the fabrication or production of selected parts or even products to high-quality suppliers. A prevailing theory suggests that standard items and commodities might be good candidates for outsourcing, but great care should be given to strategic materials. The advantages and disadvantages of sourcing from outside the company, the impacts associated with the supply networks, and an evaluation of the alternatives should all be considered. The assessment should also consider the overall goals related to supply networks: mapping the flow processes linking the suppliers and distributors; analyzing existing and potential capabilities of each supplier and distributor; identifying internal and external relationships; establishing policies, procedures, and guidelines for the interactions; setting priorities for the flow of goods and the improvements in the processes; resolving conflicts; and evaluating performance. It also includes ensuring that a supplier and distributor development process is in place, and is functioning properly.

Supply network considerations for critical items include seeking options for troublesome issues, finding alternatives for unfavorable supplier and distributor situations, determining whether to make or buy, and establishing strategic relationships to stabilize costs and/or availability problems with critical suppliers and distributors. Many companies have a tendency to focus on the prevailing aspects of the supply networks. They focus on the obvious and the immediate to the exclusion of obtaining a full understanding of vulnerabilities associated with supply networks, and how to mitigate the underlying risks.

Often assessments fail to consider the more in-depth aspects of the long-term viability of the suppliers and distributors, or whether they have any inherent flaws that could lead to problems in the future. For instance, pending laws and regulations may heighten the difficulty or cost of certain materials like heavy metals or other toxic substances. Such problems may reflect not only on the suppliers or distributors but on the producers of the end products as well. Strategic leaders have to be concerned that problems in the supply networks do not become their problems, because they did not understand the breadth and depth of the situation, and take proper precautions. This includes ensuring that the company is engaging credible and trustworthy entities in the supply networks. In the final analysis, supply network assessment goes beyond ensuring that requirements are met. It also involves protecting the goodwill, reputation, and strategic position of the company and the business unit. Reputation can be damaged by the inappropriate or illegal actions of the entities that strategic leaders select.

Assessing the implications of related industries

Related industries include manufacturers and marketers of complementary products and services, providers of software and information, and many others whose outputs help to reinforce the value and benefits that customers derive from the SBU's own products and services. Many authors and practitioners are also called "complementors." Related industries usually provide positive outcomes that are important, if not critical, to the proper functioning and use of the SBU's products and services. The most obvious example, but one that is usually taken for granted, is the complementary relationship between automobile producers and the petroleum industry. Petroleum companies are part of a related industry that supports automobile manufacturers with vital complementary products essential for customers. Without gasoline, diesel, or other fuels cars would be just expensive stationary devices of seats, radios, CD players, etc. without much value, utility, and of course mobility. Moreover, related industries are often essential for success. For example, Disney World depends on the airline industry to provide the means to get customers to Florida and rental car companies to provide them with local transportation.

Complementary products and services are often designed and developed by companies that are completely independent of the efforts of the primary producers. They scan the business environment to discover opportunities that fit their strategic perspectives and product portfolios. There are numerous situations and many examples. For example, leather goods manufacturers make bags and gear for all types of devices from cameras to computers. Other examples include ancillary products that make the primary products more valuable and easier to use. Printer manufacturers make digital cameras and PCs more effective by making it easier for customers to immediately print their results. Electrical surge protectors safeguard primary electrical devices like computers by eliminating usage concerns due to power loss and supply problems. In such cases, many of the complementary products already exist and just have to be adapted to fit new situations. Moreover, in most of the cases, especially those where the primary producers had no input, the companies in related industries are fully responsible for their actions and outcomes. However, there are often formal and informal relationships where one company supports the other through marketing efforts or information exchange.

The primary producers may link with companies in related industries on a formal basis to create added value for customers by providing a full package of products and services. Enhanced value creation can be achieved through the integration of the efforts of the primary producers and those of the complementary products. Such integration theoretically allows two or more companies to optimize the overall package so that it is better linked, and provides more benefits with fewer negatives. "Wintel", one of the most famous of such links, is an informal tie between Intel and Microsoft – they collaborate to develop mutually aligned microprocessor and operating systems that function best together. Another example is Apple's alliance with AT&T in the distribution of the iPhone.

Related industries are important, if not critical, but great care has to be exhibited to ensure that there are no undue risks being assumed by either party. Closer relationships with the companies in the related industries require the parties to assume greater responsibilities for direct and indirect effects and impacts, and the implied duties to mitigate the inherent difficulties to the extent possible. GM has designed cars capable of using E85 (85% ethanol). It has implied responsibilities to ensure that E85 is used safely and that the producers are providing the appropriate fuel. It needs to coordinate with producers of E85 to assure that it is used safely and effectively.

The assessment of related industries is similar to the assessment of the supply networks, except the focus is on examining the players instead of the choices, and the essence of the relationships between the parties. It involves a comprehensive analysis of the capabilities of related industries and how well they are able to provide support mechanisms. The most important items include:

- Identification of the main strategic related industries;
- Determination of critical implications;
- Prioritization of requirements in terms of the importance to the success of the business;
- Analysis of concerns and vulnerabilities;
- Assessment of risks to businesses.

Given the broader perspective of related industries, the assessment is more open-ended and it is more difficult to define precisely who should be studied and what the impacts and implications are. However, in many situations, the strategic players in the related industry are relatively easy to determine. For example, car manufacturers are working with Shell-Hydrogen to help develop a hydrogen fuel infrastructure for the potential applications of fuel-cell based vehicles.

Identifying the critical companies in related industries and determining their importance are central to understanding what has to be done to improve the complete package of the offering, and requisite support services. SBU leaders can then decide whether to have related industries provide some aspects of

the package, to form partnerships with selected companies in related industries to ensure that the packages are complete and fulfill the requirements,
or to take on the responsibilities themselves. Each has advantages and disadvantages. The advantages for taking direct responsibility for outcomes are
that strategic leaders can theoretically control the strategic initiatives under
the management of the SBU, and ensure that proper solutions are provided.
The main disadvantage is stretching the resources of the SBU and potentially
entering business activities that are not core to the success of the organization,
or where it lacks the knowledge, capabilities, and resources to be successful.
Cooperation among the parties may optimize each of their capabilities and
objectives. The disadvantage of integrated actions includes the assumption of
responsibilities for the actions of the other parties which may lead to problems,
including risks and liabilities. The advantage of the independent approach is
that the SBU usually does not assume potential liabilities and risks. The disadvantages of independent actions include outcomes which may be random
and a complete solution may not be available.

As with supply networks the assessment must include a full understanding
of the associated vulnerabilities and a determination of how to mitigate the
risks. For instance, if two complementary companies are too closely linked,
the problems of one may spill over to the other – or customers may retaliate
against both if they believe that the links restrict their options instead of
creating better solutions. Care must be taken to ensure that the approaches
are perceived to be positive and beneficial to customers. Management has to
ensure that the solutions are appropriate and that customers still have viable
alternatives. The purpose is to create better solutions, not to restrain customer
options or their prerogatives.

Assessing the implications of the infrastructure

Assessing the infrastructure is not very common in most strategic management approaches, because the external infrastructure is often assumed to
be more than adequate, at least in the developed countries. However, such
assumptions may be poor ones in many developing countries and even in
the developed countries there may be concerns due to terrorism, maintenance inadequacies, or failures to keep pace with technological changes. For
instance, highway congestion makes the automobile less valuable in such circumstances even though the manufacturers provide high-quality and reliable
products.

The publicly owned and quasi-public external infrastructures include Internet communications, the airways, the highways, the waterways, sanitation

systems, water systems, and atmosphere, etc. The privately-owned external infrastructure includes telecommunications, energy systems, railroads, shipping, buses, and numerous means of transportation. The precise fit into specific categories is not critical, but the means and mechanisms to support businesses and customers are very important. Infrastructure supports the production and distribution of goods and makes serving markets more cost-effective. One of the main strategic advantages that most companies enjoy today is the relatively low costs of long-distance transportation. The transportation networks add valuable contributions that facilitate movement. For example, the emergence of Netflix, a one-day delivery service for DVD movies relies on the low cost and reliability of an efficient US postal service, and growing residential broadband access.

The infrastructure also provides the means to handle, transport, process, and eliminate the wastes and pollution generated during the production of the products or during the applications. The infrastructure offers producers and customers ways to improve their ability to communicate with each other, increasing speed and reliability and enhancing overall product and system quality.

The infrastructure supports the value delivery system and provides the means to link key players. It provides real and virtual networks that link suppliers, producers, and customers so that they can acquire the requisite information, goods, and services.

Assessing the infrastructure involves examining the system requirements of the SBU as they relate to the infrastructure, and making determinations about the adequacy of the infrastructure to support the requirements. The assessment can take the form of a functional analysis to ascertain the quality and reliability of linkages. A critical infrastructure supports requirements. For instance, a critical step is to identify the viable means and mechanisms available to support the requirements of the SBU (i.e. highways, airlines, and ships).

The second step is to perform a functional analysis of the requirements. The analysis includes a determination of the scope of the system available, the quality of the resources, the effectiveness of the solutions, the risks associated with usage, and the cost-effectiveness of the outcomes. It also describes and assesses the sophistication of the capabilities and constraints of the infrastructure. It provides an understanding of what the infrastructure can do and cannot do.

The third step is to prepare a synthesis of the functions into a comprehensive view of how the capabilities and constraints support or limit the viability of using a specific aspect of the infrastructure. For example, if railroad cars are selected to move toxic gas like chlorine, what are the implications? Can the systems support the requirements for safe and low-cost transport? Are there constraints that have to be managed or limit the applications? The analysis would include every facet of the transport system to ensure that it can safely meet the requirements. If it cannot meet the requirements, some other solution must be determined. In certain cases, where there are no viable solutions, the assessment suggests that such products are not worth producing and other solutions should be explored.

Assessing the infrastructure is open-ended, and it is difficult to articulate a general approach that would fit even a majority of the situations. A general assessment involves a comprehensive analysis of the capabilities of the infrastructure and how well it is able to provide the support mechanisms. The most important actions are to:

- Identify main resources and support structures;
- Determine critical implications;
- Prioritize requirements in relation to the importance of business success;
- Determine concerns and vulnerabilities, and assess risks.

The infrastructure plays a vital role in supporting the strategic decisions of business leaders. The infrastructure provides physical links to customers and distribution channels. It includes the means to complete the network of activities for obtaining the raw materials and getting the product into the hands of the customers. The assessment of the infrastructure provides strategic leaders with the confidence that their solutions are viable and can be implemented successfully. This is necessary when dealing in emerging markets.

Strategic analysis: Internal capabilities and resources

The distinction between capabilities and resources is a critical one, especially in preparing strategic analysis. It is important to separate the two. Capabilities, intellectual capital, and human skills and talents are much more difficult to duplicate. For instance, there are thousands of football stadiums around the world, but there are only a handful of players who have the football skills and talent of a Pele. Resources are usually more commonplace than human capabilities. While resources are often viewed as scarce and require capital to acquire, the requirements for resources are easier to contemplate and even obtain. Moreover, they are relatively easy to duplicate. For instance, Wal-Mart has hundreds of superstores, each modeled after the previously successful ones.

Assessing the core competencies and capabilities

Core competencies are the powerful strengths and capabilities that are unique to the organization, and are difficult for others to emulate. C. K. Prahalad and Gary Hamel define core competencies as "the collective learning in organization, especially how to coordinate diverse production skills and integrate multiple streams of technologies."[14] Core competencies are great to have, but they may be difficult to maintain. Whereas during the 1990s corporate and strategic leaders viewed core competencies as a way to determine where they should focus their attention (i.e. on areas in which the businesses enjoyed core competencies), the strategic perspective today is less certain. While it makes sense to invest in businesses that are strong and where the company has huge advantages, it is often not clear how long those advantages will last, and whether they will be as meaningful in the long term. As the business environment changes more quickly, new technologies, processes, and business practices may undercut the benefits of the core competencies of an organization. In a world of rapid change, it may be risky to assume that today's core competencies will be viable tomorrow. For example, if cars powered by fuel cells become viable, what happens to the value of the car industry's knowledge of internal combustion engines?

Core capabilities are similar to the notion of core competencies, except that they are not necessarily unique. While the SBU may enjoy many exceptional core capabilities, it can be assumed that other companies echo these strengths. Capabilities are distinctively human in nature, and are not resources in general. Capabilities relate to people and the intellectual capital of the organization. This is a critical distinction, since people are unique. They can move from company to company. If their contributions are lost, they are not easily replaced.

The purpose of a core competencies and capabilities assessment is to determine whether there are sufficient capabilities in specific areas to formulate and implement strategy and action plans. Table 6.5 provides an overview of some of the main elements of a competencies and capabilities assessment. It highlights some of the critical questions pertaining to the understanding of the current situation and determining future requirements.

The assessment includes the quality of the overall intellectual capacity and the number of people necessary to achieve critical mass. It also includes a general overview examining the adequacy of the existing capabilities and a determination on what additional capabilities are required in the future. While the assessment is often based on examining the current situation and trends, it should also provide some perspective on what has to be improved,

Table 6.5 Competencies/capabilities assessment – selected questions pertaining to the understanding of the current situation and determining future requirements

Primary factors	Understanding current situation	Determining future requirements
Competencies Technical Marketing Production Finance Intellectual capital Development Relationships	What are the core competencies of the organization? What are the sources of the competencies? Are the core competencies powerful enough to obtain or maintain sustainable advantages? How are core competencies protected? What is their expected longevity?	Do they provide a power position? Do they have to be enhanced? How can they be exploited to gain advantage? What are the risks and vulnerabilities? What can be done to mitigate risks and vulnerabilities? Do people have the mindset to be leaders?
Capabilities Technical Marketing Production Finance Intellectual capital Development Relationships	Does the organization have the knowledge, skills, and capabilities necessary to carry out all facets of its mission? What are the essential capabilities of the organization? What qualities does the organization enjoy? Do people respect the core values of the corporations? What are the organization's capabilities to innovate? Are all of the essential critical areas covered by robust capabilities?	What are the strengths and weaknesses of the organization's core capabilities and what has to be improved to meet future needs? Can the organization enhance existing capabilities and develop the requisite new capabilities to meet new requirements? What is its ability to learn and what is its learning rate?
Leadership Executive Strategic Operational	What are the strategic leadership capabilities of the organization? Does the organization have them leaders and people who are innovative and can create sustainable solutions?	Can the strategic leadership be significantly improved? Does management have the mindset to lead change? Are leadership and personnel development programs adequate to meet the future needs?

enhanced, or changed. The big weakness of most capability assessments is that they focus too much on the existing situation and not enough on future scenarios.

Whereas many businesses focus on their core competencies and try to determine their strengths and weaknesses, it is also crucial to determine the overall core capabilities of the enterprise. Analysis must ensure that they meet the requirements of the external dimensions, and are aligned with the challenges of the business environment. It is great to have several unique core competencies, but if the rest of the organization or extended enterprise is deficient in several areas, then the advantages may be nullified and the overall results are actually net-negative. It is imperative that the organization enjoys a complete array of capabilities that are balanced and powerful across the business spectrum. Moreover, great care has to be taken when focusing on core competencies and outsourcing those areas that are deemed to be less important. The business environment is highly dynamic, and core competencies are quickly emulated in many cases. An organization's position of power may be quickly reduced. For instance, giants like GE and Motorola became six-sigma companies with outstanding quality capabilities. But, many other global corporations were also quick to adapt six-sigma quality capabilities. Indeed, many core competencies have only a short life span and advantages are quickly lost.

Moreover, seemingly tangential areas may become critical requirements. Managing suppliers was once relegated to relatively low levels in the operating system, but today it is usually viewed to be of great strategic importance as most large companies depend on supply networks to provide a large percentage of the inputs for products and services, especially if they engage in extensive outsourcing. Thus, supply chain management moved from a seemingly insignificant process to one that had strategic significance.

Strategic leaders have to reflect on both the organization's strengths and weaknesses of their organizations. The old philosophy was to exploit the competencies and strengths, and minimize the importance of weaknesses. Now, strategic leaders not only have to think about ways to protect the core competencies and strengths of the organization, but also to find ways to overcome the weaknesses. In today's business world as much attention has to be given to addressing weaknesses if the organization is to prosper. Certain weaknesses may become the Achilles' heel that prevents the company from achieving lasting success. In some cases, a small number of unchecked weaknesses may cause significant barriers to success or even outright failures. Imagine a great soccer (football) team with ten world-class players who have to depend on a totally inept goalie that is last in the league at preventing the other teams from scoring. The skill, competencies, and efforts of the ten great players are nullified by the incompetence of the one. Likewise in business, a small number of weaknesses can cancel out many of the organization's great strengths. For instance, the perceived inability of American car manufacturers to design fuel-efficient and reliable cars has offset the effectiveness and success of their improvements in costs and quality.

Capabilities include specific areas like research and development, product design and development, marketing know-how, manufacturing skills, financial management, and administration. Capabilities involve people and how they develop ideas and insights, and convert them into realities. The capabilities of the organization are the intellectual means for translating opportunities into positive outcomes, and turning challenges and threats into neutral or even positive possibilities. Assessing these intangibles is often difficult because future outcomes are impossible to predict, especially those associated with radical innovations. Imagine assessing the value of the work of such geniuses as Thomas Edison, Nikola Tesla, and the research and development team at Bell Labs that invented the transistor prior to their inventions and the acclaim they realized. Many such people are deemed to be failures until their great breakthroughs.

The knowledge, skills, and capabilities of the organization are among the most important strengths and assets, yet they are among the most difficult areas to judge. Often there are overarching skills and assets that make the organization successful. The focus has to go beyond core capabilities in engineering, marketing, production, finance, and other critical areas. All capabilities have to be examined including the ability to think out-of the-box, be creative, be compassionate, and lead change. Moreover, the perspectives must contemplate how core capabilities are enriched over time through learning and the acquisition of new talent. Strengths can be measured in terms of the qualities of the intellectual capital of the organization and the number of talented people in each of the main arenas. Actual determinations are usually qualitative rather than quantitative. The value and contributions of leaders and people are difficult to measure with precision.

Several of the qualitative measures look at motivation, and the mindset of employees on doing the best they can. Having a positive mindset leads to an organizational willingness to learn, and take on new challenges. It involves individuals accepting the core values of the organization, and being ready to defend them. It also involves being innovative and taking risks to improve and expand the possibilities.

Enterprise-wide strategic leadership (ESL), as discussed in Chapter 3, must be an essential core capability. Poor or self-interested leadership is often a significant factor in the demise of many organizations. Like the profound negative impact of having a poor goalie, incompetent leadership often has dire consequences for the fortunes of their organizations. Good companies with good people are sometimes led by people without expertise in leadership or willingness to subordinate their own personal goals. These situations often result in poor outcomes for everyone.

Assessing the leadership capabilities of an organization is one of the most arduous yet crucial tasks associated with strategic analysis. It is difficult for executives and boards of directors to objectively determine the capabilities and potential contributions of key strategic leaders. There are often many reasons for the lack of short-term performance. The incumbent may be relatively new in the position and the strategies and action plans need time to come to fruition. On the other hand, entrenched strategic leaders who constantly promise great achievements that are seemingly imminent but are never achieved are often given too much leeway. There are no simple answers.

Moreover, there are the common practices of focusing on short-term achievements rather than a more reflective and balanced approach on both short-term outcomes and the long-term prospects. The history of most businesses suggests that many strategic leaders gave too much attention to the short term and not enough to the long term. Assessing leadership is fraught with many challenges including pressures on the responsible individual (the person doing the assessment) or the governing parties (executives and boards) to placate the person being assessed, or to postpone dealing with problems, or the lack of objective methods and criteria for making impartial assessments. It is difficult to precisely define what strategic leaders are supposed to do and whether they are on track or not in fulfilling their responsibilities. This is at least a problem in the short term. However, if negative results continue into the long term, much damage may be done, and many of the problems may become irreversible. The challenges are endless. Great organizations are driven by great people and good leaders. Indeed, corporations and SBUs are social organizations dependent on the people that lead them, and the people that contribute to their success.

Assessing the vital resources

Resources are the assets of the organization that are used to transform ideas, concepts, and inputs into outputs and outcomes that sustain the businesses and contribute to success. They provide for the conversion of inputs into outputs; or they are the inputs, outputs, or conversion devices themselves! Resources are things; they are property. They can be acquired, owned, and sold. They are rarely unique and in most cases can be replaced if damaged or lost. While resources can be scarce, especially in a given circumstance, they are often replaceable by converting one form to another. The most obvious is the exchange of money for goods.

While the precise distinction between tangible and intangible resources is not critical, it is often the latter that differentiates the former from just being static and having commodity status to a dynamic and highly valuable means to create extraordinary value. Resources include the portfolios of businesses, the technology platforms, product lines, and support services of the organization. They are the assets that are owned and controlled by the SBU. They are the means for accomplishing the end results. Technologies, patents, products, processes, and even business units may also be viewed as resources.

Resources are the means to achieve the objectives of the organization. They include plant and equipment, facilities, buildings, inventories, and money. They also include the input into production of products or for providing services. They are the outputs that can be sold to other producers or end customers. They may help to determine the overall value of a business(s) and the ability to transform inputs into desirable outputs and successful outcomes. However, resources tend to be static in terms of usefulness and strategic value. It is how they are combined and used to create value that makes them power assets in achieving the goals of the organizations. Only value-added resources contribute to customers' needs, requirements, and success as discussed in Chapter 1. For example, Toyota invented lean production and lean business practices to focus on value-added activities and eliminate waste and non-value-added resources.[15]

Assessing the value of resources is less complicated than that of core capabilities, but it is still difficult to fully determine their usefulness. The assessment has to reflect on both the quantitative and qualitative aspects. Quantitative assessment focuses on the number and size of the resources. In some cases, having a lot of certain resources, typically deemed to be good, is actually a long-term deterrent. For example, GM had overwhelming production resources during the 1950s and 1960s causing executives at the time to assume that those assets were so powerful that GM would be successful regardless of the competitive actions of Ford and Chrysler. As discussed earlier, Toyota had such a weak position in relation to resources that its strategic leaders realized that they had to change the nature of their production system. It turned a weakness into a strategic advantage using lean methods. GM did not contemplate these challenges because its views were masked by the seemingly overwhelming strengths of its huge resource base and formidable product portfolios.

Simply examining resources on the basis of quantities or strengths and weaknesses is not only a static perspective, it can also mislead strategic leaders to think that they have advantages when none exists. During most of the twentieth century US Steel perceived that it had enormous strengths because of its manufacturing capacity to produce steel. But by the 1970s much of its capacity was obsolete and its strength in numbers became a weakness.

Qualitative assessment focuses on the value of resources and their contribution in obtaining strategic advantage. It focuses on the long term to ascertain for how long the resources are expected to be valuable. It recognizes that almost everything has a life cycle and that today's assets can become tomorrow's liabilities. Qualitative assessment tends to be more subjective, but potentially more realistic about the true value of the resources.

At the SBU level, resource assessment should focus on the value, quality, and effectiveness of the resources in terms of the strategic direction and the opportunities and challenges in business environment and market spaces. The assessment relates to the outside world, especially in the long term. Table 6.6 provides an overview of the main elements of a resource assessment. It highlights some of the critical questions pertaining to understanding the current situation and determining future requirements.

The history of business is replete with stories of once powerful companies that exploited the short term to an extreme, leaving themselves vulnerable to the wind of change. In today's business world, with ever-present vulnerabilities to changing technologies, needs, requirements, and expectations, optimizing present positions with disregard for the long term is often a prescription for disaster. It is the duty of strategic leaders responsible for the strategic analysis to ensure their resources are aligned with the present and the future.

Strategic leaders often try to optimize their resources and productive assets. However, the notion of optimization is more relevant at operating levels where the time horizon is generally shorter and the power of the prevailing positions can be expected to be maintained during the time horizon – usually five years or so. It becomes more difficult to think in terms of optimizing the present situation as the time horizon is extended to the long term. Historically, most of the attempts by strategic leaders to optimize their present position have usually resulted in sub-optimizing the future ones. For example, NCR, a powerhouse in mechanical cash registers and other machines, was unprepared as the business world changed from mechanical to electronic devices.

Table 6.6 Resource assessment – selected questions pertaining to the understanding of the current situation and determining future requirements

Primary factors	Understanding current situation	Determining future requirements
Tangible Strategic Financial (Money) Businesses Property Operational Informational	What are the most vital resources? Are there sufficient financial resources to take advantage of the opportunities and deal with the challenges? What are the most important plant and equipment, facilities, and physical assets? What are advantages and disadvantages of the businesses? Product lines? What are the most important assets? What are the strengths and weaknesses/advantages and disadvantages of the product delivery systems/operations? Is the information system responsive to the needs of the organization?	What is the projected life cycle of the vital resources? What are the expected cash flows and other sources of funds? What are the expected additions, subtractions, and new technology-based capital improvements or expansions? How can the business and product lines be exploited to gain strategic advantages? What are the risks and vulnerabilities? What can be done to mitigate risks and vulnerabilities? What is required to keep pace with changes in the business environment and market spaces?
Intangible Strategic Businesses Property Operational Informational	What are the most important intellectual properties? Patents? What are the most crucial intangible assets? Reputation? Goodwill? What are the most critical technologies, know-how, and knowledge bases? What are sources of information and knowledge?	What is the expected life of the intellectual properties? How do the intangible resources have to be improved? Can the organization enhance existing technologies and develop new technologies to meet future requirements?

Assessing business portfolios and key relationships

At the SBU level, the power and longevity of business portfolios and product lines are among the most important considerations. It is imperative that strategic leaders configure business units properly so that the core capabilities, vital strategic resources, and management systems are aligned with their mission, scope, and core strategies from an internal perspective; and the opportunities and challenges in the business environment and market spaces from an external one. In *Leading the Revolution*, Gary Hamel identified configuration as one of the essential components in linking the strategic resources (which includes capabilities from his perspective) with the core strategy of the organization.[16] While his notion of configuration relates to internal integration, the configuration of business units has to include how it is aligned with the external dimensions of the extended enterprise and the partners and allies that support the strategic actions.

Most existing businesses are configured on the basis of their historical missions, technologies, products, and markets. The logic and definition vary considerably from a focus on the underlying technology(s) to the types of customers served. For example, Google's incredible success is predicated on its system that quickly provides access to the information that people want. Google uses technology to create value for people by facilitating their efforts and saving time.

Peter Drucker in his famous *Harvard Business Review* article, "The Theory of Business" outlined four main specifications about businesses:[17]

(1) The assumptions about the environment, mission, and core competencies must fit reality.
(2) The assumptions in all three areas have to fit one another.
(3) The theory of business must be known and understood throughout the organization.
(4) The theory of the business has to be tested constantly.

Drucker's points fit the importance of assessing business portfolios. The logic of the businesses has to be aligned with the needs and expectations of the business world. Reality changes every day, some days the changes are minuscule and other days they are dramatic. For instance, the terrorist attacks on September 11, 2001 instantly and dramatically changed the business environment. On the other hand, the significant increase in crude oil prices from $10 per barrel to over $140 occurred between the years 1998 and 2008. Both have radically changed many of the underlying assumptions about the underpinnings of business. Such changes along with all of the other large and small variations and trends require ongoing reassessments of the fundamental characteristics of what businesses are, and what they should be. Such analyses are the precursor to strategic formulation – this is covered in Chapter 7.

Assessing business portfolios involves examining each business and its product lines to determine how well they fit the needs and expectations of the business environment, and what the strengths and weaknesses/advantages and disadvantages are. The purpose is to ascertain the attractiveness of the business portfolio and determine its viability for the future. Some of the most attractive businesses today are actually on the decline, requiring either substantial innovations and reinvestments or even some form of divestment or elimination. On the other hand, some of today's unattractive businesses may have great prospects for the future, if they can be carefully developed into powerhouses. For instance, most alternative energy projects and the quest for renewable energy sources came to an abrupt halt in the 1990s when crude oil prices bottomed out at $10 per barrel. Today, these options are some of the most exciting business opportunities in the energy sector.

The business portfolio may include other forms of value creation and money-making activities. Relatively new ventures are often separated into a category in which the market and financial expectations are low for the short term because their objectives and actions are focused on the long term. It is useful to make such distinctions, because if such ventures are assessed on the basis of traditional financial terms, they might be terminated as underperforming assets or they do not meet the criteria for acceptable performance. For example, a business unit of UTC is developing fuel cells for automobiles and power generation. While the business unit has sold products and has generated revenue, the main thrust is to improve the power output and the economic feasibility of the technologies so that they can be applied on a large scale in the major markets for moving sources (vehicles) and stationary power (electricity). Such new ventures in commercial development may represent the future positions of the corporation and are not expected to make a contribution in the short term.

The business portfolio may also include knowledge-based endeavors that leverage the value of the intellectual property of the company. While such activities might not be considered businesses on their own, it is useful to classify them as a separate category. Knowledge-based endeavors include licensing patents to other corporations to obtain fees and royalties. It also includes providing technical expertise, training, education, and other related services. Again, these categories could be classified as service businesses, but they are really a special group, because in these categories the important value-added components are providing the underlying intellectual property of the services (i.e. the delivery of the education).

In cases involving knowledge-based endeavors, most of the investments (costs) associated with the intellectual properties are sunk. There are high upfront investments but the ongoing costs are low. Although the profits may appear to be large, strategic leaders have to reflect on the investments made across the full spectrum of the businesses and think about what the proper returns should be. For example, one of the classic blunders in making money on intellectual property involved RCA selling an open-ended license to use its color TV technologies. RCA made a good profit on the transaction, but it compromised its strategic position in the color TV business that eventually resulted in RCA withdrawing from the business. However, IBM successfully manages the development and marketing of its intellectual capital that generates more than $900 million per year.[18]

Businesses must also be assessed on the basis of the power and effectiveness of the strategic relationships that they enjoy. External partnerships and alliances provide strategic assets that supplement the capabilities, resources, and portfolios of the SBUs. Partnerships and alliances include formal arrangements with strategic suppliers, key distributors, companies that provide complementary products and services, and a broad array of others that support the strategic actions of the SBU. They are the collaborative, ongoing arrangements that link the external organizations together for mutual benefit. The scope of partnerships and alliances extends well beyond the transactional basis of doing business, and beyond the contractual relationships between the parties of the extended enterprise. Most of the relationships with the entities of the extended enterprise often do not rise to the level that could be considered as partnerships or alliances because they are really arm's-length market-related (transactional) relationships in which each party is protecting its own turf and not thinking about mutual benefits. Such relationships are typically limited to the commercial contributions and support activities that are specifically defined in buyer–seller relationships established through contractual arrangements. These relationships are often narrowly defined, specific in nature, and may be confounded and conflicted by the other relationships that some of the suppliers and distributors have with the competitors of the SBU.

Strategic partnerships and alliances, on the other hand, usually involve forming relationships based on mutual interdependencies, trust, and shared or linked actions. But, the parties remain independent. Partnerships and alliances can take the form of well-defined yet limited arrangements that are highly focused on one or more objectives, legally binding formal arrangements for sharing resources, capabilities, operations, and/or developments, informal agreements that are based on working arrangements and trust, joint ventures with formal links between the entities, and numerous other mechanisms. They usually provide mutual benefits that provide the logic for long-term relationships.

The most obvious informal partnerships involve supporting the establishment of new ventures or the development of market potential where the parties have complementary interests that provide win–win situations. For example, eBay is very happy to have informal relationships with individuals and companies that use its services to sell previously owned products over the Internet. This is particularly powerful in those situations where the primary developer does not have the capabilities or resources (usually money) to orchestrate the full commercialization of the new venture.

Other situations include two or more competitors to the extent that it is legal to form alliances to support their mutual goals, to offset weaknesses, to build critical mass, or to achieve a more powerful position. This is common practice in the airline industry where numerous national and/or international competitors have formed alliances with airlines in distant countries to provide their customers with a complete network of routes so that passengers can travel across the globe using different airlines, but enjoy the benefits of common ticketing and frequent flyer miles on their primary carrier. In such cases, the advantages must outweigh the disadvantages and the threat of competitors usurping power from their positions must be minimal. For example, US Airways, United Airlines, Lufthansa, and others have formed the Star Alliance so that customers can travel more broadly and obtain the advantages of traveling using a single carrier. Most of the members of the Star Alliances are strong competitors in their home or regional markets but are weak global players. The alliance allows each to gain a more powerful global presence without risking losing their positions in their primary markets.

The strategic logic for most partnerships and alliances is to enhance the positive aspects without incurring significant risks to their businesses or threats to their positions. The logic at the SBU level is typically characterized by one or more of the following:

- Sharing of information, knowledge, and resources to gain power, and understand critical success factors to learn how to achieve success, and to improve performance.
- Combining capabilities and resources to improve the economics and/or market potential of strategic actions, activities, or transactions, and to leverage assets so that positions are enhanced and threats are reduced.
- Supporting or linking the development and deployment of new businesses, technologies, and/or products through improving speed, leveraging of capabilities, reducing investments, and expanding market potential. This includes reducing the financial risks associated with research and development or the establishment of new ventures through cost sharing.
- Supplementing the capabilities and resources of the organization especially in areas where the business unit does not enjoy strength or a powerful position. This includes achieving economies of scale and becoming profitable sooner than if acting alone.

- Providing a critical mass of capabilities, resources, and complementary products and services across the extended enterprise so that all customer needs and expectations are supported.
- Reducing competitive intensity through the merging of efforts by certain competitors, especially those with complementary products and services or ones that do not compete head-on.

In each of the categories there are potential dangers. Sharing information and knowledge always runs the risk of others misusing or misappropriating the disclosures. This is particularly worrisome if relationships are abruptly terminated because of conflicts between the parties. Combining capabilities and resources is likewise a concern if the individual parties lose their capabilities to act independently in the affected areas. Threats to other parties or their weaknesses in areas that they are suppose to support each other can negatively affect the fortunes of the parties. Becoming codependent is the overall concern. Supporting the codevelopment of new technologies and products may result in inefficiencies that cost more money and take more time unless the parties are aligned and can integrate their product development processes.

Using the advantages gained through others' resources and capabilities has to be coordinated so that true savings are realized and economies of scale are obtained for all of the participants. There are always long-term risks when companies that are competitors or those that serve the same customers join forces to achieve selected or narrow objectives. Individual short-term objectives may be aligned but there are always threats that long-term objectives will diverge, one or more of the parties will attempt to gain a superior position, or someone will act inappropriately. As military history tells us, today's allies may become tomorrow's enemies.

One of the most crucial reasons and expected benefits of alliances is the addition of complementary products and services to provide the whole array of offerings that markets require and customers expect. This is critical when success depends on customers obtaining a full package of complementary products and services and the complete package cannot be provided by a single entity. For instance, producers of video game devices often encourage others to develop games for their systems to provide customers with more choices when using the producers' devices.

Companies may form partnerships and alliances to enter markets that they do not have the resources or knowledge to address on their own. In many cases, global corporations have difficulties entering markets in developing countries because they do not understand the cultural aspects of the lay of the land, the rules of the game, or lack a sense of the intangible requirements,

Table 6.7 Business portfolio assessment – selected questions pertaining to the understanding of the current situation and determining future requirements

Primary factors	Understanding current situation	Determining future requirements

Portfolios
Businesses
Geographic
   coverage
Product lines
Ventures
	What are the most critical businesses?
	What are the scope and geographic coverage of
	   the businesses?
	What are the critical strengths and
	   weaknesses/advantages and disadvantages of
	   the businesses?
	What is their expected longevity?
	How can the advantages be sustained?
		Do they provide a power position?
		Do they have to be enhanced?
		How can they be exploited to gain
		   advantage?
		What are the risks and vulnerabilities?
		What can be done to mitigate risks and
		   vulnerabilities?
		What new businesses have to be added?
		What businesses have to be eliminated
		   or sold off?

Relationships
Partnerships
Alliances
Consortia
Coalitions
Linkages
	What are the most critical strategic
	   relationships?
	Does the organization have the right
	   partnerships and alliances to ensure success?
	Do the relationships make strategic sense and
	   fit the strategic logic?
	Do the objectives of the parties align with the
	   objectives of the organization?
	Do the entities have the same principles,
	   values, and beliefs?
	Are there significant cultural differences?
	Can the entities work together successfully?
	Are partnerships and alliances stable?
	Are the performances of the parties acceptable
	   and are the parties trustworthy?
		What partnerships and alliances are
		   required to supplement the
		   businesses?
		How do the existing partnerships and
		   alliances have to change/improve to
		   keep pace with the strategic
		   direction of the SBU?
		Are the partnerships and alliances
		   sustainable and capable of creating
		   long-term value?
		Are they moving in the strategic
		   direction of the SBUs?

and/or the means and mechanisms for doing business. There are often invisible barriers that the outsiders do not adequately prepare for. For instance, global corporations often use joint ventures to set up businesses in Russia because it is extremely difficult to determine what has to be done to comply with all of the formal and informal requirements in a country that has had to undergo significant changes and shifts over the last decade where the economy is still turbulent and full of uncertainty.

Table 6.7 provides an overview of the main elements related to assessments of the business portfolio and of strategic relationships. It highlights some of the critical questions pertaining to the understanding of the current situation and determining future requirements.

Companies may also form partnerships and alliances to comply with mandates that seemingly do not provide any strategic or competitive advantages. For instance, many companies in the EU formed consortia to comply with the directive for taking back electrical and electronic wastes at the end-of-life.[19] Hewlett-Packard (HP) realized that "take-back" requirements are an essential part of its value system as end-of-life responsibilities flow back to the producer. In order to comply with the directive and to minimize the costs associated with compliance, HP formed an alliance with Braun/Gillette, Electrolux, and Sony to leverage their combined resources and efforts.

The assessments of business portfolios and partnerships and alliances are also open-ended and must be tailored to the situation. This is particularly true for partnerships and alliances where each tends to be based and built on the unique characteristics of the relationship. Assessing the business portfolio is more complicated than just examining capabilities and resources. It requires a more comprehensive approach to determine the power, value, and longevity of the capabilities and resources. The analyses are prepared on the basis of the requirements of the existing businesses and the expectations for the assumed time horizon for the planning period (typically five to ten years).

The assessment examines each of the business and/or product lines to ascertain the current strategic position and the prospects for growth and development. It explores the geographic coverage of each one. The analysis might take the form of a simple strength and weakness assessment and/or a determination of the main advantages and disadvantages of each. New ventures and new businesses should also be assessed to understand how they fit with the mainstream businesses and product lines.

The assessment of businesses involves determining the areas where the organization enjoys a power position and realizing what has to be done to enhance it – exploit the positives and reduce the negatives. The focus may also include understanding what new businesses are required and/or what existing businesses should be eliminated or sold off.

Assessing partnerships and alliances involves a similar view except that the analysis includes all of the partnerships, alliances, consortia, coalitions and strategic linkages. It starts with an identification of all such relationships and prioritizes the importance of each in the present and in the future. The assessment links the relationships with the businesses and explores the advantages and disadvantages. It reflects on the purpose and power of each relationship, determines the logic for each and how well the alignment is working.

Box 6.1 Johnson & Johnson: How its credo connects context with reality

Johnson & Johnson (J&J) is a diversified health care company with leading products and services in pharmaceutical, medical devices, and consumer segments. In 2005, J&J had revenues and net income of $50.5 billion and $10.4 billion, respectively.[1] J&J is one of the most innovative companies in the industry spending $6.3 billion on R&D in 2005.[2] Incorporated in 1887, J&J has a long history of developing and marketing successful products that range from antiseptic dressing for surgical procedures and later band aids (1921) to baby powder (1890) and leading over-the-counter pharmaceutical products like Tylenol.[3]

J&J has a long history of applying science and understanding the pressing needs of society and health care practitioners to discover new solutions for humankind, and its business prospects. The founders, Robert Wood Johnson and his brothers, invented numerous products to make surgical procedures safer from infections by providing sterile dressings, clothing, and related materials. This tradition continues to the present. J&J has been guided by well-established values for more than sixty years. William C. Weldon, Chairman of the Board of Directors and CEO, reiterated J&J's core values and principles:[4]

Johnson & Johnson is governed by the values set forth in Our Credo, created by General Robert Wood Johnson in 1943. These principles have guided us for many years and will continue to set the tone of integrity for the entire Company. At all levels, the employees of Johnson & Johnson are committed to the ethical principles embodied in Our Credo and these principles have been woven into the fabric of the Company.

J&J is widely recognized and respected. In 2006, it was listed as one of the Global 100 Most Sustainable Corporations by Innovest Strategic Value Advisors. J&J has been included in the Dow Jones Sustainability Index since 2000.[5] The listing is earned through demonstration of best-in-class performance pertaining to sustainability. J&J was also assessed by independent financial index company (FSTE) for inclusion as a constituent of the FSTE4Good Index Series.[6] Strategic leaders focus on the external context as the primary driver for making strategic decisions. J&J has a powerful legacy of understanding the needs and expectations of the external dimensions. Its first and foremost responsibilities according to the Credo are to customers, the employees, the communities, and lastly the stockholders. External context from all of the upstream providers of goods and services to downstream customers, stakeholders, and related parties are critical forces in driving J&J's strategic direction. J&J incorporates input from all of the external stakeholders and internal participants into the strategic analysis and strategy formulation. External entities provide valuable insight about needs and expectations, emerging issues that require attention, and the requisite objectives and business strategies. J&J's vision of global responsibilities was expressed in its 2003 Sustainability Report:[7]

Caring manifests itself in our corporate giving, as we reach out to support social and public health programs as well as medical educational initiatives around the world. Through these efforts, we strive to help establish structures that will bring lasting improvements, not just short-term relief. Our corporate contributions are an investment toward a healthy global future.

This report delves into each of these three aspects of J&J as a caring, sustainable organization – caring for communities, people, and the global environment. Our commitment to these global responsibilities is not an afterthought or a sidelight, secondary to our main business functions. It is embedded in the J&J culture and lies at the heart of our health care mission. In fact, it is one of the four overarching principles that have contributed to guide our strategic thinking about the future:

- our decision to be broadly based in human health care;
- to manage our businesses through a unique and dynamic decentralized system;
- to manage our businesses for the long term; and
- to pay constant attention to the ethical requirements of Our Credo responsibilities to patients, employees, communities and shareholders.

Going forward, J&J has identified four imperatives that inform our management decisions:

Innovation – finding innovative health care product solutions that improve the lives of people around the world.

Collaboration – fostering dialog, teamwork and shared expertise across our many technology platforms and businesses to maximize our effectiveness.

Flawless execution – using process excellence techniques, such as root cause analysis and tracking of critical metrics, to continually improve our operations, and following a global strategy of beyond compliance, establishing high internal performance expectations.

Leadership and people – providing professional development opportunities for a highly skilled and diverse workforce, deeply rooted in our Credo values.

These four principles and four management imperatives are the cornerstones of our overall corporate strategy at J&J. As a broadly based, decentralized global organization that is financially strong and highly respected, we have the capacity and the responsibility to make meaningful improvements in the world. J&J is working to harness our organizational power – especially the strength of our people and partnerships – to make those improvements and reach our ultimate goal: Healthy People, Healthy Planet, and Healthy Futures.

J&J thinks about the long term and how to achieve strategic positions that are sustainable and successful. It uses innovation to discover new technologies and product platforms that reinforce its ongoing success. It uses collaboration as the key to link everything together. Strategic leaders know that great plans are meaningless unless the enterprise can execute them at the highest levels of performance. They know that success is derived through people and that financial outcomes are derivatives of great strategies and executions. J&J's leadership realizes that articulated principles are not flowery statements but real management constructs that define what success is intended to be, guide people to obtain success for the company, and light the way for sustainable success over time.

J&J focuses on the customer, the employee, the community, and the stockholder, in that order. Its more inclusive approach ensures that all stakeholders are considered and that opportunities are discovered. Strategic leadership for several generations has so ingrained the ideals of the Credo into the hearts and minds of the employees that it remains visible and tangible on a daily basis to influence decision making and execution. The simplicity of the Credo provides a solid foundation for employees at all levels when they are engaged in contributing to the success of the company. The Credo serves everyone well, given that the nature of J&J's businesses are complex and involve risks and uncertainties.

Notes

1. J&J Annual Report 2006.
2. 2005 Sustainability Report, p. 44.
3. www.jnj.com/our_company/history/history_section_htm "Early Years – Our History."
4. www.jnj.com/Investor Relations/htm – Message from our Chairman and CEO.
5. 2005 Sustainability Report, p. 44.
6. *Ibid.*
7. 2003 Sustainability Report, pp. 8–9.

Summary

Business leaders use a well-established strategic management framework that has significant links with the external business world. They also have well-defined ways of doing business, and an established flow for conducting business. The system includes governance for ensuring that roles and responsibilities are executed properly, and that the organization performs its mission to the highest degree possible.

Strategic management also involves SBP for the future. While the prevailing situation is often adequate, strategic leaders must ensure that the organization embraces change and is prepared to make transitions and transformations to enjoy an even better future and achieve sustainable success. While there may not be a definitive starting point, strategic leaders periodically review the existing situation and reflect on the strategic management framework for making decisions. Such reflections may lead to a thorough examination and a reconfiguration of the framework. The framework maps out the strategic logic of the SBU, its scope, baselines, and process. It defines and articulates the management constructs of the organization. It also reflects on existing business models, systems, and structures.

The strategic management framework provides the strategic leaders and their staff with a basis for conducting a strategic analysis of the internal aspects of the SBU and the external realities that it has to deal with. The strategic analysis consists of three main parts: an analysis of the external dimensions; an analysis of the internal aspects; and the interrelationships between the two. The basic approach is to determine the opportunities for enhancing the SBU's position, and assessing how it can take advantage of those opportunities. The intent of strategic analysis is to determine and articulate the strategic options that are available. Strategic options lay out the possibilities for objectives, strategies, and action plans.

The intent of this chapter is to lay the foundation for strategy formulation and implementation. Great strategies and outstanding execution are based on a comprehensive understanding of reality as an overarching perspective, followed by creative strategic leadership with insights and imagination to transition and transform the prevailing realities into a more sustainable future.

References

Bossidy, Larry and Ram Charan (2004) *Confronting Reality: Doing What Matters to Get Things Right.* New York: Crown Business

D'Aveni, Richard (1994) *Hyper-competition: Managing the Dynamics of Strategic Maneuvering.* New York: Free Press

Freeman, R. Edward (1984) *Strategic Management: A Stakeholders' Approach.* Boston, MA: Pitman

Hamel, Gary (2000) *Leading the Revolution.* Boston, MA: Harvard Business School Press

Liker, Jeffrey (2004) *The Toyota Way: 14 Principles from the World's Greatest Manufacturer.* New York: McGraw-Hill

Tolstoy, Leo (1963) *Anna Karenina.* New York: The Modern Library

NOTES

1 Product delivery systems focus on their extended enterprises and operational management.

2 Leo Tolstoy, *Anna Karenina* (New York: The Modern Library, 1963, p. 3).

3 Gary Hamel, *Leading the Revolution* (Boston, MA: Harvard Business School Press, 2000, pp. 65–70).

4 *Ibid.,* pp. 71–77.

5 *Ibid.,* p. 78.

6 Larry Bossidy and Ram Charan, *Confronting Reality: Doing What Matters to Get Things Right* (New York: Crown Business, 2004, p. 3).

7 *Ibid.*

8 Stakeholders are individuals or groups that are directly or indirectly affected by strategies, systems, structures, operations, and/or processes of the SBU. They do not obtain direct economic benefits like customers do.

9 R. Edward Freeman, *Strategic Management: A Stakeholders' Approach* (Boston, MA: Pitman, 1984).

10 For instance, until recently, Dell had maintained an effective business model selling PCs direct to customers.

11 Richard D'Aveni, *Hyper-competition: Managing the Dynamics of Strategic Maneuvering* (New York: Free Press, 1994, p. 21).

12 *Ibid.,* pp. 21–22.

13 *Ibid.,* p. 28.

14 C. K. Prahalad, and G. Hamel, "The Core Competencies of the Corporation," *Harvard Business Review,* May–June 1990, pp. 79–91.

15 Jeffrey Liker, *The Toyota Way: 14 Principles from the World's Greatest Manufacturer* (New York: McGraw-Hill, 2004). *The Toyota Way* provides a rich level of detail on Toyota's principles and system for lean.

16 Gary Hamel, *Leading the Revolution*, p. 78.

17 Peter Drucker, "The Theory of Business," *Harvard Business Review*, September–October 1994.

18 IBM 2006 Annual Report, p. 27.

19 Directive 2002/96/EC of the European Parliament and of the Council dated January 27, 2003.

7 Strategic formulation – options, mission statements, and objectives

Introduction

Strategic formulation is a complex, vibrant element of the strategic management process. It involves exploring options, determining the mission, selecting objectives, and crafting business strategies and action plans. The leaders of strategic business units (SBUs) discuss, analyze, and objectively consider all of their strategic options as they engage in strategic formulation. This is accomplished in concert with the comprehensive strategic management framework, and based on the results of the strategic analysis as discussed in the previous chapter. The overarching aim is to chart the course for the future and transition and/or transform the business unit into a more successful entity through strategic business planning (SBP), enterprise-wide strategic leadership (ESL), and effective decision making.

SBU leaders often start the strategic formulation by laying out the available strategic options. The question: which ones make the most strategic sense? While strategic leaders often have a good pulse on the realities of their business world, studying and discussing options provide a good segue from the laborious details of strategic analysis to the excitement of strategy formulation. For example, Microsoft, with its numerous strengths, powerful positions, and huge financial resources, has an incredible number of strategic options. It has the resources to become involved in scores of new businesses, new ventures, radical developments, and improvement programs – even acquiring companies outside its traditional business arena. Its effort to acquire Yahoo! for approximately $44 billion is an example of its commitment to improve its position in Internet searches and become a leading player.

Developing strategic options is not about predicting the future, or even forecasting possible events. It is a management method used to shed light on the possibilities of the future, and to provide ways to understand some of the main implications of the driving forces of change. Conditions and trends in the business environment and market spaces are charted out, and translated into strategic options for the business unit. These strategic options are tested based on what could or might happen over time.

The determination of strategic options is intended to follow a scientific approach to link the interrelationships between external opportunities and internal means, to explore what can be done to brighten future prospects, and to realize extraordinary value. Some of the main categories of these options include growth, development, improvement, investment, and learning. They also include potential mergers, acquisitions, and the divesture of businesses. The main perspectives also focus on the organization's internal capabilities and resources to take advantage of the current and future situations, and to set the stage for crafting realistic business strategies and objectives.

Strategic formulation also involves developing new or revised mission statements, formulating new business objectives and strategies, and deciding upon the action plans and initiatives that segue into strategic implementation. The culmination of the strategic formulation is a strategic evaluation of the decisions to determine how well they fit the context and strategic management and operations. The main questions asked during the strategic evaluation often focus on whether the strategies are logical and achievable from both external and internal points of view, and whether the organization, the strategic partners, and the external contributors and recipients understand and agree with the revised mission statements, strategic objectives, and business strategies. Likewise, the strategic evaluation attempts to ensure that there is general acceptance before strategic leaders give their approval for implementation. The strategic evaluation concludes the strategic formulation or SBP phase (the inner loop depicted in Figure 6.1) of the strategic management process and initiates the transition to strategic implementation (the outer loop depicted in Figure 6.1) and the subsequent execution by the whole of the SBU and the value delivery systems. Strategy formation is discussed in Chapter 8 and strategic implementation and execution are discussed in Chapter 9.

The chapter includes the following main topics:
- Identifying the essential elements of strategic formulation and how strategic leaders translate the insights and understandings gleaned during strategic analysis into objectives, business strategies, and action plans.
- Determining the strategic options that make business sense when examining the opportunities and challenges in the external business environment and matching them with the internal capabilities and resources of the SBU and the extended enterprises.

- Formulating new mission statements to keep the purpose and aims of the SBU current with its external context and internal capabilities and resources.
- Determining business objectives and targets, and ensuring that planning process meets needs, mandates, and expectations of the business environment.

Strategic formulation

Strategic formulation is at the heart and soul of the strategic management process. It builds upon the foundation of the strategic management framework, and the strategic directions that have been initiated by the vision of the corporate executives. Strategic formulation involves the intellectual exercises and process elements to examine how the SBU can create extraordinary value in good times and bad. This includes those times with positive circumstances or diminishing opportunities. It explores how the company can achieve sustainable success even in situations where there are significant deficiencies and gaps. In such situations strategic leaders have to think about creating more powerful capabilities and positions to overcome constraints and limitations. For example, in the 1970s, European aircraft manufacturers were at a significant disadvantage in competing against Boeing. They joined forces and established Airbus, which became a very effective competitor. Airbus combines the strengths and advantages of the partner companies that make it easier for the strategic leaders to take advantage of strategic options, formulate aggressive business strategies and action plans, and achieve more favorable results.

Strategic formulation involves dramatically increasing the prospects for success by systematically improving every aspect of the SBU based on sound theories and practices. Strategic formulation also focuses on developing new capabilities, resources, and means to exploit opportunities and mitigate challenges. It is a dynamic construct that necessitates going beyond simply making improvements to the existing business situations; it involves creating a dramatically enhanced reality through new means, mechanisms, and outcomes. In the 1980s and 1990s management constructs like total quality management (TQM) focused on continuous improvement. Today, strategic leaders must also focus on continuous development and radical change. They must outperform expectations across the enterprise and time. Success is never guaranteed and it requires ongoing commitments and efforts to obtain sustainable success.

The precursors to strategic formulation include examining and revamping (if necessary) the critical elements of the strategic management framework, and understanding the external context and the internal capabilities through strategic analysis, as discussed in the previous chapter. The strategic management framework and strategic analysis are critical parts of the strategic management process, developed to establish a solid foundation for managing the business units and leading change. In most business situations they are the crucial upfront phases in the strategic management process that provide the underpinnings for making strategic decisions about the future. They provide strategic leaders with the knowledge; understanding; insight; creative thoughts; ideas and concepts; and the theories about determining the strategic options, assessing the merits of the options, and selecting objectives, business strategies, and action plans. These are among many of the most important considerations for leading change and creating a brighter more productive and sustainable future.

The upstream phases of the strategic management process can be – and are often performed – by professional strategists and strategic analysts who have been specifically tasked with creating or reinforcing the framework, and providing the intelligence and analyses for understanding reality. They set the stage for strategic formulation. In very large organizations, they are specialists who spend most of their time on SBP, strategic formulation, and strategic implementation. While such professionals set the stage through analysis, in most large businesses the actual strategic formulation of objectives, strategies, and action plans is, or should be, the domain of strategic leaders.

Strategic formulation is the high-level responsibility of SBU leaders. It is not a periodic function, but the life blood of strategic leaders who should be engaged in it every day. It is dynamic and requires constant reflection and ongoing efforts. It is a mistake to think about it as just planning.

SBP often is viewed as a cycle with an inception and culmination, but in reality it is part of the continuum (forming plans) for strategically managing the SBUs. Strategic leaders have to continuously think in terms of crafting strategies and implementing them. There are no precise starting and ending points. Moreover, as large companies and SMEs become more complex and sophisticated, it requires more time to ensure that the strategic formulation unfolds properly.

In the real world many large companies and small and medium-sized enterprises (SMEs) have two-year, three-year, and even five-year planning cycles. The time frame depends on the dynamics of the business environment, and the effects of change on the company and the SBUs. The more turbulent the

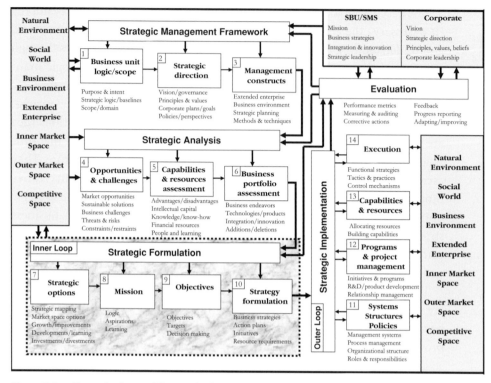

Figure 7.1   The main phases of the standard strategic management process

business environment, the more often strategic leaders need to address their strategies and action plans. Remember, SBP is not just about developing plans; it is about creating and enjoying sustainable success. Strategic formulation is a pivotal aspect of SBP. Figure 7.1 maps out the main phases of the standard strategic management process with specific emphasis on the key subsets of each phase and essential elements.

The elements identified in Figure 7.1 highlight some of the most important considerations. The figure indicates essentially the same flow and elements as the strategic management process mapped out in Figure 6.1. The two figures are essentially identical, except that the depiction in this chapter is a simplification showing the main elements in a linear layout, without showing the interactions that are necessary for achieving success in the real world.

In Figure 7.1, strategic formulation is specifically identified as a critical phase of the process. The intent is to indicate its importance, and emphasize its centrality in strategic management. However, it must be recognized that every element is important. As discussed, great strategies with poor execution result in poor outcomes. Likewise, great execution of poor strategies usually results in poor outcomes. There are many ways to fail, but it usually takes great leadership, well mapped-out processes, and concerted efforts and hard work to succeed.

The strategic management process is dynamic and iterative. Many elements are worked on concurrently, and the efforts are often based on different time frames. For instance, strategic leaders may be developing new business strategies and action plans for the current cycle, while the functional units are working on programs from the previous cycle. Indeed, great care needs to be taken to ensure that everyone is in synch, regardless of one's position in the overall process. Most importantly, the phases are not equal in time duration or in terms of the efforts required to achieve the desired outcomes. Every phase and the elements therein are critical to achieving success.

Strategic formulation is linked to the upstream side of the strategic management process through the determination of strategic options. Strategic options are the culmination of strategic analysis and are the ingredients for crafting business strategies. Likewise, action plans and initiatives are the culmination of the strategy formulation, and become the essential ingredients for the organization in its quest to achieve results through the ongoing elements in the strategic implementation phase.

Strategic formulation is typically straightforward because fewer people are involved, and those involved generally have the expertise to complete their assignments in a professional manner. Implementation and execution are usually more difficult with the addition of many more people whose knowledge and experience are often less sophisticated in terms of strategic management and the people involved usually are more practical. One of the reasons why implementation and execution tend to be more difficult is because the people throughout the organization lack a frame of reference for implementing strategies and actions. Often they did not participate in the formulation phase so they do not understand the logic used to craft them. In some cases, the most profound aspects of strategy formulation are kept secret for competitive reasons.

Many businesses still use the big "DAD" type approach during strategy formulation. This approach was described by Lawrence Susskind and Jeffrey Cruikshank as a tool for resolving problems.[1] DAD stands for "Decide, Announce, and Defend." While Susskind and Cruikshank used the DAD approach in the context of environmental problems and dispute resolution, strategic leaders often use it in strategic formulation. With the DAD approach, it is easy to decide what to do since only a small number of leaders are involved. However, problems during implementation may arise, because most of the people in the organization had no input, or little context. Resistance to change often results when others do not have a voice in the upfront phases of the process. This is typical when strategic leaders make decisions without any input from the organization. After the decisions are announced, a lot of time is spent defending the logic of the decisions. While strategic leaders may ultimately convince people within the organization that the decisions are sound – or simply force them to take the requisite actions – the process is neither effective nor efficient. And, if complete buy-in is not obtained, both implementation and execution are often sub-optimal. Even without any resistance, time may be lost while strategic leaders engage in explaining and re-explaining the underlying aspects of the decisions and/or what the people in the organization have to do.

The alternate method is the small "dad" approach. This features engagement and involvement throughout the strategic management process. The acronym for small "dad" stands for "**d**iscuss, **a**nalyze, and **d**ecide." Many people are engaged in the upfront phases; they have a chance to assess the pros and cons of choices; then the strategic leaders and the organization decide upon the best choices. While unanimity on final decisions is rarely the case, a more favorable response is usually the result when people are given a chance to voice their views and understand the logic behind the decisions. The additional time taken during strategic formulation becomes time saved during implementation, which may more than compensate for the investment. While each strategic situation has its own particular requirements and mandates for confidentiality, an open, honest, and participatory process encourages higher performance. Moreover, the added insights often result in better outcomes. Insights from diverse participants may bring alternative perspectives that shed light on the positive or negative effects and impacts that may open the door to additional options or flaws in strategic thinking. Occasionally, strategic leaders are unaware of barriers to success, yet these are well understood by managers and/or contributors at lower levels of the organization.

Determining strategic options

Background on strategic options

Determining strategic options is the precursor to strategy formulation. It attempts to assimilate the knowledge gained from the strategic analyses of the external dimensions and the internal aspects, combined with the insights gained from the strategic leaders and other contributors. Several schools of thought exist on how to determine strategic options. One is that they are driven by opportunities; another is that they should be based on core competencies and capabilities; a third is based on an "industry attractiveness and company strength" matrix; and a fourth involves open-ended perspectives on what could be done.

In reality, strategic options should be determined using all of the information, knowledge, analyses, and insights available. Focusing on perceived opportunities and challenges is sensible. In the long term, the fortunes of the organization are driven by the external dimensions regardless of the internal aspects. However, the difficulty in using this approach alone is that the organization may not have the competencies and capabilities to take advantage of the opportunities. The changes in the external environment may be moving in a different direction from the traditional core capabilities of the organization. The organization might be in a poor position relative to the developing opportunities and changing directions. It then has to make dramatic improvements in its competencies and capabilities through learning and experience.

Focusing on core competencies and capabilities is also sensible since they are the strengths of the organization, and the power of its strategic positions. However, those competencies may not be in concert with new opportunities in the business environment either. Thus, the organization runs the risks of investing in areas where it has strengths, but those that are unimportant to the dynamics of the market spaces, or the external opportunities. This school of thought is somewhat the opposite of the first one.

The "industry attractiveness and company strength" matrix attempts to integrate the two schools by examining the attractiveness of opportunities (markets) and the power of the capabilities of the organization (its position). The theoretical concept is based on the notion that the organization should focus on market spaces where there is a convergence of its internal strengths and market or industry attractiveness. While this seems to make sense, the elements of assessment mechanisms are narrow and static. They address the prevailing situation using several key criteria. This included examining markets in terms of size, profit and growth potential, and stability among others. It also included examining company strengths in terms of market share, quality, customer loyalty, and return on investment among many others as well.

The Boston Consulting Group (BCG) matrix, also called the product portfolio matrix, was one of the simplest approaches in the third category for determining strategic options and/or investments.[2] It compared an organization's relative market share in a business to the industry's growth rate. The matrix consists of four categories or quadrants. The theory suggests that if the organization enjoyed a high market share and the industry had a high growth rate, then that quadrant was an attractive area for investments. This category was deemed to be the "stars." On the opposite side in the quadrant of low growth and low market share, the organization's position is deemed to be unattractive and should be divested. This category is called the "dogs." In areas where the organization had high market share but the industry growth rate was low, the theory suggests that the organization should exploit the cash flow from such "cash cows." The other quadrant is called "question marks," since it was not clear what to do when the markets were attractive, but the organization was weak. Such approaches are simplistic at best, and a little dangerous, since they are based on a static view and often lead to faulty conclusions about what strategic moves to make. While the BCG matrix originated in the 1970s, it is still being taught in many business schools today.

A more advanced approach for determining strategic options or alternatives is called "strategic position and action evaluation" (SPACE). It uses a four-factor dimensional model that compares the organization's financial strength and competitive advantages versus the industry strengths and environmental stability. Each of the dimensions includes key elements used to determine the strength or power of the situation. Figure 7.2 depicts that model and provides the key factors for each of the dimensions.[3]

The strength or power of the internal or external situation is determined by examining the key elements and ranking them to obtain a score. The SPACE model involves assessing the factors for each of the dimensions as presented on the graphic in the corners, and determining from the factors whether the business should be aggressive, conservative, competitive, or defensive. While the strategic positions and action evaluation are based on quantitative and qualitative analysis of the factors, much of the perspectives are subjective. Worse, the assessments are based on a static view of the existing situation. However, the SPACE model represents a giant leap forward from the simplistic thinking of the BCG model which often led companies down the wrong path by killing off or milking to death businesses that would be extremely attractive in the future.

The SPACE model's main weakness is that it is also prescriptive. It suggests strategic alternatives based on the prevailing conditions, rather than mapping out the most viable options – yet leaving the door open for other creative approaches as well. Given the following sections that cover a more contemporary view of strategic options, the details of the SPACE model and the strategic alternatives identified in Figure 7.2 are not fully covered. (See reference noted in endnotes for additional information. The SPACE model

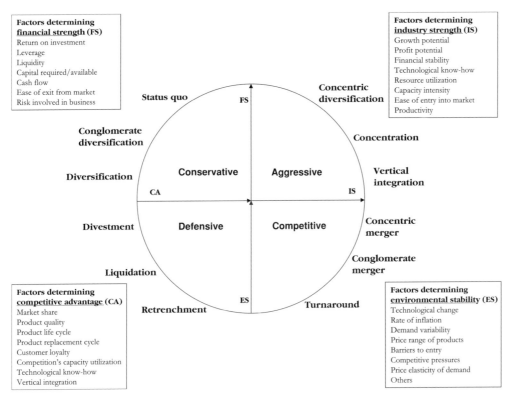

Figure 7.2 SPACE Model – continuum of strategic alternatives

was used by GE and Shell during the 1970s to provide insights about strategic options.)

The strategic assessment of strategic options is not as simple as determining an organization's position relative to market opportunities or focusing on core competencies. Moreover, most situations are usually dynamic. Powerful positions can quickly give way to weak ones; conversely, poor conditions may give rise to great opportunities. Think about the implications of energy. Less than a decade ago, energy investments were viewed as unattractive, and many businesses failed to consider making improvements or developing new sources of energy because strategic leaders believed that most of the options were not economically feasible. Taking a static view rather than a long-term perspective often forces strategic leaders to misread the business situation and make poor decisions.

Understanding the implications of the strategic options is complex and difficult to generalize. The fourth school of thought involves more open-ended approaches. It requires strategic thinking, insight, and imagination. It involves using the internal and external assessments, insights gleaned from analyses and scenarios, and imagination about what could be done and what has to be done to achieve success. It takes reflections on the whole business environment and all of the opportunities and challenges across the entire extended enterprise to determine the power and limitations of the capabilities and resources. Most importantly, it links the external requirements and expectations (opportunities and challenges) with the internal capabilities and resources and those of the extended enterprise and examines the business prospects in the current period and in the future.

Strategic options from an external perspective include exploiting new opportunities, neutralizing or eliminating threats, mitigating or reversing challenges, and creating or exiting businesses. Strategic options from an internal perspective include leveraging capabilities and resources, exploiting the power positions of the businesses, product lines, and/or the extended enterprise, building new capabilities and adding strategic resources, and eliminating the gaps between the aims and objectives and the realities of the current capabilities and resources. It is not sufficient to simply match core capabilities and resources with opportunities in the markets or the business environment, and exploit the strengths and power positions as long as possible. Eventually, everything changes. The use of such simple approaches often leaves the organization vulnerable to shifts in the business environment, and change in the market spaces. This is evident in how US Steel's overwhelming strategic advantages have been stripped away over time through changes in the markets, and the rapid development of the competition. Even on an absolute basis if "Steel" is just as capable as it once was, its relative strength has declined in comparison to other sophisticated players across the world. It can be argued that companies like Steel were not aggressive enough during their glory days and let the others catch up.

The "maintaining the status quo" or "wait and see" options are prescriptions for disaster. Likewise taking a conservative approach is also risky, since competitors are improving and new competitors are emerging all the time. It is a dynamic world where the best options usually involve being aggressive – ensuring not only continuous improvement, but also continuous developments.

Mapping out select strategic options

The strategic options for SBUs are heavily influenced by the strategic direction of the company and its vision for the future, as well as the values, beliefs, and desires of its strategic leaders. While it is always difficult to precisely determine how strategic options are identified, it is clear that the grand strategies, directions, and policies of corporate leaders are important precursors for understanding the fit and desirability of the strategic options.

In simple terms, strategic options relate to improvements, developments, growth, investments, divestures, and to learning (i.e. transitions and transformations). Large businesses typically employ most of the main options as they fine-tune the existing strategic performance, expand their reach in space and time, and increase the power of the organization. Unless the organization is making significant progress, it is actually falling behind.

Strategic options are determined through strategic analysis and plain old strategic thinking. The foundation for developing strategic options may be based on highly quantitative approaches as discussed under strategic analysis, or qualitative approaches based on mental models of what could be done providing the right means and mechanisms are in place. The latter generally involves out-of-the-box thinking about what could be, if the business unit is aggressive in leading change. In either case, the status quo is not an option. The perspective is based on how aggressive strategic leaders have to be. The answers to developing the strategic option for the strategy formulation choices are not prescriptive or pre-ordained. Unlike past theories that were based on the existing strengths and weaknesses, opportunities and threats (SWOT) of the organization, the approaches used to determine the strategic options must be much more dynamic. They have to be holistic to the extent possible, and include the extended enterprise as part of the strategic thinking and decision-making process. The main strategic options include:

- *Growth/expansion* – focuses on exploiting current capabilities, resources, and business portfolios, and using them to expand upon the prevailing opportunities and challenges. This includes moving into new market spaces using the strategic positions, core capabilities and resources of the organization.
- *Improvements* – focuses on making incremental and/or ongoing improvements to current capabilities, resources, and business portfolios, and finding better ways to take advantage of opportunities and challenges through derivatives, enhancements, and related additions to the SBU and extended enterprise.
- *Developments* – examines the potential for new opportunities across space and time using out-of-the-box thinking, determines the requisite capabilities and resources necessary for organic developments to achieve sustainable

success, and creates the means and mechanisms necessary to orchestrate success.

- *Learning* – explores opportunities and threats, and strengths and weaknesses, determines the requisite new knowledge and organizational capabilities to exploit opportunities and mitigate threats, and creates an organization where learning and knowledge are sources of gaining sustainable advantages and ongoing success.
- *Investments* – examines the potential for new opportunities across space and time using out-of-the-box thinking, determines the requisite means and mechanisms for making external joint ventures, acquisitions, and mergers, and creates the ability to make dramatic, if not radical changes to the business units and its extended enterprise.
- *Divestments* – explores opportunities, challenges and threats, and the advantages and disadvantages of the business portfolios, determines the businesses that are no longer viable or fit the strategic direction of the SBU, and involves taking appropriate action to ensure that the business unit has the most advantageous mix of businesses and that potential weaknesses do not detract from the successes.

Aggressive growth is a viable option and works best at the intersection of positive opportunities and positive internal strength. Growth and geographic expansion are common options for most businesses, especially those that are relatively young and have not reached their full potential. However, great care has to be used as maturity approaches, because the markets may become saturated. More of the same often results in less success, not more success, as markets reach maturity. Moreover, risks may increase as companies expand using the same underlying approaches. As Wal-Mart expanded across the US it used its proven formula for selling good products at affordable prices to people with modest incomes. It also increased the size and scope of some of its new retail outlets to employ improvements. The newer superstores are both discount and food stores. Growth and expansion options must be carefully considered, ensuring that the company does not become vulnerable to change.

The best opportunities for improvement options are often found where keeping pace with change demands that the internal aspects be strengthened. This is a commonplace option that most companies deploy. Indeed, in a world of rapid change, the importance of continuous improvement is well understood. However, continuous improvement may not always be good enough. It simply allows the business unit to keep up with competitors and peers but not make any gains in real terms. For instance, in the financial arena if inflation is 3% and an individual gets 3% interest on his investment, the result in real terms is just staying even before taxes. In business operations, if all producers improve productivity by 3% per year and your business only improves by 2%, then it fell behind by 1% relative to the competitors. Improvements are the most viable when the underlying factors are favorable and stable, and there are no overwhelming difficulties. Great care has to be used to determine that simple improvements are improving the situation.

Development options involve broad arenas where the opportunities are mostly positive, but the internal aspects may require radical innovations and/or dramatic changes, especially when there are negative aspects that have to be mitigated quickly. Developments are designed to enhance one's prospects in the business environment, strengthen the core capabilities and resources of the organization, and overcome weaknesses and vulnerabilities in the business unit and its extended enterprise. They involve aggressive actions to reconfigure the prospects. Development options are especially important when the perceived value and benefits of expansion and/or improvement are marginal, or when the business situation is not very favorable. In such circumstances doing more of what was previously done may not bear fruit, or even with good gains the situation remains poor. For instance, the improvements made by Bill Ford at Ford Motor Company (FMC) during his tenure as CEO did not result in significantly enhanced outcomes, and FMC continued to have difficulties. FMC did make significant improvements, but the rate of improvement was not sufficient to keep ahead of changes in the market spaces. Development options involve a broad array of change, innovations, and radical moves to enhance the external and internal dimensions. They require extraordinary results.

Learning options are appropriate for all of the possibilities. Accelerated learning may turn weaknesses into strengths and disadvantages into advantages. Rapid learning and the acquisition and deployment of new knowledge may be the quintessential strategic option that covers the full array of internal and external aspects. In a world of rapid change learning provides the intellectual capital to outpace change and to build new competencies before they are absolutely necessary. While core competencies and capabilities are critical for success, it is the ability to create, enhance, and change the competencies that is essential for success. Moreover, as requirements and expectations become more complex, strategic leaders and their organizations have to exhibit many more competencies in many different areas of endeavor. Gone are the days when strategic leaders could function adequately based on competencies in one or two areas like finance and marketing. Learning is most often combined with one or more of the other strategic options to provide more comprehensive

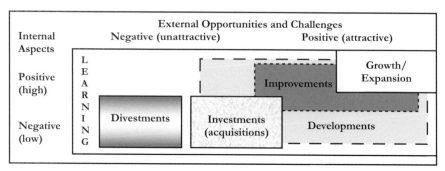

Figure 7.3   A relative mapping of select strategic options

and balanced outcomes. Indeed, learning is usually part of the other strategic options.

Investment options may cover all of the spaces as well, but are among the best when the opportunities are unclear and the internal strengths are less favorable. They typically involve buying other companies or businesses, especially in cases where there are needs to enhance business portfolios and the internal capabilities and resources are limited. Investment options, especially those associated with buying outside companies, also make strategic sense when strategic leaders have to move quickly, and cannot wait to develop internal capabilities and resources.

Divestures involve similar strategic options, except that both the internal and external aspects are clearly unfavorable or untenable. Divestures involve selling off or spinning off existing businesses. This makes the most sense in mature businesses that are very weak and management does not have the time or financial resources to make radical changes. It also makes sense when the potential is so low that even with dramatic results the overall performance would still be unacceptable.

Figure 7.3 provides a relative sense of the relationships between the broad categories of strategic options, and their relationship from internal and external perspectives.

The perspectives of strategic options indicated in Figure 7.3 are neither intended to be definitive nor prescriptive, but to highlight the main areas where each of the strategic options is the most advantageous. Please note that the layout is intended to provide a relative sense and not absolute one. Moreover, growth and expansion are lumped together in the graphic, even though there are subtle differences, explained later.

The intent of determining strategic options is to map out the available alternatives across space and time while avoiding the tendency to be presumptuous or prescriptive. The approach considers as many strategic options as possible without restricting strategic thinking, or the imagination of the strategic leaders. If the strategic leaders constrain their thinking and assessment based on how the strategic options are aligned with the core capabilities/competencies of the organization, many of the most exciting possibilities might not be considered or may be quickly eliminated. Many strategic options may be viable and a fit if leadership and the organization are willing to invest into new developments or new learning to build the requisite competencies and capabilities.

In exploring strategic options, the approach should be open-ended; as many options are considered as possible. It is important to remember that strategic options are not strategies, although there may be overlaps in the categories. Strategic options are simply a mapping of the available choices. The approach is not to formulate strategies, but to identify and articulate what is desirable and possible. The more options available, the more power leaders have, and the more likely they are to make good strategic choices.

Strategic options are usually manifested at the intersections between the internal dimensions and positions, and the external dimensions and realities. For instance, core competencies do not present viable options by themselves unless they are aligned with external opportunities. Determining strategic options is the end point of strategic analysis and the beginning of strategy formulation. The critical distinction is that determining strategic options does not require intense decision making – while crafting strategies does.

The main categories of strategic options

Growth and improvement options

Growth is both a strategic option and a business objective. It usually involves doing more of the same, except being more aggressive or on a broader scale. Growing the existing businesses is a natural choice for strategic leaders. Identifying areas of opportunity where the organization has strengths (capabilities and resources) and focusing the organization toward growth in those areas is a frequently used option. It is not only the most obvious option; it is one of the easiest to deal with. For instance, under Ray Kroc McDonald's grew its hamburger chain from a few stores in California to a national force, and then an international giant in the fast food industry. It enjoyed great success as it replicated its stores in location after location for more than fifty years. It focused on growth using its core competencies in selecting locations, and designing focused fast food restaurants with quick meals at affordable prices. However, growth opportunities eventually leveled out as customer preferences changed, and evolving weaknesses, like the lack to attention to the nutritional value of the food, negatively affected long-term potential and near-term performance. Competition from other types of establishments replicated McDonald's' success, and fragmented the fast food market into many segments from traditional hamburger places to taco and sandwich joints.

While most scholars and business leaders understand the implicit and explicit benefits of growth, there are inherent concerns about what growth options implies. The main concern is expanding the businesses based on business approaches that may have reached their natural limits, or that the weaknesses or vulnerabilities of the organization are compounded as the businesses expand. During the 1990s, GM and FMC expanded their offerings of sport utility vehicles (SUVs) to take advantage of the craze for larger, plusher vehicles. This approach was successful as fuel prices dropped and consumers focused on luxury and size. However, growing their businesses in this area increased GM's and Ford's vulnerabilities to rising energy prices and shifting consumer preferences. Today, both companies are rethinking their options trying to find new directions for achieving success.

Growth options require a comprehensive assessment of the positive and negative aspects of the business. The positives are often the strengths – these must be understood so that they can be fully exploited. Knowing the weaknesses and inherent flaws, and mitigating them to the greatest extent possible are also crucial for exploiting the growth options. For mature businesses, weaknesses often become the limit to potential growth, and barriers to ongoing success. For example, Wal-Mart's growth has slowed significantly as its traditional customer base has leveled out, and more affluent customers seek more up-scale surroundings. Moreover, it appears that some of Wal-Mart's strengths may be becoming weaknesses. Its focus on cost reduction has a related down-side. Wal-Mart is embroiled in litigation with state governments over the treatment of employees – even becoming a topic in the 2008 presidential campaign trail. The result is that some customers are buying their goods at other retailers like Target and Costco.

Growth is also about expanding the value proposition. People want value for their money. As businesses grow, they reach out to new customers, but may not find customers who enjoy the same value proposition as existing customers, even though the company assumes that the value proposition remains the same. For example, Europeans may not have the same appreciation for fast food as Americans. Fast may mean added value for the typical American customer, but a net loss for a European family that may prefer to dine with their friends, and enjoy leisurely conversation to complement their food at more traditional restaurants, guesthouses, and pubs. In this example the benefits of fast food are out-weighed by ambience. Understanding and responding to such differences are critical for deploying growth options.

Growth options include an examination of opportunities in open market spaces that are not traditionally served by the business. This includes moving into new geographic areas. Most obvious is international expansion. Typically, the organization looks for markets similar to their existing markets. Again, great care has to be taken to discover the requisite requirements for achieving success in new market spaces. Selling existing products in developing countries often leads to problems, since the products were designed and developed for a different set of market conditions. In the case of Nestlé, there were problems with its infant formula in Africa because mothers there did not know how to sterilize the water and prepare the milk.[4]

Determining the constraints and limitations of the businesses is a critical factor. Most opportunities have limitations that play out over time, especially for mature markets that have become saturated. The opportunities decline in intensity and growth becomes harder to achieve. It is a reoccurring phenomenon that eventually happens in most industries. Change can be the result of many factors. The existing and emerging competitors usually diminish the rewards of the business. As technologies and products mature, they often become commodities with a concomitant decline in margins and profitability. Changing factors in the social, economic, and environmental underpinnings may also limit the potential for growth. For instance, increasing energy costs and an international focus on carbon dioxide emissions may lead to a decline in the use of large automobiles. Understanding the risks and vulnerabilities that might limit growth is critical.

Growth and improvement options are often complementary, differing by a matter of degree. Improvement options involve strengthening positions by improving advantages and offsetting or eliminating disadvantages. They may involve improvements to existing technologies, products, operations, and process to overcome potential limitations. Unlike the theories associated with core competencies that focus on strengths, improvement options recognize that incremental innovation, if not dramatic technological and product improvements, can simultaneously shore up weaknesses, and respond to new opportunities. It is particularly critical in those situations where a large gap exists between evolving conditions and trends in the business environment, and the strengths of the organization. For example, FMC enjoyed a historic strength in its pick-up truck line, which served customer needs in the 1990s when demand favored trucks. Today, consumers are looking for greater fuel efficiency, and smaller cars. Dramatic improvements leading to the production of more efficient cars may be necessary to regain its position and return to profitability.

Improvement options usually focus on existing markets and customers. The approaches include:

- How to strengthen product lines and positions;
- How to reduce weaknesses and shortcomings;
- How to exploit near-term opportunities; and
- How to eliminate the prevailing vulnerabilities.

They focus on finding ways to make improvements via the near-term business prospects. These are usually through the lens of continuous improvement to the organization and the extended enterprise.

Development and learning options

Development options involve the more radical alternatives for addressing opportunities and challenges. They involve what "could be," instead of "what is." The basic approach begins by examining the whole of the market spaces, not just the existing markets, and assessing the entire extended enterprise, not just the internal organization. Development options are harder to visualize because they are usually dependent on actual developments to fully comprehend the magnitude of potential gains. The personal computer (PC) provides a vivid example. In 1981, at a cost of $7,000 the PC was principally a specialty device used by businesses to prepare repetitive documents, like proposals and invoices.[5] Twenty-five years later it is a staple commodity used in almost every sector of the economy from businesses to classrooms in colleges and universities.

Development options involve very aggressive approaches that include addressing new markets with new businesses. It also involves developing new-to-the-world technologies that have the potential to solve many of the underlying problems experienced by social, economic, and environmental sectors of society. Development options also attempt to make dramatic changes that enhance the prospects for the future. They include creating new business ventures to replace obsolete ones, or to take advantage of new opportunities through new business approaches like serving people in developing countries with solutions that fit their needs. They are particularly good options for weak players who are not enjoying success in their current markets. If a company is particularly weak given the prevailing situation, then one of the best options is to change the nature of the game. For instance, Southwest Airlines (SWA) was a relatively small airline that was less well endowed than its competitors. It created a business model that minimized the need to acquire different types of planes and gates at the largest airports. By concentrating on low cost and superior services on a narrow front, SWA found opportunity outside of the hub-and-spoke model used by the larger airlines. Southwest serves the smaller less-congested airports using a standard aircraft, the Boeing 737. Development options may overlap areas where growth and improvement options are also mapped out. Therefore, they often represent options within options.

On the negative side, development options represent areas in which aggressive actions are necessary to overcome situations where the opportunities seem to be thin. Such areas are typically viewed by strategic leaders as being ill-suited for strategic action, but they should not be categorically dismissed. For instance, markets for consumer products that are unrelated to the basics of life (food and shelter) in many of the poorest countries are very small. As stated above, most of the large global companies have not developed the requisite means and mechanisms for serving such markets. Yet, such markets could be large because the needs are great. They require extraordinary solutions for translating the external conditions into new business opportunity, and transforming the internal aspects into power capabilities, resources, and product lines that are aligned with those new opportunities. However, such approaches are not easy to exploit.

Generally, the intent of development options is to leapfrog expectations of the markets, and strategic positions of the competitors. If improvements provide incremental gains, development options are intended to make significant gains. Developments may change the nature of the competitive scene. Like the impact of digital cameras on the businesses related to photography, development options are best when the product portfolio has become commoditized or the organization's position is very weak. In such cases, the prevailing situation is unattractive, and the best alternative is to break out of the mold.

Development options may include starting new business ventures within the SBU in the form of a new value delivery system or as an adjunct to the SBU. While such options are often called corporate entrepreneurship, they involve complex initiatives to start new business units within the SBU. Development options may also overlap with areas where investment options make sense. This is appropriate because development options and investment options have similar aspects. Both require significant new investments to create what does not exist within the SBU umbrella. Development options focus on solving the problems from an internal perspective, while investment options rely on an external perspective. The latter is discussed in more detail in the second subsection.

Learning

Learning is an overarching perspective. It covers all of the space mapped out in Figure 7.3 and it is one of the most fruitful areas from a time perspective. Learning is always appropriate, and usually results in gains. The key is to select the right areas upon which to focus. Answers to this question typically revolve around how much learning is required to make the necessary gains. One of the most important challenges involves assessing the learning required to develop opportunities for the business unit.

Learning is most critical during early stages of the life cycle. It is during this time where overall knowledge is relatively low, and the potential for enhancement is great. During the early stages learning is rapid, and efforts are usually rewarded with a dramatic increase in capabilities and benefits. As the business situation matures, new learning becomes more difficult and costly, but always appropriate. However, great care has to be exhibited. Learning more about obsolete technologies, products, processes, and methods provide little, if any, long-term benefit. Indeed, learning may shift toward the more innovative areas during the later stages of the life cycle. As the business arena matures, it may face the possibilities of breakthrough technologies that make learning more about old technologies less valuable. Again, knowing what to learn is a critical factor.

Learning options provide dual benefits: they can enhance the positives and overcome the negatives. Rapid learning can propel organizations from last place to first place in a short period of time. For instance, GE Medical Systems (GEMS) had lagged behind in the development of X-ray technologies for medical systems. It was so far behind that its products were non-competitive. GEMS focused on magnetic resonance imaging technologies to overcome weaknesses in providing equipment for medical establishments, and leapfrogged into a competitive advantage. GEMS has expanded its knowledge base and used learning at higher rates than others to great success. Not only did it catch up, it converted business weaknesses into strengths.

Learning expands knowledge. Knowledge has become one of the most important strategic advantages. Learning options generally concentrate on the future, and what is required to take advantage of the opportunities that lie ahead. Learning options are especially powerful in the realm of technological change and the creation of new technologies. New technologies have the power to overcome the core competencies and capabilities of the dominant corporations, and provide opportunities for newcomers to assume a commanding position. Organizations that can acquire new knowledge and expand upon it gain powerful positions in the new realities. Learning options cover the gamut from: (1) improving the existing knowledge base; (2) maintaining supremacy by staying ahead of the learning curve; and (3) inventing new knowledge that makes the world of yesterday obsolete and creates whole new business arenas. Learning options are complex. They are about understanding what the choices are, not about making them.

Investment and divestment options

Investment (acquisition) options examine external solutions to solve internal weaknesses and limitations and achieve sustainable solutions. Investments usually entail buying other businesses, acquiring outside technologies or products, and/or linking with other organizations through partnerships, alliances, or joint ventures. The approach is to overcome internal weaknesses quickly by acquiring outside capabilities and resources. Investment options may overlap with other options to provide strategic leaders with a wider array of choices.

As internal limitations indicate the need for change, businesses have two main choices: they either have to increase the power of their positions through investments (external or internal), or get out of the business. Given adequate time and if the external factors and opportunities are reasonably favorable, then development options may make sense. However, if time is of the essence, the acquisition of more favorably positioned companies may be the preferred way to overcome internal weaknesses. Investment options are not the opposite of development options. They can be done in tandem, where the organization can strengthen its position through external investments and internal developments to create viable positions.

Divestment options usually involve areas of severe weaknesses, where the opportunities both in the present and in the future are bleak. Divestment options are broad and difficult to categorize. They include areas that require dramatic solutions. In strategic terms these include selling or spinning off businesses, shutting down operations, forming joint ventures with others, and restricting the scope of the business to the most advantageous areas. Again, great care has to be taken to avoid upsetting customers, and ensure that ethical and legal responsibilities are fulfilled. For example, IBM chose to spin off its printer business to a separate company, Lexmark, to ensure that its customers would continue to obtain the benefits that they had enjoyed. IBM shareholders continue to have the benefits of ownership, and the strategic leaders of IBM were able to concentrate on more favorable opportunities.

Transferring ownership of the business using various mechanisms, or selling it altogether is an effective way to provide customers with ongoing solutions and at the same time protect the goodwill or reputation of the corporation. When IBM sold its PC business to Lenovo (a Chinese company) it was able to recover some of its investment, and obtain some of the benefits from the potential success of the Chinese company. On the other hand, Intel simply exited its memory chip business in 1986 when it realized that its position was no longer viable. Intel was able to do this because its previous customers had already found new suppliers. While these examples are actually strategic *actions*, they represent some of the strategic *options* that the companies had in dealing with their business situations.

Investment and divestment options are often seen as polar opposites. The former suggests that the organization can take positive action to participate in opportunities and challenges that arise. The latter explores the options for dealing with extremely negative positions – especially those with untenable situations.

Forming mission statements

Most businesses have a specific, well-defined mission, articulated in written form. The mission is generally the purpose, the aim, and/or the intent of the business. Relative to the business unit, the mission identifies, defines, and communicates the strategic logic of the business unit, its reasons for being, and in some cases its aspirations. It describes the scope and reach of the organization and what it hopes to accomplish. The mission and the primary roles and responsibilities of the strategic leaders should resonate with each other.

The mission of the business unit should be reevaluated periodically to ensure that it is aligned with the business environment and the capabilities and resources of the organization. Like other strategic management constructs, the mission can become obsolete or stale. Often there is drift in the stated mission over time as opportunities, challenges, threats, and/or new capabilities and resources move the strategic direction of the company and/or SBU into new market spaces that the original mission does not adequately cover. The stated mission may become woefully inadequate in terms of the conditions and trends, reflecting the realities of early times that were simpler and easier to manage.

Many businesses have mission statements. Good mission statements should be as comprehensive as possible in defining the business unit, its involvements, commitments, and expectations with regard to the business environment, market spaces, customers, stakeholders, other recipients, employees, partners, external contributors, and shareholders. The messages should be accurate, open, and honest, and used to inspire people within the organization and enterprise about how to engage and communicate with outsiders about the true essence of the business unit and what it expects to accomplish. Unfortunately, some are typically broad and ill-defined descriptions of intentions, or flowery statements about products and services. Worse, many mission statements are written as marketing messages, and do not properly convey the purpose and true positions of the business units.

James Collins and Jerry Porras, in their *Harvard Business Review* article, "Building Your Company's Vision," suggest that the core purpose or mission should be as follows:[6]

[The] Core purpose, the second part of core ideology [it defines the enduring character of an organization], is the organization's reason for being. An effective purpose reflects people's idealistic motivations for doing the company's work. It doesn't just describe the organization's output or target customers; it captures the soul of the organization . . . In identifying purpose some companies make the mistake of simply describing their current product lines or customer segments.

The core purpose or mission is the reason for existence and the long-term aim of the organization – which is never ending. It is the enduring motivation and justification for being in the business and the overarching perspectives of "who we are," "what we are doing," "why we are doing it," "how do we do things," and "where we are going." While the core purpose is intended to be timeless, it is important to recognize that the purpose of the organization and its *raison d'être* must evolve over time. The management constructs used to convey the messages must be dynamic and robust.

The first question to answer is the definition of the internal and external dimensions of the enterprise. It defines the scope from an external perspective, and the breadth and depth of the business unit. The second question focuses on the strategic direction and intended actions. The third question involves strategic logic and fit. The fourth question pertains to values, behaviors, policies, and practices. The last of the questions relates to future expectations and direction.

The notions of purpose and mission should be proactive and provide people both inside and outside the organization with a clear picture of what it is trying to pursue and achieve. The mission should be stated in terms of what the organization aspires to be, and how it relates to the external and internal dimensions of the organization.

Mission statements are more and more difficult to keep current in many industries because the rate of change usually outpaces the capabilities of strategic leaders to update their determination about what business the business unit is in. While constant updating is probably unnecessary and unwarranted, it is important to ensure that mission statements are accurate, and reflect the real world and the aspirations of the organization. In some cases, it may be better to eliminate formal mission statements if they are either so trite that they are meaningless, or that they are so out of touch with reality that they are misleading.

Moreover, many SBUs are more diverse that ever, requiring each segment to have its own mission statement. While it should be possible for strategic leaders to develop their own mission statements, it is not as easy as it may sound. Most formal SBU mission statements require corporate approval, consensus with other SBU leaders, and agreement within the organization itself, all of which takes time and effort to accomplish. The problem is that in some cases, the investment of time, effort, and money may be difficult to obtain. Just as complicated is the problem of reaching consensus without significantly compromising the final mission statements (i.e. they become so generic that they do not mean much). However, where there are such difficulties it may be advantageous to bring the specific challenges to the forefront so that the opposing points of view can be heard and resolved. Through discussions and debates a richer understanding may be reached with more cohesion within the organization.

Forming or updating the mission and/or mission statements is a critical part of strategic formulation. The effort ties back to the salient points established under the umbrella of the strategic management framework. Some of the most important strategic decisions are related to the strategic logic and scope of the SBU. They determine the parameters that establish the reach of the SBU based on geographic, market, and technological aspects, and social, economic, environmental, and financial perspectives. The mission statements should provide some clarity regarding purpose and intent. Indeed, intent is one of the most important aspects because it conveys a sense of direction, not just one of being.

The mission and/or mission statements may be formed, reformed, or transformed before or after the determination of the strategic options. Each approach has advantages and disadvantages. The main advantage for doing it before is to have a "clean sheet" when assessing and deciding what the mission should be. The main disadvantage of developing a mission statement too early in the process is that the insights and observations identified during the strategic option step would not be available to facilitate discussions and decision making. Thus, the time, effort, and effectiveness in articulating new or revised mission statements are not as efficient, productive, and/or as successful as they could be. The main advantage for changing the mission or preparing the mission statement after the assessments of strategic options is that strategic leaders have additional insights and knowledge about opportunities and challenges. The main disadvantage is that they may continue to shape their thinking based on the prevailing situation rather than what the SBU should be doing.

Regardless, the reflection on the mission should include views and perspectives on what the mission ought to be, not just based on what the mission is and how it can be changed. Again, the questions focus on how much change is necessary or required. The efforts should take a broad perspective unencumbered by the attractiveness of short-term opportunities or the prevailing business situation that may be very favorable, but have "rain clouds" on the horizon. Indeed, one of the main difficulties in traditional strategic management is that there is too much focus on the short term, when everything is attractive, and not enough attention is paid to the long-term prospects. For example, most of the petroleum companies are surely satisfied with their current business performance with record profits. They realize that petroleum reserves are declining, but the present financial projections are mostly optimistic with peak production not occurring until well in the future. Great care should be exercised to ensure that the mission statements themselves do not overly constrain the future goals and strategies.

Reforming and transitioning the mission statement usually involves incremental change that modifies the prevailing case to reflect changing realities. The difference between them is the degree of change. Transforming a mission statement involves making radical changes that are intended to create more opportunities to discover new realities. While neither is inherently good or bad, strategic leaders may wish to have a more open-ended agenda and express a more aggressive perspective.

As the world changes, opportunities shift and strategic leaders have to revise the mission (and mission statements) accordingly. Figure 7.4 provides a simplified view of strategic perspectives on changing mission statements.

A key question on changing the mission of the business involves how far from the current mission is appropriate. The greater distance that the strategic leaders have to go, the greater the challenges, but the greater the possible rewards. Again, it is often a question of time, money, people, and resources. It is also a matter of the prevailing opportunities and challenges. In

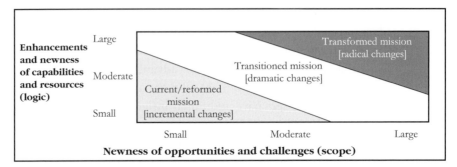

Figure 7.4   Simplified view of changing the mission statements

the broadest sense, as a business matures, opportunities become scarcer. Over time, business units, their competitors, and others have exploited most of the prevailing opportunities in the immediate business environment and market spaces that have significantly reduced the potential to create extraordinary value. Most great opportunities eventually become commonplace business prospects involving commodities and generic offerings. For instance, in the 1980s, the market for PCs created fortunes for Intel and Microsoft. Today, the margins have shrunk dramatically, and all but the latest models are commodities that are readily available at discount houses like Wal-Mart.

The layout provides a relative sense of categories and types. If the changes in external opportunities and requisite changes in internal resources are relatively small, then current mission statements may suffice with minor modification. Most businesses typically make evolutionary changes to their missions. Occasionally, they make a significant change.

Moderate to significant changes in opportunities and challenges and/or moderate to large changes in the requisite capabilities and resources suggest that mission statements may require dramatic or radical changes to reflect these new realities. Such changes involve the two other categories, transitioned and transformed. The former involves dramatic change based on the prevailing realities. The latter typically involves creating a more radical reality based on technological innovation or radical changes like new business model(s).

The transitioned mission involves making more complicated changes to the internal and external dimensions. For example, during the 1990s Toyota transitioned from a strategic focus on high quality, reliability, affordability, and customer satisfaction to a higher level of sophistication that included all of its previous attributes and capabilities with improved value propositions, enhanced value delivery, increased focus on fuel efficiency, and reduced pollution and emissions. The imperceptive changes did not provide immediate benefits to the business units, but as the business environment changed, especially due to increased fuel costs, Toyota's strategic position improved dramatically. Toyota's success is not due to good luck but solid strategic thinking about what its mission should be and what people expect.

Transformed missions are the most complex, and often take years to orchestrate. They involve radical changes that focus on new-to-the-world opportunities and challenges and require new capabilities and resources. Small companies and start-ups are often engaged in such endeavors. Although small companies face enormous challenges, they usually have several significant advantages that large companies do not share. Smaller companies do not have to worry about their existing investments in positions and/or assets that might be rendered useless if the changes are successful. They do not have to write off prior investments or lay off employees. Nevertheless, global corporations can, and may have to, make a radical change to their mission even if the prevailing businesses are still making money. IBM is a good example of a company that has undergone significant changes in its mission over the last century. It has changed from a tabulator equipment manufacturer, to a computer hardware and service integrator, to the service and solution provider of today. While the IBM story is more complicated and richer than can be articulated in a single sentence, it is clear that IBM's strategic leaders have transformed the missions of their businesses many times during its history.

Businesses may use all three approaches. The norm may be evolutionary change to adapt to the changing business environment. However, periodically the situation may warrant making dramatic or radical changes to mission statements. The intent of the construct in Figure 7.4 and related discussions is to provide guidance for strategic leaders who are reflecting on how they should modify their mission(s) and mission statements. Most mission statements are intended to guide the organization toward sustainable success, not to mandate specific objectives or strategies. The revised mission statements may include an expanded external scope or enhanced strategic logic of the business unit or both. However, the changes do not have to be implemented instantaneously – they can occur over a considerable period of time or even in a series of phases that may take decades to realize.

Selecting business unit objectives

Business unit objectives represent the desired outcomes that the organization wants to achieve. Based on the precepts of the balanced scorecard (see Chapter

2) objectives should cover the most critical areas of concern for the SBU leaders. They should include both external and internal perspectives:

External	**Internal**
Value proposition	Value creation
Market success	Organizational capabilities and knowledge
Customers' and stakeholders' success	Learning and systems developments
Value delivery	Processes' improvements and best practices
Growth potential	Financial performance and rewards
Sustainable success	Shareholders' wealth

They should also include broad topics like corporate social responsibility, sustainable development, and protection and preservation of the natural environment. Moreover, strategic leaders should establish objectives for both sides of the value proposition. In my book, *Sustainable Business Development: Inventing the Future through Strategy, Innovation and Leadership,* selected categories for setting objectives are identified based on the value proposition – improving the positive aspects and mitigating the negative ones.[7] This implies the strategic leaders should set objectives on improving their businesses, technologies, product/market positions, quality, and value-added among many others as well as reducing, if not eliminating, negative impacts such as waste streams, toxic substances, environmental degradation, resource depletion, human health concerns, and a whole host of others.

Business objectives should inspire people to achieve outstanding results. And, a realistic time frame should be created based on the existing or expected capabilities and resources of the organization. Stretch goals are great, but if they are unattainable, the organization may become frustrated and fail to achieve even the minimum level of accomplishment.

Setting business objectives is an art form. It requires vast knowledge of the external context and internal capabilities, resources, and business portfolios. Those who select the business objective have to combine imagination, insight, and instinct about business in general – and their businesses in particular.

Formulating business objectives is part of the strategic management process that has to be based on the upstream strategic analysis, the assessments of situations, future expectations, and the realistic options that are available. Weak objectives usually lead to weak performance. Business objectives should fit the strategic needs of the businesses in the present, and challenge the organization to create extraordinary value, exceed all expectations, and achieve sustainable success.

Strategic leaders should ensure that there are sufficient numbers of inter-related objectives, so that efforts and achievements are not skewed toward a narrow set of outcomes. Just having financial objectives is usually a primary concern. If strategic leaders focus solely on financial outcomes to the exclusion of more broad-based objectives, then the ensuing strategic decisions may be skewed toward short-term profitability at the expense of other critical objectives and long-term success. Moreover, a limited number of related objectives makes it easier for people to manipulate short-term results. For instance, if the objective is to increase return on assets (net income divided by total assets), management can realize the objective by increasing net income (profits) or decreasing total assets. Indeed, cash flow or profitability can remain flat while meeting or exceeding the objective for return on assets simply by selling off assets necessary for future expansion. A short-term win may be achieved through the attainment of a single objective; however, without the counterbalance of broader perspectives it may mean a less sustainable long-term position. Balance is critical both in terms of the broader perspective and time frame. In the past, many business leaders unwittingly sacrificed long-term success by focusing on short-term results.

Setting business objectives should involve participation from a broad array of strategic leaders, professionals, and important contributors of the business unit as well as by external partners like select customers and suppliers. They should be directed and guided by the corporate vision, and strategic direction and mission of the SBU. Moreover, business objectives are a subset of the corporate goals and objectives, and should be internally consistent and externally driven. Even those objectives that relate to internal aspects like learning and process improvements are ultimately pursued for the purpose of achieving external goals.

Business objectives usually define content, level of achievement, and time frame. They may also be open-ended or well defined (closed). Open-ended objectives have content, but usually lack a specific definition of the required level of achievement and a definitive time frame. Open-ended objectives are typically used to convey a sense of purpose, cohesion, and direction. They are usually high-level goals used by corporate or senior management at the business unit level to set the stage for the myriad of objectives that often exists in very large organizations. They transcend daily aspects with the theoretical perspectives based on the corporate vision and the desire of strategic leaders to create a more ideal business situation. Again, the notion of sustainable success is an open-ended objective. It is both theoretical and practical – providing an overarching sense of what the organization is trying to achieve. However, it lacks detail and specificity. Other examples include "being the best in the industry," "having the highest quality and performance," "achieving world-class status," and "being best in the world."

While such objectives have meaning and are understood by most people, they can be misinterpreted – as they can mean different things to different people. Strategic leaders have to provide specific interpretations to ensure that people across the enterprise are fully aware of their intent. One of the major problems often experienced by companies is when their open-ended business objectives are used for external purposes like promoting the image of the business. For instance, how are outsiders to view a statement by a business that suggests it wants to be the "best in the world" but the current reality is not even close? For example, Shell Oil has promoted its sustainable development paradigm and its social, economic, and environmental objectives in numerous advertisements. People on the outside often take such open-ended business objectives out of context, and demand proof that the strategic leaders are following the intent of the objectives. The results may be mixed, as Shell is seen as one of those petroleum companies who make a lot of money by pushing oil products. Strategic leaders have to ensure that the rhetoric meets the reality, especially when the reality is mostly based on the old paradigm.

Yet, opened-ended objectives may be appropriate if they are supported by highly aggressive business strategies. Open-ended objectives are useful for communicating an overall intention to make transitions and transformations in the structure of the business and its purpose.

Well-defined or closed-ended objectives not only have content, they have specific targets for achievements and a definitive time scale for achieving desired outcomes. The typical well-defined objective should be stated in the following terms: what is to be achieved, when it is to be realized, and what level of accomplishment is desired. The content should be realistic, and relevant to the business. It often is expressed in the form of a target with specified content, timing, and process. The target should involve a significant challenge that is achievable and rational. It should be accomplished within a time frame that requires diligence and process improvements.

Objectives are usually nested in a hierarchical structure where corporate objectives establish the framework for business objectives and business objectives set the stage for operational and functional objectives. Figure 7.5 depicts

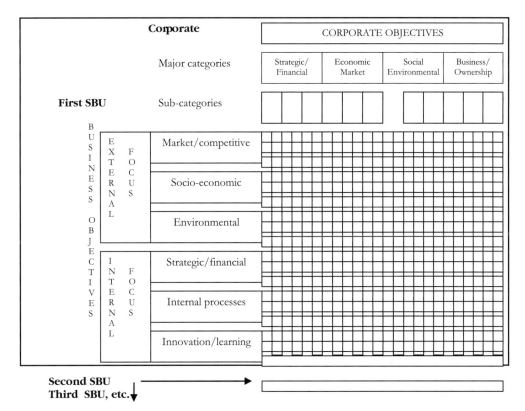

Figure 7.5   Interrelationship between corporate and business objectives

a simple portrayal of how business objectives might be linked to overall company objectives.

This is not to suggest that every business objective has to be perfectly aligned to one or more corporate objectives. There may be specific requirements of the business unit that are not linked to corporate objectives or the overall strategic direction. The matrix indicates that business objectives should support corporate objectives, and major categories of objectives that can be further divided into sub-categories.

In many situations, business objectives can be identified as having an external focus or an internal focus. While strategic leaders should use caution to ensure that internal objectives are related to external realties, the classification scheme helps convey the intent and purpose of a given objective. Moreover, objectives can be identified as short-term or long-term. These two terms are difficult to precisely define, because the usage is dependent on context – fast-paced business environments versus slow-paced ones. Objectives can be further classified as enhancing positive outcomes based on opportunities and challenges, or correcting or eliminating negative aspects based on threats and vulnerabilities. Setting business objectives should be based on a solid understanding of the business environment and the market spaces. It takes strategic analysis into consideration including the opportunities, challenges, capabilities, and resources of the organization. Strategic leaders should also examine the available strategic options, and the needs and expectations of the whole enterprise from customers, stakeholders, and partners to employees and shareholders.

Strategic leaders must select business objectives with outcomes that are balanced. It is imperative that the selection of business objectives does not implicitly force decision makers into making unwanted tradeoffs or sacrificing long-term benefits and sustainable success. For instance, if the main objective is to maximize financial aspects, then decision makers may subordinate long-term market success, social responsibilities, and environmental protection as they try to achieve the stated objectives. In many organizations good people do everything they can to achieve their stated objectives. However, when these are flawed there are often conflicts, sending the organization down the wrong path or struggling with mutually opposing objectives. For instance, in the days before six-sigma thinking, people worried about adding costs in order to produce high-quality products that would affect the objective to maximize profits. In many such situations, decision makers often focused on profitability at the expense of quality.

Business objectives must focus on meaningful areas where capabilities and resources are available, or can be developed or acquired in a reasonable amount of time through learning or acquisitions. Attaining consensus with and within the leadership group and ensuring that there is fairly wide range of acceptance is important. For instance, some objectives like financial ones may have acceptance from the marketing leaders, but there may be whole groups of functional management in the areas like production, operations, or even finance that may disagree. In such situations, the senior leader may have to question whether or not there is broad-based agreement, or whether certain factions expressed agreement because the objective is favorable from their perspective.

Benchmarking peers and competitors, or ascertaining what the customers and stakeholders expect is another approach to determine business objectives. If the benchmark study indicates that the best-in-class or even best-in-world companies are achieving success at a given level, then the organization should strive to outperform them. Selected objectives should be tailored for the organization if benchmarking information is used.

Business objectives have to be in alignment with organizational capabilities and financial resources, and acceptable to the people who have to implement the ensuing strategies. For instance, a company with strong principles pertaining to sustainable development or social responsibility may not be willing to maximize profits at the expense of customers, society, or the natural environment. On the other hand, if most of the strategic leaders have employment contracts that include financial incentives for increasing profits or on an annual basis, their motivation may be skewed toward the financial objectives that provide near-term results, regardless of the social, economic, and environmental implications.

Business objectives can be stated in qualitative and quantitative terms. Good objective statements include both, indicating what the objective is, the target for its accomplishment in quantitative terms, and the time frame in which it is expected to be achieved. Moreover, good business objectives should be based on measurable objectives over time. While open-ended objectives are usually difficult if not impossible to measure, well-defined business objectives can be measured on a periodic basis. There may be reluctance on the part of certain strategic leaders to precisely specify the objective and target in quantitative terms if they are fearful of not being able to deliver the results. This is a particular concern if people could lose their jobs or suffer financially. For instance, uncertainties about whether the SBU will receive requisite resources, support mechanisms, and/or the full commitment of the leadership may mean that responsible leaders are only willing to make general statements about the objectives they expect to obtain.

Business objectives can be selected on the basis of a variety of management constructs. Appropriate categories for selecting objectives are provided in Peter Drucker's key results areas as discussed in Chapter 2. In reality, strategic leaders may combine the constructs and use the categories that fit their situation the best. As stated, business units should define a reasonable number of objectives from different categories so that results are not skewed toward one area. Depending on the size of the organization, its capabilities and resources and commitment to making change, strategic leaders should have between eight and sixteen main objectives for each SBU. While there is no magic formula for determining the right number, the theoretical perspective suggests that a representative list of business objectives from each of the key categories requires at least eight objectives – one or two pertaining to financial aspects, the same about market space objectives, and additional objectives covering people, internal processes and learning, social, economic, and environmental factors, and competition. While there are no absolute limits, it can be argued that beyond a certain number of objectives people lose a sense of priority. A way to avoid confusion is to put the main objectives into categories, and identify sub-objectives within each of the categories. If further clarification and/or delineation are required, then subsets of the sub-objectives can be developed. Regardless, it is important to provide a sense of the fit and logic of the objectives and what they mean to the organization. If the objectives are categorized properly, employing the use of sub-objectives, then people within the organization and the enterprise intuitively know the priorities and can act accordingly.

The selection process can be orchestrated using top-down, bottom-up, or a combination of the two along with numerous team-type approaches. The most effective way to start might be with the "must do" objectives as required by corporate and/or the strategic leaders of the SBU. These are generally the top-down approaches. They might be followed by the desired objectives of the organization based on the insight and knowledge of the personnel and operating leaders. These might be viewed as bottom-up or middle-up objectives. After culling out the suggestions from the organization and combining them with the "must do" objectives, SBU leaders might establish a broad-based team of strategic leaders, managers, and knowledgeable professionals to think "out-of-the-box" about what should, or could be accomplished, and then propose objectives that guide the organization to the desired ends.

Theoretically, such approaches would allow the whole of the organization to provide input and have a say in the process, build consensus, and provide mechanisms for strategic leaders to reach out beyond the obvious to select business objectives that create sustainable outcomes. James C. Collins and Jerry I. Porras's *Built to Last: Successful Habits of Visionary Companies* (1994) suggests that companies should establish Big Hairy Audacious Goals (BHAG).[8] Collins and Porras believe that BHAG engage people. It is tangible, energizing, highly focused.[9] Objectives should not only set the stage for what has to be accomplished, but also serve the means to inspire people to achieve great outcomes and sustain their future.

Great companies usually achieve their objectives because the people are dedicated and work hard to fulfill their responsibilities. Therefore, it is incumbent upon strategic leaders to ensure that people are working on the right objectives. Strategic leaders not only have to select the right objectives, they have to properly specify the objectives so that their colleagues are directed toward the right results, and are encouraged to take expeditious pathways to get there.

Ultimately, strategic leaders have to determine the business objectives and articulate them throughout the organization and enterprise. Table 7.1 provides

Table 7.1 Examples of externally focused and internally focused business objectives

Objectives	Specifications	Potential concerns or vulnerabilities
Externally focused		
Market-related Value creation	Create new-to-the-world products that exceed the needs of the existing new market spaces and increase the revenue stream of such endeavors by $10 million by 2012.	The organization has to make improvements on the basis of market needs and the customers' perception of what creates value and success. Creating value requires dramatic developments, not just continuous improvements.
Value proposition	Improve the value of product "A" by 10% within two years through increasing efficiency and decreasing emissions.	Must ensure that the objective is sufficient to meet or exceed the expectations of customers and stakeholders during the time horizon.
Customers served	Expand market reach into areas not being served by the business unit make product more affordable and in line with the needs of market spaces.	Reaching out to new markets, especially those that are fundamentally different than traditional markets, requires a concerted effort and dedication that takes years to initiate and launch.
Customer success	Decrease overall customer problems and complaints from 3% to less than 1% by 2011 and improve customers' value proposition.	The expected results in the short term are small in comparison to the potential in the long term. It usually takes ongoing commitments to improvements to realize compounded gains.
Customer satisfaction	Improve customer relationships by increasing the number of alliances with customers by 50% within three years.	Building customer relationships takes many years of sustained efforts and outcomes to create the trust necessary for customers to become loyal.
Affordability	Improve the price to performance of all products by 15%, increase product longevity by 50%, and reduce operating expenses by 2012.	Product redesign development programs take several years to complete and it may take many years before customers realize the improvements.
Competition related Market share	Increase the market share in selected market segments by 20% by 2012 through improved value proposition.	Aggressive actions without enhanced capabilities, improved cost structures, and better resources may result in just more rivalry and not gains.

(cont.)

Table 7.1 (*cont.*)

Objectives	Specifications	Potential concerns or vulnerabilities
Competitive position	Move 10% of the businesses toward new market spaces that have less competition and more opportunity.	In a world of intense competition it is difficult to find new opportunities, and if one does find such market spaces, they quickly attract attention.
Competitive advantage	Decrease the intensity of competitive actions by exploring more complicated customer requirements where there is little competition and achieve 10% of revenues through such actions by 2012.	Serving the most difficult customer requirements or even the most difficult customer requires enhanced capabilities and new innovation. Such actions require more sophisticated management constructs and more aggressive leadership.
Social/stakeholder Connectedness	Increase the connections with the local communities and provide full disclosure of the impacts due to operations.	It may be easy to build connections with people in one's home country but it is often difficult to do the same across the world.
Stakeholder satisfaction	Expand stakeholder involvement by twofold within two years; solicit input and provide feedback.	The number of stakeholder groups involved with the SBU is only one facet of success; often the most challenging groups are not engaged.
Social responsibility	Dedicate people and money toward reducing poverty everywhere.	These are long-term objectives that take decades of commitments to realize improvements.
Economic Economic development	Promote economic development in the region and local communities dedicating at least 10% of purchases to businesses in region within two years.	Increasing the scope of responsibilities necessitates expanded thinking within the business units. People have to be educated to think beyond the traditional focus on markets and customers.
Sustainable development	Improve the economic conditions of the people supporting the business unit by ensuring they are treated fairly and are able to make a reasonable wage or obtain a fair profit.	This is an open-ended objective that is desirable but difficult to orchestrate and measure. Moreover, it most likely is a moving target that requires constant adjustments as the economic conditions change.
Environmental	Reduce air pollution by 50% over the next five years; continue to reduce air pollution by 50% every five years.	Most global corporations have made incredible improvements over the last decade; it may require new technologies to make further improvements.

Table 7.1 (*cont.*)

Objectives	Specifications	Potential concerns or vulnerabilities
Pollution prevention	Reduce the amount of toxic substances used in the production of products by 90% over next ten years.	Long-term objectives require concerted programs to ensure that appropriate results are achieved on an ongoing basis.
Sustainable development	Support global initiatives on climate change and reduce carbon dioxide emissions to pre-1990 levels by 2012.	Global initiatives often require corporate actions, not just those of SBUs; however, the SBU can improve its consumption of energy.
Internally focused *Strategic* Growth	Grow existing business portfolios 20% by developing two new businesses during the next five years.	Growth is important. It is also important to make improvement to the underlying capabilities of the organization.
Reputation/image	Enhance image and reputation within three years.	Broad objective that is difficult to measure and achieve.
Leadership	Improve brand and business unit recognition and image by increasing exposure in global community.	Requires multifaceted efforts to make improvements across all dimensions.
Financial Value creation	Increase the contribution of the business and product portfolios to creating wealth.	It often involves making radical changes to the businesses that enhance the positives and eliminate the negatives.
Cash flow	Improve the cash flow of the business or product lines by 10% within two years.	Could be a good objective but is short-term oriented. What happens after one year?
Return on assets	Increase return on assets by 10% each year over the time horizon.	It is very broad. It can be achieved by reducing assets rather than improving net income.
Margins	Reduce structural costs by 5% per year over the next five years, including materials from suppliers.	Requires immediate and ongoing results. May induce people to make the wrong reductions, like in quality and important features.
Profits	Increase profitability by 10% per year for the next ten years.	Long-term objective that gets more difficult to achieve without new strategic initiatives.
Revenues	Grow revenues 10% per year for the next five years.	If served markets are only growing by 5%, then new markets must be found.

(*cont.*)

Table 7.1 (*cont.*)

Objectives	Specifications	Potential concerns or vulnerabilities
Innovation Patents	Increase the number of new patents from 500 to 750 per year by 2012.	Patents are not always a measure of success. Many patents have limited commercial value.
Product innovation	Increase the new product development programs by 50% within three years.	If the business environment is changing dramatically, technological innovation may be necessary, not just product innovation.
Cycle time	Reduce product development cycle by 10% or two months each new cycle.	Cycle time reduction is important but not at the expense of thoroughness.
Learning Training	Ensure that 100% of employees have received adequate training in the primary roles and are provided at least 40 hours of new training per year.	The number of hours spent on training does not always translate into learning or new knowledge. Great care has to be used to ensure that training programs are effective.
Development	Improve employee satisfaction through education programs that are fully supported by the company.	Education and development programs should focus on the requisite future capabilities of the organization, not just the current needs.
Internal processes Quality	Improve overall quality of products and processes by reducing defects from 1,000 per million opportunities for defects to 100 per million by 2012.	It becomes more and more difficult to achieve the next level as quality is improved. The low-hanging fruit is easy. The upper reaches require extensive efforts and new methods.
Productivity	Improve productivity and efficiency by 5% per year for the next ten years.	Process improvements require knowing what processes need to be improved.
Effectiveness	Improve resource utilization rates by 20% within two years.	Effectiveness involves working smarter and uses assets better; must focus on right processes.
Connectedness	Expand linkages with suppliers and improve relationships with top 100 suppliers within two years.	Success requires mutual success across the enterprise. Helping suppliers may require development programs.
Cost reduction	Outsource all non-strategic fabrication within ten years.	Outsourcing does not always result in improved cost structures; new costs may appear.
Risk reduction	Reduce the risk of accidents, spills, and injury by 20% within three years.	Risk reduction should involve every process and improvements should be made quickly.

a typical list. It is sub-divided into externally focused and internally focused objectives. In both areas the perspective should be on enhancing the SBU's relationships with the external dimension. Making internal improvements should be driven by the needs and expectations of the business environment, the markets, customers, and stakeholders.

The objectives might also be sub-divided into short-term and long-term categories, and those focusing on the positives as well as the negatives. The table includes specifications for the objective; they should include content, expected level of achievement, and time frame. In an actual situation, more specificity should be given to help guide its execution. Moreover, the more quantitative the objectives are, the easier it is to measure the ongoing performance and attainment. It is usually easier to formulate business objectives based on the context of a real world situation as indicated in Table 7.1. The categorization of objectives provides meaning and a sense of logic and fit.

The table also identifies potential concerns or vulnerabilities related to the objective. Every objective has the potential to be misinterpreted or to cause the organization to move in the wrong direction. Strategic leaders have to think through the implications of each objective to ensure proper wording. Moreover, if the objectives are too broad, they may be initiated through the wrong strategies and action plans. For instance, if the objective is to improve profits, it might drive cost reductions that negatively impact quality or reliability, or drive the outsourcing of strategic processes to potential competitors. Achieving an objective in the short term may come at the expense of increased vulnerability to the emerging competition. On the other hand, if the objectives are too narrow and specify precisely what is required, then flexibility becomes constrained, and the organization loses freedom to meet changing business conditions. For instance, a specific business objective might define the improvement of existing products by a certain percentage. In this example, the organization may become locked into a perceived sense of importance based on the objective, instead of what is important for the marketplace. In the world of cell phones, size reduction was a critical aspect until the proliferation of features and functions became the new mantra.

The list is not intended to be exhaustive. It is illustrative of some of the business objectives that could be selected in each of the main categories. Others may be equally or even more important. Moreover, strategic leaders have to decide how many and type of objectives they should have.

The categories may be listed in different order depending on their importance. Market-related objectives are among the most critical for sustainable

Internally focused objectives		Externally focused objectives										
		Market-related		Competition-related		Social/stakeholder		Economic		Environmental		
		Short	Long	Short	Long	Short	Long	Short	Long	Short	Long	
Strategic	Short											
	Long											
Financial	Short											
	Long											
Internal processes	Short											
	Long											
Innovation	Short											
	Long											
Learning	Short											
	Long											

Figure 7.6   Matrix view of objectives with external and internal foci

success. Creating value and ensuring customer success often have a direct relationship with the sustainable success of the business units. Attention to corporate social responsibility and related contributions to economic and environmental well being are likely to be critical. Financial and strategic objectives are often derivatives of success with external-focused goals. Moreover, innovation, improving internal processes and organizational learning are crucial in setting the stage for realizing all of the other objectives of the organization. Figure 7.6 depicts a general scheme showing a two-dimensional matrix of SBU objectives.

The matrix presents possible interrelationships although not all internal- or external-focused objectives are linked. There may be several stand alone objectives. For instance, strategic leaders may wish to reward certain employees for outstanding performance for work they did to help their colleagues.

As indicated, every business objective carries with it potential concerns, limitations, and/or potential vulnerabilities. Very aggressive business objectives must have a realistic time horizon. Results often follow the "hockey-stick" phenomenon which implies that very few gains are realized in the short term and most of the gains are made as a result of the ongoing commitment and investments in related strategies, action plans, and initiatives. It may take five years to reach the point where true gains are being made, and ten years before the most significant outcomes are realized. One of the main difficulties these objectives face is that they are very difficult to track since very little apparent progress is made during the early years. It is akin to growing corn. The farmer tills the soil, plants the seeds, watches the stalks grow, and months later, finally sees corn husks develop. Months of investment and labor culminate with the harvest and sale of the crop – but there are no guarantees. Many variables along the way can influence the final outcomes – extreme weather conditions, devastating storms, destruction by insects, and poor economic conditions.

Likewise in the general business situation, if the cost structures follow the experience curve, where costs decline as the volume of products produced increases, then short-term objectives may be difficult to achieve since the most significant gains are made in the longer term due to the compounding effects of ongoing cost reductions. In such cases, it is difficult to state objectives that require identical annual outcomes. For instance, an objective of reducing overall costs by 5% per year across the next five years for an entire product portfolio may be impossible to achieve if it includes new product introductions with higher entry level costs. Indeed, such objectives on their own might cause management to focus on existing products and defer new product development. On the other hand, the reverse could be true if improvements are made through efficiency gains within the operations or the supply networks. In such cases, it may be easy to make improvements during the early years where there are many opportunities to make dramatic gains especially if the conditions at the beginning are very poor (the concept of the low-hanging fruit). However, once the low-hanging fruit has been picked, it may become more difficult to achieve the next level of efficiency and cost savings. Many companies during the 1980s with extremely poor quality, especially those with three-sigma quality (theoretically having 66,000 defects per million opportunities for defects), were able to make significant quality improvement as they moved toward four-sigma (6,000 defects). However, the challenges became increasingly more difficult as they approached five-sigma (233 defects) and eventually six-sigma quality (3.4 defects).

Strategic leaders have to be especially cautious when specifying growth objectives, as with other positive improvements. Growth objectives become increasingly difficult to achieve as the base expands. In the case of eBay it was relatively easy for their revenue stream to grow by more than 60% per year from $431 million in 2000 to over $3.2 billion in 2004. However, with today's significantly higher base, outstanding performance is difficult to achieve. Even with ongoing large gains, the rate of growth usually declines. Home Depot typifies this, after posting gains in net earnings that improved from $2.6 billion in 2000 to $5.8 billion in 2005. Yet, its shares in price/market capitalization have languished, most likely because its rate of growth in revenue declined from 17% in 2001 to 11% in 2005.

For objectives on improving negative impacts, business objectives that are based on the notion of a half-life may work well. The construct is simple and easy to specify. It simply states that the impact will be reduced by 50% during the time horizon. The same objective can be stated for the future periods as well. For each objective, strategic leaders only have to specify the base and the time horizon. For instance, if a business unit generates 2,000 metric tons of waste per year, then the objective becomes a 50% reduction or 1,000 metric tons by the end of the time horizon, which could be specified as five or ten years. The objective can be repeated until it is feasible to eliminate the negative effects or impacts completely.

Business objectives set the tone and specify the strategic intent of what is to be accomplished. They are also pivotal in setting the stage in the formulation and selection of business strategies. For instance, if the business objectives are designed to stretch the organization, then concomitant business strategies must be similarly aggressive. Business objectives and strategies are linked, and are really part of the overall strategic direction for the business units.

Box 7.1 Google Inc.'s aggressive mission for preeminence

Google has quickly become one of the best-known words, brand name, and company in the world. It has aggressively led change in the Internet search business and upstaged successful predecessors like Yahoo! Google Inc. was founded by Larry Page and Sergey Brin in September 1998 to commercialize their search engine technologies. Originally named "BackRub," Google Inc. was financed by $100,000 and $1 million investments by Andy Bectolsheim and family and friends, respectively.[1] Page and Brin realized that although they had limited funds, their success would be predicated on an aggressive move to the lead. They concentrated on perfecting and introducing the most outstanding search engine yet seen. They framed the development in terms of basic business philosophies like "never settle for the best." Their view as expressed by Page is as follows:[2]

"The perfect search engine would understand exactly what you mean and give back exactly what you want." Given the state of search technology today, that's a far-reaching vision requiring research, development and innovation to realize. Google is committed to blazing that trail. Though acknowledged as the world's leading search technology company, Google's goal is to provide a much higher level of service to all those who seek information, whether they're at a desk in Boston, driving through Bonn, or strolling in Bangkok.

To that end, Google has persistently pursued innovation and pushed the limits of existing technology to provide a fast, accurate and easy-to-use search service that can be accessed from anywhere. To fully understand Google, it's helpful to understand all the ways the company has helped to redefine how individuals, businesses and technologists view the Internet.

Google's impressive growth and success can be attributed to its quest for perfection and its contributions to the success of its external clients and constituents. Google's relentless pursuit of success and perfection is characterized in the "ten things Google found to be true."[3]

1. Focus on the user and all else will follow.
2. It's best to do one thing really, really well.
3. Fast is better than slow.
4. Democracy on the web works.
5. You don't need to be at your desk to need an answer.
6. You can make money without doing evil.
7. There is always more information out there.
8. The need for information crosses all borders.
9. You can be serious without a suit.
10. Great just isn't good enough.

The "ten things" continue to shape strategy formulation and guide strategic leaders through the maze of Internet opportunities and challenges. Often new companies get overwhelmed with exciting growth and all of the possibilities for making money. Google understands that success is based on doing a few things exceptionally well, instead of just outperforming the competitors in a marginal way. Perfection is difficult to copy. Google understands reality and works on sharing the reality with the world. Its mission is clearly stated as follows:[4]

Our mission is to organize the world's information and make it universally accessible and useful. We believe that the most effective, and ultimately the most profitable, way to accomplish our mission is to put the needs of our users first. We have found that offering a high-quality user experience leads to increased traffic and strong word-of-mouth promotion. Our dedication to putting users first is reflected in three key commitments we have made to our users:

• We will do our best to provide the most relevant and useful search results possible, independent of financial incentives. Our search results will be objectives and we will not accept payment for inclusion or ranking in them.
• We will do our best to provide the most relevant and useful advertising. Advertisements should not be an annoying interruption. If any element on a search result page is influenced by payment to us, we will make it clear to our users.
• We will never stop working to improve our user experience, our search technology and other important areas of information organization.

We believe that our user focus is the foundation of our success to date. We also believe that this focus is critical for the creation of long-term value. We do not intend to compromise our user focus for short-term economic gain.

Google has been successful in developing its business based on its philosophies and mission statement. In 2004 it raised $1.7 billion in its initial public offering of shares and obtained $4.3 billion in a second offering in 2005. It has leveraged the initial investments and its public offerings into one of the most valuable corporations in the world. Its market capitalization exceeds $142 billion as of Mach 26, 2007. It meteoric rise to prominence has been due to its focus serving its clients, the advertisers, and its users with the best results possible. Revenue growth has been tremendous, from $19 million in 2000 to $10.6 billion in 2006. Its gross margins are about 30% over the decade. Its revenue growth is outstanding, though the rate has decreased in recent years. In 2006 its net profit margin was 29% – stellar, when you look at another Internet success story, Amazon, whose margin was 1.8% by comparison.

Google is a successful company; however, there are no guarantees. Just as it usurped the lead from Yahoo! and now earns more profits in a quarter than Yahoo! does in a year, there are emerging companies like Suidoo, Sproose, and Mahalo, or existing ones like Microsoft that develop new technology, or use a different approach to satisfy customer search needs, and create a better platform. Moreover, there are currently numerous difficulties that include copyright infringement cases and lawsuits about the open use of materials.

Strategic leaders have to map a course into the future that is guided by Google's philosophies and fundamental beliefs. They have to be aggressive and develop new capabilities and businesses. They must also be careful not to waste resources on trying to do everything that comes along. Making the right choices in keeping with opportunities and realities is central to future success. The challenges going forward will become more complex and more difficult to sort out.

Notes

1. www.google.com/corporate/milestones.html.
2. www.google.com/corporate/tenthings.html.
3. *Ibid.*
4. Google Inc., Form 10-K, December 31, 2006, p. 1.

Summary

Strategic formulation involves the conversion of information, knowledge, and analyses into perspectives, insights, and constructs about what can be done, what has to be accomplished, and what strategies are necessary for achieving success. The front-end parts of strategic formulation involve understanding the business world and mapping out the strategic options available to the leaders of the SBUs. The process unfolds in a logical sequence to identify the most appropriate strategic options. Each business is unique; therefore, it is incumbent upon strategic leaders to reflect on the choices they have and to gain a specific perspective that is not generic.

Strategic options are choices that strategic leaders have to lead change, and realize their objectives. Strategic options include the following categories: growth, expansions, improvements, developments, learning, investments, and divestments. Each has its own specific characteristics and fit in terms of strategic direction. Each has advantages and disadvantages which are critical in recognizing that there are few if any generic approaches that are prescriptive. The theoretical view suggests that it is the role of the strategic leaders to map out strategic options and understand their fit to the realities of the SBUs.

Growth and expansion options are prevalent and often involve doing more of the same except in different geographic locations. They usually are the simplest to understand and select because they are supported by the core competencies and capabilities of the organization. They also involve serving the same or similar customers based on well-established requirements and expectations.

Improvement and development options are essential for keeping pace with or ahead of change. The notion of continuous improvement is widespread and practiced by most businesses. However, if the business situation is changing dramatically or the underlying capabilities are weak, then continuous improvement may not be good enough. Development implies making dramatic or radical changes. Continuous development is a burgeoning notion that suggests in a fast-paced world simply making improvements is not enough. Businesses must develop outstanding new products and technologies to sustain their strategic positions.

Investment options pertaining to acquisitions, mergers, joint ventures, and/or new business ventures are appropriate when the business units have weaknesses in certain markets or in the business environment. Investments are often a faster way to overcome strategic weaknesses especially when time is of the essence. Divestment options are the most relevant when the situation is irrecoverable or it is not worth the time, money, and efforts to overcome all of the problems.

Based on strategic options and the realities of the business environment, strategic management periodically reaffirms or refreshes the mission of the business unit. The mission and the related mission statements provide the organization with its purpose, aims, and sense of direction. It tells people what they should engage in and why the effort and commitment is important.

Selecting the business objectives has a direct tie to formulating strategies. The business objectives should be linked to the corporate objectives, being a subset of the overall corporate objectives and the grand strategy of the corporation. They should be balanced from both an internal and external perspective. Indeed, the main focus should be on markets, customers, stakeholders, and society. Moreover, business objectives should reflect the underlying principles of sustainable business development and include those related to social, economic, and environmental imperatives. The internal objectives should be connected to the external so that positive gains are shared across the enterprise. The main internal objectives include strategic positions, financial rewards, internal processes, innovation and learning. Internally focused objectives are often derivatives of external objectives. For instance, making money and being financially successful usually make customers successful and keep stakeholders happy. Selecting objectives involves critical decision making that requires not only balance, but also great insight into what has to be done and what can be accomplished. Trying to do more than what is possible may lead to disaster; likewise failing to be aggressive and outpace peers and competitors may also lead to vulnerabilities.

Strategic leaders must reflect on the objectives that they establish to ensure that they are proper. Great organizations usually achieve their objectives. However, if the objectives are not established properly, any achievements are significantly reduced in value and benefits to the businesses.

References

Collins, James and Jerry Porras (1994) *Built to Last: Successful Habits of Visionary Companies.* New York: Harper Business Essentials

Guth, William D. (1985) *Handbook of Business Strategy.* Boston, MA: Warren, Gorham, & Lamont

Rainey, David L. (2006) *Sustainable Business Development: Inventing the Future Through Strategy, Innovation and Leadership.* Cambridge, UK: Cambridge University Press

Rowe, Alan, Richard Mason, and Karl Dickel (1982) *Strategic Management and Business Policy: A Methodological Approach.* Reading, MA: Addison-Wesley Publishing Company

Susskind Lawrence and Jeffrey Cruikshank (1987) *Breaking the Impasse: Consensual Approaches to Resolving Public Dispute.* New York: Basic Books

NOTES

1 Lawrence Susskind and Jeffrey Cruikshank, *Breaking the Impasse: Consensual Approaches to Resolving Public Dispute* (New York: Basic Books, 1987, p. 260). Their note states that the "decide-announce-defend" approach was first used by Dennis Ducsik.

2 William D. Guth, *Handbook of Business Strategy* (Boston, MA: Warren, Gorham, & Lamont, 1985, p. 65). S. K. Johnson, the author of the chapter, outlines several of the prevailing portfolio matrices or models.

3 Alan Rowe, Richard Mason, and Karl Dickel, *Strategic Management and Business Policy: A Methodological Approach* (Reading, MA: Addison-Wesley Publishing Company, 1982, pp. 155–164).

4 http://shell.ihug.co.nz/~stu/milk.htm. Nestlé has instituted various initiatives to deal with the difficulties but concerns still exist.

5 In 1981, the PC industry gained in stature with the introduction of the IBM PC based on an 8088 or 8086 computer chip. IBM adopted an open architecture to facilitate software development of the many potential applications. In February 1982, Intel introduced the 80286 chip. At the end of 1984, IBM introduced the AT. It ran on Intel's 80286 microprocessor, which was significantly faster than the older chips. The AT was also a multi-user machine that allowed several people to operate remote terminals at the same time. Compaq's response to IBM's move was to design and introduce its own 80286 personal computer. In October 1985, Intel introduced the 80386. On September 9, 1986, Compaq unveiled the Deskpro 386, the first PC based on Intel's 80386 chip. In April 1987, IBM introduced the first four models of the new PS/2 system, containing 3.5 disk drives and proprietary technology. In August 1989, Intel introduced the 80486 microprocessor. In March 1993, Intel introduced the Pentium chip.

6 James Collins and Jerry Porras, "Building Your Company's Vision," *Harvard Business Review*, September–October 1996, p. 68.

7 David L. Rainey, *Sustainable Business Development: Inventing the Future through Strategy, Innovation and Leadership* (Cambridge, UK: Cambridge University Press, 2006, pp. 121–125).

8 James Collins and Jerry Porras, *Built to Last: Successful Habits of Visionary Companies* (New York: Harper Business Essentials, 1994, pp. 23–200).

9 *Ibid.*, p. 94.

8 Strategy formulation – business strategies and action plans

Crafting business strategies and action plans are among the most crucial aspects of the strategic management process. While the front end of strategic formulation requires incredible analyses, insights, and imagination, the harmonization of business strategies and action plans requires more than intellectual exercises and hard work. It involves a team effort to affirm the strategic analyses, understand the implications of the future, and know what is necessary to realize the desired future state. It is based on the intellectual capacity of strategic leaders and the organization to ascertain the best strategies in the context of both the theoretical possibilities and the practical realities.

The crescendo of strategic formulation necessitates that strategic leaders become fully engaged in deliberations over strategic options and business objectives, and in the selection of the best business strategies. It involves making difficult decisions that establish the strategic agenda for the future and determine the pathways to success. It also involves translating the strategies into action plans and initiatives so that the selected strategies can be validated in light of the capabilities and resources of the organization and the real world. Strategy formulation is not about either-or outcomes, but holistic perspectives about strategic decisions to create sustainable success.

Business strategies focus on the plans and actions of the business unit or those of a small and medium-sized enterprise (SME) to create value and achieve sustainable success. In a large company they are a subset of the overall corporate strategy. They involve what should be done, not necessarily how to do it. Deciding on the "what" includes the "why." It provides the logic and plan while articulating the "how" involves functional and operational approaches for the lower levels of the organization. The former is the responsibility of the strategic leaders, the latter of functional and operational leaders. Often there is confusion about what business strategies are and what functional and operational strategies are. While it is not always possible to discern the exact differences between them and the distinctions may not always have a significant influence on the outcome, it is important that strategic leaders focus their attention on higher level strategy formulation and do not spend all of their time concerned about lower level functional strategies. The latter generally involves short-range tactics like product pricing, outsourcing, advertising, and procurement.

Occasionally, critical functional or operational strategies become strategic requirements. For instance, ensuring health and safety is usually deemed to be part of the operating system, but if there are catastrophic failures and employees are killed or injured, such matters become strategic. Therefore, it is difficult to generalize and specify who is precisely responsible for each of the areas. It is clear that if the strategic leaders focus too much of their attention on lower level strategies, they may fail to pay enough attention to the higher level business unit strategies and vice versa. Moreover, if they delegate everything and assume that lower level management is empowered by such approaches and is fully able to act appropriately, there may be disconnects between the levels. Strategic leaders must provide direction, decision making, and oversight. Oversight is critical regardless of the actual approaches. Strategic leaders have a duty to ensure that strategies and actions plans are properly crafted and implemented.

Business strategies are the pivotal step in the strategic management process, tying the upstream aspects of reflection and analysis of the external and internal dimensions to the downstream aspects of implementation and execution. Without appropriate and effective business strategies most organizations would be adrift in an ocean full of exciting possibilities without a compass, a rudder, or an understanding of what is desirable and doable. Simply knowing about wonderful opportunities and having great capabilities and resources does not translate into strategic direction and actions. It takes competent and committed strategic leaders, dedicated functional management, and knowledgeable practitioners to translate opportunities and challenges into desired outcomes.

The chapter explores a myriad of business strategies that are used by companies, especially business units and SMEs. They include generic, preemptive, expansion and growth, market space and competitive, and diversification strategies. Each category has a number of subsets that are designed to reflect a given context or specific situation. The various strategies are discussed from a general perspective based on the notion that strategic leaders in their setting should decide what the best strategies are for the prevailing and expected business conditions and trends. The discussions are based on the presumption that there are no pre-ordained strategies for a given situation as there are too many variables involved and the situations often change quickly. Moreover, each company is unique.

Strategic leaders are the architects of the future. Their insights, imagination, and intellectual capabilities orchestrate change and create favorable results. They are the critical decision makers. If strategy formulation were prescriptive, then anyone or anything could formulate a business strategy – even a computer. Strategy formulation needs experienced, dedicated leaders to decide on the correct course of action and position the organization for success.

Strategy formulation also includes selecting action plans that convert business strategies into initiatives and then actionable programs that can be implemented by the organization. Action plans involve defining what has to be done, detailing who is expected to be involved, and when the actions are expected to be carried out. It also involves matching resources to requirements and ensuring that the organization has the capability to implement the strategies. The chapter includes the following main topics:

- Crafting business strategies that have strategic fit, that are challenging and take the organization beyond its comfort level, and that are exciting and actionable.
- Selecting and developing action plans and initiatives.
- Evaluating the results of strategic formulation.

Crafting business strategies

General perspectives on business strategies

Business strategy involves the art and science of crafting, selecting, and developing planned approaches to translate the stated business objectives into definitive directions and to realize desired outcomes through actionable plans. The primary focus is on determining how the business unit serves its selected current and future markets and customers and how it positions itself to be successful in the market spaces. The focus is also on fulfilling the broader social and environmental obligations and responsibilities.

Business strategy involves decision making which orchestrates the transition and transformation of the organization into what it wants to be in the future. Business strategies should be proactive to exceed the expectations of markets, customers, stakeholders, and other constituents; to surpass or render irrelevant the strategies, actions, and achievements of the competition; and to outperform the aspirations and expectations of shareholders, the board of directors, and/or the executive management team.

Business strategies may be classified as short- and long-term strategies that focus on the overarching objectives of the company and those of the business unit. However, business strategies generally focus more on the long term while operating and functional strategies focus more on the short and intermediate term. The former are discussed in this chapter while the latter are discussed in Chapter 9.

The precursor is to determine how well the existing business strategies are working. This involves a qualitative and quantitative assessment of the current fit, strategic logic, scope, value creation, and net contributions of each of the existing business strategies. As the business environment changes and the strategic direction of the business unit is modified, the prevailing business strategies may become out of synch or even obsolete with the realities of the business world and the company; therefore, those business strategies have to be reinvented, reformulated, or replaced. Moreover, if the business and financial performance and results pertaining to the prevailing business strategies are inadequate, or opportunities and challenges have changed dramatically, then the strategic logic of the existing business strategies may have to be revised to reflect the new realities.

The scope or reach of the business unit is an essential determinant in formulating business strategies. As the scope of the businesses expands, new opportunities, challenges, and vulnerabilities enter the scene. The business strategies likewise have to change to include additional perspectives, requirements, and realities. For example, as McDonald's expanded internationally its business strategies changed to include the cultural aspects of serving meals in countries like France where drinking wine during a meal is the norm. While such perspectives may seem to be operational, they involve profound changes to business strategies and actions.

The existing business strategy should be examined to determine how well it fulfills the objectives and realities of the business unit. The key question is how well can they contribute to value creation and sustainable success. If the resultant outcomes are successful and exceed objectives and expectations, then the business strategies may be sufficient, or just require simple modifications to go forward. On the other hand, if there are significant gaps between what is being achieved and what is required via the objectives and expectations, then new business strategies may be warranted. Ultimately, each business strategy should be judged on the basis of how well it contributes to success of the company and the business unit and the attainment of the business objectives. It is crucial to keep in mind that the measure of success is on future expectations, not just the present situation. Everything may seemingly be in accordance with the expectations and the current financial results may be great, yet the future prospects could be on the decline and the long-term strategic success questionable.

The formulation of new business strategies focuses on the creation of favorable situations and sustainable advantages for the business unit. It includes improving the capabilities, position, and power of the organization and its relationships within the extended enterprise and its ability to sustain success. The central perspectives are on the positive means and mechanisms to create value across the enterprise and satisfy customers, stakeholders, suppliers, distributors, employees, shareholders, and all of the other constituencies. It also involves understanding the prevailing and potential issues, problems, and challenges and finding the best way to resolve, dissolve, or eliminate them.

These categories of business strategy have many subsets. Some of the most prominent include generic strategies, preemptive strategies, expansion/growth strategies, market space/competitive strategies, diversification strategies, and turnaround strategies. There are also many special cases of corporate strategies that may be developed and executed at the strategic business unit (SBU) level. They include acquisitions, divestitures, collaborations, and many others. Some of the most important perspectives include enterprise integration, relationship building, timing, uncertainties, risks, and vulnerabilities. The categories listed do not include the older notions of reactive strategies like maintaining the status quo or reacting to change (wait and see) since they are not consistent with the principles of proactive strategic management. Moreover, it is highly questionable whether those types of strategies are relevant in a fast-paced business world. They are often a prescription for failure.

Generic business strategies

Background

The notion of generic business strategies permeates most of the traditional books on strategic management. While there are a number of versions, most of these constructs are based on Michael Porter's three generic strategies: overall cost leadership, differentiation, and focus.[1] As discussed in previous chapters, his seminal work revamped strategic thinking during the 1980s and has endured for more than two decades. There are numerous examples of each of the generic strategies and how they have contributed to successes in the past, but there are also concerns about their viability in today's business world because they are often emulated or duplicated by competitors resulting in commoditized situations.

Overall cost leadership involves achieving a low-cost position across the value chain and even the whole value delivery system to compete with rivals. It implies that the low-cost position may allow the strategic leaders to undercut the competition and to gain a dominant market share. Many Japanese companies used cost leadership to gain entry into the US markets during the 1970s and 1980s. Today, Wal-Mart has obtained a low-cost position in retailing by using its integrated value system to reduce costs and gain a superior competitive advantage.

Differentiation involves creating distinction and producing advantages through value-added attributes that are hard for others to emulate. It usually includes providing tangible and even intangible benefits to customers that are valuable or even unique. The brand names of well-known products and their stellar reputations are among the most powerful. Historically, Mercedes differentiated its position on the basis of superior product designs, high-level features, high-quality materials, and superior customer support services. Of course, the Mercedes name and the fact that it is a status symbol helped to sell cars. GE, Pratt & Whitney, and Rolls Royce make jet engines that have a great reputation. It is difficult for new companies to compete in this market because brand name and reputation play a critical role in purchasing decisions.

Focus involves selecting narrow market segments where the business can enjoy specific advantages. It allows businesses that are weak overall to concentrate on narrow fronts or market segments where they may be strong or have a differential advantage. For example, Nucor Corporation became a viable steel producer by starting as a niche player making low grade rebar. The large competitors paid little attention. However, over time, Nucor was able to move from being a niche player in the US steel industry by focusing on making steel from scrap metal and providing products to regionally based customers. It leveraged those successes to become the industry leader. It used its strength and above-average profitability in low-end markets during the 1980s and 1990s to become a technologically sophisticated producer of highly valued strip steel which is sold to automobile and appliance manufacturers. It successfully avoided significant competition in the early years by selling products that were at the extremes of the large markets and were not very attractive to the large integrated steel producers.

Each of the generic strategies has advantages and disadvantages as discussed below. They also involve risks and uncertainties, especially during turbulent times. Generic strategies need support systems and relationships if they are to become more distinctive and powerful.

Perspectives on low-cost leadership

A low-cost leadership strategy means obtaining a relatively high, if not the best, market share. It employs low-cost structure through economies of scale, high capacity utilization, and high volume to obtain cost reductions. Cost structures tend to decline for many products as the cumulative number of products increases. Costs are usually not linear with respect to production volumes; as the number of units increases, the cost per unit generally decreases at a non-linear rate. With higher volumes the fix costs associated with certain processes and activities including the expenditures for design and development, overheads for production facilities, and investment in information systems are absorbed by a larger number of products, thus lowering costs on a *pro rata* basis. In addition, the "experience or learning curve" suggests that as people gain experience in production and/or work processes, the time needed to produce a unit declines.

Low-cost providers must be very efficient and effective, and typically have to operate at close to full capacity so that unit costs remain low and other costs elements are minimal. The strategy can work well; however, it is often susceptible to economic downturns, new entrants into markets, strategic innovations and business models developed by competitors. The reliance on excellent capability utilization is one of the most critical vulnerabilities associated with low-cost leadership. Poor capacity utilization diminishes cost-effectiveness and the strategy becomes less viable.

Low-cost leadership is also obtained by reducing costs within the value chain. New product designs can provide exactly what the customer needs and expects without the extra features and functions that increase cost structures, but do not provide additional benefits or enhanced customer satisfaction. This approach requires great knowledge about customer expectations and what contributes to value-added. For example, the Toyota Camry has most of the essential specifications that customers want without frills and costly extras. Southwest Airlines and Jet Blue are renowned for their no-frills, "provide just what the customer is seeking" approach that is very cost-effective and gives customers essential benefits at low prices. Low-cost producers and providers can initiate several approaches to enhance their strategic positions. Indeed, they must be very aggressive in continuing to maintain low-cost leadership as competitors discover their secrets and emulate their positions. This requires optimizing the entire strategic management system (SMS) and value delivery system to achieve low costs. Lean production is also one of the most advantageous ways to eliminate economic and environmental waste, reduce cost structures, and mitigate vulnerabilities associated with an overreliance on high-volume production.

The value delivery system can provide rich opportunities for reducing costs. Cost leadership can be enhanced or obtained by having favorable relationships with suppliers and distributors who are also low-cost providers. Low-cost leadership necessitates gaining competitive advantages through cost structures that are difficult to obtain and/or replicate. This is typically the case when more cost-effective materials or parts are used before other producers and competitors become aware of the situation. The notion of outsourcing to suppliers or "off shoring" to low-cost suppliers in China and India may fit some of these perspectives, but again great care must be exercised since the approaches may not be sustainable and can easily be copied. The difficulty with initiatives like outsourcing from a strategic perspective is that competitors quickly follow and negate the advantages. Moreover, off-shore suppliers themselves may become competitors.

Eliminating the need for some of the supporting entities in the value delivery system is an effective way to reduce costs and make it difficult for less able competitors to follow. For example, Wal-Mart eliminated many intermediaries and lowered the overall cost of acquiring goods. Reconstructing the value delivery system is another effective way to improve cost structures. Such actions include eliminating distributors and even retailers and selling direct to consumers or end users. Amazon.com was an early innovator in using the Internet. Low-cost leaders that have optimized cost structures must continue to seek out other areas for improvement. They must also seek ways to reduce the costs of owning and operating products from a customer's perspective. For example, the Boeing 777 and 787 are more than 20% more efficient than earlier models.

Overall cost leadership works well when the products and services are essentially commodities and the driving force is price. When the commodities are difficult to differentiate and only the primary benefits of the product or service provide value, customers seek to maximize the value proposition by obtaining the most cost-effective solution. For instance, basic food products like milk and bread are commodities that customers buy routinely on the basis of price; they do not care about fancy extras or even who the producers are.

The vulnerabilities associated with low-cost strategies include engaging in severe competition where margins are depressed to levels where no one makes a suitable profit. For instance, even with the great acclaim given to Southwest Airlines' low-cost business model, from a financial perspective, the firm is just an average performer when compared to businesses in other industries. The airline industry engages in intense competition because of high fixed operating costs. Any attempt to obtain incremental revenue by lowering prices depresses the profitability of every competitor.

Another vulnerability is that lower costs often result in lower prices with spiraling downward effects. Customers may gain value from lower prices; however, this makes it difficult for producers and providers to make more than average profits and have cash flow available to make improvements, refinements, or enhancements that increase customer value. For instance, the prices for personal computers continue to fall as the cost of the hardware and peripheries decline. Even Dell is having difficulty maintaining profitability in an age of low-cost products with outstanding attributes that typically exceed customer expectations. Dell has changed its business model, but cash flow may not improve.

One of the most serious risks implicit in any strategy, especially a low-cost strategy, is the possibility of failing to achieve the intended leadership position. Being stuck in the middle of the pack without a defensible strategic position or sustainable advantage often results in failure. A long-term risk associated with overall low-cost leadership strategy for businesses based in developed countries is that emerging companies in China and India may become the global low-cost producers in the future. Current low-cost leaders may find it difficult to compete against such entities on the basis of cost and price. Emerging companies in developing countries may be the developers, producers, and providers of most of the global commodity products because they will be able to achieve economies of scale, high capacity utilization rates, and enjoy enormous volume-related advantages.

Perspectives on differentiation

Differentiation strategies are the most appealing when customers have the financial wherewithal and desire to pay for extra benefits, features, and functionalities. Differentiation requires that customers and stakeholders recognize and appreciate the added value of any extras and enhancements. The added value provided must then be translated into above-average margins and higher net profits. Such strategies work well when customers are willing to pay a premium for customization. While most differentiation strategies are underpinned by the value proposition, differentiation is highly dependent on providing gains for customers that justify the added premium.

A differentiation strategy must combine unique benefits to customers with unique advantages for the producer/provider as well. Customers obtain tailored products that better meet their needs and expectations without having to customize the products themselves as they might have to do with generic products. The business unit has the potential to obtain higher margins and customer loyalty, as the desirable outcomes are not as broadly available with commodity-type products and services. For example, Toyota launched a hybrid Camry in 2006. The car offers higher fuel efficiency than the standard Camry; however, customers have to pay approximately $3,000 more for the differentiated version. In the current period of uncertainty about energy costs, many customers may be happy to pay more for cars to reduce any vulnerability associated with fuel availability and expense. Toyota is enjoying short-term success based on this differentiated position given the limited numbers of hybrid models available for customers, especially from competitors. Toyota's lead in hybrid-drive technology is expected to continue for several years as competitors try to catch up.

Differentiation is more complex and difficult to orchestrate than cost leadership because the related strategies take numerous forms. Prevalent forms include incorporating technological sophistication, multifaceted features and functions, exceptional reliability and longevity, superior service and support, outstanding environmental stewardship, and high-quality products. Key to success is using the value proposition to understand the underlying aspects and requirements for success. Customers want high value. Improving positive and reducing negative aspects associated with technologies, products, services, and processes provide the means to create better solutions for customers and stakeholders.

The more difficult it is for competitors to duplicate differentiated positions the more effective the strategies generally are. While cost leadership typically depends on simplicity and "bare bones" approaches, the success of differentiation depends on a well-honed understanding of complexities and value-added requirements to create unique solutions. The more complex positions are more difficult to assess, understand, copy, and implement. However, complexity does not always mean more complicated solutions. Complex systems can be used to simplify solutions, making outcomes more desirable and workable from the customers' point of view. For example, Siemens makes devices that operate at extreme temperatures and in harsh environments. While these devices employ sophisticated technologies and elaborate engineering, they are fully automated and controlled to simplify operation and maintenance. The capability to manage complexity simplifies the lives of customers and allows Siemens to gain an advantage over its competitors.

Differentiation is also achieved through the efforts of the entire extended enterprise. Highly integrated extended enterprises can provide exceptional quality, fast delivery, excellent support services, customized information flow, and tailor-made solutions. For example, book publishers, including Cambridge University Press (CUP), let customers buy just the chapters in a book they want. CUP allows instructors to custom select text from various college textbooks for use in courses. By tailoring the textbook to the specific needs of the instructor and students, the publisher can provide the required chapters, case studies, and other materials. The final product may have additional costs since it has to be assembled from a variety of sources. But, the customized solutions avoid economic and environmental waste by providing just what is required to fulfill needs of the user (the student) and the customer (the instructor). The solutions can include products from other companies and even those from other publishers or competing media.

Differentiation requires distinction and a sense of uniqueness. This necessitates exploiting core competencies and high-level capabilities to design and develop products, services, operations, and processes that provide customers and stakeholders with attributes and/or solutions that are not readily available from other sources. While customized products and services are often more costly than those available from low-cost leaders, customized products typically provide more value and are often less costly to own and operate. Saving money on the application side provides customers with more powerful solutions that usually do not affect the producer/providers overall margins and profits. For instance, new cell phones now have multiple features and functions including the ability to phone, receive and send e-mails, text messages, take and send digital pictures, and have access to social networking sites (e.g. Facebook) via the Internet. These cell phones provide customers with flexibility and more freedom of action, and are a prime example of differentiation by compiling various sources of technological media.

There are numerous ways to differentiate products and services for customers without having a negative effect on financial success. These approaches include providing additional tangible and intangible aspects. Adding enhanced tangible features and functions makes products easier to use, and less costly and burdensome to own (including end-of-life disposal).

Intangible ways of eliminating the worry about owning complex products is an excellent way to gain advantage. For instance, guaranteeing products and services for their lifetime or providing an extended warranty is a functional strategy that could have strategic significance when used as a way to differentiate between competitive positions. Businesses with high-quality defect-free products and processes should offer guarantees that are more than twice the industry norm. In October 2006, GM announced a ten-year or 100,000-mile warranty which is now amongst the best in the industry. Imagine the strategic advantage if GM or any other producer had the competency, capability, and confidence to increase their warranty to fifteen years and 150,000 or even 200,000 miles without taking a huge financial risk because their products were so superior. Competitors would find it difficult to follow quickly unless they had similar high-quality capabilities, products, and processes. These strategies lead to highly differentiated advantages from the industry norm where customer concerns about product quality and reliability are manipulated by selling expensive extended warranty contracts. Such short-term functional strategies work when customers have few choices. However, these same strategies often work against companies in the long term as customer loyalty slips. If the producer does not believe in product quality, why should customers assume the risks? Other approaches used to gain competitive advantage through differentiation include:

- Improving the value proposition using more positives and fewer negatives; provide more value through enhanced features, functions, and benefits as well as reduced costs, defects, burdens, and impacts.
- Increasing information flow and educational methods to provide the knowledge needed to use products and processes. This is especially true for technologically sophisticated hardware and software such as electronics, computers, and video games. This also applies to providing information for the safe and appropriate use of chemicals and mechanical devices as well as the requisite prevention and protection aspects for health and safety and environmental issues and problems.
- Translating customer uncertainties into understandable benefits that each individual can appreciate. If each buyer has specific requirements, then a differentiated approach has to respond to these customer needs including how the customer should buy, use, or interact with the product.
- Maintaining flexible systems and structures so that products and processes can quickly adapt to meet changing requirements and expectations.

Imitation by others of functions and features not based on truly unique competencies and capabilities is a vulnerability of differentiation strategies.

Other difficulties include failing to achieve a sufficient increase in the value proposition, lacking ways to convince customers that the unique or customized attributes, benefits, and/or solutions are sufficiently valuable and powerful, and failing to translate any extra value into financial and sustainable success. In today's business world, customers often want premium products and service; however, they are not willing to pay more for them. A risk to differentiation strategies, especially those employing premium pricing, is that customers drive all the competitors to achieve the same results. Customers wait until prices fall to more reasonable levels and then buy the features or functions they want. This is a particular concern in situations where customers do not have to act immediately. This phenomenon is at play in many high-tech product areas like plasma and LCD TVs, digital cameras, and cell phones. Prices are normally high during the introduction stage. However, they decline rapidly as quantities sold or the number of competitors in the market increases. Another difficulty involves poor communication processes to educate potential customers about the advantages provided via differentiation. For instance, the product may have better attributes, but customers can not discern the value of the differences between the options.

Differential advantages are difficult to acquire and even harder to keep. If there is a significant time lag between deploying strategies and obtaining financial benefits, then there may be insufficient time to capture extraordinary rewards before competitors try to appropriate their share of the business. One of the major threats in today's business climate is that the window of opportunity to capitalize on strategies, investments, and new developments is often extremely small resulting in inadequate returns. This is a particular concern with high-tech products like cell phones that are based on rapidly changing technologies. Many new products have a short life span and are quickly replaced by other new products that trump the advantages of their predecessors.

Perspectives on focus

Strategic focus is the third generic strategy. It implies a narrow perspective on select market niches where the business unit can enjoy advantages that are not available in the broader market. This approach is usually employed by smaller companies or weaker businesses. Strategic focus works well when the target market segment fits into the domain of the business unit. Orange growers' cooperatives in Florida are competitive in the production and sale of orange juice because they focus all of their capabilities and resources on that endeavor. Dunkin' Donuts and Starbucks are successful providers of coffee and complementary products and services. However, both stay away from broader forays due to competition in the full service restaurant businesses. Pizza restaurants are a good example of focus in terms of products provided and customers served.

The key to success for strategic focus is to ensure the market niche is large enough to support the objectives of the business. However, this same market segment usually has to be small enough not to garner the attention of mainstream competitors in larger markets who have the resources to overwhelm smaller players. Focus usually requires a balancing act that can be difficult to maintain, especially by the business units of large companies.

Main vulnerabilities to strategic focus include the introduction of new technologies and products, the significant decline or growth of the niche market, and the threat of more powerful competitors seeking opportunities as their principal market segments become saturated and intensely competitive. Highly specialized market niches are always susceptible to technological change, new products and processes, or other sources of innovation. The famous "buggy whip" producers fit this perfectly. No matter how well producers designed and manufactured their products, the needs evaporated and the category declined. This situation is even more obvious today as technological change drives markets and customers. For instance, powerful thumb drives replace floppy disks, MP3 players and iTunes replace compact discs, and thousands of technological changes and product innovations cause existing products and services as well as the strategic positions of the producers and providers to decline if they are unable to change. Market niches like the general store, drive-in movie theater, and the home delivery of milk simply disappear while few people think about the implications – or in many cases even notice.

The threat of market decline is always present, but the opposite situation is also a significant threat to those utilizing a focus strategy. If the market segment grows substantially, there may be new competitors trying to obtain a share of the market. Small or narrow market segments may not be worth pursuing because of limited revenue streams and profitability. The situation can change dramatically if the market potential expands and isolation is replaced with more attention and competition. For example, Volkswagen enjoyed great success in America when it was the prime supplier of small cars. It served a relatively small niche that was viewed as unprofitable by the "Big Three American producers." Everything changed after the oil crises of the 1970s when small cars became a critical segment and many other competitors, especially from Japan, entered the mix. Volkswagen had difficulties adapting and its strategic position declined.

Focus strategies require commitment and staying the course for a significant period of time, say ten to twenty years. For example, Nucor remained in the sub-structure of the steel industry for more than twenty years as it grew in strength and capability. Its strategic leader, Ken Iverson, had the patience and wisdom to stay the course. Focus strategy may also require low-cost leadership in specific areas or product differentiation to keep competitors out of the organization's market spaces. Again, Nucor is a good example. It combined its niche position with a powerful low-cost strategy. While Nucor used a focus strategy to grow in isolation, integrated giants like US Steel and Bethlehem paid little attention. As new processing technologies allowed for more cost-effective production of more valuable steel products from scrap metal, Nucor was on the cutting edge of change.

Focus is the most difficult generic strategy for large companies to use because the outcomes are often dictated by market segments and not by the aggressiveness of the organization. For instance, if a business unit is serving a focused market niche growing at 2% per year, this makes it difficult to compete and grow at 10% because the firm is constrained by strategic choice and is unwilling to engage in severe competition.

Overall implications and trends

Applying generic strategies often has a fundamental flaw. As the name implies they are generic and offer a limited range of choices intended to fit a broad array of businesses. The notion of generic strategies suggests that businesses can be successful if they select the right generic strategy from the ones available. To have just three overall strategies that are appropriate for millions of businesses around the world seems implausible. Consequently, with only three generic choices the effectiveness of each strategy is limited because competitors easily become aware of what that strategy is.

When Porter articulated generic strategies during the early 1980s, businesses often viewed the world in terms of an "either-or" mentality. At that time strategic leaders had to decide what strategy to select: low-cost leadership, differentiation, focus, or a combination of them all. Today, with technological change and sophistication, intense competition, and the increased power of customers and stakeholders, market spaces are much more complicated. Simplicity is inherently good; however, it may not be realistic in this more complex business world.

Many large companies have combined generic strategies into a "super generic strategy." The term incorporates facets of the three generic strategies. Many companies enjoy low-cost leadership positions while also having highly differentiated products for each market segment. While such a strategy is not in the traditional sense of what focus means, the strategy includes treating each market segment as if it were the focus. For example, Toyota has numerous business units and product portfolios within its large umbrella of cars offering choices for customers of all backgrounds, ages, and locations. Toyota tries to be the low-cost leader in every segment based on lean business concepts. It produces numerous models tailored to the needs of specific customers so they can obtain the right solution for their needs. This approach enhances the value proposition because customers do not have to buy extras they do not want. The Lexus, Toyota, and Scion product lines are specifically designated to divide the larger car market into manageable segments where each brand is viewed as important and gets proper attention. While there are always products or product lines that get more management attention or are viewed as more critical to financial success, Toyota executes strategies that combine the three generic strategies. While generic strategies are still used, most businesses adapt business strategies customized to their unique situation.

Preemptive strategies

Underpinnings, philosophies, and categories

Preemptive strategies are proactive approaches for leading change and taking the initiative to aggressively move on opportunities and challenges in the business environment before such actions are expected or become obvious. Preemptive strategies necessitate changing and even disrupting industry or market space norms through fast-paced, hard to duplicate strategic actions that provide distinctive and sustainable advantages for first mover, fast follower, or strategic change leaders. Preemptive strategies eschew the notions of reacting to change or anticipating changes only slightly ahead of the necessity for action. Preemptive strategies imply that strategic leaders seek out every opportunity to forge positive changes and exploit new opportunities before customers or competitors understand the implications.

Preemptive strategies require extremely assertive actions in making dramatic or radical improvements to the external and internal dimensions of business units. This includes the main elements of the extended enterprise as well as strategic and operational management systems. Being aggressive does not mean increasing the rivalry among competitors; it does mean taking every opportunity to make profound changes that advance the well being of customers, the extended enterprise, the organization, and all of the key contributors.

Table 8.1 Selected preemptive strategies[2]

Construct	Spatial strategies	Temporal strategies	Mass and energy strategies
Strategic management system (Level)	*Systems integration* – Integrating the entire system from the depths of the supply chain to the far reaches of customers and secondary markets; linking the end of products and enhancing product and material recovery and reuse	*Systematic change* – Reinvigorating the strategic management system with new or improved clean technologies, products, and processes; leading change through innovation and integration of the value system across time to meet future needs and achieve sustained competitive advantage; leading positive changes.	*Substantial transitions* – Adapting new ways of achieving positive outcomes; reinventing capabilities and resources to meet the future and not just exploiting the prevailing situation; ensuring that social, economic, and environmental factors are considered; being socially responsible and ethical.
Operating system (Level)	*Synthesis* – Integrating the product delivery system with suppliers and customers to minimize disruptions and negative impacts and consequences, eliminate wastes and pollution, reduce losses, and improve efficiency and effectiveness.	*Synchronization* – Linking capabilities, resources, outcomes, and strategic direction with the needs, requirements, and expectations of constituencies over the life cycle of products and processes; enhancing responsiveness over life cycles and exceeding expectations.	*Superior satisfaction* – Creating distinction and uniqueness that support viability and long-term success; satisfying customers, stakeholders, and constituencies with positive outcomes; providing total satisfaction to society, customers, stakeholders, employees, and shareholders.

The strategic logic is also on making significant improvements to existing systems and creating new developments that eliminate the underlying problems and difficulties of the prevailing situation. Improvements include initiatives like reducing defects through six-sigma quality management and enhancing lean business practices. New developments include creating clean technologies and new-to-the-world products that enhance customer satisfaction and eliminate waste and pollution. Preemptive strategies focus on dramatically enhancing value creation and improving the value proposition.

Preemptive strategies usually involve the full integration of the whole enterprise into a seamless and highly assertive value delivery system (holistic management system) that is fully capable of planning and executing every action at the highest level of quality and performance. Most importantly, preemptive strategies involve strategic innovations that significantly or radically improve underlying technologies, products, and services. These include inventing and validating clean technologies, developing and delivering more valuable solutions, enriching and exploiting improved process capabilities, and reinventing the strategic management system and value delivery system with outstanding intellectual capital, capabilities, and resources. Preemptive strategies involve transitions and transformations to the next level of achievement and sustainable outcomes.

Preemptive strategies are not simply more aggressive than generic strategies; they are based on a management mindset that revamps the old line of thinking about what businesses should engage in and how they should conduct their affairs. They involve out-of-the-box thinking about how to move closer toward perfection and obtain the best solutions for customers and stakeholders, and to build enduring relationships with all of the essential contributors and recipients. Strategic thinking shifts from the competitive spaces of the past to preempting the market spaces and creating the business enterprise of the future. This includes integrating the extended enterprise into a complete system, leading change to secure sustainable advantages, and using all of the capabilities and resources in the most effective and least damaging ways.

Creating a preemptive strategy means taking every opportunity to reconfigure space, time, and realities into more favorable outcomes. Table 8.1 provides an overview of the main categories and elements of preemptive strategies. It lists the main areas related to the strategic management system and their implications at the operating system level.

Preemptive strategies do not mean exploiting markets and customers through fancy marketing campaigns or shrewdly convincing customers to buy flawed products and services. They mean moving away from the old paradigms of using single-sided marketing approaches to sell as many products as possible to ill-informed customers to the more philosophical, ethical, and socially responsible approach of disclosing both sides of the value proposition. Dual-sided means informing customers and stakeholders about the positive aspects such as features, functions, and benefits as well as negative implications like waste generation, potential burdens, and the possibility of defects. It is more open, transparent, and honest. Dual-sided management does not disadvantage the strategic leaders that are open and honest since it is in keeping with what customers truly want – great solutions supported by full disclosure. Dual-sided management provides advantages to such leaders as full disclosure is in line with reality and preempts early-stage problems or prevents them altogether. It preempts problems and difficulties. Today, it is very easy for customers and stakeholders to check on the veracity of statements and public disclosures by companies and claims made in marketing campaigns. The Internet makes it possible to simply "Google" to find what you want to know to make an informed decision about a given product. Moreover, the media around the world have stories about companies and their strategic leaders being queried about potential abuses via stock options,[3] bribery or "under the table" funds.[4] When the truth comes out, the consequences are usually severe.

General perspectives

Preemptive strategies focus primarily on designing, developing, delivering, and supporting the best solutions to ensure customer and stakeholder success and creating systems to reinforce success. Providing ways for customer and stakeholder success – not just satisfaction – is expected to be one of the dominant objectives and metrics of the future.

Preemptive strategies include occupying prime positions in existing market spaces and discovering new market spaces as discussed in the "Blue Ocean Strategy" in Chapter 5. For instance, Microsoft and Intel have the most advantageous positions in personal computer (PC) businesses. They have maintained great success for more than twenty-five years in a business arena where most of the players have failed and even giants like IBM have capitulated. Microsoft's position in particular is extremely successful because others cannot emulate its power and entrenched position in numerous market segments around the world. However, completely new technologies may someday change the situation to the possible detriment of Microsoft. Moreover, other factors like antitrust actions, especially those in the European Union (EU), may cause difficulties.

Preemptive strategies are based on fundamentals that underpin opportunities and challenges and require decisive and early action. They include exploring all of the options available and to select the most advantageous approaches. Preemptive strategies are usually not constrained by competitive positions or actions and allow business leaders and strategists many degrees of freedom. Think about IBM's missed opportunity to preempt Microsoft during the early 1980s and become a key player in PC software. Now, imagine anyone trying to preempt Microsoft today. Not to suggest that this situation is impossible, but given the prevailing conditions this will not happen unless there are wholesale changes in technologies, markets, customer expectations, and attitudes.

Preemptive strategies involve exploiting new opportunities before they are recognized by existing and emerging competitors, new entrants, or entities in related industries. Theodore Levitt discussed in his famous 1960 *Harvard Business Review* article, "Marketing Myopia," that strategic leaders must be proactive:[5]

The usual result of a narrow preoccupation with so-called concrete matters [i.e. profit possibilities of low-cost production and a strategic focus on products and growth] is that instead of growing, the industry declines. It usually means the product has failed to adapt to constantly changing patterns of consumer needs and tastes, new or modified marketing institutions and practices, or to product developments in competing or complementary industries. The industry has its eyes so firmly on its own specific product[s] that it does not see how it is being made obsolete.

... Management must think of itself not as producing products but as providing customer-creating satisfaction [success]. It must push the idea (and everything it implies and requires) into every aspect of the organization. It has to do this continuously and with the kind of flair that excites and stimulates the people in it.

In short, the organization [management] must learn to think of itself not as producing goods and services but, as buying customers, as doing the things that will make people want to do business with it [providing and creating value through customer solutions and ongoing success].

Levitt made his comments in a period dominated by American giants, corporations like GM, AT&T, IBM, NCR, Pan Am, RCA, and many others. Taken on a broader scale, his comments apply to many companies and business leaders of today. Their thinking is also narrow and their strategies focus too much on existing market demand, financial requirements, and competitive landscapes. Levitt observed that most of the preemptive changes and actions were made by those outside the traditional industry. He indicated that strategic leaders in those industries were slow, if not unable, to engage in preemptive moves. This allowed others to lead change because strategic leaders within the industry were myopic. They focused on selling products and making money instead of creating extraordinary value, providing the best possible solutions, building enduring systems and relationships, and achieving sustainable success.

The theoretical proposition is that if an organization's strategic leaders do not preempt the prevailing situation someone else will. Their inability to act using broader perspectives is expected to negatively affect the fortunes and even the survival of the organization or at least the business unit. The notion that change is slow and that the status quo can be maintained is old thinking that is almost impossible to visualize today.

Preemptive strategies include taking actions to transition or transform the business unit's positions into more favorable ones. The major categories include:

- Revamping how the business unit addresses market spaces and outperforms competitors or makes them irrelevant.
- Enhancing the extended enterprise and making it more enduring and successful.
- Creating new technologies, developing new products, and enhancing innovation processes – focusing on solutions.
- Developing and improving value delivery systems, especially by eliminating negative impacts and economic and environmental wastes.

Strategic leaders shape their perspectives of markets and select advantageous market segments to optimize a business unit's capabilities, resources, and overall position. Management can preempt market opportunities by revamping how the business units provide solutions to customer and stakeholder needs and expectations. Developing preemptive opportunities involves understanding the implicit and explicit requirements of customers and stakeholders. This involves taking action – aggressive action – to provide significantly more than what is expected. This includes making radical changes to the business model that provides unique benefits to the business unit.

As discussed earlier, the notion of a "super generic strategy" can be viewed as a preemptive strategy for exploiting market space opportunities. This requires providing the best value proposition by including affordability and sustainability, creating superior products, services, and benefits, building trust and integrity through respected brand names and company behaviors, and establishing customer relationships for mutual gain. The theory involves optimizing solutions and building enduring relationships that are based on creating value without trade-offs or compromising long-term potential for short-term gain.

Fundamental approaches

The fundamental approach focuses on creating awareness about solutions, building credibility among players, gaining acceptance by potential customers, and expanding market reach to those historically without access to the solutions. Preempting market spaces also means addressing underlying needs and expectations to enhance customer ability to effectively and efficiently use and benefit from the new solutions. For instance, Dow Chemical's product stewardship program provides the information and knowledge customers need to safely use Dow products. This saves customers time and money in obtaining information and training people. The program also reduces risks associated with product applications and the probability of adverse situations.

A preemptive strategy includes seeking first mover advantage to gain access to new materials and components, technologically sophisticated production equipment, processes, methods, and superior logistics. These upstream enhancements require finding and securing more cost-effective means and mechanisms to provide the ingredients for products and services. Obviously, one approach is to discover and deploy low-cost manufacturing in low-wage countries. However, care must be taken to avoid creating other vulnerabilities as the desire for low costs can overwhelm the decision-making process. A broader perspective may result in unique outcomes. Preempting supply networks with enhanced linkages and relationships can result in new solutions that are more difficult to copy. For example, Mercedes has integrated its suppliers many tiers deep into the supply chain.

There are also downstream ways to create preemptive positions. One of the most effective superior positions is to build capacity or occupy positions that are hard to copy. This is analogous to occupying the high ground in military situations. For instance, GE is acquiring water resources around the world because it realizes that water is expected to become a critical resource in the future. Likewise, Wal-Mart positions stores in locations that are unfavorable for others, but still allow Wal-Mart to attract customers from adjacent urban and suburban areas.

Creating new technologies and developing new products and processes are effective methods for changing market spaces and competitive positions. Radical new technologies can provide the means to wipe out the strengths and superior position of market share leaders and reshape competitive landscapes. New, clean technologies provide better solutions with more benefits and fewer distractions. Likewise, successful new-to-the-world products often provide superior benefits and value proposition. This is especially true after they have acquired critical market mass and costs are reduced through increased volume.

Technology and product development are ways to reverse weakening positions and establish leadership positions in market spaces that are dominated by entrenched companies. Moreover, these developments are especially appropriate for companies that are disadvantaged in the prevailing situations. For example, market share leadership in photography would have been difficult for another organization to usurp from Kodak and Fuji without a dramatic change in technology. However, with digital technologies there are new leaders and more competitors are participating in the market segment.

Preemptive strategies require identifying emerging opportunities before others do, thinking out-of-the-box about what solutions can and/or have to be, recognizing how to develop and deploy these solutions through preemptive moves, and understanding the ongoing actions necessary to sustain position. All require imagination on the part of strategic leaders about how to preempt the prevailing situation and inspire the entire organization to form strategies that achieve extraordinary results. Preemptive strategies go beyond the norm and expect and attempt to create sustainable advantages. While preemptive advantages are not permanent, they are enduring and can be enhanced over time as the organization continues to pursue aggressive approaches.

Expansion and organic growth strategies

Expansion strategies

Expansion and organic growth strategies focus on increasing the economic underpinnings and financial activities of the business unit by expanding the means and mechanisms for producing more of the prevailing outputs. Expansion strategies are traditional business approaches that simply take a formula, business strategy, or business model which has proven to be successful in one market segment to reach out to other markets segments or to drill further into the existing segments. Expansion strategies focus on markets and customers. They are often based on geographic reach where strategic leaders replicate achievements in previous market segments into new ones. Historically, fast food restaurants, coffee shops, retailers, soft drink companies, bookstores, car dealers, and others follow geographic expansion strategies.

Expansion strategies involve penetrating existing markets in more depth and breadth and moving to new market segments. The former is typically referred to as market penetration, while the latter is typically known as market development. Both are usually based on narrow perspectives using existing capabilities and resources tailored to existing product portfolios. Generating more revenues and profits through marketing and operations are usually the key objectives. Moreover, strategic action plans often concentrate on functional strategies and/or tactical approaches like advertising and promotion. Such strategies are usually deemed logical, low risk, easy to execute, and fundamentally sound because they are based on previous experiences and structured on known processes and practices. Most expansion requirements are well defined and the people within the organization are capable of creating another version of what has been successful using the same schemes. The keys for successful execution depend on providing an outstanding value proposition, understanding the critical factors for success, and having the marketing skills, financial resources, and the managerial talent to develop and deploy the added operational aspects.

The power of expansion strategies arises from simply mapping out the details for strategic actions and developing the requisite capabilities and resources for implementation. The requirements are usually a logical extension of existing organizational knowledge and behaviors. The risks include becoming more entrenched within narrow product, functional, and operational realities. While doing more of the same makes intuitive sense, such actions without reflection on the implications can increase the business unit's vulnerabilities to market dynamics and technological changes. Market conditions and trends are always changing as social, political, economic, and environmental realities affect customers and stakeholders.

Assuming that markets are static or that there is an underlying demand for existing products is a very risky perspective. For instance, circa 2002–2004 many food processing companies and others engaged in providing food products were caught off guard by the rapid growth of the "low-carbohydrate," weight-watching phenomenon. People's view and acceptance of high-calorie, high-fat foods like hamburgers, French fries, doughnuts changed radically. Many successful companies like McDonald's and Krispy Kreme had to rethink their business strategies and operational tactics because their customers questioned the nutritional value of their products.

Expansion strategies, especially those that do not change basic products, and existing business models that simply march into new markets, require significant assessments and periodic evaluations to assess the viability of the approach. This is a concern, especially when the focus is on products and services, not on solutions. There must be ongoing analysis of the business environment regarding the soundness of internal means and mechanisms to ensure that all defects, impacts, and burdens are identified, corrected, and mitigated as quickly as possible. The logic is simple. Flawed methods and weak approaches are easy to correct or modify during the early stages of expansion.

They become more difficult and costly to correct or solve as problems increase and the outcomes of the expansion strategies mature. Careful development means mitigating problems early in the process. For example, Toyota was very careful during the introduction of the Prius to monitor the performance of their customers' experience. Toyota's leaders involved with the Prius realized that it is relatively easy to repair 20,000 cars with an unexpected defect. However, it would be extremely costly to do the same for two million or more cars. The norm for most expansion strategies is usually just the opposite. The strategic leaders want to expand quickly often using a "cookie cut" approach. For instance, fast food companies typically build thousands of similar stores in their home country and then often use the same model throughout the world. Imagine discovering a significant defect, impact, or problem after tens of thousands of stores have been built and each has the same fundamental problem.

Organic growth strategies

Organic growth strategies are similar to expansion strategies except they include organic developments like creating additional product forms and/or versions, developing updated products and services, and improving ways of reaching and satisfying customers and stakeholders. Organic growth strategies may also involve taking on new market segments while adding new products and services through market penetration and market extensions.

The underlying premises to organic growth strategies are to exploit business opportunities closely related to the prevailing mission of the business unit and to leverage the core strengths and strategic positions of the organization. Growth strategies have many variations from systematic additions to the operating base to the development of new markets and customers and improvements to existing ones. Changing the capabilities, resources, and portfolios of business units in the pursuit of exponential growth involves highly leveraged incremental improvements, and ongoing developments in capabilities, resources, products, processes, and operations. Exponential growth is much more aggressive than simple expansion and can take the forms of preemptive strategies except they are usually narrowly defined in terms of the conventional mission of the organization. For example, Google is a company that is focused on a growth strategy. It is building a large portfolio of inter-related services that help Internet customers to find what they are looking for.

Organic growth strategies often go beyond market aspects and take a slightly broader perspective. They focus on increasing the scope of businesses to improve both short-term and long-term prospects, especially financial returns and rewards. Like expansion strategies, the strategic logic appears easy to defend and the risk factors are deemed low because of the direct links to the organization's prevailing capabilities, resources, and market experiences and know-how. Conditions and trends are accommodated since organic growth strategies involve adjustments via improvements and developments to reduce vulnerabilities.

Emerging industries and high growth markets are natural situations for growth strategies, especially where the opportunities are large enough that competitors do not have to engage in severe competition. Organic growth strategies are also a good fit for relatively young businesses with favorable external conditions and trends for rapid growth. Organic growth strategies focus on doing more of the same except better. Mature and declining industries and markets are not very conducive to aggressive growth strategies. For example, car companies view markets in China in terms of aggressive growth strategies; however, markets in the US are characterized as mature with severe competition.

International expansion and growth strategies

International expansion and growth are special versions of expansion and growth strategies. However, the addition of unfamiliar social and cultural aspects and their implications plays a much more important role in formulating and implementing such strategies. Competing in international markets requires changing the strategic mindset by reflecting on cultural, demographic, and market differences between the home markets and international ones. Strategic leaders cannot assume that conditions are similar to their existing markets; nor can they assume that successful approaches in one country will work equally well elsewhere.

A major mistake is to assume that successful products can be introduced to an unfamiliar market in a distant country without adapting them to market requirements and conditions, especially those relating to legal and cultural aspects. There are very few truly global products and most products have to be customized for local tastes, preferences, and expectations. For example, Wal-Mart learned that Germans want culturally sensitive approaches, not just "Americanized" ones.

Strategies based on international growth and expansion have been in use for centuries. Large global companies can have operations and sales in more than 100 countries. International strategies are a sensible way to increase revenues, profits, and market reach; however, great care is necessary when deciding how to accomplish objectives and achieve prescribed results. International strategies include: exporting to foreign markets; licensing foreign companies to produce and sell the company's products; building in-country production and marketing capabilities; franchising operations; and forming joint ventures with national or local companies to strengthen competitive advantages and mitigate inherent weaknesses. Each approach has advantages and disadvantages.

Exporting is usually easier to do and involves fewer in-country risks. The financial implications are often favorable because the business unit is simply leveraging existing capabilities and resources. Investments and commitments are generally low and if the strategy does not work, withdrawal without significant losses is relatively easy. However, simply exporting end products designed for conditions in one country and exporting them to other countries without customizing them are becoming more and more difficult to carry out. A lack of commitment to the international market is usually apparent and often leads to poor results or short-term success until the local producers or other global competitors make in-country commitments. Moreover, structural requirements may have to be in place to do business in a country or region. There may be rules and regulations that require specific modifications, adaptations, and certifications if the business wants to sell its products in certain markets. This is especially the case when exporting to the EU. For instance, international marketers of chemical products may have to test all of their products to ensure the company complies with EU directives. Such directives tend to keep out marginal players – those who want just to import products and sell through distributors.

Franchising can work well for global branded products and services where the local company (the franchisee) has distinctive advantages. The franchiser generally has to be well respected, have a solid brand, and a global reputation. The franchisee must have good market connections and know the underlying requirements for doing business such as understanding social, political, cultural, and economic underpinnings. Fast food companies are prolific franchisers because their strengths and basis for competing are intangibles that are not easily copied and usurped. Basic formulas for hamburgers, coffee, sandwiches, etc. are well known and are essentially commodities, but the power associated with name recognition is difficult to duplicate – at least in the short term. For example, the value associated with McDonald's' brand name and golden arches are critical aspects that are impossible to garner without obtaining them from McDonald's or getting similar intangibles from a principal competitor. There are numerous examples of successful franchises like

Starbucks and Dunkin' Donuts but great care has to be taken because the business world is changing and the preferred global brands are also changing.

Building in-country capabilities and resources is a powerful way to obtain competitive advantage and show commitment to the markets. This requires substantial investment and long-term dedication to make the investments pay. Developing capabilities that are specifically designed for a given country requires a comprehensive understanding of the country's cultural, social, political, economic, and environmental concerns, issues, and mandates. The advantages of such strategies include the ability to customize products, processes, and operations by including local suppliers into the enterprise that enhance preferences associated with buying locally, the use of local talent to fine-tune the connections with the indigenous population, and the possibility of having low-cost operations. The disadvantages include the potential difficulties of achieving economies of scale, not having sufficiently trained employees or resources to control operations, uncertainties associated with the political structure of the country, and the risk of investment losses due to social and political changes or a breakdown in stability.

Large investments in foreign countries can have many positive aspects for a firm. These include producing products at lower cost and penetrating local markets based on an actual presence in the country. There are many variations to the approaches including having smaller operations in several countries to diversify the risk of a large investment in a single country. There are advantages and disadvantages for the various strategic choices. The main theoretical advantage is to spread investments across a broader scope (i.e. diversifying the portfolio). However, there are vulnerabilities to international expansion and growth strategies. Stability is always a concern. The potential for social and political upheaval is always a consideration with the resulting loss of the positions and investments.

Expanding into countries with uncertain political and legal systems and structures is risky. Strategic leaders must quickly learn the laws and regulations underlying political realities. Understanding the legal aspects in advance is easier than learning the political realities through research and experience. For example, Shell Oil was hit with numerous charges of violating environmental laws in Russia during 2005 and faces a significant loss of strategic position in oil exploration and production. The details are not clear; however, the government is sovereign and most likely will prevail if it chooses to do so. It is usually within the power of the government or the political leaders to nationalize foreign operations or to invoke special requirements, fees, taxes, and/or penalties unexpectedly. Historically, there have been many examples of companies losing all of their holdings due to government actions or new political leaders changing the rules of game. For example, the Persian government nationalized the oil fields of the Anglo-Persian Oil Company (British Petroleum or more accurately BP Plc) in 1923. While strategic leaders may know what the laws and regulations are, they also have to understand the sources and implications of political mandates and social interruptions. Great care must be exercised to ensure investments remain safe and secure. Another potential disadvantage is the dilution of capabilities and resources where it is difficult to obtain critical mass in any one location. For example, Union Carbide had difficulty getting skilled workers with the knowledge necessary to operate its plant at Bhopal. While the tragedy that followed the 1984 release of methyl isocyanate gas that killed thousands in the local community had many causes, the events might have been different if workers had been more knowledgeable and had been able to respond to the catastrophe.

Historically, the large companies, especially the multinationals, selected relatively stable and politically sound locations when making global investments. For most of the twentieth century US companies invested in Europe and Japan and vice versa. Such approaches were generally successful because the markets were fairly similar and since World War II the political and social conditions were relatively stable in the developed countries. During the last twenty-five years, European and Japanese companies made large investments in US manufacturing plants. BMW built a multi-billion dollar plant in South Carolina to produce sport utility vehicles primarily targeted at the US market. Toyota has invested billions in US manufacturing, including a recent plant in Alabama to produce its Tundra truck line.

Having operations in multiple countries supports the ability of a company or business unit to expand and/or grow without saturating home markets. When a company builds plants and creates new positions in the home markets of competitors this may interfere with the competitors' extremely favorable conditions and home market dominance. This action can take away their ability to exploit their home markets to subsidize highly competitive international markets like the US. For example, many Japanese companies have very advantageous home market positions where they get premium prices. Premium pricing generates extraordinary margins at home, so they can be more competitive in the US and the European Union.

Forming strategic alliances and/or joint ventures, especially with indigenous companies, is an effective way to gain access to foreign markets without taking on the roles, responsibilities, and risks of company-owned operations. Both provide the means and mechanisms to mitigate the uncertainties and risks of making forays into new market spaces where strategic leaders: (1) do not have the information to make knowledgeable decisions; and (2) they are unfamiliar with business and market requirements as well as the cultural expectations of customers, stakeholders, and political leaders. The strategic logic includes strengthening the business unit's capabilities and resources when taking on new unfamiliar market conditions by using external entities, improving access to the underlying social, political, and economic realities through allies and partners, reducing the level of commitment a "go it alone" approach requires, leveraging the resources and capabilities of allies and partners to benefit the extended enterprise, and learning and sharing with others who have specific knowledge, insights, and information. Strategic alliances and joint ventures allow combined forces to establish a more sustainable market share position, produce the dominant or standard form of products and services, and reduce potential competition since partners can become competitors.

Strategic alliances are based on cooperative agreement(s) between two or more companies on well-defined objectives and target areas for the mutual gain of the parties. There are many forms of alliances including a domestic company working with a global corporation to develop local markets, two or more companies that require size and strength to address established national or regional markets, and multiple companies working together to supplement each other's strengths and offset each other's weaknesses.

Joint ventures (JVs) are legal entities – duly organized corporations that are jointly owned by the principals. JVs usually have very specific missions and business operations dedicated to the underlying reasons for forming the joint venture. Airbus Industrie (Airbus) is an example of a joint venture between British Aerospace, Aerospatiale, and Daimler-Benz Aerospace AG which combined their strengths and achieved a critical mass to compete with the dominant world competitor, the Boeing Aircraft Company.[6] Without the creation of the JV it would have been difficult for the principals to achieve success on their own.

The major risks involving strategic alliances and joint ventures include partnering with entities that do not share your principles and values, failing to achieve the critical mass necessary for success, and sharing confidential information and knowledge that can be used against the organization if the strategic alliance or joint venture breaks up. Assuming that partners and allies will always help to strengthen or solidify a business situation does not always turn out to be true. Forming relationships and supporting collaborations can consume more time, effort and money than what is generated from business ventures or required on a stand alone basis. For example, Caterpillar and

Mitsubishi Heavy Industries spent more than ten years trying to develop hydraulic shovels based on a combined design from the two companies. Each might have accomplished the end result on their own with less cost and effort. Philosophical and economic difference caused many delays and ultimately cost both companies more money than initially anticipated.

Overall assessment

The main concern with expansion and growth strategies involves concentrating too much on existing circumstances and focusing on a narrow front instead of a more balanced approach to orchestrate multiple areas of change as well as develop new technologies, new-to-the-world products, and new business models. Risks include being attacked by new competitors from developing countries that have cost advantages, like emerging companies from China, shifting market dynamics that favor other enterprises, and an increasing rate of obsolete technologies and products, especially in old-line companies. Using prevailing approaches as markets and products mature makes it more difficult to grow and expand. Obtaining and sustaining competitive advantages becomes increasingly difficult and strategic positions erode to the point that above-average profits are difficult, if not impossible, to obtain. Products become commodities over time, yet customers continue to expect more benefits for less money and superior outcomes with fewer defects, burdens, and impacts. Interestingly, the latter provides opportunities for making ongoing gains and capturing competitive advantages even in mature situations. In most situations related to mature products, market producers and providers can maximize the positive aspects before they can minimize the negative aspects. There are always opportunities; strategic leaders just have to know where to look for them. Strategic leaders must examine the full scope of opportunities and concentrate on those with the most profound impacts.

Market space and competitive strategies

The underpinnings of market space and competitive strategies

Market space strategies are directed at primary economic and social forces of business units. They address markets, customers, stakeholders, and competitors. Market space strategies include those focused on served markets, new markets, and new developments. Competitive strategies, derived from market space strategies, deal with competitors and the competitive landscape. The strategic logic for market space strategies is straightforward. The main purpose of most businesses is to provide great solutions for customers and stakeholders and to obtain mutual benefits and rewards from positive exchanges. Positive exchanges include customers receiving excellent value and outcomes from the solutions as well as satisfaction and success, while the business unit generates cash flow and profits and associated tangible and intangible gains. While there are always potential problems and negative aspects for the parties, the economic objectives of the transactions and relationships should involve mutual gains and enduring success.

Market-related strategies pertain to existing market conditions and trends and are based on "win–win" concepts that create value for all parties and encourage collaborative and respectful behaviors. New market space strategies involve creating and building new market opportunities through product and market developments which includes developing new business ventures.

Competitive strategies are really a subset of market space strategies because competitors are determined by markets selected. Unless the SBU chooses to provide products and services (i.e. the solutions for the selected market), concerns about competitors in that market or market segment are minimal. Moreover, the form and substance that competition takes is dependent on the strategic choices of the SBU's leadership. For example, as Dell Computer sold its products directly to consumers it avoided direct competition; therefore, it did not have to struggle for retail shelf space or worry about who paid for carrying the inventory. But, all that has changed since Dell revised its business model to sell products through retailers like Wal-Mart, Staples, and Best Buy.

Competition is an expected result of selecting markets and serving customers. In most markets there are similar companies with their own strategies trying to obtain their share of economic outcomes such as transactions, revenues, profits, etc. Competitive strategies focus on successfully dealing with competitors so as to neutralize or minimize their effects on the SBU's market space strategies.

Theories about competitive strategies are often derived from military strategies of the past. Military strategies generally pertain to winning battles and destroying the enemy. Numerous theoretical strategists took military strategies and converted the context to business situations. Sun Tzu's *Art of War* constructs are often used as the basis for many competitive strategies. They are based on Tzu's views and strategies for waging war. The main concern about such military-based strategies is that business is not about war and when companies engage in severe competition generally everyone loses. The US airline industry is a good example of destructive competition where even the most powerful companies suffer losses. Even before September 11, 2001, most of the airlines were in financial difficulty. In war, the losers may be vanquished; however, the winners are often significantly bloodied in the foray and require years to recover. For instance, the Soviets won the battle of the "Eastern Front" during World War II, but their losses were staggering. Moreover, most historians agree that the Allies won World War I, but when the situation is examined in terms of casualties and negative impacts the answer becomes fuzzier – or, it becomes clearer that no one really won!

Market space strategies

Assuming that business is about success in market spaces, then the primacy of market space or market-based strategies is intuitively obvious. Note that market space is a more inclusive perspective of market challenges and opportunities than market-related strategies (also referred to as market-based strategies). The market space strategies include both served markets and latent markets, called respectively the inner and outer loops of Figure 5.3. The outer loop includes ill-defined new-to-the-world markets as well as non-traditional markets, including those that represent significant opportunities in developing countries, but those that require significant changes in perspectives and strategies to bring to fruition.

The distinctions between the inner loop and outer loop market spaces are important because many of the greatest opportunities of this century are expected to be in new markets, especially in developing countries that require substantial development. Over the next few decades the gross domestic product (GDP) of the rest of the world is expected to make significant gains and by circa 2040 achieve parity with the G7 countries.

Market space strategies are complex because they involve making dramatic changes to the prevailing situation, especially by enhancing served markets and addressing new markets. Such strategies involve improving existing solutions and initiating new developments to internal capabilities, resources, portfolios, systems and operations of the SBU, the power of the extended enterprise, and the external realities of the business environment and market spaces. Market space strategies include many of the strategic approaches discussed earlier under preemptive strategies (as many preemptive strategies are also market space strategies).

Market space strategies are aggressive business strategies. They go beyond making incremental improvements to prevailing market conditions and trends as is the case with generic strategies; or, even those associated with expansion and growth strategies normally used to secure advantages in well-defined situations. Most of the latter strategies and related strategic advantages, if any, are usually duplicated by others quickly. Over time most exciting market situations and powerful competitive positions are relegated to common ground. Most markets mature faster today than in the past and competitive advantages start eroding once major competitors understand what they need to do to level the playing field. While there are still examples of companies that can maintain their strategic advantages for decades like Microsoft (Windows), Intel (Pentium), Anheuser-Busch (Budweiser), and Procter & Gamble (Ivory Soap and Tide), the normal situations in most industries are rapid changes in competitive advantage and market leaders being replaced by new leaders who are subsequently threatened by others. Even growth and expansion strategies that are very powerful during the introduction, growth, and early maturity stages of the product's life cycle typically "run out of steam" during the mid and later stages of maturity and decline. With digital information, rapid transfer of information, a global supply base, and accelerated technological innovation, existing competitors and emerging companies can quickly overcome their weaknesses and negate the leaders' strengths through aggressive strategies, fast actions, acquisition of capabilities from competitors (i.e. competent knowledgeable people), and the sharing of resources in the extended enterprise. For instance, a major disadvantage of outsourcing is that less and less of what the business unit does is proprietary and thus available to others who wish to copy the formula.

Market space strategies are appropriate for breaking out of competitive traps of the past and finding new ways to achieve success. They are useful during any stage of the life cycle; however, they are most compelling as markets reach maturity and many of the simpler approaches have run their course. Therefore, market space strategies focus on changing the status quo and disrupting the market scene through revamping technologies, introducing new products, enhancing market conditions, and negating the competitive advantages of the players. They also involve opening new market segments that have large market opportunities and new life cycles.

Opening new markets or market segments is especially advantageous for businesses stuck in the doldrums of mature and declining markets or those that are "stuck in the middle" with few prospects of overcoming the numerous leaders ahead of them. Jack Welch's famous directive to the strategic leaders of GE's businesses to be "one or two" in their markets or industries is based on the realization that if a business is not a top market share leader it is difficult to be successful and the challenge to move to acceptable positions is often too expensive or not worth the investment. Welch's strategic thinking on market share leadership may have been stimulated by the strategic analysis and insights of his predecessor, Reginald Jones. Jones became a superstar after successfully determining what GE should do with its mainframe computer business. He recommended that GE exit the mainframe business because it would require substantial investment to modernize the technology and operations just to get to the break-even point. Moreover, he suggested that GE had better opportunities to make money with the billion plus dollars required.

The prevailing market space strategies are characterized using three main categories: (1) market-related strategies involving improvements and developments to enhance positions for success in served markets; (2) new market space strategies involving strategic moves into new markets or those that the business had not previously addressed, and strategic actions to develop the means and mechanisms for success; and (3) competitive strategies involving strategic actions to overcome competitive threats and challenges and to mitigate the strengths of competitors. Each is based on strategic perspectives, strategic thinking, and actions at the SBU level. Note the important difference: market space strategies involve high-level business strategies not functional strategies involving marketing and operations.

Most market space strategies focus on improving the business unit's strategic positions and capabilities for success in existing or new markets. While there are subtle distinctions between what is strategic, functional, or operational, in this context it is clear that market space strategies focus on the longer term and attempt to gain sustainable advantages.

As discussed above, many companies muddle the distinctions between market-related strategies with competitive strategies. To make matters worse, competitive strategies are viewed as more crucial than the market-related strategies. Rather than viewing markets and customers as essential economic forces, many strategic leaders concentrate on defeating competitors and winning battles.

Market space strategies view markets as opportunities and view those opportunities from the perspectives of the recipients of the solutions. Therefore, the producers of products and providers of services are the ways and means to provide solutions. The primary purpose of market space strategies is to satisfy needs, wants, and expectations by creating successful outcomes and making the recipients successful in their related endeavors.

Market-related strategies

Market-related strategies focus on the prevailing markets and any logical enhancements. These often require product improvements and developments to satisfy changing needs and expectations of existing and new customers. These enhancements include new product development based on specifications from customers and stakeholders as well as market developments to create awareness and marketplace acceptance. Enhancements also include market extensions based on existing markets.

Market-related strategies include many of the approaches classified previously as generic, preemptive, expansion, or growth strategies. The market-related strategies concentrate specifically on how to improve a business's position in existing markets. Market-related strategies, especially in mature markets and industries, require careful analysis and critical strategic thinking about strategic options. If companies can continue to improve their value proposition by improving benefits and reducing costs and impacts, then the market situation can be viewed as positive even though conventional thinking suggests otherwise.

Strategic leaders must examine all possible options and avoid using narrow perspectives such as the old simplistic Boston Consulting Group (BCG) model as discussed in Chapter 7.[7] Market-related strategies are neither obvious nor prescriptive. Moreover, occasionally counter-intuitive approaches work very well. For instance, GE invested half a billion dollars in their appliance business to make it a successful star performer. Conventional thinking would have suggested that it was a "cash cow."

Market-related strategies focus on opportunities to enrich markets and customers through decisive actions to enhance capabilities, resources, and portfolios of the organization and its extended enterprise. Such strategies include: (1) developing new technologies and products to provide greater value; (2) integrating the extended enterprise; (3) curing defects and impacts across the enterprise; and (4) creating new means and mechanisms for providing the best possible solutions. While there are many definitions, market-related strategies involve making improvements and investing in new developments that dramatically change the underlying market structure and performance.

Market development strategies are high-level approaches to create awareness and acceptance, respect, connections, and applications for the SBU's solutions. While such factors can be accomplished through generic, expansion and growth strategies, the specific agenda for market-related strategies is to link customers with the solutions of the SBU and have these links endure over time. First and foremost, strategic leaders must create and build awareness and acceptance by providing compelling evidence that their solutions are more valuable than other choices. Please note that this requires real attributes that satisfy customers with tangible and intangible benefits and provide the necessary information to use the products and services successfully (product stewardship). Some specific actions include developing clean technologies, enhanced products, support services, risk-free offerings, end-of-life take-back services, and eliminating customer concerns about risks and losses. Conversely, constructing fancy marketing campaigns that spin the positive aspects and avoid the negatives are not viewed as constructive approaches.

Developing respect in the markets is critical for achieving lasting advantages. Respect is built through honesty, integrity, and openness. Respect is enhanced by having high-quality products and services that are affordable and reliable – those that are augmented by full disclosure. Respect is also achieved through credible brands and positions that are supported with an enterprise committed to customer success. Respect includes ensuring that messages are fundamentally correct and convey the full story about the solution. It means that marketing is dual sided and does not overly portray the positive aspects and not tell the truth about negative aspects that always exist.

Connections involve building solid relationships with customers for the long term. That customer loyalty is enhanced when there are deep relationships is difficult to prove. However, it makes intuitive sense that customers will remain loyal to those companies with professional or even personal relationships. Companies like Siemens have replaced the old notions of marketing with a more dynamic approach based on customer relationship management. Customer relationship management is a more profound form of marketing and operations that focuses on the external perspectives, especially the application aspects.

Applications focus on how customers buy and use products and services. The strategic approach is a form of mass customization where each customer receives the product or service in a unique way. This reverses the older perspective of creating products and then tailoring them to customer requirements. The starting point is the customer with design and delivery based on specifications the customer selects. While this approach is relatively new and difficult to achieve in every sector, there are many examples of where the approach is successful. Dell is well known for the customization of its products – customers select the options they want. Another more poignant example is how customers can specify the color of a GM car from a broad array of colors, not just from a limited list. While this appears to be a small point, studies conducted by GM suggest that customers often buy their cars from a competitor because they did not like the color choices from GM.

Market extension strategies address new market segments within the overall existing market structures by developing new and/or improved products to fulfill the specific needs and expectations of those market segments. The basic approach is to identify specific requirements and then provide significantly better solutions to customers in that market segment than what is available from traditional producers and providers. Note that unless the strategies involve aggressive action and improvements, any approaches are really just expansion strategies.

The strategic logic of market extension is multifold. Market extension includes broadening the value system to enjoy the economies of size (i.e. more effective utilization of manufacturing assets, sales force, supply networks, etc.), leveraging the power of the organization's reputation and brands, reducing the pressure of narrowly focused competitors, and increasing overall business opportunities including revenue streams. Moving into new market segments related to existing ones is viewed as a relatively low risk strategy because many of the capabilities, resources, and product portfolio requirements are known and familiar. The variations in market conditions and circumstances are usually modest and the changes in processes, practices, and behaviors of the SBU are relatively easy to adapt to gain requisite proficiencies.

New market space strategies

New market space strategies could be viewed as diversification because they involve new markets and new products. However, they are not pure diversification since new markets typically have commonalities with existing markets and new products have similar underpinnings to current products. For instance, moving into non-traditional markets and modifying product portfolios to fit the requirements in developing countries require changes in market perspective and new product development. These strategies necessitate taking substantial risks in developing the means and mechanisms for success. Indeed, there are two broad categories of new market space strategies: (1) wholly un-served markets; and (2) new-to-the-world markets. The former focuses on a radical market development to transform the capabilities and resources of the whole extended enterprise to be in alignment with the realities and challenges of un-served market segments, especially those in developing countries. This category represents significant opportunities in geographical regions where economic development has lagged. The strategy includes addressing untapped markets and finding solutions for them. New-to-the-world markets generally involve radical technological innovation to create new solutions that revolutionize existing markets or create new ones.

New market space strategies require extensive learning on an accelerated basis and significant transformations to the way business is conducted. The main concerns include the ability of the SBU to obtain capabilities and knowledge for achieving success in unfamiliar business environments and the organization's adaptability to function and perform in new and arduous conditions. The people engaged in such endeavors have to develop a mindset that allows them to understand and manage change, and its associated problems and difficulties, and to quickly overcome any barriers to success.

Competitive strategies

Competitive strategies may be necessary in commodity-related market segments where it is difficult if not impossible to gain competitive advantage or differentiate one's position. Competitive strategies involve approaches taken to deal with or compete against competitors. Competitive strategy often connotes that strategies are developed and based on rivalry among the participants including the struggles between producers or service providers and their customers. If the presumption is that business is about winning battles among competing forces, then competitive strategy has primacy. However, as discussed through out this book, competition is a positive and vibrant economic force that drives businesses toward improvements and developments that enrich prospects for customers, stakeholders, shareholders, and other constituents. Competition is an essential part of the free enterprise system and tends to make markets more efficient and effective since participants, especially customers, can choose from a broader array of choices.

The more choices one has the more power an individual may have over the situation. Likewise in business, competition provides customers with the ability to discern what the best solutions are among many options. Economic competition is beneficial in the long term since it often allows successful players to become more competent and capable. However, intense rivalry is often a destructive force especially when players became antagonistic. It becomes counter-productive when the energies are spent on fighting and destroying rather than creating and building.

According to Henry Mintzberg and James Brian Quinn, renowned strategists from McGill University and Dartmouth College, respectively, competitive strategies involve plans, patterns, positions, and perspectives.[8] They include the when and how of what you plan to do, where your organization's strategic position will be in the future, as well as how to respond when you get there. Mintzberg and Quinn made important distinctions between generic strategy and competitive strategy. They suggest:[9]

Competitive strategy, in contrast with generic strategy, focuses on the differences among firms rather than their common missions. The problem is it addresses not so much "how can this function be performed" but "how can we perform it either better than, or at least instead of, our rivals?" . . .

Competitive advantages can normally be traced to one of three roots: (1) superior skills; (2) superior resources; and (3) superior positions. In examining a potential advantage, the critical question is "What sustains this advantage, keeping competitors from imitating or replicating it?"

They make important points that competitive strategies are related to how the business unit compares to competitors, how it plans to engage them, take appropriate action to prevail against the competitors' counter actions and initiatives, and obtain and sustain viable and successful positions in product/market areas.

Competitive strategies depend on timing, the nature of the intended actions, and the types of moves – offensive and defensive. In each category there are many variations and interrelationships; however, each can be characterized in four main areas that follow:

- Timing-related strategies – the innovative leader, fast follower, and imitator (copycat).
- Position-based strategies – market share leader and occupying prime position.
- Offensive strategies – attacking and flanking.
- Defensive strategies – protecting and repositioning.

Each type of competitive strategy is, or can be, linked with other categories. For instance, the fast-paced innovative leader strategy can use innovations to become market share leader. Some competitive strategies can have elements similar to preemptive and generic strategies, except where the focus is on markets and customers and on beating competition, respectively. Regardless, the primary motivation for most competitive strategies is to achieve competitive advantage over rivals to gain superior competitive positions and success.

Fast-paced innovative leader strategy involves using technology, product, and process development to change the underpinnings of competition through rapid innovation using superior development capabilities, resources, and speed to market. The purpose is to beat others to market with new products and services that generate above-average profits and provide customers with immediate satisfaction. Such strategies can be viewed as preemptive. The approach is often daring and involves significant technological, product, and market risks. Leadership necessitates blazing new pathways that are full of trials and tribulations that require insight, imagination, rapid learning, and resolutions to manage and overcome. Intel is a good of example of an innovative leader by succeeding and maintaining leadership over several decades. However, the leader must be careful not to make too many strategic mistakes. Often leaders get sidetracked and lose in the long term. For example, both K-Mart and Wal-Mart were founded in 1962 as discount stores. K-Mart was an early leader, but was not able to sustain this because it did not innovate as quickly as Wal-Mart and built too many stores in poor locations using less sophisticated approaches.

The fast follower strategy is similar to fast-paced innovative leader except the approach involves a slightly more conservative tone. The fast follower uses superior competitive intelligence to track, understand, and improve upon the successes and failures of leaders. The strategy acknowledges it is easier, less costly, and often safer to follow the successfully established trail of the leader as long as the delay is short and any disadvantages caused by the delay are compensated by additional knowledge and learning gained through intelligence and observations. Cost avoidance, lower risks, and fewer mistakes more than offset any potential challenges associated with being second or third. Such strategies work extremely well when the cost of leadership is high, the probability of multiple failures is significant, and the ability to achieve leadership from behind is likely. Many Japanese companies used such strategies during the 1980s. More recently, Schick used fast follower strategies to compete with Gillette in the "multi-blade" battles during Gillette's introduction of the Mach III razors and blades. Schick was able to catch up to Gillette with a significantly lower investment. It used resources more effectively to seek competitive advantage over Gillette via further developments of four-blade and five-blade razors. However, there is always the risk the fast follower will never gain leadership or even a foothold. After two decades, Microsoft still enjoys overwhelming advantages over competitors, who still find it difficult to emulate Microsoft's success even though most of the product/market situations are now mature.

The imitator strategy usually involves waiting until the market structure, product designs, and competitive know-how are broadly known and/or part of the public domain. The competitors can easily replicate the requirements to compete at low cost. The imitator simply takes what others develop and tries to enjoy the fruits of their work and risk taking with minimal investment and risk. Such strategies are deployed to achieve a low-cost position as the imitator tries to take market share from the leaders and followers by offering the most cost-effective products and services. Such strategies work when products and services are commodities. An imitation strategy is usually employed and works best during the later growth and early maturity stages of the life cycle. They are viewed as low risk since investment is low; however, if the competitive positions are undifferentiated and commodity based, the potential to earn above-average margins is low or non-existent.

Imitator strategies may work in certain industries such as the pharmaceutical industry where the market potential is still significant after proprietary and highly successful products come out of patent protection (e.g. Prozac). At that point anyone can manufacture the product based on publicly available information. The basic risk of imitator strategies is that a firm may have to engage in severe competition where success is marginal and in many cases no one really succeeds. However, imitator strategies are viable for companies tailored to be low-cost producers or providers who have exceptionally low operating costs. Imitator strategies are used by companies in China and India for many product and service sectors where they have differential advantages in low-cost production.

The market share leader strategy is a competitive strategy with an economic and technological basis. Leading market share strategies are based on the theories and practical experiences in providing market-related and financial advantages of broad awareness, economy of scale, and good cash flow. The presumption that superior market share is positively correlated with financial success is usually valid. However, the correlation is not automatic as there are numerous exceptions. The advantages of market share leadership tend to decline as markets mature. They can even turn into disadvantages as demand decreases. Then, the market share leader is stuck with excess capacity and unabsorbed expenses. For example, in the airline industry the market share leaders are not financially successful or stable. The smaller niche players like Southwest Airlines and Jet Blue are successful because they have carved out well-defined and distinctive positions that are easier to manage with more cost-effective approaches. The presumption that size improves a firm's position has to be validated for most situations. Think about the difficulties at Ford Motor Company with its proliferation of product lines and manufacturing capacities, but its inability to find sufficient customers to buy its products and generate extraordinary cash flow.

Market share leadership is critical during the early stages of the life cycle where building awareness and acceptance is of utmost importance. During the introduction and growth stages customers and stakeholders form opinions that often last for decades. Historically, people obtain a lot of information from other customers via word of mouth and base their own purchasing decisions on the opinions of family members, friends, and neighbors. Today, this situation is even more pronounced with the rapid flow of information over the Internet. The early and mid-term market share leaders have huge advantages because they have many more customers spreading the word. If word of mouth is positive, market share leaders gain momentum and often quickly outdistance the laggards. While such situations do not always result in successful outcomes, market share leadership is a powerful strategy for achieving enduring success; at least the company has the ability to control its destiny. While the evidence is not conclusive, a market share leader is usually successful until they stumble and allow competitors to catch or bypass them.

Occupying the prime market position or geographical locations are powerful competitive strategies. Rather than trying to be all things to all people, this strategy focuses on achieving success in the most advantageous market segment(s). It is similar to the generic strategy of focus; however, it selects the best positions or locations based on all of the options. Industries and markets have categories or segments that offer advantages and better opportunities. Many of the best examples are in high-end markets. For example, Mercedes-Benz in the pre-Daimler Chrysler days was very successful in the luxury car segment. The focus was on elite customers who wanted sophisticated automobiles and were willing and able to pay the price. This resulted in high margins and limited competition since few competitors could offer similar solutions. Duplicating the designs was easy; however, it was much more difficult to create the brand's recognition and elite status. In addition, certain geographic locations are more prestigious and renowned as well as more profitable. For example, Calvin Klein, Victoria's Secret, and other exclusive fashion houses have built their brands and reputations on success in glamorous locations like Paris, Hollywood, and Milan.

Prime positions offer significant advantages because they are easier to defend. This is akin to occupying the high ground in military battles. Any efforts can be concentrated on a smaller number of objectives pertaining to the market or competitive situation. For example, BMW focuses on the luxury car segment with a sporty flair.

Many of the aforementioned competitive strategies can be considered either offensive or defensive since there are significant overlaps between categories and numerous distinctions are possible. Moreover, the more aggressive offensive strategies could fall in the categories of preemptive strategies. Indeed, the differences between offensive and preemptive strategies are subtle in many cases. The main difference is that preemptive strategies do not usually depend on the competitive situation and prevailing competitive position, but on the requirements of market spaces. As discussed earlier, preemptive strategies focus on the company's strategic direction and desire to achieve ongoing success. Many so-called offensive and defensive strategies used by businesses are really operational strategies formed and executed (or should be) by the functional groups. Launching hard-hitting marketing campaigns or cutting prices may be viewed as offensive strategies. However, they are really functional approaches that should be orchestrated at lower levels of the organization. Business unit competitive strategies should not be based on means (capabilities, resources, and positions) and mechanisms (processes, practices, and methods) that are easily duplicated by the competition. For instance, price cutting by one competitor in the airline industry often leads to price cutting by other competitors leaving everyone in a worse state than before. On the other hand, creating new products to secure advantages in growing market segments is more difficult to instantaneously duplicate; thus, they are business strategies.

Offensive competitive strategies are developed and employed to secure, enhance, or maintain business advantages in specific arenas and to stave off competitors. They are often used to win competitive battles and to gain overwhelming strategic positions ahead of competitors. Examples include Microsoft in software, Wal-Mart in retailing, and BMW in automobiles. Remember that time changes everything and many of yesterday's competitive leaders like GM, Sears, and United Airlines have struggled to keep pace with the demands of today.

Direct offensive strategies are common and include many sub-categories. Attacking rivals directly is an obvious approach. This involves taking competitive action to capitalize on the strengths of the attacker and/or to negate the strengths, advantages, and initiatives of primary competitors (the defenders) or exploit their weaknesses. Good direct offensive business strategies are difficult for competitors to respond to and gain momentum against. They involve building capabilities, resources, and business or product portfolios by making significant improvements ahead of competitors and initiating development programs that distance a business unit from competitors. These approaches are the dramatic actions that lead to competitive advantages not replicated in the short term. They include changes in mindset about how to engage the competition and how to achieve success. As an example, Airbus changed the competitive scene in commercial aircraft in the 1980s by using new designs with sophisticated technologies. Boeing took many years to incorporate advanced technologies in its designs like "fly by wire" and other more cost-effective electronic controls. Airbus was able to make large increases in its market share during the ensuing years.

In business, attacking strategies include frontal or direct assaults. Both must be conducted in ways to provide huge benefits without incurring negative consequences. Attacking strategies do not make sense if outcomes include winning at a high cost or achieving only a small increase in competitive advantage. Pyrrhic victory involves a competitive engagement that is not worth winning. To achieve real wins, competitors using attacking strategy often attempt to obtain overwhelming advantages with minimal damage, but these approaches are difficult to achieve in the real world. Specific to the soft drink businesses, both Coca-Cola and Pepsi engage in frontal attacks against other competitors. They use their power, influence, and total strength-based brands, production economies, distribution efficiencies, rapid inventory turns, and technological sophistication to gain shelf space in retail outlets and to disadvantage other competitors. The famous "cola wars" between Coca-Cola and Pepsi where the two companies supposedly fought for market share during several decades can also be viewed as how two giants use very aggressive campaigns to subordinate weaker competitors. They use their position and power to reduce the effectiveness and exploit the weaknesses of smaller companies. For instance, Coca-Cola and Pepsi introduced an expiration date for their products. Both know their products sell in a matter of days, whereas the products of smaller competitors may stay on shelves for many weeks. They gain advantage at no real costs. These comments are not intended to imply that Coca-Cola and Pepsi were in collusion or their actions were inappropriate. Each was intent on gaining market share and they were very aggressive in their actions. Key to the success of their strategies was that the companies achieved successful outcomes regardless of who actually obtained the highest market share.

Flanking strategies are generally used by businesses that are not the most powerful in the industry or market. Flanking strategies are effective when the flanker understands the main weaknesses of competitors and exploits those weaknesses without confronting the competitors' strengths. Business is full of stories of smaller or weaker companies successfully flanking the power and positions of more endowed competitors. The approach generally involves finding an opening where competitors are not as well positioned, powerful, or entrenched. There is always some weakness that can be exploited. Finding this weakness is a necessary ingredient to achieve success. For example, in microprocessors, AMD was able to build a strategic position by concentrating on the low margin side of the PC market. Therefore, AMD avoided much of

Intel's superior power by taking on less profitable opportunities. Low margin opportunities are not always less attractive because they are often high volume situations. Remember the successes of the Model T and the VW Beetle.

Competitors using flanking strategies can exploit ploys, such as appearing to make frontal attacks in certain main markets and then concentrating their efforts on select market segments that are not well fortified. The European and Japanese automobile companies successfully invaded the US market by selecting segments that were not well defended. For instance, US companies were very weak in small car design, production, and cost-effectiveness. This allowed the Japanese companies in particular to gain a foothold in the small car segment and gain respect in the minds of consumers. Then, over the long term, Japanese companies leveraged their successes in the small car segment to other categories.

A newer offensive strategy is the concept of rapid mobility. The strategy involves moving rapidly to take advantage of changes in the marketplace, and requires the capability to quickly occupy new positions as they evolve and change again as market dynamics require. Indeed, in some cases the strategy involves foregoing permanent positions altogether and having a rapid deployment capacity that allows the business unit to take on new opportunities expeditiously and shed old positions that lose viability. Moving rapidly entails flexible capabilities and resources that can be reconfigured quickly, as well as not being burdened with obsolete assets. For example, Amazon.com gained business success in retailing by eliminating much of the "bricks and mortar" associated with building retail stores. The firm developed a web-based retailing experience and moved quickly across many product categories to more successful ones. While this approach was not always successful, and it required many years to achieve financial success, the company succeeded because it was not weighed down by commitments to unsuccessful investments. Mistakes were made, but most of the effects and implications were short term.

Defensive strategies usually involve building walls or barriers around the SBU's position. There was a historical tendency to build defensive walls around cities, countries, and businesses to keep out invaders or intruders. Building defensive mechanisms has an alluring appeal since barriers appear to provide protection and reduce vulnerabilities. Defensive mechanisms seem to make sense for those that have achieved and want to protect their incumbent success, status, power, and/or wealth from those that are hungry and looking for success. However, care must be used since there are always ways around the best defenses.

Defensive positions rarely succeed in the long term and opponents generally figure out ways to defeat any barriers or defenses. From the Greeks using deception in the destruction of Troy to the circumvention of France's Maginot Line in 1940 by the Germans going through Belgium at the beginning of World War II, most walls, barriers, and defensive strategies are successfully defeated by attackers who seek rewards beyond the barriers. Numerous management constructs attempt to create barriers to competition. While barriers such as high capital investment and high market share make it more difficult for competitors to succeed, there are few true barriers over the long term. Defensive strategies usually depend on maintaining the status quo where there is a well-established order. This situation is difficult to imagine in today's business environment.

The difficulty with defensive business strategies is that they are static approaches in a dynamic world. Protecting market share and trying to keep existing products secure in market segments becomes more and more difficult to maintain over time. The attackers continually probe to find weak spots and to break through vulnerabilities. Often the attackers just wait until the defense mechanisms break or wear down naturally. As an example, many of the defensive castles of Europe during the Middle Ages simply became obsolete over time. Gunpowder and cannons added another dimension to the battlefield with the capabilities to shoot over and through stone walls. While it may take many years to completely disintegrate, the business defenses of today often start to decay sooner rather than later. For example, Google did not take long to overcome the strong hold that Yahoo! had on Internet search engine users. Yahoo!'s strong market position and market share were insignificant against Google's powerful capabilities.

Holding strategies can also be used to protect existing positions. Holding strategies usually depend upon getting reinforcements within a specific time frame. The objective is to buy time until their new and more exciting technologies and/or products are available. For example, when Microsoft (X-Box 360) or Sony (Play Station 3) introduced new products, other competitors did everything they could to keep their customers from switching to the new products.

Repositioning simply involves moving to positions that are easier to achieve success. For example, Toys 'R' Us reinvented itself as Kids 'R' Us as the company was more successful in providing products for very young children instead of the broader spectrum toys for children of all ages. Repositioning is effective when the prevailing situation becomes untenable from a market or competitive perspective. Repositioning is used in situations where the overall market attractiveness has declined and is not going to recover in the foreseeable future. This strategy is also useful where competitors have preempted all of the prime areas and few options are available to a company thinking about repositioning. "Ask Jeeves" is an example of one of the many original search engines that have declined due to the dominance of Google. "Ask Jeeves" is trying to reinvent itself as "Ask" by focusing on more specialised searches.

Diversification strategies

Diversification strategies are the broadest and most difficult category to characterize properly. They run the gamut from creating new businesses to acquiring other companies. As with other business strategies there are many conceptual and strategic overlaps. This increases the difficulty of discerning exactly what fits into the category of diversification strategies.

In the conventional sense, diversification involves spreading out business portfolios, the scope of investments, and inherent and underlying risks. Diversification theory suggests a broader scope reduces vulnerabilities to change, difficulties, or losses to any one business. Diversification can include extending into disparate new business fields and/or taking on a greater variety of served product–market segments and business activities. Traditional economic theory suggests that a broader portfolio of businesses or product lines improves the position of the business unit by having more options and lower vulnerabilities than any one business or product line.

Diversification strategies are usually undertaken during the late growth and early maturity stages of an SBU's primary endeavors. This is especially true as opportunities in existing markets slow down or as the continuation of growth or expansion strategies increase the business risks of having too much investment or business activity along a narrow front. This is especially a concern in turbulent markets or if significant market changes are occurring.

The history of business is replete with stories of extremely successful companies that suffered a decline because they limited their potential by narrowly defining their businesses. Levitt, in his famous "Marketing Myopia," discussed how railroads got into trouble because they focused on railroads instead of fulfilling the transportation needs of passengers and freight customers.[10] Other examples include NCR, a leader in mechanical cash registers, which was still focusing on the older technologies when transistors became dominant in their product markets, and IBM, the market share leader in mainframe computers in the early 1990s, which was losing money because market demand for hardware had declined.[11] In each case, the companies were too heavily invested in their major line of business and chose not to engage in businesses that seemingly distracted them from their main focus and traditional money-making endeavors.

The objectives of diversification include increasing the scope of the business unit, creating more value, expanding into new areas for growth, and reducing the risks and vulnerabilities of the existing narrow perspective. Diversification strategies frequently used by strategic leaders are employed to increase overall business potential, enhance cash flow and profitability, and reduce vulnerabilities to having too narrow product portfolios.

Diversification strategies generally involve opening up new lines of business to reduce the vulnerabilities of participating in narrow fronts, developing new business opportunities to offset declining growth in traditional areas, pursuing business potential that allows the company to leverage assets, capabilities, and resources across a broader front, and finding new-to-the-world opportunities that provide exciting financial and market rewards.

Diversification is a double-edged sword as there are many positive and negative consequences. Too often diversification, especially in unrelated fields, leads to greater uncertainties and ill-defined situations where strategic leaders are unable to understand or fail to appreciate what is required to be successful. For example, ITT under the leadership of Harold Geneen built a conglomerate that included Sheraton Hotels, Wonder Bread, Hartford Insurance as well as telephone equipment, industrial products, and others. Geneen's diversification strategy was short lived because such a wide range of businesses became more and more difficult to manage and keep pace with reality, especially after Geneen left ITT.

Many companies and business units run into difficulty when they expand beyond their comfort level, sphere of influence, and knowledge base. Diversification is more than just developing and delivering a new product or creating a new business venture. It implies acquiring all of the knowledge, information, connections, and relationships with associated extended enterprises. This often means creating an entirely new extended enterprise and all of the requisite dimensions must be developed to have a complete and effective value delivery system.

Diversification makes sense when a business in a single line or concentrated in a relatively small arena is boxed in by competitors or disadvantaged by customer or supplier power. For example, producers like Lego and Stanley Tools are concerned with the loss of power in negotiating with customers like

Wal-Mart because such a large account represents a significant portion of their businesses. Suppliers can use diversification strategies to extricate themselves from weak positions by finding new, more successful market spaces.

There are many mechanisms for diversification. The categories of diversifications are typically subdivided into those related to existing businesses and those unrelated and essentially new to the company. Related diversification involves developing new products for new markets where the company can use existing capabilities and resources to achieve end goals. Related diversification means that common linkages are used to improve performance and financial results or reduce investments and risks of a business venture. This generally involves leveraging existing capabilities and resources for new product–markets, sharing well-respected brand names across multi-product lines that are not the same, and using a common extended enterprise with different product categories. For example, Toro makes counter-seasonal products such as lawn tractors and snow blowers. While the products and markets are substantially different, Toro leverages the brand name and most of the manufacturing and operational resources. Microsoft's venture into gaming via X-Box opened up new business horizons outside of the software business, yet allowed Microsoft to use some existing areas of expertise.

Unrelated diversification involves increasing the scope of business areas new to the business unit. Unrelated diversification means that the underpinnings, connections, and relationships are essentially new and that few existing areas, capabilities, and resources can be leveraged. The logic is to reduce dependence on prevailing businesses and to find new ways to earn cash flow and sustain the business unit.

Some of the unrelated diversification strategies include acquiring a preexisting business from other companies or buying the whole company. They also include forming a joint venture with partners and allies, starting new ventures within the confines of the business, and investing internally in technological innovation to create new-to-the-world technologies and products. While the latter is a variation of starting a new business venture, the main difference is that a new venture commonly uses existing technologies or technologies licensed from others, referred to as corporate entrepreneurship. Technological entrepreneurship develops new-to-the-world technologies within the firm via a research and development center. Many possibilities for new ventures exist; however, many new businesses are often based on some nuance and are not just dependent on technological innovation. For instance, most of the variation between coffee houses is predicated on speed of delivery, décor, or special circumstances, such as wireless Internet access. For example, Starbucks is as much about surroundings and social aspects as it is about coffee and food.

Special business strategies

Special business strategies are developed to meet the requirements of special situations, conditions, or circumstances. There are numerous business strategies beyond the ones discussed above. Special business strategies include those pertaining to start-up companies and businesses in emerging industries. They also include strategies pertaining to acquisitions and divestitures and strategies for dealing with maturity and decline, especially when related to a turnaround because of poor performance.

The special case of corporate entrepreneurship is not covered because the focus of the book is on existing companies. Moreover, strategies pertaining to corporate entrepreneurship for starting new ventures involve extensive discussions requiring an entire book to cover the subject matter. The second special case, a turnaround, is a prevalent situation that necessitates special treatment and is summarized in this section. The same is true for the third area pertaining to acquisitions and divestitures.

Obviously, turnaround strategies are best avoided in the first place. Turnaround strategies are invoked when the business situation is imperiled usually because financial performance has degraded. The tipping point is difficult to identify and detail. Strategic leaders are usually aware of such situations; however, they often wait too long for strategic moves, stopgap measures, or market changes to take hold. Turnaround strategies are generally used when the shareholders or corporate executives run out of patience or time.

Businesses get into trouble for a myriad of reasons. To drill back in time to ascertain what happened and what causes led to the effects, impacts, and consequences are often impossible. Some of the main causes include increasing costs and expenses due to too many non-value-added activities and actions and poor decisions and investments as discussed in Chapter 1, forming business strategies that are out of synch with reality, and having strategic leaders who are overly optimistic or pessimistic.

Being aggressive is a positive that is based on the real world aspects; being overly optimistic is often foolish. This often happens when the demand for products and services slows down and the strategic leaders continue to assume that the growth rate stays the same. Costs and operating expenses continue to rise, but revenues and profits stay flat or even decline. Another cause is losing a market position or competitive edge that made the organization successful. Such situations are especially true for companies that have enjoyed great success in the past. These firms try to maintain the prevailing situation that provides the financial success shareholders and investors expect and demand. For instance, high growth rates with high profitability are easier to achieve during the growth stage of an industry or company. However, these characteristics become more and more difficult to maintain as the customer base expands and markets mature. Think about how Wal-Mart can continue to grow and maintain profitability at its historical growth rate and financial performance. For most mature businesses, the best choices for growth and expansion were selected during the early years. As the years progress, strategic leaders are often faced with poorer and poorer choices if they want to maintain historical financial performance. Also, strategic leaders and people in the organization may become more conservative from a strategic perspective, yet less frugal as they enjoy the fruits of earlier successes. They allow costs and expenses to escalate, spending on unnecessary items like big sales commissions, outrageous perks, or plush surroundings during successful times without thinking about the long-term implications. They fail to mitigate small problems before they escalate into larger ones. For instance, waste mitigation and management adds to expenses in the short term; however, such practices can avoid environmental damage, regulatory responses and penalties, and expensive cleanup costs. Leadership's diminishing focus lets the organization become less productive and effective. Leadership may fail to keep the management systems and structures current or in synch with the business environment. One of the biggest problems overall is to maintain control, especially over operating expenses and unnecessary expenditure. This often happens to very successful companies as their growth rate begins to slow down. For example, in 2006 eBay's operating expenses increased by 43% while its increase in revenue slowed to a rate of 31%. If this is allowed to continue, profitability may become constrained.

Highly successful businesses can lose their innovative spirit and entrepreneurial mindset as strategic leaders, managers, and employees become sedentary because they do not perceive the pressing need for continuous developments, strategic innovations, and leading change. They become risk averse in the belief the ongoing businesses have low risks and strategic innovations have high risks. Interestingly, maintaining the status quo can be just as "risky" as developing and commercializing innovations. The former may have low short-term risks but negative future rewards whereas the latter often has significant near-term risks, but typically has greater long-term potential and rewards. Again, there are no prescriptive approaches that guarantee positive results.

Poor management, lack of attention to change, the inability to satisfy customers and stakeholders, and inadequate operations and poor execution are some of the typical causes of difficulties and problems that result in failure. Business problems eventually manifest themselves in financial terms. However, difficulties can exist for years before they have a discernible impact on financial performance. By the time cash flow and profitability indicate there are huge problems and challenges, the probability of a successful turnaround is significantly lower and the recovery process involves a multiplicity of dramatic actions.

Turnaround strategies involve resolving a crisis, achieving stability, and transitioning or transforming the business into a sustainable enterprise. For most situations this is not a matter of going back to the glory days of the business, but involves going forward to achieve improved results and sustainable success. Solutions lie in the future not the past. This usually involves changing the mindset of strategic leaders. They have to adapt to new approaches and become much leaner and more dedicated to the future success of the organization.

Peter McKiernan, head of the School of Management at University of St. Andrews in the UK and an expert in corporate turnarounds, identifies their six distinct stages: (1) causes; (2) triggers; (3) diagnostics; (4) retrenchment; (5) recovery; and (6) renewal.[12] Finding and alleviating the cause(s) is a critical first step in understanding what to do and how to proceed. Triggers are the tipping points that involve dramatic negative changes in the business situation, going quickly from an acceptable yet unexciting situation to one that is totally unacceptable. Diagnosing causes leads to a better understanding of the situation; however, it may not always lead to innovative solutions for resolving the issues at hand. The problems may be so entrenched that they have to be managed within the context of the recovery. For instance, unfunded benefits for retired employees at many of the old line corporations in the US have to be paid. Retrenchment involves scaling back, making changes, and restructuring. Recovery and renewal involve making transitions and transformations to new sustainable strategic realities.

Resolving a crisis means preventing the loss of cash commonly referred to as "stop the bleeding." Strategic leaders have to analyze the business situation in detail to discover the causes and eliminate them. This is not easy because there are usually many interrelated and confounding causes. Simple break-even analysis does not work because the break-even point will shift as changes are made. Causes usually develop over many years of neglect, failure to recognize changes, and the inability to take strategic actions in response to changing markets.

Some of the initial strategies and tactics in a turnaround situation include cost cutting, selective tightening of product lines, pruning product–market segments, and retrenching into more favorable positions. These approaches to reduce the bleeding are viewed as negative reactions to improve cash flow and profitability. As discussed, businesses often allow excess costs and expenses to creep into the financial aspects of their operations. These include carrying too much inventory to keep production running smoothly, providing excessive benefits to sales people, and paying bonuses for senior leaders regardless of performance. They often have more product lines than necessary to support customer needs and expectations. New lines are often added without thinking about the implications on the existing ones or how they will be integrated and sustained over the long term. Such actions make the overall business portfolio less profitable and attractive as more capacity is added to serve the same market potential; costs escalate while financial success goes down. Profits and cash flow remain the same or decline as sales are spread over a larger portfolio.

In a turnaround situation markets can often provide the evidence why the previous or prevailing strategies, initiatives, and actions were unsuccessful. Turnaround strategies involve making changes, improvements, and repositioning. They suggest new approaches must be taken, including external and internal changes. Simply running through a litany of possible actions is not the answer. Turnaround strategies have to be tailored to the situation. While business literature indicates that there are generic strategies to follow, most turnaround situations are one of a kind, requiring a unique strategic response.

Responsible leaders must formulate and implement a new game plan. They should designate a turnaround leader(s), one with the expertise and willingness to make dramatic changes and improvements. This individual must have an entrepreneurial mindset, and the leadership capabilities to overcome resistance to change in the organization and the ability to reshape its culture. Such a leader must be decisive and move quickly because time is of the essence. If the business is hemorrhaging cash, often there is a predetermined point where the situation can no longer be tolerated, the organization is no longer viable, or recovery becomes impossible.

Some typical actions include selling off assets and product lines, shutting down operations or outsourcing processes, laying off employees, firing strategic leaders and certain managers, eliminating expenses, reducing costs and expenditures, and establishing stringent controls. However, care must be exercised when selecting such actions. Selling off product lines/businesses may be necessary for survival but often involves selling the most profitable parts which makes recovery and renewal more of a challenge.

Selling off or shutting down operations and product lines may transfer valuable know-how and potential profitable operations to outsiders or future competitors. Laying people off often results in a loss of intellectual capital and know-how. The intellectual capital of the business usually exists in the minds of employees; with wholesale reductions, substantial amounts of existing knowledge and know-how may leave with them. For instance, a substantial part of the failure from business process reengineering was the lack of appreciation of the value of people. Reducing expenses and making capabilities and resources scarcer may exaggerate the very causes of decline. Simply tightening the flow of money in an organization with stringent controls may cause people to be less innovative. While financial controls are important regardless of the situation, great care has to be taken during a turnaround not to exasperate the problems by making changes that are difficult to orchestrate. This is especially true when people believe it is already too difficult to obtain approvals for new initiatives and programs or to implement them. These approaches can make a bad situation worse when people stop pursuing innovative ideas and only worry about ways to save money. The very actions meant to lead an organization toward recovery and renewal may stymie the possibility for a turnaround and brighter future.

Acquisitions at the SBU level are employed to augment the business and related operations. Such acquisitions generally do not involve buying unrelated businesses; that is the responsibility of corporate management. The main purposes of SBU-level acquisitions are to strengthen or protect core businesses, improve the salient aspects of a business, and diversify into related areas not easily or cost-effectively developed through organic means.

Divestitures are made upon recognizing the business unit or operation is not performing and will not do so within a reasonable investment or time frame. Divestitures are made when assets, positions, and efforts do not fit the strategic direction and no longer make strategic sense. Business areas that lack the proper attractiveness given other available opportunities can also warrant divestiture. Divestitures are sometimes forced on an organization when the business situation is no loner viable. For example, Intel exited the memory chip business to focus on microprocessors. Intel's market share had deteriorated to less than 5% – its position was no longer worth the effort.

Acquisitions and divestitures are complicated management constructs that involve strategic, human resource, legal, and financial management considerations as well as a host of other social, economic, and environmental considerations. Each subject is a specialty that requires in-depth analysis, strategy formulation, and program execution.

Strategic action plans and initiatives

Action plans

Action plans and initiatives provide links between strategy formulation and strategy implementation just as strategic options are the links between strategic analysis and strategy formulation. Identifying action plans and initiatives is a precursor to the evaluation stage as to whether the overall strategic business plan and business objectives and strategies are achievable within the organization's capabilities and limitations.

Action plans translate related strategies into actionable programs. They provide the framework for (1) implementing high-level improvement and development programs; and (2) investing into creating, acquiring, or developing new businesses or ventures. Action plans require specific investments into distinct programs managed at a high level by strategic leaders who fulfill the organization's strategic direction. Action plans fit the business unit mission and company's vision and are directly linked to strategies that are critical for achieving sustainable success. The financing of action plans is often allocated from the capital budgets of business units.

An action plan is a skeletal form of an implementation program. Action plans guide the pathway from formulation to implementation by providing broad aspects without getting into particulars. Action plans involve identifiable means related to one or more strategies to achieve specific outcomes (i.e. new businesses, technologies, products, etc.). They provide strategic leaders with details about whether there are sufficient resources and capabilities to achieve desired results. Preparing and evaluating action plans focus on ensuring that resources and capabilities are available and appropriate to implement selected strategies and achieve objectives. If the strategies and objectives are not attainable, then adjustments to the objectives, strategies, and/or time horizon must be made before the whole organization gets involved (e.g. it might be decided that the objectives and strategies can be successfully implemented and accomplished in five years, not three). The adjustments would involve some combination of scaling back objectives, modifying strategies, or extending the time horizon.

Action plans include the connections to strategies and objectives, the main elements or steps necessary for the implementation process, the desired actions including expected start and end dates, responsible individuals, and most importantly, the capabilities and resources required. These elements usually involve any financing required to complete each of the other elements in the process.

Action plans are similar to subsequent related action programs except that they identify and detail the high-level aspects for evaluating certain resources as well as determining the feasibility of strategies and actions. During strategic implementation action plans are converted into more detailed action programs. Action plans have some of the same elements as action programs. However, they do not drill into sub-elements, develop a specific schedule, involve detailed budgets, assign lower level responsibilities and other project management details. Indeed, project management requirements are part of implementation and are usually under the control of the program management. The number and type of action plans are directly related to business objectives and strategies. However, there are useful categories to identify where action plans for the organization are employed and translated into specific action programs. Strategic areas that business units develop action plans for include:

Internally focused actions

- Research and development for creating and developing new-to-the-world technologies.
- Product development for commercializing new products, services, and processes.
- Creating and launching new business ventures.
- Investing into new capital equipment.
- Building new production and assembly lines.
- Sustaining the success of customers and stakeholders.
- Developing new strategic leaders.
- Outsourcing operations and processes.
- Spinning off or selling existing businesses.
- Changing the strategic management framework including the business model.

Externally focused actions

- Buying and integrating intellectual property.
- Integrating the extended enterprise through enhanced relationships and new partners.
- Acquiring external businesses
- Buying external assets and resources.
- Forming strategic alliances and partnerships.
- Forming joint ventures.
- Creating coalitions and collaborations within the extended enterprise.
- Building relationships with non-economic stakeholders and society.

The list is not comprehensive, nor is it in order of relative importance. It obviously could include more items. Action plans should be linked to strategies where one or more action plans are required to implement the strategy and achieve objective(s).

Many businesses simply eliminate using action plans and proceed directly to developing action programs. While such an approach seems sensible, this short-cut presumes the viability of all of the action plans and that each can and will be funded. The notion of an action plan is akin to developing and assessing a concept in a well-run integrated new product development process. The logic realizes that some of the candidates may have to be modified or screened out before the remainder are fully developed. It may be a waste of time and money to fully articulate the action program before strategic leaders have carried out a final review of the action plans. Action plans are much easier to articulate than the resultant action programs. The former produces the essence of what has to be done, while the latter provides the details.

Action plans are critical for large organizations because strategic leaders and key decision makers often cannot devote the time and effort to guide the development of all of the action programs on a real-time basis. There are many variations for developing action plans as well as determining initiatives. There is always the possibility that the strategies chosen are correct; however, if the wrong action plans have been implemented, they must be changed or modified.

A one- or two-page synopsis can provide the salient points for each action plan. The key is to provide sufficient detail so decision makers can review, modify, and approve or reject the plan. The format used should provide a balanced perspective of the action plan as summarized in Table 8.2.

The review process is highly dependent on the specifics of the business enterprise, and dictates of strategic leaders. The review determines whether there are compelling reasons why the business unit should invest into an action

Table 8.2 Simplified format for summarizing action plans

Key elements	Essential questions or concerns
1. *Description*	Describe the action plan and the essential elements. How does it fit the strategic direction and logic of the organization? Who is expected to be the overall program leader?
2. *Objectives and strategies*	How does it relate to and meet the business objectives and strategies? What is the target market segment(s) or specific reason for developing it? How does the action plan fit the businesses and what are the main benefits?
3. *Business environment, market aspects, and competition*	What are the most important driving forces in the business environment? Identify the most important business conditions and trends. What are the most important market considerations? Who are the most important competitors? What are the expected competitor responses?
4. *Critical factors for success*	Identify the most important factors for achieving success. Identify the means and mechanisms required for success. What are the required capabilities and resources?
5. *Main barriers to success*	What are the most critical limitations? Who or what stands in the way to success? What are the barriers?
6. *Main financial considerations*	Estimate the expected investments or required funding. What are the expected rewards?
7. *Risk factors*	What are the most significant risks?
8. *Time line*	Determine the expected development cycle. Identify the expected launch and completion dates.

plan. The review is a positive approach used to enhance the probabilities of developing successful action plans. In most situations, a hierarchy of criteria is used to determine acceptance of the plan. In general, the following guide criteria are used to determine the value, feasibility, and acceptance of an action plan: strategic fit and logic, importance of opportunities, links to objectives and strategies, size of investment and associated potential rewards, and lastly the complexity and significance of expected outcomes.

Once each action plan has been fully developed and properly articulated, the entire portfolio is summarized and reviewed. Financial considerations are often the most critical factors in making final determinations. Given that action plans are linked to objectives and strategies, they are important and critical to success. Final questions relate to the organization's capabilities and financial resources for carrying out all of the action plans. Some of the key questions are:

- Is the business unit capable of fulfilling the requirements?
- Are the funds available to support all of the action plans?
- What are the projected revenues and cash flow over the planning horizon?
- Can the rewards and discounted cash flow returns exceed the strategic objectives and fulfill the intent of the business strategies given the assumed risks?

The strategic response to these questions depends on the number of action plans, total investment required, and availability of funds over the time horizon. The strategic leaders decide what will be done, when each action plan is to be initiated, and how much is allocated to each action plan. In addition, most strategic leaders have their own format for such decision making. The approach can even be *ad hoc*, or certainly appear that way, where strategic leaders make most of the determinations based on their experience and judgment.

Strategic initiatives

Strategic initiatives follow a path similar to action plans. However, initiatives involve plans, programs, and/or projects that the organization undertakes to transition or transform capabilities and resources to a higher level. Strategic initiatives are more system and process focused in dealing with the capabilities and resources of the firm. Strategic initiatives are critical high-level endeavors that change the underpinnings, approaches, methods, and techniques for making dramatic improvements or creating a new paradigm.

Strategic initiatives are also derived from business strategies driven by external forces including changes in markets, customer demand, legislation and regulation, among others that require internal change management programs. For instance, the six-sigma quality initiatives at corporations such as Motorola and GE are internal improvement programs that originated from the external world of customers and competitors.

Strategic initiatives follow the strategic logic of the vision and mission, and are the means and mechanisms for empowering an organization through broad-based actions. Unlike action plans that require top-down direction due to capital investments and board level attention, strategic initiatives can be bottom-up or middle-up-down approaches that allow functional management and employees across the organization to make a significant contribution to the plans, framework, and processes before execution. For example, 3M is famous for its bottom-up approach in launching initiatives to improve the underpinnings of the firm. The Pollution Prevention Pays (3P) Program at 3M is based on grassroots initiatives to improve environmental performance. 3M has saved over $1 billion over the last thirty years from 3P initiatives.

Similar to action plans, the number and type of initiatives are directly related to business objectives and strategies. Strategic areas where business units can develop initiatives include:

Initiatives to build or enhance strengths, capabilities, resources, and approaches

- Institute sustainable business development paradigm.
- Renew management constructs and frameworks.
- Build new core competencies and capabilities.
- Learn new knowledge, skills, and approaches.
- Establish new systems, processes, and practices.
- Enhance quality, reliability, and effectiveness of products and processes.
- Build customer and stakeholder relationships.
- Make incremental improvements.
- Integrate the extended enterprise.
- Improve capacity and effectiveness.
- Enhance information systems.
- Support social systems and structures.

Initiatives to mitigate weaknesses, vulnerabilities, and barriers

- Eliminate non-productive assets, businesses, and operations.
- Reinvigorate the spirit and commitment of the organization.
- Improve resource utilization and avoid resource depletions.
- Form coalitions to solve complex issues like global warming.
- Eliminate toxic substances.
- Reduce or eliminate environmental impacts.
- Clean up pollution and wastes; eliminate non-productive approaches.
- Create waste reduction and prevention approaches and product take-back systems.

Again, the list is not comprehensive or in order of importance and could include many more items. Strategic initiatives must be linked to strategies required for implementation as well as to achieve objective(s). Initiatives are easily converted into implementation programs with the additional details necessary to ensure that they are. The added elements include scheduling, assignments of roles and responsibilities, team formation, work breakdown structure, determination of quality and performance standards, reporting and control mechanisms, and support. The most important elements pertaining to initiatives during the later stages of strategy formulation are: (1) the time frame for starting and completing each initiative; and (2) the resources required for execution. Like action plans, money is a principal concern including the total amount of money all of the strategic initiatives will require on an annual basis.

Strategic evaluation – inner loop

The final step in strategic formulation is to sum up the required resources and make adjustments if the requirements surpass available capabilities and resources during the time frames for implementing the action plans and initiatives. While some companies wait until implementing strategies to determine required resources and how they are obtained, it is best to do so before final commitments are made, at least in a summary manner. This kind of thinking ensures that strategic leaders understand their responsibilities to provide resources and to avoid lost time and embarrassment when they realize that additional funds must be obtained from internal or external sources. If funds are not available, then senior management will need more time to secure the necessary funding or modify the objectives and strategies.

Limited or lack of funding is a significant barrier to success and puts the people engaged in implementation and execution at a disadvantage and leads to inefficiencies and ineffectiveness. Such problems result in inconsistencies within the strategic management process that should be resolved during strategic formulation. Determining the required resources and actual allocation of resources are fundamental elements that bridge the formulation and implementation loops.

Strategic evaluation involves assuring that strategic decisions are sound and the implementation game plan is in place so that the process continues seamlessly and the desired results are obtained. Strategic evaluation examines the implications of the objectives, strategies, action plans, and initiatives including assuring strategic fit, understanding and mitigating potential risks, and gaining acceptance across the organization and with corporate management. The intention is to facilitate implementation and execution. Strategic evaluation gets everyone on the same page before strategies and plans are formally adapted and communicated to the internal organization and external parties. This is especially significant when disclosures are made to shareholders, the investment community, customers, stakeholders, and important constituents. Once action plans and initiatives are announced this signals senior management's commitment to their completion.

Should significant changes occur, especially if the intensity of the action plans and initiatives is diminished, management will have a lot of explaining to do to shareholders and other constituents. For example, FMC had to delay its sustainable development programs because of the firm's worsening financial conditions in 2005. Strategic leaders had to reverse some of their previous commitments.

Strategic fit simply involves assuring the right action plans and initiatives have been selected and the desired outcomes will lead to sustainable success. While failure is always possible, achieving success – the ultimate objective of the business – is also a concern. For example, FMC has introduced many new models in the US over the last few years. The action plans have been implemented successfully, but the overall outcomes have not led to the desired improvements in strategic positions.

Risk assessment and risk mitigation are also important elements of strategic evaluation. While each action plan and initiative may have had its own risk assessments and risk mitigation steps, a broader perspective of risk is taken during strategic evaluation. Specifically, strategic evaluation examines the risk implications of the whole strategic business plan. While there are a myriad of risks, they are usually based on uncertainty, the possibility of failure, and the inability to act and perform adequately. This will result in losses, liabilities, and damage, especially to the reputation of the corporation. Uncertainty is due to a lack of information and knowledge about the implications of decisions and any unexpected or uncontrollable future changes in the business environment. Risk areas include technological, social, political, economic, market, stakeholder, environmental, and financial aspects that influence the firm.

Technological risks include not understanding the implications of prevailing technologies, investing in the wrong technology, or making significant mistakes while developing or using technology. For example, during the 1980s GM invested heavily in robotics. This proved to be the correct decision, but the implementation of the technology was less than fully successful. There are always inherent and unavoidable risks with any selected technology including the negative side of environmental impacts. Technological risks involve design defects and a failure to meet generally accepted standards. These include failures to include certain necessary features, apply technical specifications, or produce proper outcomes. There is also the potential failure to provide adequate information, instructions, or warnings about the appropriate application of a technology.

Social risks involve dramatic changes to social systems and structures. The world changes quickly and people can be forced to abandon old methods and behaviors and adapt new ones. Such changes can make plans obsolete before they are implemented, especially when there is a significant time delay between strategic formulation and strategic implementation. This suggests that a concentrated and well-orchestrated strategic management process must unfold as quickly as possible. Yet, the practical side and reality of the business world often means that the process is time consuming and full of potential delays.

Political risks involve changes in the business environment's political structure, political instability in a given region or country, and new laws and regulations that affect strategic positions. Political risks are far-reaching and can have quick and devastating effects.

Economic and market risks are associated with uncertainties about conditions and trends in market segments as well as overall business environment. Markets are never completely understood leading to difficulties or misinterpretations, false assumptions, and missed opportunities. Market requirements can change during the formulation stage, thus requiring new solutions instead of the anticipated ones.

Stakeholders play a critical role in achieving success. Under certain circumstances the acceptance of stakeholder group(s) is imperative for success. The views of a single or multiple stakeholder groups can change quickly from positive to negative, creating barriers that were not envisioned.

Environmental risks are complex and range from problems with pollution and waste management to the depletion of resources and the destruction of the natural environment.

Financial risks are traditionally the concern of strategic leaders. Financial implications are used to monitor the potential success of business strategies and action plans. Financial risk is often viewed in terms of the probability of losing money, taking on liabilities, or having business failures. Financial risk is broader than just investment risks, since business failures influence the entire corporation by damaging its reputation or impacting other SBUs.

Strategic evaluation is continuous, not just a one-time event. Strategic evaluation is used to ensure strategies are implemented properly and that outcomes are in line with requirements and expectations.

Box 8.1 Nestlé and its strategic formulation

Nestlé is the world's largest food company. Its headquarters are in Vevey, Switzerland. It was founded in 1867 by Henri Nestlé who successfully developed a food for babies who were unable to breastfeed.[1] In 1905, Nestlé merged with the Anglo-Swiss Condensed Milk Company. It is truly a global corporation with operations in most countries.

Nestlé is driven by its customers and stakeholders. One of its primary strategic themes is "Nutrition, Health and Wellness." Rather than viewing the growing customer preferences for more nutritious foods as a threat to its businesses, Nestlé is taking advantage of changing attitudes and is transforming itself focused on the well being of people. Peter Brabec-Letmathe, Chairman of the Board and CEO, understands that the changes in the market spaces around the world offer opportunities for his company:[2]

We have a responsibility to provide consumers with high quality, highly nutritious products regardless of where we are selling our products, and regardless of the price point at which we are selling them. We believe that those on lower incomes have as much right to high quality, high nutritious food as those on higher incomes and, in fact, have an even greater need: their food spend is often not discretionary; it is often all they can afford.

Brabec-Letmathe believes that the greatest opportunities lie in creating more value for customers especially in the food, beverages and nutrition businesses. The company plans to enhance its leveraging of resources, to increase the speed of its innovations, to provide consumers with better communications, and to improve the quality and effectiveness of its products for people. Most importantly, strategic leaders want to make dramatic improvements in execution. Planning and execution are to be guided by the company's business principles. Nestlé is committed to the following business principles in all countries, based on local legislation, and cultural and religious practices:[3]

- Nestlé's business objective, and that of management and employees at all levels, is to manufacture and market the company's products in such a way as to create value that can be sustained over the long term for shareholders, employees, consumers, business partners and the large number of national economies in which Nestlé operates.
- Nestlé does not favour short-term profit at the expense of its successful long-term business development, but it recognises the need to generate a healthy profit each year in order to maintain the support of our shareholders and the financial markets, and to finance investments.
- Nestlé recognises that its consumers have a sincere and legitimate interest in the behavior, beliefs and actions of the company behind brands in which they place their trust, and that without its consumers the company would not exist.
- Nestlé believes that, as a general rule, legislation is the most effective safeguard of responsible conduct, although in certain areas, additional guidance to staff in the form of voluntary business principles is beneficial to ensure that the highest standards are met throughout the organisation.
- Nestlé is conscious of the fact that the success of a corporation is a reflection of the professionalism, conduct and the responsible attitude of its management and employees. Therefore recruitment of the right people and ongoing training and development are crucial.
- Nestlé operates in many countries and in many cultures throughout the world. This rich diversity is an invaluable source for our leadership. No single document can capture every legal obligation that may be required in each of these countries. Indeed, there may be conflicting legal requirements. Nestlé continues to maintain its commitment to follow and respect all applicable local laws in each of its markets. If an interpretation of anything contained in this document

is construed as contrary to local laws, such interpretation should not be followed in that country.

Based on these principles Nestlé has established high-level business strategies that cut across several of its business units. These strategies are intended to realize opportunities and transform the company into an even more powerful entity so that it can sustain success as the world changes. The following are selected examples of the innovative strategies:[4]

- Focus on "popularly positioned products" for people living in developing countries like China, India, Indonesia, and Brazil who have limited incomes. Affordability and availability are the key drivers.
- Lead in consumer communications with transparent labeling systems that disclose the positives as well as the negatives.
- Use cutting-edge research to develop optimal solutions for special situations like baby foods and use innovative technologies to improve the nutritional value of products.
- Make strong brands even stronger and healthier.
- Use R&D expertise to create and launch new big brands; to focus on fewer bigger projects that lead to faster and more profitable innovations.

Nestlé has aggressive business strategies to expand its reach into new market spaces that represent attractive growth. It is a leader in sustainable development and "carries out its global responsibility by taking a long-term approach to strategic decision making."[5] It is making significant business investments in developing countries, especially those in Africa. It has made a commitment to helping human development to improve their quality of life.[6]

Nestlé has had several difficulties over the years with consumers using its products improperly, especially mothers preparing infant formula with contaminated water, and with suppliers of cocoa using illegal labor practices in Africa. However, Nestlé has taken aggressive actions to mitigate such problems. It is an innovative leader in water management and stewardship.[7] It complies with the standards of the World Health Organization and adheres to the International Codes of Marketing Breast Milk Substitutes.[8] It is a leader in protecting the well being of indigenous workers and ensuring that its suppliers conform to human rights and internationally accepted labor standards. It supports the UN Global Compact and promotes "Shared Value Creation", a keystone of its social responsibility.

Notes

1. www.nestle.com/allabout nestle/history.htm.
2. Nestlé Management Report 2006, p. 3.
3. Nestlé Corporate Business Principles, p. 5.
4. Nestlé Management Report 2006, pp. 27–45.
5. The Nestlé Sustainability Review, 2002, p. 7.
6. The Nestlé commitment to Africa, 2005.

7. The Nestlé Water Management Report, 2007, and Nestlé and Water: Sustainability, Protection, Stewardship, 2003.
8. The Nestlé Sustainability Review, 2002, pp. 41–42.

Summary

Strategy formation involves the critical decision-making steps of strategic formulation. The front end of strategic formulation takes the output of strategic analysis and converts the accumulated information, knowledge, views, perspectives, and insights into strategic options relevant to the SBU. Based on the vision and strategic direction articulated by executive management and insights and observations from strategic analysis and strategic options, strategic leaders reaffirm, refine, or reinvent the mission of the business unit. Changes are usually subtle unless there are profound reasons for making more significant changes. Strategic leaders then reflect on the whole business environment to ensure they have an accurate view of reality. In today's business environment with ever-present change, doing nothing or making small improvements can be as risky as making audacious moves. Resting on one's laurels in very dynamic situations like consumer electronics, telecommunications, computers, and software is a prescription for disaster. There are numerous books on how the fast and nimble outclass big and powerful organizations. In a business world of change more conservative or less aggressive actions provide opportunities for competition to become the new leaders of the future.

Selecting business strategies requires strategic thinking about the effects, impacts, and consequences of strategic decisions and how they will drive the organization toward achievement and sustainable success. The thought process involves solving the theoretical problem of having strategies that are easy and achievable relative to strategies that are too difficult and unobtainable. Business strategies must challenge the organization to stretch beyond its normal capacities to realize extraordinary outcomes while at the same time not demanding results that go beyond reason. Human beings can produce incredible short-term outcomes by going beyond this breaking point; however, they may damage themselves in the process. The proper approach is to have business strategies that produce extraordinary value and outcomes on an ongoing basis without endangering the capabilities of the organization.

Crafting superior business strategies is the crux of strategy formation. While business strategy selection is linked to the strategic options and realities of internal and external conditions and trends, strategic leaders must be assertive without being combative. They must realize their business objectives and simultaneously ensure that customers, stakeholders, partners, and other constituents are successful.

The best strategies are ones that provide sustainable advantages and produce exceptional results and enduring success. Winning in the short term at the expense of long-term success is folly as this usually involves giving back most of the gains at some time in the future. These approaches often cause adverse reactions from external forces to make winning going forward more difficult.

The main categories of strategies discussed in the chapter have advantages and disadvantages. Generic strategies are simple and easy to understand and manage. However, the consequence is they are relatively easy for competitors to duplicate and trump. The generic implies that they are used by many companies and may not offer any advantages.

Preemptive strategies focus on producing extraordinary value and achieving successful outcomes before everyone else. This is based on the concept of being ahead of the pack and aggressively staying ahead over time. Christopher Meyer, author of *Fast Cycle Time* and *Blur*, stated that for business there is only one rule – "Rule 1: The competitor who consistently, reliably, and profitably provides the greatest value to the customer first, wins ... There are no other rules."[13] While sustainable success is the critical factor for succeeding, Meyer's rule and preemptive strategies for the most part are on the same page.

Expansion and organic growth strategies are logical approaches for companies with unexploited opportunities. These strategies are usually linked to the core capabilities, resources, and know-how of business units. Expansion and organic growth strategies typically involve doing more of the same, such as more related products, services, and stores. The main advantage is that the pathway is well established, people know what to do, and expected results are presumed predictable. Expansion and organic growth strategies are fairly successful for companies that have not reached maturity. These strategies are especially effective during the growth stages of industries or markets. However, great care is necessary as prevailing situations mature. A disadvantage is that conditions and trends eventually change where doing more of the same creates diminishing returns.

Market space strategies are important since the economic driving force of businesses involves the markets they serve and customers they satisfy. Market strategies are more important than competitive strategies because of their direct focus on economic objectives. Market space strategies (it is important to reiterate) do not involve functional or lower-level strategies of marketing and operations. The main advantage of market strategies is that they deal with the essence of a business unit because they focus on customers and their success. Markets are ever-evolving and associated strategies must be continuously updated to keep pace. Unlike preemptive strategies that are intended to aggressively precede change, market space strategies are developed in concert with change.

Diversification strategies are the most varied as they range from creating new business ventures to acquiring outside companies. The usual purpose is to break out of established patterns to create new or better opportunities. They are important to consider for mature businesses that have already exploited most of the low-hanging fruit. The main disadvantage of diversification strategies is the inherent risk of taking unfamiliar actions and initiatives that the organization is unprepared or ill-equipped to handle.

Strategic leaders then translate the selected objectives and strategies into action plans and initiatives. The purpose is to determine if the business unit has the capabilities and resources to pursue the chosen strategies and objectives. Action plans and initiatives are easier for people in the organization to implement and execute. Strategic formulation involves why, what, and when. Strategic implementation determines who, how, and how much. Both are critical. Without great strategies implementation and execution are an endless series of trial and error. Without implementation and execution great strategies are meaningless and produce nothing. In business, great strategies are important; excellent execution is the difference between good and great.

References

Faulkner, David and Andrew Campbell (2003) *The Oxford Handbook of Strategy*. Oxford, UK: Oxford University Press

Gerstner, Jr., Louis (2002) *Who Says Elephants Can't Dance?* New York: HarperCollins

Guth, William D. (1985) *Handbook of Business Strategy*. Boston, MA: Warren, Gorham, & Lamont

Meyer, Christopher (1993) *Fast Cycle Time: How to Align Purpose, Strategy and Structure* for Speed. New York, NY: Free Press

Mintzberg, Henry and James Brian Quinn (1996) *The Strategy Process: Concepts, Contexts, and Cases*, third edition. Upper Saddle River, NJ: Prentice Hall

Porter, Michael (1980) *Competitive Strategy: Techniques for Analyzing Industries and Competitors*. New York, NY: Free Press

Rainey, David L. (2006) *Sustainable Business Development: Inventing the Future through Strategy, Innovation and Leadership*. Cambridge, UK: Cambridge University Press

NOTES

1 Michael Porter, *Competitive Strategy: Techniques for Analyzing Industries and Competitors* (New York, NY: Free Press, 1980, p. 35).

2 David L. Rainey, *Sustainable Business Development: Inventing the Future through Strategy, Innovation and Leadership* (Cambridge, UK: Cambridge University Press, 2006, p. 170)

3 www.internetnews.com/bus-news/article.php/361817. In an article written by David Needle dated July 5, 2006 the author quoted company sources saying that there was an internal investigation to uncover any irregularities in stock options granted to executives between 1997 and 2001. The article indicated that Apple "had been notified of derivative lawsuits filed against in the United States District Court of the Northern District of California and the Superior Court of Santa Clara County."

4 http://business.guardian.co.uk/story/0,,2054490,00.html. In an article written by David Gow dated April 11, 2007 the author indicated that Henrich von Pierer, chairman of the Siemens board was fighting calls for his resignation over his role in the company's €500 million corruption scandal.

5 Theodore Levitt, "Marketing Myopia," *Harvard Business Review*, July–August 1960, pp. 45–56.

6 In 1999, Aerospatiale and Daimler-Benz Aerospace AG formed the European Aeronautic Defense and Space Company (EADS). In 2001, Airbus was incorporated as a JV with EADS and British Aerospace owning 80% and 20% of the shares, respectively.

7 William D. Guth, *Handbook of Business Strategy* (Boston, MA: Warren, Gorham, & Lamont, 1985, p. 65). S. K. Johnson, the author of the chapter, outlines several of the prevailing portfolio matrices or models.

8 Henry Mintzberg and James Brian Quinn, *The Strategy Process: Concepts, Contexts, and Cases,* third edition (Upper Saddle River, NJ: Prentice Hall, 1996, pp. 10–15).

9 *Ibid.*, p. 59.

10 Theodore Levitt, "Marketing Myopia," *Harvard Business Review*, July–August 1960, pp. 45 and 56.

11 Louis Gerstner, Jr., *Who Says Elephants Can't Dance?* (New York, NY: HarperCollins, 2002, p. 357). IBM's net income was minus $5.0 billion and minus $8.1 billion, in 1992 and 1993, respectively.

12 David Faulkner and Andrew Campbell, *The Oxford Handbook of Strategy* (Oxford, UK: Oxford University Press, 2003, pp. 763–764). Peter McKiernan wrote Chapter 26, "Turnarounds."

13 Christopher Meyer, *Fast Cycle Time: How to Align Purpose, Strategy and Structure for Speed* (New York, NY: Free Press, 1993, p. 9).

9 Strategic implementation and execution

Introduction

Strategic implementation is the downstream side of the strategic management process. It focuses on converting business strategies into desired outcomes through systems, organizational structures, program design and development, resource allocations, and various other means and mechanisms. It also includes ongoing or periodic strategic analysis, strategy implementation, and strategic evaluation.[1]

The strategic implementation process involves the outer loop of the overall strategic management process as portrayed in Figure 6.1. It links the front end inner loop of strategic formulation with the operating levels of the organization that are usually responsible for execution.

When taking place during strategic implementation, strategic analysis involves the ongoing or reaffirmation of the assessment of the business environment, market spaces, and internal aspects to determine whether significant changes have occurred or are expected to occur. As time marches forward the analysis conducted during strategic formulation may become outdated. Systematic reflection is required to ensure that if significant changes have occurred, they are considered by the strategic leaders and are incorporated in subsequent decision making. Strategic leaders can then modify the business strategies or adapt the implementation processes to reflect the new realities.

Strategic implementation is interrelated with strategy formulation and an essential part of enterprise-wide strategic management (ESM). It focuses on high-level management constructs to do the following: (1) reinvent, modify, and/or adapt the management systems; (2) restructure or improve the organization; and (3) provide the means to upgrade and refine the support mechanisms that are necessary to achieve results.

Strategic implementation includes promulgating policies, establishing procedures, determining best practices, setting performance standards, and forming management controls. It also involves establishing the mechanisms for guiding operations management and the lower levels of the organization in the execution of the business strategies and action plans. The mechanisms include the functional strategies, the tactics, operations, processes, practices, and specific activities taken by the whole organization to obtain results and sustain success. They involve the operating system and how it executes and achieves results.

Strategic evaluation entails management oversight to monitor progress and keep the implementation processes functioning properly on track. This is done through systems integration, change management techniques, auditing, risk assessment, and administrative controls like budgets and reporting. While most of the actual activities are performed by operational management, strategic leaders are responsible for maintaining control.

Execution focuses on operational level actions and activities of the business unit and its operating systems to achieve results, make progress, take corrective action, and realize continuous improvements. Execution also involves the roles and responsibilities of operational management to inspire people and recognize and reward them.

Strategic implementation and execution are difficult and complicated because they include many more elements of the management systems and organization. The specific approaches are more fragmented than those approaches pertaining to strategic formulation. They are more dependent on how the organization operates in the real world.

People engaged in strategic implementation and execution are pressed to do double duty. They usually have to perform their day-to-day operations and tasks in addition to the requirements that have to be fulfilled to implement and execute business plans and strategies, especially those at the higher levels like designing or redesigning the management systems. They do not have the luxury of stepping outside of their normal activities to focus exclusively on implementation and execution. They have to do both, and often the pressing needs and requirements of the present overwhelm the situation and cause strategic implementation and execution to suffer.

Moreover, there are more people engaged in strategic implementation and execution than in strategic formulation. This makes the management process more arduous. Unlike formulation, one of the main difficulties associated with implementation and execution is that many of the people involved are ill-informed about the overall strategic management process, the genesis of the business strategies, action plans, and initiatives, and are poorly trained for the roles and responsibilities associated with implementation and execution.

The challenges are daunting, but the rewards can be great for organizations that integrate the front end of strategic formulation with the back end aspects of strategic implementation. This chapter includes the following main topics:

- Reflecting on the underpinnings of strategic implementation.
- Developing the means and mechanisms to implement business strategies.
- Selecting performance metrics and evaluating strategic outcomes.
- Identifying and examining the tactics, techniques, and methods for executing strategies.

Underpinnings of strategic implementation

General perspectives on strategic implementation

Strategic implementation and execution are often lumped together and are usually viewed as being interchangeable. Such thinking distorts the importance of each and how they translate business strategies into outcomes and gains for the organization and its extended enterprise.

Strategic implementation primarily involves improving, changing, and adapting the management systems and organizational structure(s) so that they are aligned with specific business objectives and strategies. While such strategic initiatives are not always required after the selection of new business strategies, the strategic leaders should always reflect on how well the management systems and organizational structure match the new strategies. There is often a presumption that existing designs are more than adequate, but in a fast-paced business world almost everything requires reflection, adaptation, modification, and occasionally radical change. Moreover, strategic leaders should collectively examine the management systems and the critical processes to ensure that there are definitive approaches for deciding what should be done internally and what is more appropriate for external entities to do. This is an important element that should be basis of the strategic assessment of the organization's capabilities and resources and whether the specific elements are critical factors for success. This logic leads to whether to outsource processes and activities or not.

The strategic decisions and actions about the design, configuration, and processes of the strategic and operating management systems are the precursors to changes in the organization structure and are the most essential initial steps of strategic implementation. This includes modifying or redesigning the strategic management process and framework (see Chapter 6). It may also include designing or redesigning the business concept or business model if there is a definitive one. Many strategic leaders had not thought about the importance of the business framework or concept until recently when formal business models have become a more important management construct for identifying and managing the underlying aspects of the business unit and its connections with the extended enterprise.

The strategic management framework, business model, and/or management systems outline how the people within the organization and those of the extended enterprise are linked and integrated, how all of the elements contribute to success, how the actions and activities interact and flow across space and time, and how all of the relationships and interfaces are managed. They connect the internal and external dimensions into a unified view of how all of the elements are interrelated.

The organizational structure is an expression of how people and their roles and responsibilities are interconnected and interrelated within the business unit. It also provides a sense of the functions, actions, and tasks that the people are expected to perform. In today's more dynamic business world, it is critical that the organizational structure is flexible and accommodates change quickly and effectively. The organizational structure is more than a framework of reporting relationships between subordinates and superiors. It should convey a sense of importance and meaning for every individual position, group or department, team, and subsystem, and ensure that the incumbents at every level are valuable contributors to the success of the whole. This should include links with the extended enterprise.

Based on the need to modify management systems (or business models) and the organizational structure, the design, development, and implementation of the action programs are vital to ensure that the business strategies are put into effect and are managed and controlled properly. Generally, the most critical facets of the action programs are mapped out during strategic formulation, specifically during the determination of strategic action plans as discussed at the end of Chapter 8. Action programs include high-level investments in research and development, new product development, plant and equipment, new business ventures, acquisitions, divestitures, and the human resources that are critically linked with one or more of the business strategies. Management also has to translate the strategies, action plans, and initiatives from strategic formulation into actionable programs that can be managed, tracked, and completed. For both action programs and initiatives, the key to success is to ensure that people know: (1) what has to be done; (2) why the strategies and actions are important; (3) when they are expected to be executed; (4) who is responsible for execution; and (4) what results are expected.

Resource allocation, a major responsibility of senior management, is often ill-defined and poorly executed. One of the most critical responsibilities of strategic management is to ensure that the organization and its people have the necessary and appropriate capabilities and resources to perform. Otherwise, action plans and programs are useless. Many strategic leaders want exceptional results, extraordinary performance, and great success but fail to do their part in providing the necessary ingredients to realize those outcomes. They minimize investment because they believe that lower investments improve the internal rate of return or reduce financial risks if results are less than what is desired. Often they fail to invest enough in the people or provide adequate resources, yet they press their employees to achieve more than can be reasonably expected.

A simplified framework for strategic implementation

The means and mechanisms associated with implementation can be articulated in numerous ways. For many of the elements it may not matter what the sequences are, but how well they are managed. However, there are some critical elements with precursors that must follow a logical progression. As discussed above, it is crucial that strategic leaders initiate actions to adapt, improve, or radically change the management systems before they engage in the design or redesign of the organization structure. From that point going forward there are several alternatives for laying out the implementation framework. However, it is important to separate the implementation elements related to the means from those related to the mechanisms. The former involves strategic leaders with input from lower levels, whereas the latter is principally the domain of both strategic leaders and functional managers. While such distinctions are more often the case in the breach than in the norm, strategic leaders must define the management level that is responsible. The underlying principle is to ensure that there are individuals designated as the responsible leader for each major element and sub-element associated with implementation.

Figure 9.1 provides a simple framework of the major elements of strategic implementation sub-divided into the means, the mechanisms, and evaluation. The main elements of the means are shown on the right of the graphic. The major elements of the mechanisms are shown on the left. Evaluation cuts across the whole – top to bottom, left and right sides of implementation.

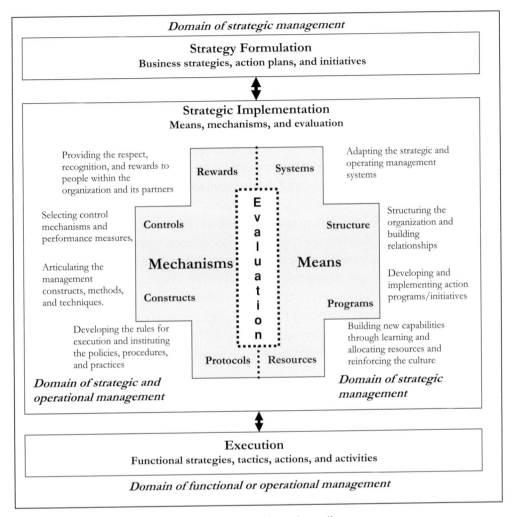

Figure 9.1   The main elements of strategic implementation and execution

The framework provides a simplified perspective. The elements depict the big picture of strategic implementation. The picture is not comprehensive, because depending on the actual situation and the complexities of the business unit, there may be more important elements than those identified. Please note that related details involve the links within the strategic management processes pertaining to the implementation and execution of business strategies, not the underpinnings or components of the operating systems.

The right side involves dealing with the aforementioned systems, structures, programs, and resources. The left side involves most of the operational aspects of implementation. Based on the total set of strategies (business and functional), strategic and/or operational management modifies the tactics and protocols used to guide the organization in performing tasks and activities. Success is achieved by using standard protocols that include procedures, best practices, methods, and techniques.

Procedures are most useful in stable business environments since they provide guidance and well-defined routines. In stable environments these approaches may have reasonable life spans that do not require ongoing modifications. However, in dynamic business environments they may become a barrier to change. Great care has to be used to ensure that appropriate choices are made.

Operational and functional management drive many of the processes and practices for directing the organization in its quest to realize its objectives and business strategies. They are the architects of the functional strategies and the tactics of the organization and the value delivery systems to achieve operational results. These lower-level strategies are really subsets of the business strategies that are critical for making the actual improvements and accomplishments, and fulfilling the requirements of the day-to-day operations. They have a shorter time horizon than business strategies and are more easily duplicated by competitors.

Establishing control mechanisms and selecting performance measures are critical elements of evaluation that are necessary to keep the organization on track, and for monitoring results. Control is a fundamental management construct that is always difficult to determine. Too much may stifle creativity and innovation. Too little may result in sloppy execution, inadequate performance, and the possibilities of failure.

Performance measurement is an ongoing process used to monitor progress and make adjustments and modifications if necessary. It is vitally important for strategic leaders to collect feedback on progress and have a real-time knowledge about the probabilities of obtaining success. Moreover, performance measurement ties the operational aspects and execution back to the strategic management process. This becomes even more important as the strategic business planning cycle matures and the next cycle of strategic formulation approaches as it is often risky to develop new business strategies based on the assumption that the prevailing strategies are working.

Rewards and recognition, especially when provided by strategic leaders, help drive the organizational culture, teams, and individuals to become more aggressive and seek out further gains. Achievements, outcomes, and successes have to be understood, put into context, and built into the next planning cycle.

Additionally, the people responsible for obtaining positive outcomes must be recognized and rewarded for their accomplishments.

Evaluation is the centerpiece that provides ongoing feedback to senior management and operational managers about successes and failures in real terms. It involves taking immediate action to correct deficiencies and cure problems before they become entrenched and have the potential to derail sustainable success. Evaluation involves all of the positive steps to help people during implementation and execution. While the conventional view was based on management control, enlightened management would ensure that success is achieved because all of the ingredients have been provided and people have the means and mechanisms to perform properly. This is reinforced by the philosophy of the late Dr. W. Edwards Deming that more than 90% of the difficulties are due to systems, not people. Evaluation is about how well management systems are performing and ensuring that difficulties are discovered quickly and that corrections and adaptations are made with diligence and speed. It is important to realize that problems, difficulties, and even failures are normal, especially with unfamiliar requirements, actions, and activities. They just have to be resolved expeditiously. Moreover, failures are learning experiences that can be tolerated in many situations if they are discovered early and corrected immediately.

Execution is even more difficult to precisely map out since the number of variables expands as the focus shifts from business strategies to the functional or operational strategies and tactics. It shifts from high-level strategic thinking to the day-to-day activities and week-to-week actions of doing and achieving. Moreover, there is often a fine line between what is strategic and what is operational. It is important to be able to distinguish between the two. As the level of detail drills further into the organization and the operational levels, the strategic management process fades and the operational management processes come into perspective. If strategic management usurps the power and authority of operational and functional management, the organization loses flexibility and tends to become overly controlled and rigid. It often requires much more time to make changes and to respond to pressing issues, as well as opportunities.

Theoretical aspects of strategic implementation

In the business literature, strategic implementation has been the weak sibling of strategic formulation. Academics and business scholars have been more inclined to study strategic formulation because it is considered to be a more significant and exciting subject matter than what can be developed from the more mundane realities of the everyday business world. While it is always difficult to generalize, the implications and impacts of strategic implementation are often confounded by the multiplicity of variables, and complicated by many causes and effects of changes in the business environment. Moreover, it is difficult to articulate universal approaches since there are so many variations. It is nearly impossible to develop generic models pertaining to implementation and execution. Each company has to invent unique models or approaches for implementing and executing business strategies.

Strategic implementation is not only more diverse, but the related management constructs are more complicated and difficult to map out using simple diagrams. Moreover, strategic implementation involves many more groups of people: academics studying business strategy; business leaders, economists, social scientists, psychologists, behaviorists, and plethora of others that focus on the emotional, organizational, operational, and strategic aspects of a wide variety of business leaders and practitioners who are engaged in the real world of business practices. The theories may be well established but they are scattered across the many disciplines of management and the roles of professionals and practitioners.

Academics and theoretical strategists understand the power of management theories and strategic management constructs. Good leaders shape perspectives and decision making on the theoretical underpinnings, and then try to determine how the latter fit or explain the real world. Deming was one of the most influential management gurus who espoused the importance of theory. In his book, *Out of the Crisis,* he stated:[2]

Experience alone, without theory, teaches management nothing about what to do to improve quality and competitive position, nor how to do it. If experience alone would be a teacher, then one may well ask why we are in this predicament. [U.S. companies in the early 1980s had extremely poor quality and did not have the knowledge on how to get out of their problems.] Experience will answer a question, and a question comes from theory. The theory in hand need not be elaborate. It may be only a hunch, or a statement of principles.

Basic management theory comes from principles and high-level strategic thinking. It involves doing what is right based on the underpinnings of sustainable business development (SBD), corporate social responsibility (CSR), and other management constructs dealing with the fundamentals of good management. It is difficult to prove the validity of these constructs, but as

Deming said pertaining to quality management they are inherently correct; just implement them and the results will provide the evidence.

The underlying purpose for theoretical propositions is to have logical perspectives for decision making, and to avoid having to rely on trial and error or intuition. While some situations may require strategic leaders to depend on their instincts, these should only be used in those cases where the more formal approaches are not appropriate, or are proven to be unworkable or unreliable.

Operational leaders tend to eschew theory and want to find practical approaches for solving their problems. Moreover, they may have a desire to keep the solutions as simple as possible to facilitate implementation. They want the processes associated with implementation and execution to be straightforward and easy to understand. These perspectives are seemingly sensible but care has to be exercised to ensure that management does not overly simplify the processes, especially in complex situations. Such decision making often makes the actual execution by practitioners more complicated. It is imperative that leaders at all levels accommodate the complexities of the business world as discussed in the earlier chapters and ensure that the implementation and execution are as straightforward as possible. Complexity should be handled by the leaders who are the most well equipped to manage it.

Practical aspects of strategic implementation

A general perspective for improving strategic implementation is to divide it into three main categories: the means, the mechanisms, and evaluation as shown in Figure 9.1. Each of the three categories can be managed effectively, and the leadership roles and responsibilities can be assigned to individuals who have the intellectual and experiential background, knowledge, skills, and capabilities to carry out the tasks. Such architecture provides for a systematic way to ensure that the downstream side of the strategic management process is managed in the most effective manner possible. While it is useful to identify three categories, it is also imperative that the strategic implementation process is fully integrated across the extended enterprise and linked effectively to formulation and execution.

Strategic implementation is often disjointed in many business units because it is fragmented into disciplines rather than being interdisciplinary and interconnected. Many organizations tend to have specialists handle requirements instead of broad-based teams of capable individuals who are dedicated to solutions and long-term success.

Relying upon a few leaders or specialists to be responsible for implementation and execution may facilitate decision making and actions, but it may also lead to the big "DAD" syndrome. In such situations, a small group of people decide what is necessary and appropriate, and quickly reach consensus amongst themselves on what has to be implemented and how it must be done. Such approaches are efficient and timely, but usually the rest of the organization is unaware of what has to be done and is not cognizant of how and why the decisions were made. These limitations may lead to problems downstream, especially during execution. The first few steps in the process are easily completed, but the downstream activities are often fraught with challenges that slow implementation and execution.

Specialists have expertise in a narrow field and usually perceive problems and solutions in that context rather than taking a broader view of the whole organization. For example, oil industry experts may view the depletion of petroleum in terms of finding more oil reserves instead of the broader perspectives of conservation and renewable energy technologies. While specialists contribute to understanding the depths of the issues, their contributions should be equal to the perspectives of those with a breadth of expertise. Implementation and execution should be guided by both theoretical and practical approaches. Such management constructs should be lean, easy to understand and manage, yet include all of the essential ingredients for achieving sustainable success. Most importantly, there must be a management system(s) and business model with explicit processes that people in the organization can easily follow to perform their responsibilities and actions.

People within the organization must acknowledge what has to be done, by whom, when it is to be accomplished, and what the expected results are expected to be. Generalists may be good team leaders and frame the implementation and execution processes that facilitate the actions and activities of all of the people from various disciplines or functions to become knowledgeable, participate in the process, and contribute to success.

Given that implementation and execution take more time than it takes to formulate strategy, it is imperative that flexibility and adaptability be built into management constructs. In a dynamic world with profound changes occurring on an accelerating basis, stability is important but adaptability is the key to survival. One of the main challenges in developing new technologies that take five or more years to develop is to keep ahead of the changes in the business environment and ensure that the development program is on the cutting edge.

The roles of strategic leaders in implementation

The strategic leaders of the organization are responsible for ensuring that the decisions made during strategy formulation are converted into extraordinary value for everyone. They must also ensure that significant outcomes result in the conversions or translations without delays or losses. In many ways the links between strategy formulation and strategy implementation are akin to flow through a nozzle. The nozzle is the smallest point in the process where the intensity of the actions increase dramatically until the flow is well beyond the nozzle. This is the crescendo for the strategic leaders who must ensure that the management systems and the organizational structure are aligned with the new strategies and that people in the organization are capable of performing at the highest levels and have the requisite capabilities and appropriate resources.

R. H. Hayes, Kim Clark, and Steven Wheelwright in their research on large development projects indicate that management's ability to influence a development project's outcome is very high during the early stages of a new development, yet most senior management only become significantly involved during the later stages.[3] This is generally explained by the fact that senior management historically followed the flow of money. For most programs the majority of the money is spent toward the later stages, but most of the significant decisions are made during the early ones. Likewise, strategic leaders must contribute their influence and knowledge to ensure that strategic implementation gets off to a fruitful start by contributing guidance and oversight. Often it is too late to make contributions after implementation starts to flounder during the mid-stages.

At the beginning of strategic implementation, strategic leaders should organize their efforts, finalize the resource allocations, structure the organizational approaches to manage activity, and initiate the action programs. These are vital areas for establishing the foundation for strategic implementation and engaging the whole organization. This is the critical period when strategic leaders have to show their commitment to strategies, action plans, and initiatives and provide the organization with the tangible and intangible means and mechanisms to take action and achieve results. They must demonstrate their willingness to support the practitioners. The employees across the organization must know that senior management is working with them and will provide the ongoing support. This is an example of "walking the talk."

Figure 9.2 illustrates the theoretical flow. It portrays the critical role that strategic management plays in linking formulation and implementation. After

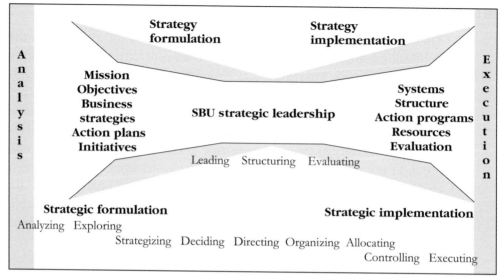

Figure 9.2   A representation of the linkage between formulation and implementation

formulating the strategies, the strategic leaders lead change by structuring the solutions and evaluating the ongoing actions and activities. To preclude constraints and delays, strategic leaders must continue to play a significant role in getting strategy implementation into full gear.

Strategic leaders have an ongoing responsibility to ensure that strategic implementation is properly controlled and results are evaluated over time to provide feedback on accomplishments in light of the objectives and to modify, adapt, or correct actions if performance fails to meet expectations. The details of strategic implementation, the means and mechanisms, are discussed in the next two sections.

Strategy implementation – the means

Adapting the management systems

The management system(s) bridges the gap between strategy and structure. It facilitates strategy implementation and provides a flexible framework for people to perform the appropriate actions, activities, and tasks associated with the business strategies. While crafting strategies often seems to be the most intellectually stimulating and reorganizing the organizational structure the most challenging, strategic leaders who want to implement successful strategies should also focus their attention on developing, validating, and deploying effective management systems to enable their people to be successful. Thomas Peters and Robert Waterman Jr. in their benchmark book, *In Search of Excellence,* outlined seven critical factors for success.[4] They suggested that strategy and structure were the hardware while the other five elements were the software. Their research determined that:[5]

any intelligent approach to organizing had to encompass, and treat as interdependent, at least seven variables: structure, strategy, people, management style, systems and procedures, guiding concepts and shared values (i.e. culture), and the present and hoped-for corporate strengths and skills.

These seven elements were simplified as McKinsey's Seven 7s: structure, strategy, staff, style, systems, shared values, and skills. The importance of systems changed the implementation mindset from Alfred Chandler's "structure follows strategy" to a richer view that strategy is implemented through management systems supported by organizational structure. The Seven 7s really involve strategy followed by systems followed by structure. Systems and structure include staff, skills, style, and shared values.

Peters and Waterman did not arrange the elements in the order of importance or flow. However, in most strategic situations the management system is the glue that links strategies with structure and provides the pathways toward implementation and execution. Moreover, it identifies and maps out the processes that are used to guide people (staff) in obtaining the desired outcomes.

Strategic planning is the game plan for the future based on what the business unit wants to become, along with its principles, values, and beliefs. The game plan is also based on the overarching purpose of the business unit and its perspectives on how it can achieve success. Strategies are backed by policies either from corporate or SBU management that articulate the overarching guidelines/mandates for implementation and execution.

Figure 9.3 depicts a modification of the McKinsey framework showing the critical role management systems play in strategy implementation. It suggests that systems follow strategy and then they are followed by structure, which should be based on the processes and requirements of the systems.

Designing a management system is generally easier to realize and map out than developing a new organizational structure. The system is more than software; it prescribes the flow of actions, tasks, and activities through well-defined and established processes that provide direction, links, and protocols. It provides the essential constructs for both implementation and execution and connects the strategic with the operational. People within the organization

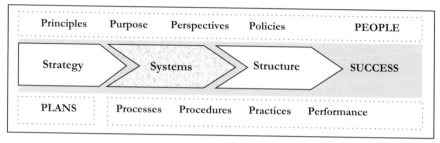

Figure 9.3   The role of management systems in strategy implementation

are provided with direction, guidance, and oversight necessary for proper implementation and execution.

A management system is a flexible construct that can be adapted to new situations much more easily and quickly than the organizational structure. The configuration of the processes, the specifications of those processes, the selection of the practices, and the actual work elements are determined by the required outcomes and expected performance, not just by how people are supervised or what the reporting relationships are. In a management system, people may be organized according to an organizational structure, but that structure does not have to articulate how they perform that work – the system and processes do that. For instance, people may work in autonomous teams with various reporting relationships.

The management systems define the work flow, the links, and the requirements; the organizational structure maps out the relationships amongst the people. While in a classical sense, the strategy, systems, and structure are distinct but interdependent, in a modern view they are interrelated and interwoven, especially systems and structure. In the innovative organization of the future there may not be organizational structure at all, just flexible teams of people who operate within the management system and work on projects, programs, and processes until completion or until the next transition and/or transformation. People become the essence of the system, not the organization.

From a strategic business unit (SBU) perspective the two main categories are the strategic management system and the operating system. Today, many business units have separate management system constructs for quality, environmental management, production (especially with lean management), information, and accounting and finance. While these separate management systems facilitate the design and application of the individual systems, they tend to make integration of the whole more difficult and may sub-optimize overall results. Often people within each separate management system try to optimize their piece of the whole rather than the whole itself.

A management system includes the essential internal dimensions of the business unit or subset thereof, and articulates how they are linked and function together. It provides the framework for integrating the entire value delivery system into a holistic entity that creates value for customer, stakeholders, and all of the entities of the extended enterprise and for shareholders, employees, peers, partners, and allies of the organization. A management system can also take the form of a business model that identifies, defines, and links all of the internal and external dimensions in the value system. It includes the various processes that lead to the execution of business strategies, actions plans, initiatives, and operations of the business unit.

An all-encompassing business model includes the strategic management system and processes, the operating system(s), and all of the links with the external dimensions. The former includes the strategic management framework, process, and details discussed in Chapter 6. The latter includes all aspects of the operating system and the extended enterprise involving designing, developing, producing, delivering, and providing solutions for customers, stakeholders, and other entities in the commercial arenas of business. Business models involve the whole value delivery system with the extended enterprise and the elements of market spaces and the business environment.

Management systems are usually complex. They involve numerous variables that are difficult to fully articulate and have many complicated interactions that are challenging to fully comprehend and manage over time. This is especially true for large companies with far-flung business units that have hundreds or thousands of different products and services. Trying to map out such complicated processes and relationships in a relatively simple flow diagram is almost impossible beyond laying out the skeleton forms.

A management system is intended to define the business in terms of purpose (mission), logic (strategic direction), scope (domain), and processes and relationships. It provides a framework that pertains to the internal and external dimensions of the whole enterprise and their interrelationships. The management system may have one or more subsystems and specific processes for each major requirement.

The management system includes all its sub-processes and essential processes of the business unit. The management system may also take the form of the interrelationships among the internal and external dimensions. The management system should be expressed in terms of the entities, relationships, interfaces, critical elements, key processes, and roles and responsibilities. It

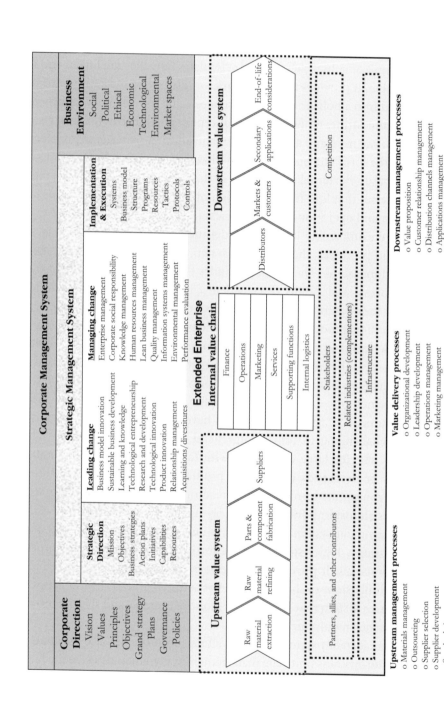

Figure 9.4 A portrayal of the elements of a management system

should link the relationships between the entities and articulate the critical processes for the people of the business unit to follow and manage. It provides a sense of the strategic formulation elements and the implementation and execution processes. It is imperative that the management system and all of the processes be developed from an application perspective, not just a theoretical one. The management system should be tailored to the business unit's external context (i.e. its business environment) and be guided by the directives of corporate management. Since the primary purpose of a management system is to facilitate implementation, it should focus on the real world aspects of the market spaces and the extended enterprise.

Figure 9.4 provides the essential aspects of the strategic management system depicting the corporate management directives on the top left and the external drivers of the business environment on the top right. The management system includes all elements of the value chain and the value system, both upstream and downstream. The inclusive perspective is the value delivery system; the narrower perspective is simply the value system.

The embedded corporate management system was described in Chapter 1. The strategic management process was described in Chapters 6 to 8. The extended enterprise was described in earlier chapters.

The most important high-level role and responsibilities of strategic leaders are shown above the elements of the extended enterprise which flow from the upstream dimensions on the left to the downstream dimensions on the right. The dimensions of the value (delivery) system are shown with the internal value chain as they are integrated into the enterprise. The most important processes for leading and managing change in the enterprise are listed below the elements of the extended enterprise. The lists are not intended to be comprehensive.

Strategic leaders are ultimately responsible for the design, development, and deployment of the high-level strategic management systems and in many cases the operating systems. Strategic leaders must ensure that the selected management system fits the strategic logic and purpose of the business unit. There is a tendency for some strategic leaders to adapt management systems that are based on software packages which provide a comprehensive perspective of all of the actions of the organization and integrate all of the flows, especially the flow of financial information. But such "canned" approaches are designed for the general cases, not necessarily the needs of an individual organization. For instance, SAP, the German software company, has been successful selling and installing its enterprise management software. While SAP's system software is comprehensive and ties most of the functions, operations, and processes together, the adapting organization has to modify its management systems and processes to accommodate the software rather than the software being adapted for the user.

A management system always exists. It may be formal and well articulated or very loose, especially for start-up companies. It can be argued that most discernible management systems are those of companies with a single line of business, where all of the elements fit a single management system that includes the strategic and the operational. However, for large global businesses the realities of the world tend to confound how the elements fit together and there are many variations. While there are standardized or generic approaches like the ISO 9000 series of standards for quality management, a management system should be an organization's construct for managing processes, actions, and activities. Done well, it transforms inputs and actions into outputs and realities that meet the business objectives of the organization and create value for customers, stakeholders, shareholders, and other constituents. Generic management systems may be fine for special areas like quality, environmental management, social responsibility, or information flow, especially for managing flows and outcomes based on specifications derived by customers or stakeholders. For instance, automobile manufacturers want all of their suppliers to have the same quality standards and quality management systems; therefore, QS9000, a variant of ISO 9000, is mandated for suppliers. Likewise, many corporations only want to deal with companies that are fulfilling their environmental management obligations; therefore, they require ISO 14000 certification.[6] But, the intent of a management system is to be holistic and all encompassing.

Designing the organizational structure

General design aspects

Organizational structure is the arrangement of people within the organization and describes how they are linked to management systems. Chandler stated that:[7]

Structure can be defined as the design of the organization through which the enterprise is administered. This design, whether formally or informally defined, has two aspects. It includes, first, the lines of authority and communications between different administrative offices and officers and, second, the information and data that flows through the lines of communications and authority. Such lines and such data are essential to assure the effective coordination, appraisal, and planning so necessary in carrying out the basic goals and policies and in knitting together the total resources of the enterprise.

Today's organizational designs focus on building core capabilities – concentrating knowledge and learning to have the critical intellectual capital for exceeding the objectives and expectations of the business unit. While Chandler viewed the organizational structure as the means for implementing strategies, it is important to recognize that organizations of today are more horizontal than vertical. In discussing enterprise-wide management in my book on SBD, the following comments about organizational structure are made:[8]

Chandler focused on the notion of the enterprise as the primary management level, which fits well with enterprise management methodologies. However, organization design is distinct from just the hierarchical structure. It relates to the architecture of the relationships between the people of the organization. In his studies of General Motors, Mobil Oil, Du Pont, Sears, and others, Chandler described vertical structures where lines of authority and communications between the levels were created essentially for planning and execution. The concept of aligning (or knitting together) capabilities and resources and integrating the whole enterprise is also a key element in the structure. Linking the organizational elements within the business unit and with the extended enterprise is critical for achieving the right structure.

Structure links the management levels and subunits within each level. The organizational structure articulates the reporting relationships, the authority, and responsibilities of each management position. It is the means for translating direction into action. The organizational structure is ultimately designed on the basis of the strategies and systems. The longevity of a given organizational design depends on sustaining the capabilities of human resources and the building of new knowledge and competencies through experience and learning. It is critical to keep the capabilities and competencies in synch with the strategic direction of the corporation and the business units. Organizational structure also defines how teams and individuals are organized and deployed to effectively manage programs and actions. The construct of teams runs the gamut from co-located teams of cross-functional members to virtual teams that lack physical contact.

The structure also coordinates the information flow to deploy people in response to the strategic direction. Communication is frequently blamed when the organization fails, but, more often it is the lack of integration, the inability of management to coordinate the efforts, and the lack of attention to long-term objectives that causes failure. Communication is the effect, not the cause of success or failure.

As discussed in earlier chapters most businesses prior to the railroads were relatively small and privately owned. Their organizational structures were simple and typically involved the owners as the strategic leader with a small cadre of functional managers. However, the far-flung operations of the railroads required more sophisticated structures with managers in remote locations who were responsible for the distinct units scattered across the system. The senior management of the early railroad enterprise tended to organize the operations using a professional organizational model borrowed from the military or government administration. Basically, they employed the "bureaucracy" form of structure with well-defined job descriptions, roles and responsibilities, reporting relationships, lines of authority, division of labor according to functional skills, and permanent status. The typical organization was subdivided into leaders, line management, staff, and workers. The leaders made the decisions, the line implemented the decisions, and staff members were the advisors. The workers were the instruments for execution. The bureaucrat form worked exceptionally well because it was stable and people became very efficient as they did the same job day after day, month after month, and year after year. People did change jobs through promotions but the process was slow and easily managed. The great strength of the structure was also its biggest weakness. It encouraged stability and the status quo. It was a good vehicle for managing the existing system, but was not set up to either encourage change or to deal with it. During the nineteenth century the railroads generally flourished. But when they were challenged during the twentieth century they were unable to accommodate change and declined.

The theory of organization is rich in intellectual underpinnings and has many variations. It is not the purpose of this discussion to examine the historical developments, but to highlight several of the prevailing types of organizations and to explore their fit within strategic implementation. While there are numerous types of organizational design, the focus herein is on the following: (1) functional; (2) divisional; (3) matrix; (4) network; (5) project; and (6) virtual. Within each there are also variations, and today's large companies and/or business units generally have adapted one of the types or a variation thereof to fit the unique requirements of their businesses. Distinctive types of organizations tend to be structured to fit their business environments, strategic positions, size, uniqueness, technologies and product portfolios, capabilities, resources, knowledge, and level of integration with the extended enterprise.

Keep in mind that these discussions pertain to the organizational structures of business units, not those of large corporations. The organizational structure of most corporations is more complicated and typically involves structures dealing with far-flung businesses in multiple countries, subsidiaries, wholly owned independent companies, divisions, joint ventures, and the like. There may be holding corporations, matrix organizations with divisions within divisions, and numerous other forms. General Electric, for example, is divided into sectors with divisions and business units.

The functional form

The bureaucratic structure of the railroads evolved into a functional organizational type for small companies. The functional organization was relatively simple and easy to understand and manage. The work was divided according to the functions or disciplines of the people performing the work. The organization was structured by departments and tended to be highly centralized with the leaders/managers of the departments reporting to the general manager/strategic leader of the company. The structure was hierarchical with reporting relationships that flow from the top to the bottom.

The functional organization evolved over the years with more interactions between the levels of management. Figure 9.5 depicts the typical structure and relative advantages and disadvantages.

The strategic leader(s) made the decisions, and the information flowed through the organization to the managers and workers who were engaged in carrying out the orders. The command and control style of management was predominant. As the strategic leaders gave the orders and attempted to control the outcomes, the employees followed without being involved in providing input or understanding the logic behind the decisions. Their job was to do what they were told to do.

A functional structure generally provides mechanisms for building strong expertise within the functions and knowledgeable leadership of the functional areas. Functional organizations work well in highly stable situations where the work can be mapped out according to the disciplines and the amount of interaction is minimal. The main difficulties include slow communication across the organization and poor coordination of multifaceted work that is dependent on the many functions. Functional organizations need highly capable and knowledgeable strategic leader(s) who can integrate the efforts of the functional managers and departments.

Divisional form

The divisional structure became necessary for many businesses as their organizations grew in size and complexity. The organization can be structured according to the markets served, product lines, product types, geographic locations, and/or brands. The whole company may also be structured in the

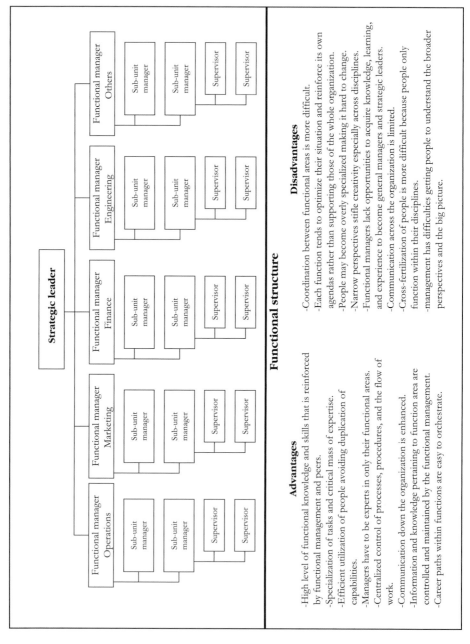

Strategic leader

- Functional manager Operations
- Functional manager Marketing
- Functional manager Finance
- Functional manager Engineering
- Functional manager Others

Under each: Sub-unit manager, Sub-unit manager, Supervisor, Supervisor

Functional structure

Advantages

- High level of functional knowledge and skills that is reinforced by functional management and peers.
- Specialization of tasks and critical mass of expertise.
- Efficient utilization of people avoiding duplication of capabilities.
- Managers have to be experts in only their functional areas.
- Centralized control of processes, procedures, and the flow of work.
- Communication down the organization is enhanced.
- Information and knowledge pertaining to function area are controlled and maintained by the functional management.
- Career paths within functions are easy to orchestrate.

Disadvantages

- Coordination between functional areas is more difficult.
- Each function tends to optimize their situation and reinforce its own agendas rather than supporting those of the whole organization.
- People may become overly specialized making it hard to change.
- Narrow perspectives stifle creativity especially across disciplines.
- Functional managers lack opportunities to acquire knowledge, learning, and experience to become general managers and strategic leaders.
- Communication across the organization is limited.
- Cross-fertilization of people is more difficult because people only function within their disciplines.
- management has difficulties getting people to understand the broader perspectives and the big picture.

Figure 9.5 Functional structure and its advantages/disadvantages

same way but at a higher level. At the SBU level, the divisional form is usually based on product–market segments or lines and brands. Each of the divisions has its own functional organization and acts semi-autonomously from the other divisions. There may be sharing of knowledge that is common across the divisions such as technical know-how and engineering capabilities. For example, Pratt & Whitney (P&W), a division of United Technologies Corporation, has three main portfolios (product lines) that serve specific groups of customers based on P&W's gas turbine engine technologies – technologies that have been adapted to the needs of the individual market segments. The product lines include military engines, jet engines for commercial aircraft, and gas turbines for stationary power. Each unit is a profit and loss center and reports separately within P&W.

Figure 9.6 depicts the typical divisional or decentralized structure and provides a listing of some of the advantages and disadvantages. In a divisional structure, authority is decentralized and strategic leaders of each of the divisions or product lines have the power to make strategic and operational decisions affecting their units. This form was a natural transition for large business enterprises whose size made the functional form unwieldy. It actually subdivided the whole into several distinct parts each of which had its own functional organization. It was first used by large diversified corporations like DuPont and General Motors, to improve the focus on the market spaces and ensure that it was given the proper attention. The divisional form was further refined into the prevailing concept of strategic business units that are driven by their mission and business strategies.

The main advantage of the divisional form is in having a strategic leader or general manager at the head of each of the divisions with a broad understanding of the whole, and who makes decisions based on the market and business perspectives, not just the strengths of the internal functions. The main weakness is that the critical capabilities and resources have to be delineated within the divisions and sharing scarce resources becomes more difficult. For instance, in a functional organization the most talented engineer is in the engineering department. In a divisional form it becomes more difficult to figure out how to handle this unique resource.

Project or program form

Project or program structure is a relatively simple form that focuses on one or more programs that are critical for organizational success. It may be used as the sole structure in the case of a business unit that is based on project-type businesses like architectural firms or consulting companies which provide

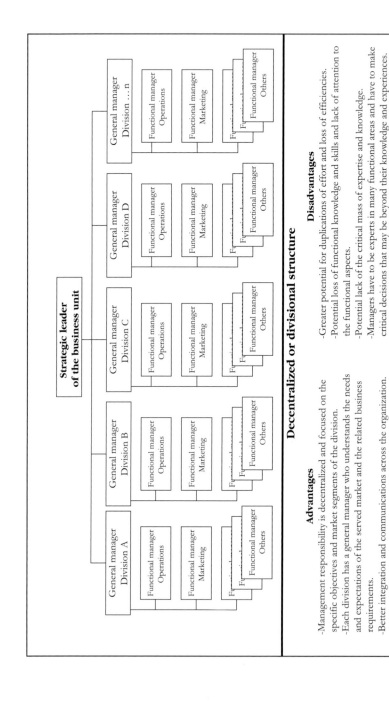

Strategic leader of the business unit

- General manager Division A
  - Functional manager Operations
  - Functional manager Marketing
  - Functional manager Others
- General manager Division B
  - Functional manager Operations
  - Functional manager Marketing
  - Functional manager Others
- General manager Division C
  - Functional manager Operations
  - Functional manager Marketing
  - Functional manager Others
- General manager Division D
  - Functional manager Operations
  - Functional manager Marketing
  - Functional manager Others
- General manager Division ... n
  - Functional manager Operations
  - Functional manager Marketing
  - Functional manager Others

Decentralized or divisional structure

Advantages

- Management responsibility is decentralized and focused on the specific objectives and market segments of the division.
- Each division has a general manager who understands the needs and expectations of the served market and the related business requirements.
- Better integration and communications across the organization.
- Accountability and easier measurements of the performance of the division through financial reporting and management attention.
- More flexibility and ability to change to the needs of markets or changing conditions and trends in the business environment.
- The causes of difficulties and problems are easier to detect.
- Broader-based organizational capabilities and easier to develop general manager and strategic leaders.

Disadvantages

- Greater potential for duplications of effort and loss of efficiencies.
- Potential loss of functional knowledge and skills and lack of attention to the functional aspects.
- Potential lack of the critical mass of expertise and knowledge.
- Managers have to be experts in many functional areas and have to make critical decisions that may be beyond their knowledge and experiences.
- General managers have little incentive to share information and lessons learned across the divisions.
- Potential for control problems as each general manager decides what to do and how to do it; strategic leaders(s) have to have broad experiences, capabilities, and knowledge.
- Cultural aspects have to support the integration of people across the organization.

Figure 9.6 Decentralized or divisional structure and its advantages/disadvantages

project-oriented services for their clients. Project structure may also include team-based organizations that develop new technologies and products. There are many variations – from a substructure within one of the other organizational structures to whole businesses being managed in a project or program format.

The project form is well suited for leading change and involves flexibility and adaptability. The whole organization can focus on the project or program or be divided into groups or teams that are responsible for one or more of the programs or projects. The main advantages are flexibility, adaptability, and simplicity. The main disadvantages are that such structures are often too simplistic for a complex organization and they can lead to duplication of resources and people. Project and program structures are really special cases that fit organizations that are in business on managing projects.

Matrix organizational form

The matrix organizational structure was developed during the mid twentieth century to obtain benefits from both the functional form and the divisional or program/project forms. While it should not be viewed as a compromise structure, it is suited for business situations that involve complex businesses and ones that necessitate highly skilled and technologically sophisticated people who are generally scarce. It is often selected because there are insufficient numbers of people with high-level skills and capabilities to meet the requirements across all of the product lines or even business units. Such situations usually involve product lines and market segments that are complex and risky. Business units engaged in these situations have to ensure that their designs and systems are safe and meet all of the standards, codes, and government regulations at levels that may even go beyond the typical six-sigma quality management paradigms. For instance, designing, producing, and constructing nuclear power plants is very complex, requiring technologically sophisticated engineering and technical talent. The people involved are usually functioning at the forefront of their fields of expertise. Such people are rare and most organizations cannot afford to have them working on just one project. These critical people must be shared which might lead to a functional form of organization. Yet the strategic leaders of such businesses have to have a project or program form to assure that the proper attention is given to each program/project. Thus, the organizational solution is the matrix organization.

Figure 9.7 depicts the typical matrix structure and lists some of the advantages and disadvantages.

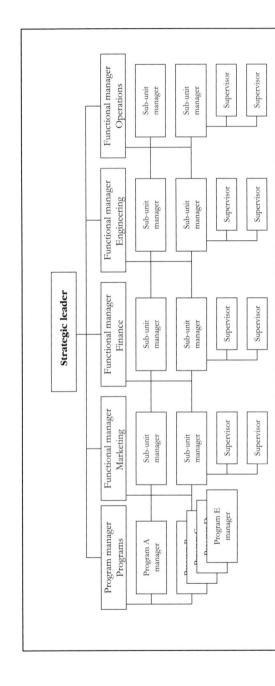

Matrix structure

Advantages

- Designed to meet the requirements of program, market, or geographic area without specifically dedicating people to just those specific areas.
- Has advantages of both functional and divisional forms.
- Efficiency and effectiveness can be achieved through sharing of functional capabilities.
- Program management can obtain expertise from a broader array of people across the functional areas.
- Decisions can be made based on input from the functional experts and the program management and provide checks and balances.
- Employees have a broader view of the business strategies.
- Easier to cross-train people and prepare for change.

Disadvantages

- Employees may have two bosses leading to confusion and conflicts.
- Coordination becomes more difficult as people are assigned work for functional and program areas.
- Scheduling people across many programs is complicated and often leads to commitments that can not be realized.
- Strategic leader may have difficulties clarifying lines of authority and responsibility.
- Each manager may try to optimize his or her own positions at the expense of the whole.
- Changing priorities lead to inefficiencies and complications.
- People may not have time for training and learning.

Figure 9.7 Matrix structure and its advantages/disadvantages

The matrix structure is actually a hybrid of the functional, divisional, and project/program forms. It is often viewed as a flexible form that can be tailored to fit the specific business situation. There are numerous variations, including those that combine geographic, program, and product line focus with functional and many other combinations. Matrix structures are typically used by large business units that have many overlapping product lines and lines of businesses. They are relatively straightforward to design and develop, but are much more difficult to manage. The interplay between the responsible managers often creates problems within the organization and much time and effort may be required on an ongoing basis to rectify problems that seemingly never get resolved. Managers may spend a lot of time sorting out who is responsible for the various activities and actions.

The main advantages include the focus on key requirements and the sharing on limited resources. The main disadvantages are the complexities involved in having multiple bosses and the potential in conflicts between them and the difficulties associated with establishing priorities.

Virtual structure

A more recent addition to the list of organizational structures is known as the network or virtual structure. Both are characterized as lean organizations that are linked to an extended enterprise in a way that minimizes internal resources and capabilities. Only the most essential competencies and capabilities are maintained within the organization. The approach avoids investing in assets and resources unless they are absolutely necessary. Outsourcing is employed to fulfill the rest of the mission requirements and achieve objectives.

Network and/or virtual structures necessitate connectedness with external entities, especially supply networks and partners. They maximize the use of contributors outside the organization to accomplish most of the business's essential elements. For example, Nike uses about 500 manufacturing companies around the world to produce its products. It focuses on the essentials of marketing and product development. Virtual organizations also leverage resources in the public domain. They use the infrastructure and related industries to avoid costs and achieve their objectives. eBay is a virtual organization which depends on millions of people spending time and effort to conduct business using its system. eBay makes money based on the hard work of entrepreneurs who are engaged in building their own businesses.

The main advantages of networks and virtual organizations are: (1) they are easy to form; (2) they tend to be cost-effective; and (3) can be modified rapidly if the business environment dictates change. The main disadvantage is the potential for others – including partners and contributors – to usurp those same opportunities if they can duplicate the value proposition(s) and eliminate the primary player, their former partner. Moreover, there is always the potential for the primary player to be held responsible for the actions, mistakes, blunders, and omissions of its partners. For example, Nike has been criticized in the past for the poor labor practices of its suppliers. It has had to intervene to ensure that its surrogates are not abusing their employees, using child labor, or being unethical. Such problems are more likely to damage the reputation of Nike than the actual perpetrators of the unethical practices.

The continuing evolution of business unit organizations

Organizational structures have evolved over the last 100 years from vertically integrated structures responsible for all activities, to virtual organizations that try to minimize the internal organization and their employees. Moreover, business unit organizations tend to evolve over the course of their life cycle. Typically, they start out as functional organizations, and change into divisional forms as they grow more complex. While there is not a linear path toward increasing complexity as the business units get larger, many organizations often select some variation of a matrix structure to achieve the most results with the lowest investment.

The organizational structure must continuously evolve to match the rapidity of change and the strategic innovations of the organization. A strategic leader who fails to keep his or her organization current with the realities of the business environment and market spaces may end up with structures that are stodgy and lack the capability to improve, develop, or change in advance of their peers and competitors. The more demanding the business environment, the more dynamic the organizational structure must become.

Today, organizations arranged horizontally across the extended enterprise are better adapted to a more turbulent business environment and are much more capable of change. There is no such thing as the perfect organizational structure. It is incumbent upon strategic management to continuously reflect on the organizational structure, and to outpace change, rather than be forced to catch up with the demands of a changing environment.

The design of the organizational structure should match the degree of change in the business environment, and the expected life cycle or time horizon of the business strategies. Stable conditions and trends and long time horizons are generally easier to manage and require steady transitions like continuous

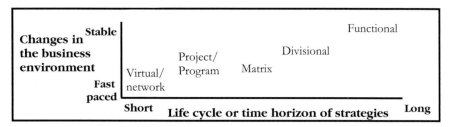

Figure 9.8   Organizational structure based on change mechanism and time horizon

improvements and incremental change. Rapid change and short time horizons necessitate flexibility, adaptability, and mobility. Good designs also need to accommodate innovative and aggressive actions to lead change.

The types of organizational structure mapped out in Figure 9.8 provide a relative sense of how each type fits into the grand scheme based on life cycle and/or time horizon and degrees of changes. The types suggested are the standard approaches. It is a misnomer to overly emphasize standard organizational types. Most organizations tailor their structures to best accommodate their strategies and systems. Moreover, there are many additional types and configurations that are not mentioned in this section. And, there are counter-intuitive approaches that may provide superior results.

Keep in mind that people are essential for successful strategic implementation. They have to be organized in a systematic way that provides guidance in the execution of the strategies. While there are no absolutes in organization design, there are basic guidelines. The organizational structure should provide for the integration of the people and the subunits in which they work. It should support their tasks and be as adaptable as possible to the needs of the individuals, groups, teams, and overall organization. It should be designed to meet the prevailing conditions and trends, yet flexible enough to adapt as changes occur. It should support the external dimensions as well as link the internal dimensions. Most importantly, it should reinforce the value propositions of the business unit, ensure connectedness with the extended enterprise, facilitate value delivery, and support execution.

Leading change through implementation programs

Designing and developing implementation programs involves insight, imagination, creativity, and thoroughness. Leaders are the champions, the sponsors

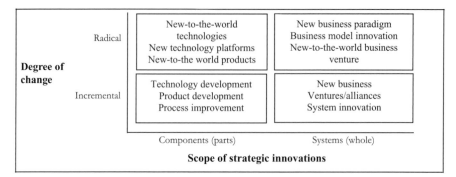

Figure 9.9   Selected types of innovation programs supporting implementation

(providing resources, especially money), and the head architects of the implementation programs. They are among the most important contributors, especially through strategic innovation. Such innovations include new processes, products, technologies, management systems, and business models. The key questions often focus on the type of innovations and a matter of degree – what kind? what purpose? and how much?

Strategic innovation involves the critical elements of planning, organizing, directing, designing, developing, demonstrating, and deploying. Investments of time, money, and effort are required from the start to realize the downstream rewards. Strategic innovations are typically divided into categories that are based on the degree and scope of the changes. In simple terms, these programs involving strategy implementation can be categorized using a two-by-two matrix. The degree of change can be divided into incremental (transitional) and radical (transformational). The scope can be divided into components (products and technologies) and systems (the management system and the business model). The actual categories vary depending on the industry and circumstances. For instance, in the service sector the focus may be on processes and systems, not products.

Most of the implementation programs fit into one of these categories. A relative sense of the categories and their fit is illustrated in Figure 9.9.

In general, programs involving incremental innovation include product and technology improvements that are usually based on well-known management constructs that are relatively easy to articulate and use. Most businesses have well-defined protocols and processes to develop new products, and improve existing technologies. Large businesses engage in such efforts routinely and their people are experienced in developing and implementing the related programs. Even the more complicated programs involving technology developments are based on well-established methodologies that are used frequently enough so that people follow prescribed processes.

Incremental improvement programs for systems development are also based on established methodologies. Over the last two decades, business process improvement has become one of the most frequently used protocols. With the advent of total quality management (TQM), six-sigma quality methods, and lean business practices, most employees – especially in large corporations – are engaged in making process improvements.

New ventures based on existing technologies and products are still an art form and many large companies have difficulties in getting such ventures established even though they are based on known inputs and requirements. Moreover, many business leaders and professionals are not as familiar with the requirements for starting whole new businesses. One of the most frequent approaches in this category is establishing a new business in a foreign country. These efforts require people experienced in developing new-to-the-company market-related programs and new businesses. These efforts require rapid learning and the modification of methods to fit the specific market and business conditions.

Forming strategic alliances is also a specialized area which requires the contribution of strategic leaders and professionals. The methods vary considerably from situation to situation and typically require many specialists like lawyers and financial consultants to negotiate arrangements and produce agreements that are legally sound and business appropriate.

Radical innovation programs are much more difficult to define. Project management techniques are required to develop methods implementing the programs. In most businesses, these kinds of programs are relatively rare and most of the people in the organization have limited, if any, experience with radical innovation. In developing new-to-the-world technologies and products, or even making dramatic improvements via new technology platforms, most business units have highly specialized research and development centers. The responsibilities and actions for such efforts are usually carried out by experienced professionals and technical specialists often dedicated to such programs. Many variations exist for implementing radical technological innovation. Project management and R&D management are among the most popular management constructs.

The most complicated implementation programs concern those involving radical innovations to the business model(s) and those engaged in starting new-to-the-world business ventures incorporating new-to-the-world technologies. While most businesses only occasionally engage in such programs, they are becoming more important areas of strategic management because of the rapidity of change in the business environment. Not only do products and technologies have shorter life cycles, businesses in general – even whole paradigms – are likewise impacted by the enormous changes that are occurring on a global scale. It is becoming harder and harder for strategic leaders to keep ahead of change.

Strategic innovations, especially more radical ones, require out-of-the-box strategic thinking. Gary Hamel, author of *Leading the Revolution*, suggests several design rules for such cases involving radical innovations:[9] (1) unreasonable expectations; (2) elastic business definition; (3) a cause, not a business; (4) new voices; (5) an open market for ideas; (6) an open market for capital; (7) an open market for talent: (8) low-risk experimentation; (9) cellular division; and (10) personal wealth accumulation. While Hamel has his own interpretation of the design rules and he applies them across the full scope of strategic innovation, some of them are also important in the development of new-to-the-world technologies and new paradigms.

Unreasonable expectations imply that out-of-the-box achievements can be realized and that the unthinkable is possible. The business world has changed dramatically over the last decade through radical inventions and new mechanisms. Businesses of today are often limited by their inability to think about the future. An elastic definition of the business supports radical innovation. The broader horizons in both space and time provide insights about how to create new realities to achieve success. One of the most compelling aspects of management constructs as discussed in this book is the broad view of the business environment and how strategic leaders can take advantage of the exciting new opportunities.

Strategic leaders can inspire the organization to create extraordinary value by extending the reach of the organization and its purpose beyond the obvious financial goals. A truism may be stated: "Give people an overarching reason for achieving success." The principles of ESM offer the logic that people need to integrate their personal and professional objectives with those of the business to create win–win situations for society, stakeholders, employees, managers, and shareholders. People want to be proud of the organization they work for, and live and breathe the objectives, strategies, and actions. Unfortunately, too many strategic leaders have narrow objectives that focus mostly on their own success and possibly the success of shareholders rather than the whole organization and enterprise, and the future.

The dramatic improvements based on TQM and six-sigma quality techniques are proof that success can be enhanced when more people participate in the processes. Inclusiveness is a key to success. By bringing in new voices, you enrich the innovative process by obtaining new insights and perspectives. This is particularly important when making radical innovations throughout the whole system. Everyone can contribute to a better understanding of what can be done and how to do it. The grassroots levels of the organization have ideas about improvements that are obvious to them, but not always apparent to the strategic leaders.

Creativity is a critical success factor. Openness to new ideas, new ways of doing things, new sources of capital, both intellectual and financial, and new people is a way to expand the scope and opportunities of the business unit. Breaking out of the old way of thinking is a fundamental ingredient in managing strategic innovation, developing new business models and even new paradigms. Challenging all assumptions and perceptions is one way to find new approaches for leading change. They can, and often do, change. For instance, most shareholders want growth because they perceive this as the only way to create value and profits. But there are many ways to create exceptional value including eliminating wastes, increasing benefits, decreasing costs, and providing success.

An entrepreneurial mindset is critical for making radical changes, especially to the business model. Changing the business model is usually perceived to be extremely risky because the whole organization might be affected and everything in it and everything it touches. Engaging in experiments involving smaller portions of the whole allows innovation to surface without risking everything. The inherent risks of radical innovations can be moderated by subdividing the efforts into smaller packages based on a product line that can be implemented, tested, and validated before proceeding to the next one.

Extraordinary value creation is more likely when the gains and rewards are spread across the organization and even the enterprise. If everyone stands to gain, everyone is more likely to contribute. If a few people obtain the gains and everyone else gets little or nothing, the others quickly learn that they are just benefiting the strategic leaders or the company and may be less enthusiastic about their contributions. Hamel also had some additional tenets about the new innovation agenda:[10]

- Everyone can help build innovative strategies.
- Rule-busting innovation is the way to win.
- Unconventional business concepts create competitive advantage.

- More of the same is high risk.
- There's no correlation between size and profitability.
- Innovation equals entirely new business concepts.
- Strategy is easy only if you are content to be an imitator.
- Change starts with activists.
- Our real problem is instrumentalism.
- Diversity and variety are the keys to innovation.

Radical innovation can become the means to break out of extremely competitive situations. Although radical innovations are risky, the status quo may be just as risky if not more so. As time marches on prevailing approaches become obsolete. Failing to innovate at a level sufficient to exceed the dictates of the business environment is a recipe for disaster. One of the most frequent strategic mistakes is a reliance on incremental innovations that are insufficient to gain sustainable advantages.

Business model innovation is one of the remaining bastions for achieving competitive advantages that is not fully utilized. Product innovations and new technologies may provide marginal benefits in long-term competitive advantages due to imitation. The most important factors to consider when thinking about business models are: value creation, the uniqueness of the positions and capabilities, the fit with the market spaces, the successes provided, and the longevity of the competitive advantages. Paradigm changes are also crucial to make radical innovations and enhance the prospects of the organization. Please note that this subject is so extensive that it is beyond the scope of this book.

Building new capabilities and managing resource allocations

Building new capabilities and allocating resources are among the most arduous challenges of strategy implementation and the most open-ended. During strategic analysis the competencies and capabilities of the organization are examined and articulated. Many of the most compelling opportunities, strategic options, and the related business strategies often necessitate enhancements to the competencies, capabilities, and resources of the organization. Augmenting the organization with people who have the requisite capabilities and aligning them with the new business strategies are among the early tasks required during implementation. Such efforts also involve developing new proficiencies among the existing management and staff to match the needs of the management system and organizational structure in executing the programs, actions, and activities.

Great strategies and action plans may be doomed to failure unless there are enough people with the right knowledge, skills, and talents to orchestrate implementation and to ensure that it unfolds properly. If strategic formulation is about intellectual capital, then strategic implementation is about human capital. Moreover, the best management systems, organization structures, programs, etc. are meaningless without dedicated, informed, experienced, knowledgeable, and hard-working people. People are the critical factor in transitioning or transforming an organization and in achieving sustainable success.

Great organizations have ongoing development programs that are continuously updating the skills and knowledge of the organization. These are constantly adjusted to reflect the needs of the organization and the dictates of the business strategies. In a world of rapid change, core capabilities, even core competencies, tend to shrink over time as other businesses replicate and then surpass them. Highly capable organizations become stagnant, descend quickly to the ranks of the average, and then sink into mediocrity.

Retaining highly capable people and recruiting new talent to add new requisite skills are essential to have the right human capital for implementation. When developing people or adding new ones it is important to ensure that they understand and can use cutting-edge management constructs and technical techniques – those that are in concert with future requirements, not the prevailing or even obsolete methods. In today's business environment some of the most important human attributes include adaptability, broad-based knowledge, and the ability to collaborate with superiors, peers, and subordinates; these include being energetic and pleasant, and having in-depth skills. On the other hand, some of the negative attributes that become dissuaders are arrogance, self-centeredness, inability to work in teams, failure to learn, dictatorial behaviors, and unethical practices. Great people are the foundation on which success is built. Inappropriate behaviors and people with poor attitudes sow the seeds of decline, despair, and even destruction.

One of the most important ingredients in building a highly competent and capable organization is to establish an innovative culture that encourages creativity, out-of-the-box thinking, and grassroot initiatives for positive changes. Cultural enhancements are among the most difficult elements to devise and successfully accomplish. Cultural changes focus on enhancing the core values and principles of the organization and ensuring effective cross-functional integration. They require the chemistry of the organization to be in synch with the vision and ethical standards of the corporation and the mission and strategies of the business units to ensure that people perform according to the overall game plan.

The culture of the organization reflects its personality and character. Successful businesses focus on creating an enterprise-wide culture to ensure a unified approach across functions, relationships, and entities. The approaches that strategic leaders use to hone an organization's culture or "the way they do things and achieve extraordinary results" include: providing opportunities for learning and gaining experience through education and training, encouraging proper behaviors and practices, ensuring accountability, promoting fairness and honesty, recognizing commitment and performance, and providing excellent compensation and rewards. Yet, crucial elements that are often ignored include ensuring proper internal communications about strategies and their implementation (especially at the grassroots levels), recognizing the achievements of all the people within the organization, and encouraging innovative thinking and risk taking. The actions of people often reflect the management style of their strategic leaders. If an effort to innovate leads to failure that is severely punished, then the motivation to try something new tends to dry up. If the credit for successes is not shared, or strategic leaders fail to recognize the contributions of key participants, then the leaders will lose the support of those people who are critical for implementation and execution in the future.

Allocating resources is a fundamental role of business leaders. When these are lacking, strategy implementation is usually impossible. Managing resource allocations can be divided into two main categories: those pertaining to high-level systems, structures, programs, and capability developments, and those involving execution of the actions and the day-to-day operations.

From a financial perspective, most implementation actions involve capital budgeting and the funding of action programs, and most execution activities involve operating budgets and the funding of the operating systems. Capital budgeting includes the allocation of funds for research and development programs, new product development, management development, and new ventures. Capital budgeting emanates from the high-level decisions made by strategic leaders during the strategic management processes and the theories used by financial management leadership in the allocation of funds. The former has been discussed throughout the book. The latter are based on well-known concepts, methods, and techniques used to determine the cost of capital and calculate returns on investments.

Operating budgets are based on standard cash flow determinations matching the requirements for funds with the sources of cash. Again, these are not discussed here, given that such methods and techniques are well established and are adequately covered in financial management texts.

Managing resource allocations also includes non-financial resources. Some of the most important areas include assigning portions of manufacturing capacity to new products, providing training facilities for employees' training, and leveraging existing operating systems to new business ventures. The list of such examples is extensive.

Strategy implementation – the mechanisms

Establishing policies and adopting best practices

The major mechanisms of implementation process involve the policies, guidelines, and practical aspects for supporting the action plans and helping to turn action plans and initiatives into realities. While they involve practical aspects, they remain fairly high-level approaches that facilitate execution. They reinforce guiding principles, provide methods and techniques, incorporate control mechanisms, and include ways to recognize and reward achievements.

Policies are the prescribed courses of actions and high-level guidelines for implementing strategies. They delineate rules for engagement, limitations on actions, and codes for proper behaviors. Policies are the mechanisms used to communicate what is acceptable and what is not across the entire organization. Policies are multifaceted and include those that pertain to the whole company (corporate) and those that affect only the individual business unit. Strategic leaders of business units, at least in decentralized organizations, usually have the authority to set policy as long as they do not contradict their corporate policy. The scope of these policies is often limited to the affairs of the business unit.

Policies can also be directives that facilitate decision making by lower-level operational managers. Such policies standardize routine decisions at functional levels. Lower-level management obtains some level of autonomy to make certain decisions without higher-level approval. Thus, such policies function both as tools for flexibility and of control. They also ensure that fairness is exercised across the functional and/or operational aspects of the organization since everyone is expected to follow the same rules.

Well-written policies can have the effect of speeding up decision making on routine matters, since the rules are clearly spelled out. Uncertainty is reduced by using standard approaches and well-understood protocols, principles, and ethics. Policies provide a sense of acceptable behavior. They should enhance, not restrict. They guide people, but should be flexible enough to allow adaptive approaches.

Policies are normally authorized by strategic leaders. However, a broader group of leaders, managers, and supervisors representing various parts of the organization should be consulted whenever possible. More diverse participation provides opportunities for the outliers to introduce additional insights into the discussions and be vested in the implementation. It also offers better approaches for handling control and accountability. Like many management approaches, policies that are too loose may fail to protect the vital interests of the business unit and cause unnecessary risk. On the other hand, overly stringent policies may reduce freedom of action and the ability to respond to pressing situations. Too little may undermine the proper governance of the business unit; too much may stifle creativity and flexibility. As discussed in Chapter 7, the small "dad" approach may be useful in developing policies where most of the constituents in the organization have an opportunity to have a voice in the decision-making processes. Again, the theory is that people are more likely to accept the final decisions (policies) if they understand the underlying logic and have a chance to contribute whether or not the outcomes are exactly what they wanted.

In most organizations, policies are intended to endure over time and apply to everyone. They are occasionally modified to reflect organizational changes, but are usually broad enough that they are not tied to the prevailing situation, but rather the underpinnings. For instance, the principles, values, and acceptable behaviors of a business unit usually do not change if there are changes in strategies and direction. Most of the underpinnings are timeless and help to establish the foundation of the organization.

Procedures, on the other hand, are established methods for accomplishing the outcomes of processes. They are developed specifically for the process, and explain the desired flow of activities and how to achieve results with a minimum of time, effort, resources, and costs. The focus of a procedure is on both efficiency and effectiveness. Procedures provide a step-by-step mapping out of the process so that any individual knows actually what has to be done, the required sequences, and the expected outcomes. Procedures are less stringent than policies and apply only to those engaged in the given process.

Procedures are generally devised for processes that are repetitive. They are the most useful and appropriate in those situations where the efforts are ongoing and there is an expectation that the activities are expected to continue for some time. For instance, the assembly of products in manufacturing follows a process that is repeated time and again. Each cycle is identical to the previous one, as each product is a duplicate. Well-thought-out and established procedures facilitate the work flow and enhance the quality of the work. Quality standards like ISO 9000 are based on establishing procedures that are religiously followed to ensure that tasks and activities do not deviate from the prescribed approaches.

Procedures are much easier to change and are typically the domain of the functional management group responsible for the processes. One of the main principles of quality management – continuous improvement – indicates that improvements should be made on an ongoing basis as better ways are discovered through learning and experience, and that such new ways should be adapted as soon as possible. Given that procedures generally affect only those engaged in the process and those who provide input or receive output, the number of people who are, or should be, involved in making changes is usually small and manageable. It is desirable and often necessary as in the case of ISO 9000 to have a formal process for making changes that can be imitated, developed, and completed quickly.

Practices define how the actual work elements are performed. They typically apply to work that is performed repeatedly and there are established processes and procedures for doing the work. Practices are discovered and enhanced through experience and knowledge. Establishing the accepted practices and instilling them into the processes are the domain of functional management. Functional leaders can improve the processes by increasing the outcomes in terms of the inputs. If best practices cannot be obtained within the organization, then benchmarking may provide options for achieving the requirements to make the systems as powerful as possible.

Benchmarking is one tool used to determine what the best practices are by examining other operations, organizations, and businesses. Benchmarking goes beyond obtaining intelligence about competitors. It includes examining processes and practices in related industries and related situations in which analogous processes are used, especially if superior results are achieved. External practices can be uncovered using many different approaches, both formal and informal. Formal approaches generally involve systematic research on what is happening in the external environment. Informal approaches involve learning from others as more information becomes available.

Best practices usually relate to management systems and their key processes. They are the most effective and proven ways of accomplishing tasks and carrying out the requisite actions to achieve outstanding, sustained results. Best practices are based on the realities of the situation including the capabilities and competencies of the people and resources that are available. They should be difficult to obtain (i.e. not trivial) and most importantly, difficult for competitors to duplicate. The long-term approach is to obtain a set of unique practices that provide the business unit with significant advantages.

Best practices are not just simply improvements, but often involve radical developments to the core capabilities and methodologies of the organization. Innovative practices that are not quite proven, but which have shown great promise for dramatic improvements may result in extraordinary value and outcomes. Without the inclusion of innovative approaches and ongoing developments in the practices of the organization existing best practices can become stale and eventually obsolete. Therefore, it is imperative that new ways of achieving results are continuously sought. This fits the notion of continuous development, especially where the change mechanisms are radically different from the previous approaches.

Adapting best practices should make the systems and processes more reliable, effective, efficient, and easier to use and manage. They should enhance quality and reduce problems. Best practices should move the systems and processes more toward the ideal with more benefits, fewer harmful effects, and lower vulnerabilities and risks.

Great care has to be exercised to ensure that practices taken from others fit the unique aspects of the organization. Every organization is different, described by its own culture and ways of doing things. Simply adopting practices without adapting them may lead to problems and the potential of failure. With that said, it is also important to recognize that in a fast-paced business world, no organization can develop everything on its own. Best practices wherever they may be found have to be explored, assessed, and deployed if they fit.

Selecting and communicating the main management constructs

Management constructs are theoretical and practical models, methods, and techniques. They are a relatively new strategic perspective that runs the gamut from simple ideas about how activities lead to the production of existing and new products, to more detailed approaches that lead to the creation of new products and technologies. They may even include more elaborate models for integrating the whole business and its extended enterprise, including all of the management systems and processes. The former involves the components of the systems while the latter includes all aspects of the system and the linkages with the extended enterprise. Moreover, based on the principle of inclusiveness, the latter includes the design, development, and deployment of a model of the strategic and/or operations aspects of the business unit, its subsets, and their connections.

A management construct is intended to be a representation, an assessment, and a perspective of the external and internal dimensions of business situations, and include many of the elements discussed throughout the book. For instance, the management construct would provide guidance on how to view and analyze the business environment – what is included in the analysis and the methods and techniques used in the analysis. It might be a part of the whole or the whole itself.

Strategic leaders provide guidelines through the selection of appropriate management constructs. Management constructs combine concrete aspects – information, data, knowledge, and experience – with the theoretical thinking about the opportunities, challenges, constraints, resources, and portfolios of businesses systems, technologies, and products and services. Management and practitioners use these constructs to depict their view of reality and their understanding of the scope of the enterprise for improved decision-making to create better solutions. They provide the tools for selecting the best approaches.

A comprehensive list of the most significant management constructs might include thousands of quantitative and qualitative techniques, methods, and management constructs running the gamut from a simple two-dimensional matrix such as conventional price-to-performance concepts to more sophisticated models like ESM and SBD.

The pressing needs for making informed and well-thought-out decisions and implementing those decisions in timely way has existed throughout history. Today, the pressures for more sophisticated management constructs have increased dramatically as the business environment becomes more turbulent and capable of rapid change. These factors magnified by global trade are among the most profound effects causing an ongoing evaluation of the suitability of the prevailing management constructs. It is often not a matter that the older approaches are obsolete, rather it may be that they do not fit the situations.

With a broader and more complex scope it is much more difficult to map out all of the networks, interrelationships, and dependences. While there has always been a healthy tension between having management constructs that are comprehensive and having ones that are simple and easy to understand, strategic leaders have to ensure that the management constructs used are appropriate and provide the right answers and best solutions.

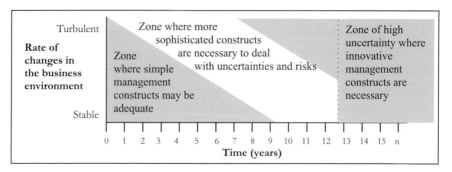

Figure 9.10   A relative sense of the applications – simple and sophisticated management constructs

The notion of simplicity and ease of use dominated management thought for most of the twentieth century. Simple management constructs are useful for situations with limited scope and short time frames. They are generally inadequate for truly assessing and understanding the business environment and market spaces, especially in the long term. Thus, more complicated approaches are needed because of globalization, increased technological sophistication, shortened product life cycles, and other changes in the business environment. Today, senior management cannot afford to make trade-offs between thoroughness and ease of use. The demands and challenges are great; management constructs must measure up to the needs and fulfill the requirements of the situation. Figure 9.10 provides a relative sense of whether simple management constructs can be used or more sophisticated approaches are necessary.

Simple constructs are those that examine the prevailing situation. They tend to view the business environment in static terms. For instance, the traditional strengths, weaknesses, opportunities, and threats (SWOT) analysis is used extensively to examine the prevailing business conditions. It provides reasonable insights providing the business environment and the rate of change are stable and slow, respectively; the prevailing technologies are dominant and unchanging; product innovations are incremental; the economic and social conditions are stable; and the perspectives focus on the near term. Simple management constructs include many of the well-known ones like SWOT analysis, industry analysis using Porter's five forces, the power of core competencies, and discount cash flow analysis. However, as the business environment becomes defined by change, especially in the technological and economic aspects, such simple management constructs are less effective and the assumptions made in developing the constructs are usually not valid.

On the other hand, if the business environment is turbulent and there are enormous changes in the technologies, social, political, and economic conditions and trends, and there are radical changes in many of the other variables, then more sophisticated management constructs like those discussed in this book should be used. While this is a theoretical perspective and it is not based on absolute values, it does provide guidelines about what types of management constructs should be used. It can be argued that the current business environment is unstable and market conditions are turbulent (i.e. a mid-range situation that has reasonable social and economic stability, but relatively high levels of technological and political uncertainties on a global basis). With that said, higher petroleum prices and more uncertainty in financial markets may make the situation worse.

More sophisticated management constructs have to be more inclusive, and drill back to the social world and natural environment, if necessary, to examine more of the underpinnings of change. Most importantly, they must examine all assumptions and eliminate those that are no longer valid. For instance, many management constructs assume that the dominant technologies of the prevailing situation will continue to shape the market forces in the future. Such views are often true, but when conditions and trends become more turbulent, the prevailing technologies may become obsolete or fail to provide the required solutions. In such cases, more sophisticated management constructs have to be used to understand the forces of change and to adequately consider the implications of the driving forces of change. The more sophisticated management constructs include ESM, SBD, six-sigma quality, strategic innovation, the extended enterprise, and sustainable solutions. As the strategic situation becomes more turbulent, strategic leaders should contemplate not only expanding the scope of their strategic framework, but they should also develop an inclusive business model that integrates all aspects of the external and internal dimensions.

Instituting control mechanisms

Strategic control is a broad topic that cuts across every facet of strategic management. It is a critical component of ESM, and transcends the elements of the strategic management process. It is a general management responsibility that includes protecting assets, achieving financial goals, maintaining financial and intellectual resources, keeping the operations and activities safe from harm or doing harm, obtaining high levels of quality and performance, and providing good management discipline through the proper delegation of authority. It begs questions like: how safe is safe? or how much control is appropriate?

Strategic control is a fundamental element of all management that dates back to Henri Fayol in the literature and actually much earlier from the practical side. It involves the management's responsibility to ensure that the organization performs in accordance with its mission, meets its objectives, and manages and functions within generally accepted practices. This includes ensuring compliance with all laws and regulations, and providing requisite information to shareholders, governments, and other important constituencies, and minimizing and mitigating risks.

Strategic leaders at all levels have fiduciary responsibilities to safeguard the well being of the company to ensure its sustainable success and to advance its prominence, reputation, and social, economic, and ethical standing in the communities (global to local) in which they do business. They have a duty of care to ensure the proper governance of the organization. Strategic leaders focus on long-term shareholder value creation, the financial wherewithal, the intellectual capital and capacity, and the proper allocation of resources.

Strategic control implies keeping the strategic and operations management systems and processes within defined parameters so that positives are achieved and negatives are avoided or mitigated. Managing strategic and financial risks and ensuring health and safety are critical responsibilities of strategic leaders that cut across every operation and activity. While the focus is generally on high-level aspects of the SBU, strategic leaders are ultimately responsible for everything and they must keep in mind that failures in the operating systems can also derail the strategies and good work of the organization. For instance, BP plc and Lord Browne were widely acclaimed for their efforts to transform the corporation using the principles and precepts of SBD. It was recognized by the Dow Jones Sustainable Index as a leader in the petroleum industry in 2002–2003. In its Sustainability Report 2003, BP states that "sustainability means the capacity to endure as a group by renewing assets, creating and delivering products and services that meet the evolving needs of society, attracting successive generations of employees, contributing to a flourishing environment and retaining the trust and support of customers, shareholders and communities."[11] However, during 2005–2006 it had a disastrous fire at its Texas City refinery and ran into several severe problems that detracted from its rhetoric about SBD. BP also had to shut down its Alaska pipeline for weeks because it had failed to ensure that the proper maintenance had been carried out.

While the conduct and performance of the operating systems are normally viewed as tactical, they can become strategic if the consequences of actions or inactions result in severe negative situations. Clearly if people are injured or killed the implications are strategic, and have critical implications that reach beyond the scope of business. Moreover, when the consequences of action, or failure to take action, have broad impacts that resonate across the company and its reputation, then strategic leaders have to consider them as impinging on the well being of the whole and ensure that strategic controls are in place to protect both the people and the well being of the company and the extended enterprise, the assets of the corporation, shareholder value, and sustainable success.

Strategic control includes proper governance of the organization. Governance extends to value delivery systems, maintaining control of resources and other inputs, managing strategic risks, and providing measures to determine the potential to realize the desired outcomes. Each category is critical and requires ongoing effort to affect positive results. However, these are amongst the most challenging because they are open-ended, requiring broad-based attention. Unlike many of the elements of the strategic management process that have end points and can be fulfilled, strategic control requires ongoing diligence and commitment. The proper governance of any organization is always difficult to exactly define. From a business unit perspective it involves the proper conduct of the strategic management process; it is all-inclusive. And it includes the proper function and control of the value delivery systems through functional strategies, tactical plans, budgeting, policies, and agreed-upon management constructs. While strategic leaders have to provide the organization with sufficient flexibility to allow people to perform their duties and tasks on a timely basis, good governance implies that there are enough safeguards and oversight to ensure that everyone operates within acceptable practices and that assets are sufficiently protected.

Strategic control and good governance involve giving direction to subordinates who may need help in executing their responsibilities. Strategic leaders have to provide people with the knowledge, capabilities, and resources to carry out their strategies and action plans. They allocate financial resources and provide the mechanisms necessary to ensure that money is not only available in accordance with the needs and requirements, but it is properly used and accounted for. Strategic control also involves managing the relationships of the organization; legal aspects of contracts and compliance with laws and regulations. There are a myriad of government mandates that extend from financial accounting and reporting to health and safety regulations that require oversight from management.

Controlling, managing, and mitigating risks are crucial to good governance. Risks are ever-present, and involve strategic, financial, market, stakeholder, compliance, and operating aspects. Strategic risks include failing to implement business strategies and achieve desired outcomes, being unable to develop action programs or achieve results, damaging the image and reputation of the business, and suffering losses of positions or assets. Financial risks generally involve losses in valuation, decline of assets, decreases in cash flow and profits, and other financial instruments. They also involve a failure to cover the cost of capital of the investment and the money used in the conduct of the businesses. Moreover, risks are an essential part of business given that there are always uncertainties and unforeseen events. If everything was known and deterministic, then all of the competitors and non-competitors alike would be able to maximize their situations as well as resulting in little advantage for anyone. But business does involve risks. Strategic leaders who can mitigate, reduce, or eliminate risks are generally in a preferred situation.

While most businesses have control systems that focus on financial aspects, these systems tend to be lagging approaches that examine decisions and results afterwards and then try to sort out the causes of the problems and the required solutions. They are really strategic evaluation, not strategic control. The latter focuses on being proactive and ensuring that implementation and execution are achieving the desired outcomes. Control is about taking action and ensuring that they result in acceptable outcomes on a real-time basis. The former focuses on examining the course of events and outcomes, and determining whether everything is proceeding in accordance with objectives, strategies, programs, standards, lines of authority, approval, financial mechanisms, policies, principles, and best practices among many other mechanisms.

The strategic management process and related elements are actually part of the mechanisms used for strategic control. As strategic leaders follow the process they:
- Learn what has to be done via strategic analysis;
- Map out what they plan to do through strategic formulation;
- Establish the means and mechanisms for achieving results and success through strategic implementation; and
- Carry out the actions and obtain results through execution.

Strategic leaders monitor the process and the outcomes along the way by selecting and using performance measures. These provide ongoing feedback about how well the organization is performing via formal information systems and management reports. Management reports often focus on financial results, but they should include all critical measures so that a balanced perspective is provided so that corrective actions, if necessary, can be effected immediately.

Strategic leaders have to decide what measures should be used to monitor ongoing results. These measures should provide direct and ongoing feedback on a real-time basis. Measures provide early warning about whether the strategic management process is tracking properly and that the business unit will be able to implement its business strategies and achieve its objectives. The measures provide indications about the probabilities of achieving success and the insights about what corrective actions may be necessary to get the process back on track if there are difficulties. Measures are used to track the progress of the development of the management systems, the structuring or restructuring of the organization, the development of the action programs, and all of the other aforementioned means and mechanisms necessary to implement and execute the business strategies.

Measures should determine the progress in terms of a balanced view of satisfying expectations of the business environment and meeting internal requirements. The measures should be linked to business objectives and monitor the most crucial variables with respect to market space, value creation, uniqueness of strategic position, and financial viability. There are numerous measures that can be used. The broad categories include:

- Value creation and sustainable success;
- Timeliness and the time horizon;
- Money and rewards; and
- Risk and uncertainty.

Value creation is an essential parameter for measuring business success. It is a broad but powerful measure. It defines and determines the ultimate purpose of the business enterprise. If you can create value, you create success. Value drives customers and the solutions they seek. Customer success often translates into business unit success.

Time is one of the most important measures. The quicker the organization can formulate and implement its business strategies the more likely it is to realize desired outcomes. While there is not a perfect correlation, it is obvious, especially in turbulent times, that the faster the business unit can implement the requisite means and mechanisms and be thorough at the same time, the less likely that changes in the business environment will be disruptive. Many organizations have the right strategies and the best means and mechanisms to get results, but they are simply too slow during execution and they are trumped by others. Measures of time relate to the other critical aspects as well. For instance, the failure to implement programs properly may allow competitors to be the first to the market with new technologies or products, giving them the advantages of being first to the market.

Money is always a powerful measure. Finance and economics are significant factors in determining success or failure. If cost structures are higher than expected, the competitive position and the customer-derived value may be reduced dramatically. As prices are forced upward, the value proposition suffers, reducing the viability of the product from a customer's perspective. Higher prices often translate into lower sales volume and revenues. If markets are constrained, lower volumes translate into higher costs, lower profits and cash flow. All of these factors have negative effects on the return on the investment and the financial well being of the business unit.

Risk deals with uncertainty about the future, or a lack of information about the present. There are always risks associated with capabilities of the organization and uncertainties of the business environment. For instance, new products may have defects leading to product liability claims. The product or the production processes may have environmental impacts, affecting stakeholders and creating compliance and legal problems.

Strategic leaders often use business objectives and goals as the primary measures to track potential outcomes. Objectives become the mechanisms to ascertain if implementation and execution are tracking on course. If the actual values are in line with the expected outcomes, then it is assumed that there is a high probability that implementation and execution are within an acceptable range. However, if one or more of the measures and/or objectives are trending toward an extreme point, it indicates that the variance to the established plan is drifting out of control. Measures are intended to provide instantaneous feedback while evaluation is used to make periodic determinations about expected outcomes.

Developing reward mechanisms

Developing reward mechanisms may be the last element of the major mechanisms but it is not the least important. Rewards involve remuneration for the value that people create, encouraging right behaviors and best practices, instilling positive reinforcements for achievements, aligning people toward the strategic direction, and motivating individuals and teams to focus on the business objectives and expected results. In the context of the business unit, rewards are mechanisms to achieve positive outcomes in the future as well as recognizing accomplishments in the present or the past.

Rewards can provide incentives for management, employees, and teams, but they are usually not as structured as the typical incentives for executive management. Incentives are motivational techniques used to realize selected goals, especially by executives, whereas rewards are encouragements for obtaining desired positive outcomes. For executives and certain strategic leaders, rewards are generally provided in the form of well-documented incentives for achieving a narrow set of goals specific to the organization's shareholders. The typical incentives for senior management include an increase in remuneration in salary, bonuses, and stock options predicated on improving share price or market capitalization of the corporation, improving net income and return of equity, and other, very specific, financial targets. While incentives may make sense to the current shareholders and the board of directors, they often lead to some short-term gains at the expense of long-term ones.

In the business units, rewards provide recognition of achievements, and encourage future efforts toward long-term sustainable success. Rewards are given on the basis of individual effort and team-based approaches as well. They are more than just incentives for achieving selected objectives; they are part of a balanced strategic management approach that includes fairness in sharing in the glory of the achievements and inducements across the organization for making extraordinary contributions. They should include all aspects of the organization from the top down and across the extended enterprise. It is not only right and proper that all participating employees are duly recognized and rewarded, but it makes the positive realities of the situation more sustainable.

Poorly administered rewards can have negative outcomes in the long term by limiting significant contributions of those who go unrecognized. Remember that it is human nature to pay attention and figure out what the true incentives are and then act accordingly.

Table 9.1 provides a matrix of rewards in terms of time horizons and the organizational elements.

Rewards should provide special recognition for extraordinary achievements and outcomes that result in positive gains for the whole, and are sustained over the longer term. Great care must be exercised to ensure that gains in one area are not achieved at the expense of losses in others. Playing zero-sum games should be discouraged. Making trade-offs should be avoided. If teams are used for developing new products, then team-based rewards should be

Table 9.1 Examples of incentives and rewards

	Immediate	Longer term	Intangible
Strategic leaders *Managers*	Enhanced total compensation Better benefits	Bonuses Profit sharing More autonomy	Promotion Recognition Awards
Professional staff *Employees*	Improved base pay Better benefits	Promotion Performance pay Bonuses Flexible benefits Enhanced work environment	Respect Recognition/ commendation Learning Development Training Awards
Team based	Provided performance pay	Team bonuses More input in decision making Enhanced roles Quality of work	Self-directed leadership Mobility Recognition/ commendation Higher status Flexible work hours

given. For example, Ken Iverson used team-based recognition and rewards as a mechanism to achieve a superior performance at Nucor Steel. Now the former CEO, Iverson had tremendous respect for the company's managers, professionals, and workforce. He knew that people, not machines, produce results. He developed a reward system that recognized achievements biweekly if the production teams outperformed the standard requirements. He paid bonuses to workers on the basis of the team effort each pay period. If the team performed above expectations, then the whole team shared in the bonus. If the team failed to exceed the standards, then no one on the team got a bonus.

Michael Armstrong and Duncan Brown in their book, *Strategic Reward: Making It Happen*, suggest that there are considerations to take into account when examining the effects of rewards on organizational performance:[12]

1. It must be recognized that reward strategies will only affect performance if they work (i.e. they are implemented effectively by all concerned, especially line managers).

2. The extent to which reward strategies and policies on their own can make an impact may be more limited than early US exponents of the concept believed.

3. Reward strategies work best if they are integrated with other HR strategies, so that there is a coherent approach with mutually supporting policies and practices.

Their suggestions are in keeping with the discussions pertaining to strategic implementation in this chapter. Success is achieved through the integration of the means and mechanisms available to strategic leaders to ensure that business strategies can be successfully carried out. Strategic leaders have to inspire people to produce extraordinary results. However, they cannot expect that people will continue to perform if all of the glory, recognition, and rewards go to a small cadre of senior management. Even worse is an environment where strategic leaders get the glory if success is achieved and others get the blame if failures occur. Strategic leaders need to share the accolades as soon as possible and to the greatest extent possible if they want to continue success over the long term.

Strategic leaders should consider providing incentives and rewards for entities in the extended enterprise that perform above expectations and are integrated with the management systems of the business unit. While care has to be given on how such incentives are developed and how the rewards are provided, the concept of sharing in the success often promotes ongoing success.

Evaluation

Evaluation is a critical part of the strategic management process. The approaches and metrics used to evaluate business units and their product delivery systems include continuously monitoring progress, auditing, and providing feedback to senior management. Performance evaluation is a fundamental management responsibility that relates to overall governance and to the strategic management process.

Monitoring progress includes many of the mechanisms discussed under control mechanisms. It involves preempting problems before they happen, and taking actions to dissolve the underlying potential difficulties that may result in unacceptable outcomes and impacts. Strategic leaders must focus on leading change and adapting the business unit to its new realities through transitions and transformations.

Traditional metrics like profitability, cash flow, return on sales, customer satisfaction, on-time delivery, yield, quality, efficiency improvements, productivity gains, cycle time reduction, and market share provide measures of success for value delivery systems but may not provide leading indicators that indicate how well their strategies are working. Most of the aforementioned that measure functional and operating levels are lagging indicators that describe what has happened over some period of time but they do not usually provide early warning on the lack of progress or existing difficulties. Strategic leaders need leading indicators to determine whether overall progress is sufficient to keep the organization on track. Leading-edge metrics may be used. Although more difficult to ascertain, they provide a greater sense of how well the organization is implementing and executing the strategies in real time. Leading indicators include an evaluation of the degree of increased integration, the amount of organizational learning, the degree of innovativeness, and a sense of value creation. These are challenging metrics to create, which may require numerous subsets to effectively develop a meaningful understanding of reality.

The performance evaluation validates decision making and provides confidence that the business strategies are on track. It also offers insights about the actions required for meeting targets and objectives or for taking timely corrective actions if necessary. The performance evaluation system measures actual performance against the expectations of customers, stakeholders, the community, the regulatory agencies, and other constituencies. It focuses on how well the strategic management system is meeting objectives and targets, implementing strategies, obtaining desired outcomes, mitigating risks, and achieving competitive advantage and business success.

Strategic auditing is a technique used to ascertain performance on a periodic basis. It is used by strategic leaders to determine how well lower level managers are performing their roles and responsibilities for implementing and executing the strategies and objectives of the business unit, as well as how they are carrying out their functional and operating strategies. Executives ensure that audits are performed on the SBUs across the whole company. The board of directors may engage outside organizations to perform audits.

Strategic leaders delegate many of the elements of the action programs to subordinates who are expected to deliver the desired outcomes. Such managers are often given several degrees of freedom in executing the programs, but periodic audits by the strategic and/or corporate leaders ensure that implementation and execution are being managed properly, prudently, and in accordance with the control mechanisms.

Auditing is a management control technique that allows managers at all levels flexibility of action with the knowledge that there is oversight by higher level management that may periodically review the decisions and actions. Audits are lagging control mechanisms that are used to examine past performance, and to determine whether the decisions and actions were appropriate and proper. The overall purpose is to ensure that everything is on track and to discover ways to make improvements if possible. While many people view audits as negatives, they should be perceived as helpful, at least in the context of good management, using best practices to improve future performance.

There are many types of audits that include financial audits that are certified by an independent auditing firm working for the board of directors and executives of the corporation to ensure compliance with various regulatory requirements, to numerous audits of the businesses, operations, and products and processes. The latter includes audits of health and safety, compliance with environmental laws and regulations, product safety and liability, community health and well being as it relates to production facilities, and a host of other areas. Strategic leaders and their professional staffs may also audit the strategic management process itself. Such audits might examine each element of the process and the boldness of the resultant strategies and strategic direction.

Execution

The operating system

The operating system(s) and value delivery system include the functional and operational areas of the business unit. Generally, the operating system is the lower level management system designed and constructed to carry out the mission of the business unit. There are often specifically designed systems with defined roles for all of the participants to execute business strategies. It is critical for people to understand that the value delivery system/product delivery system encompasses more than manufacturing or operations. It includes all of the internal functional areas. Typically, they include supply network management, production, assembly, marketing, service support, finance, and the complementary areas that support the action plans.

As discussed earlier, many large companies historically used a de-coupled, hierarchical approach for managing the organization that included operations management of the value delivery system on the bottom, and corporate and strategic business management at the top. Traditional business models often limited the scope of the framework to facilitate decision making and simplify the interactions. Organizational reporting linked decision makers with those who executed through a vertical multilayered structure that required many interactions between management up and down the chain of command. The mechanisms were thorough, but usually slow. They consumed enormous amounts of time and resources. The strength of the methodology was the ability to focus on the specific elements within the organization and obtain solutions. Senior management was responsible for specifying the objectives, strategies, and action programs. Functional or operational management carried out the programs. The functional areas were central to the operating system. Each part was developed and optimized as if it was an independent component. While examining the parts separately facilitated decision making within the defined context, the integration of the parts into a true system became challenging. The strength of the approach became the weakness. Due to the lack of integration at the operating level, senior management had to play a significant role in resolving difficulties within the system. While this is a broad brush of the historical situation, it is clear that most businesses optimized the functional areas and had difficulties integrating the whole.

The operating system is the core operating level. It concentrates on existing conditions and meeting the market, production, technical, and financial requirements of the organization. It is usually supported by the product and process innovation capabilities for updating and improving performance. The core operating level is usually supported by well-established management constructs that produce results through well-defined processes. The historical construct for managing the operating level focused on the resources deployed within the system and the organizational elements engaged in converting inputs into outputs.

The value delivery system incorporates the internal functions and links them with the extended enterprise. It focuses on the tactical approaches for achieving results. The value delivery system and the operating system focus on: (1) market opportunities, customer wants and needs, and stakeholder expectations; (2) product attributes, product and process specifications, product innovation, and marketing requirements; (3) the interrelated effects of customers, consumers, stakeholders, related industries, and competition; (4) day-to-day operations, functional strategies, and tactics; and (5) the use of fundamental management methods for making sound business decisions. These areas should be aligned with its mission, business strategies, and objectives.

Functional strategies and tactics

Functional strategies and tactics involve translating inputs into outputs that are valuable and desirable solutions. Generally, outputs are designed, produced, marketed, and distributed for customers who require solutions to their social and economic needs and wants. The solutions are usually the goods and services that are sold through markets that provide cash flow for the business enterprises. This is an oversimplification of the complex processes that are generally involved in the conversion processes that start with raw materials, energy, labor, and capital and result in customer relationships and the exchange of goods for money. The functional strategies involve the direct transactions with the entities of the value delivery system and the extended enterprise as they carry out the economic mission.

Functional strategies are the crucial approaches used in each of the primary internal dimensions of the operating system. Traditional primary internal dimensions include production, marketing, finance, human resource management, product development, supply network management, and essential support functions like information management. Other critical areas may include legal, stakeholder management, asset management, waste management, and government relationship management.

The functional strategies usually focus on the short and intermediate terms, and deal directly with the operating aspects. They are often confused with business strategies or are given higher levels of importance by strategic leaders who elevate day-to-day functional strategies and decisions to levels where they cannot produce effective or enduring results. While pure definitions are impossible and the actual importance of functional strategies is dependent on the situation, one perspective suggests that they are really the tactical decisions that are made by operating managers to effectively deal with the short term.

Functional strategies and tactics are actually moves and emergent approaches used by managers to handle the prevailing situations in the most effective way possible. As managers read the business environment they form actions for immediate execution. They reflect upon the realities of the situation and take into account the resources and capabilities of the organization and its value delivery system. Actions are generally based on relational and transactional approaches that translate business unit plans and strategies into realities. They have a relatively short time horizon, and are highly adaptive to meet the specific needs and requirements of the prevailing business environment. It can be argued that functional strategies focus on the near term based on the internal and external dimensions of the value delivery system and its extended enterprise, while tactics involve the immediate response to the pressures of the present at ground level.

Functional strategies and tactics like business strategies are subsets of the higher level strategies with one great exception. While corporate and business strategies are planned and orchestrated through strategic analysis, strategic formulation, and implementation, functional strategies, and to even a greater degree tactics, are emergent management approaches that are formed on a short time horizon to meet the realities of the present and near term. They are based on the knowledge, experience, and presence of the functional management engaged in the prevailing situations.

Functional strategies and tactics involve making specific decisions about the product delivery system and its relationships to its business landscape. They are highly focused on the value delivery system but driven by the immediate forces that the managers have to manage and satisfy. Table 9.2 lists some of the categories and specific areas that might be considered under the banner of functional strategies and tactics.

The list is not intended to be comprehensive but illustrative. It is not the purpose of this text to provide a detailed discussion of the functional strategies and tactics, nor of all of the techniques and methods used in the execution of business on a real-time basis. The managers and supervisors who engage in day-to-day actions have to be adaptive and creative in the fulfillment of their roles and responsibilities.

Functional strategies and tactics are always susceptible to market forces. They may be easily copied by others and are usually not a source of competitive advantage since competitors typically use same tactics. For instance, pricing strategies are often touted as being a source of gaining advantages over the competition but in most cases they are easily emulated. With that said, pricing may be more than a functional strategy if the company enjoys a low-cost position that its competitors cannot replicate for a year, two, or more as in the case of Wal-Mart. Regardless, even when there are significant benefits from functional strategies they generally are not sustained over time. For example, Hewlett-Packard uses new product introductions as mechanisms to stay ahead of competition. Even with its outstanding track record of successful new products it usually gains only short-term advantages with each new product. However, its innovation strategies of continuous new product development do give it competitive advantages at the business unit level.

As the strategic management process flows from the upstream elements of formulation to the downstream ones involving execution, the process becomes more focused on real-time aspects, but in that light the elements have to be more adaptive and emergent and based on less on planned approaches and more on the management's abilities to adapt.

Table 9.2 Listing of functional strategies and tactics

Functional strategies	Specific aspects	Considerations
Markets	Target markets and customers	Segmentation, locations, sophistication, relations
	Value proposition	Value creation, customer success, affordability
	Basis of competition	Pressures, power, positions, know-how, adaptability
	Driving forces	Social, economic, technological, political, ecological
Value system	Supply network connections	Capabilities, resources, knowledge, relationships
	Stakeholders	Positions, power, requirements, mandates, interests
	Related industries	Support, linkages, relationships, positions, value
	Infrastructure	Support, logistics, technological sophistication
	Competitors	Number, power of leaders, size, strategies, actions
Product line	Product line mix	Mix of products, depth, breadth, scope, life cycle
	Uniqueness of positions	Power, differentiation, quality, value, sophistication
	Designs Cost structures	Knowledge, insights, developments, sustainability inputs, conversion processes, volumes, overheads
Marketing	Product strategies	Brands, sophistication, quality, reliability
	Pricing strategies	Premium, affordable, market-based, discounts
	Promotion and advertising	Theme, message, media, timing, honesty, clarity
	Distribution channels	Direct, retail, wholesale, intermediaries
	Customer service and support	Responsiveness, service support, quality, timeliness
Operations	Production capabilities	Volume, processes, utilization, sophistication
	Capacity and planning	Facilities, locations, layouts, scope, scheduling
	Processes and equipment	Lean production, machines, technologies
	Supply management	Procurement, outsourcing, relationships
	Quality management	Process control, quality outcomes, six-sigma
	Workforce management	empowerment, labor practices, methods, polices
	Waste management	Pollution prevention, waste reduction, compliance
Finance	Costs of capital	Funds, approvals, metrics, sources, uses
	Revenues and cash flow	Sales, cash flow, margins, profits, returns
	Budgeting	Costs, expenses, investments, cycles, controls
	Financial control/reporting	Accounting, accuracy, control, audits, reports
Management	Leadership	Inspiration, authority, responsibilities, talents
	Entrepreneurship	Creativity, knowledge, experience, insights
	Management and commitment	Competencies, risk-taking, flexibility, people skills
Human resources	Recruitment and retention	Nature of work, pleasure, compensation, benefits
	Training and development	Knowledge, learning, skills, opportunities
	Work processes	Structure, processes, flexibility, adaptability
	Rewards and recognition	Respect, awards, promotions, new positions
Information	Information system	Structures, linkages, networks, support, services
	Hardware and software	Technologies, data processing, automation, design
	Security and recovery	System, processes, backup, protection, procedures
Development	New products and services	Product development, process improvements
	Capabilities enhancements	Alliances, partnerships, cross-functional teams
	Research/knowledge creation	Learning, building, creating, new ventures

Program management

Functional managers institute the actions and activities that result in achievements and the attainment of the objectives. Program managers are the individuals who are specifically tasked with the execution of the implementation of the action program. Depending on the type of organization they may also be the functional managers per a functional organization, or they may be program managers as in a matrix organization.

Regardless, they are the professionals and/or entrepreneurs that follow the script laid out by strategic leaders via business strategies and action plans and the implementation processes. However, in most cases, they have some flexibility to make appropriate decisions to adapt the plans and programs to fit the changes in the business environment and market spaces as time unfolds. Without the ability to modify the action plans, the whole process would become static, frozen in the moment that the plans were formulated. This would cause implementation and execution to drift out of synch with reality.

Execution must be both rigorous and adaptive. Uncertainty and ambiguity are ever-present, so the flexibility to make changes in the plans as the situation requires must be a prerogative of management. As the process moves deeper into execution, the knowledge, capabilities, creativity, self-reliance, and adaptability of the functional and program managers increase in importance. It is impossible to specify every detail associated with execution. Moreover, it is undesirable since rigidity tends to stifle creativity making managing more difficult, not easier.

Functional and program managers focus on deployments, actions, and accomplishments. A capable organization is one that understands what has to be done and how to do it, has the resources to execute, and possesses the willingness to engage and succeed. Such an organization often uses collaborative teams that have the skills, capabilities, and behaviors, and use best practices, methods, and techniques to realize desired outcomes.

Functional and program managers have the knowledge to solve problems and the integrity to create balanced solutions. They are responsible for challenging their staff people to exercise their abilities to the greatest degree. They resolve conflicts within the organization and with partners as soon as possible. They understand that decisions are critical and involve risks. They are willing to take responsibility for their decisions and take any criticism for results that are less than expected. They also encourage others to be innovative and create the sustainable success.

Summary

Strategic leaders have to be the architects of change and the masters of interdisciplinary and interorganizational actions, initiatives, and programs. They have to focus on the future of the organization through strategic implementation and execution. Implementation involves setting the stage for deployment and action. Execution involves the actual carrying out of the business strategies.

Strategic leaders have to have the capabilities to orchestrate the design and development of new management systems, organizational structures, and program management methodologies. They have to build organizational capabilities and provide the resources for proactively inventing the future of the organization. These are the means for achieving results. They are supported by the mechanisms, which include: developing the rules for execution and instituting policies, procedures, and practices; articulating the management constructs, methods, and techniques; selecting control mechanisms and performance measures; and providing recognition and rewards, and enhancing the culture of the organization.

Strategic leaders generally delegate most of the actual execution of the business strategies to functional and program managers who are responsible for ensuring that the whole organization is engaged in achieving results. They also are responsible for obtaining the near-term objectives and functional strategies of the product delivery system.

Strategic formulation involves intellectual capital. Strategic implementation involves physical, human, and financial capital. Execution involves all of the above and a lot of hard work. Sustainable success is the result of enduring efforts. Great outcomes do not just happen; they are created by the leadership and the people of the enterprise.

References

Armstrong, Michael and Duncan Brown (2006) *Strategic Reward: Making It Happen*. London, UK: Kogan Page

Chandler Jr., Alfred (1962) *Strategy and Structure: Chapters in the History of the American Enterprise*. Cambridge, MA: The MIT Press

Deming, W. Edwards (1982, 2000) *Out of the Crisis*. Cambridge, MA: The MIT Press

Hamel, Gary (2000) *Leading the Revolution*. Boston, MA: Harvard Business School Press

Hayes, Robert H., Kim B. Clark, and Steven C. Wheelwright (1988) *Dynamic Manufacturing: Creating the Learning Organization*. New York: Free Press

Peters, Thomas and Robert Waterman Jr. (1982) *In Search of Excellence: Lessons from America's Best-run Companies.* New York: Harper & Row Publishers, Inc.

Rainey, David L. (2006) *Sustainable Business Development: Inventing the Future through Strategy, Innovation and Leadership.* Cambridge, UK: Cambridge University Press

NOTES

1   The strategic implementation process includes the elements discussed. Strategy implementation is one of the most important elements of the strategic management process. Strategy implementation specifically addresses the management constructs for turning business strategies into executable actions.

2   W. Edwards Deming, *Out of the Crisis* (Cambridge, MA: The MIT Press, 1982, 2000, p. 19).

3   Robert H. Hayes, Kim B. Clark, and Steven C. Wheelwright, *Dynamic Manufacturing: Creating the Learning Organization* (New York: Free Press, 1988, p. 279).

4   Thomas Peters and Robert Waterman Jr., *In Search of Excellence: Lessons from America's Best-run Companies* (New York: Harper & Row Publishers, Inc., 1982). Peters was a former McKinsey principal and Waterman was a director of McKinsey and Company at the time.

5   *Ibid.,* p. 9.

6   ISO 9000 has become an international reference for quality management requirements in business-to-business dealings, and ISO 14000 focuses on enabling organizations to meet their environmental challenges. The ISO 9000 family is primarily concerned with "quality management." This means what the organization does to fulfill:
   - the customer's quality requirements; and
   - applicable regulatory requirements, while aiming to
   - enhance customer satisfaction, and
   - achieve continual improvement of its performance in pursuit of these objectives.

   The ISO 14000 family is primarily concerned with "environmental management." This means what the organization does to:
   - minimize harmful effects on the environment caused by its activities, and to
   - achieve continual improvement of its environmental performance.

7   Alfred Chandler Jr., *Strategy and Structure: Chapters in the History of the American Industrial Enterprise* (Cambridge, MA: The MIT Press, 1962, p. 14).

8   David L. Rainey, *Sustainable Business Development: Inventing the Future through Strategy, Innovation and Leadership* (Cambridge, UK: Cambridge University Press, 2006, pp. 647–670).

9   Gary Hamel, *Leading the Revolution* (Boston, MA: Harvard Business School Press, 2000, pp. 244–271).

10   *Ibid.,* p. 280.

11   Sustainability Report 2003, BP plc, London, p. i.

12   Michael Armstrong and Duncan Brown, *Strategic Reward: Making It Happen* (London, UK: Kogan Page, 2006, p. 47).

10 Reflections and concluding comments

Introduction

As discussed throughout the book, enterprise-wide strategic management (ESM) is a more inclusive, more sophisticated, and realistic strategic management framework for leading change in complex business situations. ESM is based on several key premises. One of the most important is that the overarching goals are to create extraordinary value and achieve sustainable success. Extraordinary value and sustainable success are developed and achieved through enterprise-wide strategic leadership (ESL), holistic thinking, proactive business strategies, strategic innovations, and outstanding implementation and execution.

In today's business environment, strategic leaders have to reach out beyond the traditional perspectives of "supply and demand" approaches and the narrow focus on competitors, the markets, and customers. They have to engage, interact, and understand the whole business environment and market spaces. This includes critical driving forces of the social/human world and the natural environment. These broader perspectives result in the ability to lead change and to discover, develop, and deploy enhanced solutions to take advantage of the opportunities and to resolve or eliminate many of the problems facing businesses and humankind. Most importantly, they provide critical insights for future business prospects, long-term financial success, and sustainable business performance.

Despite the ever-growing complexities of large companies, the accelerating intensity of competition, and the threats from emerging competitors in developing countries, the business world of today is still vibrant and full of opportunity. However, most of the exciting opportunities go beyond traditional markets or those associated with conventional competitive strategies. In developed countries many markets are mature and the possibilities of achieving extraordinary results are becoming more limited and difficult to obtain. Most of yesterday's innovative products have become commoditized. They have been replicated many times by competitors. Many large companies are finding not only that there are numerous competitors, but many of these competitors also have the same advantages, competencies, and capabilities that were once the sole domain of the most elite corporations in the world. Most global companies produce high-quality products and operate sophisticated management systems. Gaining and keeping competitive advantages based on product–market positions, marketing, manufacturing, and financial strengths are hard to realize, and even harder to maintain. Even when large companies and their strategic business units (SBUs) have such advantages they face stiff pressure as global competitors can match or surpass the products and benefits being offered. Moreover, the driving forces have expanded from competitive and market pressures to include a broad array of requirements, mandates, and expectations. Success is predicated on satisfying all of the external entities including the demands and expectations of stakeholders, governments, and society.

ESM and ESL involve seeking out broader perspectives and reaching out beyond the prevailing situations. Today's strategic leaders have to constantly be aware of the true needs, wants, and expectations of people wherever they may be and provide the best solutions possible, ones that holistically fulfill the underlying objectives. This requires a combination of holistic and creative thinking with great insights and reflections about the external dimensions (context). Holistic thinking and its related management constructs are among the most critical prerequisites for achieving enduring success. Holistic management requires an inclusive approach, linking essential elements of the value delivery system into a comprehensive management system for decision making and leading change. Holistic management involves integrating the extended enterprise and creating solutions that are sustained over time for all key entities. The extended enterprise is central for developing and implementing effective business strategies and action plans. In today's business world, enterprise-wide capabilities and resources are necessary for orchestrating and ensuring sustainable success.

Creative thinking is the springboard to enjoying enormous business opportunities. For instance, consider the more than two billion people around the world who live on two dollars per day or less. They need basic products that fit their circumstances – those that are affordable and easy to use without depending on an existing support infrastructure. Literally billions of people have money but it is limited and they must use it wisely. They need products that are specifically designed and priced for their needs. Such products have to meet local conditions and reflect the needs of the indigenous people; hence, opportunities!

Strategic leaders are the architects of the future and the key decision makers of the organization and business enterprise. They determine and realize the strategic direction through the choices of business objectives, strategies, and action plans. They have to be insightful and aggressive. Strategic leaders have to select business strategies that dramatically improve the positives and eliminate the negatives. The related actions and initiatives must have outstanding potential for changing the business world for the better and making the enterprise more successful and sustainable.

Successful business enterprises provide great solutions. Strategic leaders must think in terms of the solutions that people want and need, not just the products and services that they produce and sell. Anything that provides an enhanced solution, one that is better than the existing choices, may have the power to change the prevailing situation. While not all strategic innovations prove to be great solutions, a leadership mindset that emphasizes enhanced options and better choices that fit the customers' situation opens the door for greater customer satisfaction and success. Indeed, sustainable customer and stakeholder success is also a critical factor for the company's success.

People want to be successful and enjoy their personal and professional lives. Providing customers and others with success and successful outcomes is an important part of the overall solution or "total solution." Strategic leaders must tailor their solutions to their customers and stakeholders. For instance, people in developed countries want to purchase washing machines that consume less electricity, water, and detergent yet provide better cleaning with less wear and tear on clothes. On the other hand, there are millions of people living in developing countries who cannot afford the kind of devices that require electricity and installation services. They may be happy to have clothes washers that rely on manual operations. The manually operated washing machine is a relic in countries like the US but it may actually save time and labor in the market spaces lacking an external infrastructure. A manual washer may be a preferable alternative to using river water to wash clothes using methods that are thousands of years old. Affordability may be hastened by the community making the purchase and the devices being shared by several households. The solution has to be couched in the context of the users and their applications, not just based on the perceptions or objectives of the producers. The strategic management mindset has to shift from producer-centric to market-centric and/or enterprise-centric.

Sustainable success depends on strategic positions, systems, solutions, and relationships that are comprehensive and interconnected – those that provide extraordinary value. It is enhanced when the systems, solutions, and relationships are difficult for others to duplicate. As the basis for the solution moves from products and processes to systems, structures, and relationships, the solutions become more holistic and integrated, thus fully articulated; competitors and others have to follow suit if they wish to stay in the game. But, copying enterprise-wide value delivery systems and fully articulated solutions involve more expansive approaches and more complex strategies and actions. Some of the competitors may make the efforts and investments, but many will not or cannot. Most importantly, the innovator/integrator forces the others to play his or her game. If sustainable solutions are based on holistic management and systems integration, then it becomes more difficult for competitors to achieve the same sustainable success. While it is not impossible to be successful using conventional competitive advantages like core competencies, products, or processes, the probabilities of succeeding using simplistic and/or narrow approaches are expected to decline. As the requisite solutions become more and more sophisticated, strategic leaders must use the whole business enterprise to obtain the desired results and sustainable success. Toyota, for example, bases its strategic position on cutting-edge technologies and products, like hybrid-drive vehicles, yet it is its integrated system that provides its competitive advantages and success. Toyota's leaders realize that their suppliers and suppliers of suppliers are integral to its overall success. Moreover, success is predicated on the capabilities of all of the contributors and how well recipients enjoy the solutions. Toyota knows that it has to provide the best value proposition.

ESM is more comprehensive than traditional strategic management systems. It includes the full scope of all of the critical entities that are necessary to create and provide solutions. It includes the extended enterprise and other critical aspects of the business environment, social world, and natural environment. An effective management framework like ESM involves integrating all of the forces and entities that drive change for success. It also highlights the critical interfaces between the entities and ensures that the requisite needs, expectations, requirements, and mandates are fulfilled.

Theories and methods pertaining to ESM are being developed, expanded, and improved by strategists in large companies and small and medium-sized enterprises (SMEs). It may take decades for most companies and their strategic leaders to obtain the sophistication necessary to compete on the basis of ESM and have fully articulated approaches that include comprehensive considerations about the business environment, the social/human world, and the natural environment. The promise of a fully integrated business enterprise offers hope that business leaders can discover the opportunities and challenges, create exceptional value, and achieve sustainable success.

This chapter discusses the future directions of ESM and offers some concluding comments.

Future direction of ESM

The business world has changed dramatically since the demise of the Soviet Union and the liberalization of trade in North America, the European Union (EU), and the Pacific Rim. The notions of first, second, and third worlds have given way to the more modern view of the global economy in terms of developed countries (the US, most of the EU, Japan, and several others), newly industrializing countries (such as China and India), and the developing countries (typically the poor countries in South Asia and sub-Saharan Africa). While there are many other classifications, it is clear that the global business environment has changed radically over the last two decades as billions of people around the world want to share in the wealth that people in developed countries generally enjoy.[1]

Globalization has improved the abilities of people to connect with each other and participate in economic activities that would have been impossible or too costly just ten or twenty years ago. The Internet has made communications and the sharing and use of information and data widely available and virtually free on a per use basis. Computers and advanced telecommunications technologies like fiber optics, satellites, and cell phones have expanded the reach of people and their ability to conduct business efficiently and effectively from remote locations. Moreover, logistics and transportation costs have improved dramatically allowing goods to be produced far from customers cost-effectively.

The prevalent view is that the world is shrinking as technologies and innovative methods, especially telecommunications and logistics, provide new ways to lower costs and make products and services more valuable and attractive to the consumer. There has been a proliferation of new products and technologies and mass customization is seemingly a key to success. While there is no doubt that the geographical scale of the world has shrunk, in reality the business world has expanded many times over the last twenty years. With the obliteration of the notions of the first, second, and third worlds, the business environment of the global corporations, other large companies, and even SMEs has increased dramatically. The global market of potential consumers has increased dramatically from about 1 billion people, those living in the developed countries, to 3–5 billion people, especially potential consumers living in the newly industrializing countries like China and India. Moreover, the number of people who might be deemed as customers has tripled if not more so; it can be argued that most of the people in the world are now potential customers.

From a business perspective the world without the old barriers of Iron Curtain and restrictions on trade opens up phenomenal opportunities. Larger populations of people participating in the economic exchanges mean more customers and more opportunities for businesses. While most of the attention to date has been on low-cost labor that has driven down costs, strategic leaders must also recognize that new market spaces are being expanded as people in developing countries seek to improve their living conditions and the quality of their lives. With a more interconnected and fast-paced world, strategic leaders must pay more attention to the social, economic, and environmental aspects that impinge on their businesses. They must take a broader perspective and expand the scope of their strategic thinking and business boundaries to include more of the dynamics of the business environment, the social/human world, and the natural environment.

An added leadership imperative is to assume increased responsibilities for the actions, outcomes, and impacts of the entities of the extended enterprise, not just one's own organization. Strategic leaders must become more aware and involved with the broader communities of people, and actively play positive roles in helping to solve some of the more critical problems affecting humankind. The potential effects and impacts of the forces of change on the natural environment and participation in reducing the negative aspects of humankind's relationship with nature cannot be left to governments alone. This does not mean that strategic leaders have to assume responsibilities for the social well being of all people or that they should usurp the roles and responsibilities of the political leaders and government agencies. It does mean that in a more complex and interconnected world where the lines of demarcation between business, social, economic, and political agendas become cloudy, strategic leaders have to collaborate with leaders in other fields to deliver the best possible solutions for humankind and preserve the natural environment at the same time. It is an implicit responsibility that stems from the fact that everyone contributes to social, economic, and environmental problems; therefore, everyone has a shared responsibility in helping to create solutions to meet the needs and expectations of people without degrading or destroying the planet, regional ecosystems, and the well being of humankind.

ESM, ESL, strategic thinking, and sustainable success require a generational outlook that meets the needs of the present while ensuring that there are sufficient resources and effective solutions for future generations. This also implies that leaders across all endeavors mitigate the negative impacts on the social and natural world.

The premises are simple, and have been articulated for generations in almost all cultures and their beliefs and philosophies. They involve the historical perspective of the categorical imperative and the contemporary view of sustainable development. They include the concept of universal ethics that all businesses must follow and that there are absolute standards of behavior within the context of respecting the cultural aspects of all people. It implies that strategic leaders have a "duty of care" to protect society and humankind, to engage in business activities that are legal, ethical, and moral, and to promote fair and honest outcomes for the present and in the future.

Business leaders must ensure that their decisions lead to appropriate solutions for the people involved, and use of the resources properly and efficiently. Moreover, they do have a duty to minimize resource depletion and environmental degradation, to avoid destructive behaviors, and to mitigate negative effects. It is proper and just to use resources to satisfy needs of the present, but it is unacceptable and unwise to overuse or waste resources, or to create pollution that requires future generations to engage in expensive remediation projects, or to suffer the adverse impacts and negative consequences. These premises make social, economic, environmental, and financial sense. The overuse of resources, the generation of waste streams, and other inefficiencies and wastes cost money which reduces cash flow, profits, and returns. Moreover, creating environmental problems may save money today, but often result in liabilities that are much more costly to solve in the future.

These premises and enhanced business opportunities are interrelated. Solving human-related problems and eliminating environmental burdens and impacts are often the genesis for business-related opportunities. Increased social, economic, and environmental responsibilities underpin outstanding strategy formulation, implementation, and execution that allow strategic leaders to outperform their peers and competitors. They enhance relationships with customers, improve employee morale, lower the inherent risks of doing business, and increase shareholder confidence that the strategic direction and operations are on the right track. And, they lead to shareholder wealth creation.

Most importantly, ESM focuses on minimizing the causes, effects, and impacts that might damage the reputation of the company and its business units. Strategic leaders take years to build value and wealth for shareholders, all of which can be quickly decimated if the goodwill and reputation of the organization are besmirched. For example, Merck, the US pharmaceutical giant, was often regarded as one of the most admired corporations in the world. Nevertheless, its strategic position and market capitalization were seriously affected when its failures in the Vioxx story became widely known.

ESM and the management constructs thereof are essential for leading change in the significantly more complex business environment of the twenty-first century. With global expansion there are many new and emerging competitors who have inherent advantages that are difficult to handle if the basis of strategic management is still centered on the three generic strategies of low-cost leadership, differentiation, and niche or competitive strategies concentrating on beating or destroying competitors. Such simplifications are just too elementary for large global companies and even SMEs to rely on for achieving sustainable success. Companies and their business units must be more sophisticated, and provide great solutions and success for all of the contributors and recipients of the solutions. Such approaches then provide sustainable advantages and enduring outcomes.

The underlying basis for achieving success is shifting from the products and services to the total solutions and from just satisfying customers to developing and enjoying enduring customer and stakeholder relationships. It also goes from having core competencies within the organization to having a unique enterprise-wide value delivery system that outperforms expectations, and from defeating the competitors to creating extraordinary value based on the uniqueness of the whole enterprise. Moreover, sustainable success is based on having a holistic perspective of the social, economic, and environmental underpinnings that provide opportunities and result in financial, organizational, and strategic success.

Concluding comments

ESM is a holistic strategic management construct. It focuses on the social, economic, and environmental underpinnings of the business environment, the opportunities and challenges of the market spaces, and the well being, development, and sustainability of the extended enterprise(s) and the business unit(s). It represents a fundamental shift in strategic thinking and perspective from concentrating on the producers' view of the business landscape and the rivalry among the competitors to understanding the economic and social needs and expectations of the markets, customers, and stakeholders, and the broader ecosystems.

The center of attention moves in a profound way from the internal perspectives of the producers of products and/or services to the customers and stakeholders and to the market spaces – the essence of the economic force of the business world. While the notions of industries and company-centric management constructs made sense during most of the twentieth century, they are no longer as viable. The focus is on solutions, systems, and relationships. Customers need more than products and services. They really want and expect the best solutions. They may be willing to buy the existing products and services – but only until more beneficial solutions become available and accepted.

The strategic management constructs of today, especially those pertaining to the global business environment, must be dynamic, have a broad scope, and create, develop, and deliver solutions that encompass the needs and expectations of all of the entities of the market spaces and extended enterprise. The most important shift in strategic management thinking is moving from a narrow perspective to a much broader and more inclusive one – ones that encompass the full scope of the extended enterprise.

ESM involves the creation of total value for the whole enterprise and ensuring ongoing success for all of the entities and individuals. ESM with the principles of sustainable development offers business leaders the theories, constructs, methods, and practices that can result in sustainable success. Contemporary strategic leaders must be visionaries who create a more viable and productive reality using extraordinary means and mechanisms to go beyond making simple improvements. While the concept of continuous improvement is useful, it often results in outcomes that are insufficient for truly keeping ahead of expectations and requirements. More and more products and services are becoming (or have become) commodities; even those based on high-tech approaches like cell phones become commonplace. Having a good product is not good enough. Businesses must have the best solutions, ones that create extraordinary value through the efforts of the whole extended enterprise.

Sustainable solutions are based on the intellectual capital, capabilities, resources, and strategic positions of the whole enterprise, not just the internal dimensions of the business units. Not only has the emphasis turned to creating and delivering the best solutions, but it is on providing customer success and

Table 10.1 Perspectives on the critical factors of strategic management

Critical factors	Narrow perspectives	Broad perspectives of ESM
Business paradigm	Producing good products and enhancing quality and outcomes through continuous improvement	Creating total value and sustainable success through ESM, ESL, and sustainable development
Business focus	Producing/selling products, making money, and creating shareholder wealth	Ensuring stability and the well being of the whole, providing the best solutions possible, and creating value and success
Market focus	Providing good products and achieving customer satisfaction	Ensuring customer and stakeholder success and building relationships
Competition	Engaging in industry rivalry, prevailing in the ensuing battles, and achieving market share leadership	Outperforming expectations through enterprise-wide integration and making competitors irrelevant
Economic drivers	Providing products and services that meet customer needs	Providing sustainable solutions that exceed the expectations of everyone
Social driver ethics	Providing employment opportunities, and contributing to society through charities and good business practices	Being socially responsible for the decisions and actions of the enterprise and helping to resolve social difficulties
Environmental drivers	Ensuring full compliance with government mandates and preventing pollution	Eliminating degradation, depletion, impacts, and burdens, and protecting the well being of the natural environment
Internal drivers	Building core competencies of the organization and exploiting the strengths of the organization	Creating the most capable extended enterprise and developing unique strengths and mitigating the weaknesses
Management constructs	Creating competitive advantages of the business for achieving financial success	Creating a unique business model that outperforms all others and has extraordinary and sustainable advantages
Enterprise-wide strategic leadership	Command and control mechanisms to obtain results and performance; "do as I say not as I do."	Leading change and ensuring that everyone across the enterprise is successful; being part of the team

having enduring relationships. The focus must also be on ensuring stability and creating an environment of well being and success. Table 10.1 summarizes some of the critical factors for achieving success discussed throughout the book. It identifies the narrow perspectives of traditional strategic management and the broad perspectives of ESM. Please keep in mind that perfect solutions are a distant dream that require concerted efforts, investments, and dedication.

ESM is not about wishful thinking about ideal situations, it is about reality. Strategic leaders at all levels must engage in more sophisticated strategic management paradigms that recognize the legitimate and pressing need to make dramatic transitions and transformations in their enterprises. They must do everything possible to provide the best solutions and to inspire people to achieve greatness in every endeavor.

ESM extends from the widest and deepest aspects of the business situation to most profound leadership qualities for managing enterprises. The scope is broad and solutions are multifaceted. The approach is to build solid relationships across the enterprises that endure. It is based on strategic innovations that transition and transform the whole enterprise into a strategic position that creates value, achieves success, and makes competition irrelevant.

ESL involves the essential roles and responsibilities of strategic management at all levels. It involves creating the vision of the future, positioning the organization to realize that vision, and inspiring the people to transform existing capabilities into world-class competencies and capabilities. Strategic leaders engage people throughout the organization to build the knowledge, capabilities, and actions necessary to support the transitions and transformations to a richer reality. They are responsible for setting the strategic direction, policies, principles, and values and for providing governance, reporting, and ethical behaviors. Moreover, they have the overall responsibility for ensuring that the corporation and the business units meet their objectives, performance criteria, and social responsibility.

The world has changed radically over the last twenty years; the challenges are enormous and the opportunities are staggering. However, success is never guaranteed. The world is more complicated than ever before and many of the simple approaches have already played out. Strategic management constructs of today have to be more innovative, creative, and sophisticated. In a complicated world it is incumbent upon strategic leaders to manage complexity at strategic management levels where there is the required intellectual capital. ESM focuses on handling complexity at strategic level and providing simpler approaches at the operating levels. However, ESM is not a magic bullet that will put an end to difficulties and problems. It is not the end but the beginning; it is about rekindling the fires and passions within the enterprise to be great and provide for the well being of the whole.

The world is expanding into a rich mosaic that is both exciting and scary. People in developed countries enjoy an unprecedented quality of life, affluence, and well being. While there are millions of people in developed countries still living at the margins, the social, political, economic, and technological systems and structures have created and produced incredible successes for the fortunate people lucky enough to live in the industrialized nations. But the economic elites are a minority of the world's population. There are billions of people around the world who aspire to join the ranks of the economic elites.

Thomas L. Friedman's book, *The World Is Flat*, has enjoyed great success and provides an insightful view of globalization.[2] But, the business world is neither flat nor round. It is multidimensional in space and time. Businesses have created, developed, and deployed sophisticated technologies, products, and services that provide solutions for a broad array of needs and expectations. Yet, there are innovative solutions necessary to fit the requirements of billions of people around the world who do not have access to the prevailing products, have the wherewithal to buy them, or the means and mechanisms to use them. One of the most exciting opportunities of this century is to expand the benefits of the businesses to the developing countries. This will enrich the people in those countries and provide companies with great opportunities to obtain sustainable success.

Dramatic changes and improvements can and must be made to include everyone in the benefits and rewards of the economic prosperity. ESM necessitates that strategic leaders embrace ESL and create value for their shareholders, customers, stakeholders, and society. ESM means sustaining success in the present and in the long term.

References

Friedman, Thomas L. (2005) *The World Is Flat: A Brief History of the Twenty-first Century*. New York, NY: Farrar, Straus and Giroux

NOTES

1 While most people in the developed countries have reasonable, if not excellent, living conditions and quality of life, there are still people living at the margins. However, many of the people who are classified as poor may be better off than most people in the poorest countries in the world.

2 Thomas L. Friedman, *The World Is Flat: A Brief History of the Twenty-first Century* (New York, NY: Farrar, Straus and Giroux, 2005).

Index